EUROPEAN HISTORICAL DICTIONARIES
Edited by Jon Woronoff

Historical Dictionary of Denmark

Alastair H. Thomas and
Stewart P. Oakley

European Historical Dictionaries Series, No. 33

The Scarecrow Press, Inc.
Lanham, Maryland & Oxford
1998

SCARECROW PRESS, INC.

Published in the United States of America
by Scarecrow Press, Inc.
4720 Boston Way
Lanham, Maryland 20706

4 Pleydell Gardens
Kent CT20 2DN, England

British Library Cataloguing in Publication Information Available

Library of Congress Cataloging-in-Publication Data

Thomas, Alastair H.
    Historical dictionary of Denmark / Alastair H. Thomas and
Stewart P. Oakley
        p. cm. — (European historical dictionaries series ; no. 33)
    Includes bibliographical references.
    ISBN 0-8108-3544-4 (alk. paper)
    1. Denmark—History—Dictionaries. I. Oakley, Stewart P.
II. Title. III. Series: European historical dictionaries ; no. 33.
    DL105.T46   1999   98-38071
    948.9'003—dc21   CIP

⊖™ The paper used in this publication meets the minimum requirements of
American National Standard for Information Sciences—Permanence of
Paper for Printed Library Materials, ANSI Z39.48–1984.
Manufactured in the United States of America.

To Janet Thomas,

for her patience and support,

and to our sons

Simon and Andrew.

CONTENTS

PREFACE

Work on this *Historical Dictionary of Denmark* was begun by Stewart P. Oakley, professor of Scandinavian studies at the University of East Anglia, Norwich, England. He took important planning decisions on the titles of many of the entries and wrote many of them in the first half of the volume. His entries are initialed SPO. Tanya Oakley and Kate Kalbag helped him, and their help is acknowledged. Stewart Oakley's invaluable historical scholarship is at the core of this book. Its completion serves as a memorial to his career as a scholar of Danish history and literature.

Following Stewart Oakley's death in 1995, the dictionary was taken over, the entries revised and completed, and the volume carried through to publication by Alastair H. Thomas, Professor of Nordic Politics at the University of Central Lancashire, Preston, England. His entries are initialed AHT. He has also extended the scope of the dictionary to include many brief biographies of politicians and of contributors to the musical, literary, cultural, academic, scientific, and commercial life of Denmark.

In any project such as this, inclusion or omission of topics is a matter of judgement. But the intention has been to give English-speaking readers the means to become familiar with the lives and achievements of the many great Danes who have contributed to the development of their country and its culture. That interest can be taken further with the Bibliography.

Acknowledgements

My involvement in this project was suggested by Professor Clive Archer. Staff at the Danish Institute in Edinburgh were helpful in supplying information and answering questions. Frands Schjødt Pedersen suggested useful sources. Annette Scheel sent information about Greenland at short notice. Joanne Kirk helped with the page-layout.

Greenland at short notice. Joanne Kirk helped with the page-layout. The University of Central Lancashire gave me a semester of research leave and funded travel and living costs in Denmark. The Institute of Political Science of the University of Copenhagen made available accommodation during May 1998. Hans Jørgen Nielsen helped to arrange this and he and his wife Bodil made me welcome, while staff in the Institute's Library answered questions helpfully. Rikke Blak Kjeldal checked the Danish in the text. Grete Edelmann, hospitable as ever, has encouraged my interest in Denmark and the Danes for the past half-century. They all contributed to the successful completion of this book, and my thanks go to them all — although, as always, final responsibility for the content rests with the authors. AHT

EDITOR'S FOREWORD

Denmark is one of the smaller European democracies. On a world map it is hardly noticeable, a promontory and some islands north of Germany and south of the Norwegian-Swedish peninsula — though it achieves greater geographical prominence when the large but sparsely populated territories of the Faroe Islands and Greenland are added.

On older maps it would have been easier to find. The realm of King Knud (or Canute, 1018-1035) included England, most of Scotland including the North Atlantic isles, Norway, and the southern and western coasts of Sweden. Two centuries later the Danish empire included all the southern Baltic coast and conquests in Estonia. Queen Margrethe I's Kalmar Union (from 1397) united the three crowns of Denmark, Norway and Sweden. From the 17th century Denmark had colonial possessions in the West Indies, West Africa, and India. But by 1866 even Southern Jutland (recovered in 1920) had been lost and Christian IX (king 1863-1906) had little more than his progeny to support his unofficial title of "the father-in-law of Europe." Today Denmark, with its thriving capital, Copenhagen, is peaceful, progressive, and prosperous (the second-richest European Union country after Luxembourg), and individual Danes continue to make their mark in the world.

This *Historical Dictionary of Denmark* does justice to the term "historical". It covers the older, more "glorious" periods when Denmark was a force to be reckoned with and mixed freely in European politics and wars. It presents the earlier rulers and explains the conditions of the times. But it also provides ample coverage of the modern and contemporary eras, with less prominence for kings and queens and more for the politicians and political parties, the trade unions and other organizations that run the country. The subjects covered reach well beyond politics and warfare into the economy, society, and culture (art, music, literature, and religion) with, of course, a look at the wel-

xi

fare state and at Danish relations with other countries and the European Union. This is buttressed by a chronology, an introduction, several useful appendices, and a substantial bibliography.

This volume was initiated by Stewart Oakley, one of the most eminent British specialists on Scandinavia, whose many books included *The Story of Denmark*. After Professor Oakley passed away in 1995, the work was continued by Alastair H. Thomas, Professor of Nordic Politics at the University of Central Lancashire. He has also written extensively on Denmark, Scandinavia, and Social Democracy. His next book is *Nordic Democracy in the New Europe*. This *Historical Dictionary of Denmark* benefited greatly from the complementary interests and perspectives of two fine scholars who have managed to provide a picture of a country which, while small, certainly matters.

Jon Woronoff
Series Editor

NOTES TO READERS

The letters Æ, Ø, and Å, in that order, follow Z at the end of the Danish alphabet. For the convenience of English-speaking readers, in this Dictionary they are sorted as Ae, O, and A, respectively. These letters are pronounced: æ like ea in b*ea*r; ø like ea in *ea*rly or like u in b*u*rden; and å like aw in cl*aw*. Danish is notoriously difficult to pronounce, but some guidence may help with place-names etc. D sounds as in English at the start of a word, but after an accented vowel as *th* in *th*is; for example Odense is pronounced O*th*ense with a short final e. *J* always sounds as a short *y* (unless there is a French derivation, as in *ajour*, up-to-date). W is little used, but is pronounced *v*.

When a person is known by other than his full first name(s), this is shown in the Dictionary by underlining. For example, **ANDERSEN, HANS CHRISTIAN** is known to Danes as H.C. Andersen; **ESTRUP, JACOB BRONNUM SCAVENIUS** is known as J.B.S. Estrup; and **GRUNDTVIG, NICOLAJ FREDERIK SEVERIN** is known as N.F.S. Grundtvig.

Where a publication is mentioned in a Dictionary entry, a translation of the title has generally been given, and the following convention has been adopted:

P.V. Glob, *Mosefolk* (1965, *The Bog People*, 1969) shows that the book was published in Danish in 1965 and in English in 1969.
P.V. Glob, *Højfolket* (1970, People of the Burial Mound) shows that the book was published in Danish in 1970. The translation of its title (without a date) implies that there is no English language edition (but see also the Prehistory section in the Bibliography).

We have aimed to be consistent in spelling of names. But a difficulty arises where, for example, a name originates in another language. For example the Danish royal house of Oldenborg originates with the

German dukedom of Oldenburg. Similarly, the Danish spelling of Slesvig is used to refer to the duchy, the southern part of which is now part of the German *land* of Schleswig-Holstein. Individuals with French or German origins have had Danish careers — Prince Henrik for example: Danish spellings are used unless there is clearly a non-Danish context, for example the Danish royal house of Oldenborg, but the Count of Oldenburg.

Words in bold indicate a cross-reference to an entry on this topic elsewhere in the dictionary.

ABBREVIATIONS
AND ACRONYMS

AC	Akademikernes Centralorganisation, Central Organization of Professional Employees (literally of university graduates)
AD	Anno domini (Latin), of the Christian era.
AEK	Atomenergikommissionen, Atomic Energy Authority (= DAEK)
AMPA	Amager Partisaner, Resistance Group in World War II
AOF	Arbejdernes Oplysningsforbund, Workers' Educational Association
A/S	Aktieselskab, joint-stock company
AS	Akademikernes Samarbejdsudvalg, cooperation committee of professionally qualified occupations
ATP	Arbejdsmarkedets Tillægspension, Employment Supplementary Pension
ATV	Akademiet for de Tekniske Videnskaber, Academy for Technical Sciences
BC	before Christ
bn.	billion = 1,000 million (in Danish milliard, mia.)
BOPA	Borgerlige Partisaner, communist-dominated resistance group in World War II
c.	circa, about
cand.	candidatus (male) candidata (female), graduate.
cand. act.	candidatus actuarii, graduate actuary
cand. agron.	candidatus agronomiae, graduate in agriculture
cand. art.	candidatus artium, graduate in a minor subject in connection with a major subject, e.g., cand. jur. et art., graduate in law and a minor subject

cand. brom.	*candidatus bromatologiae*, graduate in food science
cand. geom.	*candidatus geometriae*,
	graduate in geodesy and cadastral science
cand. hort.	*candidatus hortonomiae*,
	graduate in landscape gardening or horticulture
cand. jur.	*candidatus juris*, graduate in law
cand. lact.	*candidatus lactonomiae*, graduate in dairying
cand. ling.	*candidatus linguae mercantilis*,
merc.	graduate in business languages
cand. mag.	*candidatus magisterii*,
	graduate in Arts in major and minor subjects
cand. med.	*candidatus medicinae*, graduate in medicine
cand. med. vet.	*candidatus medicinae veterinariae*,
	graduate in veterinary medicine
cand. merc.	*candidatus mercaturae*
	graduate in business economics
cand. oecon.	*candidatus oeconomiae*, graduate in economics
cand. pharm.	*candidatus pharmaciae*, graduate in pharmacy
cand. phil.	*candidatus philosophiae*,
	graduate in arts in major subject only
cand. polit.	*candidatus politices*,
	graduate in public administration
cand. polyt.	*candidatus polytechnices*, graduate in engineering
cand. psych.	*candidatus psychologiae*,
	graduate in applied psychology
cand. scient.	*candidatus scientiarum*,
	graduate in a major science subject
cand. scient.	*candidatus scientiarum politicarum*,
pol.	graduate in political science
cand. silv.	*candidatus silvinomiae*, graduate in forestry
cand. soc.	*candidatus socialium*, graduate in social sciences
cand. stat.	*candidatus statisticae*, graduate in statistics
cand. theol.	*candidatus theologiae*, graduate in theology
CB-	Civilt brandværn,
organisation	Civil defense organization in World War II
CD	Centrum-Demokraterne, Center Democrats
CF	Civilforsvaret Civil Defense
CFF	Civilforsvars Forbundet, Civil Defense Union
CFK	Civil Forsvars Korps,
	Civil Defense Corps from 1949

CO	Statstjenstemændnes Centralorganisation, Central Organization of Civil Servants
DA or DAF	Dansk Arbejdsgiverforening, Danish Employers' Federation
DAÆ	Dansk Andels Ægeksport, Danish Egg Export Committee
DAEK	Danmarks Atomenergikommissionen (= AEK)
DAG	Danmarks Andelsgødningsforretning, Danish Co-operative Fertilizer Society
DAL	Danske Arkitekters Landsforbund, National Association of Danish Architects
DASF	Dansk Arbejdsmands- og Specialarbejderforbund, Danish General and Semi-skilled Workers' Union
DB	Danmarks Brugsforening, Retail Co-operative Society of Denmark
DDH	Det Danske Hedeselskab, Danish Heath Society
DDL	De Danske Luftfartsselskab, Danish Aviation Company
DFDS	Det Forenede Dampskibs-Selskab, United Steamship Company
DGL	Danmarks Grundlov Denmark's Constitution
DIF	Dansk Idræts Forbund, Danish Sports Federation or Dansk Ingeniørforening, Danish Engineers Association
DJ	Dansk Journalistforbund, Danish Journalists Federation
DK	Standard abbreviation for Denmark, or Danske Kvindesamfund Danish Women's Society
DKB	Dansk Kvinders Beredskab, Danish Women's Reserve
DKF	Det Kooperative Fællesforbund, Union of Urban Co-operative Societies
DKP	Danmarks Kommunistiske Parti, Danish Communist Party
Dkr	Danish *krone*, plural *kroner* the unit of currency
DLAM	Dansk Landbrugs Andelsmaskinindkøb, Danish Farmers' Co-operative Machinery Purchasing Society

DLF	Danmarks Lærerforening, Danish Union of Teachers
DMS	Danske Missionsselskab, Danish Missionary Society
DNSAP	Danmarks Nationalsocialistiske Arbejderparti, Danish National Socialist Workers' Party
DONG	Dansk Olie og Naturgas, Danish Oil and Natural Gas
dr.	doctoral graduate. See Universities for explanation of the status of this degree.
DR	Danmarks Radio, Danish State Radio
DRK	Dansk Røde Kors, Danish Red Cross
DS	Dansk Samling, Danish Rally (political party)
DSB	Danske Statsbaner, Danish State Railways
DSU	Danmarks Socialdemokratiske Ungdom, Danish Young Social Democrats
DTH/DTU	Danmarks Tekniske Højskole (Universitet after 1995), Technical University of Denmark
DUI	De Unges Idræt, (Social Democratic) Youth Sports organization
EC	European Community
EEC	European Economic Community
EF	Europæiske Fælleskab, the European Community
EFTA	European Free Trade Area
e.g.	*exempli gratia,* for example
EMU	Economic and Monetary Union
exam. art.	*examinatus artium,* Arts graduate in minor subject only
EU	European Union
FA	Finanssektorens Arbejdsgiverforening, Association of Employers in the Finance Sector
FCU	Forsvarets Civiluddannelse, Training for Civil Employees in Defense
FDB	Fællesforeningen for Danmarks Brugsforeninger, Danish Cooperative Wholesale Society
FDF/FPF	Frivilligt Drenge- og Pige-forbund, Voluntary Boys' and Girls' Association
FN	Forenede Nationer, United Nations
FP	Fremskridtspartiet, Progress Party

FPU	Fremskridtspartiets Ungdom, Progress Party Youth organization
FR	Fællesrepresentationen for danske Arbejdsleder- og Funktionærforeninger, Joint Council of Danish Supervisors' and Technical Officers' Societies
FTF	Fællesrådet for danske tjenstemands- og funkionærorganisationer, Joint Council of Danish Public Servants' and Salaried Employees' Organizations
g	gram
GATT	General Agreement on Tariffs and Trade (predecessor of the World Trade Organization)
GDP	gross domestic product
GNI	gross national income
GNP	gross national product
g.r.t.	gross registered tonnes
HB	Hovedstadens Brugsforening, Greater Copenhagen Cooperative Society
HD	Handelsvidenskabelig Diplomprøve, Diploma in Business Economics
HFO	De danske Handelsforeningers Fællesorganisation, the joint organization of Danish trade associations
Hipo	Hilfspolizei, Danish auxiliary police assisting occupying German forces during World War II
HK	Handels- og Kontorfunktionærernes Forbund i Danmark, Shop and Office Workers' Union
IA	Inuit Ataqatigiit, Inuit Brotherhood; Greenlandic political party
IFU	Industrialiseringsfonden for Udviklingslandene, Industrialization Fund for Developing Countries
IM	Indre Mission, Home Mission
JAF	Jydsk Andels-Foderstofforretning, Jutland Co-operative Feedstuffs Society
KF	Konservative Folkparti, Conservative People's Party
KFUK	Kristelig Forening for Unge Kvinder (YWCA)
KFUM	Kristelig Forening for Unge Mænd (YMCA)
KGH	Den Kongelige Grønlandske Handel, Royal Greenland Trade organization
km	kilometer
Kr F	Kristeligt folkeparti, Christian People's Party

KTAS	Københavns Telefon Aktieselskab, Copenhagen Telephone Company
KU	Konservativ Ungdom, Young Conservatives
lic.	*licenciatus*, holder of an advanced postgraduate degree approximately equivalent to Ph.D. in UK or US. This degree can be obtained in all faculties.
LO	Landsorganisationen i Danmark, Trade Union Congress
LOF	Liberalt Oplysnings Forbund, Liberal Education Association
LS	Landbrugernes Sammenslutning, Agricultural Association
m	meter (measure of distance). million.
mag. art.	*magister artium*, Master of Arts, MA
mag. scient.	*magister scientiarum*, Master of a science, including anthropology
mag. scient. soc.	*magister scientiarum socialium*, Master of Social Sciences
MF	Medlem af Folketinget, Member of the Folketing
NATO	North Atlantic Treaty Organization
OECD	Organization for Economic Cooperation & Development
ØK	Østasiatisk Kompani, East Asiatic Company
OL	Olympiske lege, Olympic Games
RB	Ritzaus Bureau, Danish Press Bureau
RUC	Roskilde Universitetscenter, Roskilde University
RV	Radikale Venstre, Radical (social) Liberal Party
SALA	Sammenslutningen af Landbrugets Arbejdsgiverforeninger, Union of Agricultural Employers
SAS	Scandinavian Airlines System
S, SD	Socialdemokratiet, Social Democratic Party
SF	Socialistisk folkeparti, Socialist People's Party
SFU	Socialistisk folkepartis Ungdom, Socialist Peoples Party's Youth organization
SiD	Specialarbejderforbundet i Danmark, Union of Semi-skilled Workers in Denmark
SOE	(British) Special Operations Executive
status quo ante	(Latin) the situation at the start
WEU	Western European Union
V	Venstre, Denmark's Liberal Party

CHRONOLOGY OF
DANISH HISTORY

c. 14000 BC - c. 3000 BC	Old Stone Age
c. 11000 BC	Bromme Culture
c. 3000 BC - c. 1500 BC	New Stone Age
c. 2700 BC	Megalith Graves
c. 2000 BC	Boat Ax Culture
c. 1500 BC - c. 500 BC	Bronze Age
c. 1300 BC - c. 1000 BC	Trundholm Sun Chariot
c. 1000 BC	Egtved Grave
c. 800 BC - AD 100	Celtic Iron Age
c. 200 BC	Dejbjerg Wagon
c. 100 BC	Gundestrup Bowl
c. AD 100 -500	Roman Iron Age
c. AD 400	Hjortspring Boat
c. 500-c.800	Migration Period
c. 800- c. 1050	Viking Period
793	Danish raid on Lindisfarne (northwest England)
878	Danelaw established in England
c. 900	Hedeby active
960	King Harald "Bluetooth" baptized
c. 975	Trelleborg fort built

xxi

1658	Treaty of Roskilde
1661	Absolute monarchy established
1665	King's Law drawn up
1671	West India and Guinea Company established
1671	Titles of count and baron introduced and Order of Dannebrog revived
1675-1679	Scanian War
1676	Fall of Griffenfeld
1677	Battle of Køge Bay
1683	Danish Law
1688	Great land survey published
1700-1720	Great Northern War
1702	Serfdom (*vornedskab*) abolished
1721	Hans Egede's missionary expedition to Greenland
1722-1723	Holberg's Comedies
1733	*Stavnsbaand* (adscription) introduced
1741	Conventicle Act
1770-1772	Struensee in power
1784	*Coup d'état* by reforming administration; the "Great Reforms" begin
1786	Great Agricultural Commission appointed
1788	Adscription (*stavnsbaand*) abolished: liberation of the peasantry
1792	Slave trade abolished (with effect in 1802)
1801	First Battle of Copenhagen
1807	Copenhagen bombarded by British
1813	State bankruptcy
1814	Loss of Norway by Treaty of Kiel
1835-1836	First meetings of Consultative Assemblies for Holsten, Slesvig, Jutland, and the Islands
1841	First public State accounts
1844	First Folk High School opened in Rodding
1847	Copenhagen-Roskilde railway opened
1848	End of absolute monarchy
1848-1850	First Slesvig-Holsten War
1849	June Constitution
1852	Treaty of London
1857	Sound tolls (*Øresunds tolden*) abolished
1864	Second Slesvig-Holsten War: both duchies lost to Germany

1866　July Constitution restores power to the monarch
1868　Esbjerg harbor constructed
1870　United Liberal Party formed
1871　Social Democratic Party founded
1874　Iceland granted a constitution
1882　First cooperative dairy founded in Hjedding
1901　Change of System introduces
　　　parliamentary government
1905　Radical Liberal Party formed
1915　Revised Constitution and universal suffrage
1916　Conservative People's Party formed
1917　Danish West Indies (Virgin Islands)
　　　sold to the United States
1920　Easter Crisis. South Jutland restored.
　　　Danish-German boundary fixed.
1924　First Social Democratic government
1928　Århus University started teaching
1929-1940　Social Democratic and Radical Liberal majority
　　　coalition
1931-1933　Denmark and Norway dispute Eastern Greenland
1933　"Kanslergade Agreement" between Social Democrats,
　　　Radicals and Liberals;
　　　K.K. Steincke introduces new social welfare codes
1939　24 June: Danish-German non-aggression treaty
1940　9 April: German forces occupy Denmark
1941　United States establishes bases in Greenland at Thule,
　　　Søndre Strømfjord, etc.
1943　29 August: Germans seize control of administration
1944　"Siege of Copenhagen" in June;
　　　Iceland declares independence
1945　5 May: Denmark liberated
1948　23 March: Faroe Islands granted home rule
1949　4 April: Denmark joins NATO
1953　5 June: new Constitution takes effect;
　　　First meeting of Nordic Council
1957　Denmark and Norway refuse NATO tactical nuclear
　　　devices on their territory
1959　15 February: Socialist People's Party formed
1960　1 July: Denmark joins European Free Trade
　　　Association (EFTA)

1966 Odense University begins teaching
1967 2 June: restrictions removed on sale of pornographic
publications
1972 14 January: accession of Queen Margrethe II
1972 Progress Party formed
2 October: referendum on European Economic
Community (EEC) membership
Roskilde University Center begins teaching
1973 1 January: Denmark joins EEC
4 December: "earthquake" election
1974 7 October, trial of Mogens Glistrup opens
1978 Voting age reduced to 18
1981 November: Mogens Glistrup sentenced to four years'
imprisonment for fraud (reduced to three years on appeal in June 1983)
1985 1 January: Greenland leaves the EEC
1989 26 May: homosexual couples permitted to marry
1992 2 June: referendum rejects Maastricht Treaty
1993 14 January: Schlüter government resigns over Tamil
Affair and is succeeded by Poul Nyrup Rasmussen
(Social Democrat)
18 May: referendum accepts Maastricht Treaty, with
four Danish reservations, converting European Community to European Union (EU)
1995 Prince Joachim marries Alexandra Christina Manley
of Hong Kong
1996 Copenhagen: European City of Culture
1997 Denmark proposes a UN Human Rights Commission
resolution critical of China
1998 11 March: parliamentary election gives narrow
majority to Poul Nyrup Rasmussen's Social Democrat
+ Radical Liberal government.
April: the Faroe Islands elect a majority in favor of a
more limited relationship with Denmark.
7 May: the Nyrup Rasmussen government, with
Liberal and Conservative support, imposes a settlement of an 11-day general strike and lock-out, the first
time this has been necessary since 1985.
28 May: referendum ratifies EU Amsterdam Treaty

INTRODUCTION

Denmark: Geography and People

The Kingdom of Denmark is made up of Denmark itself, the Faroe Islands, and the island of Greenland. Denmark *(Danmark)* consists of the peninsula of Jutland *(Jylland)*, a northward extension of the North European Plain with a southern border shared with Germany, and 482 islands, of which fewer than a hundred are inhabited. The total area of mainland and islands is 43,093 square kilometers (16,619 square miles). The whole country is low-lying, the highest point being only 173 meters (568 feet) above sea level. The Faroe Islands *(Foröyar* in the Faroese language) consist of 21 islands far out in the North Atlantic between Shetland and Iceland, with a total area of 1399 square kilometers (540 square miles). Greenland is the largest island in the world, with an area of 2,175,500 square kilometers (840,000 square miles), of which only about 342,000 square kilometers (132,000 square miles) is free of the ice-cap that covers the rest.

The largest of Denmark's islands are (in descending size): Zealand (Sjælland*)*, separated from Sweden to the east by the Sound (Øresund); Funen (Fyn) to the west of Zealand and separated from it by the Great Belt (Store Bælt) and from Jutland by the Little Belt (Lille Bælt*)*; Lolland to the south of Zealand; Bornholm in the southern Baltic; Falster and Møn, between Lolland and Zealand. The main island of the Faroes is Stremoy.

Denmark's climate is temperate and changeable, and while its only commercially valuable mineral deposits are clay and lime used in the building industry, a large proportion of the land is suitable for agriculture. Danish agriculture, largely organized in small family farms, has since the later 19th century been highly efficient and productive, especially in its dairying and livestock sectors, and until the 1960s agricultural produce made up the bulk of the country's exports. Since then

1

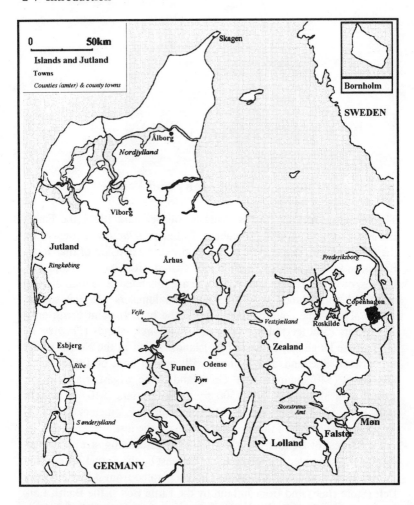

MODERN DENMARK
showing neighboring countries, Jutland and the larger islands,
counties (amter), Copenhagen and some major towns.

these have been overtaken by manufactured goods and services. In both the Faroe Islands and Greenland the population is heavily dependent on fishing for its livelihood. The 1992 population of Denmark is 5,162,1262. Over 3 million Danes live in urban settlements, half of them (1,337,114) in the capital of Copenhagen (København), a seaport on the east coast of Zealand. Other large towns (in order of size) are Århus (200,188) in eastern Jutland, Odense (138,986) on Funen, and Ålborg (113,599) in northern Jutland. The 1990 population of the Faroe Islands is 47,449 with 14,682 in the chief town of Thorshavn (Tórshavn). Greenland's 1992 population is only slightly higher at 55,385. Its capital of Godthåb/ Nuuk on the southwest coast has a population of 12,233 and all but about 2,500 of the remaining population live in scattered settlements along the west coast of Greenland.

The only significant minority in Denmark itself are the German-speakers in southern Jutland. The pure Inuit (eskimo) of Greenland are outnumbered by Greenlanders of mixed Inuit and Danish blood. The vast majority of inhabitants of the kingdom are members of the national Lutheran Evangelical Church (although for many this membership is only nominal).

History
Prehistory
There is evidence of human presence in the area of modern Denmark even before the onset of the last Ice Age 100,000 years ago, but continuous occupation did not begin until about 10,000 BC when hunters moved in from the south in the wake of the retreating ice sheet. The Old Stone Age lasted until about 2,500 BC. Toward its end, the land sank to give the country something like its modern shape. Agriculture began to be practiced in the succeeding Later Stone Age, which also saw the erection of the stone monuments or dolmens (*kæmpehøje*) still common in the Danish countryside today. The Bronze Age (1500-500 BC) was marked by close trade relations with the Mediterranean, in which amber from the southern Baltic coast played an important part. It was a period of considerable wealth leading to the emergence of a powerful ruling class. A decline began with the early or "Celtic" Iron Age, when the climate deteriorated and links with the south were broken by the westward advance of the Celts. The older trade links were reestablished at the beginning of the Christian era, and many artifacts

from the Roman world reached Denmark. With the fall of the Roman Empire in the West there was again a cultural decline, but at the end of the 8th century, a king of the Danes named Godfred is recorded as defying the advancing power of the Franks with a defensive wall (Dannevirke) across the neck of southern Jutland. The Danes and their land of Danmark are first recorded about this time, although it is not known whether they were yet united under one king.

Vikings

In the Viking Age, which lasted from the 9th until the middle of the 11th century, organized Danish armies ranged over much of western Europe and settled in eastern England, where they formed the Danelaw. This was reconquered by the kings of Wessex in the course of the 10th century, but at the beginning of the 11th the English throne was seized by Knud (Canute the Great), who from 1018 to 1035 ruled over both England and Denmark, and for a brief time also parts of Norway.

The Danes were converted to Christianity after 960 during the reign of King Harald "Bluetooth," and in 1104 the Scandinavian Church was made a separate province under the archbishop of Lund in Scania, lands which were Danish until the 17th century but since then have been southern Sweden. Close cooperation between the Church and the Crown enabled the Crown to grow in power. After a period of civil war in the first half of the 12th century, the age of the Valdemar kings (beginning with Valdemar I in 1157) saw the expansion of Danish power eastward along all the southern Baltic coast to beyond the river Oder. This power collapsed under Valdemar III (1202-1241), and for a time the realm was at the mercy of German nobles. Royal power was limited by the emergence of a group of politically ambitious nobles in Denmark, who exploited the fact that the Danish crown was elective and in 1282 imposed on King Erik Klipping a charter, on which was modeled the accession charters of kings until the mid-17th century. Stability returned with the reign of king Valdemar IV "Atterdag" (1340-1375).

Denmark also had to deal with the rising economic power of the Hanseatic League of German merchants, and it was partly to counter this that the opportunity of two vacant thrones was taken in 1397 to unite the three kingdoms of Denmark, Norway, and Sweden in the Kalmar Union. The main architect of this was King Valdemar's able daughter Margrethe, and the Union, throughout its history of over a century, was dominated by Denmark, the richest of the three countries and the one through which European influences flowed into the rest of Scandinavia. Many Swedish nobles were wary of Danish dominance and on several occasions during the 15th century broke away from the Union and chose their own king. A final attempt to crush Swedish resistance in 1520 by king Christian II led to the definitive establishment of Swedish independence. Norway remained under the rule of Copenhagen until 1814, however.

Missionaries of the Reformation had already penetrated Denmark, and won considerable support in the larger towns. The Crown regarded the new movement with caution until a dispute over the succession to the throne after the death of King Frederik I led to a civil war (the Count's War, Grevens Fejde) and the victory of Frederik's son, the Lutheran duke Christian, who was crowned king as Christian III and immediately set about imposing a Protestant church settlement throughout his new realm. In the middle of the 16th century the collapse of authority in the eastern Baltic led to a power struggle involving Denmark, Sweden, Russia, and Poland (the Northern Seven Years' War). From this Denmark emerged in 1570 as still the most powerful maritime power in the Baltic, but financially and economically exhausted.

Relations with Sweden

By the beginning of the 17th century Denmark's position was being seriously threatened by Sweden, and the young and ambitious King Christian IV persuaded his reluctant Council to attack Sweden with the ultimate objective of reviving the Kalmar Union. The resultant Kalmar War (1611-1613) brought little benefit, but the outbreak of the Thirty Years' War in Germany in 1618 seemed to offer a new opportunity to balance the rising power of Sweden under Gustav II Adolf (Gustavus Adolphus). King Christian countered the advancing Imperial Catholic forces but was defeated at the battle of Lutter in 1626 and had finally to withdraw from the struggle in 1629. Sweden saw the field open and answered Danish intrigues to limit its gains with an invasion from the south in 1643. Denmark was defeated and had to surrender territory at the peace in 1645. This series of defeats in foreign policy considerably weakened the power of the monarchy, and when Christian IV was succeeded by his second son as Frederik III in

1648 the new king's power was severely restrained. Within 10 years, however, the Crown had regained some room for maneuver.

When the Swedish King Charles X became embroiled in Poland in the mid-1650s, Denmark went to war with him in the hope of wreaking vengeance. Charles struck back, invading Denmark from the south. He managed to cross the ice between the Danish islands during a particularly severe winter and forced a peace in 1658 which deprived the Danish king of central Norway and all the lands he had previously held in Scania to the east of the Sound. Charles had less success when he attacked again: the Maritime Powers of Britain and the United Provinces of the Netherlands imposed a compromise peace in 1660, by which central Norway was returned to Denmark but the Sound was divided between Denmark and Sweden. Denmark's power in the Baltic was never regained. Ironically, however, the war greatly strengthened the power of the monarchy. The Estates assembly declared it hereditary and in 1661 it was also decreed absolute. So it remained until the middle of the 19th century.

Absolute Monarchy
The introduction of absolutism was followed by a large-scale reform of central and local government to give the crown greater control over its servants, but in an attempt to solve serious financial problems the Crown sold a large part of its land-holdings both in Denmark and Norway. Consequently for the first time the middle class gained a stake in the land market. Foreign policy remained hampered by the need for subsidies, but at the end of the 17th century alliances were concluded with Saxony and Russia in preparation for an attack on Sweden to destroy its Baltic supremacy. The Great Northern War began in 1700, but Denmark had to withdraw almost immediately under pressure from the Maritime Powers and a swift Swedish counter-attack across the Sound. Denmark did not re-enter the struggle until after the defeat of the Swedish King Charles XII in Russia in 1709 and got little more out of the peace settlement in 1720 than the acquisition of the whole of the duchy of Slesvig (German Schleswig).

The destruction of Swedish power meant that Russia was now the leading power in the Baltic, and the possession of Slesvig caused several crises (including the threat of war in 1762) in relations between Russia and Denmark, until an agreement (the *mageskifte*) was reached in 1773 by which Russia gave up claims to Gottorp lands in Holsten

(German Holstein) and recognized the Danish crown's full right to both Slesvig and Holsten, in return for a Dano-Russian defense agreement, which committed Denmark to counter Swedish expansion. Except for a brief war against Sweden in 1788, reluctantly undertaken to fulfill this treaty obligation to Russia, Denmark managed to remain at peace until the end of the 18th century.

Absolute government changed character in the course of the 18th century. While in the earlier part kings ruled as well as reigned, in the middle years royal power began to slip into the hands of powerful ministers like J.H.E. Bernstorff. This development led to a crisis in the early 1770s, when the German doctor J.F. Struensee managed to acquire such influence over the mentally sick King Christian VII that he was able to exercise a virtual dictatorship in the kingdom for some 18 months, during which he tried to turn Denmark into an ideal state in the spirit of the French Enlightenment. He was overthrown by conservative forces and sent to the scaffold, while the young English queen Caroline Matilde, whose lover he had been, had to leave the country.

The succeeding regime, led by Ove Høegh-Guldberg, undid most of Struensee's work, though Guldberg ruled much as his predecessor had done. He was overthrown in 1784 in a coup d'état by the young Crown Prince Frederick, aided by a number of reforming ministers led by A.P. Bernstorff. The new government now used royal power to institute a series of reforms which much improved the lot of the Danish peasant, who was freed in 1788 from the restrictions of movement which had been imposed 50 years earlier. Many peasants began to acquire their farms and the labor services owed to landlords by those who remained tenants were either regulated or wholly commuted.

In this way Denmark was cushioned against the social unrest which threatened many countries in the wake of the French Revolution. While Danish overseas trade suffered during the wars against Revolutionary France, Denmark managed to avoid being drawn into the conflict for some time. To protect its trade it joined the Russian-led Armed Neutrality League, but was compelled to leave this in 1801 by Britain's attack on the Danish fleet in Copenhagen harbor. As French armies drew closer to the Danish border, Britain became apprehensive that the large Danish fleet would fall into Napoleon's hand. In 1807 Britain demanded that the fleet be surrendered for the duration of the war. When the Danes refused, Copenhagen was besieged and bombarded, and the British seized the Danish fleet. Denmark immediately allied with France and declared war on Britain. The war proved disastrous: Danish overseas colonies were occupied and Denmark's trade brought to a halt. In 1814 a Swedish army under Marshal Bernadotte appeared on the southern borders of the kingdom and Denmark agreed to make peace. By the consequent Treaty of Kiel, Denmark surrendered control of Norway to the Swedish crown in exchange for Swedish Pomerania (exchanged soon after for the small duchy of Lauenburg south-east of Holsten).

Slesvig-Holsten

No sooner had the country begun to recover from the effects of the Napoleonic war, than it was faced with the problem of rising German nationalism to the south. The German-speaking population of Holsten demanded the union of the duchy and the half-Danish Slesvig with a united Germany. The "Schleswig-Holstein Question" was to figure in European politics for the remainder of the century and to embroil Britain, Russia, and other great powers, as well as Germany and Denmark. The British prime minister Lord Palmerston once commented that "only three people ever understood it: the Prince Consort, who was dead; a German professor, who had gone mad; and himself, but he had forgotten."

Many Danes responded to the German demands by proposing the separation of Holsten from Slesvig and the union of Slesvig with the kingdom (the "Ejder Policy"). The problem became closely linked to the demands of liberals in Denmark for an end to the absolute powers of the monarch and the grant of a constitution with a popularly elected parliament. King Frederik VI agreed in the mid-1830s to set up four elected provincial consultative assemblies, but he refused to grant a constitution because of the delicate position of the Duchies, torn between Danish and German allegiance.

The hand of his successor King Frederik VII was forced in 1848 by a revolt of the German-speakers of Slesvig-Holsten and a countering surge of Danish nationalism. In the face of this he agreed to surrender his absolute powers and called a popularly elected constituent assembly, which in 1849 agreed to a constitution with a two-chamber parliament (*Rigsdag*) chosen on a wide franchise of male voters. The king retained the power to appoint his ministers.

The revolt in the Duchies was crushed in the First Slesvig-Holsten War, but Denmark had to agree not to unite Slesvig to the kingdom. This left the problem of the relationship of the Duchies to the king-

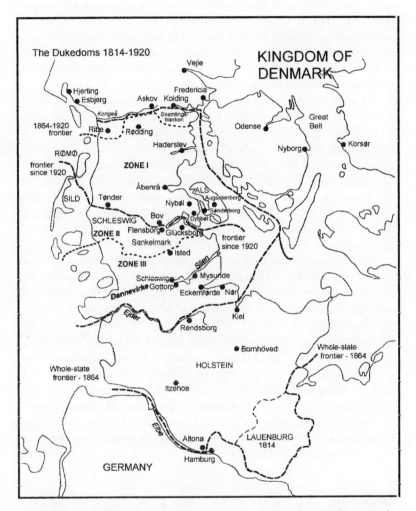

The Dukedoms 1814-1920

KINGDOM OF DENMARK

Vejle

Hjerting
Esbjerg

Askov   Kolding
Fredericia

Kongeå
Skamlings-
banken

1864-1920
frontier

Ribe
Rødding

Odense

Great
Belt

RØMØ
frontier
since 1920

Haderslev

Nyborg

Korsør

ZONE I

Åbenrå

ALS

SILD

Tønder

Nybøl
Augustenborg
Sønderborg

SCHLESWIG

Bov
Dybbøl

ZONE II
Flensborg
Glücksborg

Sankelmark

frontier
since 1920

Isted

ZONE III

Slien

Schleswig
Mysunde

Dannevirke
Gottorp

Eckernförde   Nør

Eider

Kiel

Rendsborg

Bornhöved

Whole-state
frontier - 1864

Whole-state
frontier - 1864

HOLSTEIN

Itzehoe

Elbe

Altona

LAUENBURG
1814

Hamburg

GERMANY

Southern Jutland, showing the duchies of Slesvig, Holsten and Lauenburg, the 'whole-state' frontier of 1864 (which incorporated the duchies into the Danish state), the frontier of 1864-1920 (following the disastrous loss of territory in the second Slesvig-Holsten War), the three zones of the 1920 referendum, and the line of the post-1920 frontier.

dom. Various forms of joint constitution were tried during the 1850s, but failed until in 1863 a constitution was approved which defied international agreements by uniting Slesvig and Denmark. Prussia and Austria replied by declaring and winning the Second Slesvig-Holsten War. At the peace settlement Denmark lost both Duchies, amounting to about one-third of the country's productive land.

The conservative forces who came to power seized the opportunity to introduce a new constitution in 1866 which changed the composition of the Upper House to make it less democratic. The rest of the century was taken up by a bitter struggle between governments of the Right, supported by the Crown and the Upper House, and a Lower House increasingly dominated by Liberals. A compromise between the more moderate elements on both sides was concluded in 1895, but the Right remained in office until 1901, when the overwhelming victory of the Liberals at the polls forced the king to agree to appoint a Liberal administration. This was the Change of System.

The later part of the 19th century witnessed considerable economic and social changes in Denmark. While the basis of the economy remained agrarian and the growing industrial sector was orientated strongly to agricultural produce and the home market, grain cultivation was unable to compete with cheap imports from the American prairies and gave way to animal husbandry as the most characteristic form of production. Small farmers organized themselves very successfully in cooperatives to meet the competition of the large landowners and produced high-quality butter and bacon for the British and German markets. After 1860 many Danes joined their fellow-Scandinavians in emigration to North America, but the impact of emigration was less in Denmark than in Norway or Sweden, due partly to the smoother growth of population.

Democracy
The last third of the 19th century was dominated by the growing challenge to the conservative regime, supported and held in office by the power of the monarch. The Left (Venstre) was a loose alliance of Liberals united by their demands for voting rights and for a government responsive to majority opinion in a democratic lower house, the Folketing. Venstre remained the name of the Danish Liberal Party, and should not be confused with the socialist left. They were countered by the Right (Højre), an alliance of land-owners, state officials and

merchants which took the name Conservative People's Party from 1916. Democracy came eventually with the Change of System in 1901. Very soon thereafter, the four main parties of the modern party system were in place: Social Democrats, Radical Liberals, Liberals, and Conservatives.

Denmark remained neutral during World War I and benefited from Germany's defeat by regaining control of southern Jutland and the northern part of Slesvig (*Sønderjylland*) after a referendum in 1920. The 1920s was a decade of political instability, as no single political party could gain sufficient support to win control for any length of time. But in 1929 a Social Democrat and Radical Liberal cabinet was formed under Thorvald Stauning which remained in office throughout the 1930s. It was soon faced with the economic crisis of the Great Depression, to which it reacted by concluding a pact with the Liberals (the Kanslergade Agreement of 1932) by which the Liberals agreed, in exchange for protection of agricultural prices, to support government controls over the economy and a social welfare program which laid the foundation of the welfare state.

Occupied in World War II
In spite of a non-aggression pact with Germany signed in June 1939, German forces occupied Denmark on 9 April 1940 simultaneously with an attack on Norway, to which Denmark was a vital stepping-stone. Little resistance was possible and surrender came within a few hours. The fiction was adopted that Denmark was being protected against an invasion by the Allies and consequently the Danish government was allowed to remain in office. Even the Danish armed forces were not disbanded, and an election was held in early 1943. At first there was little active opposition to the Occupation, but in time discontent with the demands of the occupying forces and with the government's apparently supine policy led to the growth of an active resistance movement. When the government did not quell this, the Germans issued an ultimatum in August 1943 which led the cabinet to resign and to a German takeover, although Danish civil servants continued to run the administration. In 1944 Copenhagen was briefly "besieged" by German troops, but in the face of the Danes' opposition, they had to give way to most of the demands of the Resistance.

Iceland had been granted a constitution in 1874, with home rule in 1904, and in 1918 independence under the Danish monarch. During

World War II the island was occupied first by British and then by US forces. In 1944 Iceland declared itself an independent republic, in fulfillment of well-developed intentions but to the disappointment of King Christian X. In 1948 the Faroe Islands were granted home rule. Immediately after the surrender of the German occupying forces in May 1945, a broad "national" government was formed under Vilhelm Buhl which included Resistance representatives. After elections on 30 October this was replaced by a cabinet led by the Liberal, Knud Kristensen. But two years later he had to resign after a vote of no confidence over his personal advocacy of a referendum to revise the frontier in Slesvig. Negotiations with Norway and Sweden to form a purely Nordic defense union broke down, and the minority Social Democrat cabinet took Denmark into the North Atlantic Treaty Organization (NATO) in 1949, a founder member with Norway and Iceland. Sweden and Finland remained neutral.

A Modern Constitution
Constitutional reform had already been under discussion before the war, and in 1953 a new constitution was approved in parliament and by referendum. Its main features were the abolition of the Upper House (*Landstinget*), the adoption of the office of Ombudsman and the recognition of parliamentary government, which Denmark had enjoyed in practice since the "Change of System" in 1901. Greenland was incorporated into the kingdom. The new single chamber *Folketinget* contained two representatives from the Faroes and, for the first time, two from Greenland, which had gained its own elected council in 1950. At the same time, the principle was enacted of female succession to the throne.

In spite of help through the Marshall Plan, Denmark's economy faced considerable difficulties throughout the 1950s, dependent as it was on exports to countries themselves recovering only slowly from the war, and politics was largely dominated by economic considerations. The Social Democrats remained by far the largest party but never had a majority and when in office cooperated with other parties, especially the Radical Liberals, to carry through their program. Building on plans laid down in the 1930s, they created one of the most comprehensive welfare states in the world, although at the cost of high taxation.

The economy improved in the 1960s and Denmark's dependence on agriculture lessened, while the industrial sector became as large and the service sector of the economy grew rapidly. The British market remained important, however, so Denmark followed the British lead in relations with the Common Market, and at the beginning of 1960 joined the European Free Trade Association (EFTA).

The student unrest of 1968 in France was prefigured in Denmark with opposition to the rather outdated courses on offer and the deferential attitude expected toward the highly formalized professorial regime in the universities. The outcome was a very liberal structure which gave students a right to one-third of the seats on all committees, with the other two-thirds divided between academic and administrative staff. The same currents of change in family and social patterns gave rise to attempts to establish alternative societies. Sometimes starting with summer camps, some for women only, and sometimes taking the form of occupations of empty buildings, one of the most durable attempts survived for over 25 years in a large vacated Copenhagen barracks, renamed Christiania.

Also starting among students, but soon extending more generally throughout society, were demands for women's equality with men. Voting rights for women had been granted in 1915, and the social reforms of the 1930s brought considerable advances for women. The demands of the 1960s women's movement were for economic equality, in terms of both equal pay and equal status at work and in society. Legislation followed in the 1970s, and by 1994 the proportion of women in the cabinet was 35 percent, a significant gain symbolic of their advance in other aspects also.

In the late 1960s the debate about democracy led to extensive reform of the structure and functions of local government around 1970. At both county (*amt*) and district (*kommune*) levels the number of units was greatly reduced by amalgamation. The *kommuner* became both the principal tax-gatherers and the main providers of social assistance, primary and secondary schools, libraries, primary health services, roads and water supplies, while the counties (*amter*) were responsible for hospitals, further education, major roads, and the like.

Nordic Council and European Community

In 1952 the Danish prime minister, Hans Hedtoft, inaugurated the first meeting of the Nordic Council. This move came in reaction to and soon after the disappointment of failed negotiations to form a Nordic defence alliance which would have included Denmark, Norway, and Sweden but was preempted by the formation of the North Atlantic Treaty Organization (NATO) and the decisions by Denmark and Norway to join it. The Nordic Council brings together parliamentarians from the five Nordic countries of Denmark, Finland, Iceland, Norway, and Sweden and the territories of the Faroe Islands, Greenland, and the Åland Islands. Later a Nordic Council of Ministers and a secretariat were added. Entirely intergovernmental in its activities and with no federal intentions, this organization has done much to develop a web of integrative links between the member countries. Especially in the spheres of education, culture, and research it has encouraged the growth of inter-Nordic links and fostered cooperative activities. By harmonizing legal, commercial, and welfare regulations it has greatly simplified trade and population movements within the area. Indeed Turner and Nordquist (1982) termed it *The Other European Community*.

In 1972, after a referendum resulted in a large YES majority for membership of the European Community (EC), Denmark joined, as did Britain and Ireland. Denmark, like Britain, has been reluctant to see further integration beyond the Economic Community which it joined or toward "ever closer union." The EC issue cut across the Social Democratic Party, while the taxation necessary to pay for the highly developed welfare provision increased a sense of frustration with the state and its officials. The oil-price-induced recession added further to voters' worries. At the 1973 "earthquake" parliamentary election the party system fragmented. Old minor parties revived and three new parties entered the Folketing; one of these, the populist Progress Party formed by the tax lawyer Mogens Glistrup, won 16 percent of the vote and overnight became the second-largest party in a Folketing in which suddenly 11 parties were represented, while all the established parties lost support.

The period 1973-82 saw a succession of narrowly based governments, briefly under the Liberal Poul Hartling and in 1975-82 led by the Social Democrat Anker Jørgensen. These used the well-established pattern of consensus in Danish politics to draw parliamentary support from the established parties and from the new Center Democrats and Christian People's Party for centrist policies which limited the growth of the tax burden while preserving the main elements of welfare provision.

Anker Jørgensen ran out of ideas to deal with the country's economic difficulties and was succeeded in 1982 by Poul Schlüter, the first Conservative prime minister since 1901, in close partnership with the Liberals and with cabinet support from the small parties of the center. In just over a decade of office, the Schlüter cabinets presided over a strengthening economy. Although attracted by the rhetoric of Ronald Reagan's economic nostrums and Margaret Thatcher's commitment to "roll back the state," Schlüter's ministers were constrained by the need to work together in coalition and by the lack of a parliamentary majority, which required them to seek Radical Liberal and sometimes Social Democratic support for their economic and social policies. These constraints were made abundantly clear in over one hundred parliamentary defeats on European Community, NATO, and environmental issues at the hands of a center-left majority which included the Radical Liberals, the Social Democrats, and the Socialist People's Party.

Schlüter's cabinet resigned at the start of 1993 on charges of maladministration arising from the long-running Tamil Affair and was succeeded by Poul Nyrup Rasmussen at the head of a Social Democrat plus Radical Liberal cabinet which at first also included the Center Democrats and the Christian People's Party, reviving the partnership of the 1930s and 1950s and reasserting the importance of social democracy in Danish politics. In its last year, the Schlüter government had seen the Maastricht Treaty of European Union narrowly defeated by Danish referendum voters. Within five months of taking office, and helped by agreement on a national compromise spanning all parties except the extremes of left and right and by acceptance of four Danish derogations at the Edinburgh Council of Ministers in December 1992, the Nyrup Rasmussen government saw the Danish electorate endorse the Treaty by a comfortable majority at a second referendum.

The Modern Danish Economy

Lacking resources of raw materials (at least until the exploitation of North Sea gas since the 1970s), the Danish economy was historically dependent on its important agricultural sector. Until 1880 this employed over half the working population, and over 30 percent until 1930. By 1960 the proportion had fallen to 19 percent, and decreased further to 10.6 percent in 1970 and 7.7 percent in 1981. Manufacturing has employed a third or more of the workforce since 1940.

Because of the belief by Danish politicians that it would be difficult or impossible to find international finance for a deficit on the balance of payments, Danish economic growth during 1950-57 was below the Organization for Economic Cooperation and Development (OECD) average (as it was also in Belgium and the United Kingdom), and by the end of the period foreign net debt had been almost eliminated. Thereafter there was full employment, and economic growth was remarkably strong, averaging 4.4 percent, until the first oil-price crisis of 1973-74. By contrast, during 1973-82 the average annual growth rate was only 1.5 percent, insufficient to offset the growth in the labor force. With the recession after the second oil-price shock of 1979-80 the economy deteriorated: unemployment approached 10 percent of the workforce; the balance of payments deficit on current account remained high; the budget deficit grew alarmingly.

In 1982 the new Schlüter government announced a policy of reconstruction with the following elements: first, an incomes policy which would no longer include automatic indexation of wages; second, a tighter fiscal policy, to be achieved partly by trimming public-sector budgets and partly by taxing pension savings; third, a firm exchange-rate policy which rejected the previous pattern of recurrent devaluations and aimed to improve business confidence, and so reduce inflationary expectations and interest rates. The latter was accompanied by relaxation of foreign exchange controls which made it easier for Danes to buy securities abroad and foreigners to buy Danish assets. Helped by falling rates of inflation and interest internationally, lower oil prices and an appreciating dollar, the Danish economic recovery in 1983-86 was remarkably strong. Economic growth averaged 3.4 percent per year and the current account improved in 1983 and 1984 as a result of improved price-competitiveness in previous years. Business confidence also improved: together with falling interest rates and improved profits. This led to a sharp rise in private-sector investments from the end of 1983. Employment also improved, mainly in the private sector, and unemployment fell to 8.1 percent in 1986.

The strong economy continued into the 1990s, with expansion of gross domestic product at about 3 percent per year until late 1995, when it slowed as international growth weakened. Economic policies aimed at reducing structural unemployment and placing public finances on a sound long-term basis achieved a large measure of success. One of the four Danish opt-outs from the terms of the Maastricht Treaty of European Union was from the obligation to join the Economic and Monetary Union (EMU), in order to retain some control of national economic policy, but for most of the 1990s Denmark met the EMU criteria for a well-managed economy.

In the first five years, 1993-97, of Nyrup Rasmussen governments, Danish private consumption grew by 18 percent. About 14 percent of this arose from growth of total disposable real income and the remainder from decreased private savings from a previously very high level. Public sector consumption was 12-13 percent higher, partly due to growth in the number of day-care institutions. The gross national product grew by about 15 percent but the tax burden did not fall. Increased production and lower interest rates meant that the average Dane saw a distinctly improved standard of living, while the number of people in work grew by 120,000 since 1992. Of these, 85,000 were in the private sector and 35,000 were in the public sector. Net exports fell each year except 1996, but competitiveness remained largely constant. As a result there was a sharp fall in the balance of payments surplus from 24.5 billion Dkr in 1992 down to 4.1 bn Dkr in the 12 months to 1 November 1997, a worsening of 20 bn Dkr over five years. (*See* Appendix 6: Economic Data.)

The Nyrup Rasmussen government and the nonsocialist opposition agreed that the tax burden should not increase further, and indeed should be reduced, but they disagreed about how quickly to do so. They also agreed not to push ever more people out of the labor market and into dependency on transfer benefits, but disagreed on how to do this. The tax burden depends partly on the level of public services and partly on the number of people on transfer benefits. Public services improved markedly in 1993-97. The government pointed to 130,000 new child-care places for 0- to 9-year-olds, taking the total to c. 480,000. Almost 10,000 more elderly people had been housed, in addition to the 60,000 already housed. Total spending on hospitals in fixed prices grew in the five years by 13 percent to c. 36.6 billion Dkr in 1998. The problem was to ensure that the municipalities that are responsible for these services did not simply increase spending and taxes without also seeking savings, as they had been compelled to do in 1985-89. The rapid growth of municipal spending in 1995-97 had surprised the government. Employment in the public services increased. This meant that taxes rose, especially on incomes and employment, which limited demand for labour, especially in services and in firms that compete abroad.

Nyrup Rasmussen called an election in March 1998, six months before the end of the Folketing term and, with the inclusion of the Faroes and Greenland representatives in the calculation, emerged with a one-seat majority in the Folketing. His coalition of Social Democrats with Radical Liberals continued in office, relying on the socialist block (the Socialist People's Party and the Red-Green Unity List) for parliamentary support, but also expecting support from the two small parties of the center, the Center Democrats and the Christian People's Party. The Liberals held their ground but the Conservatives lost 11 of their 27 seats. The Danish People's Party won 13 seats in the first election it had contested, on a campaign against *foreigners* (refugees and immigrants) and against *the foreign* (the European Union) which had attracted most of the vote which previously went to the Progress Party. (*See* Appendix 4: Party Shares of Votes, 1890-1998.) Following the election, the leaders of the Liberal and Conservative parties both resigned, the Liberal because he had led his party for 14 years, and the recently chosen Conservative because his party had lost heavily. The responsible opposition had lost leadership and coherence. The Nyrup Rasmussen Social Democratic and Radical Liberal government was reshuffled and continued in office with socialist support but with the alternative of support from the center-right and so with more room to maneuver.

The Faroe Islands Economy
Fishing is the mainstay of the Faroes economy. In the 1980s the Faroe Islands banks lent generously and fishermen invested heavily in boats and equipment, while the government invested heavily in harbors, roads, and tunnels. Purchases of consumer goods also increased rapidly. Investment reached almost 50 percent of gross national product and the balance of payments deficit reached over 20 percent of GNP. These expansionary conditions ended in the late 1980s. In 1988-93

GNP fell 30 percent in real terms as a consequence of the earlier economic policy. The Faroes government reduced subsidies, while over-fishing brought a drop in fish landings and exports. The result was deep recession. Within a few months in 1992-93, unemployment reached 25 percent. In a society of 47,000 people, there were over 1,000 forced house-sales, and a net 10 percent of the population emigrated, mainly to Denmark. Average income had been slightly higher than in Denmark, but it fell to under 70 percent. The annual Danish subsidy to the Faroese economy in the mid-1990s was c. 15-20 percent of the Faroes' GNP.

Before long the Faroese banks were looking to the Danish government for support to guarantee their viability. Den Danske Bank, the largest of the Danish banks, took a minority share-holding in Sjóvinu-bankin, which the Faroes home-government had reconstructed in 1992 and then held a majority share-holding. In return, through the Finance Fund of 1992 the Faroes government became a major shareholder in Føroya Banki, of which until then the largest shareholder had been Den Danske Bank. Soon afterward the Faroes home-government found major liquidity problems with Føroya Banki. By October 1993, just seven months after the exchange deal, the Faroes government had to take up loans of over 1.8 billion kroner in Denmark for the Finance Fund to keep the two banks afloat. One third of this was to cover the loss in Føroya Banki. The two banks were merged. The Faroes government contributed a total of almost 3 billion kroner. Together with its coverage of guarantees on investment loan losses, it owed the Danish state 6 billion Dkr, plus interest at market rates.

The implications for the Faroese people were dire. They soon came to believe, mistakenly, that the Danish government had pushed the Faroes government into taking over Føroya Banki without telling them (what Faroes people believed Danish ministers and civil servants knew) that Føroya Banki was insolvent. When a Danish newspaper in Spring 1995 published details of the bank transfer, the Danish Folketing started an investigation, though not the judicial inquiry that the Faroese government had unanimously called for.

The issue continued to reverberate in Danish politics as questions were asked about how much prime ministers Poul Schlüter and Poul Nyrup Rasmussen had known in advance about the deal with Den Danske Bank. The prime minister is responsible for such aspects of policy in the Faroes and Greenland as are not transferred to the home-governments in the respective territories. Just as the Tamil Case brought down the Schlüter government at the beginning of 1993, the Faroes bank case threatened confidence in the Nyrup Rasmussen government. It survived, but Nyrup Rasmussen conceded that his government had been ill-informed in its decisions, and that the Faroese people were due "suitable compensation." With improved fish catches, by 1998 the Faroe Islands' economy had recovered significantly and unemployment was down to 10 percent, although there were still worries about fish stocks. The recovery was more soundly based because it did not rely on borrowing against government guarantees.

The Greenland Economy

Greenland depends very heavily on fishing. Frozen shrimps are its largest export. With fish fillets, shellfish and other fish products, these constitute over 95 percent of the country's exports. Previously there was some mineral export but this ceased in 1991. Most household goods are imported, as are intermediate goods (part-processed), and come from Denmark mainly, but in smaller quantities from the UK, Japan, and other countries. There has been a persistent balance of trade deficit during 1986-96, sometimes amounting to as much as 40 percent of exports, except in 1989 and 1990 when there were small surpluses.

The development of the GNP (corrected for inflation) has been very uneven since 1980. In 1980-87 there was significant growth, with a figure over 12 percent in 1987. The growth rate fell sharply from 1988 to almost 10 percent shrinkage in 1990 and remained negative until 1993, producing an absolute fall in GNP. There was positive growth of 5 percent in 1994 and 3 percent in 1995. Nevertheless, the economic setback was reflected in subsequent bankruptcies, with a peak of 93 in 1994 and 47 in 1995. Price levels are about 18 percent higher in Greenland than in Denmark. Taking this into account, GNP and, therefore, also the value of production per head is over 40 percent lower in Greenland than in Denmark.

The whole economy of Greenland is small and is easily affected by individual enterprises. Thus the accounts of 1993 to 1994 reflect the reorganization of TELE Attaveqaatit to the limited company Tele Greenland A/S. Its contribution to the GNP was 66 million kroner in 1993 and 215 million kroner in 1994, almost all the difference attributable to a changed accounting basis.

Income tax was introduced in 1975 and from 1979 an additional 'land tax' (landsskat) is payable by all residents in Greenland. There is no value-added tax, but import tax and vehicle tax are levied. There is a tax based on turnover on shrimps caught but not landed for processing in Greenland. The home-rule government took over taxing responsibility in 1980. The tax burden (total taxes as a percentage of GNP) rose from 17 percent in 1980 to 33 percent in 1993. This compares to 48 percent in Denmark in 1992. Greenland depends on a significant annual subsidy from Denmark, estimated for 1997 at 2.6 billion kroner.

In proposing its 1997 budget, Greenland's home-rule government set out its major objectives as: increased freedom of trade, via tight management of expenditure and reduction of government debt; no increase in the tax-burden on commerce; structural improvements to reduce costs and prices; and greater transparency for social infrastructure costs. This implied a move from a centrally directed economy to greater reliance on market forces. It was hoped that the economy would become less reliant on fishing, with the development of the economy producing growth of incomes and a reduction of unemployment from 6 percent to 3 percent over the next ten years.

THE DICTIONARY

-A-

ABEL (1218-1252). King of Denmark 1250-1252. The second son of King **Valdemar II**, he became duke of Slesvig in 1232 and in 1237 was married to Mechtild, daughter of count Adolf IV of Holsten. Soon after his father's death in 1241, Abel fell out with his elder brother King **Erik IV**. Civil war followed. The two brothers became temporarily reconciled in 1244 and even planned a joint crusade in Estonia, but in 1246 fell out again when Erik planned to invade Holsten. Abel took the part of his relatives there. Abel's invasion of the kingdom was repulsed, however, and a fresh reconciliation followed. Fighting broke out again in 1250. Abel was defeated, but on a visit to the king in Slesvig, he had Erik seized and murdered. Swearing his innocence, Abel was elected king and crowned in Lund. During a reign which was the shortest recorded for any Danish king, Abel proved himself a capable ruler who maintained good relations with his southern neighbors but came into conflict with both Norway and Sweden. He died fighting the Frisians, who had refused to pay the tax he demanded of them. He was buried in Slesvig. His sons Erik and Valdemar died young. SPO

ABELL, KJELD (1901-1961). Author. Born in Ribe, he graduated *cand. polit.* in 1927, then worked in Paris and London as a painter and decorator until 1934. In *Melodien, der blev væk* (1935, The Lost Tune) he castigates the petit bourgeoisie. Sensing the fascist threat, his play *Anna Sophie Hedvig* (1939) acclaims the active and if necessary violent fight against injustice. From 1949 his theme became the contrasts of loneliness and fellowship, as in his play *Vetsera blomstrer ikke for enhver* (1950, Vetsera Doesn't Flower for Everyone), abandoning the realistic style for a more imaginative one. AHT

ABILDGAARD, NIKOLAJ A. (1743-1809). Painter. Born in Copenhagen, the son of a draughtsman, he entered the **Academy of Arts** in 1764, spent 1772-77 in Rome on a stipend, and returned to become a professor in the Academy in 1778. He served as its Director in 1789-91 and from 1801 until his death. One of the finest graphic artists of his time, he was the leading exponent in Denmark of early neoclassical style and many of his themes were taken from the Classical world. Abildgaard was also strongly influenced by the art of the Italian Renaissance and favored literary themes (e.g., from Norse mythology and Shakespeare) and historical subjects. The most outstanding of the latter were the murals depicting incidents in the history of the house of Oldenborg in the Knights Hall in **Christiansborg Palace** which he painted in 1778-91. All but three of these were destroyed in the fire of 1794 but are known from surviving sketches. Abildgaard was also a designer of interiors and furniture and was responsible for several of the rooms in **Amalienborg Palace**, and for the Column of Liberty (*Frihedsstøtten*) in Copenhagen to celebrate the emancipation of the Danish peasants in 1788. The base of Norwegian marble supports an obelisk of Bornholm sandstone and allegorical figures of Loyalty, Patriotism, Courage and Husbandry. The great painter Christoffer **Eckersberg** was one of his pupils. SPO

ABSALON (c.1128-1201). Bishop of **Roskilde** 1158-1191 and Archbishop of Lund 1178-1201. Born in Fjenneslev in mid-Zealand, the son of the great nobleman Asser Rig and member of the powerful Zealand family of Hvide, as a child he was a companion of the later King **Valdemar I**. After studying at the University of Paris, in 1158 he was elected bishop of Roskilde. During the 1160s he assisted King Valdemar in his ruthless crusades against the heathen Wends, which ended in 1169 with the capture of their stronghold on Rügen, their conversion to Christianity, and their submission to the Danish Crown. On land by the **Sound** (Øresundet) to his bishopric, Absalon had the fort of Havn constructed in 1167, around which developed the city of **Copenhagen**. Royal favor gained him the archbishopric, which he was allowed by papal dispensation to hold together with his bishopric. In 1180 and 1182 he put down peasant uprisings in Scania caused by his harsh enforcement of the bishop's tithe. During the reign of Valdemar's successor, King **Knud IV**, he appears to have acted as virtual regent. In 1184 he led the forces which compelled Boguslav of Pomerania to swear allegiance to the Danish crown and went on to force the Mecklenburg princes to do the same. Absalon was buried in the church of the family monastery of Sorø, which he had richly endowed. He claimed to have inspired both Svend Aggesen and **Saxo Grammaticus** to write their Danish histories. SPO. *See also* **Valdemar II.**

ABSOLUTE MONARCHY or **ABSOLUTISM,** a system of government under which the monarch reigns without reference to a council or advisers or any kind of popular assembly. This system prevailed in Denmark during 1661-1848. After defeat by Sweden in the war of 1657-60, King **Frederik III** secured the support of the **Estates** of Clergy and Burghers in declaring the monarchy hereditary rather than elective. This rid him of the restrictions placed on him by the nobility in his **Accession Charter**. In 1661, after the Diet had dispersed, the monarchy was declared absolute and no further meeting of the Estates was called. The sovereign's new powers and the order of succession to the throne were elaborated in the **King's Law** of 1665. Although **Christian V, Frederik IV,** and **Christian VI** exercised their powers personally, under **Frederik V** and **Christian VII** in the later 18th century they were wielded by powerful ministers such as the **Bernstorffs** and **Struensee** rather than by the king himself, while **King Christian VII** was not capable of conducting the government because of mental illness. After the death of **A.P. Bernstorff** in 1797, crown prince Frederik assumed more and more personal responsibility and, after his accession as King **Frederik VI** in 1808, he used the war situation to dispense with his council, but. had to recall it with the return of peace. In 1831, in face of a rising tide of liberalism, he agreed to establish elected provincial **Consultative Assemblies** in the Kingdom and the Duchies. As a result of the upheavals in Germany, **Frederik VII** finally declared himself a constitutional monarch on 21 March 1848, with powers defined in the constitution of 1849. SPO. *See also* **Government, Monarchy.**

ACADEMY OF ART, ROYAL DANISH. Originally a private society of artists, it was granted royal patronage in 1754 by King Frederik V as Det kongelige Skildre- Bildhugger- og Bygningsakademi (Royal Academy of Painting, Sculpture and Architecture) and granted quarters in **Charlottenborg Palace** in Copenhagen where it remains. In 1814 it was renamed the Royal Academy of Fine Arts (Det Kongelige Akademi for de Skønne Kunster, or Kunstakademiet). Its Council of 36 members is responsible for advising the government on artistic matters and for supervising the training of artists in the Academy's schools of painting, sculpture, and architecture. A new charter of 1959 established a separate administration for the schools with a rector and council. SPO.

ACCESSION CHARTER (*Håndfæstning*), the charter limiting the powers of the monarch which had to be agreed to by every king from **Erik V** in 1282 until the institution of **absolutism** in 1661, as a condition of his election to the throne by the noble council (**danehof**). Like the English Magna Carta (with which it is often compared), it was mainly concerned with the privileges of the nobility, such as their monopoly of high office and exemption from taxation, but (again like Magna Carta), it originally laid down the principle that no one should be imprisoned without due process of law and originally promised that a meeting of the danehof should be held every year. The Charter agreed to by King **Christian III** in 1536 limited the right of habeas corpus to the nobility, but omitted their right of rebellion, which had been included in the Charter since the accession of King **Hans** in 1483. The last Charter was that agreed to by King **Frederik III** in 1648. It was also the most stringent, allowing the king to do little without the consent of the council. SPO

ADELER, CORT (1622-1675). A Norwegian-born naval officer, he became a Danish *generaladmiral* (the second-highest naval rank) after many years of service in the Dutch and Venetian fleets. He expanded the fleet and engaged in overseas trade. He was ennobled in 1666 and became director of the newly established **East India Company** in 1670. When the war in **Scania** started in 1675 he led the entire Danish fleet against Sweden. AHT

ADLER, HANNA (1859-1947). Teacher. The daughter of a wholesaler, in 1892 she was one of the first two women to graduate *cand. mag.* in physics. Following a visit to the USA, in 1893 she founded the first Danish coeducational school, with classics and modern streams. The school has been administered by **Copenhagen** city council since 1918, with the name Sortedam Gymnasium. AHT

AFRICA, DANISH POSSESSIONS IN. A Danish-Africa Company for trade with the Guinea coast was first set up by the Dutch merchant Jon de Willum in 1625. In 1658 merchants from the town of Glückstadt on the Elbe and from **Copenhagen** were granted a monopoly of African trade by **Frederik III**, provided that they administered the Swedish fort of Carolusborg on the Gold Coast (now Ghana), which the Danish King had acquired the previous year. They built the forts of Frederiksborg (1659) and Christiansborg (1661) as their trading posts. Frederiksborg was acquired by Britain in 1685 after the governor had failed to repay the loan for which it was security. Christiansborg became the headquarters of a lucrative trade in slaves destined for sugar plantations in the **Danish West Indies**.

West African trade was opened to all Danish subjects in 1735 and Fredensborg (1736) and Augustaborg (1787) were added. In 1754 the West Indies-Guinea Company was dissolved and its assets taken over by the Crown. A new company was founded in 1765, but 10 years later it also went bankrupt. Governor Kiøge occupied the Dutch possessions on the nearby coast during the American War of Independence and successfully defied Dutch efforts to regain them when peace returned. He subdued the coastal tribes east of the Volta river and built the forts of Prinsensten (1784) and Kongensten (1783) to control them. When the slave trade was abolished in 1803, the economic value of Denmark's African possessions rapidly declined and in 1818 the Danish crown tried to sell them to the United States as a home for freed slaves. In 1849 they were finally sold for £10,000 to Britain, which Denmark had assisted in the Ashanti Wars. SPO, AHT. *See also* **Carstensen, Edward.**

AGGERSBORG see TRELLEBORG FORTS

AGRARIANS see FARMERS' PARTY

AGRICULTURAL ASSOCIATION (Landbrugernes Sammenslutning, LS) was a right-wing movement of farmers set up in Jutland in 1931 to demand State assistance during the agricultural crisis. Policy was discussed at annual Farmers Meetings. It was responsible for organizing the **Farmers' Protest** in 1935. Its demands were voiced in parliament after 1936 by the **Farmers' Party.** In 1940 it concluded a pact with the National Socialists (Nazis) and adopted a pro-German stance during the Occupation, which lost it many members. Its chairman, **Knud Bach**, was sentenced in 1947 to five years in prison for collaboration. Attempts to revive it after the war met with little success. SPO

AGRICULTURAL COUNCIL, THE, (Landbrugsrådet), was founded in 1919 to coordinate the work of the Federation of Danish Agricultural Societies and the Federation of Danish **Cooperative** Societies, and from 1939 also the specialist agricultural export organizations. During 1932-39 the Danish Smallholders Associations took the place of the Agricultural Societies. The Associations again became members in 1976. As the collective voice of Danish **agriculture**, it represents Danish agriculture in Europe and abroad and is a major influence on national agricultural policy. SPO

AGRICULTURAL PRODUCER COOPERATIVES see COOPERATIVE MOVEMENT

AGRICULTURAL REVOLUTION. Traditional peasant agricultural practices began to change in the later 18th century with the freeing of the peasantry from ties to the landowners and the extension of **enclosure.** These changes helped to create a class of independent small farmers willing to innovate. In the mid-19th century, grain production for the international market boomed, but imports of Russian and American grain after 1870 brought a slump in prices and a change to animal produce, in particular to butter and bacon for the British market. To meet competition from the large landowners, the smaller producers organized in the cooperatives which have remained characteristic of the Danish farming industry ever since. SPO. *See also* **Cooperative Movement** and contrast **Industrialization**.

AGRICULTURE. In the absence of other natural resources, Denmark has always been heavily dependent on the produce of its soil. In 1901, 41 per cent of employment was in agriculture. This proportion was 21 per cent in 1950, 13 per cent in 1950, 8 per cent in 1970, and 5 per cent in 1993. In the 16th century the most important agricultural export was cattle from **Jutland**, fattened on noble estates before being shipped to the Netherlands and northern Germany. This declined in the 17th century, when a period of depression began which lasted into the early 18th century. Cattle were sorely affected by plague in the middle decades of the century, but at the same time a rise in grain prices then revived interest in agriculture and encouraged the introduction of new techniques, especially on the larger estates. Peasant agriculture, which had changed little since the Middle Ages, was encouraged by the growth of peasant proprietorship and the spread of **enclosures** from the late 18th century.

After a difficult period during and after the **Napoleonic Wars**, Danish grain-growing enjoyed a boom in the middle years of the 19th century, but the fall in grain prices as a result of the imports into western Europe of larger and larger quantities of American and Russian wheat in the 1860s began a shift to animal husbandry. Smaller farmers began to organize in **cooperatives** to produce bacon, butter, and dairy produce, especially for the British market, and Denmark became a net importer of fodder cereals. There were 185,000 farms in 1951, but by 1993 consolidations had reduced the total to 74,000, mostly family run and with a median size of 20-30 hectares. SPO, AHT. *See also* **Cooperative Movement**.

AHLEFELT, FREDERIK (1623-1686). Grand Chancellor (*storkansler*). The son of a Count, at first he entered the service of the state in the duchies of **Slesvig-Holsten**. He was regent (*statholder*) in Copenhagen 1661-63 and then in the duchies . After **Christian V** became king in 1670, with **U.F. Gyldenløve** and P. Schumacher (**Griffenfeld**), he was among the leaders of Denmark. After their fall from power in 1676 he was appointed grand chancellor, in charge of policy both at home and abroad. In shifting alliances with France and other powers he sought to isolate the duke of Gottorp, who favored Sweden. AHT

AIR FORCE see DEFENSE

AIRLINES see SCANDINAVIAN AIRLINES SYSTEM

AKTUELT, until 1959 *Social-Demokraten*, then *Det Frie Aktuelt*. The paper was first published in 1871. Its sharply critical commentary on the society did much to establish both the **trade union** movement and the **Social Democratic** political party. It continues to be owned by the trade union movement, but in 1987 its freedom and independence were established in the hands of the editor in chief. In 1998 it moved to a new building at Kalvebod Brygge 35-37, Copenhagen. AHT. *See also* **Press**.

AKULLIIT PARTIIA is a small Greenlandic center party, formed in 1991 and led by Bjarne Kreutzmann, which aims to privatize the large enterprises owned by the Greenlandic home-rule authority. AHT. *See also* **Greenland**.

ALBERTI, PETER ADLER (1851-1932). Liberal politician. He was the son of Christian Carl Alberti (1814-90) who founded the Zealand Farmers Savings Bank in 1856. He graduated *cand. jur.* in 1873 and qualified as a supreme court advocate in 1881. He was vice chairman (1875-84) and chairman (1890-1908) of the Savings Bank. He was elected to the **Folketing** in 1892 as a Moderate Liberal, having defeated the radical **Viggo Hørup**. As minister of justice in Liberal cabinets 1901-08 Alberti introduced corporal punishment for assault and sexual offenses, against strong radical opposition. In July 1908, amid rumors of financial irregularities, he left the government. In September he confessed to fraud in the administration of the savings bank and of the Butter Export Association amounting to 15 million kroner and was sentenced to eight years' imprisonment in 1910. **J.C. Christensen**, who had defended Alberti in office, resigned from the premiership, and his **Liberal Reform Party** lost heavily in the election of 1909 as a result of the scandal. An attempt failed to impeach Christensen for not investigating Alberti's affairs. SPO, AHT

ÅLBORG (spelled **AALBORG** until 1947) is Denmark's fourth-largest city and second-largest port and an important industrial center (ship-building, cement, distilling, tobacco, and textiles) with a population of 157,270 (1993). Situated on the south side of the Limfjord in northern **Jutland**, it is known to have existed as a town by the end of the Viking period and was granted a charter in 1342. King **Hans** was born and died there. During the **Count's War** in the early 16th century, it sided with Count Christoffer and was defended on his behalf by the adventurer "Skipper" Clement, who used it as a base to raid along both sides of the Limfjord. For this the town was severely punished by the victorious forces of King **Christian III** led by Johan Rantzau, who had many of the defenders killed and Clement executed. By the 17th century Ålborg was again flourishing as a center for the herring trade, and it remained Jutland's largest town and the second largest in Denmark until overtaken by **Århus** in the mid-19th century.

The magnificent six-story house of one of its merchants, Jens Bang from 1623-1624 still stands as a memorial to its prosperity; restored in 1920, it now contains a pharmacy on the ground floor. The cathedral, dedicated to the English St. Botolph, is from the late 15th century but with remains of the earlier Romanesque building and much restored and rebuilt. The town's castle of *Ålborghus* was restored in 1539 and a northern wing added in 1633. The 15th-century Monastery of the Holy Spirit (*Helligåndsklosteret*) still serves as a home for the elderly. The city is linked by a road bridge, built in 1933, a railway bridge, and a tunnel to the large industrial complex of Nørresundby (population 37,000) on the north side of Limfjord with its 13th-century church and the prehistoric cemetery of Lindholm Høje. SPO

ALLEN, CARL FERDINAND (1811-1871). Historian. The son of a migrant Scottish silver-plater, he graduated *cand. theol.* in 1836. He wrote *Håndbog i fædrelandets historie* (1840) as a history of Denmark from a national-liberal perspective. The incomplete *De tre nordiske Rigers Historie 1497-1536* in 5 volumes (1864-72, History of the Three Nordic Kingdoms) ends at 1527 but is a comprehensive account of **Christian II**'s reign. AHT. *See also* **Historiography**.

AMALIENBORG PALACE in **Copenhagen** has been the official residence of the Danish royal family since 1794. Designed by Nikolaj **Eigtved** in Rococo style as four identical noblemen's residences around a central square in the new Frederikstad, they were completed in 1749-60 and named after an earlier building on the site that was destroyed by fire in 1689. An equestrian statue of **Frederik V** by J.F.J. Saly was placed in the square. The colonnade in neoclassical style uniting two of the buildings was constructed in 1794 to designs by C.F. Harsdorff. The palace became a royal residence after **Christiansborg** was destroyed by fire. Two of the palaces are occupied by the royal family, and the Schack Palace to the south is Queen **Margrethe II**'s residence. The other two are used for state and official functions. SPO AHT. *See also* **Copenhagen**.

ANCHER, ANNA (1859-1935). Painter. Her childhood home in **Skagen**, Brøndum's Hotel, became the center for the leading painters of the 1870s. The surroundings and the local fishing activity inspired her initially naturalistic and later coloristic paintings. AHT. *See also* **Skagen School**.

ANCHER, MICHAEL (1849-1927). Painter. Born in **Bornholm**, he studied at the Academy in Copenhagen then lived for the rest of his life in **Skagen**. Local fishing and his wife Anna's family provided the motifs for pictures of daily life and more personal family portraits. AHT

ANDERSEN, ALSING EMANUEL (1893-1962). He was the politician son of Frederik Alsing (1862-1936), a shoemaker who became a highly influential trade unionist, a founder of the Social Democrat (SD) Federation, a member of Copenhagen City Council from 1901, its chairman of Finance 1914-1933, and who worked closely with Thorvald **Stauning**. Alsing graduated *cand. mag.* in languages in 1917. Stauning appointed him Secretary of the SD Federation in

1917, Secretary of the SD parliamentary group in 1918, and its chair 1932-35. A member of the **Folketing** from 1929 until his death, his administrative ability brought extensive influence. A frequent representative at international labor conferences, he was a member of the Socialist Workers' International executive 1929-35, warned of the Nazi danger, and welcomed immigrants. In the 1920s he expounded the traditionally neutral SD stance on foreign policy, but in the 1930s worked closely with Stauning to develop a new defense policy leading to the 1935 Congress resolution to end unilateral disarmament. This was not enough to deter the German invasion of 9 April 1940, for which as defense minister (1935-40) he had to answer. He briefly re-entered the cabinet in 1942 as **V. Buhl's** finance minister.

Throughout the 1940-45 German occupation his first priority was survival of the SD party organization as an independent means of defense, whatever the outcome of the war, and his 1943 party newsletter defended collaboration and characterized the Resistance as chauvinist and communist. As a contact with the Freedom Council he contributed to its postwar program, *Fremtidens Danmark* (Future Denmark) (*see* **J.O. Krag**). Appointed interior minister in 1947, he resigned after 10 days under Conservative, Liberal, and Communist pressure regarding his role in 1940, but calls for his impeachment were not supported by the parliamentary investigation which finally reported in 1955. He used his linguistic talents for international cooperation: in 1929-35 on the SD Labor International executive, and in 1948-57 in the Danish United Nations delegation. His son Niels Alsing Andersen (1920-) became the member of Copenhagen City Council responsible for hospitals in 1974. AHT

ANDERSEN, CARL CHRISTIAN (1849-1932). Politician. Born in Copenhagen, he completed his apprenticeship as cabinet-maker in 1868 and joined the cabinetmaker's section of the new Internationale in 1871. As a co-founder of the Cabinet and Chairmaker's Trade Union in 1872 and chairman 1873-84, he recruited extensively. His practical and realistic outlook was diametrically opposed to **Pio's** romantic and revolutionary socialism. From 1877, with C. Hørdum and P. Holm, he was the force behind reorganization of the executive of the **Social Democratic** (SD) press and a member of the SD Federation 1878-1931. As manager from 1886 of the Workers' United Bakery in Copenhagen he was a pioneer in the growing **co-**

operative movement. He sat in the *Landsting* from 1890 as one of its first two SD members, and was an elected member 1918-32. From 1902 he was chairman of the Star brewery, a co-operative started in 1900 by the **trade unions**, supported by the Sugar Workers and the Bakers' Unions, which did well in the 1920s. At the height of his powers he typified democratic working class instincts; in his later years he was a respected elder statesman of the Danish labor movement, with 50 active years' experience of its trade union, political, and cooperative wings. He presided over SD congresses (1876-1931) as a tactician who led more by example than by words, a man very much at the center of his party. AHT

ANDERSEN, HANS CHRISTIAN (1805-1875). Novelist, poet and writer of fairy tales. Born in **Odense** the son of a poor shoemaker, H.C. Andersen (as Danes usually refer to him) left home at age 14, after his father's death and his mother's remarriage, to seek his fortune in **Copenhagen**. His love of the theater and a fine voice secured him a place in the dance and song school of the **National Theater**, and in 1822 he won the patronage of Jonas Collin, a director of the Theater, to whose family he remained close throughout his life. Collin enabled Andersen to secure sufficient formal education to matriculate in 1828, the year after his first poems were published. Andersen's first work to secure widespread notice was his autobiographical novel *Improvisatoren* (1835, *The Improvisatore*, 1845). In the same year that this appeared (1835), he published his first fairy tales, on which his fame now largely rests. Nearly 160 of these continued to appear throughout his life. He also wrote five more novels, plays, and poetry and several autobiographies, of which the most important is *Mit Livs Eventyr* (1855, 1877, *The Story of My Life*, 1871, 1880). Several travel books reflect his extensive wandering, which took him as far as North Africa. In Sweden he fell in love with the singer Jenny Lind, a love not returned. He never married and, in spite of the great fame which he enjoyed, was a lonely and often despondent figure. He is commemorated in **Odense** by a museum and in Copenhagen by the name of a boulevard running southeast from the Town Hall Square and by a statue in Kongens Have, the park surrounding **Rosenborg Castle**. SPO

ANDERSEN, HANS NIELS (1852-1937). Businessman. Born in Nakskov, **Lolland**, he was for some years a seaman and a captain of one of the King of Siam's trade-ships. In 1884 he founded the import and export firm Anderson & Co. in Bangkok. In 1897 he founded and ran the **East Asiatic Company**. This company developed agencies around the world with shipping, plantations and financial activities. During **World War I** he tried to serve Danish interests in Britain. In 1901 he worked for the **Change of System** and the formation of **Deuntzer's Liberal** government, and in 1920 for the dismissal by King **Christian X** of **Zahle's Radical Liberal** government. AHT. *See also* Order of the **Elephant**.

ANDERSEN, KNUD BØRGE (1914-1984). Social Democrat (SD) politician. He graduated *cand. polit.* in 1940 from Copenhagen University, where he chaired the Student Society and got to know **Jens Otto Krag**. From 1935 he worked in the State Radio talks department, which he headed from 1948 to 1950, also teaching at Krogerup Folk High School under the influence of **Hal Koch**. He was then principal of Roskilde Labor High School from 1950 to 1957. He edited the SD journal *Verdens gang* (The Way of the World) 1953-58, making it more lively and committed. Following Hans **Hedtoft's** death he was elected to the **Folketing** (1957-70 and 1973-82), where he quickly took leading roles as principal SD parliamentary spokesman from 1962 to 1964. He was on the committee to draft the party's program of principles in 1961 and a member of all subsequent program committees until he retired. In parliament his interest centered initially on education and cultural policy; outside parliament he chaired AOF, the Labor Educational Association, and *Arte*, its counterpart for theater and music. As minister of education in Krag's 1963-68 cabinets he supervised implementation of the 1958 school reforms during the "educational explosion." He was also responsible for introducing the Højere forberedelseseksamen (Hf, Higher Preparatory Exam) and supervised the development of 1968 legislation on recreational education. In 1971 in **Krag's** third cabinet he was foreign minister during EC entry negotiations, continuing as such in Anker **Jørgensen's** 1972-73 and 1975-78 cabinets, showing particular interest in the Third World and speaking for freedom movements and racial equality, sometimes to the annoyance of the opposition but supported by a parliamentary majority. He was Folketing Chairman (Speaker) during 1978-81. His versatile ability to take on new political tasks and get to the heart of the matter contributed to the labor movement, but he tended to ignore civil service advice. As well as numerous newspaper articles, with J.O. Krag he wrote *Kamp og fornyelse: Socialdemokratiets indsats i dansk politik 1955-71* (1971, Struggle and Renewal: the SD Contribution to Danish Politics 1955-71) and the autobiographical *I alle de riger og lande: oplevelser i 70'ernes danske udenrigspolitik* (1983, In All the Realms and Countries: Experiences of Danish Foreign Policy in the '70s). AHT

ANDERSEN, VILHELM (1864-1953). Literary historian. He graduated *cand. mag.* in Danish, Latin, and Greek in 1888 and became professor of Danish literature at Copenhagen University 1908-1930. He rehabilitated national and romantic literature after its devaluation by **G. Brandes**, e.g., in volume 3 of *Illustreret Dansk Literaturhistorie* (1929-34, Illustrated Danish History of Literature). He sought to show the ancient Roman influence on European literature and to focus on the person of the author behind the work in his analysis. AHT

ANDRÆ, CARL GEORG (1812-1893). A politician and mathematician, he was a member of the Constitutional Convention of 1848-49, ending his career in parliament and cabinet as council president (prime minister) 1856-57. In the mid-1850s he developed the single transferable vote method which was the first ever proportional election system. It was used in elections from 1861 onward, and is still the basis of the current Danish rules. AHT

ANKER, PETER (1744-1832). Colonial official. Norwegian born, after extensive travels in 1783 he was appointed Danish-Norwegian consul in London. In 1786-1806 he served as governor of Danish possessions in East India (*see* **Asiatic Company**), retiring on pension to his farm, Øraker, near Oslo. As governor he was incorruptible and pursued a flexible policy of neutrality toward other conflicting colonial powers. AHT

ANSGAR (ca. 801-865). Bishop. As a Benedictine monk he was appointed by his monastery Neue Corvey in Saxony as a missionary to the North, but hardly reached the Danish border. Following a successful stay at Birka in Sweden in 829-831 he became archbishop of Hamburg-Bremen with charge over northern missionaries. He appears to have held Christian services on visits to Hedeby and Ribe, but the new belief did not survive and left no trace. Only in the Middle Ages was he recognized as "apostle of the North." AHT

APPLIED ARTS AND DESIGN, MUSEUM OF (Kunstindustri museum), was established in 1890 by the Ny-**Carlsberg** Foundation in the Rococo building in Bredgade, **Copenhagen**, which was built in 1757 as the Frederik Hospital to designs by Niels **Eigtved** and **Laurids de Thura**. It displays European arts and crafts from the middle ages to the present, plus some Chinese and Japanese artifacts, with the main emphasis on living-room furniture and fittings, including porcelain, glass, silver, textiles, furniture, and jewelry, including modern Danish design. AHT

ARCHAEOLOGY. As early as 1595 Anders **Vedel** supervised the excavation of mounds in the Danish countryside, but in Denmark the science was really born in the early 17th century, when Ole **Worm** described the first of the **Gallehus** horns to be discovered and asked clergymen to record local monuments. In 1754 a law offered a reward to finders of objects of value, which were to be held in the royal Kunstkammer, which already housed Worm's and other collections. In 1807 the Royal Commission for the Preservation of Antiquities (Den Kongelige Commission til Oldsagers Opbevaring) was established and the first museum of antiquities (The Royal Museum of Northern Antiquities) was opened to the public in Trinity Church in **Copenhagen**. Nine years later, the young Christian Jürgensen **Thomsen** (1788-1865) was appointed the Commission's secretary. A brilliant lecturer, Thomsen made the royal collections (housed from 1832 in **Christiansborg** and often referred to as The Old Nordic Museum) a popular attraction and first classified them into Stone Age, Bronze Age, and Iron Age according to a theory already familiar but never before applied to material objects in chronological sequence. The second great figure in 19th-century archeology was J.J. Worsaae (1821-1885). Appointed inspector of monuments in 1847, he pioneered archaeological techniques and first divided Thomsen's Stone Age into Old and New. He worked on excavations with King **Frederik VII**, a keen archaeologist. Worsaae became director of the Old Nordic and the Ethnographic Museums and the Royal Chronological Collection in Rosenborg Castle in 1866, after serving as minister of culture in 1874-75.

His pupil Sophus **Müller** succeeded him as director of the museum (from 1892 the **National Museum**) and laid a firm basis for advances in the 20th century, including an excavation plan for the museum. Prominent among later Danish archeologists has been Johannes Brøndsted (1890-1965), professor of Nordic Archaeology at the University of Copenhagen from 1941 to 1951, when he also became director of the National Museum. His three-volume *Danmarks Oldtid* (1938-40) remains a standard work of reference. After the National Museum in Copenhagen, the most important collection of archaeological finds, including **Grauballe Man** is housed in the mansion of Moesgård outside **Århus**. Among the best known archaeological finds in Denmark have been the beautiful flint dagger from Hindsgavl on Funen, the well-preserved Bronze Age woman's costume from Egtved in southern **Jutland**, the Bronze Age trumpets known as *lur*, of which there are some 35 examples, the Early Iron Age "Bog Men" of Grauballe and **Tollund**, the Iron Age gold horns from **Gallehus**, the silver bowl from **Gundestrup**, and the late Viking Age ships found at **Skuldelev** in **Roskilde** Fjord in 1962. SPO. *See also* **Museums; Prehistory**.

ARCHITECTURE. The earliest Danish buildings were of wood. The first stone structures were churches in Romanesque style from the 10th century. Of these only the foundations remain, but some later Romanesque churches from the 12th century survive in **Jutland**, above all the cathedral of Ribe from 1176. The oldest remains of a secular building are of a tower near Farum on **Zealand**, which dates back to around 1100. The foundations of the original castle of Copenhagen under the modern **Christiansborg** date from some half a century later. Brick was introduced as a building material about this time and soon became popular for churches (e.g., Kalundborg Church and the later **Roskilde** Cathedral). The Gothic style was introduced in the 13th century. The round **Churches** of **Bornholm**, **Zealand** and **Funen** were constructed as fortresses against the **Wend**ish pirates who harassed the Danish coasts at that time.

The Dutch Renaissance style appeared under royal patronage in the middle of the 16th century with **Kronborg Castle** at **Elsinore**, and reached its peak in the reign of the great builder-king **Christian IV**, when something like a national style developed for the first time (e.g. The **Exchange** and **Rosenborg Castle** in Copenhagen and **Frederiksborg Castle** in northeast Zealand). The style can also be seen in the many brick manor houses constructed (often on earlier foundations) by newly affluent nobles in the 16th century, e.g., Hasselagergård on Funen and Gisselfeld on Zealand. As elsewhere, so in Denmark the Baroque style seen in **Charlottenborg** is associated with the introduction of royal absolutism, but Dutch influence remained strong until the 18th century, when central European trends came with E.D. Häusser, architect of the first **Christiansborg**.

In the middle of the 18th century the Rococo style manifested itself in the work of Niels **Eigtved**, responsible for the mansions which make up **Amalienborg** in Copenhagen. Before the end of the century this had been overtaken by Neoclassicism, seen, for example in the colonnade at Amalienborg by C.F. Harsdorff (1735-1799). The Great Fire of Copenhagen in 1795 provided opportunities for Harsdorff's pupil **C.F. Hansen** who was commissioned to design the second Christiansborg as well as a new Town Hall. After a somewhat lean period in the mid-19th century, a revival began with Copenhagen's City Hall, designed in 1892-1905 by Martin **Nyrop** (1849-1921) and the best Danish example of National Romanticism. After World War I the favored style was classical (e.g. Hack Kampmann's Police Headquarters in Copenhagen of 1919-24). Functionalism in the 1930s is represented by Kay Fisker's Århus University and by the early work of **Arne Jacobsen**. A unique product of this period is the Grundtvig Church at Bispebjerg in Copenhagen, begun as a memorial to N.F.S. **Grundtvig** in 1921 to designs by P.V. Jensen **Klint** but not completed until 1940 by Kaare **Klint**. The Bauhaus-influenced Edvard **Heiberg** designed many of the large pre- and post-war housing developments around Copenhagen. During the 1950s, Japanese and American influences are evident, for example in Jørgen Bo's and Vilhelm Wohlert's **Louisiana** and the atrium houses ("Kingo Houses") near **Elsinore** by Jørn **Utzon** (b.1918), while Fisker and Jakobsen continued to produce public buildings of high quality and interest. More recently Utzon has won fame for the Sydney Opera House and the younger Henning Larsen for the Saudi Arabian Foreign Ministry building in Riyadh. Larsen also designed the buildings for Copenhagen Business School (Københavns Handelshøjskolen). SPO, AHT. *See also* **Bindesbøll, Gottlieb; Copenhagen; Herholdt, Johan Daniel**.

ÅRHUS (AARHUS before 1947, a spelling which the Univeristy has retained). The second-largest city of Denmark, a port and industrial center (light shipbuilding, engineering, food products, textiles, brewing), was founded in the middle of the 10th century on the river of the same name in eastern **Jutland**. It became a bishopric as early as 948 and received a town charter in 1441. It grew only slowly in early modern times and even at the beginning of the 19th century had a population of only some 4,000. Its rapid expansion came with the development of the harbor and the arrival of the railway in the later 19th century, when it overtook **Ålborg** in size. It now has a population of over 270,000. Its cathedral, dedicated to St. Clemens, is the longest church in Denmark and dates originally from the early 13th century but was almost completely rebuilt in Gothic style in the 15th century by Bishop Jens Iversen Lange and was last restored in 1921-27. It and the much older Church of Our Lady (*Vor Frue Kirke*), the original cathedral from the early 12th century, are the only medieval buildings to have survived the numerous fires which the city has suffered. It contains a fine reredos by the **Lübeck** sculptor Bernt Notke from 1479.

Århus Town Hall, faced with Norwegian marble, is one of the monuments of modern Danish architecture. It was designed by **Arne Jacobsen** and Erik Møller and built in 1938-1942. The **University** of Aarhus dates from 1928 and is housed in yellow brick buildings designed by **Kay Fisker**, C.F. Møller, and Povl Stegmann. In *Den Gamle By* (The Old Town), founded in 1909, Århus has one of the finest open air museums in Scandinavia, with some urban buildings brought from other parts of Denmark as well as from Århus itself. In the fine Museum of Prehistory, now housed in the mansion of Moesgård outside the town, may be seen **Grauballe Man**, one of the most famous of the 'Bog People'. Århus numbers the astronomer Ole **Rømer** among its sons, and the **Heath Society** was formed there in 1866. SPO, AHT

ARMY. From the end of the Middle Ages until the early 17th century, the Danish Crown depended for land defense largely on the feudal cavalry provided by the nobility (*rostjeneste*) and the royal estates and on fortress garrisons. Under **Christian IV** (king 1588-1648) these were supplemented by hired foreign mercenaries and a peasant militia, for which all farms were grouped into "files" (*lægd*). At the end of the reign the total force numbered over 25,000. In 1671 four cavalry regiments of some thousand men each were formed to be supported by designated royal estates (*ryttergods*), and in 1701 the peasant militia was reorganized to provide a force of 15,000. This was abolished at the beginning of the reign of **Christian VI** (king 1730-46) but resurrected in 1733 in connection with the institution of the *stavnsbånd*.

A national army was set up in 1803 of 35,000 front line troops, each serving with the colors for six years, and liability to serve in it was extended in 1829 beyond the peasant class to certain other categories such as sons of schoolteachers, though substitutes were allowed. Universal liability of Danish males to military service came with the constitution of 1849. Defense became an important political issue after military defeat in the Second **Slesvig-Holsten** War (1864), when the Conservative administration sought to improve the defenses of **Copenhagen**, while the **Liberal** opposition wanted a more flexible approach with more reliance on the mobile militia, and more radical elements such as the small **Social Democratic** representation called for an end to all armed forces as of little use against a great power.

Denmark was neutral in World War I. Calls for disarmament grew in the early 1920s and there were considerable reductions in the size of the army in 1932. Under the **Social Democratic** and **Radical Liberal** administration in power 1929-40, there was only improvement in quality in the face of the threat from the South, and although some frontier units did put up heroic resistance on the first day of the German occupation in April 1940, the Danish army was at that time in no position to oppose the enemy. It was allowed to continue in being until the German takeover in August 1943, when it was disarmed and all its officers briefly interned.

The army in 1996 had a peacetime strength of 19,000, including about 3,900 civilians and about 6,900 conscripts, most of whom serve for 9-12 months. The wartime strength is about 60,000. It is organized in five mechanized infantry brigades, including the Danish Reaction Brigade. There are 24 helicopters, half equipped with anti-armor weapons and half for observation and liaison. In addition there are local defense units organized in infantry battalions, plus artillery battalions and support units. The men of the latest annual service groups form the troops of the line, while those of the previous years form the local defense and the reserve.

The Home Guard (*Hjemmeværnet*) was set up in 1948. Its personnel serve voluntarily and number about 66,000 persons, 52,000 in the army home guard, 4,400 in the navy home guard, 7,800 in the air-force home guard, and 1,800 in the service corps. Denmark joined **NATO** in 1949, and armed forces have since worked within its framework. SPO, AHT

ARREBO, ANDERS CHRISTENSEN (1587-1637). Author. A priest, he graduated *magister* in 1610 and was appointed bishop of Trondheim in 1618 but was dismissed in 1622 for alleged immorality. In 1626-37 he was parish priest of Vordingborg. His verse work, in late renaissance style, *Hexaëmeron*, depicts the Creation with sections on Danish and Norwegian landscape and is considered the most important 17th-century poem in Danish. AHT

ARUP, ERIK (1876-1951). Historian. He graduated *magister* in 1901 and in 1916-47 was professor of history at Copenhagen University. In addition to trade histories and historiographic critiques he wrote *Danmarks historie* (vol. I, 1925; II, 1932; III published posthumously in 1955), ending in 1660. AHT. *See also* **Historiography**.

ASIATIC COMPANY (Asiatisk Kompani). Founded in 1732 to govern Denmark's Indian possessions, it was granted a 40-year monopoly of trade with China. In 1772 the company was reformed and lost its trading monopoly. Five years later, its possessions were bought by the Crown for 272,000 riksdaler. The company continued its trading activities, but it never fully recovered from the seizure of all its ships by the British in 1807 and in 1843 was dissolved and its assets sold by auction. SPO. *See also* **East Asiatic Company; East India Company; India, Danish Possessions**.

ASSER (c. 1059-1137) was created bishop in 1089 and in 1104 the first Nordic archbishop with his seat in Lund and 22 bishops in his care. He had Lund cathedral built. AHT

ASTRONOMERS, DANISH see BRAHE; LONGOMONTANUS; PETRUS; RØMER. See also VEN.

ATASSUT, a liberal political party whose name translates as the Link, was founded as a movement in 1978. It became a political party in 1981 and has been the main opposition party of **Greenland** since then. It favored home rule and also wished Greenland to remain in the European Community. Its representative in the **Folketing** sits with the **Liberal Party**. In the election of 1991, it obtained 30.1 percent of the vote and 8 of the 27 seats in the island's Landsting. SPO, AHT

ATOMIC ENERGY COMMISSION, Atomenergikommissionen **(AEK),** was established by the Danish government in 1955 to develop the peaceful use of nuclear energy for the benefit of society. It was abolished in 1976. In 1981 the consolidated electrical utilities Elsam and Elkraft reported that it would be feasible for the high-level radioactive by-products from a nuclear power station to be stored underground, but this was contested by the Danish Geological Research unit. In 1985 the **Folketing** resolved that future energy planning should not include nuclear energy. AHT

AUGUST, BILLE (1948-). Film director. He trained at the Photo and Documentary Film School in Stockholm 1967-71, and at the Danish Film School 1971-73. He was strongly influenced by the Swedish film director Ingmar Bergman and has worked extensively in Sweden as well as in Denmark and Hollywood. Of over 15 films, *Pelle the Conqueror* (1987), based on **Martin Andersen Nexø**'s epic, was awarded the Golden Palm at the 1988 Cannes Festival, and the Golden Globe for the year's best foreign film in Hollywood in 1989. He has been awarded many other prizes in Denmark, Norway, Sweden and the United States. See also **Film Industry.** AHT

AUGUSTENBORG is the name of the house of dukes (*hertuger*) of Slesvig (to Danes, Southern Jutland) from duke Ernst Günther

(1609-89), who married Augusta of Holsten-Glücksborg, to Augusta Viktoria (1858-1921) who married Wilhelm II of Germany (1859-1941), kaiser 1888-1918. In 1844 various groups in **Slesvig** and **Holsten** agreed to support the claim of duke Christian of Augustenborg to inherit the two duchies, as the Danish male line of inheritance seemed likely to die out with the then crown prince Frederik, who later became **Frederik VII**, king 1848-63. While Danish law permitted female inheritance, the law in the two duchies did not — so the claim was an attempt to separate the two duchies from the Danish monarchy. In 1846 King **Christian VIII** issued *The open letter on the succession*, which stated that Slesvig, as a Danish entailed estate which had been incorporated in 1721, had the same law of succession as the **King's Law** had determined for the Kingdom. If succession via the male line should die out, this allowed for inheritance via close female relatives. The open letter was intended to secure that the Danish Kingdom and the Slesvig duchy would continue to have the same ruler. This view was opposed by the German-speakers in the two Duchies, a situation which led directly to the two **Slesvig-Holsten** wars of 1849 and 1866. AHT

AUKEN, SVEND GUNNARSEN (1943-). **Social Democratic** politician. The son of two medical doctors active in politics, he graduated *cand. scient. pol.* in 1969 from Århus University with a thesis on Danish labor relations, studying also at Washington State University and in Paris. He lectured in political science at Århus University until 1989. He was elected for SD to the **Folketing** in 1971, at once actively opposing Danish **European Community** (EC) membership. He developed close links with the trade union movement and was on the executive committee of Landsorganisationen (the national confederation of trade unions) in 1977 and 1983-87. He was chairman of the powerful parliamentary Labor Market committee 1975-77. In the parliamentary SD party he rose rapidly, becoming vice-chair in 1975, and party spokesman ("floor-leader") in 1977. He was a close adviser to Prime Minister **Anker Jørgensen** as minister for labor 1977-82, with responsibilities which included negotiating incomes policy. With SD in opposition from 1982, he was party spokesman from 1983, vice-chairman of SD in 1985, and succeeded Jørgensen as chairman after the 1987 election, the third since 1979 in which SD's support declined. He was chairman of the

Socialist International, 1988-92. He has written in Danish extensively, including an OECD report on French youth unemployment (1984), and on defense, the EC, the trade union movement, economic policy, and Marxism. He failed to unite the components of the labor movement against attacks on the **welfare state** from the right or against the significant **Socialist People's Party** on the left, and was replaced as party leader in April 1991 by **Poul Nyrup Rasmussen**, in whose government he served as environment minister 1993-4 and as Environment & Energy Minister from 1994. AHT

AXEL, Prince (1888-1964). The son of Prince Valdemar (sixth son of **Christian IX**) and Princess Marie, his naval career culminated in appointment as admiral in 1958. He pursued a parallel business career from 1921 in the **East Asiatic Company** as a director from 1927 and chairman from 1938. In 1940 he was considered for prime minister of the nonparty government proposed by Knud **Højgaard**, but this came to nothing. He was the International Olympic Committee's representative in Denmark, 1932-58. AHT

- B -

BACH, KNUD (1871-1948). Politician and landowner. From a landowning family, he helped to found Landbrugernes Sammenslutning (LS, the **Agricultural Association**) and was its national chairman, 1931-44. His attempt in 1940 to deal with the German occupiers separately from the Danish government, and the close relations of LS to the Nazis, brought a five-year prison sentence after **World War II**. AHT

BACH, OTTO (1839-1927). Painter. The self-taught son of a grocer, he painted portraits, animals, and historical scenes such as *Tordenskjold in Marstrand* (1875), *The Knight's Conspiracy from Finderup Barn* (1882), King Christian IV's Coronation Procession 1596 (1887) and his nature paintings, e.g. *A Pair of Horses outside an Inn* (1878). This established him as one of the most popular naturalistic painters of the time. He was professor of painting at the **Academy**, 1887-1909. AHT

BAGGESEN, JENS (1764-1826). Author and poet. He studied theology at Copenhagen University and was appointed a professor there in 1790-1814, but lived for long periods abroad, during 1800-1806 in Paris and in 1811-13 in Kiel as a university professor. His early publications were clever satires in the style of Ludwig **Holberg** and Johann **Wessel**. He supplied the libretto for the opera, *Holger Danske* by Friedrich **Kunzen**, but its 1789 performance was unsuccessful. His major work, *Labyrinten* (1792-93, The Labyrinth) is a visionary and atmospheric description of a journey to Germany and France, written with a subjectivity and ecstatic emotionalism in which the subjectivism of Jean-Jacques Rousseau is apparent. In the 1810s he launched a polemic against Adam **Oehlenschläger**, describing him as poetically deaf and spiritually dumb. Supported only by N.F.S **Grundtvig**, in 1820 he left Denmark in disappointment on another of his travels. Although uneven in quality, some of his poems are insights into the mind of someone who lived a tortured and homeless existence. AHT

BAJER, FREDRIK (1837-1922). Politician, husband of **Matilde Bajer**. The son of a priest, he began a military career, but taught from 1865, and was a Swedish translator in 1871-1907. In 1872-95 he was a Liberal member of the **Folketing** and with his wife helped to found Dansk Kvindesamfund (**Danish Women's Society**) in 1871 and Kvindelig Læseforening (Women's Reading Association) in 1872. His interest in peace led to the founding of Dansk Fredsforening (the Danish Peace Society) in 1885 and he helped found the World Peace Bureau, of which he was chairman, 1891-1907. He was awarded the **Nobel** Peace Prize in 1908. AHT

BAJER, MATILDE (1840-1934). Politician, wife of Fredrik **Bajer** and one of the pioneers of the **women's movement**. After helping to form the **Danish Women's Society**, she helped form the more po-

litically active but short lived (1886-93) Kvindelig Fremskridts-
forening (Women's Progress Association). AHT

BALLE, NICOLAE EDINGER (1744-1816). Bishop. Born in Nakskov, the son of a deacon, he graduated *cand. theol.* in 1765 then
studied abroad. He was a professor at Copenhagen University, 1772-
83, then bishop of **Zealand** until 1808. He is best known for his
school catechism, *Balles lærebog* (1791 and many later editions).
He was attacked vigorously by adherents of the "old beliefs," although conservative in his views and a defender of biblical Christendom against the anti-church and deistic currents of the time.
AHT

BALLET is the performing art for which Denmark has the highest
international reputation. Its modern history dates back to the foundation in 1771 of a ballet school in the **Royal Theater**, although
dance had been taught there from the Theater's foundation. The first
ballet master was the Frenchman Pierre Laurent. But it was his successor, the Italian Vincenzo Galeotti (1733-1816), who came to **Copenhagen** in 1775 and danced until he was 77, who first gave Danish ballet an international reputation. His ballet *Amor og
Balletmesterens Luner* (Cupid and the Ballet-Master's Whims) is
the oldest still performed anywhere in its original form. Antoine
Bournonville (1760-1843) settled in Denmark from Vienna and was
ballet master in 1816-23. Of the 50 or so ballets which he created, a
number, like *La Sylphide*, are still performed. Even more important
for the art's development is his son **August Bournonville**, who
dominated the art in Denmark for some fifty years (1829-77). A
somewhat lean period followed until the arrival on the scene of
Harald Lander, ballet master at the Theater in 1932-51. Thanks to
his training and choreography Danish ballet acquired a reputation
after **World War II** which it has retained and which was extended
to London and Paris by Frank **Schaufuss** (1921-97). The most famous of Lander's pupils was Flemming Flindt (1936-   ), ballet
master in 1966-78, who introduced the American style of dance into
Denmark; since leaving Copenhagen he has spent much of his time
in the United States. In 1988 an international ballet festival in Co-

penhagen inaugurated the Hans Christian Andersen Ballet Award for the world's best ballet performance. Peter Schaufuss (Frank's son) was artistic director in 1995-96 of the 90 dancers who form the Royal Danish Ballet. SPO, AHT. See also **Knudåge Riisager**.

BANG, BERNHARD (1848-1932). After passing veterinary examinations in 1873 he lectured at the national Agricultural College (Landbohøjskolen), researching and publishing on diseases of cattle and gaining a world reputation for his work on tuberculosis. AHT

BANG, (JENS) GUSTAV (1871-1915). Social Democratic (SD) theorist and politician; husband of **Nina Bang**. He graduated from Copenhagen University in Nordic philology, 1890 and *dr. phil.* 1897 with a thesis on *The Decline of the Old Aristocracy* of the 16th and 17 centuries, which he attributed to biological degeneration. His interest in socialism and in Marx's theory of history began as a student and he became the most important Danish socialist theoretician of his time. From 1896 Bang wrote for *Social-Democraten*, with weekly "Monday articles" to popularize Marxist ideas from 1905. His most important books were *The Breakthrough of Capitalism* (1902), *The Future Socialist State* (1903), and *The Capitalist Social Economy* (1912). *Kirkebogstudier* (1906, Studies of Church Records) described working class conditions of the 17th century. He viewed SD as a class party which would abolish class conflict through dictatorship of the proletariat. Simultaneously Bang defended SD reformism in practice, considering reforms to be the necessary precondition for the revolutionary seizure of power by the working class. Elected to the **Folketing** 1910-1915, he integrated without difficulty into the party's practical politics and did not use his position for more radical measures. His writing attracted considerable notice and helped to develop the left-opposition, but was of little significance to SD in the longer run. AHT

BANG, HERMAN (1857-1912). Novelist, poet, and playwright. Born on the island of Als, where his father was a parish priest, he gave up his legal studies at the University of Copenhagen to write for the stage. Having had little success with this, he turned to journalism, and his first published work (in 1879) was a collection of his newspaper articles. A novel published in the following year was confiscated because of its sexual content. In 1884 Bang began four years of travel in central Europe, during which he began to attract attention as a writer. A number of his novels are autobiographical and all his writing is pessimistic in tone, influenced perhaps by consciousness of his homosexuality. He died in Ogden, Utah, while on a lecture tour of the United States and is buried in the Western Cemetery (Vestre Kirkegård) in **Copenhagen**. SPO

BANG, NINA (1866-1928). Politician and wife of **Gustav Bang**. The daughter of a future minister of war, she graduated *cand. mag.* in history (1894) and researched 16th century shipping and trade in the **Sound**. She wrote for *Social-Democraten* and other newspapers from 1898 and was elected to the Danish **Social Democratic Party**'s national executive committee in 1903. She was elected to Copenhagen City Council 1913-18 and to the *Landsting* from 1918. As minister of education in Th. **Stauning**'s first SD government (1924-25), Bang was the first woman cabinet member, working with commitment for greater democracy in schools. Although one of the first women active in Danish politics, she considered women's issues merely a part of the general political conflict. She translated *Marx: Wage Labor and Capital* (1900), wrote *Karl Marx: His Life and Work* (1918) and (with Emil Wiinblad), *The Life and Struggle of the Working Class: Selected Articles by Gustav Bang* (1915). AHT

BANG, PETER (1900-1957). Manufacturer. The son of a confidential clerk, he trained as a smith in 1921 and an electrical engineer in 1924. In 1925 he formed the company Bang and Olufsen A/S with Sv. Olufsen (1897-1949), developing radio, audio, and television equipment of world-renowned design. AHT

BANG, PETER GEORG (1797-1861). Politician. He graduated *cand. jur.* in 1816 and was professor of law 1830-45. He was a member of the **Roskilde Consultative Assembly**, legal adviser

1845-1848 to **Christian VIII**, member of the **Constituent Assembly** (1848), member of various cabinets 1848-53, prime minister (Konseilpræsident) and interior minister 1854-56, and minister for the monarchy's common interior affairs 1855-56. He sought to build bridges between the **Ejder**-Danes (*see* **Slesvig-Holsten**) and supporters of the unitary state, and between conservative (monarchist) and **liberal** (democratic) views on the **constitution**. AHT

BANKING. Denmark's first private bank, officially entitled Kiøbenhavnske Assignations- Vexel- og Laanebank but usually referred to as Kurantbanken, was founded in **Copenhagen** in 1736 on the initiative of the newly created College of Commerce and was granted the right to issue notes backed by silver. The bank became more and more involved with the making of loans to the state and was finally taken over by the Crown in 1773. It was succeeded in 1791 by a new private bank, Danmarks og Norges Spendbank, but this was overshadowed by the Depositokursen formed in 1799 with the same right to issue notes.

Following the declaration of national bankruptcy in January 1813, a new State Bank (Rigsbanken) was established with funds provided by a 6 percent tax on property. Three years later this became the privately owned National Bank (Nationalbanken i Kjøbenhavn), supervised by the minister of justice as bank commissioner and with a crown nominee among its six directors. Denmark's first savings bank (Fyens Disconto Kasse in **Odense**) had already appeared, and the first true commercial bank investing in industry followed in Odense in 1846, although local branches of the National Bank had already begun to do this. A new stage began in 1857 with the founding by the industrialist **C.F. Tietgen** of Privatbanken i Kjøbenhavn, the first bank whose customers could make payments by check. The economic boom of the 1870s led to the formation of a number of large banks in the capital, e.g., Den danske Landmandsbank (The Danish Farmers' Bank) in 1871 and Kjøbenhavns Handelsbank (Copenhagen Bank of Commerce) in 1873. Provincial banks also multiplied, and by 1908 there were 119 in Denmark. *See also* **Alberti**.

The economic crisis immediately after World War I caused a number of Danish banks to fail. The collapse of Landmandsbanken in 1922 with a loss of 500 million kroner led to a special government inquiry which revealed extensive unsecured speculation by many leading figures, but blamed and imprisoned the managing director **Emil Glückstadt**. Not until 1928 were the bank's affairs again in order. The following year the managing director of Folkebanken (The People's Bank) was also found guilty of embezzlement and his bank forced to close. In 1925 Andelsbanken failed and in 1928 Privatbanken also faced difficulties.

The National Bank remains a 'self-owned' institution and acts as central bank, as holder of the nation's reserves and with the currency-issuing monopoly. Difficulties for Kronebanken in 1984 and 6 July Bank in 1987 were resolved by take-overs, and the latter crisis led to establishment of the Depositors' Guarantee Fund, Indskydergarantifonden, which covers a depositor's losses up to 250,000 kroner. At the end of 1989 the two largest commercial banks, Den Danske Bank and Handelsbank merged and were soon joined by Provinsbank. The new *Danske Bank* was consequently the largest in Scandinavia. There is also a thriving savings-bank (sparekasse) sector. Some 200 banks are registered, but Den Danske Bank, Unibank and Bikuben accounted in 1993 for two-thirds of total assets. SPO, AHT.

BARDENFLETH, CARL EMIL (1807-1857). Politician. The son of an officer, in 1827 he graduated *cand. jur.* In 1841 he was appointed to take charge of the court of his childhood friend Crown Prince **Frederik (VIII)** and in 1843-48 as *stiftamtmand* (prefect) of **Funen**, of which the prince was governor. In March 1848 he influenced **Frederik VII** to accept the change to constitutional monarchy to counter the opposition in **Slesvig-Holsten**. He joined the ensuing cabinet as justice minister 1848-51 and as minister for Slesvig to 1851-52, but his relationship to the king cooled when he criticized the king's relationship to Countess **Danner**. AHT. *See also* **Constitution**.

BARTHOLDY, CHRISTIAN (1889-1976). Priest. The son of a priest, he graduated *cand. theol.* in 1912 and served in various country parishes. As chairman of the Indre Mission (Inner Mission)

1934-59 he was a sharp and feared castigator of the Danes' godlessness and the indolence of the priests of the national church. AHT. *See also* **Vilhelm Beck.**

BARTHOLIN, RASMUS (1625-1698). Scientist. Born in **Roskilde,** the son of Caspar Bartholin the Elder (1585-1629), who was professor of Latin, medicine and theology at the University of **Copenhagen,** Rasmus studied in Leyden, France, and Italy before becoming professor of mathematics in Copenhagen in 1657 and a year later of medicine. He was rector of the University in 1666, 1674, and 1683. He is best known for his discovery in 1669 of the double refraction in Iceland spar. SPO

BARTHOLIN, THOMAS (1616-1680), the anatomist brother of Rasmus. Born in **Copenhagen,** Thomas studied for 10 years (1637-47) in various European universities, including Leyden, Padua, and Basel, before being appointed in 1647 to the chair of mathematics in Copenhagen. He became professor of medicine in 1654, when he was also for the first time rector of the university and published his discovery of the human lymphatic system, for which he is most famous. Although he may have been preceded by the Swede Olof Rudbeck, Bartholin was the first to publish his results. He was largely responsible for the production of Denmark's first pharmacopoeia in 1658, and in 1667 he founded his university's first zoological museum. He was allowed to retire to his estates from lecturing in 1660. Many of his manuscripts were destroyed when his house burned down in 1670. His son Caspar the Younger (1655-1738) was appointed professor of Medicine in Copenhagen three years before his father's death. SPO

BAUNSGAARD, HILMAR (1920-1989). **Radical Liberal** politician and prime minister. Born in Slagelse, he held various business appointments including the management of the Merchants' Central Purchasing organization, 1947-61, and entered parliament in 1957. He was his party's chairman in 1960-61 and 1964-68 and was minister of commerce in Viggo Kampmann's and Jens Otto Krag's **Social Democrat**-Radical Liberal coalitions in 1961-64. Pursuing a center-seeking strategy, when the 1966 election produced a majority for the socialist block, he led his party away from its traditional alliance with the Social Democrats toward one with the non-socialist parties. As prime minister in 1968-71 he headed a coalition of his own party with **Conservatives** and **Liberals**, the first Radical to hold the office of prime minister since 1920. His government ended censorship of pornography and presided over the introduction of pay-as-you-earn income tax, but failed to curb the rising costs of welfare. He retired from politics in 1974. SPO, AHT

BECK, VILHELM (1829-1901). Priest, *cand. theol.* 1855. As chairman from 1881 of the Indre Mission (Inner Mission) he opposed Grundtvigianism and any form of biblical criticism. AHT. *See also* **Bartholdy, Christian; Church, Danish; Grundtvig, N.F.S.**

BECKER, KNUTH (1891-1974). Author. The son of a failed landowner, at the age of eight he was placed in a care home. At 15 he became a farming pupil, then an apprentice smith, eventually owning a machinery firm. From 1934 until his death he lived from his writing. His best-known work is the series of novels (1932-56) about Kai Gotsche, partly autobiographical, which depicts the struggle of boy and man to find himself despite adult oppression, hypocritical church moralizing, and odious militarism. AHT

BEGTRUP, BODIL (1903-1985). Diplomat. Her father was a judge and her mother a mathematics teacher. She graduated *cand. polit.* in 1929 and that year joined the committee of the Danish Women's National Council, becoming vice-chairman, 1931-46, and chairman, 1946-49. From 1946 she was a member of the Danish United Nations delegation, particularly concerned to advance the cause of women. From 1949 she held various diplomatic appointments, becoming the first Danish woman to achieve the rank of ambassador. AHT

BENNEDSEN, DORTE MARIANNE (1938-). **Social Democratic** (SD) politician. The daughter of Bodil and Hal **Koch,** she graduated *cand. theol.* in 1964 and served as assistant priest, 1965-68. She was general secretary of the Danish Youth Council (Dansk Ungdoms Fællesråd) 1968-71, and chairman of the Consumer Council (Forbrugerrådet) 1974-79. She represented SD in the Folketing from 1975 and was the youngest member in Jens Otto **Krag**'s and Anker **Jørgensen**'s cabinets as Minister for Church Affairs 1971-73 and as Education Minister 1979-82 in Jørgensen's cabinet. From 1984 she was chairman of the Nordic Association (Foreningen Norden) and a member of the **Nordic Council**. AHT

BENTZON, NIELS VIGGO (1919-). Composer. He taught at the Conservatoire in Århus. His music fuses something of the lean, rhythmic neoclassicism of Stravinsky, the contrapuntal vitality of Hindemith, and the diatonicism of **Carl Nielsen**. His 620 compositions include works for piano, organ, chamber groups and orchestra, an opera and six ballets. He has also exhibited his paintings and drawings and received many Danish awards, including Artist of the Year in 1994. His fourth symphony (*Metamorphoses*, 1949) ranks with **Holmboe**'s sixth and seventh as arguably the finest Nordic symphonies. His *Kronik om René Descartes* (Op. 337) was premiered in 1975. AHT

BERG, CHRESTEN (1829-1891). Liberal politician, teacher, and journalist. Born near Lemvig in northern **Jutland** in a farming family, he began his life as a cowherd, but qualified as a teacher in 1850 and taught in Kolding in 1852-61 and in Bogø in 1861-74. He was an outstanding teacher, who did much to politicize the rural population of Denmark in the later 19th century. He first entered **parliament** in 1866 and was one of the founders of the United Liberal Party in 1870. In 1872 he led a bitter Liberal attack on the Conservative regime. Following the split in the Liberal Party in 1877, Berg lost his place on its executive committee and with **Viggo Hørup** formed a more radical group. He was one of the architects of the *visnepolitik* (withering policy) against the administration, by which government bills were lost in committee. In 1883 he was elected speaker of the **Folketing**, but two years later he and two other radicals were sentenced to six months' imprisonment after a police chief had been forcibly removed from the platform from which Berg was to speak in Holstebro. He strongly opposed any reconciliation with the Conservative administration, and his sudden death undoubtedly removed one of the main obstacles to this. He ran no fewer than 12 newspapers, of which six survived under his heirs. SPO. *See also* **Liberal Party.**

BERGH, RUDOLF (1824-1909). Medical practitioner. The son of a doctor, he qualified *cand. med.* in 1849 and practiced in **Copenhagen** hospitals, specializing in sexually transmitted diseases. In 1885 he took the initiative to found Vestre Hospital which became a leading center for the treatment of such diseases, especially among prostitutes. The hospital was renamed after him in 1910. AHT

BERING, VITUS JONASSEN (1681-1741). Seaman and explorer. Born in Horsens in **Jutland**, he entered the Russian navy in 1703 and was made captain of the fourth grade in 1715. By 1724 he had risen to the first grade and was sent in 1725 by tsar Peter the Great to investigate the easternmost part of Siberia. During his six-year voyage Bering discovered the straits which bear his name and so proved that there is no land bridge between Asia and America. In 1733 he set out to map the same area, including Alaska and the Aleutian Islands. He wintered on Kamchatka in 1740-41 and there founded the town of Petropavlovsk. Soon after this, however, he was shipwrecked and died of scurvy on what is now Bering Island. He bequeathed his property to the poor of Horsens. SPO

BERLING, CARL (1812-1871). Newspaper publisher and court official. In 1836 he took over the family printing business. Berling became closely attached to the court of **Frederik VII**, with whom he had been friends since their youth, and Frederik married his lover, subsequently Countess **Danner**. Berling's defense of her against the many who considered her relationship unsuitable isolated him politically. As a consequence he left Denmark in 1859. AHT

BERLING, ERNST HEINRICH (1708-1750). Printer and publisher. Born in Mecklenburg or Lauenburg, he learned his trade in Lauenburg, moved to **Copenhagen** in 1731, and in 1733 set up his own printing firm on Store Kannikestræde. In 1747 he was made printer to the Court and the following year successfully petitioned the Danish crown for permission to publish a newspaper in the capital. The first copy of what became Denmark's famous newspaper *Berlingske*

Tidende appeared as a twice-weekly on 3 January 1749. *See also* **Press**. SPO

BERLINGSKE TIDENDE is a Conservative Copenhagen daily newspaper and the oldest Danish newspaper still being published. Founded in January 1749 by the printer and publisher **Ernst Berling** as a continuation of the *Extraordinare Relationer* founded by Joachim Wieland, under the title *Kjøbenhavnske Danske Post Tidender*. It appeared at first only on Tuesdays and Saturdays. In 1808-31 it was an official government organ with the title *Det Privilegerede Statstidende*. Its circulation suffered from Denmark's economic difficulties after the Napoleonic Wars, but by 1831 it could be published daily, and from 1840, when it was the *Berlingske Politiske og Avertissement*, it also appeared on Sunday. By 1845 it had both morning and afternoon editions. Under the 20-year editorship of Mendel L. **Nathanson** from 1838, the paper's circulation rose to 9,000. In 1903, when it lost its monopoly of official notices, its morning edition could sell 15,000 copies. This had increased to 84,000 by 1925. It acquired its present title in 1935 and by 1963 had a circulation of 171,000. It faced difficulties in the 1970s, exacerbated by a five-month-long strike in 1977 and in 1982 faced closure. It recovered to enjoy a circulation in weekdays of about 133,000 and on Sundays of some 193,000 in 1996. Its afternoon tabloid offspring *B.T.* first appeared in 1916, developing a circulation in 1996 of 155,000 for its weekday editions and 190,000 on Sundays. SPO, AHT. *See also* **Press**.

BERNSTORFF, ANDREAS PETER (1735-1797). Statesman. Son of an official at the court of Hanover and nephew of **J.H.E. Bernstorff**, he entered Danish service in 1758 under the patronage of his uncle. He instituted reforms on the latter's estates on **Zealand** and followed him into retirement when his uncle was dismissed in 1770. He was recalled to office after the fall of **Struensee** in 1772 and the following year he became Danish foreign minister. As such, he followed a policy of close cooperation with Russia, and in 1780 carried Denmark into Catherine the Great's Armed Neutrality League to protect the trade of neutral powers during the War of American Independence. A separate agreement with Britain on the definition of contraband which angered the Tsarina led, however, to his dismissal at the end of the year. After the coup d'état in 1784 led by Crown Prince Frederik, Bernstorff resumed control of Denmark's foreign policy and was indeed the leading member of the new reforming administration. He entered reluctantly on war with Sweden in 1790 in fulfillment of Denmark's treaty obligations to Russia after the Swedish attack. He concluded an agreement with Sweden in 1794 to defend the two countries' trade. He died in office. SPO

BERNSTORFF, CHRISTIAN (1769-1835). Politician. The son of a landowner and politician, by 19 he was already a diplomat, serving in Stockholm 1794-97. Then he was foreign minister until 1810 and a member of the privy council (*gehejmestatsraadet*). His policy of neutrality in the Napoleonic Wars only partly succeeded. In 1812-16 he was ambassador in Vienna, 1816-18 in Berlin. In 1818-35 he was foreign minister of Prussia. AHT

BERNSTORFF, JOHAN HARTVIG ERNST (1712-1772). Statesman. Born in Hanover in a family of distinguished landowners and officials, he entered Danish state service in 1731 after an extensive "Grand Tour" of Europe. After a number of diplomatic postings, including the prestigious French embassy, he was in 1751 given charge of Denmark's foreign affairs, which he continued to direct for the next 19 years, favoring neutrality. He was also largely responsible for the country's economic policy, which he conducted in an orthodox mercantilist spirit, seeking the development of state-supported industry and trade. After surviving a crisis in Dano-Russian relations in 1762, Bernstorff concluded an alliance with the new tsarina Catherine II in 1765, which envisaged a final settlement of the dispute over the lands of the duke of **Holstein-Gottorp** in Holstein, a dispute which had dogged Danish foreign policy since the late 17th century. The Russian alliance added fuel to the attacks of his jealous rivals at court, and in 1770 he was dismissed by **Struensee** after the failure of an expedition against Algiers for which he was held responsible. He died in Hanover. SPO. *See also* **Holstein-Gottorp; Russia; Sweden**.

BERNTSEN, ARENT (1610-1680). Author. The son of a Norwegian cooper, he worked as a clerk and in various official posts, settling in 1644 in **Copenhagen**. In 1650-55 he published *Danmarckis oc*

Norgis fructbar Herlighed (The Fruitful Pleasure of Denmark and Norway), the first systematic topographical description of the two Kingdoms, combined with a detailed handbook of estate administration. AHT

BERNTSEN, KLAUS (1844-1927). Politician. The son of an estate-owner, he became an unqualified free-school teacher, later a high school teacher and head. Elected to the **Folketing** 1873-84 and 1886-1926 to represent the **Liberals**, he was interior minister 1908-09, prime minister and defense minister 1910-13, defense minister 1920-22, and minister without portfolio 1922-24. His main achievement was the preparation of the 1915 **constitution**. AHT

BIBLE. The earliest translation of the New Testament into Danish was made in 1524 by Hans Mikkelsen, the Malmö merchant who had advised King **Christian II** and who had followed the king into exile the previous year. Copies of the work were smuggled into Denmark from Christian's court at Lier. After the establishment of Lutheranism by King **Christian III**, a translation of the whole Bible, based on Luther's German version was prepared and published in 1550. The most important contributor to this was **Christiern Pedersen**. In 1607 a version which went back to the original sources was prepared by H.P. Resen, and further revisions were made in 1736, 1819, and 1871. A new version of the Old Testament, the first to benefit from the "new criticism", was approved in 1931 and a new version of the New Testament in 1948. A fresh translation of the New Testament appeared in 1974. A Danish Bible Society (Det Danske Bibelselskab), inspired by its English equivalent, was founded in 1814. It met competition in the later half of the 19th century from a Danish branch of the British Bible Society, which, among other things, supplied bibles to Danish troops during the Second **Slesvig-Holsten** War in 1864. SPO

BIEHL, DOROTHEA (1731-1788) wrote plays in the style of Ludvig **Holberg** and translated comedies, the most important of which was *Don Quixote* (1776-77). Her reputation rests on her stories of court life, bordering on scandal, and memoirs *Mit ubetydelige levnedsløb* (1787, *My Unimportant Life*, 1909). AHT

BILLE, ANDERS (1600-1657). Politician. The son of a **Jutland** nobleman, he began a military career at 19, first in German and then in Danish service, attaining the rank of field-marshal (*rigsmarskal*, five-star general) in 1642. He worked energetically but without success for a more effective **army** and died of wounds suffered during the Swedish capture of Frederiksodde. AHT

BINDESBØLL, GOTTLIEB (1800-1856). Architect. In 1817 he qualified as a builder of mills, then as an architect at the **Academy of Art**, then lived abroad 1834-38, mostly in Rome, becoming professor of architecture at the Academy in 1856. His designs include the **Thorvaldsen** museum (1839-47), houses for the Doctors' Association at Østerbro (1854), and the Agricultural College (1856), all in **Copenhagen**. He was the father of Thorvald Bindesbøll (1846-1908), who graduated from the Academy as an architect in 1876 but is best known for his decorative ceramics, with their distinctive asymmetrical snaking ornamentation. AHT

BING & GRØNDAHL see PORCELAIN, ROYAL DANISH

BIRCK, LAURITZ VILHELM (1871-1933). Economist and politician. A merchant's son, he graduated *cand. polit.* in 1893 and *dr. polit.* in 1902 and was professor at Copenhagen University from 1911 in macroeconomics and finance, writing economic theory from a social-conservative critique of commercial life. He was elected to the **Folketing**, 1903-10 and 1918-20, initially for the Right and then as a **Conservative**, breaking with the party in 1920 when it sought to annex **Flensborg** to Denmark. AHT

BIRKEDAL, VILHELM (1809-1892). Priest. After graduating *cand. theol.* in 1834, he served the parish of Ryslinge in **Funen** from 1849, from 1868 free of the national church. As a churchman he was a Bible-orthodox follower of N.F.S. **Grundvig**. He was an energetic proponent of **Scandinavianism**, a Danish boundary on the **Ejder**, and strong national defense. AHT

BISSEN, HERMAN VILHELM (1798-1868). Sculptor. Born in **Slesvig** of a **Holstein** farmer, he spent a lengthy period in Rome where he was influenced by **Thorvaldsen**, with whom he worked closely. He is considered the leading sculptor of Danish nationalist themes, including *The Danish Soldier after Victory* (Fredericia, 1858), *Frederik VI* (in **Frederiksberg** Garden, Copenhagen 1858), *The Lion of Isted* (Isted, 1863, then displayed in Berlin 1864-1945 and since in Tøjhusmuseet (Armory Museum) in Copenhagen, and the equestrian statue of *Frederik VII* (1873) in the square of **Christiansborg**, Copenhagen, which was completed by his son Vilhelm. AHT

BJERREGAARD, JYTTE RITT (1941-). Politician. Born in **Copenhagen**, she trained as a teacher 1964, matriculated in classical languages 1966, and taught in comprehensive schools 1964-1970, then lectured at Odense Teachers' College. In 1966 she married the historian Søren Mørch. Her parents, a carpenter and a bookkeeper, were active communists but she only became active in politics on completing her education. She was a **Social Democratic** (SD) parliamentary candidate 1969, and was elected to the **Folketing** from 1971, where she was a member of the Finance Committee, 1971-73 and 1974-75. From 1969 she chaired SD's education policy committee, her main area of interest. She opposed Danish EC entry in 1972 and supported the student movement, so was thought left-wing. Bjerregaard served as education minister in the **Jørgensen** governments of September to December 1973 and 1975-78, seeing through long-planned reforms of comprehensive schools, changes in the government of universities, and the regulation of access to higher education. Questions about her expenses on an official visit to UNESCO in Paris led to her resignation, but she returned to the cabinet 1979-81 as minister for social policy. A frequent, competent, and controversial speaker, she attracted opposition from left and right which often gave way to acceptance of her views. She was chair or vice-chair of the SD parliamentary group 1982-88, but in 1987 lost to **Svend Auken** in the contest for SD leadership in succession to Jørgensen. She chaired the Danish European Movement 1992-94 and in 1995 was appointed the Danish member of the European Commission headed by Jacques Santer, in charge of environmental policy. AHT

BJØRNBAK, LARS (1824-1878). Politician. The son of a teacher who himself qualified as a teacher in 1843, he was influenced by the rationalism of his time and rejected the Grundtvigian-influenced high school. In 1857 he founded an agricultural college in Viby, south of Århus with an entirely informative of education program. Unsuccessful as a **Liberal** candidate for the **Folketing**, he campaigned against **Scandinavianism** and for Danish disarmament. AHT

BJØRNER, JOHANNES LAURITZ (1869-1954). Politician. The son of a sawmill owner, he learnt the same trade and worked as a lumber-merchant. He helped found the Henry George Association in 1902 and the **Justice Party** in 1919. In books and lectures he campaigned for a free economy and a single land-tax. His wife Signe (1877-1958) shared similar political interests. Following a stay in the United States of America 1880-94, on her return to Denmark she was educated at Askov Folk High School, where the two met. She was secretary of the Henry George Association 1910-47 and of the Party in 1919. AHT

BLICHER, STEEN STEENSEN (1782-1848). Short-story writer and poet. Born near **Viborg** and educated largely at home by his father, a clergyman and author of theological and topographical works, he studied at the University of Copenhagen from 1799. As a student he was seriously ill but cured himself and gained employment for a time as private tutor on the island of **Falster**. He graduated *cand. theol.* in 1809 with distinction and married his uncle's 17-year-old widow. It did not prove a happy marriage. In 1811, in financial difficulties, the couple took over his father's glebe, and three years later he published his first collection of poems. In 1819 he secured a living near his birthplace. Still in financial need, Blicher there began to write realistic tales strongly colored by the Jutish countryside, in which he traveled widely, some in the local dialect. His fame as one of Denmark's greatest writers of short stories largely rests on these stories, e.g. *En Landsbydegns Dagbog* (1824, *Journal of a Parish Clerk*, 1945), *Hosekræmmeren* (1829, *The Hosier's Daughter*, 1945), or *Præsten i Vejlby* (1829, *The Minister of Vejlby*, 1945). His collected stories were published as five volumes in 1833-36, and as a collection of ballads and dialect tales, *E Bindstouw* (1842, In the Spinning Room). His collection of poems *Trækfuglene* (1837, Migratory Birds) focus on life's brevity with beautiful simplicity but without sorrow. A rather neglectful parish priest, he was pensioned off just before his death. SPO, AHT

BLIXEN, KAREN (-FINECKE) (1885-1962) was a short-story writer who also used the pen-name Isak Dinesen. Born at Rungstedlund, north of **Copenhagen**, into a wealthy family, after her father's suicide when she was 10 she was raised by puritanical relatives. She sought escape at the age of 29 by marrying Baron Bror von Blixen-Finecke, after an affair with his half-brother Hans. With him she moved to Kenya in 1913 to run a coffee plantation near Nairobi in the area later named Karen after her. Her marriage was dissolved in 1925 and she fell in love with the English adventurer Denys Finch-Hatton. After he died in a flying accident, the coffee factory burned down and the plantation failed financially, she had to return to Denmark in 1931 where she lived with her mother. Blixen published *Seven Gothic Tales* in 1934 (*Syv fantastiske forœllinger*, 1935). This collection was written in English, as was much of the rest of her work: *Winter's Tales* (1942), *Last Tales* (1957). Her African experiences form the basis of several of her books, the best known being *Den Afrikanske Farm* (1937, *Out of Africa* 1937), filmed in 1985 starring Meryl Streep and Robert Redford and awarded several Oscars. In the book she shows the deep sympathy for the native people which set her apart from the racist white community. Another of her stories, *Babette's Feast* (1950) was also filmed successfully. She was one of the inspirations of the literary journal *Heretica* (1948-54). She was buried at Rungstedlund, where she was born and where she wrote many of her stories. A museum was opened at Rungstedstandvej in 1991. SPO, AHT

BLOCH, CARL (1834-1890). Painter. A merchant's son, he studied at the **Academy of Art** from 1849. Beginning as a painter of landscapes and genre pictures of scenes from the west coast of **Jutland** and, following a stay in Italy 1859-66, of everyday scenes from Italian life, he is best known for his historical paintings such as *Niels Ebbesen and Count Gert* (1868), *Christian II in Sønderborg Prison* (1871), and his depiction of the dying Chancellor Niels Kaas handing over the keys to **Christian IV**'s Kingdom (1880). AHT

BLUHME, CHRISTIAN ALBRECHT (1794-1866). Politician. The son of an officer, he graduated *cand. jur.* in 1816 and followed a career in the central administration. He was appointed minister of trade in March 1848 but resigned in November. He was foreign minister 1851-54 and also prime minister 1852-53, continuing as foreign and prime minister 1864-65. In the 1850s he worked to retain the duchies in the state, and in 1864-65 to obtain the best peace terms for Denmark after the defeat of 1864. AHT *See also* **Slesvig-Holsten**.

BOHR, NIELS (1885-1962). Atomic physicist. The son of the professor of physiology Christian Bohr (1855-1911), he was professor at the University of Copenhagen 1916-55, where in 1913 he had already constructed a basic model of atomic structure. In 1920 he established the Institute of Theoretical Physics, which he directed until his death, and was awarded the **Nobel Prize** for physics in 1922. In 1940 he published the principle of atomic fission, which was the theoretical basis of the atom bomb. In 1947 he had the rare distinction as a commoner of being awarded the Grand Cross of the **Order of the Elephant**. He was appointed chairman of the Danish Atomic Energy Commission in 1957. His son Aage Bohr was also awarded the Nobel Prize for physics (jointly) in 1975. SPO

BOJSEN, FREDERIK (FREDE) (1841-1926). Liberal politician. He graduated *cand. theol.* in 1864 and the following year founded a **folk high school** on the island of **Møn**, which elected him to **parliament** in 1869. In 1878 he split the Liberal Party by agreeing with **Estrup**'s Conservative cabinet to support the budget and eight years later sought a way out of the confrontation which had brought political life in Denmark to a standstill. As one of the leaders of the moderate wing of the **Liberal Party**, he was largely responsible for negotiating the 1894 compromise that moderated the bitter political conflict which followed the reactionary constitution of 1866. He left parliament in 1901 and spent his later years as headmaster of Rødkilde Grammar School. SPO. *See also* **Change of System**.

BOMHOLT, LAURITS JULIUS (1896-1969). **Social Democratic** (SD) politician. He graduated *cand. theol.* in 1921 then taught from 1923 at the Labor High School in Esbjerg, becoming its head in 1924 at age 28. He was also a journalist for the *West Jutland Social Democrat*, edited the SD Youth movement's paper *Red Youth* 1924-

30, and was a popular speaker at youth meetings. He was the major influence on the party's cultural policy, supporting the May 1934 party program *Denmark for the People* which shifted SD's focus from a class party to a "people's party," a change crucial to SD's future development. He edited *Culture for the People* (1938), linking SD to the earlier national culture. Bomholt was an elected member of **Esbjerg** town council 1933-41 and on the executive committee of local SD organizations, representing Esbjerg continuously in **parliament**, 1929-68. He was parliamentary chairman (Speaker) 1945-1950 and 1964-68, and was a member of the Radio Council from 1934, chairing it 1940-53, except while education minister, February to October 1950; education minister again 1953-57, and minister for social policy 1957-61. As education minister he was responsible for radio and TV and shifted policy from the bland to the controversial; he also presided over reforms of apprentice education, improved education grants, and established the Language Council (1955), the Arts Fund (1956), and the Library School (1956). As Denmark's first minister of culture he increased funding for art museums, the Film Fund, libraries, the arts, and research. He wrote *Danish Poetry from the Industrial Revolution to the Present* (1930), linking history to social conditions. He also wrote *Arbejderkultur* (1932, Labor Culture), a programmatic work influenced by the Danish Liberal leader **Viggo Hørup**, by Soviet Russian theoreticians, and by German socialists which posited a new cultural ideal grounded in the worker's sense of reality and rejected the previous bourgeois culture, including Christian observances, in effect setting out the principles of a socialist culture policy. In addition he was the author of three novels, *Længsel* (1944, Longing), *Blomstrende grene* (1947, Flowering Branches), and *MF* (1962), the latter illustrating SD life in a provincial town; five volumes of autobiography (1954-61); a collection of poems *Kakkelvers* (1965); and a widely acclaimed novel, *Guds knægt* (1966, God's Lad). His development of a culture policy drew to the party many leaders of opinion from science, the arts, and culture. AHT

BORCH, OLE (1636-1690). Polymath. The son of a priest, he studied at Copenhagen University where in 1660 he became professor of philology, botany, and chemistry, and from 1664 of medicine, following a period of study abroad. His principle achievements were to establish the study of Latin based on classical studies, and in botany and medicine to expand knowledge of healing plants. AHT

BORDING, ANDERS (1619-1677). Poet. The son of a doctor, he acted as a tutor to various noble families. His poems include *Lærde kvinders forsvar* (1647, A Defence of Educated Women) in support of the spiritual equality of women. From 1665 he wrote professionally, publishing the first Danish monthly journal in verse, *Den danske Mercurius*, from 1666 until his death. AHT

BORGBJERG, FREDERIK HEDEGAARD JEPPESEN (known as F.J.) (1866-1936). **Social Democratic** (SD) politician. Raised by his merchant uncle in **Copenhagen**, he studied theology and was initially influenced by the educational ideas of Bishop **Grundtvig**, which were rooted in Danish culture rather than grammar school classicism. He moved on to Darwinism, Tolstoy, radicalism, and then socialism as the logical consequence of cooperativism, and was one of the first intellectuals to influence and lead the labor movement. Borgbjerg began writing in 1890 for *Social-Demokraten* (the SD newspaper) as "A peasant student"; a country wide speaking tour in 1892 plus his organizational ability helped to elect eight SDs to parliament in 1895. A member of parliament 1898-1936 and member of Copenhagen City Council 1898-1913, he led the SD press campaign during the great 1899 lockout, persuading members to accept the **September Agreement**, which formed the framework for subsequent negotiated industrial relations. He wrote *Socialdemokratiets Aarhundrede* (The Century of SD) with C.E. Jensen 1901-3 and worked hard in the 1903 SD party Congress to end the alliance with the **Liberals**. In 1908 he developed the party's positive relationship to the producer **cooperative movement**, but failed to include consumer cooperatives because **Stauning** wished to retain the many small shopkeepers who supported SD. He was the leading editor of *Social-Democraten* 1911-24 and 1926-29, worked hard for constitutional reform 1912-15, and was active in negotiations on Icelandic home rule in 1918. In the 1920 Easter Crisis King **Christian X** dismissed the **Radical Liberal** government although it still had a majority, ostensibly because of its views on the German border: Borgbjerg used *Social-Democraten* to proclaim this a coup d'état, since the labor movement feared that the king would lose them the democracy gained in the 1901 **Change of System**, as the Employers' Federation threatened general lockout. A general strike was called, and his preemptive publication helped to win it support; the unions achieved a negotiated settlement. He was minister of social affairs 1924-26, and education minister 1929-35, establishing Aarhus University and parents' councils for schools. He contributed greatly to Danish SD's expansion and its intellectual development, adapting well to negotiation and compromise. Overshadowed in the party leadership by Stauning after 1920, he remained loyal to him and to the party, at his best when large ideas or important decisions were at issue. AHT

BORGE, VICTOR (1909-). Actor and pianist. He was born in **Copenhagen**, the son of Bernhard Rosenbaum, the master of the royal orchestra, and was educated at the Royal Danish Music Conservatoire and in Vienna and Berlin. He made his debut as a pianist in 1926 in Copenhagen and in review in **Århus** in 1933. Later he built a career in films in Denmark and Sweden, then left from Petsamo, Finland, for New York in 1940. He appeared in Bing Crosby's radio show in 1941 and in 1942 was named "radio discovery of the year" by the press. He built a highly successful career in radio and television in the USA and became a US citizen in 1948.

Borge's musical talents brought engagements with major orchestras and world tours as soloist and conductor. His musical productions included Mozart's *The Magic Flute* for Cleveland Opera Co. in 1979 and at the **Royal Theater,** Copenhagen, in 1992, and Bizet's *Carmen* in London's Royal Opera House, Covent Garden, in 1986. But he is best known for his one-man shows of Comedy in Music (his New York show in 1953-56), a theme which he pursued under various titles for the next three decades. With Robert Sherman he wrote *My Favorite Intermissions* (1971, Danish and Swedish editions, *Noder og Unoder*, 1972) and *My Favorite Comedies in Music* (1981, *Musikomik*). He has also written *Smilet er den korteste afstand* (1997, The Smile is the Shortest Distance).

In 1965 he founded the Thanks to Scandinavia Fund for students from the four Nordic countries to study in the USA, and has endowed scholarships at Connecticut University, at State University of New York, and at Dana College, Nebraska. In 1985 he founded a Danish Music Fund in memory of his parents. Borge has been awarded honorary membership of the Royal Danish Orchestra and the **Absalon** Prize on Copenhagen's 800-year jubilee in 1967. He was given Doctorates of Music from Butler University, Indianapolis, Indiana (1970), Dana College, Nebraska (1976) and Connecticut University (1983) and a Doctorate of Humane Letters from Luther College, Decorah, Iowa (1985). His 75th birthday was celebrated with a charity concert with the Royal Choir in Copenhagen City Hall in 1984, and he was awarded the **Hans Christian Andersen** Prize in 1995. He has also been awarded the Variety Club's Big Silver Heart (1984), the Ellis Island Medal of Honor (1986), and the James Smithson Medal (1990). AHT

BORNHOLM is an island in the Baltic with an area of 58,831 hectares (227 square miles) and a 1991 population of 45,690. Its main town is Rønne with 14,315 inhabitants. A center of trade since prehistoric times, it is traditionally the original home of the Burgundians and appears at the end of the 9th century as 'Burgendaland'. Bornholm has been part of the Kingdom of Denmark at least since the end of the **Viking** Age. In the early Middle Ages it belonged to the archbishop of Lund, who in the middle of the 13th century built the great fortress of Hammershus, now under the protection of the National Museum. Its other outstanding medieval monuments are the four Round Churches, of which Østerlars (from about 1150) is the largest. It came under the control of the Crown in 1522 but was mortgaged to Lübeck in 1525 and, in spite of attempts to recapture it in 1535 during the **Count's War**, did not return to Danish control until 1575. Occupied by the Swedes in 1645 and granted to them by the Treaty of **Roskilde** in 1658, it was liberated when the islanders captured Hammershus Castle and gave the island back to **Frederik III** in 1660. At the end of **World War II** it was occupied by Russian troops after the German garrison refused to surrender and following a severe bombardment of the towns of Rønne and Nexø. The Russians did not leave until March 1946. The island has its own flag — the **Dannebrog** of Denmark with a green instead of a white cross on a red ground. SPO. See also **Churches, Round.**

BØRRESEN, HAKON (1876-1954). Composer. The son of a grocer, he learnt piano, cello, and music theory from an early age. His violin concerto (1904) was widely played. His greatest success was his one-act opera, *Den kongelige gæst* (1919, The Royal Guest), based on Henrik **Pontoppidan**'s story — by 1964 it had been performed 134 times at the **Royal Theater**. His opera *Kaddara* (1921) has a Greenlandic theme. In addition to three symphonies, he wrote for the theater and ballet. He spent his summers at **Skagen,** writing *Prelude* in honor of its 500th anniversary as a market town. He was a leading figure in Danish musical life for the first half of the 20th century and was chairman of the Danish Composers' Association (Dansk Tonekunstnerforening) for 25 years from 1924. His efforts for Nordic cooperation were rewarded by membership of the Swedish Music Academy and honorary membership of the Norwegian Composers' Association. Strongly influenced by late romanticism, he was uninfluenced by **Carl Nielsen**'s break with these ideals. AHT

BORUP, JOHAN (1853-1946). The son of a priest, he graduated *cand. theol.* in 1877 and then taught high school. In 1891 he founded a high school for ladies and gentlemen with a nonuniversity curriculum in buildings by Frederiksholms Kanal in **Copenhagen**, from 1916 named Borup's High School. This was the first **folk high school** in the city. AHT

BOURNONVILLE, AUGUST (1805-1879). Dancer, choreographer, and founder of the Danish ballet tradition. Son of Austrian-born ballet-master Antoine Bournonville (1760-1843) at the Royal Theater in **Copenhagen**, he first appeared on the stage at the age of eight and studied in Paris before returning to Denmark to succeed his father in 1830 as ballet master at the Royal Theater. He remained at the Theater until 1877, with the exception of the periods 1855-56, when he was ballet-master with the Vienna Opera, and 1861-64, when he worked in the Royal Theater in Stockholm. Bournonville created over 50 ballets, many still performed today, including *La Sylphide, Napoli,* and *Et folkesagn* (A Popular Legend). His ballet *The Dancing School* is based on his Friday class at the Royal Theater. His *Mit teaterliv* (3 volumes, 1848-78, My Life in the Theater) is a fine autobiography. SPO

BRAHE, TYCHO (or **TYGE**) (1546-1601). Astronomer. Born in Knutstorp in **Scania** (then part of the Danish Kingdom), the son of a member of the Royal Council, he attended the University of Copenhagen and a number of universities in the German-speaking world to study law. While abroad he became more interested in the physical sciences and after returning to Denmark in 1570 set up an observatory at Herrevad Abbey in Scania, the property of his uncle. After acquiring European fame with his account of the discovery of a new star in Cassiopeia *(De Stella Nova)*, in 1576 he was granted the island of Hven (**Ven**) in the **Sound** by **Frederik II**, on which he founded the royal observatory of Uraniborg. To this he attracted research workers from all over Europe. Although he rejected the Copernican view of the universe and developed his own geocentric system, his discoveries did much to undermine the Aristotelian view of the universe then largely accepted, and he drew up the most accurate account of the heavens yet seen. He left Hven in 1597 after quarreling with the Crown, and in 1599 entered the service of Emperor Rudolf in Prague. There he was joined by the young Johan Kepler, who built on Brahe's work. He died in Prague and is buried there in the church of Our Lady of Týn. The largest planetarium in Western Europe, located in central **Copenhagen**, is named after him. Opened in 1989, it was designed by Knud Munk. SPO

BRANDES, EDVARD (1847-1931). Radical politician and writer. After graduating in oriental languages he assisted his brother **Georg** as literary and theater critic for a number of journals. Elected to the **Folketing** in 1880 for the island of Langeland, Brandes caused some scandal by proclaiming himself an atheist, much to the discomfort of the Grundtvigian wing of the Liberal Party to which he belonged. He came to represent an urban and cosmopolitan liberalism, expressed in an article he published in the newspaper *Morgenbladet* in 1883 on the occasion of the centenary of **Grundtvig**'s birth. As a result he was forced to yield direction of the paper to moderates under **Christen Berg**. The following year he and others of like mind founded *Politiken*, which rapidly overtook *Morgenbladet* in popularity. Brandes resigned from parliament after the compromise reached between moderate **Liberals** and the **Conservative** government in 1894, of which the radical members of the party strongly disapproved. In 1900 his unfavorable review of the performance of the actor Robert Schyberg in the play *Mester Geert Westphaler* led the latter to attack Brandes on Østergade in **Copenhagen**. Brandes consequently challenged Schyberg to a duel, which was fought without injury to either party in Ermelund on 10 February. Brandes gave up his editorship of *Politiken* in 1904 and served as minister of finance in the governments formed by **Carl Th. Zahle** in 1909-1910 and 1913-1920. SPO

BRANDES, GEORG (1842-1927). Literary critic and brother of **Edvard Brandes**. Born into a well-to-do Jewish family in **Copenhagen**, he studied law and literature at the University there before traveling abroad. In France he encountered the positivist criticism of Hippolyte Taine and on his return to Denmark began in November 1871 a course of lectures at his old university on Main Currents in Nineteenth Century Literature (vols. 1-6, 1872-90), which are taken to mark the Modern Breakthrough in Scandinavian literature and the beginning of the Modernist Movement which dominated the following two decades. This is characterized by rejection of late romanticism in favor of critical, realistic, and nonreligious writing. From the 1890s he increasingly developed the cult of the great individual.

Brandes antagonized conservative opinion by his anticlericalism and his political radicalism, and because of this he was denied the chair in literature at the university for which he was the best qualified candidate. He then spent five productive years in Berlin. After his return to Denmark, he introduced the writings of Nietzsche to his countrymen. He remained active into old age, but his influence waned after the turn of the century. His vast output included *Søren Kierkegaard* (1877), *Holberg* (1884), *Shakespeare* (I-III, 1895-96), and *Goethe* (I-II, 1914-15). With his brother Edvard he published the periodical *Det nittende århundrede* 1874-77 (The 19th Century). SPO, AHT

BRANDT, MOGENS (1909-1970) began an acting career in 1929 but is best known as a gastronomic journalist, from 1961 in *Politiken*, castigating bad ingredients and poor cooking techniques in his books *Det gode bord* (1963, The Good Table), *Man tager en sølvfad* (1965, Take a Silver Dish) and *Køkkenglæder* (1968, Kitchen Pleasures). AHT

BRAUER, WILLY (1916-). Politician. After elementary school he trained as a typographer, becoming chairman 1945-1962 of the **Co-**

penhagen branch of the Danish Typographic Trade Union, and was prominent in the 18-week strike in 1947 which stopped the non-socialist press and started a public debate on freedom of expression. A political wanderer, at 14 he was chairman of the Young **Social Democrats** in Odder but left SD four years later; joined the **Communists** 1940 (illegal during the 1940-45 German occupation), leaving with Aksel **Larsen** to found the **Socialist People's Party** in 1958-59. Brauer opposed Larsen's 1966-67 parliamentary support for SD and became a Left Socialist in the 1967 party split, but later ceased his party membership. Elected to Copenhagen City Council 1950-62, he headed the City's Fifth Department responsible for city transport 1962-70, overseeing the transition from trams to buses and expansion of electricity and gas supplies. He was a director from 1970 of I/S Amagerforbrænding, the Amager incineration company in the suburb east of Copenhagen, and from 1973 also of A/S Kommunekemi, a similar organization in Nyborg, responsibilities which made good use of Brauer's outstanding administrative abilities. AHT

BRESEMANN, SOPHUS HANS MADSEN DAUGAARD (1864-1945). Politician. As a youth he was an active organizer of coopers' apprentices, and in 1885 revived the Coopers Union, of which he was chairman 1886-91, extending its organization nationally and becoming its chief executive 1890-97. Bresemann was an active propagandist, both as an orator and in writing, publishing *The Coopers' Handbook: Instruction in Trade Theory and Practice* (1892) and *Boycotting* (1893). He was also editor and publisher (1893-97) of a union paper *Samarbejdet* (Collaboration) which paved the way for *De samvirkende fagforbund* (the cooperating trade unions, forerunner of *LO*) and was a representative at its first congress. He became editor of the *Lolland-Falster Social Democrat* newspaper in Nakskov 1901-28; in this shipbuilding and harbor town his efforts built SD into a force which gathered momentum at each election. He was elected 1905 to Nakskov town council — SD became the largest party in 1906 and gained a majority 1913. Bresemann was governing mayor 1914-28, the first Social Democrat to hold such office outside Copenhagen, and helped found Nakskov Shipyard, 1914. Local schools and care for children and the sick became a model for the country; roads, docks, and electricity supply were improved, and house building was expanded. He was chief executive of the borough association (Købstadsforeningen) 1917-33, but a declining local economy brought the town financial difficulties in late 1920s-33. He was a member of the **Folketing** 1913-35, where he spoke for SD on public works, social assistance, taxation, and limitation of migrant Polish labor. Attacked for his development of local socialism, he replied by writing *Kommunalt Styre i Nakskov* (1917, Local Government in Nakskov) and *Nakskov Kommunestyre* (1930-31). In print and in politics a natural fighter, he was a warm hearted defender of ordinary people and the needy. AHT

BRIDGES. In a country of 482 islands, about one hundred of them inhabited, bridge-building in Denmark has been important for improved communications. For example, the ferro-concrete road and rail Little Belt bridge between **Jutland** and **Funen**, with a total length of 1.178 km (0.73 miles), was built in 1929-35 at a cost of 32 million kroner. A suspension bridge nearby was opened in 1970 to take the increased road traffic. *Storstrømmsbroen*, which carries road and rail traffic between south **Zealand** and **Falster**, was built in 1932-37 at a cost of about 40 million kroner; at 3.211 km (2 miles): it remained the longest bridge in Europe until the 1970s. Funen was linked to Taasinge by bridge and causeway in 1962 and the link was later extended to the island of Langeland.

In the 1990s two very large bridges were under construction. The **Sound** (Øresund) link was calculated in 1990 to cost US$3.5 billion and the Great Belt link US$4.5 billion, to be recovered by tolls in both cases, but the two projects have had important employment effects for the Danish economy, as also in the 1930s when the **Social Democrat/Radical Liberal** government used bridge-building to counter economic depression. A "fixed link" across the **Sound** between Malmö (Sweden) and **Copenhagen** was started in 1988, and is expected to take road traffic by 2000. Starting with a motor and rail terminal at Copenhagen airport on the island of Amager, a 3.51 km tunnel emerges onto an artificial island 4 km long, from which 8 km of cable bridge continues to the Swedish shore. A major concern in the planning was that the link should have minimal blocking effect on the flow of water to and from the Baltic. The bridge carries cars on the upper deck and trains on the lower deck. It links together a single urban region in Denmark and Sweden (Ørestad) with the financial strength to compete vigorously in Europe.

Another fixed link of bridge and tunnel across the Great Belt between **Zealand** and **Funen** opened to rail traffic in 1997 and road vehicles in June 1998. The East Bridge here has a free span of 1.624 km and a total length of 6.8 km, the longest in the world after the Akashi bridge in Japan. It carries road vehicles, while the railway goes through a rather longer tunnel. A further 6.6 km West Bridge takes both road and rail traffic from the small island of Sprogø to Knudshoved in Funen. There are further plans for a link southward between the islands of **Lolland** in Denmark and Fehmarn in Germany. AHT

BRITAIN. Danish relations with Britain have always been close, if not invariably friendly. After the reconquest of the Danelaw by the kings of Wessex during the 10th century, **Viking** attacks were resumed at the end of that century and culminated in the election in 1016 of King Canute (*see* **Knud I**), who married his predecessor's widow and used England as his base from which to rule his North Sea empire. In the early 15th century, King **Erik VII of Pomerania**, the first king of the **Kalmar Union**, married Philippa, the daughter of King Henry IV. Later in the century King **Christian I**'s daughter Margrethe was married to King James III of Scotland in 1465, the Shetland and Orkney islands being pledged for payment of her dowry and consequently lost to Denmark when this could not be paid. This occurred in the midst of a long Anglo-Danish dispute over English encroachments on trade with **Iceland**, which was not settled until 1490. Ties with both countries were, however, strengthened by the marriage of James VI to King **Christian IV**'s sister Anne fourteen years before he ascended the English throne as King James I. The Earl of Bothwell, the third husband of James's mother, Mary Queen of Scots, had fled to Norway after his defeat in 1567. King Frederik refused requests for his extradition, but imprisoned him, first in Malmö and then in the castle of Dragsholm in **Zealand**, where he died insane in 1578.

Denmark and Britain found themselves briefly on opposing sides in 1666-7 during the Second Dutch War, but King William III hired Danish troops, who helped him defeat James II at the Battle of the Boyne in 1689. In the 18th century, although Denmark generally found it more advantageous to ally with France, who was more generous with subsidies, both King **Frederik V** and King **Christian**

VII were married to English princesses. In 1801, however, Denmark's adherence to the Russian-led Armed Neutrality League led to the first **Battle of Copenhagen** between British and Danish fleets, and six years later the Danes' refusal to surrender their fleet to Britain, who feared that it would fall into French hands, led to a three-day bombardment of **Copenhagen** by the British before they left with the Danish fleet in tow. Some bitterness was felt in Denmark at the lack of British help during the Second **Slesvig-Holsten** War, but from the later 19th century strong commercial links were forged, with Danish butter and bacon exchanged for British coal. Dynastic ties were again established by the marriage of **Christian IX**'s daughter Alexandra to Edward, Prince of Wales, later King Edward VII. Danish accession to the German demand in 1914 to mine the entry to the Baltic came only after a personal communication between the royal houses, although throughout **World War I**, Denmark was regarded by the British as being within the German sphere of influence. During **World War II** the apparent collaborationist policy of the Danish government at the beginning of the German occupation gave way to sympathy; much assistance was given to the Danish Resistance and a Freedom Council was set up in London by Danes in exile. Close relations continued through **NATO**, and Danish applications to the **European Community**, culminating in membership from 1972, were contingent on parallel applications by Britain. SPO, AHT

BRIX, HARALD (1841-1881). Politician. Working mostly in a **Copenhagen** bookseller, with his cousin Louis **Pio** and P. Geleff he helped found the socialist movement in Denmark, publishing and editing *Socialisten* in 1871-72. In 1873 he was sentenced to three years in prison for threats to the bourgeois civil order and a further four years for *lese-majesty* and defamation in *Ravnen*, in which he took a more radical line than most other socialists of the time. AHT

BROCK, NIELS (1731-1802). The son of a merchant, he learned the same trade in **Lübeck** and **Copenhagen**, where he established himself as an independent merchant, making a fortune in the late 18th century from colonial trade. He left part of his fortune to found what became Niels Brock Copenhagen Business College. AHT

BRÖMSEBRO, TREATY OF (August 13, 1645) was the peace treaty between Denmark and Sweden which ended **Torstensson's War**. It was concluded after negotiations opened the previous February between **Corfitz Ulfeld** and the Swedish chancellor Axel Oxenstierna in the frontier town of Brömsebro, south of Kalmar. By it Denmark surrendered to Sweden exemption from the payment of **Sound** tolls, the Norwegian provinces of Jämtland and Härjedalen, and the islands of Gotland and Ösel. The province of Halland was to be held by Sweden for 30 years, but was never returned to the Danish crown. The Dutch and the Swedes were freed from Elbe Tolls, and Sweden acquired Bremen and Verden from Frederik III Duke of Gottorp. The terms might have been even harsher for Denmark had not French mediation previously brought about a separate peace between Denmark and Sweden's Dutch allies, by which the Danes agreed to lower the Sound Tolls below their level in 1628. Brömsebro was also the scene of the signing of an alliance between Denmark and Sweden in 1541. SPO, AHT

BRØNDSTED, JOHANNES (1890-1965). Archaeologist. After graduating *cand. mag.* in classical languages in 1916 he began a career in the **National Museum**. In 1941 he was appointed professor of Nordic Archaeology in the University of Copenhagen, returning to the museum as director 1951-60. His book *Danmarks oldtid* I-III (1938-40, Prehistory of Denmark) is a milestone in Danish archaeological writing. AHT

BRØNDSTED, PETER OLUF (1780-1842). Archaeologist. The son of a professor, he graduated *cand. theol.* in 1802 then studied in Germany, France, Italy, Greece, and Asia Minor in 1806-13, returning to the University of Copenhagen as professor of philology and, from 1832, archaeology. On many journeys he studied ancient Greek relics and his fieldwork made new advances in classical archaeology. He described some of his trips in *Voyages dans la Grèce* (1825 ff), also translated into German but not Danish. AHT

BRORSON, HANS ADOLPH (1694-1764). Bishop and poet. The son of a clergyman Brorson was enrolled at the University of Copenhagen in 1712. He there, however, fell ill and had to return home. After recovering, he spent five years as a tutor for his uncle at

Løgumkloster, where he began to be strongly influenced by German **Pietism**. On graduating *cand. theol.* in 1721, he secured a living in his father's parish and then from 1729 in Tønder, where he translated Pietist hymns into Danish and composed some of his own. In 1739, 257 of these were published in the collection *Troens rare klenodie* (Rare Jewel of Faith). In 1741 Brorson was appointed bishop of Ribe, continuing to write religious poems imbued with a deep piety and a melancholy which reflected the loss of his 10 children when young and of his wife in childbirth. He is regarded as one of Denmark's greatest religious poets. SPO

BUHL, VILHELM (1881-1954). **Social Democrat** politician. A lawyer and financier, he was tax director of Copenhagen from 1924 to 1937. He entered the **Landsting** in 1932 and in 1937 became minister of finance in **Thorvald Stauning**'s Social Democratic and **Radical Liberal** cabinet. In this capacity he made himself famous for his pronouncement that "You should pay your taxes with joy." On Stauning's death he became prime minister May-November 1942, and made himself widely unpopular with a radio broadcast in which he labeled saboteurs as unpatriotic. Buhl was replaced by **Erik Scavenius**, but was chairman of the committee of nine which linked the heads of department to the leaders of the political parties after the German takeover in August 1943. After the end of the Occupation in May 1945 he formed a broad coalition government but left office after the serious setbacks suffered by his party in the elections in October and was succeeded by the Liberal **Knud Kristensen**. Buhl served in 1947-50 as minister for economic coordination in **Hans Hedtoft**'s first cabinet. SPO. *See also* **World War II**.

BUKH, NIELS (1880-1950). Gymnastic teacher. After working as a farmhand, seaman, and fisherman, in 1909 he passed the gymnastic teachers' examination and in 1912 qualified as a general teacher. In 1920 he founded the first Danish gymnastic high school in Ollerup and was its principal until his death. He created a rhythmic and dynamic form of gymnastics which accentuated movement, and publicized it worldwide in a series of journeys. AHT

BURMEISTER & WAIN is an engineering and shipbuilding organization, for long the largest industrial enterprise in Denmark. It has its origins in the workshop set up by the ironfounder Hans Henrik Baumgarten, which began production on Købmagergade in **Copenhagen** in 1843. He was joined by Carl Christian Burmeister (1821-1898) as a partner in 1846. Baumgarten withdrew in 1861, and in 1865 the firm was joined by the Scot, William Wain. It was reorganized as a joint-stock company in 1872 under the great entrepreneur **C.F. Tietgen** and in the same year a shipyard was built at Christianshavn in Copenhagen.

Rapid expansion began in 1908, when manufacture of diesel motors was begun, and the firm became a world leader in their application to sea-going ships. It launched the Selandia, the earliest ocean-going, motor-driven ship, commissioned by the **East Asiatic Company**, in 1912. Economic depression led to bankruptcy in 1932, but the company was supported by the state. The workplace has been a scene of labor conflict, with the first large strike in Denmark occuring in 1871. During World War II its workers did much to sabotage production for the occupying German powers. In June 1944 workers at Burmeister & Wain began the "go home early" movement in protest at the curfew imposed by the German occupiers.

A crisis in 1971 led to division of the company into two independent enterprises, one for shipbuilding (B&W Industri) and one for motor manufacturing (B&W Motor). These were again linked in 1974 when the holding company Burmeister & Wain A/S was formed by Jan Bonde Nielsen, but the restructuring did not succeed and in 1979 engine production was sold to Germany, becoming MAN B&W Diesel. In 1980 the parent company ceased trading, but orders for five new ships revived the ship-yard for a further 15 years. In 1996 its main US creditors defaulted, its employees lost their jobs, and numerous subcontractors lost heavily. In 1998 remaining B&W interests were in Energy, Contracting and Ship design. There is a museum of ships and diesel engines on the Christianshavn site. SPO, AHT

BUXTEHUDE, DIDERIK (DIETRICH) (c. 1637-1707). Organist and composer. Born in either Hälsingborg, or in **Elsinore** where his father was organist of the Mariakyrke, he became organist in Hälsingborg in 1657-60 before succeeding his father in Elsinore in 1660-68. He was then invited to be the organist of the Marienkirche in **Lübeck**, where he was visited by leading musicians of the day,

fame as an organist. Buxtehude produced two collections of trio sonatas, many fine choral works including c. 120 cantatas, as well as about 100 pieces for organ and for harpsichord and small orchestra, although only one cantata is known to have been written while he was in Denmark. His precociously inspired pupil Nicolaus Bruhns (1665-1697) died young. SPO, AHT

- C -

CABINETS. According to the **Constitution** of 1849, the king was free to choose his ministers without reference to the majority in the legislature, and for much of his reign (1863-1906) **Christian IX** relied on conservative advisers in defiance of the growing liberal majority in the Lower House (**Folketing**), although supported for much of that time by majorities in the more conservative Upper House (**Landsting**). The **Change of System** in 1901 marked acceptance by the king of the parliamentary principle, by which cabinets should not have a majority against them in the Folketing, although this was not written into the constitution until 1953. As is clear from the list of cabinets (see Appendix 2), this negative formulation of the principle is significant: not since 1913 has a single-party cabinet been able to count on a majority of votes from its own party in the Folketing, and majority coalitions are also rare. All governments have been led by one of "the four main parties", **Social Democrats, Radical Liberals, Liberals** (Venstre), or **Conservatives.** After the Change of System, Liberals formed majority governments until the **Alberti** scandal, and Radical Liberals led the country through World War I. A series of directionless minority governments during the 1920s was followed from 1929 by the Social Democrat and Radical Liberal coalition under Thorvald **Stauning** which stabilized the economy on pre-Keynesian counter-cyclical lines, carried through extensive social reforms, and laid the foundation of the Danish **welfare state.** Until 1966 there was close liaison both in and out of government between the Social Democrats and the Radical Liberals under a succession of Social Democratic prime ministers: Hans **Hedtoft,** H.C. **Hansen,** Viggo **Kampmann** and Jens Otto **Krag.** From 1968, when the Radical Liberals under Hilmar **Bauns-**

gaard led a majority nonsocialist coalition, the Radical Liberals have held a balance between the socialist parties (Social Democrats, **Socialist People's Party** and sometimes smaller socialist parties) and the bourgeois parties (the largest being the Conservatives and the Liberals). The 1973 "earthquake" election doubled the number of parties in the Folketing and made government formation a much more complex process.

Minority cabinets have been the norm, with tacit voting support for the cabinet from other parties in the Folketing, on the basis of policy agreements reached by negotiation in the important parliamentary committees. During 1973-82 cabinets were led mainly by the Social Democrat Anker **Jørgensen** and in 1982-93 by the Conservative Poul **Schlüter**, until the **Tamil Affair** compelled his resignation. Schlüter was the first Conservative prime minister since 1901. He frequently faced a hostile majority on foreign policy (so the 1980s became known as the period of footnote politics, as Denmark had to enter reservations to NATO and EC decisions) and on environmental issues, but he retained majority support on economic policy and thus continued in office. Under the Social Democrat Poul Nyrup **Rasmussen**, who succeeded Schlüter, a "national compromise" spanning from the Socialist People's Party on the left to the Conservatives on the right (and excluding only minor socialist groupings on the left and the **Progress Party** on the right) supported ratification of the **European Union**'s Maastricht Treaty and secured its acceptance in the second (1993) referendum. AHT. *See also* **Appendix 2**

CANUTE *see* **KNUD**

CARLSBERG BREWERIES. In November 1847 **J.C. Jacobsen** produced the first Bavarian-style beer brewed in Denmark in a newly built brewery at Valby (now a suburb of **Copenhagen**), which he named Carlsberg after his son Carl, who had studied brewing technologies in Denmark and abroad. The brewery became one of the largest in the world, licensing its product to producers elsewhere, and with exports to more than 130 countries. Increasing international competition brought a merger in 1970 with its main Danish rival, Tuborg, under the name De forenede Bryggerier A/S, later changed to Carlsberg A/S. Purchase of Tetley made Carlsberg-

Tetley the third-biggest brewery in Britain. An attempt by Bass to buy this company failed in 1997. AHT

CARLSBERG FOUNDATION, THE, was initiated in 1876 by the brewer **J.C. Jacobsen** with a grant of 2,200,000 kroner to support the work of the Carlsberg Laboratory, which had been established the previous year, and research in science, philosophy, and history. In 1878 it took over the administration of the National Historical Museum at **Frederiksborg** Castle and on Jacobsen's death in 1887 acquired his Old Carlsberg Brewery. In 1902 his son Carl added his New Carlsberg Brewery, the income from which went toward the setting up of a New Carlsberg Foundation for support of the arts. On the amalgamation of the Carlsberg and Tuborg breweries in 1970 it was agreed that the Foundation should hold a majority interest in the new organization. It is administered by a board appointed by the Royal Danish **Academy of Science** and owns the **Carlsberg Breweries**. SPO

CAROLINE MATILDE (1751-1775). Queen of Denmark 1766-72. Wife of King **Christian VII** and sister of King George III of England. Largely neglected by her husband immediately after their marriage in 1766, she became the lover of the royal doctor Johann Friedrich **Struensee** and bore him a child. On Struensee's fall from power and execution, she was imprisoned in **Kronborg Castle** and her marriage was dissolved. She was taken from **Elsinore** on a British warship to her brother's possession of Hanover. She died in Celle of smallpox, leaving behind a reputation for piety and good works. SPO

CARSTENSEN, EDWARD (1815-1898). Colonial administrator and brother of Georg **Carstensen**. The son of a diplomat, he graduated *cand. jur.* in 1841 and in 1842-50 served as the last governor of the Gold Coast (which became Ghana in 1957) before the colony was sold to Britain. He opposed the illegal slave trade there and prepared plans to "civilize" Africa along European cultural and moral lines. AHT

CARSTENSEN, GEORG (1812-1857), younger brother of **Edward**. He was born in Algiers, where his first impressions were of exotic scenes of light and color in oriental style. He was commissioned as an army lieutenant in 1835, then traveled in southern Europe, Africa, and America until 1838. On returning to Denmark he was a journalist, publishing entertaining weekly journals during 1839-45. In 1843 he founded **Tivoli** but quarreled with his directors and left in 1847. He attempted to found a similar park, Alhambra, but this failed. He went abroad, returning in 1855 to die soon afterward, embittered and bankrupt. AHT

CASTBERG, PETER ATKE (1779-1823). Teacher. The son of a priest, he graduated *dr. med.* 1802 and became the first principal of the Royal Institute for the Deaf and Dumb (Det kgl. Døvstummeinstitut) when it was founded in 1807. He is considered a pioneer of teaching in this field. AHT

CATHOLICISM, ROMAN see RELIGION

CAVLING, HENRIK (1858-1933) qualified as a teacher in 1881 but instead took to journalism, reporting for *Politiken* from 1886 and becoming its editor 1905-28. He redesigned the paper as many-sided in its coverage, with short, easily read articles, short leader articles, and a regular longer feature editorial article (*kronik*) often by a guest writer, a newspaper style later adopted by other papers. AHT

CAVLING, IB HENRIK (1918-1978). The son of a journalist, he developed a writing career of translations, short articles, and, later, short stories for weekly periodicals. In 1952-78 he published 57 entertaining novels, including *Arving* (1952, The Heir, filmed 1954), *Charlotte* (1954), *Askepot* (1956, Cinderella), and *A/S Palma Mallorca* (1963). AHT

CENSORSHIP. From the **Reformation** until 1770 all publications in Denmark were subject to censorship by the University of **Copenhagen**, the bishops and the police depending on their content. But already in the middle of the 18th century, under the influence of the **Enlightenment**, controls were relaxed, in practice, and in 1770 all restrictions were abolished by Johann **Struensee**. The following year, however, after a stream of scurrilous attacks in print on the minister, authors were made responsible for their writings, and in 1773, after Struensee's fall, newspapers were forbidden to criticize government acts. In September 1799, alarmed by fears of Jacobinism, the government imposed further restrictions, and from 1810 only privileged newspapers were allowed to print political news of any kind. The growth of liberalism in the 1830s led to talk of a further tightening of **press** control. In spite of the King's reassurances, the Society for the Correct use of Press Freedom (Selskabet for Trykkefrihedens rette Brug) was formed in 1835 with the newspaper *Det Danske Folkeblad* (The Danish People's Paper) as its mouthpiece. Six years later the liberal Orla **Lehmann** was imprisoned for delivering a speech criticizing the absolutist constitution. The "June **Constitution**" of 1849 promised freedom of the press, which was embodied in the Press Act of 1851. In spite of this, laws against blasphemy and obscenity remained in force, and theatrical censorship was exercised by censors attached to the **Royal Theater** and private theaters in Copenhagen and provincial towns.

Censorship of films was instituted in 1909 for cinemas in Copenhagen but elsewhere was a police matter until a national board was formed in 1914. Censorship of all publications was reintroduced by the German occupying authorities after the resignation of the Danish government in August 1943 but abolished again in 1945. Theatrical censorship was done away with in 1954. In 1967 all restrictions on the sale of pornographic writing were abolished and two years later of those on pictorial pornography. The State Film Censorship continues to examine all films which might be shown to children under 12 or 16 and classifies them accordingly. SPO. *See also* **Press**.

CENTER DEMOCRATS (Centrumdemokaterne) were founded in November 1973 by Erhard Jakobsen, following a split with the **Social Democrats**, and from 1989 they were led by his daughter Mimi Jakobsen. They won 14 seats and 7.8 percent of the popular vote in the 1973 election but then had mixed fortunes until their greatest success, obtaining 15 seats in 1981. They gave parliamentary support to Anker **Jørgensen**'s 1979-82 cabinets and were represented both in Poul **Schlüter**'s cabinets of 1982-88 and in Poul Nyrup **Rasmussen**'s Social Democrat cabinets of 1993-96. They are keen supporters of European Union (EU) membership, and see their role as a central and moderating influence able to cooperate equally with socialist and nonsocialist parties. They were closely associated with the Active Listeners and Viewers association (see **Radio and Television**) also started by Jacobsen. AHT

CENTER PARTY, Miðflokkurin, is a Faroes political party formed in 1991 following internal dissent in the **Christian People's Party** and **Fishing Industry Party**, with which it shares much, including a Christian perspective and active support for the family. Led by Alvur Kirke, in 1996 the party had two members in the Lagting (assembly). AHT

CHANGE OF SYSTEM (Systemskiftet). The introduction of parliamentary government in Denmark in 1901 with the appointment by King **Christian IX** of a Liberal government, headed by professor J.H. **Deuntzer,** after the overwhelming victory of the **Liberal Party** in elections to the **Folketing**. Parliamentary **government** was not, however, enshrined in the **constitution** until 1953. SPO

CHARLOTTENBORG PALACE in Copenhagen is on Kongens Nytorv. Originally built in 1672-83 by the Dutch architect Evert Janssen for King **Frederik III**'s illegitimate son Ulrik **Gyldenløve**, in 1700 it was bought by King **Christian V**'s widow queen Charlotte Amalie, after whom it was then named. In 1753 it became the home of the Royal **Academy** of Painting, Sculpture and Architecture, which is still housed there. Annual art exhibitions have been held there since 1807, and in 1857 the Charlottenborg Exhibition became a separate institution with its own building behind the palace erected in 1883. SPO. *See also* **Amalienborg Palace**.

CHILD WELFARE. A state orphanage was set up in **Copenhagen** in 1621, but those brought there were expected to work for their keep by manufacturing textiles, and child labor was widely used both in the countryside and in towns in Denmark before the later 19th century. The report on its employment in factories by the doctor Emil Hornemann (1810-1890) led to the earliest legislation in 1873, which forbade employment in factories of children under the age of 10 and limited the hours which could be worked by children under 14 to 6½ hours. Night work was wholly forbidden. The minimum age was raised to 12 in 1901. The law, however, was not strictly enforced and did not apply to other forms of child labor. Assistance under the Poor Law was replaced in the 1933 social reforms (see K.K. **Steinke**). Conditions for widows and single mothers were improved in laws of 1955 and 1956, and they were paid an allowance from 1959. **Family allowances** in cash were paid from 1967. SPO, AHT

CHINA, see ASIATIC COMPANY; EAST INDIA COMPANY

CHRISTENSEN, BALTHAZAR (1802-1882). Politician. The son of an officer, he graduated *cand. jur.* in 1825. As a national liberal he edited *Fædrelandet* 1839-41 and was a member of the Estates Assembly for the Islands (Østifternes stænderforsamling) 1841-48. In 1846 he helped found the Society of **Farmers' Friends**, of which he was chairman 1848-58. In the constitutional negotiations of 1848-49 he opposed restricted suffrage, breaking with the national liberals to align with the Venstre Liberals. Christensen was a member of the **Folketing** 1849-53, then of the **Landsting**, returning to the Folketing 1866-73 and from 1875 to his death. In 1872 he was the **Liberal Party** Venstre's first chairman. AHT

CHRISTENSEN, JENS CHRISTIAN ("I.C.") (1856-1930). Liberal politician and prime minister 1905-08. After graduating in 1877, he took up the teaching career which he continued until 1901. He entered the **Folketing** in 1890 and joined the radical group within the Liberal Party led by Chresten **Berg**. He strongly opposed the agreement reached with the Conservative government by a group led by Frede **Bojsen** in 1894 and gathered behind him its critics within the divided **Liberal Party** in a Liberal Reform Party (Venstre_reformparti), although its nominal leader was Sofus Høgsbro. Although only minister of education and ecclesiastical affairs (*Kultusminister*) in the Liberal **Deuntzer** cabinet of 1901-05, he was its most influential member. In 1905 he and three other members resigned to force out the minister of defense, Colonel W.H.O. Madsen. Consequently Deuntzer could not continue in office, and Christensen himself took over both as prime minister and as defense minister. Apparently unassailable in **parliament**, he chose to resign in 1908 over the financial scandal associated with his minister of justice P.A. **Alberti**. He had by then moderated his opposition to a strong defense, which alienated him from the pacifist **Radical Liberals**. He became minister of defense under Count Holstein-Lederborg in 1909 but only for so long as was necessary to see through the new defense bill. The Court of Impeachment cleared him of charges in the Alberti affair, although he was criticized for lack of judgment. He strongly influenced the new **constitution** of 1915. In 1916 he entered Carl Theodore **Zahle**'s second cabinet as minister without portfolio but withdrew in 1918 to participate in the election. He was minister of education and church affairs in 1920-22 and only retired from parliament in 1924. SPO

CHRISTENSEN, MARIE (1871-1945). Politician. The daughter of a farm hand, she worked as a maid from the age of 15. In 1899 she formed the Copenhagen Association of Domestic Servants, which she chaired until 1914. A national association was formed in 1904, which she also chaired until 1927. She played an important part in repealing discriminatory legislation in 1921. AHT

CHRISTIAN I (1426-1481). King of Denmark 1448-81, of Norway 1450-81 and of Sweden 1457-64. The founder of the **Oldenborg** Dynasty. The son of Count Dietrich of Oldenburg, he was elected to succeed King **Christopher III** on the throne of Denmark and two years later ascended the throne of Norway after the deposition of Karl Knutsson. He set about trying to build up monarchical power at the expense of the nobility and the church with no little success. A marriage alliance with King James III of Scotland against England cost his realm the Orkney and Shetland Isles, which were mortgaged to the Scots in the dowry settlement but never redeemed. But he gained the duchies of Slesvig and Holstein. In 1457 he was chosen by the Swedish nobility to succeed the again deposed Karl Knutsson, thus restoring the **Kalmar Union**, but the Swedes turned against him, and Karl was restored after seven years. When Christian attempted to regain the Swedish throne in 1471, he was defeated at the Battle of Brunkeberg. He founded the **University** of Copenhagen in 1479. Of his four children by Dorothea of Brandenburg, **Hans** succeeded him on the throne, **Frederik (I)** became king after the deposition of Hans's son **Christian II** and Margarethe married King James III of Scotland. SPO. *See also* **Kalmar Union, Oldenborg Dynasty**.

CHRISTIAN II (1481-1559). King of Denmark and Norway 1513-23 and of Sweden 1520-21. A son of King **Hans**, he was viceroy for his father in Norway in 1506-12. While there he was responsible for the death of the noble Knut Alvsson. In Bergen he met a young Dutch girl, Dyveke, who went with him and her mother Sigbrit Villoms to Denmark when Christian ascended the throne. After four years in Copenhagen, Dyveke died in 1517, and Torben Oxe, governor of **Copenhagen Castle**, was convicted of poisoning her and executed. Sigbrit was one of the King's closest advisers during 1517-23, with responsibility for finances and sometimes deputizing for him. She encouraged the King's attempts to limit the powers of the nobility.

In 1520 Christian led an army into Sweden to assert his claims to the Swedish throne against the Swedish regent Sten Sture "the Younger," whom he defeated in a battle in which Sture was mortally wounded. After Stockholm had surrendered to him, Christian tried to eliminate opposition by executing 82 leading nobles, clergy and burghers in the so-called Stockholm Bloodbath. After Christian's return to Denmark, Gustav Vasa, the son of one of his victims, raised a successful rebellion which brought the Kalmar Union to an end and ensured Sweden's independence. Christian's attempts to assert royal power in Denmark and to favor the peasants and burghers at the expense of the nobility led to a rebellion of nobles against him at the end of 1522. The King fled to the Netherlands, accompanied by Sigbrit Villoms, to seek the help of his brother-in-law, the emperor Charles V. In 1531 he accepted an invitation from the Norwegian bishops to assume the crown of Norway. But when he failed to capture the fortress of Akershus in Oslo, he was inveigled to sail south with an offer of negotiations from his uncle and successor **Frederik I**, but he was seized and imprisoned in the castle of Sønderborg on the island of Als for the next 18 years. Only in 1549 was he released and granted the county of Kalundborg for his upkeep. SPO. *See also* **Kalmar Union; Reformation**.

CHRISTIAN III (1503-1559). King of Denmark and Norway 1534-59. Born in Gottorp, the son of King **Frederik I**. He was viceroy in the duchies of **Slesvig-Holsten** at the time of his father's death in 1533. In this capacity he had introduced Lutheranism, and his claim to the throne of Denmark was fiercely opposed by the Church, which supported his Catholic younger brother Hans. The resultant division in the Royal Council led to civil war — the **Count's War** after the intervention of Count Christoffer of Oldenburg on behalf of the imprisoned **Christian II**. The war ended in Duke Christian's capture of **Copenhagen** in 1536 after a long siege. He proceeded to arrest the bishops, who were blamed for the war, and to introduce the **Reformation** in Denmark, Norway, and Iceland. The confiscation of much of the Church's property greatly improved the Crown's finances. Christian worked closely and harmoniously with his nobles, and conducted a peaceful foreign policy. He settled his differences with the emperor by the Treaty of Speier in 1544. He married Dorothea of Saxe-Lauenburg, by whom he had six children: his successor **Frederik (II)**; Magnus, whom he installed as bishop of Øsel; **Hans**, ancestor of King **Christian IX**; and two daughters. He died in Koldinghus and is buried in **Roskilde**. SPO

CHRISTIAN IV (1577-1648). King of Denmark and Norway 1588-1648. Son of King **Frederik II**, whom he succeeded at the age of 11. The consequent regency council was led by the chancellor Niels Kås. The year after his coronation in 1588 his sister Anna married King James VI of Scotland (from 1603 also King James I of England). Ambitious to counter Sweden's growing power in the Baltic and if possible to restore the **Kalmar Union**, in 1611 Christian finally compelled his council to declare war on Sweden (*see* **Kalmar War**). The Treaty of Brömsebro, however, secured for Denmark only a large ransom for the Swedish fortress of Älvsborg. During the following decade Christian devoted his considerable energies to strengthening Denmark's defenses, especially at sea, as well as to beautifying his capital and its surroundings with buildings in Dutch Renaissance style, e.g. **Rosenborg Castle**, **The Exchange**, and **Frederiksborg Castle**. His intervention in the **Thirty Years' War** in an attempt to strengthen Denmark's position in northern Germany against the advancing Imperial and Catholic forces, resulted in defeat in 1626 at the battle of **Lutter-am-Baremberge**, the occupation of **Jutland** by the Imperial and Catholic armies, and a peace settlement at **Lübeck** in 1629 by which Christian had to promise to take no further part in the war and surrender his claims to bishoprics in north Germany.

His further attempts to counter the growth of Swedish power, and negotiations with the Emperor to do so, led to a Swedish invasion from the south under Marshal Torstensson (*see* **Torstensson's War**)

and a fresh occupation of **Jutland**. Peace in 1643 brought the loss of parts of central Norway, the islands of Gotland and Øsel, and the province of Halland. Such disasters considerably strengthened the hand of the noble council, which had constantly opposed Christian's ambitious diplomacy. When his eldest son Christian predeceased him in 1647, he failed to secure the election of his second son **Frederik (III)** before his death.

His wife Anna Cathrine of Brandenburg, mother of Christian and Frederik, died in 1612, but he had 18 children by a succession of mistresses, one of whom, Kirsten Munk, he married morganatically in 1617; she left him in 1630. Among the 11 children she bore him, two daughters married the noblemen **Corfitz Ulfeld** and **Hannibal Sehested**. They formed a "son-in-law" party within the Royal Council, which came to head the opposition to the king. In spite of his failures in foreign policy (at least partly due to lack of support from his blinkered councilors) and the loss to Sweden of Denmark's leading position in the Baltic during his reign, in retrospect Christian was seen as Denmark's most popular monarch. He was a man of many talents, with an intelligent interest in music, architecture and ship building and a much wider view of European affairs than any of his ministers. He died in Rosenborg Castle and was buried in **Roskilde**. SPO. *See also* **Architecture; Copenhagen; Music; Thirty Years' War**.

CHRISTIAN V (1646-1699). King of Denmark and Norway 1670-99. Born in Flensborghus, the eldest son of King **Frederik III**, he was the first of Denmark's rulers to come to the throne as an absolute monarch. The early part of his reign was dominated by his chief minister Peder Schumacher (ennobled as **Griffenfeld**), whom he had inherited from his father. The year after his accession, the titles of count (*greve*) and baron (*friherre*) were introduced for the first time to distinguish the higher nobility as part of the absolute monarch's policy of creating a new nobility dependent on the crown. The knightly order of **Dannebrog** was instituted with the same purpose. In 1676 Griffenfeld was overthrown by his enemies. His successor Frederik **Ahlefeldt** never enjoyed the same influence but did much to repair the damage done to the Danish economy by the war with Sweden, on which Christian had embarked in 1675 against the advice of Griffenfeld and his generals. The war ended with the Peace of Lund in 1679, and the remainder of the reign was peaceful, although war threatened on several occasions because of Christian's quarrels with Sweden's ally the duke of Holstein-Gottorp, whose territories the King coveted. At the end of his life Christian concluded an alliance with Poland which anticipated the attack on Sweden which opened the **Great Northern War** at the beginning of the following reign. The first law code for the whole kingdom was introduced in 1683 (*see* **Danish Law**), followed four years later by one for Norway, and in 1688 a land survey of the whole of Denmark was successfully carried out to serve as a basis for taxation. Christian was married in 1667 to Charlotte Amalie of Hesse-Cassel. He was killed in a hunting accident, buried in **Roskilde**, and was succeeded by his son as **Frederik IV**. Of his other children by his wife, four died young. By Sophie Amalie Moth, the daughter of his tutor and the first with the official title of king's mistress in Denmark, he had three daughters and two sons: Count Christian Gyldenløve founded the dynasty of Danneskjold-Samsøe, and Admiral Ulrik Christian **Gyldenløve** fought in the **Great Northern War**. SPO, AHT

CHRISTIAN VI (1699-1746). King of Denmark and Norway 1730-46. The second son of King **Frederik IV**, he was born in Copenhagen Castle soon after his father came to the throne. He was well educated, but an intense **Pietism** was instilled in him by his tutors. It was intensified by his father's complex marital affairs, of which he strongly disapproved, and by the influence of his wife Sofie Magdalene of Brandenburg-Kulmbach, whom he married in 1721. As king he was an ambitious builder, above all of **Christiansborg,** begun in 1732. But the court itself became a rather somber place during the reign, and public entertainment was limited. To meet the demands of landowners and military advisers, male peasant tenants were in 1733 bound to the estate on which they had been born by *stavnsbaand,* or adscription, and to liability to service in a revived militia. Christian supported economic development, and it was during his reign that the first **Asiatic Company** and public bank appeared. Christian was the first Danish King for two centuries to enjoy a reign without war. He died in Hørsholm Castle and is buried in **Roskilde**. He was succeeded by his son as **Frederik V**. SPO

CHRISTIAN VII (1749-1808). King of Denmark and Norway 1766-1808. The only son of King **Frederik V** by his first marriage to the

English princess Louise, he was born in **Christiansborg Castle**. While apparently intelligent, he betrayed signs of mental instability at an early age. Soon after his accession he married the English princess **Caroline Matilde**, sister of King George III, but against the hopes of ministers this did not end his violent outbursts and quixotic behavior, which included roaming the streets of **Copenhagen** at night in the company of the prostitute *Støvlet* ("Boots") Cathrine (Anne Cathrine Benthagen, 1745-1805). In 1768-69 he traveled through northern Germany, the Netherlands, England, and France, accompanied by his new physician Johann Friedrich **Struensee**. The latter appeared to have enabled the King to behave without causing undue embarrassment during the trip, and after they returned to Denmark achieved an ascendancy over Christian which gave him for 18 months supreme power in the kingdom. For the rest of his reign, while never surrendering his absolute power, Christian was able to do little more than sign documents which were put before him during the successive regimes of Ove **Høegh-Guldberg**, and of his son, Crown Prince Frederik, who succeeded him as King **Frederik VI**. During his reign the great land reforms were carried out which laid the foundations of modern Denmark, and Denmark was drawn into the **Napoleonic War**, but the king seems to have been largely unaware of these great events. He died in Rendsborg Castle, supposedly of shock after seeing Spanish troops, from the army of Denmark's French ally, marching though the streets of the town. SPO

CHRISTIAN VIII (1786-1848). King of Norway in 1814 and of Denmark 1839-48. Son of Crown-Prince Frederik, half-brother of King **Christian VII** and born in **Christiansborg**, he was sent to Norway as viceroy (*statholder*) in 1813 and supported the bid by Norwegians for independence after their country had been transferred to Sweden by the Treaty of **Kiel**. He was elected King of Norway but had to step down after a reign of only three months. He was governor of **Funen** for a time and enjoyed a reputation for liberalism. His relations with his father were cool, but he was admitted to the Royal Council in 1831.

After coming to the throne, the complications of the situation in **Slesvig-Holsten** dictated caution, and he resisted the call of **National Liberals** for a constitution and to unite Slesvig with the kingdom. Not until the very end of his reign did he instruct his ministers to draw up the draft of a constitution. He supported agricultural and trade reforms, a new charter for the administration of **Copenhagen**, and a new law for the administration of rural communities. He died suddenly of blood-poisoning in **Amalienborg**. His marriage to his first wife Charlotte Frederikke of Mecklenburg-Schwerin, mother of King **Frederik VII**, was dissolved in 1810 because of her association with the French composer Edouard Dupuy. He had no children by his second wife, Caroline Amalie of Slesvig-Holsten-Sønderberg-Beck, the granddaughter of Johann Friedrich **Struensee**. SPO

CHRISTIAN IX (1818-1906). King of Denmark 1863-1906. Born in Gottorp, the son of duke Wilhelm of Glücksborg, he was the first ruler of the **Glücksborg** dynasty. As a young man, he served in the Danish army. It seemed likely in 1848 at the time of the accession of King **Frederik VII** that the house of Oldenborg would die out. His claim to the throne was based on descent from King **Christian III**'s younger brother **Hans**, but it was strengthened by his marriage to Louise of Hesse-Cassel, King **Christian VIII**'s niece. On his eventual accession, his ministers presented Christian with a **constitution** which would incorporate the duchy of **Slesvig** into the Kingdom, in contravention of the international agreements reached after the First **Slesvig-Holsten** War. The new King reluctantly agreed to this. After the disastrous Second Slesvig-Holsten War in 1864, and the consequent fall of the **National Liberal** administration, Christian was free to appoint a series of conservative cabinets in line with his political views, such as J.B.S. **Estrup**. These survived until 1901, with his support against growing **Liberal** opposition.

After the overwhelming Liberal success in the 1901 elections he agreed to appoint a Liberal government in the **Change of System**. In 1874 he was the first Danish king to visit **Iceland**, marking the millennium of the supposed date of its first settlement. When he died at 88 in **Amalienborg**, he was Denmark's oldest King. Of his six children, one son succeeded him as King **Frederik VIII**, and his son Vilhelm (1845-1913) became King of the Hellenes (Greece) as George I. His daughters Alexandra (1844-1925) married the future King Edward VII of Great Britain, and Dagmar (1847-1928) married Tsar Alexander III of Russia. Consequently he was nicknamed "the Father-in-Law of Europe". His other children, Princess Thyra (1853-1933) married Duke Ernest Augustus of Cumberland, and Prince Valdemar (1858-1939) married Princess Marie of Orleans. SPO

CHRISTIAN X (1870-1947). King of Denmark 1912-47. Born at Charlottenlund, the son of the future King **Frederik VIII**, he became the first future King to take the matriculation examination (*studenteksamen*) but then followed a military career. In 1898 he married Princess Alexandrine of Mecklenburg-Schwerin (1879-1952). He made himself unpopular with many of his subjects during the **Easter Crisis** in 1920, as the last Danish ruler to intervene directly in political life, but a few months later was able to ride over the old frontier between the kingdom and the duchy of Slesvig after North Slesvig had been awarded to Denmark in a **referendum** (*see* **Slesvig-Holsten**).

In the early years of the German occupation of Denmark in **World War II** Christian became a symbol of national unity, and his daily rides through the streets of **Copenhagen** made him an immensely popular figure. A fall from his horse in October 1942, which ended these, was greeted with dismay. His brief reply (*Spreche meinen besten Dank aus*) to Hitler's effusive birthday greeting to him, although his standard response to all such greetings, caused a crisis in Dano-German relations which led to the replacement on 9 November of Vilhelm **Buhl** by Erik **Scavenius** as prime minister. He refused to form a nonparty administration when this government resigned in August 1943 in the face of German demands, and Christian X became a virtual prisoner. He saw Denmark liberated in 1945 but died two years later in **Amalienborg** and was succeeded by his son as **Frederik IX**. His son Knud (b.1900) married in 1933 Caroline-Mathilde, the daughter of Christian's brother Harald. SPO

CHRISTIAN PEOPLE'S PARTY (Kristelig Folkeparti*)* was founded with help from sister parties in Norway and Sweden in 1970, largely as a reaction against the abolition in 1967-69 of **censorship**, the relaxation of abortion laws, and the introduction of sex education in schools. It failed to secure any seats in the **Folketing** in 1971 but gained seven in 1973, rising to nine and 5.3 percent of the vote in 1975. After this, however, support dwindled. It could win only four seats in 1981, at which level it remained throughout the 1980s but contributed to the cabinets formed by Poul **Schlüter** in 1982-88. It joined Poul Nyrup **Rasmussen**'s coalition in 1993 but failed in 1994 to get the requisite 2 percent of the vote necessary for Folketing representation and left the Folketing. Its limited electoral appeal did little to help it achieve its ideal of creating a Christian society. AHT

CHRISTIAN PEOPLE'S PARTY AND FISHING INDUSTRY PARTY, (Kristligi Fólkaflokkurin — Føroya framburðs og Fiskivinnuflokkurin) is a **Faroese** political party. Formerly the Progressive and Fishermen's Party, it adopted this title before the elections of November 1984. The party argues for cooperation with the European Union based on trading and fishery agreements. It supports **NATO** membership, which it sees as securing peace and freedom for the Western world. Led by Niels Pauli Danielsen, in 1996 it had two members in the Faroes Løgting (assembly). *See also* **Center Party**. AHT

CHRISTIANI, RUDOLF (1877-1960), engineer. He qualified as a construction engineer in 1900 and founded the reinforced concrete firm Christiani and Nielsen with Aage Nielsen in 1904. The firm soon established branches worldwide. Christiani represented the **Liberal Party** in the **Folketing** 1932-35 and 1939-43. See also Knud **Højgaard**. AHT

CHRISTIANIA. (1) The capital of Norway from the mid 1600s, when it was named for **Christian IV** who resited and rebuilt the city after a disastrous fire. It reverted to its earlier name of Oslo in 1925.

(2) A 34 hectare (840 acre) area of disused barracks on the island of Amager in the Christianshavn district of **Copenhagen** which was taken over by squatters and hippies seeking to build an alternative society. They founded an independent community, the "Free State of Christiania" in 1971. This was declared illegal, but all attempts to dislodge them failed, and massive external support led to eventual legalization in 1991. The inhabitants were conceded the right to use the area in return for the agreement by a full democratic assembly to pay rent and meet the cost of city services, and to maintain the building and grounds. Critics see it as a trouble-spot of crime and soft drugs and resent the high proportion of inhabitants on unem-

ployment pay or other state benefits. Supporters praise the sustained attempt to build a new type of society which voluntarily has constrained the use of hard drugs, set up a car-free community, and developed alternative energy strategies, which include recycling, composting, and solar and wind energy, while takings in bars and restaurants finance a nursery, a youth club, and other social services. AHT

CHRISTIANITY *see* **CHURCH; CONVERSION; MISSIONARIES; REFORMATION; RELIGION**

CHRISTIANSBORG in **Copenhagen**. The first building bearing this name, designed by the German architect D. Häusser, was erected in 1733-45 on the site of the old three-towered **Copenhagen Castle**. Its style combined central European baroque with French rococo. Of this palace only the Riding School and Nicolai **Eigtved**'s 'Marble Bridge' survived a fire in 1794. A new palace was begun in 1803 to the neoclassical designs of C.F. Hansen and was inaugurated in 1827. It became the home of the two houses of the **Rigsdag** in 1849. But it was still not completed when it too burned down in 1884, only the chapel remaining. The third Christiansborg, to a design by Thorvald Jørgensen, winner of a public competition, was built in 1907-28, the Rigsdag moving into its southern wing in 1918. The remainder of the building is occupied by the Prime Minister's Office, the Foreign Ministry, the Supreme Court, and state reception rooms. SPO, AHT

CHRISTIANSEN, ERNST VALDEMAR (1891-1974), politician. When he completed his training as a typographer in **Roskilde** in 1910, he had already joined the **Social Democratic** (SD) youth movement and soon became a leading member and chairman (1913-19) of the SD Youth Federation (SUF). On a visit to Russia in autumn 1918, he was strongly influenced by the Revolution, and worked in 1919 to take SUF out of SD and into the Left Socialist Party which became the **Communist** Party, which he chaired until 1927; he and others left the Communists in 1927 and rejoined SD in 1930. Christiansen wrote for *Socialdemokraten* newspaper especially on international and historical affairs until 1955 and represented SD in the Landsting 1947-53. He was assistant foreign minister in H.C. Hansen's 1955-57 government while Hansen as Prime Minister was also foreign minister. He chaired the Danish United Nations delegation 1955-60, and was on the Radio Council 1945-55 and 1957-63, working to ensure that all points of view were heard in programs. He wrote extensively, including memoirs entitled — *men det gik anderledes* (1960, — But It Happened Otherwise) and extensive contributions to the SD history, *En bygning vi rejser* (3 vols, 1954-55, We're Raising a Building). AHT

CHRISTIANSEN, JENS CARL CHRISTIAN MARINUS (1895-1963). Politician. He completed an apprenticeship as a machinist in 1916 in **Århus**, and was active in socialist youth work as cofounder and first chairman 1920-27 of the **Social Democratic** (SD) Youth movement (DsU). As a member of the SD national executive from 1922 he helped found the Workers' Educational Federation (AOF). A member of Århus town council 1929-30, he then moved to **Copenhagen** as AOF's chief executive, developing a range of activities: films, book clubs, correspondence courses, and an arts circle, with links to union organizations, high schools, universities etc., which tried to meet the need for competent political and union organization with a range of textbooks that educated SD politicians at all levels. Christiansen was elected to the **Folketing** in 1932, representing the fishing constituency of Frederikshavn 1935-63, and was fisheries minister in SD-led cabinets of 1947-50 and 1953-57. On the editorial committees of *Socialisten* and *Arbejderhøjskolen* periodicals, he wrote *Arbejdsfester* (1932, Work festivals); *Organisationskundskab* (1933, Organization Skills); *Dirigenten* (1939, The Chairman); *Tillidsmandskundskab* (1950, Shop Steward Skills); *Haandbog i socialdemokratisk Ungdomsarbejde* (1927, SD Youth Work Handbook, with Hans **Hedtoft**). With his organizational talent and his political steadiness, "Christian Culture" (his nick-name) was typical of his SD generation, although his four-square views sometimes raised a smile. AHT

CHRISTIANSEN, OLE KIRK (died 1958). Inventor and manufacturer of children's toys. In 1932 he started a woodworking business which made toys, to which he gave the name **LEGO**. His son, Godtfred Kirk Christiansen (1920-1995), worked in the business from its start, at age 12, and headed the company from 1958. His grandson, Kjeld Kirk Kristiansen (1947-), joined the management in 1977 and became president in 1979. AHT

CHRISTMAS, WALTHER (1861-1924). Author. The son of an officer, his early career as a naval officer took him on fantastic journeys to far-off lands. He originated the genre of Danish boys' stories, primarily with his popular *Peder Most* series, reprinted many times since 1901. AHT

CHRISTMAS MØLLER, JOHN (1894-1948). Conservative politician. He graduated *cand. jur.* in 1922 and was elected to the **Folketing** 1920-41 and 1945-47. He succeeded Victor Pürschel as **Conservative Party** leader in 1928 and immediately clashed with the Liberals over their proposals for reducing defense expenditure, instead seeking support for this cause from the **Social Democrats**. The new **constitution** proposed in 1939 divided the Conservatives. Christmas Møller sought to bring his party behind the proposals and when they failed to secure the necessary majority in a **referendum** in June, he resigned the chairmanship. In the coalition formed by Thorvald **Stauning** immediately after the German occupation of Denmark on 9 April 1940 he was appointed minister without portfolio and in the ministry reformed on 8 July he became minister of commerce. By October, however, he was forced to resign under German pressure and in January 1941 to resign his leadership of the Conservative Party. Christmas Møller was one of the main forces behind the creation of the opposition underground newspaper *Frit Danmark* in April 1942, and in May fled to England where he became chairman of the Danish Council (Danske Råd), representing Danes abroad. On 17 May he first broadcast to Denmark on the BBC and in September called for armed resistance to the occupation, actions which were attacked by the Danish government. Immediately after the war he represented the **Resistance** in the coalition government formed by Vilhelm **Buhl**. He opposed the party attempt to revise the Danish-German border and fought the 1947 election unsuccessfully as an independent. SPO, AHT

CHRISTOFFER I (c. 1219-1259). King of Denmark 1252-59. He was the last of the sons of King **Valdemar II** Sejr (the Victorious) to ascend the Danish throne. As prince he sided with his brother King

Erik IV "**Plowpenny**" in his struggle with his other brother **Abel**, and was elected King after Abel's death. His reign was taken up largely with conflicts with Norway and Sweden and with his own nobles and the Church, leading to open revolt in 1256. His imprisonment of Archbishop Jakob Erlandsen in 1259 brought about his excommunication, which was lifted only just before his death in Ribe, possibly of poisoning, where he is buried. He married Margarethe Sambiria of Pomerania; their son became the future King **Erik V "Klipping."** SPO

CHRISTOFFER II (1276-1332). King of Denmark 1320-26 and 1330-32. Eldest son of King **Erik V** "Klipping," he fought against his brother **Erik Menved**, against whose advice he was elected king. He attempted to renege on the promises given to the **Estates** in his accession charter. This brought a rebellion led by Count **Gert** (Gerhardt) of Holstein, who installed a descendant of King **Abel** as the puppet King **Valdemar III**. After four years Count Gert restored Christoffer but held nearly the whole kingdom in pawn and continued to rule the country in Christoffer's name. The latter spent the last years of his life in poverty on the island of Lolland and died in Nykøbing Castle. Christoffer married Eufemia of Pomerania, by whom he fathered the future King **Valdemar IV "Atterdag."** He is buried in Sorø. SPO

CHRISTOFFER III "of Bavaria" (1418-1448). King of Denmark 1440-48, of Sweden 1441-48 and of Norway 1442-48. The son of Count Johan of Bavaria, he succeeded his uncle King **Erik VII of Pomerania** on the thrones of all the Scandinavian kingdoms in turn after the deposition of his uncle, who remained a threat to him for the rest of his life. He allowed the **nobility** in all of his realms a largely free hand in government. He was married to Dorothea of Brandenburg, later wife of King **Christian I**, but had no children. He died in Hälsingborg and is buried in **Roskilde**. SPO. *See also* **Kalmar Union**.

CHRISTOPHERSEN, HENNING (1939-   ). Politician and vice-president of the European Commission. He graduated *cand. polit.* from Copenhagen University in 1965. As an economist with the Crafts Council (Håndværksrådet) 1965-70 he was a member of the

1968-69 commission investigating conditions for small businesses. An active **Liberal** as a student, he headed the Liberal high school Breidablik 1971-72, was elected to the Folketing in 1971, and was elected party national vice-chairman in 1972, chairman 1978-84, and chairman of the party's parliamentary group 1979-82. In the Folketing he used his economics expertise to propose clear alternatives to **Social Democratic** (SD) policies. In 1978 he followed Poul **Hartling** as Liberal leader and was foreign minister in Anker **Jørgensen**'s 1978-79 SD-Liberal coalition, an attempt to span the political middle ground which proved unacceptable to the trade unions. In Poul **Schlüter**'s government he was finance minister and deputy prime minister 1982-84. He also served as a state auditor 1976-78 and a member of the **Nordic Council** 1981-82. In 1985-95 he was Denmark's member of the European Commission and a vice-president. Subsequently he became a management consultant based in Brussels and advisor to the Czech government on European Union issues from 1996. His publications include *Et udfordring for de liberale* (1972, A Challenge to the Liberals); *Tanker om Danmark i det nye Europa* (1989, Thoughts on Denmark in the New Europe), and *Regeringskonferancen 1996: EU ved et Vendepunkt* (1995, The 1996 Inter-Governmental Conference: European Union at a Turning Point?). He was followed at the European Commission by Ritt **Bjerregaard**. AHT

CHURCH, DANISH. The Danish Church was defined as evangelical Lutheran at the time of the **Reformation** in 1536 and was the established church of the country until religious toleration was introduced by the 1849 **constitution**. It then became the "People's Church" (Folkekirken). Its basic beliefs were confirmed in the **Danish Law** of 1683. **Pietism**, with its accent on personal piety and good works, was introduced from Germany in the early 18th century and strongly influenced the Danish Court during the reign of King **Christian VI**. A moderately high church movement emerged among the clergy at the start of the 19th century under the influence of Bishop J.P. Mynster (1775-1854), and took the names "the Center" or the "Third Direction." In the 1960s representatives of these two groups joined in a call to revise the character of the Church as a loosely organized "People's Church", but without significant consequences. In the 19th century the greatest figure in the life of the Church was

N.F.S. **Grundtvig**, who established a liberal tradition which still predominates.

This was opposed by the pietistic evangelical Indre Mission (Home Mission) movement started in 1853 to counter the effects of sects such as the Baptists and the Mormons, which were making many converts especially among the poor. A legal change in 1868 allowed it to organize congregations independently of the formal parish structure. Strongest in the west of the country, it acts as an evangelical wing within the *folkekirke*, and has strong links with the Christian youth movements of the Kristelig Forening for Unge Mænd (YMCA) and Kristelig Forening for Unge Kvinder (YWCA).

The ritual of the Church is based on that approved in 1685, but is flexible under the guidance of the local bishop. Denmark has a strong tradition of hymn writing, in which the names of Hans Adolph **Brorson**, N.F.S. **Grundtvig,** and Thomas **Kingo** feature prominently. A new hymn book was introduced in 1953. Priests may marry, and women were admitted to the priesthood in 1948. The link with the state is maintained through the minister for church affairs (Kirkeminister), who need not be a Lutheran. The Ministry was formed in 1916, when the Kultusministerium, which had previously supervised both ecclesiastical and educational affairs, was divided. Thus the **Folketing** is the church's highest legal authority. Parish councils (*menighedråd*), of which there are about 2,100, are elected every four years and give members influence in their home parish over the appointment of a priest and the election of a bishop. The church receives state financial support. A specific church tax pays for church buildings, including staff houses, while incomes and pensions of bishops, priests, etc. are paid partly from this and partly from the Church Ministry. Some 87.4 percent of Danes are members (1994), at least nominally, but fewer than 10 percent of the population attend church regularly.

Around 1060 Denmark was divided territorially into eight dioceses (*stifter*) of the Roman church: Lund, **Roskilde**, **Odense** (covering **Funen** and all the islands as far as **Lolland**, **Falster**, Rügen and Fehmarn), Børglum (covering northwest **Jutland**, initially named after Vestervig monastery and later renamed **Ålborg**), **Viborg**, **Århus**, **Ribe** (reaching as far north as the Limfjord), and **Slesvig** (reaching north to Kolding fjord). These were subdivided into districts (*herreder*) which largely corresponded to their civil equivalents. After the **Reformation** in 1536 these were renamed deaneries (*provster*), with boundaries which changed very little until 1922, while Roskilde *stift* was renamed **Zealand** and the bishop's seat was moved to **Copenhagen**. When Lund became part of Sweden in 1658, **Bornholm** was included with Zealand. Lolland-Falster became a separate diocese in 1803, Copenhagen likewise in 1922, and Helsingør in 1961. There has been no archbishop of the Danish Church since the death of Hans Svane in 1668, each bishop being responsible for his own diocese. SPO, AHT. *See also* **Lutheranism.**

CHURCHES, ROUND. Fortress-like churches dating from the 12th century and found in Denmark on the island of **Bornholm** (with four), on **Zealand** (one near Sorø), and in **Jutland** (one at Thorsager). They served as refuges from the raids of Wendish pirates. All have very thick walls and very narrow window slits. SPO

CINEMA, *see* **FILM INDUSTRY**

CLASSEN, JOHAN FREDERIK (1725-1792). Landowner, industrialist, general. The son of a Norwegian organist, he graduated *cand. theol.* in 1744. He supplied war matériel from Norway to Denmark 1749-59 and in 1756 established a powder works and cannon foundry by Arresø canal, **Zealand**, which he named Frederiksværk after **Frederik V**, who had made the land available. The place soon became the first factory town in Denmark. The king bought the works in 1761, although Classen continued to direct it. He left his fortune to charity. AHT

CLAUSEN, FRITZ (1893-1945), Denmark's leading Nazi. Born in Aabenraa (then in German Schleswig) he served in the German army in World War I and was taken prisoner on the Russian front. After returning, he studied medicine at German universities and on qualifying in 1923 opened a practice at Bovrup near his birthplace. He joined the recently formed Nazis, Danmarks Nationalsocialistiske Arbejderparti (DNSAP), the **Danish National Socialist Workers' Party** in 1930, but its failure in the 1932 elections enabled Clausen to take over from Cai Lembke as its leader 1933-44. He was elected to **parliament** 1939-45. After the Germans occupied Denmark in 1940, he failed to persuade them to allow him to form a government to replace the democratically elected one and had to resign as leader of DNSAP in 1944. He was interned at the end of the war but died of a heart attack before he could be tried. SPO

CLAUSEN, HENRIK NICOLAI (1793-1877), politician and theologian. The son of a priest, Henrik Georg Clausen, who was the leading proponent of rational Christianity of his time, he graduated *cand. theol.* in 1813 and became professor of theology at Copenhagen University in 1822. He considered that theology should direct the church, a view sharply opposed by N.F.S. **Grundtvig**, for whom the creed was the ground of the Christian life. Politically Clausen supported freedom of the press, and later sharply opposed absolute monarchy from a **National Liberal** perspective. He was a member 1840-48 of the **Consultative Assembly**, 1848-49 of the **Constitutional Assembly**, 1849-1853 of the **Folketing**, and 1853-54 and 1855-66 of the **Landsting**. He was in the cabinet as minister without portfolio November 1848-July 1851. AHT

CLAUSEN, MADS (1905-1966). Manufacturer. He qualified as an engineer in 1927 and in 1933 founded Dansk Køleautomatik- og Apparatfabrik. Renamed Danfoss in 1946, the company developed heating controls and expanded worldwide. AHT

CLAUSSEN, SOPHUS NIELS CHRISTEN (1865-1931), poet. Born on the island of **Falster**, his father was a farmer turned journalist. After studying law for a time at the University of **Copenhagen**, Claussen became a journalist and in 1890 joined the staff of the newspaper *Politiken*, for which he wrote articles describing his travels in France and Italy. His first collection of poems appeared in 1887. After a long stay in Paris in 1905-12, he also turned to painting. He is now recognized as the leading Danish poet of his generation with a strong influence on those who followed him. His publications include *Djævlerier* (1904, Devilries), *Danske vers* (1912), and *Hvededynger* (1930, Heaps of Wheat). SPO, AHT.

CLAVUS, CLAUDIUS (1388-?), map maker. Working from Ptolemy's world map, sea charts and his own scattered knowledge, in 1427 he drew the first two maps of Scandinavia, one of which became widely current. AHT

COAT OF ARMS (Rigsvåben). The Small Coat of Arms, consisting solely of three blue lions and nine red hearts on a gold ground, dates from the end of the 12th century and derives from the family arms of the **Valdemar** Kings. The Large or Royal Coat of Arms achieved its present form in 1948, as a consequence of the independence of **Iceland**, when the Icelandic falcon was removed. It consists basically of a shield divided into four quarters with the Small Coat in the top lefthand corner, followed clockwise by two blue lions representing the duchy of **Slesvig**, a blue lion and nine hearts symbolizing the claims of kings of Denmark since the 14th century to be kings of the Goths, above a wyvern to represent the **Wends**, and three gold crowns for the Union of Kalmar above a ram for the **Faroe Islands**, side-by-side with a bear for **Greenland**. Superimposed is a smaller shield with symbols for Holstein, Stormarn, Lauenburg, **Ditmarschen**, and **Oldenburg**. The two "wild men" who act as supporters appeared first in the reign of King **Christian I**. SPO

COLBJØRNSEN, CHRISTIAN (1749-1814). Dano-Norwegian lawyer and statesman. Born at Sørum in Rømerike in Norway to a regimental quartermaster, he graduated *cand. jur.* in 1773 and the same year became advocate to the Supreme Court. He served as secretary to the **Great Land Commission** set up in 1786 to prepare the land reforms which followed and was himself largely responsible for the revision of the tenancy laws and, with Christian Ditlev **Reventlow**, for the ending of the *stavnsbånd* in 1788. As attorney general *(Generalprokurør)* in the Chancery he was responsible for drawing up many of the reforming decrees of the 1790s, but made himself unpopular for his association with the restriction of press freedom in 1799. A member of the Council of State *(Kancelli)* from 1788, he was dismissed in 1803 for his anti-aristocratic views. He became Chief Justice *(Justitarius)* in 1804, continuing until his death. SPO, AHT

COLLIN, JONAS (1776-1861). State official. He graduated *cand. jur.* in 1795 and from 1801 held appointments in the central administration. In 1805 he joined and in 1809-55 was president of the Agricultural Economic Society *(Landhusholdningsselskabet)*, a leading force in efforts to improve productivity in agriculture and forestry. As the leading patron of the **Golden Age**, he sought state support for its artists, and took the initiative for the building of the **Thorvaldsen** Museum. He also became Hans Christian **Andersen**'s friend and benefactor. AHT

COLONIES, *see* **AFRICA, DANISH POSSESSIONS IN; DANISH WEST INDIES; INDIA, DANISH POSSESSIONS IN**

COMMON MARKET *see* **EUROPEAN UNION**

COMMON COURSE (Fælles Kurs). This populist leftist political party was founded by the ex-Communist leader of the Seaman's Union, Preben Møller Hansen in 1986 to oppose Denmark's membership of **NATO** and the **European Community** and to fight for strict immigration controls. It won four seats with 2.2 percent of the popular vote in 1987, but in 1988 failed to win the 2 percent needed for representation. SPO

COMMUNIST PARTY. Founded in 1919 as the Left Socialist Party by a group of radical socialists who had broken away from the **Social Democratic Party**, the party became the Danish Communist Party in 1920. None of its members were elected to the **Rigsdag** until 1932, when **Aksel Larsen** and one other secured seats. This rose to three in 1939, when the party secured 2.4 percent of the vote. A newsletter, *Politiske Maanedsbreve*, was published from 5 October 1941, changing its name on 1 May 1942 to *Land og Folk* (Country and People): initially a means of furthering the resistance, it continued publication after the war, only closing on 21 December 1990 (see **Press**). After the German invasion of Russia in June 1941, leading Communists were rounded up and interned by the Danish police to prevent their falling into German hands. The Germans took over the camp in August 1943, when some internees managed to escape. Communists, organized in the inappropriately named "Bopa" *(Borgerlige Partisaner)*, played an important role in the **Resistance** Movement, and two members served in Vilhelm **Buhl**'s immediate postwar coalition government. The party won 18 **Folketing** seats and 12.5 percent of the vote in the 1945 elections, but lost half of these two years later and lost all representation in 1960. Two years before this, Aksel **Larsen**, its chairman since 1932, was expelled for his criticism of the hard line taken by the majority of his executive and formed the **Socialist People's Party**. The Party was again represented in the Folketing in 1973-79 with 6 or 7 seats but failed to gain any seats thereafter. In 1989 some Communists joined with **Left Socialists** and **Socialist Workers' Party** supporters to form the **Red-Green Unity List**, while a small rump, loyal to the Soviet tradition, formed the Kommunistisk Parti Danmark. SPO, AHT

CONSERVATIVE PEOPLE'S PARTY (Det Konservative Folkeparti). Political party formed on 22 February 1916 as the successor to the coalition of right-wing groups, representing big business and the larger landowners, which came together in 1876 as Højre, **The Right**. In the 1920 election it secured 19.6 percent of the vote but before World War II it only matched this success in 1926. In the 1920s and 1930s it took no part in government, but joined Thorvald **Stauning**'s broad coalition formed after the German occupation in 1940. In the early 1930s the Party's youth movement (Konservative Ungdom) adopted fascist tendencies and was consequently expelled by the Party's chairman since 1928, John **Christmas Møller**, who went on to symbolize resistance to the German occupation after he was forced out of the government and escaped to England in 1942.

After the war the party took part in the brief liberation government of 1945 and formed a minority cabinet with the Liberals under **Erik Eriksen** in 1950-53. It also joined the "bourgeois" coalition of Hilmar **Baunsgaard** of 1968-71. Suffering from leadership disputes between Erik Haunstrup Clemmensen and Erik Ninn-Hansen, its lowest-ever vote, at 5.5 percent, was in the election of January 1975, when it held only 10 seats. Under the leadership of Poul **Schlüter**, who took over in 1974, it regained support. In 1982 he became Denmark's first Conservative prime minister since the **Change of System** in 1901. In 1981-90 it led the Liberals in rivalry to be the largest of the nonsocialist parties, but the Liberals overtook them in 1994. Schlüter was succeeded as leader by Hans Engell, then in 1997 by Per Stig Møller. SPO, AHT. *See also* **Cabinets; Elections**.

CONSTITUTIONS. The 1661 constitution applied the principle of **absolute monarchy** until 1848 and this was rigorously enforced (*see* **J.J. Dampe**). Denmark's first modern constitution was approved on 5 June 1849 (the June Constitution) by a constituent assembly (Den grundlovgivende Rigsforsamling) elected the previous year. Drawing on the precedents of the 1831 Belgian and the 1814 Norwegian constitutions, it replaced the **consultative assemblies** by a parliament (Rigsdag) of two chambers: a Lower House (Folketing) directly elected by men over 30, and an indirectly elected Upper House (Landsting).

Following the First **Slesvig-Holsten** War of 1849-50, a further Joint Constitution of October 1855 for Denmark and the duchies did not supplant the Rigsdag, but provided another single chamber, the Rigsraad, to deal with affairs affecting both the Kingdom and the duchies of Slesvig and Holsten — in other words, foreign policy, defense, and finance. After protests from the consultative assemblies in the duchies, in 1858 the Rigsraad's jurisdiction was confined to the Kingdom and Slesvig alone. This was superseded in November 1863 by yet another constitution which incorporated Slesvig, with a bicameral assembly for representatives from both Denmark and Slesvig (the **Ejder** Policy). The enforcement of this November Constitution at the beginning of 1864 precipitated the Second **Slesvig-Holsten** War. As a result, the duchies were lost and the National Liberal administration fell, enabling the **Right** in July 1866 to enact a constitution to replace both the June Constitution and the November Constitution. Under this July Constitution the electorate for the **Folketing** was untouched, but 12 of the 66 members of the **Landsting** were to be appointed by the Crown. In the political battles of the later 19th century one of the main Liberal demands was for a return to the June Constitution.

After the 1901 **Change of System** a new constitution was approved in June 1915 which replaced the 12 Crown appointees in the Landsting with 18 chosen by the outgoing Landsting, granted women the vote, and reduced the voting age for the Folketing to 25. This did not come into force until the end of **World War I** in 1918. An attempt to reform the constitution in 1939 narrowly failed to gain the necessary **referendum** majority.

The current constitution was approved on Constitution Day, 5 June 1953. It abolished the Landsting, incorporated the principle of parliamentary government (accepted practice since 1901), allowed for referendums, and introduced the Swedish office of *Ombudsman*. At the same time the voting age was reduced to 23 and female succession to the monarchy was introduced. This constitution was widely supported, and its only organized opposition was from the

Independents Party. SPO, AHT. *See also* **Elections, Franchise, Parliament.**

CONSULTATIVE ASSEMBLIES. When the German Confederation was set up in 1815, with Holstein as a member, the promise was made that each of its components should have a representative assembly. The German revolutionary movement in 1830 demanded that this promise be met. Under this pressure the Royal Council in Copenhagen decided in 1831 to allow consultative assemblies in both the duchies of Holsten and **Slesvig** and also in the Danish Kingdom, so as to preserve the unity of the royal lands. The assembly (47 members) for Holstein would meet in Itzehoe, for Slesvig (43 members) in the town of Schleswig, one for Jutland (55 members) in Viborg, and one for the islands (*Østifternes stænderforsamling*, 70 members) in **Roskilde**, to which **Iceland** and the **Faroes** were also to send representatives. None of these were big towns and all were at a distance from possible sources of trouble.

The franchise and the right to be a representative were both based on property qualifications, so were heavily weighted towards the wealthy. Voting was by estates (*stænder*) in three groups: owners of large land-holdings; owners of land in towns; and smaller land-owners, including peasant-farmers. In all 2.8 percent of the population qualified, with about 75 times as many peasants as landowners per mandate, but the number of representatives ensured that no one estate could dominate.

The assemblies in Itzehoe and Roskilde first met in 1835. In Roskilde the principal discussions concerned the state budget. In the Viborg assembly, which met in 1836, there was a call for economies in state expenditure. The lawyer Orla **Lehmann** also called for a campaign on behalf of the Danish-speakers of Slesvig. In 1842 the Slesvig Assembly forbade one of its members, P. Hiort Lorenzen, to address it in Danish. This led to a furor in Denmark and the formulation by Orla Lehmann of the **Ejder** Program (i.e. the union of Slesvig with the kingdom and its border on the river Ejder). In response the Itzehoe Assembly formulated the program of **Slesvig-Holsten**ism in 1844. The 1847 elections to the Assemblies resulted in **National Liberal** victories in both Danish bodies and success for Danish-speakers in Slesvig. The Danish Assemblies disappeared with the institution of a national parliament in 1849, but those in the duchies continued, and the Itzehoe Assembly was the scene of a fierce attack on the Danish Crown in 1860. SPO. *See also* **Schouw, J.F.**

CONVENTICLE ACT of 1741 forbade religious assemblies unless permitted by or in the presence of the local Lutheran pastor. It was the result of the alarm felt by the established church at the spread from Germany since the beginning of the century of **Pietism**, which encouraged meetings of laymen for prayer and Bible reading. The Act was abolished in 1849, when religious toleration was introduced and Jews gained full civil rights. SPO

CONVERSION TO CHRISTIANITY. In Denmark this began seriously in the second half of the 9th century. In 826 King Harald Flak was baptized in Mainz in order to secure help from the German Emperor to regain his throne. He returned to Denmark with the monk **Ansgar** but was forced to flee again after only two years. Ansgar paid a further visit to Denmark in 850 and founded a church in **Slesvig**, but little further progress was made until the reign of **Harald Blåtand (Bluetooth)**, who came to the throne in 860. Harald was already a Christian and supported the work of German missionaries in his kingdom. Christianity became firmly established in Denmark under King **Knud I**, who placed English bishops in **Odense, Roskilde,** and Lund. SPO. *See also* **Church.**

COOPERATIVE MOVEMENT. Retail cooperative societies based on English models began to appear in Danish towns in the 1860s, the first shop opening in Thisted in northwest Jutland in 1866 on the initiative of the clergyman H.C. Somme, and in 1871 a national association (Fællesforeningen for Danmarks Husholdningsforeninger) was formed. Agricultural producers cooperatives were encouraged by the decline in cereal farming from the 1870s. To compete with the large landowners in the manufacture of dairy produce for the international market, on which guaranteed quality was demanded, the smaller farmers began to set up cooperative dairies, beginning in 1882 in Hjedding in **Jutland**. By World War I there were over 1,000 of these in Denmark, together with over 1500 retail societies. By this time all the main branches of Danish **agriculture** were organized in cooperatives. Cooperative bacon factories began with one in Horsens in eastern Jutland in 1887. A Danish Cooperative Wholesale Society

(Fællesforeningen for Danmarks Brugsforeninger) was formed in 1896 and a Central Cooperative Committee (Andelsudvalget) in 1899. In 1917 all cooperative bodies were brought together in the Federation of Danish Cooperative Societies (De Samvirkende Danske Andelsselskaber) under the leadership of Anders Nielsen (1859-1928). Cooperatives in large towns — particularly bakeries and housing associations — developed rapidly at the beginning of the 20th century and in 1922 formed their own central organization, the Union of Urban Cooperative Societies (Det Kooperative Fællesforbund). The Cooperative Bank (Andelsbanken), which became one of the country's largest, dates from 1909. After **World War II** a process of rationalization has considerably reduced the number of cooperative wholesale organizations. SPO

COPENHAGEN (København) (the English pronunciation is Kopenhaygen, **not** Kopenhargen, despite Danny Kaye), the capital of Denmark with a population (1994) of 1,346,289 in the metropolitan area as a whole, and 621,970 in the city itself. There was already a small settlement on the eastern side of the **Sound** at its narrowest point when the area was granted by King **Valdemar I** to Bishop **Absalon** around 1167. The bishop built a castle there and also began the construction of a church dedicated to Our Lady (*Vor Frue Kirke*). Strategically placed at the entrance to the Baltic where many sea-routes met, the settlement grew rapidly to become the most important of Denmark's trading ports. It was granted city status in 1254 and was acquired from the bishopric of **Roskilde** by the Crown in 1416. It became the administrative center of the kingdom in the early 15th century, when Danish lands in **Scania** meant that it was not on the eastern periphery of the country, as it is today.

By 1500 it had a population of about 10,000, making it by far the largest town in Denmark. It suffered a long siege during the **Count's War** 1534-36, but received much attention from King **Christian IV** a hundred years later, who beautified it with buildings such as the **Exchange**, **Rosenborg Castle**, and the **Round Tower** and added the area of Christianshavn, originally a separate town east of the inner harbor. At the end of the **Northern War** of 1657-60 it underwent a further long siege, after which King **Frederik III** rewarded it with a representative body of 32 as part of its government. In 1728 fire destroyed about 40 percent of the buildings, including the Council Hall, the **university**, and **Christiansborg** Castle. After much rebuilding on the old town plan, in 1749 a whole new area was developed as Frederikstaden to celebrate the third centenary of the **Oldenborg** Dynasty — this included the four mansions which became the palace of **Amalienborg**. In 1795 there was another devastating fire, and further damage was done in the 1807 **Battle of Copenhagen** by three-days of British bombardment preceding a brief British occupation of the city.

Beyond the walls, the pleasure park of **Tivoli** was laid out in 1843 and nearby the city's first main rail station was built on its present site in 1863-64. The ancient walls and gateways were torn down from 1872 to make way for the present ring of parks and lakes. Beyond these spread the working-class areas of Vesterbro, Nørrebro, and Østerbro, named after the west, north and east bridges out of the city where there are now suburban rail-stations. The center of the city moved at the beginning of the 20th century to what became Rådhuspladsen (Town Hall Square) with the building of the new Town Hall in 1892-1905, to the design by Martin **Nyrop**. This contains the World Clock designed by Jens Olsen and built in 1943-1955.

Copenhagen was little damaged during **World War II**, although the **East Asiatic Company** building was destroyed by the Germans in December 1944 in reprisal for sabotage acts by the **Resistance**, and in March 1945 the Shellhus, then Gestapo headquarters in the city, was bombed by the British Royal Air Force. At the end of June 1944 the city went on strike in protest against the execution by the occupying Germans of Resistance workers and other atrocities and the Germans imposed a state of siege and cut off all essential supplies. After less than a week, however, the besiegers gave in to most of the demands formulated by the **Freedom Council** and the strike was called off. The city's symbol, also used to hall-mark silver, is its ancient three-towered castle. Copenhagen was the European City of Culture in 1996. SPO, AHT

COPENHAGEN, BATTLE OF (1801) was a naval battle between Denmark and Britain. In 1800 Denmark joined the armed neutrality league with Prussia, Russia, and Sweden. Tzar Paul I was grand master of the Maltese Order. In retaliation for the British capture of Malta, Paul allied with France and in the spring of 1801 Russia and France enforced the closure of European ports to the British. Denmark was caught up by this policy when Britain threatened war unless Denmark left the pact: to agree to the British demand would invite invasion by Sweden, who had long coveted Norway. Denmark therefore rejected all offers of negotiations, prepared to defend the Norwegian coast, and placed block-ships to keep the British fleet out of range of **Copenhagen**. Serious defense was necessary to convince Russia that Denmark had not allied secretly with Britain. Early in 1801 the British seized all Danish merchant ships in British harbors and occupied Danish possessions in the West Indies and India.

In March 1801 a British fleet of 53 ships under admiral Hyde Parker was sent to the Sound. On the morning of 2 April the Danish fleet was attacked by a superior force under Parker's second-in-command, Horatio Nelson. Only when Nelson, having ignored his superior's order to withdraw, threatened to burn the ships he had captured with their crews on board did Crown Prince Frederik agree to negotiate. The British wanted Denmark to leave the League, which was disintegrating after the murder of Paul a week before the battle, but agreed to a cease-fire and 14 weeks' suspension of Danish membership. The battle was the famous occasion when Nelson failed to see Parker's signal because he put his spyglass to his blind eye. In Danish it is known as Slaget på Reden (the Battle of Reden), during which the 17-year-old lieutenant Peter **Willemoes** made himself a national hero, only to be killed in a further clash with the British seven years later. *See also* **Britain, Danish Relations with; Napoleonic Wars; Navy**. SPO, AHT

COPENHAGEN, BATTLE OF (1807). Involving a siege and bombardment of the city by the British, it originated in the fears of the British that the large Danish fleet would fall into French hands at the time of the negotiations between Napoleon and Tsar Alexander I at Tilsit. In August 1807 Britain sent a fleet to Danish waters and, through its envoy James Jackson (1770-1814), demanded the surrender of the fleet for the duration of the war. The British could offer no help against a French invasion of **Jutland**, so the government of Crown Prince Frederik refused, and 31,000 British troops under the command of General Wellesley were landed at Vedbæk, north of the capital on August 16. They met little resistance, as most of the Danish army was in the duchies with the crown prince. After a bombardment which lasted 2-7 September and caused considerable damage, the city surrendered, and the Danish fleet of 15 ships of the line, 15 frigates and over 30 smaller vessels was towed away across the North Sea. In spite of British attempts to bring about a reconciliation, including an offer eventually to return the fleet, Denmark concluded an alliance with France and on November 4 declared war on Britain. *See also* **Britain, Danish Relations with; Napoleonic Wars; Navy.** SPO

COPENHAGEN CASTLE (The Three Towers Castle) was built by Bishop **Absalon** in the middle of the 12th century but was replaced at the end of the 14th by a new "Copenhagen's House". It was made the royal residence in **Copenhagen** by **Erik of Pomerania** in 1416. **Christian IV** furnished its "Blue Tower" with an elegant spire. In this tower his daughter **Leonore Christina** was imprisoned for 22 years from 1663. The castle was extensively renovated by King **Frederik IV** in 1721-27, but it was torn down by his son **Christian VI** to make way for the first **Christiansborg.** SPO

COUNT'S WAR (Grevens fejde, 1534-1536) was a struggle for the Danish throne fought between supporters of Christian, duke of Slesvig-Holsten and eldest son of King **Frederik I**, and those who supported the deposed King **Christian II**. Also involved were the leading **Hanseatic** city of **Lübeck**, which wished to restore its position in Baltic trade, and Count Christoffer of Oldenburg (after whom the war was named), plus Mecklenburg and Sweden. The Council of State was divided between Catholics, who looked to the Catholic Prince Hans, duke of **Slesvig-Holsten**, and Protestants, who looked to the Lutheran duke Christian, so it failed to elect a successor to King **Frederik I**. Bishop Joachim Rønnow of **Roskilde**, as a member of the Council, postponed the election and tried to act as leader of the kingdom. This left an opening which Lübeck sought to exploit. Its army, led by Count Christoffer, was repulsed from Holsten but was invited by the Danish peasants and the citizens of Malmö and **Copenhagen** to assist them in a social war against **nobility** and clergy. The Count consequently transferred his troops to eastern Denmark, where he raised the banner of the imprisoned **Christian II**. King Gustav Vasa of Sweden entered the war against Lübeck, and the Danish nobility formally elected duke Christian as King **Christian III**. His general Johan **Rantzau** reoccupied **Jutland**, and in June 1535 defeated the forces of Lübeck and Mecklenburg at the battle of Oksenbjerg. Lübeck concluded peace in Hamburg in February 1536 and recognized King Christian, but Copenhagen withstood a ruthless siege until July. He imprisoned Rønnow and the other catholic bishops. His victory was the prelude to the **Reformation** in Denmark. SPO

COURTS. In the course of the early Middle Ages, the ancient popular courts or *ting,* headed by the three provincial courts (*Landsting*) sitting in Viborg (for **Jutland**), in Ringsted (for the islands), and in **Scania,** came increasingly under the influence of the Crown, whose *Retterting* became the supreme court of the kingdom. The judicial work of the Royal Council was transferred in 1660 to a new Supreme Court *(Højesteret).* For most Danes in the early modern period, the most important court was the manorial court which regulated affairs on the estate where they lived.

The judicial system was dominated by the land owning nobility, who enjoyed *hånd og halsret* or the right to administer corporal and even capital punishment in their own courts. Some large landowners had also *birkeret* under which they appointed judges in their own court, which was entirely independent of the royal county court or *herredsting.* Such private courts were more and more closely regulated by the Crown during the 18th and 19th centuries, but they were not all finally abolished until the 1849 **Constitution.** In 1805 the three *landsting* were replaced by two high courts, one in **Copenhagen** and one in **Viborg,** while in 1845 the Criminal and Police Court, *Kriminal- og politiretten,* was formed in Copenhagen to deal with criminal matters as a court of first instance.

The present system of courts in Denmark dates from the Administration of Justice Act (*Retsplejeloven*) of 1916, as amended. Under it there is a Supreme Court (*Højesteret*) in two divisions, which hears appeals before five judges. Two High Courts, *Østre landsret* sitting in Copenhagen for the islands and *Vestre landsret* in Viborg for Jutland, are courts of first instance, hearing cases before three judges. Cases defined by an upper limit of property value are heard by a single judge in one of the 84 lower courts. There was a third High Court to try appeals in Southern Jutland after the reunion of 1920. Juries were introduced into the high courts and lower courts in 1936. A judge in a lower court also has the functions of bailiff (*foged*), administrator of estates (*skifteforvalter*), and notary, and is responsible for records and registrations (*tinglysningsvæsnet*). SPO, AHT

CURRENCY SYSTEM. The first Danish coins were struck in the 9th century in Hedeby, but coins issued by Danish Kings only achieved monopoly status in the 11th century. Medieval currency in Denmark was based on the silver *mark* of 8 *øre*, each of 3 *ørtug*, with 240 *penninge* to the *mark*. In 1020 a mark was worth 216 grams of silver but had fallen in value by 1524 to 9 grams. After the Reformation the *daler* of 3 marks, each of 16 *skilling* was introduced. In 1625 the *daler* was divided into 6 marks or 96 *skilling* (each worth 0.263 g of silver). While the so-called *speciedaler* retained its value, the silver content of smaller coins was reduced so that the value of the so-called *kurantdaler* declined, the relation between the two being fixed in 1794 at 5:4. Notes, without direct exchange value to coinage, were issued in and after wars, as in 1713-28, 1745-47, 1757-95, 1799-1845, and 1914-27. In 1813, after the national bankruptcy, the largest unit of currency was made the *rigsbankdaler* (worth 0.04 grams of silver) of six marks of 16 *skilling* each or half a *speciedaler*. This was replaced in 1854 with the *riksdaler* of the same value. In 1873 Denmark adopted the gold standard, in common with Norway and Sweden, and in 1875 the *rigsdaler* gave way to the *krone* (crown) of 100 *øre*, with the *krone* defined as 0.403 grams of gold, and 20 *kroner* and 10 *kroner* gold coins were minted as standards. Smaller coins were made of silver and copper and bronze alloy. The smallest coins were minted from iron during **World War I**, and after 1920 from nickel. Aluminum and zinc were also used during **World War II**. Denmark left the gold standard in 1931, but in 1950 1 *krone* was worth 0.129 g of gold and in 1970, 0.119 g. After Denmark joined the **European Economic Community** in 1972 the value of the *krone* tended to follow the German mark at about 4 kroner to the mark. Denmark, like Sweden and the UK, decided not to join the Economic and Monetary Union (EMU) or the single European currency (Euro) when it starts in 1999, although the possibility remains of doing so later. This decision apparently strengthened the Danish *krone* against other European currencies. SPO, AHT

- D -

DAELL, CHRISTIAN (1883-1947). Merchant. After a commercial apprenticeship, with his brother Peter Møller Daell he started Daells Varehus in 1910, at first as a mail-order company but from 1912 also as a department store. "Daells" on Nørregade in central Copenhagen is widely known for its cash sales and extensive use of advertising and sales catalogs. AHT

DAHLGAARD, BERTEL (1887-1972). Politician. The son of a large-scale farmer, he graduated *cand. polit.* in 1913 and was elected 1920-60 to the **Folketing** as a **Radical Liberal**. He was interior minister 1929-40 in **Stauning**'s governments, and was concurrently economics minister and minister for Nordic affairs 1957-61 in the cabinets led by H.C. **Hansen** and V. **Kampmann**. With Jørgen **Jørgensen** he sought to place the Radical Liberals as a party of the center with a pivotal role, especially after 1945. His memoirs, *Kamp og Samarbejde* (Conflict and Colaboration) were published in 1964. AHT

DALGAS, ENRICO MYLIUS (1828-1894). Engineer and land reformer. Descended from a French Huguenot family which settled in Denmark in the 18th century, he became a military engineer. He built the main highway across **Jutland** from Randers to Ringkjøbing, and while doing this he was inspired to launch his development movement to reclaim and colonize the heathland of western Jutland which lay behind the foundation of the Hedeselskab (**Heath Society**) in **Århus** in 1866. SPO

DAM, HENRIK (1895-1976). Chemist. The son of a pharmacist, he graduated *cand. polyt.* in 1920 and *dr. phil.* in 1934. In 1943 he was awarded a half share of the Nobel Prize in medicine and physiology for the discovery of vitamin K. He was professor of biochemistry and nutrition 1946-65 at the technical university, Den polytekniske Læreanstalt. AHT

DAMPE, JACOB JACOBSEN (1790-1868). Politician. The son of a tailor, he graduated *cand. theol.* in 1809 and *dr. phil.* in 1812, then taught. In 1820 he tried to form a society to work for a free **consti-**

tution. It was infiltrated by the police who arrested him and in 1821 he was sentenced to death for seeking to overthrow the absolute monarchy, but this was commuted to life imprisonment. He was confined to the Castle in Copenhagen 1821-26 and 1831-32 and for the remaining years to 1841 on the island of Christiansø; he was then allowed to live on nearby Bornholm. Only when constitutional monarchy was declared in 1848 was he freed, after which he lived in Copenhagen. AHT

DANEHOF. The precursor of both the later **Estates** and the Royal Council of Denmark, this assembly of nobles emerged in the 13th century from the earlier meetings of the leading courtiers and landowners. According to the **Accession Charter**, agreed to by King **Erik V** in 1282, it was to meet annually. By the end of the 14th century, it was overshadowed by the more restricted Council of the Realm (Rigsråd). Its last meeting is considered to have been held in Nyborg in 1413. It was succeeded by the **Herredag**. SPO

DANIDA (the Danish International Development Agency) is the section of the Foreign Ministry which administrates state aid to developing countries. It was set up in 1972 in succession to the Secretariat for Collaboration with Developing Countries, which was established in 1962. Its work is coordinated with commercial aid and with nongovernmental organizations, the most important of which is Mellemfolkeligt Samvirke (MS), founded originally in 1944 for postwar reconstruction in Europe but more recently organizing the work of volunteers in Asia, Africa, and Latin America. Others include Folkekirkens Nødhjælp (Church Emergency Aid), originally established in 1922, and the Danish branch of the Red Cross, founded in 1876. Danish development aid in 1993 was the largest proportion of Gross National Income (GNI) in the world, at 1.03 percent, with Norway, Sweden, and the Netherlands the only others to exceed the United Nations target of 0.7 percent of GNI. (Other Western industrial countries averaged 0.3 percent and the United States only 0.15 percent). The high Danish level was attained in stages from 0.32 percent per year in 1963-73 and 0.66 percent in 1973-83. In 1996 about 50 percent of Danish aid went to UN organizations, 20 percent to the World Bank and its regional development banks, 15 percent to European Union development aid, and 15 percent to humanitarian and other assistance. Such aid has been conditional on the observance of human rights in the recipient countries. AHT

DANISH CONFEDERATION OF TRADE UNIONS (De Samvirkende Fagforbund) *see* **TRADE UNIONS**

DANISH CULTURAL INSTITUTE (Det Danske Kulturinstitut, previously Det danske Selskab) was established in 1940 to disseminate information on Denmark and to further international cultural exchange of all kinds. It is an independent institution governed by a council representative of Danish cultural and artistic bodies and political parties. The Ministries of Culture, Foreign Affairs, and Education appoint observers to the Institute board, but its funding is raised from foundations, business and local government in Denmark, and partner countries. It initiates or assists exhibitions, concert tours, lectures, Danish classes, exchanges, study tours, and seminars. There is also a job-swop, in-service training scheme for administrators, educationalists, social workers, etc., mostly for two weeks, but sometimes for up to a year. The Institute publishes literature about Denmark in the main European languages and provides an extensive information and reference service from its head office at Kultorvet 2, **Copenhagen**, and from branch offices in Edinburgh (UK), Brussels (Belgium), Hannover (Germany), Vienna (Austria), Kecskemét (Hungary), Gdansk (Poland), Riga (Latvia), Tallinn (Estonia), and Vilnius (Lithuania). AHT

DANISH EAST INDIA COMPANY *see* **EAST INDIA COMPANY**

DANISH LANGUAGE. A standard classification of European languages used by Lars S. Viktør places the south-Scandinavian Danish with north-Scandinavian Norwegian and Swedish and the insular-Scandinavian **Faroese** and Icelandic in a North Germanic group, separately from a West Germanic group formed by German, English, Dutch, and Frisian. The north and south Scandinavian languages are all mutually intelligible and could be regarded as dialects of a single language, but on sociological criteria they are the distinct languages of their national communities. The influence of Low German (Saxon) on Danish reached a peak around 1350. By 1525 a period of extensive changes in structure and sound was followed by greater stability as the written language was standardized, with the reformed church playing an important part. The development of literature around 1700 helped to form modern written Danish. Although at home it had to assert itself against Latin and German, Danish as the language of officials of state and church tended to suppress the local languages in Norway, the Faroes, and Iceland until the 19th century. Today Norwegian takes two forms, both distinct in pronunciation from Danish: *riksmål* still shows strong Danish influence, while *nynorsk* is based on west-Norwegian dialects. In the **Faroes** and **Greenland** Danish is a secondary official language, and in **Iceland** also it is taught as a required subject from primary school onward. Danish is the only official language in Denmark, and the mother tongue of all 5 million Danes as well as of the small Danish minority south of the German border.

Within Denmark early legal and religious texts, legends, and chronicles reflected local dialects, but with commerce centered in Copenhagen and the church in **Roskilde** the influence of **Zealand** started to predominate even before printing was introduced in 1482. When the **Bible** was published in 1550 its consistent orthography and its "plain Danish" style, which avoided learned Latinisms and Germanisms, were highly influential. The first grammars, which appeared in the 17th century, were based on upper-class Copenhagen speech, while comedies by Ludvig **Holberg** ridiculed the use of foreign language merely to impress. German domination declined in the late 18th century and Danish became a study in its own right in schools and in Copenhagen university. Spellings were largely standardized by 1800, although discussion continued. Rules of grammar and spelling were legislated in 1872 by Kultusministeriet, the ministry responsible for the Church and Education, and revised at intervals, most recently in Retskrivningsordbogen of 1986. Changes in 1948 included use of lower case letters for nouns (by contrast with the Germanic-influenced use of capitals). At the same time *å* replaced *aa* and was placed at the end of the alphabet after *æ* and *ø*. Dialects, once distinctive of **Jutland**, of the islands of **Funen** and **Zealand**, and of **Bornholm**, have succumbed to urbanization and rapid changes in communication, but still survive even among younger generations in west and south Jutland and Bornholm. In its numeral system, Danish places units before tens, as in German and Dutch, e.g., *femogtyve*, five-and-twenty, but a distinctive feature of Danish is that the tens from 50 to 90 are based on multiples of twenty and called *halvtres, tres, halvfjerds, firs, halvfems*, abbreviations of *halvtresindstyve* (literally "half three times twenty"), etc. *See also* **Faroese; Greenlandic; Syv, Peder.** AHT

DANISH LAW (Danske lov). Provincial law codes for **Jutland** and **Zealand** dated from the 13th century. As one of the centralizing reforms which followed the introduction of **absolute monarchy** in 1661, the first of six commissions was appointed to discuss codification of the law. Coming into force in 1683, *Danske Lov* was the first legal code for the whole Kingdom, largely a compilation in six books of existing law and practice with a large debt to the "Reces" produced under King **Christian IV**. It included prohibition of any activity to change the principle of absolute hereditary monarchy, with dire punishments including cutting off of the right hand, decapitation, or breaking on the wheel. It retained a section on sorcery, although the witch-burnings which had been common earlier in the century were declining, and the last was in 1693. Tax law and state administration was not covered. Molesworth, a critical Englishman, commented in 1694, "For justice, brevity and perspicuity they exceed all that I know in the world." Although many subsequent laws negated the Law's provisions, a number remain in force, while many of its principles are still recognized despite revisions in the 18th century. SPO, AHT

DANISH NATIONAL SOCIALIST WORKERS' PARTY (Danmarks Nationalsocialistiske Arbejderparti, DNSAP) was the Nazi political party founded in 1930 by the amalgamation of two existing fascist organizations under the leadership of Captain Cai Lembke. He was replaced the following year by Dr. Frits **Clausen**, who remained its *fører* until himself ousted in 1944. In imitation of the German Nazi Party, it formed its own storm troopers, youth and women's groups. Its membership reached 2,800 in 1935 and, after a setback in 1936, stood at 4,800 on the eve of **World War II**. While its main stronghold was in South **Jutland** with its large German-speaking minority, it also found support in northeast Jutland and parts of **Zealand** and **Funen**, but was weak in **Copenhagen**. Over a quarter of its membership were farm laborers. Its newspaper was called *Fædrelandet* (The Fatherland). In the April 1939 elections three of its members entered parliament with 1.8 percent of the vote. The decision by the German occupiers in 1940 to work with the democratically elected government caused the party much frustration, and in spite of German support it could not increase its representation in the March 1943 **Folketing** election. Party membership fell away dramatically, and in 1944 Clausen was deposed as leader. Membership was not adjudged an offense in itself after the war, but many members were tried for other offenses. SPO. *See also* **Schalburg**.

DANISH PEOPLE'S PARTY (Dansk Folkeparti). The 1994 election changed the balance within the **Progress Party** and its de facto leader, Pia Kjærsgaard (b. 1947), who had been a member of the party executive since the mid-1980s, was ousted as party spokesman. In October 1995 she and three colleagues left to form the Danish People's Party in reaction to the organizational and policy chaos of the Progress Party's national conference the previous month. They wished it to be clear that the new party's votes could be counted on by other parties — in contrast to the Progress Party's unreliable parliamentary record since it entered the **Folketing** in 1973. In the November 1997 local elections the party obtained about 6 percent of the vote, but its xenophobia attracted extensive comment. It is clearly nationalistic and opposes the European Union. AHT

DANISH RALLY (or UNITY) PARTY (Dansk Samling) was a political party founded in 1936 and led by the writer Arne Sørensen. Through its journal *Den tredje Standpunkt* (The Third Standpoint) it criticized party politics and the parliamentary system, but put up candidates in the elections of 1939 and, after the German occupation in 1940, was strongly opposed to the policy of concessions adopted by the coalition government. In the 1943 election it was the only legal party to oppose the policy of collaboration with the occupying forces, and gained three seats. It was represented on the **Freedom Council** set up in 1943; it won four seats and 3.1 percent of the vote in the October 1945 election but lost them again two years later. SPO

DANISH WEST INDIES. Now named the Virgin Islands and under US jurisdiction, St. Thomas was first acquired by Denmark in 1666. Import of slaves and export of sugar, tobacco, and cotton was handled by the West India Company, set up in 1671. In 1684 the neighboring island of St. Jan was also acquired. The plantations were worked by slaves brought from Denmark's possessions on the west coast of **Africa** under extremely harsh conditions. In 1733 a slave revolt was crushed with great ferocity. In the same year the fertile island of St. Croix was bought from the French and became the most important of the group. Its sugar supplied a flourishing refining industry in **Copenhagen**. The Crown took over the islands in 1755 and opened trade to all comers.

The islands were occupied by the British in 1801-02 and 1807-15 when Denmark and Britain were at war. Their economy declined in the later 19th century, and although **slavery** in them was abolished after an uprising in 1848, there was a further insurrection in 1878. They became a liability for the Danish government, who offered to sell them to the United States. A treaty was concluded in 1867 but was not ratified by the Senate. A similar treaty in 1902 also failed to be ratified, this time by the **Landsting**, but in 1917 they passed to US control for a price of $25,000,000. The sale was approved by 57.4 percent of the voters in the first **referendum** held under Denmark's 1915 **constitution**. SPO

DANISH WOMEN'S SOCIETY (Dansk Kvindesamfund or DK) is the earliest and most important women's rights organization in Denmark. It was founded in 1871 to campaign for the provision of independent support for unmarried women. It worked for better education for women and in the 1880s began to call for equal pay. The appeal by Georg **Brandes** for an end to double standards in sexual life led to the publication by the Society in 1885 of the journal *Kvinden og Samfund* (Woman and Society), which is still published. The Society did not take up the cause of women's suffrage until 1906. Membership reached a peak of some 12,000 after **World War II**, but was then threatened by neo-feminism and has declined. SPO. *See also* **Feminism; Women's Movement**.

DANISH WOMEN'S SUFFRAGE ASSOCIATION *see* **FEMALE SUFFRAGE**

DANNEBROG is the Danish national flag, consisting of a white cross on a red ground. Traditionally the original Dannebrog fell from heaven on 15 June 1219 to inspire the Danish forces to victory over the pagan Estonians at the battle of Lydanisse. More likely it was granted by the pope on the occasion of this crusade. It first appears as a Danish symbol on the seal of the **Kalmar Union** at the end of the 14th century, but it was already in the arms of the city of Tallinn. It is first mentioned in literature in a Swedish source of the 15th century. It was long used in the form of a split banner as a military and naval ensign. In the 18th century Danish merchant ships bore the more familiar rectangular version, which was decreed to be the national flag in 1867. Its name probably derives from the Frisian for "red cloth". SPO

DANNEBROG, ORDER OF, is the second of Denmark's two knightly orders, after the **Order of the Elephant**. Traditionally it was first instituted in 1219 by King **Valdemar II**, and was revived by **Christian V** in 1671 for 50 noblemen. Its scope was extended in 1808. Its classes are now those of Grand Commander (reserved for royalty since 1842), Grand Cross, Commander (First and Second Class), and Knight (First and Second Class). A Cross of Honor is awarded to Danish holders of the Order. The escutcheons of Grand Commanders and holders of the Grand Cross are hung in the chapel of **Frederiksborg Castle** together with those of the holders of the Order of the Elephant. Women have been entitled to receive it since 1951. Members are known as "white knights" after the red-bordered white sash or ribbon which signifies membership, in contrast to the pale blue of the Order of the Elephant. SPO, AHT

DANNER, LOUISE CHRISTINE RASMUSSEN, COUNTESS (1815-1874). Morganatic (non-noble) third wife of King **Frederik VII**. Born the illegitimate daughter of a house maid, she became a ballet dancer at the **Royal Theater** 1835-42. Her lover Carl **Berling** (the publisher) in 1844 helped her establish a dress shop in Copenhagen. He introduced her to Crown Prince Frederik, and she moved into the royal palace in 1848, changing her surname from Rasmussen to Danner. In 1849 she was created baroness and in 1850 married Frederik, having already borne him a son. On marriage she was granted the title of countess (lensgrevinde). She was politically close to the **Farmers' Friends** and so was disliked by the **national liberal** bourgeoisie. Though never acknowledged in Danish "society", she was popular with the common people, appears to have exercised a beneficent influence on her husband, and did much to strengthen the image of the monarchy. After Frederik died in 1863 she traveled much abroad. In 1873 she established a foundation in **Copenhagen**, Grevinde Danner-stiftelsen, to house poor working women. She died in Genoa, leaving a fortune of 6,500,000 crowns and the estate of Jægerpris to a charity, the King Frederik VII Foundation for the care and education of poor girls. SPO, AHT

DANNEVIRKE is a defensive wall in **Slesvig** in north Germany. Begun by King **Godfred** at the beginning of the 9th century to mark the southern boundary of his kingdom and protect the important trade route through Slesvig between the North Sea and the Baltic, it was strengthened with brick ramparts by King **Valdemar I**. After long neglect, it was strengthened at the beginning of the Second **Slesvig-Holsten** War in 1864 but was abandoned in the face of the Austro-German advance. There were unsuccessful calls for the establishment of the Danish frontier with Germany along the line of the Dannevirke in 1919 after the referendum in that year had placed it within Germany. SPO

DANSK SAMLING see DANISH RALLY

DAVID, CHRISTIAN NATHAN (1793-1874). Politician. A merchant's son, he graduated in political science from Göttingen and became professor of state economy at Copenhagen University in 1830. In 1834 he started the liberal-thinking weekly journal *Fædrelandet* (The Fatherland). Articles critical of absolute monarchy led to his prosecution: he was acquitted, but dismissed from the university in 1836. He was a member of the Estates of the Islands 1840-46, the **Folketing** 1850-53, the Council of the Realm 1855-63, of the **Landsting** 1866-70, and was minister of finance 1864-65. He was a supporter of the single state (*helstaten*) and of limited suffrage. AHT. *See also* **Absolutism**.

DEATH as a judicial **PENALTY** was used increasingly after the introduction of **Absolutism** in the 17th century but declined again in the 18th. It was last used in accordance with the civil code in 1892 and was formally abolished in 1930. It was reintroduced, amidst considerable controversy, as an exceptional measure to deal with war crimes in 1945, and 78 Danish collaborators were subsequently sentenced to death; of these 46 were executed, the first in January 1946 and the last in July 1950. SPO

DEFENSE became an important political issue in Danish politics after the country's defeat in the Second **Slesvig-Holsten** War in 1864 and became even more critical after France was defeated in the Franco-Prussian War of 1870-71. While it was generally realized that Denmark could not hope to defend itself for long in the face of a determined attack by a great power (and by experience Germany seemed the most likely), disagreements arose between (1) those who wished to concentrate on the defense of **Copenhagen** until help could be secured from an ally, (2) those who wished for a more flexible defense of **Zealand**, and (3) those who saw any expenditure on defense as a useless diversion of funds from more worthy objectives.

The first position was adopted by the **conservatives** who held power throughout 1864-1901, the second by the moderate **Liberals,** and the third by **Radical Liberals** and **socialists**. In spite of strong opposition from the Liberal majority in the **Folketing**, J.B.S. **Estrup**'s conservative government, with the backing of the Upper House and the Crown, started in 1886 to build a series of forts and gun emplacements on the landward side of the capital. Work on these ceased in 1894, as part of an agreement reached between moderate Liberals and the government.

After the **Change of System** in 1901, defense policy continued to divide the Liberals; in 1905 the newly formed **Radical Liberal Party** had a program of drastic reductions in defense expenditure which also found favor with the Social Democrats, while the Liberal leader I.C. **Christensen** drew nearer to the Conservatives and in 1909 even proposed expenditure to build forts.

The Danish army established a military flying school in 1912. Denmark remained neutral during **World War I** and this perspective remained influential subsequently. A Defense Act introduced in 1928 by the Liberal administration reduced expenditure sharply and was fiercely attacked by the Conservatives, who defeated the government on the issue. This opened the way for the Social Democrat and Radical governments of 1929-40, in which Peter **Munch** was foreign minister. This failed to secure the measure of disarmament for which it had called on taking office and with the threat of war growing in 1938 even agreed to modest rearmament. It was feared that any more ambitious measures might antagonize Germany. Alone of the Nordic countries, Denmark signed a nonaggression pact with Germany in May 1939, but on 9 April 1940 German forces occupied Denmark, taking the Danes by surprise: Danish military resistance lasted only a few hours. An underground **resistance** movement was organized from mid-1943 and made what use it could of regular forces.

After **World War II**, Denmark negotiated with Sweden and Norway for a Nordic defense pact, but when these talks broke down, joined **NATO** in 1949. Since then Danish defense policy has been largely dictated by NATO, although Denmark has insisted that during peacetime no nuclear weapons or foreign forces were to be based on Danish territory (with the exception of **Greenland**).

Since 1949 the defense budget has customarily been agreed by a broad parliamentary majority for several years at a time. The Air Force became an independent arm in 1951, to be expanded to eight combat squadrons. Since 1950-51 there has been a single minister of defense heading the unified command of **army, navy,** and air force. The period of compulsory service was set at 18 months, reduced in 1954 to 16 months, in 1964 to 14 months (or 12 months in the Air Force), and in 1977 to 9 months. In 1993 the period of service depended on the duties assigned: four months for cleaning duties in the navy and 12 months in the army, while men selected for service as sergeant or lieutenant served 18 to 24 months.

In the 1960s the army comprised a standing force of at least 13,000 men. The navy was reorganized into eight major units and the air force comprised seven combat and reconnaissance squadrons. In 1969 the command structure was further integrated and a Defense Council (Forsvarsrådet) of service chiefs was established to assist the minister. A rationalized structure for a smaller defense establishment was agreed to by the "four old parties" in 1973. The 1977 defense agreement maintained force levels on a budget linked to the cost of living. In 1982 NATO approved a six-year plan which called for increases of defense spending at a rate 4 percent above inflation, to which the Conservative-led government in Denmark responded with defense budget growth of 2 percent a year. A new defense agreement of 1989, supported by the four old parties plus the **Christian Democrats,** took some account of the end of the Cold War by closing four garrisons. The 1992 defense agreement reduced the army from 72,000 to 60,000 by 1996, with a peacekeeping force of 35,200.

The five-year defense agreement for 1995-99 was supported by **Social Democrats, Radical Liberals, Conservatives,** and **Center-Democrats,** with the **Liberals** joining in from April 1996. In addition to financial savings, one brigade and two garrisons would be closed, with a reduction of the army from 60,000 to 58,000 men, but there would be an increase in the budget for equipment purchases. A Danish International Brigade was established in 1995 with the tasks of participating in national defense, in the NATO Rapid Reaction Force, and in conflict prevention, peacekeeping, peacemaking, humanitarian, and like operations under mandate from the United Nations or the Organization for Security and Cooperation in Europe. SPO, AHT

DESIGN, DANISH, has origins in the **Royal Porcelain** factory founded in 1775 and the Royal Furniture Warehouse founded in 1777 "to spread good taste in furniture" in competition with French and English makers. The architect G.F. Hetch (1788-1864) emphasized that beauty must always depend on usefulness, the principle in his own designs of furniture, which has characterized later Danish design. The Copenhagen Exhibition of 1888 stimulated a Nordic counterpart to the romanticism of *art nouveau* and *jugendstil* that avoided the extremes of these developments and started two decades of development based on a strong sense of craft quality. **Georg Jensen**'s silver jewelry and cutlery in clear, simple shapes decorated with leaf and fruit motifs set new standards, and his workshop attracted other designers such as Johan Rohde (1856-1935) whose more austere designs were a simple synthesis of function, form, and material.

At the start of the 20th century a trend to neoclassicalism in **architecture** was another important influence. This led the architect **Kaare Klint** to concern himself with interior design and furniture, searching widely for elegant solutions which combined function and quality. The magazine *Kritisk Revy* (Critical Revue) with Poul **Henningsen** as chief editor was first published in 1926. It rejected the exaggerated aesthetical refinement of neoclassicalism, instead emphasizing social reality and an objective attitude to articles in everyday use. Henningsen himself designed a widely appreciated PH range of lighting. From 1927 the Copenhagen Cabinetmakers' Guild ran annual competitions and exhibitions for new designs which kept alive their craft skills.

Wartime studies of how ordinary people lived in their two-room apartments, together with the designs of Børge Mogensen for the Cooperative Movement's furniture store in **Copenhagen**, were the basis for the light, elegant, single pieces (rather than suites) of furniture which were increasingly bought by Danes and were successfully exported from the 1950s for their good quality and pleasing design. Hans Wegner's furniture designs for the new town hall of **Århus** set new standards, emphasizing that the design, whether of a building, furniture, or flatware, must suit the body and the eye. Made from Danish beech and Swedish birch, they were space-saving, easy to handle, and easily cleaned. Production was supported by research on materials strength and production planning at the Technological Institute, while the Danish Furniture Producers organization maintained quality control. Arne Jacobsen's Egg and Swan designs for upholstered chairs continued architectural involvement in furniture design. As an architect, Jacobsen gave his designs a hard-edged precision which came to be termed aesthetic functionalism. While much furniture production was based on established woodworking skills, designers such as Jacobsen and Poul Kjærholm used steel to achieve a strength which draws on the ideals of the Bauhaus movement of the 1920s while relating to the lightness of Japanese furniture.

For three decades, Denmark led Scandinavia in presenting a consolidated design idiom which was distinct from what was happening elsewhere in the world in its guild-quality workmanship, fine materials, and clean lines without unnecessary decoration. This 'Danish Modern' style gained a resounding success at the 1954 Milan Trienniale, while a three-year tour of the United States created a huge new market. The porcelain factories, too, developed simple designs with a minimum of decoration in the 1950s and 1960s which successfully blended artistic design with factory technologies.

A 'linear-organic' trend took up the smooth, curving forms of the Art Nouveau period, while also taking advantage of new materials and techniques: plastics, wood laminates, spun steel, and aluminum were the media for new practical designs, but were also the opening for a string of cheap imitations that lacked the verve or precision of the originals.

The silversmith Kay Bojesen established Den Permanente, the Permanent Exhibition of Danish Arts, Crafts, and Industrial Design in 1931 to show and sell the work of the many artists and craft workers who needed a shop window. By the 1980s the department store Illums Bolighus had taken over as the site for major design exhibitions of modern living, while the **Museum of Applied Arts** has a good collection of pieces from the height of Danish Modern designs of the 1950s. AHT

DEUNTZER, JOHAN HENRIK (1845-1918). Lawyer and politician, prime minister 1901-05. The son of an architect, he graduated *cand. jur.* in 1867 and was professor of law at Copenhagen University 1872-1901. After the Liberal Reform party gained two thirds of the **Folketing** seats and the Right only 8 percent in the 1901 elections, the king called on Deuntzer, newly elected to parliament, who described himself as "Liberal to a certain extent" (*Venstremand til en vis grad*), to form a cabinet reflecting the majority in the Folketing. This constituted the **Change of System**. The ministry, in which Deuntzer was also foreign minister, was dominated by J.C. **Christensen**. Deuntzer had to resign in 1905 when Christensen left the cabinet with three of his colleagues. He sat in the **Landsting** as one of the royal nominees from 1914 until his death, initially as a **Liberal** and then as an independent radical. SPO, AHT

DEVELOPMENT AID *see* **DANIDA**

DFDS (DET FORENEDE DAMPSKIBS-SELSKAB) is a shipping line founded in 1866 by the industrialist **C.F. Tietgen** by amalgamating the three largest Danish shipping lines of that time: Det alm. danske Dampskibsselskab, H.P. Prior, and Koch & Hendersen. It grew to be the group of companies operating the most important passenger and freight lines linking Denmark with the rest of Scandinavia and western Europe. Knud **Lauritzen** obtained a controlling shareholding in 1964. SPO

DINESEN, ISAK *see* **BLIXEN, KAREN**

DITLEVSEN, TOVE (1917-1976), the daughter of a stoker, earned her living from about 1940 as an author and journalist. In her novels

Man gjorde et barn fortræd (1941, A Child Was Harmed) and
Barndommens gade (1943, The Street of Childhood) she describes
the world of her childhood in Vesterbro, **Copenhagen**; these and
another four novels are in a realistic mode. She also wrote four volumes of short stories, two of essays, one of aphorisms, and eight
collections of poetry, one of which, *Kvindesind* (1955, A Woman's
Mind) deals with women's emotional life. The autobiographical
roman á clef, Vilhelms værelse (1975, Wilhelm's Room) deals with
a stormy marriage, a theme covered with remarkable candor in *Gift*
(1971, Marriage - but *gift* also means Poison). AHT

DITMARSKEN (German Ditmarschen) is an area of western Holsten
which was the scene of a humiliating defeat in 1500 of King **Hans**
I's feudal host by a peasant army raised by the inhabitants of this
fiercely independent republic. It had defied constant attempts to incorporate it into Holsten and in 1499 rejected Danish demands for
tribute and the right to build three fortresses on its territory. The
Danes invaded, but were unable to exploit their superior numbers in
the swampy ground south of Hemmingsted, where they were met by
about 500 armed peasants and put to flight, King Hans himself only
just escaping and leaving behind him the original **Dannebrog**. The
defeat revenged in 1559, when an army under Johan **Rantzau** easily
overcame opposition and compelled submission. SPO

DØSSING, THOMAS (1882-1947). Resistance worker. The son of a
farm-owner, he became a library director and during the German
occupation he helped produce *Frit Danmark* (Free Denmark) and
was twice arrested for illegal work. On the invitation of the **Free-**
dom Council he traveled to Moscow in July 1944, where he was accepted by the Soviet government as representative of "fighting
Denmark." He sharply opposed collaboration and the policy which
gave politicians extensive influence in the liberation government. He
was Danish ambassador in Moscow 1945-47. AHT

DRACHMANN, HOLGER (1846-1908). Poet, novelist, and painter.
After a stay in England he wrote *Engelske Socialister* (English Socialists) which was published in the **Brandes**-inspired collection
*Digte (*1872, Poems). His later poems such as *Sange ved havet*
(1877, Songs by the Sea) were more naturalistic. His burning love
for the singer Amanda Nilsson inspired his novel *Forskrevet* (2

vols., 1890, Pledged) and several poems, in which he refers to her as Edith. He wrote several plays, one of which, *Der var Engang* (1885, Once upon a Time) is still performed. His poem, *Du danske Mand!* (You Danish Man) was set to music by **Carl Nielsen** and is still popular. His reputation is mainly as a lyricist who introduced new forms, rhythms, and vitality into Danish poetry. See also **Skagen School**. AHT

DRAMA *see* **THEATER, ROYAL THEATER**

DREIER, FREDERIK (1827-1853). Author. The son of a lawyer, he studied medicine and in pamphlets published in 1848 campaigned for socialism, writing, and publishing a weekly, *Samfundets Reform* (The Reform of Society) in 1852-53. He is considered an isolated forerunner of the socialist movement in Denmark. AHT

DREWSEN, JOHAN CHRISTIAN (1777-1851). Manufacturer and politician. After learning the paper-making trade, in 1810 he took over his father's paper mill in North **Zealand**, developing it until he handed it over to his sons in 1844. He worked for technical improvements to agriculture. He was a member of the **Roskilde** Assembly of Estates 1834-48, of the constituent assembly 1848-49, and of the **Folketing** 1849-50. He was also a cofounder of the **Friends of the Farmers**. On the Slesvig question he was strongly nationalistic. AHT

DREYER, CARL THEODOR (1889-1968). Film director. He started a career as a journalist, but from 1912 wrote film scripts and from 1918 directed films, his first being *The President* (1919). His international reputation rests on his films including *Jeanne d'Arc* (1928), *Vredens Dag* (The Day of Wrath, 1943), *Ordet* (The Word, 1955), and *Gertrud* (1964) with an aesthetic, lingering style which brings out the film's humanistic message. AHT

DYBBØL LINES are the defensive position on the peninsula of Sundeved, near Sønderborg in southern **Jutland**, that protects the crossing to the island of Als. This was the scene of a major encounter between Danish and Prussian forces during the Second **Slesvig-Holsten** War. After the First Slesvig-Holsten War (1848-50), when there had been several engagements in the area, it was decided to build trenches and 10 forts across the headland, but work on these did not begin until 1861 and was not completed when war broke out again in 1864. After withdrawing from the *Dannevirke*, the Danes decided to try to hold the Lines in anticipation of the conclusion of armistice negotiations going on in London. But Prussian forces began shelling the position on 15 March and after 34 days launched a successful assault on 18 April. In the engagement the Danes lost some 4,700 men, of whom 1,700 were killed or wounded, and the duchies of Slesvig and Holsten. The site at Dybbøl Mølle is now a national park. SPO

- E -

EAST ASIATIC COMPANY (ØSTASIATISK KOMPANI, ØK) is the trading company formed in 1897 by **Hans Niels Andersen** as an extension of the company Andersen & Co., which he founded in Bangkok in 1884. Its original purpose was to trade between Denmark and the Far East, but under Andersen's direction it soon diversified into industry, forestry, agriculture, banking, and insurance. It commissioned from the shipbuilders **Burmeister & Wain** the world's first oceangoing motorship, the *Selandia*, which was launched in 1912. Its headquarters in **Copenhagen** were blown up by the German occupiers in December 1944 as one of several acts of revenge for the sabotage carried out by the Danish **Resistance**. It developed into one of Denmark's largest undertakings with 250 enterprises in over 50 countries. SPO

EAST INDIA COMPANY (ØSTINDISK KOMPANI) was formed in 1616. An expedition of six ships under the command of Ove Gjedde sailed under its aegis to India and founded its most successful trading post at Trankebar south of Madras in 1620. The Company went bankrupt in 1729, and its assets passed to the Crown. The **Asiatic Company** was founded three years later to undertake further Danish activity in India, which included trading posts at Calicut (1752) on the southwest coast, at Danmarksnagore (1700) and Fredriksnagore or Serampore (1755) in the Ganges delta. Trade stagnated after the 1807-14 war, and all were sold to the British East

India Company in 1845. A base on the Nicobar Islands was founded in 1756, abandoned in 1848, and taken over by the British in 1868. SPO, AHT. *See also* **India, British Possessions in**.

EASTER CRISIS (Påskekrisen) was the political crisis in 1920 when the Danish Crown acted politically for the last time. The outcome of the referendums in **Slesvig** at the beginning of the year disappointed many Danes, and opponents of the **Radical Liberal** government of Carl Theodor **Zahle** called for a general election. Support for Zahle in parliament was uncertain, and King **Christian X** sympathized with the call. When Zahle refused an election before the law was passed that would extend proportional representation to rural districts, the king dismissed his ministry on 29 March and appointed a nonparty cabinet under Otto **Liebe** to prepare for immediate elections. The king's action was widely seen as unconstitutional. The **Social Democrats** called for a general strike to begin after Easter and there were republican demonstrations outside the royal residence of **Amalienborg**. Under these pressures the king agreed to replace the Liebe cabinet with an interim government headed by M.P. Fries, which was supported by all political parties and was to await the passing of the electoral reform law before calling an election. The law was duly passed and the election was held on 26 April. As a result the **Radical Liberals** lost nearly half their **Folketing** seats, and the **Liberals**, as the largest single party, formed a cabinet under Niels **Neergaard**. SPO. *See also* **Borgbjerg, Frederik**.

ECKERSBERG, CHRISTOFFER WILHELM (1783-1853). Painter. Born in **Slesvig** and apprenticed as a painter, he entered the Royal **Academy of Art** in 1803, and in 1810 traveled to Paris, where he studied under David. In 1813 he visited Italy where he met the sculptor Bertel **Thorvaldsen**. From both he acquired the neoclassical realism which stressed perspective and detail. He returned to Denmark in 1816 and became professor at the Academy in succession to Nikolaj **Abildgaard**. Many of his portraits and pictures have maritime and historical motifs. His chief works include his portrait of Thorvaldsen (1814), the Nathanson family portrait (1818), and a historical series for **Christiansborg** Castle. He influenced a generation of Danish painters of the **Golden Age** but had no sympathy for the new Romanticism that was attracting so many younger contemporaries. SPO, AHT. *See also* **Painting**.

ECONOMIC PARTY (Vinnuflokkurin) *see* **PEOPLE'S PARTY**

EDUCATION. In the 12th century Latin schools were founded, linked to the cathedrals, where clerks and trainee priests could learn the Latin they needed in church services. As church and state came increasingly into conflict, they were able to find employment in both organizations. A law of 1521 required all children either to go to school or to learn a trade or work on a farm. In 1606 the Latin schools were designated to train future ordinands for the priesthood. After the **Reformation** the new **Lutheran** clergy gave rural children little more than a training in the catechism, and in the 17th century only state-approved textbooks were allowed. A law of church discipline of 1629 required parish priests to supervise the behavior of the children of the parish, which gave them supervision of the schoolmaster's teaching. Young noblemen were sent to **Sorø Academy** (*see also* **Herlufsholm**) to learn true Lutheran beliefs before they traveled abroad for their education, and their tutors were examined by the bishop to ensure that they held no heretical beliefs. Sorø Academy was closed in 1665, on the introduction of **absolute monarchy**, but was reopened in 1747 to allow sons of the nobility to study the law and administration of the state at the highest level without recourse to Copenhagen University.

In 1789 a School Commission looked at peasant education. It was agreed that religious instruction would develop the children into good citizens, but C.D. **Reventlow**'s rationalism was outweighed by Bishop Balle's insistence that church dogma should be taught. The resulting 1806 law set the lasting principle that all children from their seventh year until they were confirmed must be educated (but did not have to attend school): this formulation permitted the development of independent schools outside the state system. Initially school attendance was required only every second day, and older children had to attend only two days per week between 1 June until the harvest. The subjects taught were religion, writing, reading (including history and geography), arithmetic, singing, and, if possible, gymnastics. The schools were supervised by a local school commission chaired by the priest, with the landlord and some peasants as members.

The Latin schools were reorganized in 1805-09, with an eight-year curriculum and a requirement that teachers should be trained. Fees were introduced: as a result the number of pupils declined and they tended to be the children of the better off.

To train teachers, Blågård Seminarium was founded in 1791, with others following. By 1818 there were uniform regulations and a three-year course of study for teachers. In 1852 **Natalie Zahle** founded the first of many colleges for women teachers. In the 1990s there are 18 colleges that provide the four-year training.

School reform was high on the **Liberal** agenda of the 1901 first democratic government. Peasant schools for the many and Latin schools for the privileged had given the educated a hold on power which the Liberals opposed. Meanwhile expanding commerce and administration needed new office-work skills. The 1903 law on higher general schools set up a threefold system of five years of primary school (from age seven) after which pupils with book-based abilities went on to four years of middle school while the rest continued in school for two years (until the traditional confirmation-age of 14). After middle school there was either one year of study to the *realeksamen*, or a three-year course at *gymnasium*, where pupils divided between a new route of modern languages or the traditional classical languages route or a mathematics and natural sciences route. Passed with Liberal and Social Democratic support, the Social Democrats saw this as a move toward the comprehensive schools which would end social-class distinctions.

Rapid economic growth late in the 1950s drew many more women into employment and brought the 1958 school reform. This achieved equality by requiring rural children to attend school every day. All children were required to have seven years' education. Then they could either continue for two years, or enter the *real* line for three years. From the second or third year of this they could continue for three years in *gymnasium*. In the 1960s the number who chose *gymnasium* and university grew rapidly, and students were no longer an elite but a large proportion of the age group. In March 1968 they began a series of demonstrations and actions for a greater say in the content of their courses, in the vanguard of a movement which extended across Western Europe and the United States.

The 1975 Education Act made education (not schooling) compulsory between the ages of seven and 16, whether in the municipal primary and lower secondary *folkeskole* or in a private school or at home, so long as appropriate standards and an adequate range of subjects are provided. This formulation has allowed several experimental schools to develop, although 90 percent of Danish children attend the *folkeskole,* which educates almost all the children of all backgrounds and abilities together. Although from the eighth class, English, German, and Mathematics and from the ninth class, Physics/Chemistry may be studied at basic and advanced levels, there is a trend away from this streaming. Often a class will keep the same class teacher (usually the teacher of Danish) through all or most of its ten years. Class sizes may not be more than 28 and average 19, with a pupil-teacher ratio of 10.3:1. The Ministry of Education sets targets for each subject and recommends guidelines for how they are to be attained. The 1,825 *folkeskole* are financed by the *kommune* (municipality) with a small block grant from the state. There are also 408 private schools, attended by about one pupil in ten. The state pays 85 percent of the cost and the parents pay the rest.

After the *folkeskole* about 45 percent of pupils stay for an optional tenth year and 90 percent remain in higher secondary education, about two-thirds in technical or commercial schools and one-third in a gymnasium for general secondary education. The county councils administer schools at this level and raise the taxes to finance them. The gymnasium offers two lines: languages or mathematics, although there is a substantial common core including social studies, music, and modern languages, and what distinguishes the lines are pupils' choices for either Latin and Greek or Mathematics, Physics, Chemistry, and Biology. The concluding *studentereksamen* requires passes in ten subjects. Alternatively students may work for the Højere forberedelseseksam (Hf), the higher preparatory exam, with a broad core curriculum and a wide range of options, many of them taking core subjects further. Either examination qualifies for admission to higher education, although specific subjects or levels of attainment may be required.

To allow all, regardless of economic status, to enter higher education, the Youth Education Fund was established in 1952. In 1970 its name was changed to State Education Support (Statens Uddannelsesstøtte, SU). Arrangements have been amended frequently, and comprise a combination of the following: grants (not repayable); interest-free loans, repayable when the education ends; state-guaranteed loans (available until 1970) which ensured that the lender could not lose; state loans, free of interest or repayment while studying and then subject to interest at 2 percent over base-rate (available in 1970-75); and low-interest state loans, subject to interest at 3 percent below base-rate while studying and then at 1 percent over base-rate (introduced from 1988). A reform in 1996 made grants (SU) available for a total of six years (not necessarily continuously) with a possible seventh year in cases of illness, pregnancy, student political work, or change of studies. Study-loans were at 4 percent fixed interest while studying, and then at 1 percent over base rate. The size of grants depended on the student's housing situation (whether or not living at home) and the type of course studied. Loans are normally repayable with interest over 7-15 years beginning one year after the study-period ends (whether or not successfully). AHT. *See also* **Folk High Schools, Universities.**

EGEDE, HANS PAULSEN (1686-1758). Missionary. Born in Norway and trained as a priest, in 1710 he drew up a plan for the conversion of the descendants of the Norse settlers, who he believed still resided in **Greenland**. In 1719 he succeeded in interesting King **Frederik IV** in the plan. He also appealed to the merchants of Bergen for support with promises of the resultant trade. In 1721 he established a base at Godthåb/Nuuk on the west coast of Greenland, but found no trace of the Norsemen. Helped by his wife, Gertrud Rask, he set about the conversion of the native Inuit and worked on the island for 15 years, winning the trust of the inhabitants, especially by his courage during a smallpox epidemic. Gertrud died there, and he returned to Denmark in 1736 both because of illness and because of disagreements with **Pietist** missionaries who had arrived in 1733. In **Copenhagen** he founded the Greenland Seminary and in 1740 was appointed bishop of Greenland. He retired seven years later, having quarreled with the seminary. His son Poul (1708-89) continued his work in Greenland and his enterprise led to the recolonization and assertion of Danish sovereignty over Greenland, which was not internationally recognized until the 20th century. SPO, AHT

EIGTVED, NICOLAI (1701-1754). Architect. Born in Egtved near Vejle, he traveled abroad in 1723 and trained as architect and military engineer in Saxony and Poland under C.F. Poppelmann, among others. While still abroad, he was granted a military commission by

King **Christian VI** and a bursary for a study tour to Italy, where he was inspired by Italian baroque. He was appointed court architect in 1735 and as such introduced the French Rococo style into Denmark, firstly in the Prince's Palace in Copenhagen (1743-44), which now houses the National Museum. He is known chiefly as the designer of the National Theater (1748) and of the four mansions which make up the palace of **Amalienborg** and the plan (1749-54) of the new area of Frederikstad, of which they form the core. He also worked on **Fredensborg** palace and the interior of the first **Christiansborg** as well as a number of manor houses (e.g., Bregentved on **Zealand**). In 1754, just before his death, he was appointed first director of the new Royal Danish **Academy of Art**. SPO

EJDER PROGRAM *see* **SLESVIG-HOLSTEN**

ELDERLY CARE. Before the late 19th century care of the elderly was the responsibility of the family or of the parish, but in 1891 separate legislation was introduced to pay maintenance to "deserving poor" over the age of 60. In 1922 came a fixed **pension** which was no longer means-tested, though still subject to certain conditions. This was replaced 11 years later by the comprehensive package of social legislation associated with K.K. **Steincke**, under which entitlement to a pension depended only on membership of a health insurance society. A law of 1956 removed all restrictions and fixed the rate of the minimum pension at 10 percent of the average wage, while raising the pensionable age for men and married women to 67 and for single women to 62. An **employment supplementary pension** scheme (Arbejdsmarkedets Tillægspension, ATP) for wage- and salary-earners, supported by contributions from employers and employees, was introduced in 1964. **Welfare** services for the elderly, including the provision of rest homes, were the subject of legislation in the same year. SPO, AHT

ELECTIONS to the **Folketing** (the lower house of parliament until 1953 and since then the single parliamentary chamber) must be held at least every four years under the 1849 and subsequent **constitutions**, unless the house is dissolved earlier. Proportional representation was introduced in 1915 (*see* **Andræ, Carl Georg; Easter Crisis**) and extended to the whole country in 1920. Of the 175 members for the Kingdom of Denmark, 135 are chosen for 23 large constituencies by the d'Hondt method (which divides the party's vote by the number of seats it has been allocated plus one), replaced in 1953 by the modified Sainte-Laguë method (using successive divisors of 1.4, 3, 5, 7, etc.). Forty supplementary seats are allocated by the largest remainder method. The results are very closely proportional, subject to a threshold of 2 percent. Nonparty candidates are very rare, but Svend Haugaard was elected as an independent in 1994. Seats in the Folketing numbered 140 for the first two elections in 1920, but were increased to 149 for the third. In 1947 the number was increased to 150 and in 1950 to 151. Since abolition of the **Landsting** in 1953, Folketing membership has been fixed at 179, including two representatives separately elected for **Greenland** and two for the **Faroes**. SPO, AHT. *See also* Appendix 2; Appendix 3; **Cabinet; Constitutions; Folketing; Franchise; Government; Parliament**.

ELEPHANT, ORDER OF THE, is the highest Danish knightly order. It was instituted by King **Christian I** in 1464 and revived by King **Christian V** in 1693. It has only one class. The arms of its holders are displayed in the chapel of the castle of **Frederiksborg**. It is traditionally awarded to Danish princes on their eighteenth birthday. Only three Danish commoners have been awarded it in the 20th century: the philologist Vilhelm Thomsen in 1912, the founder of the **East India Company**, **H.N. Andersen** in 1919, and the atomic physicist Niels **Bohr** in 1947. Foreigners awarded the Order have included President Eisenhower, Sir Winston Churchill, and Viscount Montgomery. SPO

ELFELT, PETER (1866-1931). Photographer. From the age of 12 he worked in various photographic shops. He opened his own studio with his two brothers in 1890 and was appointed court photographer in 1900. He was known for his royal portraits and as the first Danish photographer of unposed public events. AHT

ELLEGAARD, THORVALD (1877-1950). Cyclist. Initially a bricklayer, from 1898 he cycled professionally, winning the world track sprint championship in 1901, 1902, 1903, 1906, 1908, and 1911. In addition he won the Danish Clubs *grand prix* 11 times, with 154 tandem wins with 49 partners in a 31-year career. AHT

ELLEHAMMAR, JACOB CHRISTIAN (1871-1946). Aviator and inventor. Trained as a watchmaker, he began to construct a power-driven flying machine in 1905 and on 12 September 1906 became the first in Europe to fly a heavier-than-air machine and the first in the world to fly a plane with landing wheels. He managed to stay off the ground for 42 meters on Lindholm, north of Lolland. Later he abandoned conventional aircraft, but in 1912 successfully flew a vertical-take-off helicopter. SPO

ELLEMANN-JENSEN, UFFE (1941-). A **Liberal** politician he is the son of Jens Peter Jensen, a newspaper editor and **Folketing** member, and of Edith Ellemann. He graduated *cand. polit.* in 1969. After national service in the artillery and on the defense staff he became a journalist with the **Berlingske** group, then in television current affairs and with the financial paper *Børsen*. He was elected to the Folketing for *Venstre* in **Århus** from 1977 and was the party's spokesman 1978-82. He was elected its national chairman in 1984-98. In 1982-93 he served as Foreign Minister and deputy prime minister in Poul **Schlüter**'s cabinet, often having to report to the **European Community** (EC) or **NATO** the reservations imposed on foreign policy by a hostile Folketing majority (*see* **Political Parties**). In 1985-95 he was Vice-President of the European Federation of Liberal and Democratic Parties. Under his leadership Venstre's urban following grew and in its free-market commitment the party moved to the right of the **Conservatives**. Untainted by the **Tamil Affair**, Venstre also moved well ahead of the Conservatives at the 1994 election, though some voters disliked his suggestion that the Progress Party might be included in a "black cabinet" coalition of the right. When Venstre failed to make expected gains in the 1998 election he resigned the leadership. He was awarded the Schuman Prize in 1987 for distinguished service to the cause of European unity; the Viking Award in 1992, Commander of the **Dannebrog**, 1st class, and many foreign honors. AHT

ELSINORE (Danish *Helsingør*) is a port in northeast **Zealand** with a 1994 population of 57,569 and literary associations with **Hamlet**. It stands on the Danish shore where the **Sound** is narrowest, only some three miles from Hälsingborg in Sweden, to which there is a vehicle and railway ferry. It was granted urban privileges in 1288 and the next year burned by the Norwegians. It was refounded on its present site in 1426 and at the same time the castle of Ørekrog was built by King **Erik of Pomerania** to enforce the collection of the **Sound** Tolls instituted that year. This castle was replaced in the 16th century by **Kronborg**. After a period of prosperity under King **Christian IV**, the town declined economically after the mid-17th century when Denmark lost the **Scania** provinces across the Sound, but recovered in the later 18th century, when it had a population of some 3,600. Hit by the depression following the **Napoleonic War** and the abolition of the Sound Tolls in 1857, from 1880 a new period of growth began. It has streets of well-preserved, color-washed buildings. The 15th-century St. Maria Church (*see also* **Buxtehude**) and the Carmelite monastery are among the best-preserved Gothic buildings in the world. SPO, AHT

EMANCIPATION OF THE DANISH PEASANT. In 1733 adult male peasants were tied to the estate on which they had been born by the so-called *stavnsbaand*. In the later 18th century this institution was increasingly attacked by agricultural reformers and finally abolished by a decree of 20 June 1788, with immediate effect for those under 14 and over 36, and for all others in 1800. Peasants remained liable for service with the militia, however. To celebrate the event, the citizens of **Copenhagen** commissioned the sculptor N.A. **Abilgaard** to design a column. Built in 1792-97, this stands in Vesterbrogade near the main railway station. SPO

EMIGRATION. While Denmark did not provide such a large number of overseas emigrants in the later 19th and early 20th century as other Scandinavian countries, some 350,000 Danes left the country before 1920, mostly to settle in North America. The movement reached its height in the 1880s, when nearly 84,000 took part. The heaviest concentration of emigrants came from the islands of **Bornholm**, **Lolland** and **Falster** and from northern **Jutland**. The same "pull" factors affected Danes as had affected the other Scandinavian emigrants in the period, e.g., cheap or free land in the American West after the Civil War. But a peculiarity of Danish emigration was the large number of Mormon converts who participated in it. The Danish Thingvalla shipping line began to operate between **Co-**

penhagen and New York in 1879 and transported many Danish as well as other emigrants. Emigration played a part in the propaganda of those in Denmark in the later 19th century who campaigned for the creation of small-holdings on large estates and state land. SPO

EMPLOYERS' FEDERATION, DANISH (Dansk Arbejdsgiverforening, DA). The first employers' association in Denmark was formed in the iron industry in 1885. The formation in 1898 of the **Federation of Trade Unions** was answered in the same year by the employers with the Danish Employers' and Masters' Association (*Dansk Arbejdsgiver- og Mesterforening*). The following year the two bodies became involved in a dispute which led to the **September Agreement**, which (with amendments) has regulated relations between capital and labor in Denmark ever since. In 1997 about 26,000 enterprises employing about 600,000 workers were members via 22 trade organizations. DA does not include employers in the finance sector, who are separately organized in the Financial Employers' Association (Finanssektorens Arbejdsgiverforening, FA) with about 61,000 employees or agricultural employers, who organize as Federation of Agricultural Employers' Associations (Sammenslutningen af Landbrugets Arbejdsgiverforeninger, SALA). SPO, AHT

EMPLOYMENT SUPPLEMENTARY PENSION (Arbejdsmarkedets Tillægspension, *ATP*). With effect from April 1964 most employees aged 16-66 and their employers have had to pay an annual contribution to the ATP fund. Amounts are agreed annually between employers' organizations and trade unions. For example, following a 15 percent increase over the previous year, in 1996 an employee working at least 117 hours per month paid 74.55 kroner and the employer paid 149.10 kroner per month, a ratio of 1:2. The contribution was about 1.2 percent of the average worker's wage, but was lower for public sector employees. On reaching 67 the worker received a pension (*egenpension*) from the ATP fund to supplement the universal national pension (*folkepension*). For a pensioner who paid into the ATP fund from the start and retired in 1995 the annual ATP was 13,428 kroner. From 1993 certain unemployed people were also covered by ATP. The fund was invested in the bond market and in 1994 the holdings comprised 4.8 percent of all traditional bonds and 8.1 percent of the market value of shares. AHT. *See also* **Pensions.**

ENCLOSURE. Before the end of the 18th century, most Danish peasants lived in villages with large open fields attached in which each farm had a certain number of strips. The crops grown in each field and the time of sowing and harvesting were determined by all the cultivators meeting in the village council. Land was often shared between villages and the earliest enclosure legislation in Denmark aimed at separating this. In the middle of the 18th century some reforming landlords began to consolidate their tenants' strips into small fields over which the individual farm had control. This was encouraged by a law of 1781, but rapid progress was not made until 10 years later, when landlords were permitted to pass on part of the cost involved to their tenants in the form of increased rents. In the 20 years following some three-quarters of Denmark's agricultural land was enclosed in this way. The last enclosure took place in 1861. Enclosure did not wholly destroy the village; in many cases, land was allocated in such a way as to leave many of the farms in place with their holdings stretching out behind them in a star pattern. SPO

ENLIGHTENMENT is the 18th-century intellectual and cultural movement inspired by French rationalism and English empiricism. According to its disciples, all beliefs and practices should be questioned in the light of reason and rejected if they do not measure up. In Catholic countries, it was anti-clerical and often anti-Christian. In Protestant countries, including Denmark, it did not generally get beyond the call for a "rational" Christianity. It led also to demands for practical reforms such as freedom of expression, religious **toleration**, the humanizing of the penal system, and the liberalization of economic life. Its earliest representative of note in Denmark was the Norwegian writer Ludvig **Holberg**, but via Germany it also influenced a number of Danish statesmen of the middle years of the 18th century such as **J.H.E. Bernstorff**. At the beginning of the reign of Christian VII a number of young nobles who sought enlightened reform supported the German doctor Johann Friedrich **Struensee**, who in a brief "reign" of 18 months tried to transform Danish society. But he moved too fast and his downfall brought a reaction. The reforms wrought after 1784, which included both the

emancipation of the peasants and an end to the **slave** trade, were in the spirit of the Enlightenment. SPO

ENVIRONMENT. Danes have been deeply and increasingly concerned with environmental issues at least since Jens Kampmann was nominated Anti-pollution Minister in the 1971 cabinet. Denmark was the first industrialized country to give cabinet priority to environmental policies. The Ministries of Energy and Environment were amalgamated in 1994 to promote energy efficiency and to integrate environmental considerations into all aspects of production and consumption. Departmental agencies cover Environmental Protection, Spatial Planning, Forests, Nature (with its own research institute), Energy, the Geological Survey of Denmark, and the National Environment Research Institute. For Greenland there are separate agencies for Environment Research, Geological Survey, and Mineral Resources Administration. Almost half the Ministry's staff work is in the Forest and Nature Agency, which is also responsible for cultural heritage matters.

Major concerns are air and water pollution, including acid rain, consequent on emissions from industrial processes in Germany and Poland as well as in Denmark. Industrial, agricultural, and domestic emissions affecting water quality have been the subject of extensive action. The response to the oil-price increase of 1973 was to give major incentives to improve the insulation of buildings. Denmark has been in legal conflict with the European Union because Denmark made the sale of drinks in metal cans illegal, as it is more energy-efficient to clean and recycle glass bottles. Other materials are also recycled in high proportion, and municipal systems combining rubbish disposal, power generation, and district heating add greatly to energy efficiency while also reducing harmful emissions. Danish firms are among the world leaders in production of pre-insulated district heating pipes or wind power.

Initial piecemeal policies have given way to a targeted, long-term, and holistic approach. Strategies include an environmental impact assessment before the launch of any new productive activity or transport project. All proposed legislation, action plans, or other governmental initiatives must be assessed for their environmental impact. Taxation is being shifted away from incomes and toward resource consumption. Each ministry must integrate environmental considerations into its own policy sector. The government has adopted national environmental action plans for agriculture, energy, and transport policy aimed at reducing the burdens they impose on the environment. Public expenditure on the environment was almost 2 percent of GDP in 1994. Of this, 85 percent was spent by municipal and county authorities, often in collaboration with the major organizations: employers, trade unions, industry and agriculture, and voluntary conservation organizations.

One example of environmental concern is planning for the **bridge** across the **Sound**. In the initial design it was estimated that the bridge would block about 2.3 percent of the water flow through the Flintre channel from the Baltic. By optimizing each component of the bridge, the blocking effect was reduced to 0.5 percent. A second example is part of the strategy against **unemployment**: the 1997 Finance Act committed 500 million kroner during 1997-2000 for "green jobs."

A third example is a tax on over-use of agricultural nitrogen in the 1998 Finance Act. The **Social Democrat** and **Radical Liberal** government obtained the support of the **Socialist People's Party**, the **Liberals**, and the **Conservatives**. Environment Minister Svend **Auken** argued that a tax would probably be necessary to get agricultural users to reduce the flow of nitrogen into the water system. But the Conservatives and the Liberals, with their close links to, respectively, business and agricultural interest groups, argued that methods such as running the water through water-meadows or forests might adequately reduce the nitrate levels. But neither party could afford electorally to be disengaged from the implementation agreement between the government and the Socialists, as then they could be portrayed as opposing clean drinking water and as protectors of agricultural interests that were damaging the environment. The Liberals no longer wanted to be seen as a farmers' party, and had to take care to retain their new nonfarming voters and their many voters who are active environmentalists. The then Conservative leader, Per Stig Møller, as a former environment minister, claimed the agreement as a victory for Conservative environmental policy, but warned that it implied reductions in the use of fertilizer and a tax if other methods did not work. To conform with the European Union's Nitrate Directive, the target to be achieved by 2003 is a reduction of 100,000 tons of agricultural nitrogen. Previous methods were estimated to have achieved a reduction of 60,000 tons, and the 1998 plan aimed at a further 35,000- to 40,000-ton reduction. Methods to be used included: establishing water-meadows beside lakes and rivers; designating areas for especially sensitive agriculture; using woodland slopes; better use of fodder; tighter limits on the use of farmyard manure; and increasing the ratio of land per animal so that fertilizer would be spread more widely.

These examples illustrate both the very detailed technical and practical approach adopted by Danish policy-makers, and the broad political support for environmental objectives in the parties across the spectrum from socialists to liberals and conservatives. As a result, the very small Green Party (De Grønne) has never surmounted the 2 percent threshold to obtain **Folketing** representation, and the **Red-Green Unity List** has no monopoly on environmentalist policies.

Denmark welcomed the higher priority for environmental policy contained in the Single European Act of 1987 and worked hard and successfully to have the European Environment Agency located in Copenhagen. *See also* **Museums**.

EREMITAGEN (The Hermitage) is a hunting lodge in the royal Deer Park of Jægersborg north of **Copenhagen** originally designed by Hans Steenwinckel for **Christian V**. It was redesigned by the court architect Laurids de **Thura** in Rococo style in 1734-36 for **Christian VI**. It is one of the finest examples both of Thura's work and of the Rococo style in Denmark. SPO

ERIK I (c. 1056-1103). King of Denmark 1095-1103. Son of King **Svend II Estridsen**, he was elected to succeed his brother **Oluf I** on the latter's death. In spite of having a number of mistresses, he appears to have been a pious and peace-loving man who earned the epithet "Ejegod" (Always Good) and worked closely with the Church. He helped found an archbishopric for Scandinavia at Lund (then within his Kingdom in **Scania**) and died of a fever in Cyprus on a pilgrimage to Palestine. He was succeeded by **Erik II**. SPO

ERIK II (c. 1090-1137). King of Denmark 1134-37. The illegitimate son of **Erik I**, he led a rebellion against his uncle King **Niels** and Magnus, who had murdered his half-brother **Knud Lavard**. He was elected King after victory at the battle of **Fodevig** and the murder of Niels. His ruthless treatment of all potential opposition finally caused rebellion, and he was murdered by a peasant at a *herredsting* near Ribe. He had no children by his wife, a Russian princess, but an illegitimate son became King as **Svend III Grathe.** How he gained the epithet "Emune" (Unforgettable) is not clear. SPO

ERIK III (1110-1146). King of Denmark 1137-1146. Son of an illegitimate daughter of King Erik I, he was elected king after the murder of his uncle **Erik II.** His epithet of "Lam" (Meek) suggests a weak ruler, and his reign was dominated by the archbishop Eskil. He was the first Danish king to marry a German princess, but they were childless. After laying down the crown he retired to St. Knud's monastery in **Odense.** SPO

ERIK IV (1216-1250). King of Denmark 1241-1250. The eldest son of King **Valdemar II** with Berengaria, he was in conflict throughout his reign with his brothers. In 1232 he reigned jointly with Valdemar II. His epithet of *Plovpenning* (Plowpenny) refers to the tax on plows that he imposed in 1249, which did not increase his popularity with the peasantry. He fell out with his brother **Abel,** and although the two appeared to be reconciled, Erik's murder in Slien shortly afterward was probably at the instigation of Abel, who succeeded him. He is buried in Ringsted. SPO

ERIK V (c. 1249-1286). King of Denmark 1259-1286. Son of King **Christoffer I,** he came to the throne as a minor, and until about 1270 a regency headed by his mother Margaret of Pomerania ruled in his name. His attempts to control the nobility led to their imposition on him in 1282 of the first **Accession Charter.** He was finally murdered in Finderup and buried in **Viborg.** His son by his wife Agnes of Brandenburg succeeded him as **Erik VI.** His epithet of *Klipping* probably alludes to his clipping of coinage. SPO

ERIK VI (1274-1319). King of Denmark 1286-1319. Son of **Erik V,** after a regency dominated by his mother Agnes of Brandenburg, he had to face opposition from his nobles ("the outlaws") and the clergy led by Archbishop Jens Grand, whom he threw into prison in 1294. This caused his excommunication, which was only removed on payment of a heavy fine. A costly foreign policy in Germany compelled him to impose heavy taxes and to mortgage land to nobles in

Denmark and Germany. A troubled reign is reflected in the epithet of *Menved* (Bird of Ill Omen). Of 14 children by his queen Ingeborg of Sweden, all were either still-born or died in infancy. SPO

ERIK (VII) (?-1332). King 1324-1326 and 1329-32. A son of King **Christoffer II**, with whom he shared the throne during two periods, he died as the result of falling from his horse after the defeat by Count **Gert** at the battle of Lohede. SPO

ERIK VII (or VIII) "OF POMERANIA" (c. 1382-1459). King of Norway 1388-1442, of Sweden 1396-1438, and of Denmark 1396-1439. The first king of the **Kalmar Union**, son of Duke Vartislav of Pomerania and great-grandson of King **Valdemar IV Atterdag**, as grandnephew of **Margrethe I**, he became candidate for the throne of Denmark, Norway and Sweden on the death of King **Olof II**. Not until Margrethe's death in 1412 did Erik rule the three kingdoms. He antagonized the nobility of all three by installing his own nominees in key posts, and at the same time embarked on an ambitious foreign policy aimed at regaining **Slesvig** from the dukes of Holstein which brought heavy taxation, including the **Sound** tolls and the enmity of the **Hanseatic League**. The revolt of Engelbrekt Engelbrektsson in Sweden lost Erik that kingdom in 1438, and the following year he fled to Gotland, where he remained for 10 years. In 1449 he returned to Pomerania, where he died. He married Philippa, daughter of King Henry IV of England in 1406. SPO

ERIKSEN, ERIK (1902-1972). Liberal politician and prime minister 1950-53. The son of a farm-owner, he trained as a farmer, became chairman of the **Liberal Party**'s youth organization 1929-32 and was elected to the **Folketing** 1935-68. He was minister of agriculture and fisheries in 1945-47 under Vilhelm **Buhl** and Knud **Kristensen.** He was prime minister of the coalition with the **Conservatives** which steered the 1953 constitution through parliament with **Social Democratic** and **Radical Liberal** agreement. He worked closely with the Conservatives in cabinet (thus ending the rift between them which dated from the last third of the 19th century) and would have liked the two parties to merge. He was prominent in encouraging inter-Nordic cooperation and was thrice chairman of the **Nordic Council**. SPO, AHT

ERSBØLL, NIELS (1926-   ). Ambassador. After graduating *cand. jur.* in 1955 he joined the Department of Foreign Affairs and served with the Danish NATO representation 1958-60 and with **EFTA** 1960-63. In 1964-67 he was secretary of the Danish Foreign Policy Council, Udenrigspolitiske Nævn, and for the Nordic Economic Collaboration Committee 1965-68. With the title of ambassador he headed the Danish representation to the European Communities in Brussels 1973-77. After a period in the Department of Foreign Economics (Udenrigsøkonomi) and as secretary of the government's Common Market Committee (Regeringens Fællesmarkedsudvalg) he was general secretary of the Council of Ministers of the European Union (EU) 1980-94, as such working closely with Jacques Delors as president and **Henning Christophersen** as vice president of the Commission of the EU. He was awarded the Grand Cross of **Dannebrog** and decorations from the Belgian, Finnish, Icelandic, Italian, Luxembourg, Norwegian, Portuguese, Spanish, British, German and Austrian governments. AHT

ESBJERG is a town on the west coast of **Jutland** with a 1994 population of 82,593. Although the fifth-largest town in Denmark and the largest fishing port, it was founded as recently as 1868, on a site previously occupied by only 30 inhabitants, to serve the increasingly important trade across the North Sea and is the main terminal for passenger ships from Britain. In 1874 it became the western terminus of the railway line across southern Jutland from Kolding and its harbor was begun in 1875. At this time the population was little over 1,000, but its commercial importance was such that by the turn of the century it had 13,500 inhabitants, making it then Denmark's eighth largest town. It was granted urban status in 1898. On 4 September 1939, a British plane accidentally dropped bombs on Esbjerg, killing a woman. In August 1943 it was the scene of a general strike against a German-imposed curfew which led to a series of strikes across the country and eventually to the German "take-over". In 1965 a fleet of about 550 fishing boats was based there, served by fish canneries, a fish-oil factory, and ship-yards. There is a town museum, a Fisheries and Maritime Museum, and museums of art, printing, and lightships. SPO, AHT

ESTATES, THE, are the three orders or classes forming part of the body politic (nobility, clergy, and commons) and participating in government directly or by representation. Sweden's four-chamber Riksdag (1540-1866) gave representation to nobility, clergy, burghers and peasants. In Denmark the term *stænderforsamling*, assembly of estates, was applied to the four **Consultative Assemblies,** for **Jutland**, the Islands, **Slesvig** and Holsten. AHT. *See also* **Parliament**.

ESTRUP, JACOB BRONNUM SCAVENIUS (1825-1913). Politician of the **Right** and prime minister 1875-94, and a large landowner. He was elected to the **Folketing** 1866-98, having joined the cabinet of another large landowner, count Krag-Juel-Vind-Frijs in 1865 as interior minister. As such he was responsible for the 1865 reform of the government of **Copenhagen** and of local government generally in 1867. He was one of the main architects of the foundation of **Esbjerg** in 1868. He resigned from the cabinet in 1869, but in 1875-94 headed cabinets of the Right, although the Liberals had increasing majorities in the Folketing. As such he was the leading proponent of monarchical rule against liberal demands for parliamentary democracy. When the opposition refused to approve his budget in 1877 he countered with a Provisional Budget, which renewed the previously agreed taxes for a further year. This was widely condemned as unconstitutional, but divisions among the **Liberals** finally enabled Estrup to get his budget passed. While the Liberals remained divided Estrup also succeeded in passing a number of reforms to benefit small-holders. But the Liberal Party reunited in 1882 and attacked government proposals by allowing them to wither in committee. In 1885 their attack on Estrup's budget proposals led him to issue one by decree which included new expenditures. This created a near-revolutionary situation; an attempt was made on Estrup's life, and in response he formed a special corps of gendarmes (the "light blues"). He continued to issue provisional budgets, but the first sign of a break in the deadlock came in 1891, when agreement was reached on reform of the **Poor Law**. Finally in 1894 a pact between moderates on both sides led to Estrup's resignation in favor of Baron Reedts-Thott. Estrup retired from the **Landsting** in 1898 but returned as a royal appointee and remained a member until his death. SPO, AHT. *See also* **Defense**.

EUROPEAN (ECONOMIC) COMMUNITY *see* **EUROPEAN UNION**

EUROPEAN FREE TRADE AREA (EFTA) is a trading partnership formed in 1960. Negotiations to set up a Nordic customs union embracing all the Scandinavian countries and Finland reached an advanced stage by the beginning of 1959 but were not completed by the time talks began in June between Britain, Denmark, Norway, Sweden, Austria, Portugal, and Switzerland with the aim of forming a free trade area, and it was decided in the Nordic capitals to await the outcome of these before proceeding further. The Danish prime minister **Jens Otto Krag**, having ensured that agricultural produce would be subject to special agreements between the participants, recommended membership of the larger EFTA to the **Folketing**, which, in spite of doubts expressed by the opposition parties, agreed on 15 July. The treaty was signed in Stockholm in January 1960 and ratified by the Folketing on 11 March. It allowed a major increase in trade between the Nordic countries during the 1960s. Denmark left EFTA at the end of 1972 to join the European Community (EC, *see* **European Union**, EU). Negotiations with the EC culminated in 1993 with the EFTA countries accepting the *acquis communitaires* (all the rules) of the EC and creating the European Economic Area. After Austria, Finland, and Sweden joined the EU in 1995, the only remaining EFTA member states were Iceland, Liechtenstein, Norway and Switzerland. SPO, AHT

EUROPEAN UNION (EU) was the European Economic Community (EEC), until 1986 then the European Community (EC) (De europæiske Fælleskaber or EF) until 1994. Danish attitudes to the EEC after its formation in 1957 were strongly influenced by ties with the two most important trading partners, Germany and Britain, the former in the EEC and the latter not. In 1960 the **European Free Trade Area** EFTA was formed with Denmark and Britain among the seven members. In 1961 Denmark applied with Britain to join the EEC but these negotiations broke down in 1963. In 1967 both countries again applied, again unsuccessfully, but a third application in 1971 succeeded. Danish industry and agriculture strongly favored EEC membership. In the **Folketing** in September 1972 all

Conservatives and **Liberals** and a majority of **Social Democrats** and **Radical Liberals** voted in favor and only the **Socialist Peoples Party** was solidly opposed. Despite Norway's "No" vote in September, in the **referendum** on 2 October 1972 the Danes voted "Yes" by 63.3 percent and joined what they referred to as "the Market" on 1 January 1973. The **Faroe Islands** declined to join for fear of the effects on their fishing industry, on which they rely heavily. **Greenland** joined, but strong opposition grew there, also because of fears for the future of its fisheries, and it left the EC after a referendum in 1985.

The Single European Act of 1986, creating the European Community, marked a further stage of integration. It was rejected in the Folketing by an opposition majority led by the Social Democrats and Radical Liberals. Conservative Prime Minister **Schlüter** responded by calling an advisory referendum and obtained a Yes vote of 56.2 percent. As the East/West division of Europe dissolved, Danish skepticism toward European integration began to change in the winter of 1989/90, and the EC was seen as the framework for relations with a wider Europe which could include fellow Nordic countries, remaining EFTA members and Central and Eastern European states. The Treaty of European Union, agreed by representatives of the 12 EC countries at Maastricht in 1991, was supported by a Folketing majority of 125 to 30 in December, but rejected by 50.7 percent of voters in the referendum on 2 June 1992. Closer economic and monetary cooperation was acceptable, but loss of sovereignty was the main concern of No-voters.

A "national compromise" was agreed in the Folketing by seven parties (including the **Socialist People's Party,** the Social Democrats, and the parties supporting the Schlüter government, but not the **Progress Party**), and at the Edinburgh EC summit in December Denmark was allowed to opt out of monetary integration, defense, citizenship obligations, and cooperation on juridical and internal affairs, the four issues on which the national compromise was based. In spite of a vigorous campaign by the **June Movement**, the 1992 decision was reversed in another referendum on 18 May 1993, when the Yes vote was 56.7 percent.

The 1997 Amsterdam Treaty introduced more democratic policymaking, prepared for the addition of new member-states from east-central Europe, permitted tighter environmental regulations, included a high level of employment as an objective, and added clarity in the interpretation of subsidiarity and openness. Denmark (with Sweden and the UK) decided to remain outside the Economic and Monetary Union (EMU) and to continue with only observer status in the Western European Union. Denmark signed and ratified the Schengen Agreement (ending border controls) but, with Finland, Sweden, and Greece, has not yet participated in its implementation. The Amsterdam Treaty was ratified by referendum on 28 May 1998. SPO, AHT. *See also* Appendix 5.

EWALD, JOHANNES (1743-1781). Poet and dramatist. Son of the pietistic chaplain to the Orphanage in **Copenhagen**, where he grew up until the age of 11, Ewald was then sent to **Slesvig**, and in 1758 returned to Copenhagen to study for the priesthood. As part of his plans to win the hand of his beloved, however, he joined the Austrian army, in which he served without much success for two years. He returned to Copenhagen, graduating *cand. theol.* in 1762. But his sweetheart married another, and Ewald led a bohemian life-style. Already suffering from gout as the result of his army service, this did nothing to improve his health. A mourning cantata for the funeral of **Frederik V** (1766) brought public notice. Ewald's first play appeared in 1769 and is classical in style. Subsequently he took up a preromantic idiom, under the influence of the German poet Klopstock, then living in Copenhagen. He often chose his themes from Norse legend, e.g., *Rolf Krage* (1770) and *Balders Død* (1773, Balder's Death). His lyric verse has, however, survived better than his drama. His most famous poem is the ode *Rungsteds Lyksaligheder* (1773, Rungsted's Joys), written during a two and a half year stay on the coast for the sake of his health. He eventually won popular acclaim in 1780 with *Fiskerne* (The Fishermen), his *singspiel* from which came one of Denmark's **national anthems**. But he died the following year, at the age of 37. He tried to unite **pietistic** religiosity with the ideals of the **enlightenment**. SPO

EXCHANGE, THE, (Børsen) is a building in Dutch Renaissance style near **Christiansborg** in **Copenhagen**. It was designed by the Dutch architects Lorenz van Steenwinckel (1585-1619) and his brother Hans (1587-1639), although King **Christian IV** also took a leading part and was largely responsible for the 54-m (177-feet) spire of four intertwined dragons' tails which adorns its copper roof and was based on models used in fireworks displays. Although the building was largely completed in 1619-20, much of the decoration, including the dragons, was added in 1624-25, and the eastern end was only finished in 1640. It was restored in 1745 under the direction of Nicolai **Eigtved** and the spire, which had become unsafe, was replaced during further restoration in 1775-77. The building originally had a trading hall on the ground floor with businesses and shops on the upper floor. In 1857 it was taken over by the **Wholesale Merchants' Society** and now houses the Copenhagen Chamber of Commerce. It is not usually open to the public. SPO, AHT

- F -

FABER, PETER (1810-1877). A telegraphist, he became known for his patriotic song, *Dengang jeg drog afsted* (When I Set Off) and the still-popular Christmas song, *Højt fra træets grønne top* (From the Tree's High Green Top) of 1848. AHT

FABRICIUS, OTTO (1744-1822). Priest and zoologist. He graduated *cand. theol.* in 1768 and went as a priest to **Greenland**, where his zoological studies led to *Fauna Groenlandica* (1780), the first description of arctic animals. AHT

FÆDRELANDET (**THE FATHERLAND**) (1) was a newspaper founded as a weekly by C.N. **David** and Johannes Hage in **Copenhagen** in 1834 as the mouthpiece of liberal opposition to the absolutist monarchy of the day. As such it was subjected to persistent government interference and in 1838 Balthazar Christiansen and Orla Lehmann joined its direction as protections against this. In 1839 it became a daily and the unofficial organ of the **National Liberals**. It ceased publication in 1882. (2) This was also the title of the paper of the **Danish National Socialist Workers' Party**, first published in Kolding in 1939 but later moved to Copenhagen. Its offices were seized by the **Resistance** at the end of **World War II** and used for the publication of the newspaper *Information*. SPO. *See also* **Press**.

FALCK, SOPHUS (1864-1926). Manufacturer. Trained as a gunsmith, he was co-owner of an engineering works until 1905. In 1906 he founded Københavns og **Frederiksbergs** Redningscorps, the rescue organization which later covered all Denmark with the name Falck. In 1963 it merged with Zone, becoming De Danske Redningscorps (The Danish Rescue Corps), and operates fire, ambulance, motorist, and other civil rescue services. AHT

FALSTER is one of the three large islands south of **Zealand**. The island's main town, Nykøbing F(alster), has a medieval center and an important sugar industry. From Gedser, the southernmost point of Denmark, ferries ply to Rostock in Germany. AHT

FAMILY ALLOWANCES were first introduced in Denmark in 1967 for all children under 18. Previously allowances had been made for young dependents through the tax system. The new payments were made monthly, usually to the mother, and adjusted in accordance with the cost of living. In 1977, as a measure of retrenchment, the allowance was means tested and the age limit reduced to 16 with special provision made for poorer families with children of 16 and 17. SPO. Since 1987 payment regardless of other family income has been made to all families with children, with the highest rate for children of 0-2 years of age, a lower rate for 3-6, and the lowest rate for 7-17 (which can be extended to children under 18). There is an additional allowance paid to about 171,000 children of single care givers and further allowances for children with neither parent alive, and an allowance for children whose parents are pensioners, whether on retirement or on early pension. AHT. *See also* **Pensions, Welfare State**.

FARMERS' FRIENDS, SOCIETY OF (Bondevennernes Selskab) was an association formed in May 1846 by Balthazar **Christiansen**, J.C. Drewsen, and A.F. **Tscherning** to unite the peasantry and the middle class in advancing the cause of peasant rights and a **constitution**. This followed attempts by the Crown to ban assemblies to discuss peasant rights. In the **Parliament** elected in 1849 it had strong support from the peasants of **Zealand** but was frequently divided, although generally it supported the **National Liberals'** Ejder policy before its collapse in 1864. After the conservative 1866 constitution was introduced, the Society called for the liberal 1849 constitution to be restored. Its representatives joined the United Liberals in 1870. SPO. *See also* **Liberal Party**.

FARMERS' PARTY *(Bondepartiet)* was a political party formed in 1935 as the Free People's Party (Frie Folkparti) largely from dissident members of the Liberal Party. Under this name it secured five seats in the **Folketing** and 3.2 percent of the vote in the 1935 elections. It changed its name to Bondepartiet in 1938 and won four seats in the 1939 election. It was already acquiring fascist characteristics and after the German Occupation in April 1940 these became even more prominent. It gained three seats in the 1943 election but lost all support after the end of the war. SPO

FARMERS' PROTEST, THE (1935-36). The economic depression of the 1930s was particularly damaging to Danish **agriculture**, the country's main earner of foreign currency. At the end of July 1935 some 40,000 farmers under the lead of Knud Bach marched on **Copenhagen** to appeal to the king for assistance. He simply referred them to his ministers. In spite of a record harvest, the farmers in September tried to put pressure on the National Bank by refusing to accept foreign currency, but the bank held firm. SPO. *See also* **Agricultural Association**.

FARMING see AGRICULTURE

FAROE ISLANDS (FÆRØERNE in Danish, FØROYAR in Faroese*)* are a group of 18 islands (17 inhabited) lying between Iceland and the Shetland Islands, since 1948 with self-government under the Danish crown. The name derives from Sheep Islands, and there are about 70,000 sheep on the islands, plus cattle and horses. The population at the end of 1993 was 45,347, but was declining. The capital of Tórshavn, with about one-third of the population, lies on the principal island of Streymoy. The rest of the population lives in about 100 villages. The dominant economic activity is **fishing,** which employs 23 percent of the work force. *See also* **Introduction**.

It is uncertain whether the islands were settled before the arrival of Norwegian emigrants at the beginning of the **Viking** Age at the end of the 8th century, and in the early 11th century they became subject to the Norwegian king. After the union of Norwegian and

Danish crowns in 1380, they continued to be ruled according to Norwegian law. A Lutheran bishop was appointed in 1540, but the diocese disappeared in 1557. The islands were within the diocese of Bergen until about 1620, when they became subject to the bishop of **Zealand**. Continuously from the middle of the 16th century all trade was a royal monopoly, which was only abolished in 1856. There were pirate raids in 1615 and 1616 and a visit in 1629 from Barbary corsairs, who took off 30 inhabitants as slaves.

The islands were governed by a royal bailiff (*landfoged*), appointed by the king and usually a Dane. In 1655 the Faroes were granted in fief to the royal favorite Christoffer von **Gabel**. His son succeeded him and enjoyed the same privileges until his death in 1708, after which the Crown resumed direct control and administration improved. In 1766-88 the islands became a haven for British smugglers, encouraged by the Danish authorities. After the end of the **Napoleonic Wars**, during which the British blockade caused considerable hardship, the ancient Løgting (Lagting in Danish), which had acted as both a law court and provincial assembly, was abolished.

The development of fishing in the 1830s aided the economy so that the population rose to over 8,000 by 1850. Under the June **Constitution** of 1849 the islands were given representatives in the **Landsting** and the **Folketing** in **Copenhagen**. The Lagting was revived as an advisory council in 1852. The later 19th century saw growing interest in the **Faroese language** and in the traditional ballad. A nationalist movement was led by Jóannes Patursson (1866-1946), and after his electoral defeat in 1906 a **Home Rule Party**, Sjálvstyrisflokkurin, was formed to oppose the **Unionist Party**, Sambandsflokkurin, which was in power until **World War II**. In 1936, however, they lost heavily to the **Social Democrats,** Javnaðarflokkurin. After the German occupation of Denmark in April 1940, British troops occupied the islands and established a naval base.

After the war, pressure grew for outright independence and a referendum on the issue was held in September 1946. The result was so indecisive that fresh Lagting elections were called, at which those favoring independence were defeated. But in March 1948 the Faroes were granted home rule with full responsibility for internal affairs and a high commissioner, rigsombudsmand, to represent the Danish state. The Danish Prime Minister's Department has responsibility for residual matters.

Heavy investment in the fishing industry in the 1980s led to deep indebtedness, and an economic crisis in 1989 resulted from a decline in the catch and depressed prices. In 1992 the Danish government made a large loan to prevent the collapse of the Faroese banking structure, on condition of a reduction in the fishing fleet and higher taxes. In 1993 the unemployment rate rose to 20 percent, setting off emigration, often to Denmark. The Social Democrats took office early in 1993, but after they lost heavily in elections in September 1994 they made way for a coalition led by Edmund Joensen, the leader of the Unionist Party, in which the Social Democrats were represented.

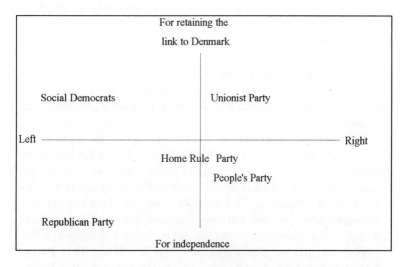

In the April 1998 election the **Republican Party** won 23.8 percent of the votes and 8 seats; the **People's Party** 21.3 percent and 8 seats, and the **Home Rule Party** 7.7 percent and 2 seats. This gave a clear majority for the parties favoring greater independence, largely as a consequence of how the Faroese banking crisis had been handled (see **Introduction**). The **Social Democrats** (of the Faroes) had 21.9 percent and 7 seats, the **Unionist Party** had 18 percent and 6 seats, and the **Centre Party** 4.1 percent and one seat. The **Christian People's Party** had 2.5 percent but no representation. The three pro-independence parties formed a coalition, with Anfinn Kallsberg of the People's Party as prime minister *(lagmand)*, intent on negotiating a new sovereign constitution. They would retain the

Danish monarchy and currency, and equal rights for Faroese and Danish citizens in each other's countries. They also wanted continued collaboration in the sectors of education, health, justice, and foreign policy. These changes would be subject to referendum. Repayment of the 6 billion kroner owed to Denmark following the banking crisis of 1992-93 (see Introduction) was renegotiated with Danish Finance Minister Mogens Lykketoft in return for Faroese support for the Whitsun 1998 package of financial stringency measures.

Since the 1940s the islands have had their own flag, a red cross with a blue border on a white ground. They remain members of **NATO** but did not follow the kingdom into the European Community in 1972. In 1990 the Faroese Academy became the University of the Faroe Islands. SPO, AHT. *See also* **Christian People's Party-Faroese Progress and Fishermen's Party; Faroese Language; Faroese Monopoly; Heinesen, William; Workers' Front.**

FAROES HOME RULE PARTY (SJÁLVSTYRISFLOKKURIN). Founded in 1906, this is the oldest of the **Faroese** political parties, from which others have splintered. With a liberal outlook, the party seeks self-government provided that it is soundly based. It wants to end the two Faroese seats in the **Folketing** and wants a directly elected *lagmand* (prime minister). AHT

FAROESE LANGUAGE is grouped with Icelandic as an insular Scandinavian language. Both originated as a **Viking**-age dialect of southwestern Norwegian, but the Faroes never developed the medieval literature of *sagas* for which **Iceland** is renowned. The Danish administration of the islands used the Danish language, while Faroese survived only as spoken dialects. A linguistic revival around 1800 occurred when the rich oral legacy of epic ballads was written down. This was followed by a Faroese bible and a translation of the Old Icelandic *Saga of the Faroese*, and then systematic collections of popular tales and legends. Demands for greater political and economic autonomy were supported by growing consciousness of a literary and linguistic culture. The clergyman and folklorist Venceslaus Ulricus Hammarshaimb codified Faroese orthography around 1850 in ways which emphasized the similarity to Icelandic and secured a uniform written language without favoring any one of the several dialects. As a result, although spoken Faroese is difficult for Icelanders and Scandinavians to understand, in written form it is easier, especially for Icelanders. There has been a restrictive attitude to exclude loan-words, especially from Danish and German. With Home Rule in 1948 it was recognized as an official language equally with Danish, and is dominant in speech and writing as the mother tongue of about 50,000 people, almost one-fifth living in Denmark. *See also* **Danish Language**. AHT

FAROESE MONOPOLY. A monopoly of trade with the **Faroe Islands** was first granted by the Danish crown in 1535 to the Hamburg merchant Thomas Koppen, who retained it until his death in 1553, when trade was again opened to all the king's subjects. It was again granted away between 1557-71 and (after a brief period when the islanders themselves enjoyed the privilege) in 1578-1619. In 1619 the monopoly was granted to the Icelandic, Faroese, and Nordland Company of merchants, but it went bankrupt in 1662. It then came into the hands of the **Gabel** family, who enjoyed it until 1709. From then until its abolition in 1856 it was run by the Danish Treasury with a resident merchant in Tórshavn to look after its interests. Until the 19th century the principal import into the islands was barley and the principal export was woolen goods. SPO

FAROES SELF-GOVERNMENT PARTY (SJÁLVSTYRIS-FLOKKURIN) **see FAROES HOME RULE PARTY**.

FASCISM. The leading political representation of fascism in Denmark between the World Wars was the **Danish National Socialist Workers' Party** (Danmarks nationalsocialistiske arbejderparti, DNSAP), formed in 1930 by captain Cai Lembke and led from 1933 by Dr. Frits **Clausen**. But the **Farmers' Party**, formed in 1934, also acquired fascist characteristics and worked quite closely with the DNSAP. Under the leadership of Jack Westergaard, chairman of the Danish Young Conservatives (Konservativ ungdom, KU) in 1932-36, this organization also became anti-democratic and even adopted shirts and jackboots. The **Conservative Party** finally secured Westergaard's replacement, and many members of KU joined the DNSAP. The National Unity Party (Nationalt Samvirke*)*, formed by the renegade Conservative, Victor Pürschel, in 1938 and the Danish Unity Party (**Dansk Samling**), formed by the ex-Social Democrat

Arne Sørensen in 1936 were both anti-parliamentary and merged in 1939. SPO

FAURSCHOU-HVIID, BENT (nicknamed Flammen, the flame) (1921-44). **Resistance** man. Brought up in the hotel trade, in 1943 he joined the Holger Danske resistance organization. An active saboteur, he also led the hunt for informers. He committed suicide on 18 October 1944, surrounded by the Gestapo. AHT

FEDERATION OF TRADE UNIONS (Landsorganisation i Danmark or LO). A central organization for **trade unions** in Denmark was created in 1898 as Det Samvirkende Fagforbund (The Cooperating Federation of Unions) with a membership of 60,000 and with Jens Jensen (1859-1928) a painter and decorator, as first chairman. It adopted its present title in 1959. While largely made up of blue-collar unions, some white-collar unions, such as the Shop Workers Union, are also affiliated. Since the **September Agreement**, it has been responsible for negotiating annual agreements on behalf of its members with the **Employer's Federation**. SPO

FEMINISM. The Feminist Movement in Denmark may be traced back to the writings of Mathilde **Fibiger** in the middle of the 19th century, but the first organization to fight for women's rights was the **Danish Women's Society**, founded in 1871. This was a middle-class movement mainly concerned with the improvement of women's educational opportunities and entry to the professions. Nielsine Nielsen (1850-1916) secured a royal decree in 1875 allowing women into the university and in 1885 was the first woman graduate as *cand. med.*; she worked as a physician. From 1888 the Danish Women's Suffrage Association (Dansk Kvindelig Valgretsforening, DK) concerned itself with political equality between the sexes. Finally in 1915 women won the right to vote. In the 1920s and 1930s feminist issues were mainly advanced as socialist (*see also* **Marie Nielsen**) and **social democratic** demands for social reform. The movement lost some of its momentum until the 1970s, when neofeminism reached Denmark in the form of the politically radical **Redstockings** (Rødstrømper), who held a large demonstration in **Copenhagen** in 1970, and Thilde's Children (Thildes Børn) who took their name from Mathilde **Lucie Fibiger** SPO. *See also*

Danish Women's Society; Women's Movement; Women's Suffrage.

FIBIGER, JOHANNES (1867-1928), the pathologist son of a medical doctor, graduated *cand. med.* in 1890 and from 1900 was professor of pathological anatomy at Copenhagen University. Based on museum researches, in 1913 he showed that cancer could be produced experimentally, for which he received the 1927 Nobel Prize for medicine. AHT

FIBIGER, MATHILDE LUCIE (1830-1872), feminist writer. Born in **Copenhagen** as the daughter of an army officer, she trained as a governess and in 1849 obtained a position on the island of Lolland. Her first novel, *Tolv Breve* (Twelve Letters), written using the penname Clara Raphael with a preface by the critic J.L. **Heiberg** was published in 1850. It strongly criticized the restrictions placed on women's opportunities for expression and development without suggesting any plan for reform, but nevertheless opened a lively public debate. Three further novels attracted little attention, but she became Denmark's first female telegraph operator and eventually managed the telegraph office in **Århus**. The neo-feminist group Thilde's Children of the 1970s was named after her. SPO

FIIL, MARIUS (1893-1944). **Resistance** man and the owner of an inn, the Hvidsten, between Randers and Mariager. His Hvidsten group, which included his wife, son, daughter, and son-in-law, received parachutists and weapons in 1943 near the inn. His execution on 29 June 1944 together with his son and son-in-law led to protests against the German occupation forces which became a nationwide "people's strike." AHT

FILM INDUSTRY. For 20 years Ole Olsen (1863-1945) traveled the Nordic region with a show of photographs and in 1899 showed the first moving pictures. In 1906 he founded Nordisk Films-Kompagni, which for a period from 1910 was the world's second-largest film company, exporting 98 percent of its production. The firm continued into the 1980s, to become the world's longest-lived film-production company. Olsen was director general until 1922, but resigned in 1924. Like Olsen, the photographer Constantin Philipsen (1859-1925) from 1898 toured all the Nordic countries with slide-shows, then in 1904 opened the first Danish cinema, the Kosmorama, in **Copenhagen**, and later had over 20 cinemas around the country. The first feature film, *The Execution*, was produced in 1903 by Peter Elfelt (1866-1931), and Nordisk Films' first international success (with about 300 copies sold abroad) was *The Lion Hunt* (1907), on big-game hunting.

From 1910 the industry flourished. *The White Slave Traffic* (1910) was sensational for its subject and its length (700 meters), while *The Abyss*, about a woman who degrades herself for the sake of a man, was the first of a genre of Danish erotic melodrama, distinguished by its sensual boldness and Asta **Nielsen**'s realistic acting. *The Temptations of a Great City* (Nordisk Films, 1911) was the story of a young man whose dissolute life puts him in debt to a money-lender, with whose daughter he then falls in love. Lau **Lauritzen** directed a string of silent farces for Paladium which sold well abroad. Valdemar Psilander (1884-1917) became the first big male star of Danish silent films. During 1911-16 he gained a world-wide reputation in the many films produced by Nordisk Films, including *At the Prison Door* (1911), *The Evangelist* (1914, directed by Holger Madsen), and *The Clown* (1916). Danish actors, trained in a tradition of naturalistic drama, helped to develop a reputation of quality for Danish films, added to their naturalistic sets and superlative photography. Light and shade were effectively used, and the acting was developed in long, well-planned scenes.

The silent-film era peaked in 1914: afterward several foreign markets were closed, and early science fiction (such as *The Sky Ship*, 1917) failed to catch the public imagination; by 1920 there was no longer a distinctively Danish style of film-making.

Peter Malberg (1887-1965) started an acting career on the stage of Århus Theater in 1907 and later appeared in over 160 films, mainly in comic roles. He was best known for the role of Balder Svanemose in *Peter the Great* (1930), filmed as *Hans onsdagsveninde* (1943, *His Wednesday Girlfriend*), but was also in the Morten Korch films and in the *Far til fire* (Father of Four) series as Uncle Anders.

Carl Th. **Dreyer** emerged as Nordisk Films' leading director in the 1920s with *The Master of the House* (1925), in which a tyrannical husband is brought to heel, but he then worked in France on *La Passion de Jeanne d'Arc* (1928) and his first sound film, *Vampyre* (1932). Meanwhile in Denmark the 1920s and 1930s were otherwise uninspired until a surge of documentaries, beginning with *Denmark*

(1935) by Poul **Henningsen**. In the 1940s Dreyer also returned home to make *The Day of Wrath* (1943), on a triangular relationship set among 17th-century witch trials.

The director Alice O'Fredericks (1900-1968) formed the company ASA in 1938, together with Lau Lauritzen, Jr. Sometimes working with others, she directed some 70 films, including *Frøken Kirkemus* (1941, Miss Church-Mouse), *Affæren Birte* (1945, The Birte Case), a series of films written by Morten Korch beginning with *De røde heste* (1950, The Red Horses) and the eight films in the *Far til fire* (Father of Four) series.

The end of the 1940-45 German occupation gave rise to serious films about the **Resistance movement**: *The Invisible Army*, directed by Johan Jacobsen (1912-72) and *The Red Meadows*, directed by Lau Lauritzen, Jr. while Theodor Christensen's *Your Freedom Is at Stake* was a documentary edited from illegal (underground) sources. This theme resurfaced in 1966 when Klaus Rifbjerg wrote and Palle Kjærulf-Schmidt directed *Once There Was a War*, depicting the occupation through the eyes of a 15-year-old. In the same year Henning Carlsen's film of the Norwegian **Nobel Prize**-winner Knut Hamsun's novel *Hunger* achieved international recognition.

The Olsen Gang was a series of 13 comedies produced by Erik Balling for Nordisk Films, centered on three petty criminals planning "the big crime." Made over the period 1968-81, the films sold well abroad and at home, in part for their ironic commentary on the Danish character. In the 1970s Balling also directed episodes of the television series *The House in Christianshavn* and the whole television series *Matador*, about a Danish provincial town in the 1930s and 1940s.

Legislation in 1965 established Filmfonden, the Film Foundation, to give financial support to the industry from a tax on film tickets and to establish a film school. In 1972 the ticket tax was replaced by direct funding from general tax and Filmfonden became the state-funded Danish Film Institute. Statens Filmcentral was formed to produce documentaries and short films, together with the Danish Film Museum, the Danish Film Workshop, and later its video counterpart. These measures were welcomed as highly progressive, and revived the film industry. In 1997 a new law centralized these activities in the Danish Film Institute.

Danish films won Oscars for "best foreign film" two years running, in 1988 with *Babette's Feast*, the film version of a story by

Karen Blixen, directed by Gabriel Axel. In 1989 the prize went to *Pelle the Conqueror*, based on the novel by **Martin Anderson Nexø** and directed by **Bille August**, who collected the Golden Palmes at the Cannes Film Festival for the same film. August's international successes make him a worthy successor to his mentor, the Swede Ingmar Bergman, although *Smilla's Sense for Snow* (1997), based on the novel by **Peter Høeg**, received disappointing reviews. Other Danish directors of the same generation include Lars von Trier (1956-) and Nils Malmros. von Trier's film *Element of Crime* (1984) attracted prizes at the Cannes, Chicago and Mannheim festivals, and *Europe* (1991) won prizes in Cannes (two), Stockholm and Gent. In 1998 the 29-year-old director Thomas Vinterberg was awarded the Cannes Jury's Special Prize for his film *Festen* (The Family Party). AHT

FINE ARTS, ACADEMY OF *see* **ACADEMY OF ART**

FINSEN, NILS RYBERG (1860-1904). Scientist. Faroese by birth, he grew up in **Iceland** and matriculated in Reykjavik at the age of 22. Hampered by chronic heart disease, he graduated *cand. med.* in 1890 and began to study the effects of light on the human body, publishing "On the medical use of concentrated chemical light-rays" in 1896. In 1895 he developed a program of light-therapy for lupus and was a pioneer of radiology. His photo-therapeutic clinic and laboratory in **Copenhagen**, founded in 1896, developed into the Finsen Institute. He was awarded the **Nobel Prize** for medicine in 1903. SPO, AHT.

FISCHER, OLFERT (1747-1829) was the naval officer who in 1801 led the Danish naval forces against the British attack at the Battle of Reden (see the Battle of **Copenhagen, 1801**). AHT

FISHING has always been an important occupation on the north and west coasts of **Jutland**, and is the most important economic activity on the **Faroe Islands**. In the Middle Ages the great herring market at Skanør on the coast of **Scania** lay within the Danish king's realms. From the end of the 16th century Danish fish exports lost importance as Dutch and English fishermen became dominant. But after the mid-19th century Danish fisheries expanded considerably again, when a growing European population and technical improvements created favorable conditions. In the 1890s motorized vessels enabled more distant grounds to be exploited, and artificial freezing more distant markets to be tapped. The Faroe Islands relied largely on wooden sailing smacks (many second-hand British vessels) until after **World War I**, but by the end of the 1930s had 10 trawlers. After **World War II** there was a further period of development with bigger boats equipped with echo-sounders and radios. The Faroese invested the profits from trading between **Iceland** and Scotland during the war so that they could soon boast the largest trawler fleet in Scandinavia, but a collapse of the market in the early 1950s compelled wholesale modernization. A new period of high investment in the 1980s led to serious economic difficulties for the islands when catches and prices fell at the end of the decade. As a condition of Danish government loans the fleet was reduced in the 1990s. Most Danish boats are small by international standards and tend to operate close to their home port, but the total catch (mostly exported) is the largest in the **European Union**. SPO

FISKER, KAY (1893-1965). Architect. Trained at the Academy, where he became professor 1936-63, he designed a series of blocks of flats in a functionalist style and was one of the architects of Århus University (1932-48), of Århus Hospital (Kommunehospital 1933), the Vestersøhus (1935-38), and Mødrehjælpen (1952), buildings in **Copenhagen**, and the Danish Academy in Rome (1965). AHT. *See also* **Architecture**; **Design**.

FJORD, NIELS JOHANNES (1825-1891). Agricultural researcher. He qualified as a teacher in 1845, then studied at the Polytechnic Institute and obtained a teaching post at the Agricultural College (Landbohøjskole) in 1858. His experiments with centrifuging, ice-storage, milk-testing, and pasteurization were very important for the change and improvement of farm production in the late 1800s. AHT

FLENSBORG *see* **SLESVIG-HOLSTEN**

FLOR, CHRISTIAN (1792-1875). Politician. He became lecturer in Danish at Kiel in 1826 and from 1836 was a leader of the Danish movement in **Slesvig**. He helped found the **Folk High Schools** in Rødding and (after the loss of Slesvig in 1864) at Askov. AHT

FLORA DANICA *see* **OEDER, G.C.; PORCELAIN**

FODEVIG (or FOTEVIG), BATTLE OF, was fought on 4 June 1134 on the southwest coast of **Scania**. It ended the civil war between King **Niels** and his son Magnus on one side and Erik I's son **Erik (II)** on the other, which had broken out in 1131 with the murder of Erik's half-brother **Knud Lavard**. At the battle, the outcome of which was largely decided by the German mercenaries, Magnus and five bishops were killed and Niels forced to flee to **Slesvig**, where he was murdered. Erik the victor was chosen to succeed him. SPO

FOG, MOGENS (1904-1990). Professor and **Resistance** leader. He graduated *cand. med.* in 1930 and was appointed professor of Neurology at Copenhagen University in 1938. He became a leading member of the Resistance group *Frit Danmark* (Free Danmark) after the German Occupation, and had to go underground in 1942 when the other leaders of the group were arrested. He was a founding member of the **Freedom Council** set up in September 1943. Arrested by the Germans in 1944, he escaped when Shell House, the Gestapo Headquarters in **Copenhagen**, was bombed by the British Royal Air Force in March 1945. He was one of the Resistance representatives in the coalition cabinet formed by Vilhelm **Buhl** on liberation. He was a **Communist** member of the **Folketing** 1945-50 and, as vice-chancellor of Copenhagen University 1966-72, was a central target of student rebellion. SPO

FOLK HIGH SCHOOLS. Inspired by the teachings of the Danish theologian N.F.S. **Grundtvig**, these schools were originally intended to inspire young rural dwellers with knowledge and love of their country, combined with a broad Christian morality. The emphasis was on oral instruction and debate and there were no examinations. The courses were residential and lasted for five winter months, when labor was less in demand on the land. The first was founded, significantly, in 1844 at Rødding in southern Slesvig, where Danish culture seemed seriously threatened by growing German nationalism (*see* **C. Flor**). After the loss of Slesvig in the Second **Slesvig-Holsten** War (1866), it was refounded at Askov in central Jutland.

But the school which became the model for many later folk high schools was founded by **Kristen Kold** with Grundtvig's help at Ryslinge on **Funen** in 1851. By 1876 4,000 pupils were attending similar schools, which from 1892 received government financial support. As more schools were established, they lost their purely rural character (see **Borup**) and increased the range of courses they offered. A new phase began with the founding in 1946 of a school at Krogerup, a manor-house near **Elsinore**, where Professor Hal **Koch** was a leading figure. There are 97 schools in Denmark, 12 for sports and gymnastics, four for pensioners and three only for the young. Courses last from a few days to months or an academic year. Some schools are associated with **trade unions**, the **cooperative movement**, or religious bodies. The folk high school idea spread to the other Nordic countries, where there are a further 300 schools, many in Finland. The one at Kungälv in Sweden emphasises Nordic themes. SPO, AHT

FOLKETING is the Danish **parliament**, which meets in **Christiansborg, Copenhagen.** (Folketing*et* = *the* Folketing.) From the 1849 June **Constitution** until 1953 it and the **Landsting** were the lower and upper houses of the **Rigsdag**. It then consisted of 100 members elected directly by men over 30. The 1866 Constitution raised the membership to 102, but made more important changes to the Landsting. The 1915 Constitution lowered the voting age to 25 and extended the **franchise** to women. Since abolition of the Landsting in 1953, the Folketing has had 179 members, including two from the **Faroe Islands** and two from **Greenland**. The voting age was lowered by **referendums** to 23 in 1953, to 21 in 1961, to 20 in 1971 and to 18 in 1983. **Elections** must be held every four years unless the prime minister requests an earlier dissolution. The constitution requires the Folketing to meet each year on the first Tuesday in October, when the Speaker (*Formand*) and four deputies are (re-)elected.

The constitution gives legislative powers to the Queen and the Folketing together, but the Queen exercises these through her ministers. Most legislation is proposed by ministers, but all Folketing members have the right to do so. The first "reading" of a Bill (lovforslag) is a debate on its principles. Details are discussed in the second reading debate, which also deals with proposed amendments. This debate may proceed directly into the third and final reading, and then to the vote on whether or not to pass the Bill. Between the readings a Bill is normally discussed in committee. At this stage interested individuals or groups may submit comments, either in writing or in person, by requesting a hearing by the committee. Otherwise committee proceedings are in private and are occasions for negotiations between the party representatives. After a Bill has been passed, it is signed by the Queen and a minister and becomes law. Unlike the "voting" parliaments of the UK or the US, but like most West European parliaments, the Danish Folketing is a "negotiating" parliament: parties customarily negotiate and reach agreements before a Bill is put to the vote, when it frequently has the support of all the "responsible" or core **parties**. SPO, AHT

FOSS, ERLING (1897-1982). **Resistance** man. In 1941-44 he illegally supplied a stream of information to Britain via Sweden. In October 1943 he joined the **Freedom Council**, and while living in Sweden from February 1944 negotiated on its behalf with Sweden. In December 1944 in London and Washington he negotiated with the Allies for recognition of Denmark as an ally. AHT

FRANCE, DANISH RELATIONS WITH. For geographical reasons alone, Denmark's political and economic relations with France have not been as intimate as relations with Germany or with Britain. The first alliance between the two powers was concluded in 1541 and involved Denmark in war with the Emperor Charles V. In the international conflicts of the later 17th century, however, Denmark generally sided with France's opponents. In 1673, after Louis XIV's invasion of the United Provinces, Denmark allied with the latter and two years later, in spite of the efforts of the pro-French chancellor **Griffenfeld**, declared war on France's ally Sweden. With the return of peace in 1679, however, Denmark swung temporarily toward France, who offered support in the Danish king's dispute with the duke of **Holsten** (Holstein-Gottorp). Disappointed in the results of this policy, Christian V drew away from France again after 1686.

At the end of the **Great Northern War** in 1720 France guaranteed Denmark's possession of the **Slesvig** territories of the Duke of Holstein-Gottorp, and Denmark sided with the Hanoverian Alliance against the Emperor formed in 1725. After the Anglo-French breach at the end of the decade Denmark maintained the link with France, who could offer much-needed subsidies. Despite his marriage to an English princess, King **Christian VII** visited France in 1768, the first Danish monarch to do so. The fall of the French monarchy in 1792 loosened political ties between the two countries, but Denmark refused to participate in any anti-French alliance. But Britain's seizure of the Danish fleet in 1807 led Denmark to conclude an alliance with Napoleon, involving adherence to his "Continental system" and Denmark continued this relationship until 1814. Having changed sides, Denmark then sent troops to participate in the occupation of France.

After defeat by Prussia and Austria in the Second **Slesvig-Holsten** War in 1864, Denmark looked to France as the best hope in the event of further attack from the south, but when France was defeated in the Franco-Prussian War of 1870-71 Denmark abandoned this policy in favor of neutrality. SPO. This took the country through **World War I** and the interwar period. During **World War II** Denmark and part of France were occupied by Germany. In its aftermath France took part in the formation of the Western European Union while Denmark sought a Scandinavian defense treaty. When this fell through, both joined **NATO**. When France and Germany took part in forming the **European Economic Community** (EEC), Denmark, with Britain, became founder members of the **European Free Trade Association** (EFTA). Both countries applied to join the European Community but Britain's application was rejected by French president de Gaulle and Denmark also withdrew. Only after his retirement in 1969 could successful applications be made, and Denmark, with the United Kingdom and Ireland, joined in 1973. This put Franco-Danish relations onto a basis of regular meetings. Until 1984 Denmark relied on France to oppose ambitious plans for European integration (*see* **European Union**). Public sentiment toward France warmed considerably following the marriage in 1967 of the future Queen **Margrethe II** to the French count who became Prince Henrik. AHT

FRANCHISE. The first elected bodies in Denmark were the provincial **Consultative Assemblies** of Estates which first met in 1836, for which a property franchise restricted the electorate to 2-3 percent of the population. The **constituent assembly** of 1848 was elected on a much broader franchise of all self-supporting men over 30 in age. The resulting June **Constitution** established a two chamber **parliament**, the Rigsdag. It retained the same voting rights for both **Folketing** and **Landsting**, excluding only those in the service of others, non-householders, and those on poor relief. This enfranchised 73 percent of men over 30 in 1849, rising to 84 percent by 1901. Voting for the Folketing was in 100 single-member constituencies, by show of hands following hustings, and the candidate won who had a plurality in the opinion of the election committee. If the committee's decision was challenged, a roll-call vote was held. Where there was only a single candidate, the vote was Yes or No. At the first election, turnout was only 32.5 percent in the 57 districts where there was a written ballot. Secret ballots replaced open voting in 1901. Elections for the Landsting were indirect, with the Folketing electorate choosing electors who then voted for Landsting members by plurality in multi-member districts. Carl **Andræ**'s version of the single transferable vote was used for Landsting elections after the 1866 constitutional changes, which restricted its composition to ensure conservative control: 12 members nominated by the crown, one elected by the **Faroese** Lagting, and 53 indirectly elected.

In 1915 universal adult suffrage (i.e., for all men and women) was introduced for the Folketing and the voting age reduced to 29, with proportional representation by the d'Hondt method for the capital and plurality elections in single-member districts in the rest of the country, with some supplementary seats to produce more proportional results overall. In 1920 proportional representation was extended to the whole country. For the Landsting the minimum age was 35 (until its abolition in 1953); for the Folketing it was 25 from the third election of 1920 and was reduced after **referendums** to 23 in 1953, 21 in 1961, 20 in 1971, and 18 in 1978. Recipients of public assistance were disenfranchised until 1961. AHT. *See also* **Elections; Women's Suffrage.**

FREDENSBORG is a royal palace in north **Zealand** built in 1719-22 by Johan Cornelius Krieger (1683-1755) in Italian Baroque style on the site of the 16th-century royal hunting lodge of Østrup. It was altered and extended several times in the 18th century by Laurids de **Thurah** and Niels **Eigtved** and finally by **C.F. Harsdorff** in 1774-76 when it was the official residence of the queen dowager Juliane Maria. The park, which retains traces of the original laid out under

King **Christian V**, gained its present form at the hands of Nicolas-Henri Jardin (1720-99) in 1756-69, embellished in 1764-84 with a collection of 69 sandstone figures depicting Norwegian, **Icelandic,** and **Faroese** peasants and fishermen by Johan Gottfried Grund (1733-96) in what is known as Nordmandsdalen or Northman's vale. The palace is used by the Danish royal family as a spring and autumn residence. From 1883 it was also the scene of regular meetings of European rulers hosted by "the father-in-law of Europe," King **Christian IX**. SPO

FREDERICIA is a town on the east coast of **Jutland** with a population of 43,587 (1990) and an important railway junction and industrial center (engineering, textiles, and food processing). Envisaged by **Frederik III** as a strategic reserve capital, it was founded as Frederiksodde in 1650 as the main fortress in Jutland, guarding the crossing to **Funen**. Military criteria enforced a grid pattern of wide streets, low buildings and high earthen ramparts. But it was captured by the Swedes in 1657 before it was completed, a bitter blow to Danish pride which intensified feelings against the nobility, who were blamed for the defeat. In 1664 it was renamed. In 1849 on 6 July (afterwards kept as Fredericia Day) it was the scene of a Danish victory during the First **Slesvig-Holsten** War, when besieging Prussian and Slesvig-Holsten troops were driven back with heavy loss. The fortifications were razed in 1909 but the ramparts remain. SPO, AHT

FREDERIK I (1471-1533). King of Denmark and Norway 1523-33. Born in Haderslevhus, the younger son of King **Christian I**, he became duke of **Slesvig-Holsten** on the accession of his elder brother **Hans** to the Danish throne in 1481. When the Danish nobles revolted against his nephew King **Christian II** in 1522, Frederik was elected to replace him. Even after securing control of his new realm, he was faced with the threat of **Christian II**. Not until the end of the reign was this lessened by the defeat of the latter's attempt to regain the throne and his imprisonment. Frederik chose to work closely with his nobles, whose privileges laid out in the royal **accession charter** he respected, and to conduct a peaceful foreign policy. In religious matters he adopted a policy of **toleration**; although he never committed himself to Reform, he protected Lutheran preachers by appointing them royal chaplains. He died in Gottorp, from where he ruled for most of his reign and was eventually succeeded by his son **Christian III** by his first wife Anna of Brandenburg. By his second wife Sofie of Pomerania he had three daughters and three sons, including Hans, who was a candidate to the throne in the **Count's War.** SPO

FREDERIK II (1534-1588). King of Denmark and Norway 1559-88. Born at Haderslevhus, the son of King **Christian III**, as a young man he was vain and ambitious. After coming to the throne he crushed the peasant republic of **Ditmarsken** before turning to the task of restoring the **Kalmar Union**, which in 1563 involved Denmark in the **Northern Seven Years' War** against Sweden. This brought his realm no gains and much material loss. After its conclusion in 1570 Frederik practically withdrew from government, leaving the administration to be conducted by his noble council and his able chancellors Peder Oxe (to 1575) and Niels **Kaas**, under whom the country recovered its strength, aided by a peaceful foreign policy. He was responsible for the building of both the castle of **Kronborg** at **Elsinore** and the first **Frederiksborg.** His health undermined by heavy drinking, he died suddenly in Antvorskov Monastery and was buried in **Roskilde.** He was succeeded by the 11-year-old **Christian IV**, his son by Sofie of Mecklenburg, whom he had married in 1572. SPO

FREDERIK III (1609-1670). King of Denmark and Norway 1648-70. Born in Haderslevhus as the second son of King **Christian IV**, he became heir to the throne on the death of his elder brother Christian in 1647. In 1621 he was elected as coadjutor-archbishop of Bremen-Verden and five years later became bishop of Osnabrück. He succeeded to the archbishopric in 1634. He made himself unpopular with the Danish nobles as military commander during **Torstensson's War** (1643-45) and had to agree in 1648 to the most binding **Accession Charter** to secure his election to the throne. With the assistance of his adviser Christoffer **Gabel** and encouraged by his wife Sophie Amalie of Brunswick-Lüneburg, however, Frederik worked to free himself from the restrictions imposed on him. The disgrace of the two sons-in-law of **Christian IV**, **HannibalSehested** and **Corfitz Ulfeldt** left the Council divided, and Frederik was largely responsible for plunging his country into war with Sweden in 1657. He was compelled to sign the humiliating peace of **Roskilde** the following year, but he greatly raised the prestige of the monarchy by directing the defense of **Copenhagen** during the siege which followed the resumption of the war by King Charles X.

Immediately after the conclusion of the final peace in 1660, the king and his advisers succeeded in persuading the commoners during a meeting of the Estates to declare the Danish kingship hereditary. The following year the king was also proclaimed **absolute**. The order of succession and the royal powers were elaborated in the **King's Law**, the final version of which was drawn up in 1665 by the increasingly powerful Peder Schumacher (**Griffenfeld**). The latter part of the reign was spent in reforming the administration and restoring the financial health of the nation, a task in which Hannibal Sehested played a leading role. Frederik died in Copenhagen of pneumonia and was buried in **Roskilde**. He was succeeded by his eldest son as **Christian V**. Another son Jørgen (George), married Anne, the daughter of King James II of England and the future Queen Anne. With his mistress Margrethe Pape he had a son Ulrik Frederik **Gyldenløve**. SPO, AHT

FREDERIK IV (1671-1730). King of Denmark and Norway 1699-1730. Born in **Copenhagen Castle** as the eldest son of King **Christian V**, he was probably the ablest of Denmark's absolute monarchs. His attack on the duke of **Holstein**-Gottorp in 1700 precipitated the **Great Northern War**. Compelled to withdraw in 1701, he kept the peace with Sweden until the defeat of Charles XII at Poltava in 1709 persuaded Frederik to re-enter the struggle. The only gain which Denmark made at the peace in 1720, however, was the Slesvig lands of the duke of Holstein-Gottorp, a legacy which was to trouble Denmark's foreign policy for the next 50 years. Although the economy and the royal finances suffered considerably from such activities, Frederik succeeded in paying more than half the debt accumulated during the long war, largely from sale of crown lands. He established a national militia in 1701, and in 1702 freed the peasantry on the eastern islands of Denmark from *vornedskab*. His reign saw cultural activities such as the Royal **Theater** and the building of the palace of **Fredensborg**. He also backed Hans **Egede**'s expedition to **Greenland**. After his death in Odense of tuberculosis, he was succeeded by **Christian V**, his son by Louise of Mecklenburg-Güstrow (1667-1721), whom he married in 1695. In 1703 he bigamously married the noblewoman countess Vieregg, but she died the following year. In 1712 the king abducted and married Anna Sofie Reventlow, again bigamously, and on Louise's death in 1721 he declared her queen, a matrimonial policy bitterly resented by the rest of the Danish **nobility**. SPO

FREDERIK V (1723-1766). King of Denmark and Norway 1746-66. Born in **Copenhagen Castle**, the only son of King **Christian VI**, he reacted strongly against the **pietistic** milieu of his father's court. He took little interest in the duties of his office, which he was happy to see exercised by his ministers, led by Adam Gottlob **Moltke** and J.H.E. **Bernstorff**, while he gave himself up to a life of pleasure. Fortunately he was well served and during a peaceful reign the economy prospered and reforms were begun which looked forward to the advances of the later 18th century. Frederik first married princess Louise, daughter of George II of England, by whom he had his successor **Christian VII** and Sofie Magdalene, wife of King Gustavus III of Sweden, and, after Louise's death in 1751, Juliane Marie of Brunswick-Wolfenbüttel, the grandmother of King **Christian VIII**. He died in **Christiansborg** of dropsy, exacerbated by excessive drinking. SPO

FREDERIK VI (1768-1839). King of Denmark 1808-1839 and of Norway 1808-1814. Born in **Christiansborg**, the only son of King **Christian VII**, his early upbringing was largely dictated by J.F. **Struensee**, who followed the teachings of Rousseau on child-rearing. After Struensee's fall (1772) Frederik's upbringing was neglected. He came to be a focus for opposition to the regime of Ove **Høegh-Guldberg** and in 1784 played a leading part in the coup d'état which brought to power a group of reformers headed by A.P. **Bernstorff**. His father's mental illness made him in effect regent, although he never adopted the title and, until the death of Bernstorff in 1797, he played only a supporting role in government. After the outbreak of war with Britain in 1807, Denmark siding with France, and his accession to the throne the following year, Frederik largely dispensed with the official council and ruled from army headquarters, though the part played by his corps of adjutants (the "red feathers") has been exaggerated. It was largely the king who was responsible for maintaining the French alliance even when Napoleon's star began to wane. The loss of Norway at the end of the war by the Treaty of **Kiel** (1814) did not diminish his popularity, but he did choose to restore the **Royal Council**.

Alarmed by the European revolutions of 1830 he agreed to set up four **consultative assemblies** for the kingdom and the duchies, which began to meet in 1834. He died in **Amalienborg** and his coffin was carried to its resting place in **Roskilde** by peasants. None of his sons by queen Marie Sofie Frederikke of Hesse-Kassel survived him and the crown passed to his cousin **Christian VIII**. Frederik had an official mistress referred to as fru Dannemand, the last in Danish history. SPO. *See also* **Napoleonic Wars; Peasant Reforms**.

FREDERIK VII (1808-1863). King of Denmark 1848-63. Born in **Amalienborg**, the only child of the later King **Christian VIII**, he was both the last of Denmark's absolute monarchs and the last of the **Oldenborg** line. His childhood was overshadowed by his mother's divorce and, while not unintelligent, he showed little interest in affairs of state and little promise as a ruler, and served for a time with the army in **Odense**. In the face of popular demands for an end to **absolutism** soon after his accession, he declared himself a constitutional monarch on 21 March. His character acquired more stability with age and with his simple bourgeois tastes, he proved to be one of Denmark's most popular monarchs. His first two marriages — to King **Frederik VI**'s daughter Vilhelmine and to Caroline of Mecklenburg-Strelitz — ended in divorce (in 1837 and 1846 respectively). His third marriage in 1849 to his former mistress, the dancer Louise Rasmussen, although created Countess **Danner** was not approved of by "society," but she was a good influence on him and helped to strengthen the monarchy in the eyes of ordinary Danish people, to whom Frederik's sudden death in Glücksborg Castle came as a great shock. He had no children, and the throne passed to his distant relative as King **Christian IX**. SPO

FREDERIK VIII (1843-1912). King of Denmark 1906-12. Born in the *Gule Palæ* (yellow palace) of Amaliengade in **Copenhagen**, the eldest son of King **Christian IX**, he was fated to be crown prince for

43 years before ruling for only six. He took his duties as monarch seriously but accepted the **Change of System** in 1901, which limited his powers by parliamentary government, and tried to remain on good terms with the **Liberal** leaders who formed the ministries during his reign. In the crisis which followed the 1909 election Frederik tried to form a nonpolitical administration, and rejected the petition by the **Right** protesting at the appointment of **J.C. Christensen** as minister of defense. He died while visiting Hamburg. Of his eight children by Louise, daughter of King Charles XV of Sweden, his eldest son succeeded him as King **Christian X**, and in 1905 his second son Carl became first king of newly independent Norway as Håkon VII. SPO

FREDERIK IX (1899-1972). King of Denmark 1947-72. Born in Sorgenfri Castle, the eldest son of King **Christian X**, he took up a naval career as crown prince. In 1935 he married Ingrid, daughter of the Swedish Crown Prince, later King Gustav VI Adolf. Of their three daughters, the eldest succeeded him as Queen **Margrethe II**; Benedikte (1944-) married in 1968 Richard, Prinz zu Sayn-Wittgenstein-Berleburg; and Anne Marie married in 1964 Constantine II, then king (1964-67) of the Hellenes (Greece). As king, Frederik IX signed the 1953 **Constitution** and the legislation under which the succession passed to his daughter rather than to his brother Knud. A popular king, his reign saw rapid restructuring and growth of the Danish economy and full implementation of the **welfare** state. SPO, AHT

FREDERIK ANDRÉ HENRIK CHRISTIAN (1968-). Crown Prince. He is the elder son of Queen **Margrethe II** and her husband Prince Henrik, and is heir to the Danish throne. Born on 26 May, he was educated in Copenhagen, also studying in 1982-83 in Normandy, France. His military education, which included service in the Royal Life Guards and the Guard Hussars' Regiment, was completed in 1989. Subsequently he completed training with the Royal Marines Special Boat Service and the Royal Danish Naval Frogman Corps, and was appointed first lieutenant of the reserve in the Navy in 1995. He studied government in 1992-3 at Harvard University, USA, spent three months as a trainee at the United Nations in 1994, and graduated *cand. scient. pol.* in 1995 from Aarhus University. His younger brother is Prince **Joachim**. AHT

FREDERIKSBERG (population 85,817 in 1990) is a **local government** district (kommune) in the center of **Copenhagen**, with its own town hall (rådhus) built in 1942-53. Frederiksberg Slot was built in 1700-1735 and used by the royal family as a summer palace. Since 1869 it has housed the Army Officers' School, but the surrounding Garden, the largest park in the capital, is open to the public and includes the Zoo and the Royal Danish Garden Society's garden. The first European tramway for horse-drawn trams was laid from Vesterport along Frederiksberg Allé in 1863, and the surrounding area developed then and thereafter. The district has six small theaters and is home to much musical and artistic activity. **K.K. Steinke** based his social reforms on his experience in the district's Department of the Poor. AHT

FREDERIKSBORG CASTLE, near Hillerød in north **Zealand**, was originally built in 1602-23 on three islands in a large lake on the site of the medieval manor house of Hillerødsholm, which had been enlarged by King **Frederik II** and of which some parts survive. Its present name dates from this time. King **Christian IV** turned it into what was intended to be the greatest Renaissance palace in northern Europe. The principal architect was the Dutchman Hans Steenwinckel the Younger (1587-1639). It was badly damaged by fire in 1665 and reconstructed by Lambert van Haven (1630-95). A much greater fire in 1859 destroyed most of the roofs and the interior apart from the chapel with its Compenius organ of 1610. But it was completely rebuilt within six years with the help of grants from the brewer **J.C. Jacobsen**. It is now the National History Museum in the care of the **Carlsberg Foundation**. Frederiksborg is also the name of the administrative county (amt) in north **Zealand**. SPO

FREDERIKSBORG TREATY (1720) is the treaty which ended Denmark's participation in the **Great Northern War**. Denmark gained the Gottorp land in **Slesvig**, under British and French guarantee, and the right to levy tolls on Swedish ships sailing through the **Sound**. This was little reward for all the expenditure in men and money, and the acquisition of the territory in Slesvig was to complicate Danish foreign policy for the next 150 years. In 1773 Russia joined Britain and France as guarantors of the status of Slesvig. SPO, AHT. *See also* **Holstein**-Gottorp; **Slesvig-Holstein.**

FREDERIKSVÆRK is a town of some 4,000 inhabitants in north Zealand on the northeast shore of **Roskilde** Fjord. It was founded in 1756 by F.J. **Classen** as Denmark's first factory town, at the time to supply the armed forces with gunpowder and cannons. Today it produces steel. AHT

FREE CONSERVATIVES (DE FRIKONSERVATIVE) were a political party formed by baron Mogens **Friis** in 1902 from the eight (later ten) members of the **Landsting** who had broken with the Right (Højre) in 1900 and wished for collaboration with the **Liberals** to stem the tide of socialism. The group disappeared with the formation of the **Conservative People's Party** in 1915. SPO

FREEDOM COUNCIL (Danmarks Frihedsråd) was a body set up on 16 September 1943 to coordinate **resistance** to the German occupation after the resignation of the government at the end of August and to represent Denmark with the Allies. It included representation from *Frit Danmark, Ringen, Dansk Samling* (**Danish Rally**), the **Communist Party,** and the (British) Special Operations Executive (SOE). Prominent members were Niels Banke, **Mogens Fog, Erling Foss,** Børge Houmann, **Frode Jakobsen,** Arne Noe-Nygaard, Aage Schoch, **Arne Sørensen,** and Flemming Muus. It declared that when Denmark was free again, it wanted a constitutional government and that traitors and collaborators would be dealt with by law. It negotiated directly with political leaders and was responsible for the demands made to the Germans during the **Copenhagen** siege in June/July 1944. In December 1944 it negotiated to form the postwar liberation government, in which it was represented by **Mogens Fog** and **Frode Jakobsen.** It then dissolved itself. SPO, AHT. *See also* **World War II.**

FREUCHEN, PETER (1886-1957). Polar researcher and author. From 1906 he took part in a series of expeditions to **Greenland.** Often writing in novel form, he described Inuit life in *Storfanger*

(1927, Great Hunter), *Nordcaper* (1929, Northern Capes), and *Eskimofortællinger* (1944, Eskimo Tales). AHT

FRIE AKTUELT, DET, *see* **AKTUELT; PRESS**

FRIIS, CHRISTIAN EMIL KRAG-JUEL-VIND- (1817-1896), politician and from the mid-1800s one of Denmark's largest landowners. He was a member of the **Landsting** 1858-80. In 1865-70 he was prime minister and foreign minister and was one of the architects of the alliance between farmers and landowners which produced the revised **constitution** of 1866. Father of Mogens Friis. AHT

FRIIS, JOHAN (1494-1570). Politician. After studies abroad, including Germany and Italy 1514-21, he was appointed to the Council of State, serving as chancellor 1532-33 and 1535-70 and becoming the leading court official of **Christian III**. He was one of the chief forces to implement the Lutheran **Reformation** and of feudal reform which greatly increased the income of the crown. He opposed Sweden and was co-responsible for the **Northern Seven Years' War** in 1563. AHT

FRIIS, MICHAEL PETERSEN (1857-1944). Graduating *cand. jur.* in 1883, he held various posts in the central government. When Liebe's cabinet was forced to resign by a general strike on the night of 5 April 1920 Friis formed a caretaker government to see the country through the **Folketing** election of 26 April, resigning on 5 May. AHT

FRIIS, MOGENS (1849-1923). Politician. After a short diplomatic career, he lived from his estate. As a member of the **Landsting** 1880-1918 he was a leader of the **Right** in its 1894 agreement with the **Moderate Liberals** (*contrast* J.B.S. **Estrup**). In 1900 he was one of "the eight" who broke from the Right to support the formation of a Liberal government in 1901 and later continued to work with them, forming a Free Conservative group in the **Landsting** in 1902 and a component of the **Conservative** People's Party when it replaced the Right in 1915. AHT

FRIKORPS DANMARK was a military unit raised after June 1941 to fight side-by-side with the Germans on the Russian front. It trained near Hamburg and suffered heavy losses in action. Its first commander was Lieutenant-Colonel C.P. Kryssing (1891-1976). He was succeeded by Captain **Schalburg** and after his death in action in June 1942 by K.B. Martinsen. It was reorganized later in the war as *SS Panzergrenadier-Regiment Dänemark*. Its first return to Denmark on home leave in December 1942 was the occasion of hostile demonstrations and many of its surviving members were punished in war crimes trials after the war. SPO

FRISCH, HARTVIG (1893-1950). Politician and cultural historian. The son of a school principal, he graduated *cand. mag.* in Latin and Greek in 1917 and *dr. phil.* in 1941, and was professor of classical languages in Copenhagen University 1941-47. He was a **Social Democratic** member of the **Folketing** 1926-50. His writings included *Pest over Europa* (1933, Plague in Europe), a reckoning with fascism and communism, and *Europas Kulturhistorie I-II* (1928 and later editions, Cultural History of Europe). AHT

FRIT DANMARK (Free Denmark), (1) was the most successful of the underground newspapers produced by the Danish **resistance** during **World War II**. It first appeared in April 1942 with a leading article by the Conservative John **Christmas Møller** on the eve of his flight to England. He and the **Communist** leader **Aksel Larsen** were the main inspirers of the publication, which had a circulation of some 150,000 copies. It was represented on the **Freedom Council** when this was set up in September 1943. After the war it became a cultural monthly review.

(2) This was also the title of a newspaper produced in London for free Danes after the German Occupation and of a postwar political movement of ex-members of the Resistance who wished to maintain its ideals against party politics. SPO

FRØLICH, LORENZ (1820-1908). Painter and illustrator. The privately educated son of a merchant, he lived in Paris and elsewhere abroad for long periods. His work included the illustrations for A. Fabricius, *Danmarkshistorie* (1852-54), **Hans Christian Andersen**'s fairy tales (1867-74), **Oehlenschlæger**'s *Nordens Guder*

(1874-83, The Nordic Gods), and over a hundred children's books in French. He was especially known for his graphic illustrations of myths. AHT

FUNEN (*Fyn*) is Denmark's second largest island after **Zealand**, from which it is separated by the Great Belt. Its area is 2,984 sq. km. (1,152 square miles) and **Hans** Christian **Andersen** dubbed it "the Garden of Denmark" for its rich soil and well-cultivated landscape. The island has a wealth of manor-houses like Brahetrelleborg (end-16th century), Egeskov (mid-16th century), Hesselagergård (early 16th century), and Ulriksholm (early 17th century). Its principal towns are **Odense**, Denmark's third largest city, and in the south Svendborg (population 26,248 in 1990). Denmark's most famous composer **Carl Nielsen** was born in Nørre Lybdelse, south of Odense. A group of Impressionist painters (*Fynboerne*) are associated with the island and have a museum devoted to their work in Fåborg. They include Peter Hansen (1868-1928), **Fritz Syberg,** and **Johannes Larsen**. In the early 20th century the southern coast and its archipelago was a great fishing area, centered on the port of Kerteminde. More recently the archipelago has attracted sailing tourists. SPO

FYRKAT *see* **TRELLEBORG**

- G -

GABEL, CHRISTOFFER (1617-1673). Politician. A land surveyor of German origin, in 1639 he became private secretary to Duke Frederik, who ascended to the throne as **Frederik III** in 1648. He gained decisive private political influence and is considered to be one of the main factors for the introduction of **absolute monarchy** in 1660-61. In 1664 he was appointed a privy councillor (*gehejmeraad*) and governor (*statholder*) of **Copenhagen**, but lost these offices on Frederik's death in 1670. In 1655 he was granted the **Faroe Islands** in fief and his son enjoyed the same privileges until his death in 1708. AHT

GADE, JACOB (1879-1963). Composer. The son of a musician and instrument dealer, as a boy with his father he played the violin at dances and in inns, becoming a musician for silent films and in cafés 1897-1931. He is best known for his *Tango Jalousie* (1925). AHT

GADE, NIELS WILHELM (1817-1890). Composer and conductor. Born in **Copenhagen** as the son of an instrument-maker, Gade studied under A.P. Berggreen (1801-10), best known for his settings of Danish folk ballads. He made his debut in 1840 with the concert overture Echoes of Ossian (*Gjenklange af Ossian*). His first symphony, based on a setting of a poem in ballad form, was first performed in 1843 at Leipzig's Gewandthaus under Felix Mendelssohn, with whom Gade worked and whom he succeeded in the Gewandthaus in 1847. Mendelssohn's romantic style was Gade's most important inspiration. On returning to Copenhagen in 1848, he was appointed chief conductor at the Musical Society, in 1858 also organist at Holmens Church, and in 1867 the first director of the Music Conservatoire (Musikkonservatorium). He composed eight symphonies, much chamber music, and many works for piano. Among his choral works, *Elverskud* (1851-53, Elf shot) is the most important. While his music is basically German Romantic in style, the influence of Danish folk ballads gives it individuality. Gade was the dominant figure of his time in Danish music, and the greatest 19th century Danish composer. SPO, AHT

GALLEHUS, THE HORNS OF, were two golden horns dating from the 5th century AD found in a field of the village of Gallehus near Tønder in southern **Jutland**, one in 1639, the other in 1743. In 1802 they were stolen from the Royal Museum (Kunstkammeret) in Christiansborg and melted down by Niels **Heidenreich**. Their appearance is known only from sketches, from which the copies now in the National Museum were reconstructed. The smaller of the two is inscribed with one of the earliest known Scandinavian runic inscriptions, reading: "I Lægest, son of Holte, made the horn." Their theft inspired the poem *Guldhornet* by Adam **Oehlenschläger** which is often seen as the breakthrough of Danish Romanticism. SPO. *See also* **Ole Worm**.

GEIGER, THEODOR (1891-1952), sociologist. German-born, he qualified as a lawyer at Würzburg in 1914, graduated *dr. phil.* in 1919, and was professor of sociology at Braunschweig 1929-33. He left Germany and was the first Danish professor of sociology 1938-52 at Århus University. His research was in the sociology of justice and morals, and in social stratification and mobility. His books include the text, *Sociologi. Grundrids og problemer* (1939, Sociology: Outline and Problems) and *Klassesamfund i støbegryden* (1948, Class Society in the Crucible). AHT

GELEFF, PAUL (1842-1928). Politician. The son of a smallholder, he qualified as a teacher in 1864 but worked as a journalist. In 1871 he was a cofounder of the International Labour Union (Den internationale Arbejderforening), the forerunner of the Social Democratic party. In 1873 he was sentenced to three years in prison for disturbing the social order. Paid to do so by the police, he emigrated to the United States in 1877, not returning to Denmark until 1920. AHT. *See also* **Pio, Louis**.

GELSTED, OTTO (1888-1968), author and critic. After leaving school he supported himself as a tutor, journalist, and writer, and became a central figure of the Danish cultural-radical movement. In the face of rising Nazism in the 1930s he opted for communism, for its theoretical promise of social equality and order. His work includes topographical descriptions, biographies of authors, e.g., *Johannes V. Jensen* (1913), artists, e.g., *Ekspressionisme* (1919), and translations: the *Iliad* and *Odyssey* from classical Greek, and the work of Sigmund Freud, Walt Witman, Bertold Brecht, and Pablo Neruda. He also wrote nature poetry as war cries in a revolutionary humanistic vein. AHT

GERHARD III, COUNT OF HOLSTEIN *see* **GERT**

GERMAN OCCUPATION *see* **WORLD WAR II**

GERMANY, DANISH RELATIONS WITH. Relations between Denmark and the states making up Germany to the south have throughout its history been close, if not always friendly. In the 12th century, emperors of the Holy Roman Empire claimed overlordship over the Danish realm and often intervened in Danish internal affairs., but after 1160 under Kings **Valdemar I** the Great, **Knud IV** and **Valdemar II** the Victorious, Danish power was extended along the southern Baltic coast. Under the latter, however, this empire collapsed, and in the early 14th century, while merchants of the **Hanseatic League** took control of Baltic trade, Holstein nobles led by **Gert** of Holstein secured control of Denmark in the shape of fiefs pledged to them by the impecunious rulers. Not until the reign of King **Valdemar Atterdag** was this yoke removed. The **Kalmar Union** between the Scandinavian monarchies was formed in 1397 partly as a protection against German encroachment, but of the Union kings who ruled Denmark, **Erik of Pomerania**, **Christoffer III** of Bavaria, and **Christian I** were all of German origin. Under Christian I the close links were established between the kingdom of Denmark and the largely German duchies of **Slesvig-Holsten** (of which the king was duke) that were subsequently to have such a profound influence on Danish foreign policy, and especially Danish relations with Germany, until the mid-19th century.

The **Reformation** strengthened Denmark's already strong cultural relations with northern Germany. Many Danish scholars and churchmen were trained at northern German universities. Many nobles from the Protestant states of northern Germany sought service at the Danish court in the later 17th century. The Danish army consisted largely of German mercenary troops, and a large colony of German craftsmen and traders established itself in **Copenhagen**. King **Christian IV** at the beginning of the 17th century sought to extend Danish influence in northwestern Germany (the Lower Saxon Circle) to counterbalance Swedish gains in the eastern Baltic, but his intervention in the **Thirty Years' War** against the Catholic emperor ended disastrously

In the later 17th century and until late in the 18th century, German cultural influence remained strong. German was the language of the army and the court until 1776, and many of Denmark's statesmen of the 18th century came either from the duchies or — like the **Bernstorffs** — north German states like Hanover and Mecklenburg, whence also came most of Denmark's queens in the period.

The rise of German nationalism in the early 19th century created a dangerous situation in the duchies and eventually in 1848 led to the first **Slesvig-Holsten** War, in which the kingdom of Prussia was involved on the side of the rebels. The status quo was restored, and many Danes supported the **Scandinavianism** movement as a shield against renewed threats from the south. This did not, however, save Denmark from humiliating defeat at the hands of both Prussia and Austria in the Second **Slesvig-Holsten** War in 1864, with the consequent loss of the duchies. The creation in 1871 of a united German Empire under Prussian leadership also placed Denmark in a potentially weak position, although at the same time Germany was one of its most important customers.

During **World War I** Denmark, although neutral, was regarded as within the German sphere of influence and in 1914 was compelled under German pressure to mine the Great Belt against any attempt by Britain to send naval forces into the Baltic. With Hitler's coming to power in 1933, the presence of a large German-speaking minority in southern **Jutland** became a potential cause of conflict. In the light of this, alone among the Scandinavian countries, Denmark signed a nonaggression pact with Germany on 24 June 1939. But in the course of **World War II** Denmark was occupied on 9 April 1940 by German forces on the pretense of protecting the country against an Allied attack. Relations between the two governments continued through their respective foreign offices until the final breakdown in August 1943 and a full German takeover, which continued until the end of the war in May 1945.

Although relations between Denmark and Germany (both West and East, and since 1990 with united Germany) have been outwardly amicable, Danes have viewed the economic and political power of their southern neighbor with some apprehension. Membership of both countries in **NATO** and in the **European Union**, organizations which include other member-states and provide a broad framework for managing security and economic and political relationships is thought safer than the unequal bilateral relationship which prevailed before 1945. SPO, AHT

GERSDORFF, JOACHIM (1611-1661). Politician. After studying at **Sorø Academy** he traveled in Germany, England, Holland, and France. He was appointed in 1648 to the Council of State (*rigsråd*) and governor (*statholder*) of **Copenhagen** and in 1652 chamberlain (*rigshofmester*). As chief negotiator, he had to sign the Treaty of **Roskilde** of 1658, by which Denmark lost **Scania**, Halland, and Blekinge. In September 1660 he opened the **consultative assembly** which made **Frederik III** the hereditary monarch and thereby paved the way for **absolute monarchy**, to which he was apparently not opposed. In October 1660 he was appointed *rigsdrost* and formal leader of the state council. AHT

GERT (GERHARD) III, COUNT OF HOLSTEIN (c. 1292-1340) was the most powerful man in Denmark during the interregnum of 1332-40. Having succeeded his father Heinrich as count of Holstein-Rendsborg in 1304, Gert aided King **Erik VI Menved** in his disastrous German campaigns, for which in 1317 he was rewarded by the impecunious king with **Funen** in pawn. In 1326 the Danish **nobles** opposed to King **Christoffer II** offered **Gert** the throne for his ward duke Valdemar of Slesvig and the post of regent for himself in exchange for military assistance. King Christoffer was forced to flee and the 12-year-old Valdemar was placed on the throne as **Valdemar III**. For his services the duke was further rewarded with **Slesvig** in fief. In 1329 divisions among Gert's Holstein allies led him to reach an agreement with Christoffer, who resumed the crown while Gert again took Funen in fief and married his sister to the king's eldest son. Duke and king again fell out in 1331, and the latter was defeated in battle and his son killed. He was consequently forced to grant the duke **Jutland** as well as Funen as security for a debt of 100,000 silver marks. After Christoffer's death in 1332, Denmark was in effect ruled by the duke and his allies. But opposition to the Holsteiners grew and on 1 April 1340 in Randers, Gert was murdered by the Jutish warrior Niels Ebbesen, who subsequently became a national hero. Holstein rule was brought to an end by Christoffer II's son Valdemar, who ascended the throne as **Valdemar IV**. SPO

GJEDDE, OVE (1594-1660), after a military education abroad, as a naval officer in 1618 led the fleet which would build the Danish trade to the **East Indies**. In 1620 he founded the trading colony at Trankebar by agreement with the ruler of Tanjore. In 1644 he was promoted to admiral and in 1645 *rigsadmiral*. AHT

GJELLERUP, KARL ADOLPH (1857-1919). Novelist and dramatist. He graduated *cand. theol.* in 1878 but his studies of Charles Darwin and Herbert Spencer and the influence of Georg **Brandes** turned him to militant atheism. From 1892 he lived in Dresden, but he shared the 1917 **Nobel Prize** for literature with **Henrik Pon-**

toppidan. Most of his writings are without substance and firm structure, but in his search for the truth he cannot be doubted. AHT

GLISTRUP, MOGENS (1926-). Tax lawyer and politician. Born on **Bornholm**, he studied Law at the universities of Copenhagen and Berkeley before in 1956 establishing a legal firm in **Copenhagen** specializing in tax law. He also taught law at the university until 1963. In an interview on Danish TV in 1971 he caused a sensation by explaining how he had helped his clients to avoid paying tax. He later launched a populist attack on the Danish government and higher **education** and in 1972 formed his **Progress Party** (Fremskridtsparti*)*, which won 28 seats and 16 percent of the popular vote in the elections of December 1973. The following year Glistrup was indicted for tax fraud and was finally, in November 1981, found guilty and sentenced to four years' imprisonment and a fine of 4,000,000 kroner. An appeal in 1983 was rejected, but the punishment was reduced to three years' imprisonment and the fine to 1,000,000 kroner. He was expelled from the **Folketing**. He was freed from prison in March 1985. Having already been replaced as party chairman, he was expelled from the party in November 1990 for indiscipline and immediately formed a new Growth Party (Trivselspartiet), which fought the ensuing election in alliance with **Common Course**. Glistrup married Lene Borup Svendsen in 1950 and has four children. SPO

GLOB, PETER VILHELM (1911-1985). Archaeologist. He graduated *cand. mag.* in 1936 and *dr. phil.* in 1945 in prehistorical archaeology, becoming professor at **Århus** University 1949-60 and State Antiquary (*rigsantikvar*) 1960-81. He led excavations in Denmark, **Greenland,** and the Arabian Gulf. His books include *Mosefolk* (1965, The Bog People), *Højfolket* (1970, People of the Burial Mound), and *Fortidens spor* (1973, Signs of the Past). AHT

GLÜCKSBORG, HOUSE OF. The Danish royal house commencing with King **Christian IX**, who came to the throne on the death of King **Frederik VII**, the last of the House of **Oldenborg** in 1863. His claim to the Danish throne was traced back to Hans the Younger of Sønderborg (d. 1622), brother of King **Frederik II** and his grandson August Filip. The elder line, descended from Hans's son

Filip, died out in 1779, but in 1825 Christian's father, Wilhelm, who belonged to the younger line of Beck, was granted the right to the castle and title of Glücksborg. Christian's claim was reinforced by his father's marriage to the granddaughter of King **Frederik V** and was recognized by the Succession Law of 1853. The duke of Augustenborg's refusal to recognize Christian's succession in the duchy of Holstein helped to precipitate the Second **Slesvig-Holsten** War. (*See* Appendix 1). The royal houses of Greece and Norway are of the same dynasty. SPO

GLÜCKSTADT, EMIL (1875-1923). Banker. He began work in Landsmandsbanken, where his father was a director, becoming a junior director in 1904 and first director in 1910. He expanded the bank's capital and during 1912-20 bought 12 banks and savings banks, so that in 1921 it was the largest Nordic bank. But stock exchange speculation and risky transactions brought the bank's failure in 1922 and he was charged with fraud. Glückstad was arrested in 1923 but died before the charge was confirmed by the court. AHT

GLYPTOTEK, NY CARLSBERG, is an art museum in Dantes Plads, **Copenhagen,** containing the collection of art begun by the brewer **Carl Jacobsen** and his wife Otilia and presented to the city in 1888. Additions were made with grants from the Ny Carlsbergfond and it is maintained by the **Carlsberg Foundation**. It has one of the largest assemblages of ancient Egyptian, Etruscan, Greek, and Roman sculpture in Northern Europe, together with French impressionist paintings and Danish art of the 19th and 20th centuries. The main building, housing the modern collections dates from 1897, was designed by Wilhelm Dahlerup, and contains a fine winter garden. The rear building with the antique collection dates from 1906 and was designed by Hack Kampmann (1856-1920). Works by Rodin and modern Danish sculptors such as **Kai Nielsen**, together with a collection of French paintings (Gaugin, Dégas), are housed in a new wing opened in 1996. SPO, AHT

GODFRED or GUDFRED (d. 810 or 811), king of the Danes. Son and successor of King Sigfrid, he gave shelter to Saxon fugitives after the conquest of Saxony by the emperor Charlemagne and in 804 rejected a call from the emperor to return them. Four years later he attacked the Obotrits in Mecklenburg, destroyed their trading center of Reric, and transferred its merchants to Slistorp (the later town of **Slesvig**). To protect this and the trade route across the neck of the Jutish peninsula, Godfred constructed a defensive wall of turf, the first *Dannevirke*. In 810 he raided the coast of Frisia and imposed a tax on the Frisians but on his return was murdered by one of his followers. He was succeeded by his nephew Hemming. SPO

GOLDEN AGE, THE, was a period of Danish **painting** covering roughly the first half of the 19th century and the height of **Romanticism**. Ironically much of this was a period of national disaster and humiliation and of economic difficulty as a result of Denmark's participation in the **Napoleonic Wars**. Its principal figures were C.W. **Eckersberg** and his pupils **Constantin Hansen** (1804-80), Christen Købke (1810-1848), Wilhelm Marstrand (1810-1873), who produced many illustrations of Holberg's plays, and Martinus Rorbye (1803-48). With these must be associated the classical lines of Denmark's greatest sculptor, the half-Icelandic **Bertel Thorvaldsen**. **Jonas Collin** secured state and personal patronage for artists of the Golden Age. The term is sometimes extended to cover the literature of the same period by Adam **Oehlenschläger**, Bernhard Severin **Ingemann**, N.F.S. **Grundtvig** and the poet and playwright Carsten Hauch (1790-1872). SPO, AHT

GOLDSCHMIDT, MEÏR ARON (1819-1887). Author. Raised in a comfortable provincial Jewish family, after leaving school he became a journalist. He edited the satirical journal *Corsaren* 1840-46, ridiculing both the **absolute monarchy** and the opposition from a radical republican perspective. He published the newspaper *Nord og Syd* (North and South) in 1847-59, asserting a more moderately conservative view. His literary works include *En jøde* (1845, A Jew), *Ravnen* (1867, The Raven), and his memoirs, *Livs erindringer og resultater* (1877, Life's memories and results) which describe the Jewish milieu, dominated by a steadily more explicit fate. *See also* **Nathansen, Henri**. AHT

GORM THE OLD (died c. 940). King of Denmark. He is the first in the continuous line of Danish rulers, but little is known of him except what was recorded on the smaller of the stones at **Jelling**, which he appears to have raised in memory of his wife Tyra and on which he is named as 'king of Denmark'. He is also named on the larger stone, set up by his son **Harald I** Bluetooth. SPO

GØRTZ, EBBE (1886-1976). The son of a Lieutenant General, when Denmark was occupied by Germany in 1940 he was the chief of the general staff, and continued to work with loyalty to the **Buhl** government's policy of collaboration. When the army was interned on 29 August 1943, he formed an underground "little" general staff and in December negotiated to coordinate military and civilian **Resistance** groups led by the **Freedom Council**. In October 1944 he was named by the Freedom Council as supreme commander of Danish underground forces in the event of regular open conflict with the occupation forces. He was defense chief in 1950-51. AHT. *See also* **World War II**.

GOVERNMENT. Denmark has been a **monarchy** since records began. Until 1661, the monarchy was elective, although from early times kings were chosen by the leading nobles from a small group of families. The monarch was assisted by high officials led by the chancellor and advised by a council of nobles, occasionally reinforced by representatives of the **estates** of nobles, clergy, burghers and peasants, especially when new taxes were to be raised. In 1661 the monarchy became **absolute** and all restrictions on the king's powers were removed. This was defined in the **King's Law** of 1665, which replaced the **Accession Charter**, to which kings had previously had to agree. The estates were no longer summoned and the Royal Council was abolished. Central administration was subsequently reformed in accordance with the collegial system.

This remained the system until the 19th century, but during the 18th century Danish government took on more of the character of a bureaucracy under which policy was made by powerful ministers such as J.H.E. **Bernstorff**. In the 1830s four **consultative assemblies**, two for the kingdom and two for the duchies, were allowed to be elected, but in 1848 absolute was replaced by constitutional monarchy, whose powers have since been defined by a series of **constitutions**. Legislative power was shared between the monarch, who appointed his ministers, and a two-chamber **parliament** or Rigsdag. Parliamentary government was recognized in practice after the **Change of System** and legally in the constitution of 1915. The up-

per house (**Landsting**) of the Rigsdag was abolished by the consti-
tution of 1953, by which Denmark is now governed. SPO. *See also*
Appendix 2; **Cabinets; Local Government; Parliament; Political
Parties.**

GØYE, BIRGITTE (c. 1511-1574). Educator. As a girl she was at
the court of Queen Dorothea (wife of **Christian III**). With her noble
husband Herluf Trolle she founded a school for the children of
noblemen at **Herlufsholm** in 1565. Although her husband died that
year and she had to move away, she continued to direct the school
until her death. AHT

GØYE, MOGENS (?-1544), the largest landowner in Denmark and a
member of one of Denmark's oldest noble families. He worked with
Christian II but helped the other **nobility** to depose him in 1523,
and later that year was made lord chancellor (*rigshofmester*) by the
new king, **Frederik I**. Following Frederik's death he worked for the
election of **Christian III**, supporting him in the **Count's War**. He
was one of the first of the nobility to support the Lutheran **reformation**. One of his daughters was **Birgitte Gøye** AHT

GRAM, HANS CHRISTIAN (1853-1938). Surgeon. In 1884 he developed a method of staining bacteria so as to differentiate them as
"gram-positive" or "gram-negative," a method adopted worldwide.
He later became chief surgeon at the Royal Frederik's Hospital, and
a professor. AHT

GRATHE HEDE was a battle fought south of Viborg on 23 October
1157 between King **Valdemar I** the Great and an army led by King
Svend III Grathe, who since 1154 had shared the kingdom with
him and with **Knud III**. Knud was murdered by Svend in August
and Knud's followers joined Valdemar. In the battle Svend's army
was defeated and Svend himself slain by peasants while fleeing from
the field. Valdemar became sole king of Denmark. SPO

GRAUBALLE MAN was one of the 160 Early Iron Age bodies preserved in bogs in **Jutland**. Peat-cutters discovered him in 1952 and
he is now displayed in the **Museum** of Prehistory at Moesgaard,
near **Århus**. He was about 30 years old and, as with many similar

finds, he had met a violent death, having had his throat cut. Analysis of the stomach contents indicates that his last meal consisted of a broth of meat and grain. SPO. *See also* **Glob, P.V.; Prehistory; Tollund Man.**

GREAT AGRICULTURAL COMMISSION (Den store Landbrugskommission), was set up in 1786 by Crown Prince Frederik, later King **Frederik VI**, following the coup d'état of 1784 to consider reform of peasant conditions in Denmark. Its leading members were Count Christian Ditlev **Reventlow** and Christian **Colbjørnson**, and its most important recommendation was the abolition of the *stavnsbaand*. *See also* **Peasant Reforms.** SPO

GREAT NORTHERN WAR (1700-1720). The war came about as the result of agreements reached between Denmark, Russia, and Saxony in 1698-99 for a joint attack on Sweden to destroy Swedish Baltic hegemony. It began with a Saxon invasion of Swedish Livonia, followed in March 1700 by a Danish invasion of the lands in **Slesvig** held by Sweden's ally, the duke of **Holstein-Gottorp**. The Swedes responded by landing an army, led by King Charles XII, south of **Copenhagen**, but King **Frederik IV** was also threatened by Britain, the United Provinces, and France, who had guaranteed the duke's possessions. By the Treaty of Travendal Frederik agreed to relinquish the occupation of Slesvig and withdraw from the war.

After the defeat of the Swedish army at Poltava in July 1709, Denmark re-entered the war in alliance with Russia and Poland-Saxony, but after defeat at Hälsingborg in **Scania** in March 1710, the main Danish army had again to retreat across the **Sound**. In 1712 Danish troops occupied the Swedish possession of Bremen-Verden but were defeated by the Swedes at the battle of Gadebusch in Pomerania at the end of the year. A Swedish invasion of the duchies of **Slesvig-Holsten** from the south in 1713 ended with the surrender of their army at Tønning in May. Treaties with Hanover and Prussia in 1715 were followed by a successful attack on Stralsund, Sweden's last possession on the southern coast of the Baltic.

A Swedish invasion of Norway in 1716 was foiled by Danish naval activity and a large army of Danes and Russians gathered on **Zealand** in preparation for an attack on Sweden over the Sound, but mistrust between the allies led to abandonment of this enterprise. A fresh Swedish invasion of Norway in 1718 ended with the death of

King Charles XII while besieging Frederikssten and the anti-Swedish coalition began to fall apart. With the help of British mediation, peace was made between Denmark and Sweden in July 1720 at **Frederiksborg**. Denmark's only gains from participation in the war were the lands of the duke of **Holstein-Gottorp** in Slesvig and the abolition of Sweden's exemption from the **Sound** tolls. SPO. *See also* **Danish Relations with Russia, Sweden**.

GREENLAND (Grønland, in Greenlandic Kalaallit Nunaat) is the largest island in the world with an area of 2,175,500 square kilometers (840,000 square miles) but a population of only 55,117 (1993), and is an overseas territory of the Danish monarchy. Its official languages are **Greenlandic** and Danish. It has its own flag: white and red halves divided horizontally with an imposed red and white globe, also divided horizontally. Its most important economic activity is fishing, but there are largely unexploited resources of oil, uranium, coal, and cryolite (a mineral fluoride of aluminum and sodium). Total Danish expenditure on Greenland in 1996 was estimated at 2,500 million kroner.

The earliest European settlement of Greenland was made by Icelanders at the end of the 10th century who established colonies on the west coast. By the end of the 14th century, when European interest in the area was renewed, these colonies had disappeared. An expedition from Denmark in 1605-07 claimed sovereignty, but not until some hundred years later did commercial and missionary interests combine in a serious attempt to make the island a Danish possession. The Norwegian clergyman Hans **Egede** obtained the backing of the Danish crown to establish a missionary station. In 1774 the Royal Danish Trade (Company) was set up and two years later given a monopoly of trade with Greenland. Interrupted during Denmark's participation in the **Napoleonic Wars**, this trade picked up again in the 1830s and the population grew rapidly. Limited self-government was granted in 1863 and extended in 1925. Gradually the traditional Inuit (Eskimo) life of hunting and fishing was superseded by modern fishing (for cod), sheep-raising, and extraction of minerals. In 1921 Greenland was finally recognized internationally as under Danish sovereignty. In 1931 Norway laid claim to northeastern Greenland and occupied part of it, but this claim was rejected by the International Court in The Hague in 1933.

During **World War II** American bases were established under an agreement made by the Danish ambassador in Washington, Henrik **Kaufmann**. A German radio station in the northeast of the island was destroyed. A joint defense agreement was signed by Denmark and the United States in 1951 allowing the continued presence of US bases and the stationing of nuclear weapons. During the Cold War these bases were important for **NATO** surveillance of the "GIUK Gap": the stretch of North Atlantic between Greenland, Iceland, and the United Kingdom through which Soviet vessels could pass into world oceans. "Defence areas" remain at Kangeerlussuaq/Søndre Strømfjord and Pituffik/Dundas — Thule Air Base.

In 1950 the Danish trading monopoly was finally ended and a popular assembly set up. The Danish **Constitution** of 1953 changed Greenland's status from colony to an integral part of the kingdom. In 1979, when the population was about 50,000, a home rule law took effect, approved by 73 percent of the voters at a **referendum**. This established a 31-member national assembly (Landsting), elected every four years, in Nuuk/Godthaab. A government (*landsstyret*) takes policy decisions. Two representatives are also elected to the Danish **Folketing**. The Danish state is represented in Greenland by the office of the *Rigsombudsmand*, an official appointed by the Danish government. During 1980-89 the home rule authority gradually took over responsibility for most policy areas, but the transfer of health care was postponed from 1989 to 1992 on grounds of cost. Subsequently only security, foreign and exchange-rate policy were controlled from **Copenhagen**. There is a University of Greenland, and in 1994 a Bishop of Greenland was appointed.

In 1972 a majority of Greenlanders voted against membership of the **European Community (EC)**, but were bound by the Danish decision to join. This added fuel to the movement for greater independence, embodied in **Siumut**, which became a political party in 1977 and won power after the 1979 election. In a referendum in 1982 Greenland again rejected membership of the EC and became from 1985 an "overseas territory" with special relations with the EC and then the European Union (EU). Siumut has remained in office throughout the 1980s, usually in coalition with another party. Siumut's main rival is **Atassut**, which favors maintaining links with Denmark and membership of the European Union. Other parties are **Inuit Ataqatigiit** and **Akulliit Partiia**. SPO, AHT

GREENLANDIC LANGUAGE is a major branch of the Inuit subgroup of the Eskimo-Aleutic family of languages. The people concerned prefer the term Inuit (meaning "human beings") for themselves, rather than Eskimo (originally meaning "those who eat raw meat"). The language was originally written around 1750 by Hans **Egede**'s son Poul and its orthography was developed by a German missionary Samuel Kleinschmidt in 1851, but in a form difficult to learn. A movement toward cultural and linguistic autonomy only developed in the 1960s and a reformed spelling was introduced in 1973. With home rule in 1979 Greenlandic became the main official language, used alongside Danish administratively and in schools. It is spoken by about 45,000 people, or some 60 percent of the Inuit population.

Whereas most languages form sentences from independent words combined according to grammatical rules, Greenlandic can build complex "sentence structures" by suffixing long chains of inflectional and derivational morphemes to a single root morpheme — so a single compound word can function as a whole sentence. For example, *sikursuarsiurpugut* translates as "we sail through the big ice", where "big ice" means "a stretch of sea dominated by big icefloes with only narrow passages of open sea to sail through." The root is *siku*, ice; the second element *sua(q)* means big, large, and two extra *r*s (*sikur̲suar-*) are added as phonetic adjustments. The third element, *siur*, means passing through; *pu* means indicative mood, and *gut* indicates first person plural, "we". AHT

GRESS, ELSA (1919-1988). Author. She graduated *mag. art.* in the history of literature in 1944 and became a sharp debater, vigorously opposing Marxism, **feminism,** and anti-Americanism. Her novels include *Mellemspil* (1947, Interplay) and *Jorden er ingen stjerne* (1956, The Earth Is No Star), but was acclaimed especially for her memoirs, including *Mine mange hjem* (1965, My Many Homes), *Fuglefri og Fremmed* (1971, Bird-free and Foreign), and *Compania* I-II (1976). AHT

GRIFFENFELD, PEDER SCHUMACHER (1635-1699). Chancellor of the Realm. Born Peder Schumacher to a German wine merchant in **Copenhagen,** he went to school at the age of four and studied at the university when only 12. He benefited from the opportunities opened to commoners by the introduction of **absolute mon-**

tour in 1663 he was appointed the royal librarian and archivist. As royal secretary to **Frederik III** he was largely responsible for drawing up the **King's Law** in 1665 and four years later became a member of the Supreme Court. He enjoyed even greater favor from King **Christian V**, who on coming to the throne in 1670 made him a member of his privy council and raised him to the nobility as Griffenfeld. The following year he was awarded the **Orders of the Elephant** and **Dannebrog**. By 1673, when he was named Chancellor of the Realm (*Storkansler*) and made a count, he was the leading influence in Danish foreign policy.

But he could not prevent the outbreak of war with Sweden in 1675 and he had made many enemies at home. The discovery that Griffenfeld had continued his links with France even after the outbreak of war with France's ally Sweden led to his arrest in March 1676 on a charge of high treason. Although the charge could not be proved satisfactorily, he was condemned to death. Only on the scaffold was this commuted to life imprisonment. In 1680 he was transferred from **Copenhagen Castle** to a less rigorous prison on Munkholm in Trondheim fjord in Norway. He died in Trondheim, where he was finally allowed to reside. SPO

GRØNBECH, VILHELM (1873-1948). Cultural historian. Graduating *cand. mag.* in Danish, Latin, and English in 1897, *dr. phil.* in 1902, and becoming professor of the history of religion in **Copenhagen** University in 1915-43, his main books were *Primitiv religion* (1915), *Religiøse strømninger i det nittende århundrede* (1922, Religious Currents in the 19th Century), *Mystikker i Europa og Indien* I-IV (1925-1932, Mystics in Europe and India) and *Hellas* I-IV (1942-1945). In these he sought to portray foreign cultures and religions from within their own preconceptions. AHT

GRUBBE, MARIE (1643-1718). In 1660-70 she was married to King **Frederik III**'s son, Ulrik Frederik **Gyldenløve**, governor of Norway. The marriage was dissolved on allegations of her unfaithfulness. In 1673-90 she was married to the nobleman Palle Dyre, but this marriage was dissolved on allegations of her affair with Søren Sørensen Møller, a coachman, whom she later married abroad. The couple ran the ferry and inn at Grønsund, Falster. Her unrestrained love-life across class boundaries, contrary to the norms of the time, has been a frequent subject of Danish literature, notably by J.P. **Jacobsen** in *Marie Grubbe* (1875). AHT

GRUNDTVIG, NICOLAJ FREDERIK SEVERIN (1783-1872). Poet, churchman, educationist and politician. Born in the parsonage of Udby near Vordingborg, Grundtvig went to school in **Århus** and in 1800 entered **Copenhagen** University, graduating *cand. theol.* in 1803. While a private tutor on Langeland an unhappy love affair caused the first of a number of mental crises. He also discovered an enthusiasm for Nordic mythology, in the interpretation of which he was a pioneer. After a further crisis in 1810-1811, from which he recovered by serving as his father's curate at Udby, he found his mission in life in seeking through both the written and spoken word to achieve a national revival. In 1822 Grundtvig moved to a preaching post in Copenhagen, but his bitter attacks on rational Christianity caused him to be silenced by the authorities and he resigned. He turned to scholarship. A series of visits to England in 1829-31, made with the help of a royal grant, made him more liberal in his political views and provided him with some of the basic educational ideals which made him the spiritual father of the **folk high school** movement, including the collegiate system which he found in Oxford and Cambridge. He developed such ideas in a number of writings in the 1830s. He advocated residential "schools for life", open to all classes of society, which would emphasize a broad Christianity and a national tradition communicated through the "living word."

Grundtvig was a member of the **constituent assembly** 1848-49, of the **Folketing** 1849-58, and of the Landsting in 1866. He contributed about 1,400 hymns to Danish religious life, as well as many secular poems. In 1839 he was appointed vicar in Vartov and in 1861, on the 50th anniversary of being called to the ministry, he was awarded the honorary title of bishop. Grundtvig was one of the most influential Danes of his time, and continued to influence the intellectual and spiritual life of Denmark long after his death. His memorial is the massive Grundtvig Church at Bispebjerg, designed by P.V. **Jensen-Klint** and completed in 1940 by his son **Kaare Klint**. SPO, AHT. *See also* **Church; Religion.**

GRUNDTVIG, SVEND (1824-1883). Oral historian. The son of **N.F.S. Grundtvig**, he graduated *magister* in 1860 and in 1869 was appointed professor of Nordic languages in Copenhagen University. His main work, *Danmarks gamle Folkeviser* (1853, Old Folksongs of Denmark) laid the ground for their systematic collection and publication, and thereby for Danish oral history. AHT

GUDFRED *see* **GODFRED**

GUILDS appeared in Danish towns in the 12th century. As elsewhere in Europe, during the Middle Ages they became dominated by oligarchies of masters who made it increasingly difficult for apprentices to progress beyond the rank of journeyman. At the beginning of the 16th century the latter began to organize their own guilds. In 1507 the Danish shoemakers guilds were accused of fraud and dissolved. This was followed in 1526 by temporary abolition of all handicraft guilds, whose monopoly was blamed for the high price of their produce. In 1620, to ease entry expensive dinners as the price of acceptance were forbidden. In 1794 a widespread sympathy strike by journeymen, protesting at the imprisonment of striking carpenters, persuaded the government to set up a commission to investigate the whole guild system. As a result, an ordinance in 1800 banned strikes. A committee was set up in 1840 to consider guilds as an impediment to free economic enterprise, under which threat the Craft Association (Håndværkerforeningen) was established. Guild monopolies were finally abolished in 1857. SPO

GULDBERG, OVE HØEGH- *see* **HØEGH-GULDBERG, OVE**

GUNDELACH, FINN (1925-1981). Civil servant. He graduated *cand. oecon.* in 1951 and pursued a diplomatic career which included appointment as vice-secretary general in 1962 and vice-director general in 1965 of the General Agreement on Tariffs and Trade, GATT. When Denmark joined the **European Community** he was the first Danish European Commissioner from 1973 until his death. His successor was Henning **Christophersen**. AHT

GUNDESTRUP BOWL is a large silver-gilt Celtic bowl probably originating in the region of the lower Danube about 100 BC, and found in Rævemosen near Gundestrup in Vesthimmerland (northern **Jutland**) in 1891. Measuring 43 cm. in height and diameter and weighing over nine kilos, it is covered with plates (five on the inside and eight on the outside) inscribed with high reliefs representing religious ceremonies, hunting scenes, and processions with both Celtic and Classical overtones. SPO

GYLDENDAL, SØREN (1742-1802), was a bookseller who began by trading books with fellow students while at Copenhagen University. Beginning in 1772 he published 1,495 titles during his lifetime and was the founder of Gyldendalske Boghandel, Nordisk Forlag A/S, the largest Danish printing, publishing, and bookselling firm. AHT

GYLDENLØVE, ULRIK FREDERIK (1638-1704). Politician son of **Frederik III** with Margrethe Pape. After a military education he was appointed governor (*statholder*) of Norway in 1664. From 1670 he was in Denmark and took part in governing the country, but had to return to Norway in 1673 following disagreement with **Griffenfeldt**. In the **Scanian War** he led the Norwegian troops against Sweden, so that the episode is known in Norway as the Gyldenløve Fight. From 1679 he governed Norway from **Copenhagen**, and retired in 1699. Following an unrecognized marriage to Sophie Urne and a scandalous one to Marie **Grubbe** he married Antoinette Augusta of Aldenburg. AHT

GYLLEMBOURG, THOMASINE (1773-1856). Author. In 1790 she married P.A. **Heiberg** but fell in love with the Swedish baron Gyllembourg, whom she married in 1801 after a dramatic divorce. She began writing short stories aged 54 on woman's role in a bourgeois family, influenced by her experience of the break with Heiberg. Her many stories have a stylistic ambivalence, combining poetic realism and aesthetic idealism and were published as *En Hverdags-Historie* (1828, An Everyday Story), *Familien Polonius* (1834, The Polonius Family) and *Nye Fortællinger* (1835-36, New Tales). Her son was J.L. **Heiberg**. AHT

-H -

HÆKKERUP, PER (1915-1979). Politician. One of a remarkable dynasty of **Social Democratic** (SD) politicians, he was the son of Hans Kristian Hækkerup (1876-1929), a newspaper editor, executive mayor of Ringsted and **Folketing** member 1920-29. His wife Karen Margrethe (née Hurup) was a Folketing member 1964-66 and 1970-81 and first deputy speaker 1971-78. Two of their three sons were also active in politics: Klaus (b. 1943) was executive mayor 1978-88 of Fredensborg-Humlebæk and a Folketing member from 1988; Hans (b. 1945) was a civil servant 1973-79, a Folketing member from 1979, and minister of defense from 1993 (continuing in the 1998 government), while his wife Lise (née Gottlieb) was a Folketing member from 1990. Per's elder brother Hans (b. 1907) was a Folketing member 1945-71, minister of justice 1953-64, interior minister 1964-68, and carried through property tax reforms, the major local government reform of 1970, and the law specifying ministers' responsibilities.

Per Hækkerup himself was chairman of the SD youth movement 1946-52 and of the International Union of Socialist Youth 1946-54. He became a Folketing member 1950-79, member of the Council of Europe's advisory assembly 1953-62 and of the **Nordic Council** 1957-62, and he chaired the 1961 Danish delegation to the UN General Assembly. As foreign minister 1962-66 in Jens Otto **Krag**'s cabinets he developed a more assertive Danish foreign policy and did much to persuade the West to take a constructive part in the European Conference on Security and Co-operation. He keenly advocated Danish **European Community** (EC) membership but criticized the 1964 proposal by nonsocialist Danish parties to negotiate without regard to the British. When the 1966 election produced a socialist majority (of **Social Democrats** plus **Socialist People's Party**), he left the cabinet to chair the parliamentary group 1966-68, giving strong leadership and holding the Social Democrats together. As economy minister 1971-73 and 1975-79 he pioneered the separation of this responsibility from the finance ministry, and died in office. AHT

HAELWEGH, ALBERT (?-1673). From unknown origins, he was the royal copper-plate engraver in 1647-73. About 250 engravings from his workshop are known, 135 of them his own work. He is best known for his portraits, often working from other artists' paintings, e.g., of **Christian IV**, **Frederik III**, of members of the Council of State, and of the Swedish Queen Christina. AHT

HALL, CARL CHRISTIAN (1812-1888). Lawyer and **National Liberal** politician, prime minister 1857-59 and 1860-63. From a **Jutland** craftsman's family, he graduated *cand. jur.* in 1833 in **Copenhagen** and soon revealed considerable oratorical talents. He was elected to the **Constituent Assembly** in 1848 and, under the 1849 June **constitution**, to the **Folketing** in 1849-81. There he organized the June Union, a middle-class constitutional party opposed to the more radical **Farmers' Friends**. This developed into the **National Liberal** party, which advocated the union of **Slesvig** with the kingdom in the Ejder policy, for which Hall spoke keenly. He joined the cabinet formed by P.G. **Bang** in 1854 as minister for the church and formed his own cabinet in mid-1857 after C.G. **Andræ** retired.

His fall from power in 1859 is attributed to the unpopularity of his National Liberals with the king's wife, the powerful Countess **Danner**. But popular opposition to the succeeding regime of C.E. Rottwit compelled King **Frederik VII** to recall him at the end of 1860. The crisis which followed introduction of the November **constitution** at the end of 1863 led the new King **Christian IX** to replace Hall with Ditlev **Monrad**. Hall remained an influential political figure, even after the Second **Slesvig-Holsten** War shattered the National Liberals. He was minister of education in the cabinet of Count Holstein-Holsteinborg of 1870-73 and continued to represent his Copenhagen constituency in the Folketing until 1881, in his later years as a supporter of the conservative **Right**. SPO, AHT

HAMLET first appears as "Amleth", the son of the viceroy of **Jutland** married to Gerutha, daughter of a king of Denmark named Rorik, in books two and three of the *Gesta Danorum,* written by **Saxo Grammaticus** around 1200. His name also occurs in the Icelandic Prose Edda. Most familiar to the Anglo-Saxon reader from the Shakespeare play, he also appears in works by the Danish writers Adam **Oehlenschläger** and Johannes **Ewald**. SPO

HAMMERSHØI, VILHELM (1864-1916). Painter. The most important of the Danish Symbolists, he is best known for his placid interiors in bourgeois milieux, many of his own home, often in black, greys and browns and characterized by their intimate atmosphere and peaceful simplicity. He trained in the **Academy of Art** in 1879-84 and then studied under Peter **Krøyer**. Hammershøi first attracted attention with a portrait of his sister in 1885, but criticism of his work by the Academy led him to join other young artists in setting up the "Free Exhibition" (Den frie Udstilling) in 1891. His younger brother Svend (1873-1948) was a prominent architectural painter and ceramist. SPO, AHT. *See also* **Painting; J.F. Willumsen.**

HÅNDFÆSTNING *see* **ACCESSION CHARTER**

HANS (1455-1513). King of Denmark 1481-1513, of Norway 1483-1513, and of Sweden 1497-1501. Born in Ålborg Castle as son of King **Christian I** and queen Dorothea of Brandenburg. In 1483 the nobles of Denmark and Norway, discontent with the attempts made by Christian to strengthen royal power, subjected Hans to the Halmstad Charter, which severely restricted his room to maneuver. But this set him the task of rebuilding the authority of the crown. In foreign policy he had only limited success: Sweden was won back only briefly, and in 1500 an expedition to crush the small peasant republic of **Ditmarsken** ended in military disaster. But he was able to create an army of mercenaries under his control and so undermined the military importance of the **nobility**. He built Denmark's first true naval force to counter those of Sweden and the **Hanseatic League.** He also sought to win the support of both the peasants and the merchants against the nobility along the lines pursued by "New Monarchs" elsewhere in Europe, a policy continued by his son **Christian II.** In 1478 he married Christina of Saxony, a devout woman, who besides Christian bore him Frans, who died of plague when 14, and Elisabeth, who married the elector Joachim of Brandenburg. The royal lands were greatly enriched following the murder of Poul **Laxmand** in 1502. Hans died in **Ålborg** and was first buried in Greyfriars church in **Odense**, but in 1805 his body was moved to St. Knuds church, where it lies beside that of his wife. SPO. *See also* **Kalmar Union; Danish Relations with Sweden.**

HANSEATIC LEAGUE was a trading alliance and merchant guild based in Lübeck, which included many north German towns and extended to Visby on the Swedish island of Gotland and as far north as Bergen in Norway. Danish Hanseatic towns included Skannør, Falsterbro and Malmö. In 1361 **Valdemar Atterdag** tried to reduce Hanseatic influence in Denmark, provoking a counter attack supported by 77 of the League's members, the largest military coalition in its history. **Copenhagen** was destroyed in 1368 and the League gained control of castles on the **Sound**. This control of Denmark was consolidated at the peace of Stralsund in 1370, which allowed the League to retain control of castles on the eastern side of the Sound for fifteen years, to collect taxes in **Scania**, and to nominate **Margrethe I** as successor to Valdemar. This was the height of **Hanseatic** influence, which ended with the **Count's War** (1534-36) and the **Reformation**. AHT

HANSEN, CHRISTIAN FREDERIK (1756-1845). Architect. At the age of 10 his mother's Court connections secured him a place in the **Academy of Art**, where he was a pupil of the Classical architect Caspar Harsdorff (1735-1799). He won the Academy's gold medal in 1779 and was granted a royal bursary to travel abroad for two years, to Austria and Italy. In 1784 he was made inspector of buildings in **Holstein**, where he was responsible for designing several churches, two town halls, and private mansions in Altona in neoclassical style. In 1791 he was made titular professor of the Academy and in 1977 was called to **Copenhagen** as chief inspector of buildings and director of architecture in the Academy of Fine Arts, with the task of designing a new **Christiansborg Palace** to replace that burnt down in 1794. This was completed in 1828, but again burnt down in 1884. He was Principal of the Academy in 1811-18, 1821-27, and 1830-33. He also designed the Old Town Hall (1816, since 1903 the City Court) on Nytorv, built in 1805-15 to replace the town hall burnt down in 1795; the capital's Our Lady's Church (1826), which contains sculptures by Bertel **Thorvaldsen**; and **Christiansborg** Castle church (1829). The C.F. Hansen medal for architecture was first awarded in 1832. His simple and monumental neoclassicism was unfashionable for most of the 19th century, but his reputation rose again in the early twentieth. SPO, AHT. *See also* **Architecture**.

HANSEN, CHRISTIAN ULRIK (1921-1944). **Resistance** man. A farmer's son, on leaving school in July 1942 he became active in the resistance movement and was one of the recipients of the first landing of weapons in **Jutland**. He was arrested by the Germans in 1944 and executed on 23 June. His prison letters were circulated illegally, widely read, and published (1945) as *A Young Danish Freedom-fighter's Last Letters from Prison 1944*. AHT

HANSEN, CONSTANTIN (1804-80). Painter. As a very young student at the **Academy of Art** he first studied architecture, then painting. He lived in Italy 1835-43, painting pictures such as *A party of Danish painters in Rome* (1837). His great murals in the main hall of the University of Copenhagen (1844-53) depict themes from ancient Greek mythology. In addition to many portraits, his best-known picture is *The Constitutional Assembly* (1864). AHT. *See also* **Golden Age.**

HANSEN, EMIL CHRISTIAN (1841-1909). Physiologist and biologist. Apprenticed as a painter, he went to university in his thirties and in 1879-1909 was leader of the physiological department of the **Carlsberg** Laboratories where his original work on yeasts was of great importance to brewing and brought him world renown among bacteriologists. AHT

HANSEN, HANS CHRISTIAN (1906-1960). **Social Democrat** politician; prime minister 1955-60. Born in **Århus** to a working-class family, as an apprentice typographer he joined the Danish Young Socialists, becoming secretary in 1929 and chairman 1933-37. Elected to the **Folketing** 1936-60, he was general secretary of the Social Democrats in 1939-41. He became a link between the party politicians and the **Freedom Council** toward the end of World War II and served as finance minister in Vilhelm **Buhl**'s coalition government formed after the 1945 liberation. He was again Finance Minister 1947-50 in **Hedtoft**'s first cabinet, then trade minister, and in Hans **Hedtoft**'s second cabinet of 1953-55 was foreign minister, the first in Denmark without a university education. After taking over as prime minister on Hedtoft's death in 1955 he continued as foreign minister to 1958 but retained the premiership until just before his death. SPO, AHT

HANSEN, JENS ANDERSEN (1806-1877). Politician. A shoemaker, with Rasmus Sørensen he started the journal *Almuevennen* (Peasant's Friend) in 1842; in 1846 this became the journal of the newly formed **Farmers' Friends**. He was a member of the **constitu-**

ent assembly of 1848-49 and of the **Folketing** 1849-77, from 1854 as the real leader of the **Farmers' Party**. With the landowners he supported the 1866 **constitution** and was a co-founder of the United **Liberals** in 1870. AHT

HANSEN, JENS <u>MARTIN</u> <u>A</u>LFRED (1909-1955). Novelist, short-story writer, poet, and critic. Born in Stevns, Hansen spent much of his youth working on farms, but he trained as a teacher and taught in **Copenhagen** before deciding in 1935 to become a full-time writer. He published two social-realist novels with a rural background, *Nu opgiver han* (1935, Now He Gives Up) and *Kolonien* (1937, The Colony). The novel *Jonatans Rejse* (1941, Jonathan's Journey) is written with a lightness of tone and a sustained joy of invention that is absent from much later work. During **World War II** he contributed to the underground press and had to go into hiding. Themes of guilt, responsibility and judgment feature in his postwar writing, e.g., in *Lykkelig Kristoffer* (1945, Lucky Kristoffer, 1974). In *Leviathan* (1950) and *Orm og Tyr* (1952, Serpent and Bull) the theme is the contest between cultural radicalism and naturalism. Hansen's most widely read novel, *Løgneren* (1950, The Liar, 1969) deals with the opposition of spirit and instinct. In 1950-52 he edited the influential literary magazine *Heretica*. SPO, AHT

HANSEN (-ANKERSTRÆDE), KARL (1865-1947). Politician. The son of a tanner, he learn the trade of coachmaker but married into a smallholding at Ankerstræde near Køge (south of Copenhagen). He was co-founder and in 1902-10 chairman of De samvirkende sjællandske Husmandsforeninger (the cooperative of Zealand smallholders' associations), playing a major part in linking the smallholders' movement to the **Radical Liberals**. AHT

HANSEN (-LUNDBY), PEDER (1801-1854). Politician. The son of a smallholder, smith, and musician, he became a smallholder and, with Rasmus **Sørensen**, one of the chief protagonists for smallholders and later for all farmers, from 1842 contributing articles regularly to *Almuevennen* (The Peasant's Friend). AHT

HANSEN, THEOPHILUS (1813-1891). Architect. The son of a fire-insurance messenger, he trained at the **Academy of Art**'s School of

Architecture in **Copenhagen** then traveled abroad, living 1838-46 in Greece and 1846-48 in Vienna. His building designs in Vienna included the parliament (1874-84) and in Greece the Academy (1869-77) and the National Library (1885-92). His style was "Greek renaissance," a mixture of renaissance and classical. AHT

HANSEN, THORKILD (1927-1989). Author. The son of an architect, he studied literary history at Copenhagen University 1945-47 but then moved to Paris as correspondent 1947-52 for the newspaper *Information*, later earning his living as author and critic. After several travel books he wrote the historical-documentary novels *Det lykkelig Arabien* (1962, Arabia Felix: The Danish Expedition of 1761-1767, 1964); *Jens Munck* (1965; North-West to Hudson Bay: The Life and Times of Jens Munck, 1970; American edition: *The Way to Hudson Bay*). His trilogy on the Danish slave trade, *Slavernes kyst* (1967, The Slave Beach), *Slavernes skib* (1968, The Slave Ship), *Slavernes øer* (1970, The Slave Islands) uncovered a suppressed dimension of Danish history. His controversial three-volume *Processen mod Hamsun* (1978, The Hamsun Trial) examines the Norwegian author Knut Hamsun's pro-German stance in the occupied Norway of **World War II** and his subsequent trial for treason. Hansen's combination of scholarship, intellect, and poetic sensibility secure him prominence among writers of modern Danish prose. AHT

HANSSEN (-NØRREMØLLE), HANS PETER (1862-1936). Politician. From a South **Jutland** farming family, in 1888 he was cofounder of the North Slesvig Electoral Union and from 1893 put the Danish case in (German) Schleswig as publisher of the daily paper *Hejmdal*. He was a member of the Prussian assembly 1896-1908 and of the German parliament 1906-19 where, in 1918, he proposed the reunification of North **Slesvig** with Denmark. In 1919-20 he was minister for South Jutland affairs in Carl Theodore **Zahle**'s cabinet, and a Liberal member of the Folketing 1924-26. He drew the border between Denmark and Germany which was the result of the 1920 **referendum**. AHT. *See also* **Slesvig-Holsten**.

HARALD I "BLUETOOTH" (BLÅTAND) (c. 940-987). King of Denmark c.940-986. Son of **King Gorm** and responsible for the larger of the two rune stones at **Jelling** on which he claimed to have converted Denmark to Christianity and to rule over both Denmark and Norway, though how far his authority stretched beyond **Jutland** is uncertain. The **Trelleborg** forts may have been constructed during his reign to assist the extension of his power. He certainly involved himself in the affairs of Norway in alliance with the earls of Lade, and may have participated in **Viking** raids on England. Toward the end of his reign, however, he faced the rebellion of his son **Svend I** "Forkbeard", who deposed him. He died in the fortress of Jomsberg at the mouth of the Oder after a battle and was buried in **Roskilde**, whose first church he is reputed to have founded. He married as his first wife the Obodrit princess Tove. His second wife was Gunhild. His daughter Tyra married King Olaf Tryggvason of Norway. The epithet "Bluetooth" may be contemporary. *See also* **Conversion**. SPO

HARALD II SVENDSEN (c. 989-1018). King of Denmark 1014-1018. Son of King **Svend I** "Forkbeard" from whom he inherited Denmark, while his brother **Knud I** inherited the Danish claim to the English crown. He supported his brother in his successful bid to win England in 1015. He never married and was succeeded by Knud. SPO

HARALD III "HÉN" (c. 1041-1080). King of Denmark 1074-1080. An illegitimate son of King **Svend II** Estridsen. On the death of the latter, he was elected by a peasant assembly at Isore on Isefjord on **Zealand** against the opposition of a party which supported his brother Knud, who was to succeed him as King **Knud II**. He conducted a peaceful foreign policy and established good relations with the Church. He is reputed to have regularized the coinage and the system of weights and measures in his realm. He married his cousin Margrethe but had no children. He was buried in Dalby in **Scania**. His epithet, meaning "whetstone", is contemporary. SPO

HARDEKNUD (1018-1042). King of Denmark 1035-1042 and of England 1040-42. Son of King **Knud I** and Queen Emma. Raised in Denmark, he took over the throne on the death of his father and, supported by his mother, laid claim also to the English throne. But he had to face the threat from his half-brother Harald and from the Norwegian King Magnus (the Good), who succeeded him on the throne after he died in London without heirs. He is buried in Winchester. SPO

HARPESTRENG, HENRIK (?-1244). Doctor. After studying abroad he wrote a herbal in Latin which he translated into Danish, and a medical text in Latin. These introduced the classical hippocratic medicine which attributes illnesses to imbalances in the four cardinal humors: blood, phlegm, choler, and melancholy or black choler. He died as a canon of **Roskilde**. AHT

HARSDORFF, CASPAR FREDERIK (1735-1799). Architect. A pupil at the **Academy** from 1754, he traveled as a student 1757-64 to Paris and Rome then was appointed professor at the academy 1766-83. He introduced neoclassicism to Denmark, supervised the rebuilding (1701-02) of **Frederik IV**'s opera house in **Copenhagen** which became the present Østre Landsret (Eastern High Court). His other buildings include **Fredensborg** (1774-76), his own house at Kongens Nytorv 3-5, Copenhagen (1780), and Erichsen's Palace (1799) on Holmens Kanal, Copenhagen, now the Danish Bank. AHT

HARTLING, POUL (1914-). Liberal politician and prime minister. He graduated *cand. theol.* in 1939 and became principal of the N. **Zahle** Seminarium (Teachers' College) in 1950. He was elected to the **Folketing** for the **Liberal Party** the same year. He was one of Denmark's representatives on the **Nordic Council** and its chairman in 1967. He supported a close alliance between the Liberals and other nonsocialist parties and became foreign minister in **Hilmar Baunsgaard's** government of 1968-71, taking a close interest in development aid. His 1973-75 minority **cabinet** offered continuity after the 1973 "earthquake" **election**. The party made large gains in the election which he called in 1975, but support promised by the Progress Party was withdrawn and he would not join the subsequent **Social Democrat** cabinet, for which he was strongly criticized. He left Danish politics to become United Nations High Commissioner for Refugees, 1978-85. He chaired the council of the Danish Centre for Human Rights 1987-89 and the Democracy Fund, 1990-95. His extensive publications include political memoirs, biographies and theology. SPO, AHT

HARTMANN, JOHANN PETER EMILIUS (1805-1900). Composer. The son and grandson of composers, he graduated *cand. jur.* in 1828 studying music concurrently and continued to develop as a composer throughout his long life. His greatest inspiration for more than 200 compositions in national-romantic style was the world of Nordic myths and sagas; their influence was especially evident in his "Nordic decade" from the mid-1830s. A central figure of Danish romanticism, he bridged the generation from Daniel Friedrich **Kuhlau** to Niels Wilhelm **Gade** and Carl **Nielsen**. His works included the music to *Guldhornene* (1832, The Golden Horns) by Adam **Oehlenschläger** for recitation and orchestra, symphonies (the first in 1835, the second in 1847-48), and the Hans Christian Andersen opera *Liden Kirsten* (1846, Little Kirsten). His many choral pieces included *Vølvens Spådom* (1872, The Prophecy of the Sibyl), but also a prolific output of simple songs and hymns, many of them settings of words by the great poet and theologian N.F.S **Grundtvig**. *See also* **Music**. AHT

HEALTH INSURANCE in Denmark originated in 1892, when the **Right** administration released state funds to subsidize private health insurance companies catering to those on low incomes, to enable them to lower their premiums and increase their benefits. This help was increased in 1922 and in 1960 the scheme, while remaining voluntary, was opened to all, although those earning more than a skilled worker's wages had to contribute to the costs of treatment. An act of 1971 which took effect in 1973 replaced the subsidized companies with a national health service. Most people (97.6 percent and increasing) who are insured in Group 1 have the right to free medical help from a general medical practitioner, who may refer a patient for free specialist care, and the right to choose their practitioner (and may change after at least six months). Group 2 insured (the rest) have free choice of practitioner and specialist but must pay a part of their fees. Prescribed medicines are subsidized.

In 1990 new rules allowed for payments to parents who gave up their job or worked part-time to care for a seriously ill child under 14. Another 1990 law, the first of its kind in Europe, made good on loss of earnings for someone caring for a close relative (for example with cancer) who wished to die in their own home, on condition that the medical prognosis is terminal. The maximum payable was normally equal to the highest wage for home help (3,000 kroner per week in 1996), plus free home-help and medicines. This benefit does not provide the right to leave from work, which must be negotiated with an employer. SPO, AHT. *See also* **Welfare**.

HEATH SOCIETY (HEDESELSKABET) was founded in **Århus** in 1866 on the initiative of Colonel Enrico **Dalgas** with the object of reclaiming the heathlands of central **Jutland** by means of afforestation, conversion into arable land and turf cutting. In 1907 it moved its headquarters from Århus to **Viborg**, where it has its own laboratory. Since its foundation it has been responsible for the afforestation of some 250,000 acres, of which it administers 31,000. SPO

HEDTOFT, HANS (1903-1955). Social Democrat politician and prime minister 1947-50 and 1953-55, known until 1945 as Hedtoft-Hansen. He trained as a printer, but became secretary of the Danish Young Socialists in 1922 and general secretary and a member of the **Folketing** in 1933. He was elected chairman of the **Social Democratic Party** in 1939, but had to resign under German pressure in February 1941 together with the party's secretary H. C. Hansen. He was minister of labor and social policy in the coalition government formed by Vilhelm **Buhl** after the liberation in 1945. As chairman of the party again, he headed a minority cabinet 1947-50 which survived the 1950 election but was soon defeated on a **Justice Party** motion to end butter rationing. He formed another minority cabinet after the 1953 election brought Social Democrat gains, but died early in 1955. In 1948-49 he worked for a Nordic defense union, but when this came to nothing he secured Danish membership of **NATO**. He was the main inspiration for the **Nordic Council** in 1952, becoming its first chairman. He took great interest in **Greenland**, setting up the reform commission in 1948 and enacting its recommendations in 1950. SPO, AHT

HEERING, PETER FREDERIK (1792-1875). Manufacturer. He qualified as a herbalist in 1814 and ran his own firm from 1818, later becoming famous for a cherry liqueur which he exported in his own ships, successively as Heering's Cherry Cordial, then Heering's Cherry Brandy, then Cherry Heering Liqueur. AHT

HEIBERG, EDVARD (1897-1958). Architect. The Norwegian-born son of a mayor of Oslo, he trained at the Academy in **Copenhagen** and in 1922-24 in Paris. He was a professor 1930-31 at the Bauhaus international academy of art in Dessau, Germany, then set up his own studio in Copenhagen in 1931. Aiming for functional social housing, he designed many of the large housing developments around Copenhagen, including Blidahparken, Ryparken, Kantorparken, Bispeparken, Voldparken, and Bellahøj. AHT

HEIBERG, JOHAN LUDVIG (1791-1860), poet, dramatist, and critic. Born in **Copenhagen** to the writers Peter Andreas Heiberg and Thomasine Heiberg (née Bunzen. *See* **Thomasine Gyllembourg**), his father was exiled in 1800 and spent the remaining 40 years of his life in Paris. Heiberg remained in Denmark with his mother and spent his youth in artistic circles. At university he began to write poetry and plays and in 1819 obtained a royal grant to travel abroad. He lived for a time with his father in Paris, where he became acquainted with French vaudeville, a combination of words, music, and dance. For a few years he was Danish teacher at the University of Kiel, and became an enthusiastic disciple of G.W.F. Hegel, whose idealistic philosophy he popularized in Denmark and which profoundly influenced his own work.

Heiberg's first vaudeville was produced in Copenhagen in 1825 to public acclaim. This was followed by other works in the same genre during the next 10 years. The most popular was *Elverhøj* (Elves' Hill) of 1828 with music by **Friedrich Kuhlau**. In 1831 Heiberg married the actress Johanne Luise **Pätges**. During these years his critical writings, often published in his own journals, to which his mother (by then married to the Swedish Baron Gyllembourg) contributed, involved him in frequent clashes with his fellow writers. In 1849-56 he was director of the **Royal Theater**, which gave him a dominant position in the cultural life of the time; indeed he was one of the greatest influences on Scandinavian theatrical life. SPO. *See also* **Romanticism; Theater**.

HEIBERG, JOHANNE LUISE (née Pätges) (1812-1890). Actress and writer; wife of Johan Ludvig **Heiberg**. She entered the ballet school of the **Royal Theater** at the age of eight, but acquired fame as an actress in over 250 different roles. She appeared on the stage first in 1823 and so impressed J.L. **Heiberg** that he wrote for her the vaudeville *Aprilsnarrarne* (The April Fools), which was produced to public acclaim in 1826. She married Heiberg five years later and dominated the Danish stage for many years. She retired from public performance in 1864, but as a producer for the National Theater in 1867-74 she introduced Henrik Ibsen to the Danish stage with his *The Pretenders*. Her memoirs, which only appeared in 1891-92, a year after her death, are among the finest of the genre in Danish. SPO. *See also* **Theater**.

HEIBERG, PETER ANDREAS (1758-1841). Author. He passed the linguistic examination in 1777 but was a writer from the 1880s. In songs, comedies, and satires and in the journal *Rigsdalersedlens hændelser* (1787-93) in a spirit of enlightenment he attacked the nobility of the authoritarian monarchy, German influences, and the problems of the time. Under a new law limiting press freedom he was convicted and banished in 1799. From 1800 he lived in Paris. He was married 1790-1801 to Thomasine **Gyllembourg** and their son was Johan Ludvig **Heiberg**. AHT

HEIDENREICH, NIELS (1761-1844). Thief. The son of a deacon, in 1788 he was sentenced to death for forging bank notes, but the sentence was commuted to imprisonment for life. He was released in 1798 and became a goldsmith and clockmaker, gaining access to the Royal Museum (Kunstkammeret) in **Christiansborg**. From there in 1802 he stole the two **Gallehus Horns** and melted them down. He was imprisoned to serve out his original sentence but released in 1840. The theft inspired Adam **Oehlenschläger**'s 1802 poem, *Guldhornene*. AHT

HEIN, PIET (1905-1996). Poet, designer, scientist and polymath. He graduated in mathematics in 1924, studied at the Royal Academy of Arts in Stockholm, Sweden, then returned to **Copenhagen** to study philosophy and theoretical physics at the Neils **Bohr** Institute. Among other things he later designed the Polygon board game and the three-dimensional SOMA cube puzzle. His greatest invention is the "super-ellipse," a rectangular oval which he first used to design the city center of Stockholm and has applied to many industrial designs. The recipient of numerous awards, Hein is committed to fostering international toleration, and to harmony between the natural sciences and the humanities. His poetry (written under the pen-name Kumbel, from Old Norse *kumbl,* a stone with inscription) is immediately accessible and has been widely translated. It takes the form of "gruks," his invented word for epigrammatic poems which concentrate a wise thought about life in a few elegant, often humorous lines, often paradoxes or puns, usually with a small illustrative sketch. In 1968 he helped to found the Danish Association for the Promotion of Discoveries (Dansk Forening til Fremme af Opfindelser). He gave the 1983 Nobel lecture: "Creative Thinking in Science and in Human Relations." His numerous awards include an honorary Doctor of Humane Letters from Yale University (1972) and an honorary doctorate from **Odense** University. AHT

HEINESEN, (ANDREAS) WILLIAM (1900-1991). Faroese novelist and poet. The son of a businessman in Tórshavn, Heinesen studied commerce in **Copenhagen,** but turned to journalism and to writing poetry. After returning to Tórshavn in 1932, he adopted the novel as his principal means of expression and produced seven between then and 1976, the best known being *De fortabte Spillemænd* (1950, *The Lost Musicians,* 1972), a "collective" novel in which the sectarian prohibitionists are confronted by the unsophisticated poor of Tórshavn. At other levels this can be read as a conflict between life and anti-life forces, or as social and economic conflict. Short stories predominate in Heinesen's work from 1957 and in the 1960s again composed poetry. The setting for his work is always his native **Faroe Islands,** although he writes in Danish and has gained recognition as a leading 20th-century Scandinavian novelist for his constant imagination and stylistic brilliance. SPO, AHT

HEISE, PETER (1830-1879) was a composer and organist who wrote chamber music, cantatas, and numerous songs and ballads in a romantic style, and the most important 19th century Danish opera, *Drot og marsk* (1878). AHT. *See also* **Music.**

HELGESEN, POVL (Paulus Helie) (c. 1485-c. 1535), a Carmelite monk, theologian, and historian. He was a sharp critic of papal malpractices and of Kings **Christian II** and **Frederik I,** but defended the church against the growing **Lutheran** reform movement of the 1520s in his *Skibbykrøniken,* a history found in 1650 walled into

Skibby church. He was the leading biblical humanist and Catholic reformer of his time. AHT

HELSINGØR *see* **ELSINORE**

HEMMINGSEN, NIELS (1513-1600). Theologian. A farmer's son, as a student he traveled to the home of **Lutheranism**, Wittenberg, where he stayed four years and was strongly influenced by Philip Melanchton. In 1545-79 at Copenhagen University he held several professorships, including theology. His numerous theological writings have a strongly moralizing tone: *Om ægteskab* (1572, On Marriage) was the basis for the Marriage Law of 1572. He was dismissed in 1579, accused of Calvinist sympathies, living his remaining years in **Roskilde** and recovering some of his influence. AHT

HENNING, GERHARD (1880-1967). Sculptor. Born in Stockholm and trained in Gothenburg, he settled in **Copenhagen** in 1909 and became a Danish citizen in 1931. At the **Royal Porcelain** Factory in 1915 and 1920-25, he produced delicate Rococo figures. Then, under the influence of **Kai Nielsen**, he began to produce the monumental female figures for which he is best known. SPO

HENNINGSEN, POUL (1894-1967). Author, architect, and industrial designer, son of Agnes Henningsen, an author who wrote in defense of the liberated woman. An advocate of simple functionalism, Poul designed a dazzle-free "PH-lamp" which sold world-wide. As a writer in the 1930s he opposed reaction and fascism, and in the 1960s as editor of the consumer magazine *Tænk* (Think) opposed consumerist advertising. He also wrote many songs which became widely known and made an important documentary film, *Denmark* (1935). AHT

HERETICA was a very influential literary journal founded in 1948 to introduce European modernism to Denmark, to counter the rationalist and realist currents of the time, and to encourage the formation of a Danish school of literature — although it prided itself on its freedom from ideological commitment. Its founders were the poet Thorkild Bjørnvig and Bjørn Poulsen, teachers at the University of Århus and most of its contributors were poets, but much of the inspiration came from **Karen Blixen**. It was edited by the novelist

Martin A. Hansen and the poet Ole Wivel (1921-) in 1950-52 and by the poet and novelist Frank Jæger (1926-77) and Tage Schou-Hansen until it ceased publication in 1954. SPO

HERHOLDT, JOHAN DANIEL (1818-1902). Architect. He trained as a carpenter but turned to architecture and was named titular professor at the **Academy** of Art in 1863. He was a Royal Surveyor of Buildings 1881-92. Responsible for the italianate University Library in **Copenhagen** (1855-61), he also designed the National Bank (1866-70) the first Main Railway Station in the capital (1863-64), and private villas, including one for **Johanne Luise Heiberg**, which established a trend. SPO. *See also* **Architecture**.

HERLUFSHOLM School is run in modern times on lines similar to an English private ("public") school with about 180 pupils and 15 staff. The manor, near Næstved, was acquired from Frederik II in 1560 by Admiral Herluf Trolle, who left it on his death in 1565 as a school for sons of the nobility "and other honest people in Denmark," which was founded soon after by his widow **Birgitte Gøye**. The original monastery buildings are ruined but the 12th century chapel was restored in 1859 by **J.D. Herholdt**. It contains memorial tablets to former pupils who fell resisting the Germans in 1940-45, including **Anders Lassen**. There is a unique 13th-century crucifix carved from a single elephant tusk. *See also* **Sorø Academy**. AHT

HEROLD, VILHELM (1865-1937). Opera tenor. He trained as a teacher and taught in **Copenhagen** from 1889 while taking singing lessons. He made his debut at the **Royal Theater** in 1893 but in 1903-15 toured the national theaters of Europe with roles in the operas of Gounod, Bizet, Leoncavallo, **Heise**, Wagner, Verdi, and Puccini. AHT

HERREDAG, THE, was a strengthened Royal Council which met as the Supreme Court of Denmark from the later years of the 15th century to the introduction of **absolute monarchy** in 1661. *See also* **Courts; Danehoff; Parliament**. SPO

HERREDSTING *see* **COURTS**

HERTZ, HENRIK (1797/8-1870). Author. He graduated *cand. jur.* in 1825 and, after travel in Italy, earned his living as a writer. He was closely associated with **Johan Ludvig Heiberg,** and especially to **Johanne Luise Heiberg** to whom many of his 54 plays are dedicated. These included satirical comedies of everyday life — *Flytte-dagen* (1825, Removal Day) and *Sparekassen* (1836, The Savings Bank); comedies such as *Amors genistreger* (1830, Cupid's Blunders), the tragedies *Svend Dyrings hus* (1837) and *Valdemar Atterdag* (1839), and the little romantic drama, *Kong Renés datter* (1845, King René's Daughter). He also wrote poems and novels. AHT

HIMMELBJERGET, a hill west of **Århus**, was the scene of an assembly called in 1839 by **Steen Steensen Blicher** to arouse national and pan-Scandinavian feelings and has been a popular venue for similar large assemblies ever since. There is now a memorial stone to Blicher on its slopes and a tower at its summit put up in 1875 to commemorate the **constitutions** of 1849 and 1866. At 147 m (482 feet) it is not as high as Yding Skovhøj, Denmark's highest point, which is 173 m (568 ft). SPO, AHT

HIORT LORENZEN, PETER (1791-1845). Politician and trader. As a member 1834-40 and 1841-45 of the Slesvig Assembly he initially worked with the German liberals against the **Slesvig-Holsten** aristocracy but from 1840 he went over to the Danish movement and in 1842 he persisted in speaking Danish despite the prohibition on doing so in the Assembly chamber. This gesture made him one of the leading representatives of the Danish-minded Slesvigers. AHT

HIRSCHSPRUNG GALLERY is a building designed by H. Storck and built in **Copenhagen** in 1911 with funds from the Copenhagen City Council to house the collection of Danish paintings, largely of the **Golden Age** and the **Skagen School**, which was donated to the city in 1902 by the tobacco manufacturer, Heinrich Hirschsprung (1836-1908). SPO

HISTORIOGRAPHY. The earliest history writing in Denmark which has survived dates from the middle of the 12th century, when an anonymous cleric composed the "Roskilde Chronicle." Svend Aggesen later in the century produced a short history of the country in Latin, while at the beginning of the 13th century **Saxo Gram-**

maticus wrote the much more ambitious *Gesta Danorum*, a history of Denmark in 16 books from the earliest times to c.1185. At the time of the **Reformation**, **Poul Helgesen** in his *Skibbykrøniken* introduced some analysis of causes, and in the reign of **King Christian III**, Hans Svaning (1500-84) produced a semi-official history of the reign of **King Hans**. He was succeeded as unofficial historiographer-royal by Anders Sørensen Vedel (1542-1616), who translated Saxo into Danish in 1575, but was overshadowed by the statesman **Arild Huitfeldt**, who continued Saxo for most of the Early Middle Ages and much of the 15th and 16th centuries. The first of the 10 volumes of his *Danmark Riges Krønike* (Chronicle of the Kingdom of Denmark) appeared in 1595. For its later sections he was able to refer to documents in the royal archives, and the accounts given by Saxo and himself were largely accepted until the 18th century.

They were then seriously questioned by **Ludvig Holberg** in his *Danmarks riges historie* (1732-35, History of the Kingdom of Denmark), which swept away much of the mythology which had previously passed for Denmark's earlier history. In the 19th century the liberal cause was most effectively championed by **Carl Ferdinand Allen** who wrote about Scandinavia as a whole at the beginning of the 16th century, while the new historiography associated with the German historian Leopold von Ranke was introduced to Denmark first by professor **Caspar Paludan-Müller** and then by professor Kristian Erslev (1852-30). The latter in particular created new standards of research by emphasizing the critical use of sources at Copenhagen University, where he was professor 1883-1916 and national archivist (*rigsarkivar*) 1916-24. In the 20th century the study of rural history, associated particularly with Professor Fridlev Skrubbeltrang, has occupied a central place in Danish historiography.

The Danish Historical Association (Dansk historisk forening) was formed in 1839, and its journal *Historisk Tidskrift* first appeared in 1840. Under the editorship of J.A. Fridericia (1849-1912) from 1897 it acquired a status to match that of similar journals in the leading European countries. SPO

Troels Troels-Lund wrote the major study of 16th-century Danish cultural history. **Erik Arup**, professor of history 1916-47 in **Copenhagen**, saw the historian's task as ordering the facts according to a comprehensive view, saw economic and agricultural history as the backbone, and argued against nationalistic and king-centered historical writing. Vilhelm La Cour's *Danmarks historie* I and II (1939-40, History of Denmark) and *Danmarks historie 1900-1945* (1950) were colored by his conservative nationalism and his engagement in the campaign to recover Southern Jutland (*see* **Slesvig**).

A radical generation of historians, with progressive views close to those of **P. Munch** and the **Radical Liberal Party**, led to publication in the 1960s of 14 volumes of *Politikens Danmarks Historie* (*Politiken*'s History of Denmark). Its 15-volume successor, *Gyldendal og Politikens Danmarkshistorie* (1988-91) strives for a more impartial perspective. A well-illustrated single-volume edition, *Danmarkshistoriens Hvem Hvad og Hvornår* (1996, The Who, What and When of Danish History) was written by Benito Scocozza and Grethe Jensen.

Historians at **Århus** University from the 1930s, led by Troels Fink, focused on Slesvig and published the journal *Jyske Samlinger* (Jutland Collections). From 1968 the introduction of a Marxist perspective led to a highly controversial dialogue, largely conducted in the pages of *Fortid og Nutid* (Past and Present). AHT

HJALF, VIGGO (1900-1985). Soldier of the **Resistance**. The son of a farmer, he joined the army and in Autumn 1943 was chief of the illegal 'mini-general staff' established by **Ebbe Gørtz**. He was accused of discriminating against Communist groups in the distribution of weapons and later brought a case against the **Communist** newspaper *Land og Folk*: as a result its editor was sentenced to three months in prison for defamation in 1960. AHT

HJELMSLEV, LOUIS (1899-1965). Linguist. He graduated *magister* in 1923, *dr. phil.* in 1932, and was professor of comparative linguistics at Copenhagen University 1937-65. His research into the general laws and structures for the development of language made him an international leader in his field. In addition to many articles his major works were *Omkring sprogteoriens grundlæggelse* (1943, Foundations of the Theory of Language) and *Sproget. En introduction* (1963, Language: an Introduction). AHT

HØEG, PETER (1957-). Author. After school at **Frederiksberg** Gymnasium and graduating *mag. art.* in literature from **Copenhagen University** in 1984, his occupations have included dancer, actor, fencer, sailor, and mountaineer. He published a highly successful thriller, *Frøken Smillas Fornemmelsen for Sne* (1992, *Miss Smilla's Feeling for Snow*, 1992, filmed as *Smilla's Feeling for Snow*, 1997); a psychological study of schoolchildren, *De måske egnede* (1993, *Borderliners*, 1993); *Forestillinger om det Tyvende Århundrede* (1988, *The History of Danish Dreams*, 1995); and *Kvinden og Aben* (1996, *The Woman and the Ape*). Acclaimed as the foremost Danish writer of his generation, he has been awarded prizes that include the Best Crime Novel in Scandinavia (1993) and the Golden Laurels for Author of the Year (1993 and 1996). AHT

HØEGH-GULDBERG, OVE (1731-1808). Statesman. Born Ove Guldberg into a middle-class family in Horsens, he became in 1761 professor of rhetoric at **Sorø Academy**. As tutor from 1764 and later secretary to the Crown-Prince Frederik, he headed the administration which took power after the downfall of Johann Friedrich **Struensee** in 1772. He was ennobled as Høegh-Guldberg and appointed secretary to the Privy Council in 1774. Of only limited imagination, he inaugurated a period of conservative stagnation rather than reaction. His only important reforms were the introduction of Danish instead of German as the language of command in the army and of the Court and in 1776 the exclusion from State employment of all who were not born in either Denmark or **Slesvig-Holsten** (*indfødsretslov*, citizenship law). He was removed from office in the coup d'état which took the Crown Prince to the throne in 1784 as **Frederik VI**, but was appointed lord lieutenant (*stiftsamtmand*) in **Århus**, holding the post until 1802 and becoming highly respected. *See also* **Christian VII**. SPO

HØFDING, HARALD (1845-1931). Philosopher. Graduating *cand. theol.* in 1865 and *dr. phil.* in 1870, he was professor of philosophy at Copenhagen University 1883-1915. He was a follower of a humanistically-based morality of happiness in which the fully formed personality was the ultimate goal of existence. In the theory of knowledge he was an empiricist: in his understanding, psychology was therefore a science of experience. His many books included *Psykologi i omrids på grundlag af erfaringen* (1882, Outline of Psychology based on Experience), *Etik* (1887, Ethics), and *Den nyere filosofis historie* (1894, The History of Recent Philosophy). AHT

HØGSBRO, SOFUS (1822-1902). Liberal politician. He graduated *cand. theol.* in 1848 but taught in high school, taking up the views of **N.F.S. Grundtvig**, and was elected for the **Liberal Party** to the **Folketing** 1858-1902. On the **constitution** he favored compromise with the **Right**, but could not accept the 1894 compromise, so joined the Reform Liberals and was their chairman 1895-1897. AHT

HØJGAARD, KNUD (1878-1968). Civil engineer. He graduated *cand. polyt.* in 1903 and worked in the USA and then with **Christiani & Nielsen** in Russia. In 1918 he founded and ran the international construction firm which became Højgaard & Schultz A/S, single-handed after his partner Sven Schultz died in 1932. The firm pioneered the use of reinforced concrete and prefabricated building modules. Its constructions include harbors in Gdynia and Funchal, district heating in Reykjavik, the **Tivoli** concert hall, and the Great Belt and Øresund **bridges**. In 1996 the company employed 2,800 and had a turnover of 3.2 billion kroner. Politically conservative, in summer 1940 he tried unsuccessfully to persuade King **Christian X** to dismiss the multi-party **Stauning** government and appoint a non-party cabinet of businessmen headed by Prince **Axel**. In 1944 Højgaard used most of his fortune to establish Knud Højgaards Fond, the foundation which owns most of the company's capital. AHT

HOLBERG, LUDVIG (1684-1754). Dano-Norwegian dramatist, essayist, and historian, born and schooled in Bergen. Holberg's father had worked his way up from peasant to noble status, but died when his son was still young, and the boy was raised by a series of relations until entering the University of Copenhagen in 1702. He eventually graduated in theology and became a private tutor in Christiansand. A lengthy stay (1706-08) in England, where he studied at Oxford University, impressed him greatly. Holberg never lived again in his native Norway but settled in **Copenhagen**, where he was appointed supernumerary professor of philosophy in 1714. In 1714-16 he traveled in France and Italy. Soon after his return he began to produce the stream of satires which first attracted public attention. In 1722 a theater opened in Copenhagen to produce plays in Danish. To this Holberg contributed *Den politiske kandestøber* (The Political Tinker), the first of no less than 27 comedies in the spirit of

Molière that he wrote before the theater closed in 1728. On these rest his fame as the founder of Danish drama, but he wrote further comedies for the **Royal Theater** after it opened in 1748. Holberg renovated Danish literature and contributed to the development of the language by ridiculing those who used Latin, French, or German to impress people and acquire prestige, thus rescuing Danish from the Germanizing influence which predominated at court. After his initial outpouring, he turned to history (he was appointed professor of history in 1730) and produced histories of Denmark-Norway which swept away many of the myths previously surrounding the subject. In the 1740s Holberg began to publish moral-philosophical fantasies and essays in the spirit of Montaigne. He never married and bequeathed his considerable fortune to **Sorø Academy**. In 1747 he was made a baron. Some of his plays still form part of the regular repertoire of the Royal Theater, the most popular being *Jeppe på Bjerget* (Jeppe of the Hill) about a drunken peasant who is made to believe that for a day he is a landlord. His tomb in Sorø church was sculpted by **Johannes Wiedewelt**. His statue sits beside the entrance to the Royal Theater SPO, AHT. *See also* **Enlightenment; Historiography; Theater**.

HOLGER DANSKE is a legendary Danish figure mentioned in the Song of Roland as Ogier the Dane who fought in Charles the Great's battle against the Arabs. He entered folk song in the 15th century via Norway. In Danish folklore he is depicted as the national hero who sleeps until Denmark is in danger; the version in **Zealand** is that he lies under **Kronborg Castle** (where there is a massive stone statue of him in a cellar). **Friedrich Ludwig Aemilius Kunzen** composed an opera entitled *Holger Danske*. The name was also used by a **resistance** group in 1943-45. Although several times depleted by arrests, the group was responsible for many sabotage actions and the deaths of about 200 informers. Its members, some 400 by the end of the war, included **Jens Lillelund**, Bent Faurschou-Hviid, and Jørgen Haagen Schmith. AHT

HOLMBOE, VAGN (1909-1996) was the most distinguished Danish composer of his generation. He was born in Horsens, **Jutland**, and studied at the Royal Music Conservatory in **Copenhagen** under the musicologist Knud Jeppesen (b.1890) and the composer Finn

Høffding (b.1899). On study visits to Berlin for tuition by Ernst Toch he met and soon married the Romanian pianist Meta Graf. Holmboe taught music at the Copenhagen Institute for the Blind for 10 years, moving to the Conservatoire in 1950 and was professor of composition there 1955-65. He taught some of the most eminent Nordic composers, including the Danes **Per Nørgård** and **Ib Nørholm** and the Norwegian Arne Nordheim. In 1947-55 he was music critic of the newspaper *Politiken*.

Like all Danish composers of his generation, Holmboe was strongly attracted to **Carl Nielsen,** of whom he is in many ways the successor, but in Romania he also became interested in the research into folk music by Béla Bartok, whose influence is evident in his chamber music. He was also knowledgeable in 17th- and 18th-century music, and belongs to the European tradition of technical skill, artistic clarity, and expressive spirituality. Besides 13 numbered symphonies and a *Sinfonia in Memoriam* (1955), he wrote a remarkable set of intertwined sinfonias for strings, *Kairos* (1960-62, Time).

The first symphony shows East European folk music influences but from the second (1938-39) onward Holmboe developed a powerful atmospheric orchestral style which combines the structural cohesion of Sibelius' later symphonies with a dynamic use of tonality deriving from Nielsen and Bartok. In the sixth and seventh symphonies (1940s) he evolved his vitally open-ended metamorphosis technique which allows the musical material, rather than a traditional format, to determine the internal structure of the work. At the same time he started on the series of 21 string quartets which rank alongside those of Bartok, Shostakovich, or Simpson and, with the symphonies, comprise his most significant compositions. Synthesis above all else was his guiding principle and can be heard clearly in his eleventh (1980) and twelfth (1988) symphonies, typically magical combinations of vigor and serenity.

Holmboe also wrote much choral music, including the beautiful Latin motets of *Liber Canticorum* (1951-84). His larger choral-and-orchestral works, such as the *Requiem for Nietzsche* (1963-64), explore dark vistas: *Sinfonia Sacra* (1941), his fourth, commemorates his younger brother Ebbe who died in a Nazi concentration camp. More playful pieces include early neoclassical concertos, the *Notturno* (1940) for wind quintet and the rollicking Concerto for Brass (1984). His books include *Mellemspil* (1961, Interlude expanded

(1988), and *Samklang*, a collection of his musical examples and Meta's photographs. AHT

HOLSØE, POUL (1873-1966). Architect. Born in Elsinore, he graduated from the **Academy** in 1903, undertook a study-trip to Italy, and settled in **Copenhagen** in 1904. During the 1920s his style was neoclassical , but he then turned to functionalism, of which his Meat Market (*Kødbyen*, 1931-34) in Copenhagen is considered to be the best example in Denmark. He was Copenhagen City Architect in 1925-43 and Principal of the Academy of Art, 1928-31 and 1937-40. SPO

HOLSTEIN (LEDREBORG), Count LUDVIG (1839-1912). Politician. The son of a landowner, he took over the Ledreborg estate on **Zealand** on his father's death in 1895. He graduated *cand. polit.* in 1866 and was a member of the **Folketing** 1872-90, initially as an independent conservative and from 1875 for *Venstre*, the **Liberal Party**, but resigned when he failed to reach agreement with the **Right**. He was prime minister briefly in August-October 1909, following the **Alberti** scandal. AHT

HOLSTEN (HOLSTEIN-GOTTORP) was a duchy with lands in **Slesvig** and **Holstein**, some shared with the King of Denmark. In 1474 Christian I got the German kaiser to agree that Holsten should be united with Stormarn and Ditmarsken and raised in status to a duchy (dukedom). The dukes traced their claims back to Adolf, younger son of King **Frederik I,** who received the lands in 1544 from King **Christian III**. A fresh division was made between the duke and the king in 1581. But relations between the two men and their successors were ill-defined and led to frequent disputes, of which Denmark's neighbors took advantage. The marriage of King Charles X of Sweden and the daughter of Duke Frederik III in 1654 confirmed Sweden's support for the duke's claims against the Danish king's attempts to gain his lands. In 1676-79 Denmark occupied the ducal lands in Slesvig, but had to leave at the peace. In 1682 came a fresh occupation, and outright annexation in 1684. The threat of war in the Baltic between Denmark and Sweden over the issue brought in the Great Powers, who in 1689 forced Denmark to restore the duke to his lands and rights by the Treaty of Altona and guaranteed the settlement.

The **Great Northern War** began in 1700 with a fresh Danish occupation of Slesvig, which soon had to be relinquished by the Peace of Travendal, however. By the Treaty of **Fredensborg**, which ended Denmark's participation in the Great Northern War, Denmark gained the Gottorp lands in Slesvig under the guarantee of Britain and France. But the duke refused to recognize the settlement and a crisis arose when he married the daughter of Peter the Great of Russia, who backed his claims. War nearly broke out again in 1762 when Duke Karl Peter Ulrich ascended the Russian throne as Tsar Peter III. His death a few months later saved the situation. His wife and successor Catherine the Great agreed, by the so-called *mageskifte* in 1773, on behalf of her son Paul that on his accession, Denmark could annex all the Gottorp territories in exchange for the duchies of **Oldenburg** and Delmenhorst in northwest Germany, which had been retained by the kings of Denmark when they ascended the throne in the 15th century. SPO. *See also* **Slesvig-Holsten**.

HOME RULE PARTY, FAROESE *(Sjálvstyrisflokkurin)*. Founded under the leadership of Jóannes Patursson in 1906 to oppose the **Unionist Party**, it has stood for the greatest measure of autonomy for the islands and for the granting to the **Faroese language** equal status with Danish there. The party split in 1939 over land reform, and a faction led by Patursson joined the Economic Party to form the **People's Party** and took a large number of **Home Rule Party** voters with them. In 1981 the party entered a center-right coalition with the People's Party and the Unionists and in 1984 a center-left coalition with the **Social Democrats**. In 1989 it was briefly a member of a new center-right coalition. It was represented in the cabinet formed in 1993 under the Social Democrat Marita Petersen and also in the administration of Edmund Joensen which took office in 1994. It gained two of the 32 seats in the Lagting in the 1994 elections and 5.6 percent of the vote. SPO. *See also* **Faroe Islands.**

HØRDUM, CHRISTEN (1846-1911). Politician. As a shoemaker, he became an active trade unionist and joined the **Social Democrats** (SD), becoming chairman 1878-82 and, with P. Holm was one of

the first two SD members of the **Folketing** 1884-87 and 1890-1909.
AHT

HORNEMAN, CHRISTIAN FREDERIK EMIL (1840-1906).
Composer. He was taught by his musician father and then at Leipzig
conservatoire 1857-60. During his lifetime he was considered the
natural successor to **Niels W. Gade** and **J.P.E. Hartmann**. He
studied at Leipzig at the same time as the Norwegian composer
Greig, but his independence of thought made him the link between
Gade and **Carl Nielsen**. His work includes cantatas and stage music. His incidental music to Holger **Drachmann's** play *Gurre* (1900-
01) is light textured, full of charming, gracious invention, and
beautifully scored. He worked for 24 years on his opera, *Aladdin*,
before its production in 1888. AHT. *See also* **Music**.

HORNEMANN, EMIL (1810-1890). Medical doctor. Even as a student he began working on epidemiology, graduating *cand. med.* in
1834 and *dr. med.* in 1839. He was a pioneer in the prevention of
cholera and the building of sound housing for workers. After the
major cholera outbreak in **Copenhagen** of 1853 he had the medical
association's housing built at Østerbro in Copenhagen, together with
other health promotion schemes. AHT

HØRRING, HUGO (1842-1909). Politician and prime minister. A
civil servant, he was appointed interior minister 1894-97 and prime
minister 1897-1900 for the last cabinet of the Right before the
Change of System. AHT

HØRUP, VIGGO LAURITZ BENTHEIM (1841-1902). Lawyer,
journalist, and radical politician. A law graduate (1867), he became
a journalist and the most effective contributor to the Liberal newspaper *Morgenbladet* after its foundation in 1873. He was elected to
the **Folketing** for Køge in 1876 and in 1878 joined **Christen Berg**
in forming a radical parliamentary group to protest against the
agreement between the **Moderate Liberals** and the conservative
administration of **J.B.S. Estrup**. In the election of 1879, for which
Hørup coined the phrase "None above and none beside the Folketing" (*Ingen over og ingen ved siden af folketinget*), the radicals
gained more seats than the Moderates. During the 1883 defense de-

bate Hørup coined the pacifist phrase "What use will it be?" (*Hvad skal det nytte?*), arguing for a "European" *Venstre* against Bøjesen's "nationalist" *Venstre*. Forced out of *Morgenbladet* in 1884, with **E. Brandes** he founded the much more influential and successful newspaper *Politiken*, editing it until 1901. Hørup lost his Folketing seat in 1892 when he opposed any agreement with the conservative administration. In **J.H. Deuntzer**'s cabinet formed in 1901 after the **Change of System**, he was minister of transport. A liberal parliamentarian, he opposed nationalism and armaments. SPO. *See also* **Press**.

HOSPITALS. In the Middle Ages the care of the sick was mainly the responsibility of monasteries. The so-called houses of the Holy Ghost found in Danish towns from the 13th century were intended for the elderly and the incurable rather than to provide medical treatment. Not until the 18th century did hospitals in the modern sense begin to appear, beginning with the King Frederik Hospital (Det kongelige Frederiks Hospital) in **Copenhagen** in 1757. But this and its immediate successors were intended for the poor who could not be treated at home and for those who it was hoped could be cured in a short time and returned to work, so their inmates tended to be young men. Provincial hospitals in the later 18th century often consisted of only a few beds and had no resident medical staff. By an Act of 1806 one or two such hospitals were to be built in every county, but not until after 1840 was much progress made in implementing this program, and by 1880 there were still only about 100 hospitals with a total of 3,800 beds in the kingdom and by 1912 there were 167. SPO

In 1975 there were 31,100 hospital beds, averaging 612 per 100,000 inhabitants, a higher average than in any of the other Nordic countries. Following developments in treatment which give greater emphasis to early discharge and day-case treatment, the total declined to 22,200 beds and the average to 427 in 1993. Active (full-time equivalent) health personnel, including physicians, dentists, qualified and auxiliary nurses, midwives, and physiotherapists averaged 1,808 per 100,000 population in 1991, of whom 989 worked in hospitals. These averages are a little lower than in Norway and Sweden but higher than Finland and Iceland. **Local government** reforms in the 1970s made most Danish hospitals the responsibility of counties (*amter*), with grant aid from the state. Some research institutes and large hospitals are controlled directly by the state, e.g., the National Hospital (Rigshospitalet) in Copenhagen, which replaced the King Frederik Hospital in 1910. AHT

HØST, OLUF (1884-1966). Painter. After various art schools, he started painting in 1909, returning to his native **Bornholm** in 1929 to become the leading depicter of the island's landscape in an expressionist and colorist style. AHT

HOUMANN, BØRGE (1902-1994). Politician, member of the **resistance**, and publisher. After school in England he worked on the state railway as a cabin boy and traffic assistant, joining the Communist Party at age 24. From 1935 he was manager of the party's newspaper *Arbejderbladet* (The Worker's Paper). From 1940 he worked on arrangements for an underground press and then illegally published *Land og Folk*. He helped to form the *Frit Danmark* (Free Denmark) resistance group and the sabotage group BOPA. He represented the **Communist Party** 1943-45 on the **Freedom Council** and was elected to the **Folketing** 1945-47. He edited *Land og Folk* 1945-55 but retired from active politics in 1958 when the **Socialist People's Party** was formed. Thereafter he ran his own publishing firm, Sirius, and brought out a series of books by and about Martin Andersen **Nexø**. AHT

HØYEN, NIELS LAURITS (1798-1870), the founder of Danish art history. In the absence of any tradition in his discipline in Denmark, he taught himself in Germany and Italy during a tour in 1822-25. He was strongly influenced by the German art historian C.F. Rumohr, who visited Denmark. He founded the Society of Artists (Kunstforeningen) in 1827 and in 1828 was made responsible for organizing the national portrait collection in the castle of **Frederiksborg** and the royal picture collection, which became the State Museum of Art. He became an associate professor in art history and mythology, championing the preservation of Denmark's artistic heritage. Høyen's lectures to the **Academy of Art** from 1829 and at the University of Copenhagen from 1856 exercised a dominating influence on the interpretation of Danish art. Rather conservative in his taste for romantic historical paintings and later for national realism, his views were too narrowly nationalistic for the healthy development of Danish art. SPO, AHT

HØYER, CORNELIUS (1741-1804). Painter. He studied at the **Academy of Art** 1755-64 and then for four years in France and Italy where he developed the skills of a miniaturist, securing appointment as court miniature painter in 1769 and also working for the Swedish, Russian and German courts. His subjects included **Christian VII**, H.C. Schimmelmann, **A.G. Moltke**, **A.P. Bernstorff** and **C. Colbiørnsen**. AHT

HUITFELDT, ARILD (1546-1609). Historian. Born in Bergen, he was sent to **Copenhagen** at the age of 10 and after traveling abroad, entered the Royal Chancery in 1570. Overwork led him to retire after only 10 years, but in 1586 he was appointed Chancellor of the Realm, a post which he retained until his death. His access to official archives allowed him to use very many sources which have since been lost. He wrote several historical works culminating in the composition in Danish in 1596-1603 of *Danmarkes Riges Krønike* (Chronicle of the Kingdom of Denmark), a history of Denmark which continued the history of **Saxo Grammaticus** until 1558, for long the standard source for knowledge of early medieval Denmark. He used his historical writing to defend the elected **monarchy**, under which the **nobility** and the King reign jointly. SPO. *See also* **Frederik II; Historiography**.

HURWITZ, STEPHAN (1901-1981). **Ombudsman**. The son of a factory owner, he graduated *cand. jur.* in 1926 and was professor of legal procedure at Copenhagen University 1935-55. He was the first holder (1955-71) of the position of *ombudsmand* (the Danish spelling), following its establishment (modeled on the Swedish *Justitieombudsman*) by the 1953 **constitution**. He did much to develop and publicize the role in Denmark and worldwide. AHT

HVIDT, LAURITZ NICOLAI (1777-1856). Politician. The son of a drysalter, he graduated *cand. theol.* in 1795 but took over the business on his father's death, reviving it in 1816 after the trade depression 1807-14 caused by the war and soon becoming the largest ship owner in Denmark. He led the liberal citizens of **Copenhagen** during the 1830s and 1840s and was a member of the **Consultative Assembly** for the Islands 1835-48. He was also chairman of the Copenhagen city council 1841-53 and in this capacity led a procession to **Christiansborg** to demand that the king change his ministers. He was minister without portfolio in **A.W. Moltke**'s government of March-November 1848 and a member of the **constituent assembly** of 1848-49. AHT

- I -

ICELAND is a large island in the North Atlantic. Since 1944 it has been an independent republic, but until then it was part of the Danish realm, with the king of Denmark as its head of state. It was settled from western Norway and from the Scandinavian possessions in the Celtic world to its south at the end of the 9th and beginning of the 10th century. Converted to Christianity in 1000, for over two centuries (the Commonwealth Period) the Icelanders ruled themselves through a unique political system without an executive head. This was also the period when the Saga literature flourished. It ended in 1262-64 when the Icelanders swore allegiance to the king of Norway. With the union of the Danish and Norwegian crowns under King **Oluf III** in 1380, Iceland came to be ruled from **Copenhagen**. In 1402 the Black Death reached Iceland and caused enormous loss of life during the subsequent three years. In 1602 the Danish crown granted a monopoly of all trade with Iceland to the merchants of **Copenhagen**, Malmö, and **Elsinore**. A third of the population was wiped out in a smallpox epidemic in 1707-09. In 1783 disaster struck again in the form of the "famine of the mist": when mount Laki erupted; about a fifth of the island's population perished.

In the early 19th century a movement for self-rule developed. In 1843 the ancient Althing, a national assembly with legislative and judicial functions which had been abolished in 1800, was restored. In 1854 the last vestiges of the trade monopoly disappeared. In 1874, on the occasion of the thousandth anniversary of the traditional date of the landing of the first Norse settler, the Alting was granted limited legislative powers and a Ministry for Iceland was set up in Copenhagen. In 1918 Iceland was finally granted home rule with only foreign policy left in the hands of the Danish government, and with the opportunity to opt for full independence after 25 years.

In May 1940 the island was occupied by British troops a month after the German occupation of Denmark. A year later they were replaced by American forces, and the United States has occupied a base at Keflavik ever since. After a referendum in 1944 full independence was declared. Since Denmark was under German occupation at the time, there was a strong feeling in Denmark that the action had been precipitate, but it was accepted. SPO

IMMIGRATION SINCE 1945. After the collapse of the Hungarian uprising in 1956, the failure of the "Prague Spring" in 1968, and during unrest in Poland around 1970 a total of some 5,000 political refugees arrived in Denmark. Labor immigration into Denmark from Yugoslavia, Pakistan, and Morocco began on a large scale in the late 1960s. They were followed by a large number of Turks, who in 1990 made up by far the largest number (27,929) of foreign citizens in the country, and of Iranians. In the mid-1980s the growing number of would-be immigrants from the Third World led to a tightening-up of regulations in 1986 and again in 1997. Immigrants tended to gravitate to the larger cities, in particular **Copenhagen**. Under pressure from the **Progress Party** and the **Danish People's Party,** government policy has been to distribute them among a number of centers. SPO. *See also* **Tamil Affair.**

INDEPENDENCE MOVEMENT, FAROESE *see* **FAROE ISLANDS; HOME RULE PARTY; PEOPLE'S PARTY.**

INDEPENDENT PARTY (De Uafhængige) is a political party formed in 1953 by some ex-Liberals who opposed the 1953 Constitution. It was led by former Prime Minister **Knud Kristensen,** who drew up its 12-point program, which included reestablishing a second parliamentary chamber, reducing state interference in economic life to a minimum, and supporting the Danish-speaking population of South Slesvig. The party also campaigned for "Christian values" and reduced government expenditure and taxation. Unlike the later **Progress Party**, it strongly supported Denmark's membership of NATO. In the 1953 and 1957 elections it had too few votes to win a **Folketing** seat, but in 1960 gained 3.3 percent of the vote and six members. In 1964 this fell to 2.5 percent and five members. It disappeared from **parliament** again in 1966, when its proportion of the vote dropped to 1.6 percent. SPO

INDIA, DANISH POSSESSIONS IN. Following the establishment of the Danish **East India Company** in 1616, attempts were made to establish trading posts on the Indian subcontinent. After unsuccessful attempts in Ceylon (now Sri Lanka), the small village of Trankebar on the Coromandel Coast south of Madras was bought in 1620 as a result of the expedition led by Ove Gjedde (1594-1660), and the fort of Dansborg was built to defend it. It grew to have a population of 3,000, while a further 20,000 inhabited the area of some 50 square kilometers which it commanded. Soon after its foundation, the Company set up smaller stations at Balasore in Bengal and Masulipatam. Trade with Asia was from 1732 controlled by the Danish **Asiatic Company**, which in 1753 secured trading rights at Calicut on the west coast and the following year gained Serampore near Calcutta, where it established the "factory" of Frederiksnagore. In 1756 an expedition from Trankebar annexed the Nicobar Islands, which were renamed Ny-Danmark. All the Company's Indian possessions were taken over by the Danish Crown in 1777 and were occupied by the British in 1801 and 1802 and between 1808 and 1815. They were finally sold to the British East India Company in 1845 for 1,125,000 rigsdaler. The Nicobar (then the Frederik) Islands were evacuated in 1848 and taken over by Britain in 1868. SPO

INDRE MISSION see **CHURCH**

INDUSTRIAL SOCIETY (Industriforeningen) is an organization formed in 1838 to promote **industrialization** in Denmark at a time when the country was recovering from the economic depression which followed the end of the **Napoleonic Wars**. The Industrial Council (Industrirådet) was established in 1910 as its executive. SPO

INDUSTRIALIZATION. With heavy dependence on **agriculture** as its most important source of exports until as late as the 1950s, Denmark's industrialization in the late nineteenth and early twentieth centuries was different from countries such as Britain, Germany, and Sweden. Its orientation to the domestic market and its organization in small production units made it more like France. Neither textiles nor iron and steel played major roles, and it developed only slowly. There was no identifiable breakthrough based on key industries, partly because of the lack of native raw materials like coal and iron. Even at the end of the 19th century Danish industry still accounted for less than 10 percent of the country's GNP. The only large-scale enterprises were in brewing, shipbuilding, tobacco production and sugar refining. There was rapid expansion in the 1890s with firms producing new electrical goods and chemicals for the home market. SPO

INDUSTRY PARTY (Erhvervspartiet) was founded in 1918 to protest against war-time restrictions. It gained one seat in 1918 and two in September 1920 but then disappeared. AHT

INFORMATION was founded by **Børge Outze** in the summer of 1943 as an underground newspaper to act as a common source of information for all **Resistance** groups. It continued publication after **World War II** as a serious evening paper in **Copenhagen** with good coverage of foreign and cultural affairs. Owned by a trust representing the employees, it is the most important Danish newspaper to remain independent of political ties. A circulation of 40,000 in 1977 had fallen to 22,963 by 1996. *See also* **Press**. SPO

INGEMANN, BERNHARD SEVERIN (1789-1862). Poet and novelist. Born in a manse on the island of Falster, he lost his father at the age of 10 and moved with his mother to Slagelse. At university in **Copenhagen** he began to write poetry under the influence of the German Romantics. His first volume of verse, published in 1811, was well received by the public. He became, however, more and more unpopular with critics like **J.L. Heiberg**, though he found favor with **N.F.S. Grundtvig**. He was strongly influenced by his experiences during extensive travels through central Europe in 1817-19; his style thereafter was less romantic and more realistic. He returned to marry his long-time sweetheart Lucie Mandix and in 1822-49 taught at **Sorø Academy**, and was for a time headmaster. Ingemann is best remembered for the hymns and historical novels which he wrote at Sorø. His novels, very popular in their day, were inspired by Sir Walter Scott and the Danish Middle Ages. His hymns, outwardly naive while spiritually profound, won him a permanent place among the great Danish Romantics. SPO

INUIT ATAQATIGIIT (Inuit Brotherhood) is a socialist political party in **Greenland**. Founded in 1978, it wants to confine Greenland citizenship to those of Inuit parentage. It opposes the 1979 Home Rule law, wants complete independence from Denmark by 2000, and stands for a progressive tax system. It also opposed European Community membership. It took part in cabinets headed by the **Siumut** leader Jonathan Motzfeldt in 1984-88 and entered the governing coalition again in 1991, when it won 19.4 percent of the popular votes and five of the 31 **Landsting** seats. SPO, AHT.

- J -

JACOBSEN, ARNE EMIL (1902-1971). Architect and designer. He has won international recognition for many buildings in a clean, functionalist style which owes little to native traditions. Born in a merchant family in **Copenhagen**, from 1919 he attended the **Academy of Art**, where **Kay Fisker** (1893-1965) was one of his teachers. From 1928 he adopted a pure functionalist style in his designs and the following year won a competition for a "House of the Future." To this period also belong the Bellavista estate (1934) and the Bellevue swimming pool (1931) in Gentofte near Copenhagen. Jacobsen then began to adopt a more individual style. In 1943 he fled to Stockholm to escape persecution as a Jew, and won fame for his textile designs. After **World War II** his buildings were strongly influenced by American architects. Among these in Denmark are the Town Halls in **Århus**, Søllerød, Rødovre (1955), and Glostrup, the SAS building and Royal Hotel in Copenhagen (1960), the first "skyscraper" in the capital, a building for the National Bank (1961-67) and many factories (e.g., at **Ålborg**), schools, and office blocks. In West Germany his designs for public buildings included the City Hall in Mainz (1970-3) and in Britain St. Catherine's College, Oxford (1970-3). Jacobsen also designed silver and stainless steel tableware and furniture, including his "Egg Chair." He was a professor at the Academy, 1956-65. SPO

JACOBSEN, CARL (1842-1914). Brewer, the son of **J.C. Jacobsen**, and a patron of the arts. After studying brewing abroad, in 1871 he founded the brewery which was known from 1882 as New Carlsberg (to distinguish it from his father's). In 1891 he opened the **Ny Carlsberg Glyptotek** and in 1892 the New Carlsberg Fund for the support of art. AHT

JACOBSEN, JACOB CHRISTIAN (1811-1887). Brewer and patron of the arts. After learning the trade in his father's brewery, he took it over in 1836. From 1847 he began producing Bavarian beer in Valby, Copenhagen. After it burnt down in 1859, he financed the rebuilding of **Frederiksborg Castle** and its conversion to a museum of national history. In 1876 he established the **Carlsberg Fund** for science and research, and left it his brewery. He was a member of the **Folketing** 1854-58 and of the **Landsting** 1866-71, generally in support of **national liberal** policy. AHT

JACOBSEN, JENS PETER (1847-1885). Novelist and poet. Born the son of a merchant in Thisted in northwest **Jutland**, he moved to **Copenhagen** in 1863 to study for university entry. Even before matriculating he began to write poetry. During his degree course in natural history, he was strongly influenced by Darwinism and in 1871 published a translation of *The Origin of Species*. He joined the circle associated with **Georg** and **Edvard Brandes** and became a close friend of the latter. In 1876, when he had returned to Thisted, he published his first great novel *Marie Grubbe*, the first important example in Denmark of the French naturalistic style. This was followed by *Niels Lyhne* (1880). Darwinism remained a potent force in his writings throughout, but these also contained strong Romantic elements. Jacobsen is one of the greatest writers of Danish Modernism, without committing himself fully to the program outlined by Georg Brandes. He has been much admired, both in the rest of Scandinavia and in Germany, and has been a potent influence on other writers. SPO

JACOBSEN, ROBERT (1912-1993) is a sculptor known internationally for his work in iron. Born in **Copenhagen** and largely self-taught, his early pieces from the 1930s used wood and were strongly influenced by German Expressionism. He began working in iron in the 1940s, at first with small pieces. He lived in Paris in 1947-62, was professor in the Academy of Art in Munich 1962-76, and then professor in the **Academy of Art** in Copenhagen until 1982. He sculpted larger objects after returning to Denmark. His structure in brick and iron on Axeltorv in central Copenhagen was erected in 1987 to mark the pedestrianization of the square. SPO

JAKOBSEN, FRODE (1906-1997). **Social Democratic** politician. He was one of the 12 children of a free-school teacher of Øster Jølby, Mors. The peasant farmers there paid for his education at Viby Cathedral School, and his outlook was deeply rooted in their values. He was politically active, from 1933 as a courier between exiled German politicians and the German resistance to Hitler. He graduated *cand. mag.* in 1939 with a thesis on "Neitzsche's conflict with Christian morality" and taught in **Copenhagen** schools. In 1941 he started and ran "the Ring" organization as part of the **Resistance** to German occupation. He cofounded the **Freedom Council** 1943-45, chairing its commando and its Arrests Committee and effectively negotiating for both **Communist** and right-wing elements of the resistance with the armed forces and the country's politicians.

By joining the Liberation government as a minister without portfolio he marked acceptance by the resistance of the revived political parties (although the converse was not equally true). He represented the **Social Democrats** in the **Folketing** 1945-73 except briefly in 1953, despite an independence of mind which sometimes put him at odds with party leaders. He served on numerous parliamentary committees but never as a minister, and was Commissioner for the Home Guard 1948-71. From the 1970s his opposition to the Vietnam War and the **European Community** brought him into increasing disagreement with his party: although a supporter of the European ideal, its institutional form left him cold. His books include *Denmark during the German Occupation* (1946), *Europa og Danmark* (1953, Europe and Denmark), *I Danmarks Frihedsråd* (1975, In the Danish Freedom Council, 2 vols.) and *Standpunkter* (1966, Standpoints). AHT

JELLING, in eastern Jutland near Vejle, is one of the most important Danish historic sites where probably the earliest Christian church was raised. It is most famous for two 10th-century rune-stones standing between two mounds. The smaller stone was raised in the reign of King **Gorm** and has a runic text which has been interpreted as "King Gorm made these marks after Thyre, his wife, Denmark's improvement". The larger stone was erected by Gorm's son **Harald**

I Bluetooth and reads "King Harald commanded these words to be made after Gorm, his father, and Thyre, his mother, that Harald who won all Denmark and Norway and made the Danes Christian." It is decorated with a dragon and a figure of Christ and was originally colored. The southern and larger mound was never used for burials, but there is a burial chamber in the northern, which may have originally contained the bodies of Gorm and his wife. The present church there dates from the 11th century, contains the oldest frescoes in Denmark, and stands on the foundations of a large wooden church with a man's skeleton buried at one end. SPO

JENSEN, (ARTHUR) GEORG (1866-1935). Sculptor and silversmith. More than any other craftsman, he is responsible for the reputation enjoyed by Danish silver design in the 20th century. Born in Rådvad, he trained as a goldsmith in 1884, then as a sculptor at the **Academy of Art** before taking up ceramics working in the factory of Bing & Grøndahl. His display of ceramics at the 1900 World Exhibition in Paris was received with acclaim. In 1904 he turned to jewelry and silver tableware in *Art Nouveau* style, with naturalistic details of fruit, leaf and insect motifs, and opened his own workshop. To this he attracted highly talented artists and designers such as Johan Rohde, Harald Nielsen, Gundorph Albertus, Jørgen Jensen, Sigvard Bernadotte, and Arno Malinowski. During **World War I** shortage of silver led him to experiment with stainless steel, which gave rise to some elegant and affordable designs of tableware such as those of **Arne Jacobsen**. His great success in the United States was assured when Randolph Hearst bought his whole exhibit at the San Francisco Exposition in 1915. His son Jørgen succeeded him as head of the firm Georg Jensen. SPO, AHT

JENSEN, JENS (1859-1928). **Trade union** leader. He was the first **Social Democrat** to be elected mayor of a Danish town. A house painter, he was chosen to be the first chairman of the **Trade Union** congress (LO) when it was formed in 1898 and was elected *borgmester* of **Copenhagen** in 1903. He was the chief architect of the 1899 **September Agreement**. A moderate, he anticipated the revisionist policies which brought the Danish Social Democrats such electoral success in the 1920s and 1930s. SPO

JENSEN, JOHANNES VILHELM (1873-1950). Poet and novelist. The son of a veterinary surgeon who practiced in Himmerland, northern **Jutland**, he entered the University of Copenhagen in 1893 to study medicine but was soon devoting most of this time to writing. He published his first novel in 1898 but later disowned this, as well as most of his early work. He traveled widely in Europe as a newspaper correspondent at the turn of the century and sailed around the world in 1902-03. His experiences led to a series of novels beginning in 1901 with *Kongens Fald* (The Fall of the King), a fine work based loosely on the fate of King **Christian II**. These reveal Jensen's strong belief in Darwinian evolution and in the revitalizing role of the Nordic race in this process. He also wrote short stories with a background in Himmerland, which he claimed to be the original home of the Goths, and developed a new genre, halfway between essays and short stories, which he called "myths." Out of these arose his most influential prose work *Den lange rejse* (The Long Journey), published between 1908 and 1921, in which he developed his evolutionary ideas. But in Danish literature Jensen is most important as a poet, introducing prose poems to Danish in 1906. He was awarded the **Nobel Prize** for literature in 1944. SPO

JENSEN, THIT (1876-1957). Author, sister of **Johannes V. Jensen**. Until she was 22 she cared for her siblings, but thereafter developed a career of writing and lecturing. Her debut was with *Den erotiske hamster* (1919, The Erotic Hamster) about a lover who breaks up a marriage; this showed the feminist concern with the conflicts between work and love, tradition and freedom, which are also revealed in her historical novels such as *Jørgen Lykke* (1931), *Stygge Krumpen* (1936), and *Valdemar Atterdag* (I-II, 1940). AHT

JENSEN, THOMAS (1898-1963). Conductor. He was educated in organ and cello at the Copenhagen Music Conservatoire 1913-15 then worked as a cellist 1917-27. Having learned conducting, he was cofounder of the **Århus** Town Orchestra, the first permanent orchestra outside Copenhagen, and in 1957-63 was attached to the Radio Symphony Orchestra. In his time, he was the foremost interpreter of the music of **Carl Nielsen**. AHT

JENSEN KLINT, PEDER VILHELM (1853-1930). Architect. He graduated as a civil engineer from the Technical University in 1877.

In 1878 he entered the **Academy of Art** to study painting, then turned to architecture, which he studied under **Johan Herholdt**. Strongly influenced by the teachings of **N.F.S. Grundtvig**, he rejected Herholdt's historicism in favor of a Danish craft tradition. He wanted, he said, to "give architecture back to the people" and regarded himself as a master mason rather than an architect. His ideas were first manifested in 1896 in the Holm Villa in **Copenhagen**. But he is most renowned for his Grundtvig Church at Bispebjerg in Copenhagen. The tower was begun in 1921 and consecrated in 1927. Meanwhile it was decided to build a complete church, in a design based on the Danish village church. This was completed by Jensen Klint's son **Kaare Klint** and consecrated in 1940. SPO. *See also* **Architecture**.

JENSENIUS, HERLUF (1888-1966). Graphic artist. He initially qualified as a teacher in 1909. He drew for the newspapers *BT* and *Dagens Nyheder*, and from 1934 until his death for *Berlingske Tidende*, with a series "From the diary of a little man" in which he philosophized on daily events. From 1935 he drew for and edited *Blæksprutten* (The Octopus). AHT

JESPERSEN, JESPER PEDER (1883-1963). Gymnastics teacher. He trained as a teacher in 1904, then reached the rank of army captain. His physical fitness program became a national institution through over 9,000 radio programs of "morning gymnastics," 1927-57. AHT

JEWS. Sephardic Jews from Amsterdam and Hamburg were allowed to settle in part of Holstein by King **Christian IV** in 1622. Some later moved to towns in the kingdom and especially to **Copenhagen**, where they established themselves as jewelers and bankers and at the end of the century were allowed to hold religious services. In 1683 immigration of poor Jews into Denmark was forbidden, though wealthy Jews could continue to secure royal permission to settle and many others entered the country illegally. By 1782 the Jewish population of Denmark was 1,830, most of them in the capital. They were forbidden to enter handicraft **guilds** or, in theory at least, to employ Christian servants, but suffered no harassment. In 1788 they were allowed to join trade guilds and were granted citizenship in 1814. Remaining discriminatory legislation was removed by the

Constitution of 1849. By then the Jewish population was some 4,000, rising to 6,000 in 1920. Others came from Russia and the Baltic republics in the 1920s and from Germany, Austria, Bohemia and Moravia in the 1930s. The writers Meïr Aron **Goldschmidt** and Henri **Nathansen** describe 19th-century Jewish life in Denmark .

In German-occupied Denmark in August 1943, the fate of Jews hung in the balance. Berlin ordered their deportation, and on the night of 1-2 October an attempt was made to round them up. But G.F. von Dückwitz, the anti-Nazi shipping attaché in the German administration in Denmark gave warning and some 7,000 were safely transported to Sweden with the help of all segments of the population. Only 481 were seized and sent to Theresienstadt, of whom 52 perished. The bishop of **Funen**, Hans Øllgaard, wrote an extremely sharp protest letter against the persecution of the Jews and had it read out in the churches of his diocese. SPO, AHT. *See also* **Arne** and **Bent Melchior, Resistance Movement; Christian Ditlev Reventlow;World War II**.

JOACHIM HOLGER WALDEMAR CHRISTIAN (1969-   ). Prince of Denmark. He is the younger son of Queen **Margrethe II** and her husband Prince Henrik, and was born on 7 June. He was educated in Copenhagen, also studying in 1982-83 in Normandy, France. His military education, which included service in the Queen's Life Guard Regiment and the Guard Hussars' Regiment, was completed in 1989 and he was appointed a first lieutenant of the reserve in the Prince's Life Guard Regiment in 1990. Thereafter he studied agriculture. In 1995 he married Alexandra Christina Manley, previously an investment advisor in Hong Kong. AHT

JØRGENSEN, ADOLF DITLEV (1840-1897). Historian. Although lacking a formal education, he taught in Flensborg until the 1864 Second **Slesvig-Holsten** War. In **Copenhagen** in 1869 he was appointed to the state archives and became official archivist from 1882. On the consolidation of the archives in 1892 he became the first State Archivist (*rigsarkivar*). As a historian he supported a **Slesvig** divided according to language loyalties. AHT

JØRGENSEN, ANKER (1922-   ). **Social Democratic** (S) politician and **trade union** leader, prime minister 1972-73 and 1975-82. An orphan, he began work as a messenger at the age of 14 and soon became involved in the trade union movement. In 1950 he became vice-chairman of the Warehouse Workers Union (Lager- og Pakhusarbejdernes Forbund) and in 1968 chairman of Denmark's biggest union, the Union of General and Semi-skilled Workers (Dansk Arbejdsmands- og Specialarbejderforbund, later SiD). In 1964 Jørgensen was elected to the **Folketing**, placing himself on the left of the party and opposing Denmark's entry to the **European Community** (EC) in 1972. After refusing several offers of a cabinet post, he was elected to succeed the pro-EC **Jens Otto Krag** as prime minister in 1972 and was elected SD chairman.

The 1973 election reduced the SD vote from 37 percent to 25 percent and fragmented the Danish party system, but as prime minister 1975-82 Jørgensen succeeded in rebuilding the SD vote and in the complicated task of building support for his succession of minority **cabinets** from the parties of the center. The 1978-79 coalition with the **Liberals** tried to span the political middle ground, but proved too much for the trade unions to accept. SD losses at the 1981 election led to resignation in 1982 and the start of a decade of governments led by the Conservative **Poul Schlüter**. On reaching the age of 65 he resigned as party chairman in 1987 and was succeeded by **Svend Auken**. Jørgensen published two books of speeches and articles, *Til venstre for midten* (1975, Left of Center) and *Styrk digerne* (1982, Strengthen the Dikes). SPO, AHT

JØRGENSEN, JOHANNES (1866-1956). Author. He initially studied natural science at Copenhagen University then took up a career as journalist and poet. Initially influenced by **Brandes**, as publisher of *Taarnet* (The Tower) 1893-94 he rejected symbolism and in 1896 converted to Catholicism. He wrote widely read and translated biographies of *St Francis of Assisi* (1907), *St. Katherine of Sienna* (1915), and *Birgitta of Vadsterna* (1941-3). His autobiography *Mit livs legende I-VII* (1916-28, Legends of My Life) is considered a prime example of the genre in Denmark. AHT

JØRGENSEN, JØRGEN (1888-1974). Politician. The son of a landowner, he trained as a farmer and ran his own farm until 1923. He represented the **Radical Liberals** in the **Folketing** 1929-60 and was education minister 1935-42 and 1957-61, and interior minister 1942-43 during the German occupation. As education minister he paved the way for unitary (comprehensive and coeducational) schools, and for the return to **Iceland** of saga manuscripts held in Danish libraries. AHT

JØRGENSEN, "KING" (1780-c. 1841). Adventurer. The son of a court clock-maker, he was sent to sea and ended in British service. Sent to **Iceland** by a well-to-do Englishman, in 1809 he proclaimed himself king and liberator from Danish domination, but was captured by a British captain and returned to England. He was later deported to Tasmania, where he died. AHT

JØRGENSEN, SEVERIN (1842-1926) was one of the chief pioneers of the Danish cooperative movement. After earning his living as a grocer, from 1868 he worked as a cooperative distributor. In 1888 he founded and directed Fællesforeningen for jyske Brugsforeninger, the Association of Jutland Co-operatives and in 1896-1913 was the first chairman of Fællesforeningen for Danmarks Brugsforeninger, FDB, a similar organization for all Denmark. He also founded the Danish Egg Export Cooperative in 1895 and the Danish Cooperative Bank, Den danske Andelsbank in 1909. AHT

JORN (JØRGENSEN), ASGER (OLUF) (1914-1973). Painter, sculptor, and engraver. Born in Vejrun near **Viborg**, he moved in 1929 to Silkeborg. In the 1930s he studied in Paris under Fernand Léger and then in **Copenhagen** with the engraver Aksel Jørgensen (1883-1957). He was strongly influenced by Surrealism and the work of the Swiss artist Paul Klee, and in 1948-51 was a founder member of the group of artists known as COBRA (COpenhagen, BRussels, Amsterdam). After 1953 he lived in Paris and Albisola, Italy, and co-founded the International Situationist Movement. Among his most famous works is a ceramic mural for the Secondary School in **Århus** (1959). His oil paintings, etchings, lithographs, sculptures, and ceramics have an abstract, colorful, often humorous style. He left many of his works to Silkeborg Museum. SPO

JUDICIAL SYSTEM *see* **COURTS; DANISH LAW**

JUEL, JENS (1631-1700). Politician. He was educated at **Sorø Academy** and then in Germany, France, and Italy. He was appointed resident in Stockholm 1662-70, where he worked for the friendship between Denmark and Sweden, which he furthered with the peace of

1679 and which ended the **Scanian War**. As president of the college of commerce from 1680 and member of the trade commissions of 1690 and 1693 he was a leader of mercantile policy. In 1680 he was appointed to the Council and in 1699 to head the Admiralty. His brother was Niels **Juel**. AHT

JUEL, JENS (1745-1802). Painter; and one of Denmark's most important artists in the 18th century. Born on **Funen**, he was initially trained in Hamburg, where he was strongly influenced by 17th century Dutch artists. In 1765-71 he studied in the **Academy of Art** in **Copenhagen** then visited the principal cultural centers of Europe. In 1773-76 he lived in Rome and in 1776-80 in Paris and Geneva. In 1780 he was appointed court portraitist and in 1784 professor at the Academy, of which he was director in 1795-97 and 1799-1801. His principal paintings, in a natural and harmonious style, were portraits of the Copenhagen bourgeoisie and nobility but he also painted many foreigners and landscapes. Two of his daughters in succession married the artist **C.W. Eckersberg**. SPO

JUEL, NIELS (1629-1697). Admiral. Like his brother **Jens** he was educated at **Sorø Academy** and then abroad, serving in the Dutch navy until 1656 and was appointed admiral in 1657. During the **Scanian War** (1676-79) he commanded the fleet that conquered Gotland in 1676 and defeated the Swedes in the battle of Køge Bay in 1677. From 1679 he headed the admiralty. His brother Jens was a politician. AHT

JUNE MOVEMENT, THE *(JuniBevægelsen)* was formed in 1992 to gather opposition to the Treaty of European Union (the Maastricht treaty). It aims to maintain opposition to a prospective "United States of Europe" which might have a common currency and armed forces and would detract from Danish sovereignty and democracy. Unlike the "Popular Movement Against the European Community-Union" (Folkebevægelsen mod EF-Unionen) formed in 1972, which wants an independent Denmark to relate to other states only on an inter-governmental basis, the June Movement accepts the Single European Market of the European Economic Community and would like it extended to all European countries, but opposes the "ever closer union" of the **European Union**. Neither movement has contested Folketing elections but both have drawn on cross-party support to achieve representation in the European Parliament, gaining four of the 16 Danish seats in 1979, 1984, and 1989, and two each in 1994. AHT

JUSTICE PARTY (Danmarks Retsforbund). This political "association" based its ideas on the theories of the American economist Henry George, whose book *Progress and Poverty* (1879) provoked widespread discussion in Denmark and led to the formation by Jacob E. Lange, Sophus Bertelsen, Professor **C.N. Starcke** and **J.L. Bjørner** of a Henry George Society, which influenced **Social Democratic** and **Radical Liberal** as well as Justice Party thinking. Henry George advocated a single tax based on land values, hence the party's alternative name of "the single-tax party." The name Justice Party comes from the second strand to the party's origin, the Retsdemokratisk Forbund formed by Severin Christensen, Axel Dam, and Christen Lambek to argue for a social ethic of highly personalized individualism and anti-collectivism. The two strands joined to form Retsforbundet in 1919, but their diversity makes it difficult to place on a left-right spectrum. The Justice Party was continuously represented in the **Folketing** 1926-60 and was considered a possible coalition partner for the **Liberals** in 1953. **H.C. Hansen** and **Viggo Kampmann** brought it into their coalition **cabinets** of 1957-60 with charge of the Interior and Fisheries Ministries, and Viggo **Starcke** (son of one of the party's founders) as a minister without portfolio. Its vigorous opposition to state intervention and its failure to achieve recognition for its single-tax policy confirmed the view that it was in cabinet to secure a majority for its partners, and it lost all Folketing representation in 1960. As the only nonsocialist party opposed to the **European Community** it returned to the Folketing in 1973 with 2.9 percent of the vote, fell below the 2 percent threshold in 1975, but returned again in 1977-81. AHT

JUTLAND (JYLLAND) is the "mainland" of Denmark, a peninsula jutting northward from the North European Plain with an area of 29,640 square kilometers (11,449 square miles). It contains Denmark's largest lake, Arresø (with an area of 40.6 square kilometers [15.7 square miles]); longest river, Gudenåen (with a length of 158 kilometers [98 miles]); highest point, Yding Skovhøj (173 m or 568 ft) and second largest town, **Århus**. Its scenery in the early 19th century has been immortalized in the novels of **Steen Steensen Blicher**, and the village at its northern tip, **Skagen**, has been the focus of an important school of artists since the late 19th century. After the 1860s the **Heath Society** worked to improve the poor heathland with its scattered individual farms that characterized much of the west of Jutland, unlike the richer east where there were some considerable estates. The poor soils of the west lead down to extensive beaches which are popular with Danes and tourists in the summer. Denmark's most important fishing centers are found on its North Sea coast. The port of **Esbjerg** was developed for the fishing fleet, for ferries to Britain and Atlantic shipping. Other fishing and ferry ports include Hanstholm, Hirtshals, and Frederikshavn. The most vulnerable part of Denmark to land attack from the south, southern Jutland was occupied by Catholic and Imperial armies in 1625-29, by the Swedes in 1657-60, and by Prussian and Austrian troops after the Second **Slesvig-Holsten** War in 1864. The border with Germany was settled by **referendum** in 1920. SPO, AHT

- K -

KAAS, NIELS (1534-1594). Politician. Of a noble family, he studied history and public law abroad. He became a secretary in the chancellery and in 1570-94 was a member of the Council of State, acting as royal Chancellor from 1570. He advocated a policy of caution toward Sweden and supporting scientists such as **A.S. Vedel** and **Tycho Brahe**. After **Frederik II** died in 1588 Kaas headed the council of state during **Christian IV**'s minority. He died at **Viborg** and was buried in the cathedral. AHT

KAAS, PREBEN (1930-1981) was an actor who won a large public following for his crazy and satirical revue numbers. In 1960-66 he appeared at the ABC theater in **Copenhagen**, and in 1969-77 was director of the Circus Revue. AHT

KALMAR UNION, named for the castle and port in southeast Sweden, was a political union between the kingdoms of Denmark, Norway, and Sweden. At its height it was the largest kingdom in

Europe. Formed in 1397 and finally dissolved in 1521, its origins lie in the union of the Danish and Norwegian crowns under the young **Oluf III** (1370-1387) in 1380. After Albrecht of Mecklenburg was deposed from the Swedish throne in 1386, the Swedish nobles negotiated with Oluf's mother **Margrethe** with a view to offering her son the throne of Sweden. When Oluf died suddenly they offered her the position of regent. The close ties between the leading families of the three kingdoms and the common threat of German economic domination made the idea of a union widely popular, and in 1397 Margrethe's nephew **Erik of Pomerania** was crowned King of Denmark, Norway, and Sweden in Kalmar, the terms of the union being defined in a Coronation Letter and a Union Letter, although these offered differing interpretations of royal power.

From early in the history of the Union, the Swedish nobility proved sensitive about their rights, which they often considered infringed by a ruler who resided most of the time in **Copenhagen**. They revolted against King Erik in 1438 and chose their own king, but the Union was restored with the election in 1440-42 of **Christoffer of Bavaria** as king in all three countries, only to be broken when, on his death in 1448, the Swedes chose a different successor to the throne. King **Hans** was again king of all three countries in 1501-3, as was King **Christian II** in 1520-21. The Swedish revolt led by Gustav Vasa in 1521 proved to be the end of the Union, although Dano-Norwegian kings did not finally abandon hopes of its revival until after the **Great Northern War**. In the mid-19th century it was the inspiration of **Scandinavianism**. SPO

KALMAR WAR (1611-1613) was fought between Denmark and Sweden and began with a Danish attack on the port of Kalmar. Disputes had arisen between the two countries over the **Sound** tolls and mutual claims in Arctic Scandinavia, but the young King **Christian IV** also dreamed of reviving the **Kalmar Union**. The Danes had the better of the fighting, but their armies could not reach Stockholm by land, and an attempt by sea was repelled. Both sides finally agreed to British mediation, and peace was concluded at **Knäred**. This required the Swedes to agree to pay an enormous ransom to secure the return of the fortress of Älvsborg, captured by the Danes early in the war. *See also* **Sweden, Danish Relations with**. SPO

KAMPMANN, VIGGO (1910-1976), economist and **Social Democrat** politician, prime minister 1960-62. He gradated *cand. polit.* in 1934 then worked in the civil service. He played a leading part in the **Resistance** during **World War II** and became secretary of its Economic Center, which planned for postwar development. He headed the Economic Secretariat 1947-50 before becoming minister of finance in Hans **Hedtoft**'s cabinet shortly before it had to resign. He then served as director of Danmarks Hypothekbank (the Danish Mortgage Bank). In 1953 he joined Hedtoft's second cabinet in his old post, continuing when Hedtoft was replaced at the beginning of 1955 by **H.C. Hansen**. In a crisis budget he introduced a value added tax (*omsætningsafgift*). After serving briefly as acting premier during Hansen's last illness, Kampmann became prime minister in 1960 of a majority administration of Social Democrats, **Radicals**, and the **Justice Party**. Because of his own heart trouble he had to hand over the premiership in September 1962 to **J.O. Krag**. He edited the social democratic journal *Verdens Gang* in 1962-66. His son Jens Kampmann was Denmark's first **environment** minister as minister for public works and pollution prevention 1971-73. SPO, AHT

KANSLERGADE AGREEMENT (1933) was a broad-based agreement between **Social Democrats**, **Radical Liberals** and the **Liberal Party** *Venstre* (thus omitting only the small **Conservative** Party) which strengthened agricultural competitiveness, extended wage agreements with a promise of no strikes or lockouts for a year, and secured support for the comprehensive reform of social legislation which laid the foundations of the Danish welfare state (*see* **K.K. Steinke**). Named after the street where prime minister Thorvald **Stauning** lived and where the negotiations were held, this agreement ended a period of instability in the 1920s, served as the foundation for broad political consensus during the depression years of the 1930s, and was the base for Social Democratic predominance through to the 1960s. AHT

KAUFMANN, HENRIK (1888-1963), diplomat. Appointed Danish minister in Washington in 1939 after a career in the Foreign Office, at the time of the German occupation of Denmark in April 1940. In common with a number of other Danish representatives abroad, he declared himself no longer bound to follow the orders of a government which was no longer free. On the anniversary of the German occupation in 1941 he concluded a treaty with the US government granting the United States of America the use of bases on **Greenland**. The Copenhagen government dismissed him and accused him of high treason, but he retained recognition as his country's representative. In 1942 he associated Denmark with plans for the United Nations, and took part as head of the Danish delegation in the 1945 San Francisco conference which led to its establishment. He served as minister without portfolio in V. **Buhl**'s liberation government, and in 1947-58 was again ambassador to Washington. SPO, AHT. *See also* **World War II.**

KIEL, TREATY OF (14 January 1814) was concluded between Denmark and Sweden at the end of the **Napoleonic Wars**, in which Denmark had allied with France. By it Denmark surrendered Norway to the Swedish crown in exchange for Swedish Pomerania. Denmark retained the former Norwegian dependencies of **Iceland** and the **Faroe Islands**, but in 1815 exchanged Pomerania with Prussia for the small duchy of Lauenburg. SPO

KIERKEGAARD, SØREN (1813-1855). Philosopher. Born in Copenhagen as the son of a hosiery shopkeeper, he began to study theology at university but fell out with his puritanical father and for a time devoted himself to a life of pleasure before undergoing a religious experience and returning to his studies. He was awarded a doctorate in theology in 1841. Breaking off his engagement at this time led to a new emotional crisis. Kierkegaard moved to Berlin and started on a long series of writings in which he outlined his main philosophical tenets, above all his theory of life's "stages": the aesthetic and the ethical, but only the "religious" could provide lasting satisfaction. This is done in novel form in *Enten/Eller* (1843; *Either/Or*, 1959). At one time he considered becoming a country parson, and strongly professed the Christian bases of his beliefs, but he became involved in bitter battles with the church establishment which undermined his health and hastened his death. He attacked Hegel's attempt to arrive at "objective" truth, which Kierkegaard claimed could lead only to personal despair, and he drew the contrast between this and "experience" which can be gone through only by each individual. These views influenced 20th-century existentialists and modern theologians. Twenty volumes of collected works (*Samlede Værker*) were published in 1963 with a further nine volumes of papers in 1968-70, and there is an extensive literature of translations and commentaries. A room in the Copenhagen City Museum is dedicated to his life and work. SPO, AHT

KINGO, THOMAS (1634-1703), poet and bishop. Born in Slangerup, the son of a silk-weaver, he graduated *cand. theol.* in 1658 and after a spell as private tutor was ordained. He returned to his birthplace as vicar in 1668. He had already published his first poem, and much more "occasional" verse followed during his years in Slangerup. In 1677 he was named bishop of **Funen** and was commissioned to compile a definitive hymn book for the Danish Church. The first part appeared in 1689, but was not approved. The task was assigned to another whose offering was also rejected, and a commission was appointed, of which Kingo became a member. He contributed some 100 hymns to the authorized book, *Aandelige Sjungekor*, which eventually appeared in 1699. One of Denmark's greatest hymn writers, his hymns are considered to be the culmination of Danish baroque poetry. He married three times. SPO, AHT

KING'S LAW (KONGELOV), a document finally approved by King **Frederik III** in 1665 which defined the succession to the Danish throne and the powers of the monarch after the introduction of **absolute monarchy** in 1661. In its final form, it appears to have been largely the work of the secretary Peder Schumacher, later **Griffenfeld**. It remained secret until 1699, when it was read at the coronation of King **Frederik IV**, and was only printed in 1709. It remained in force until 1848. By the second of its 40 articles, the king of Denmark was declared "on earth superior to all human laws and knowing no other superior of judge over him in matters spiritual or temporal save God alone," a clear statement of absolute monarchy by divine right. Frederik later became a Lutheran, but allowed no diminution of his realm nor delegation of the powers granted to him. SPO, AHT. *See also* **Monarchy; Religion**.

KIRK, HANS RUDOLF (1898-1962), novelist and critic. His father was a Hadsund doctor with radical views. He studied law at the University of Copenhagen, but soon after graduating *cand. jur.* in 1922

he turned to journalism. He joined the **Communist Party** in 1931 and from 1934 edited its paper, *Arbejderbladet*. His most popular works are his novels in a style of socially critical realism: *Fiskerne* (1928, The Fishermen), *Daglejerne* (1939, The Day-Laborer), *De ny Tider* (1939, New Times). Like other Communists, he was arrested and imprisoned in 1941 but escaped transfer to a German concentration camp in 1943. His indignation at the events of the occupation and postwar "retribution" are depicted in *Djævelens Penge* (1951, The Devil's Money) and *Klitgaard & Sønner* (1952, Klitgaard & Sons). His belief in the fundamental similarity between the ideals of Christianity and Communism is the subject of *Vredens Søn* (1950, The Son of Wrath). SPO, AHT

KLINGENBERG, POUL von (1615-1690), postmaster general. After a career as a merchant, some of it spent abroad, in 1653 he was appointed postmaster-general, and reorganized and made effective the postal service established in 1624 by **Christian IV**. He became a court-appointed supplier of war materiel, and became a large landowner from 1660 when he arranged to be paid in crown lands. His estates were unprofitable, however, and when a commission later found him guilty of defrauding the state, he lost his fortune. He resigned as postmaster-general in 1685. AHT

KLINT, KAARE (1888-1954), architect and designer. Son of the architect **P.V. Jensen Klint**, by whom he was trained, he was largely responsible for the high reputation enjoyed by Danish furniture since the 1930s. In the 1920s he set up a class in interior design in the **Academy of Arts** in **Copenhagen**, where he worked until his death. He trained his pupils in the principles of simplicity, utility and the careful choice of materials which have remained the hallmarks of Danish furniture. He also completed his father's **Grundtvig** Church in Copenhagen. SPO

KNÄRED (or KNÆRØD), PEACE OF (20 January 1613), was the treaty between Denmark and Sweden which ended the **Kalmar War**. By it Sweden surrendered all claims to sovereignty in Lappmark and promised payment of the huge sum of one million daler. Until this was paid Denmark was to retain the fortress of Älvsborg, which protected Sweden's only outlet to the North Sea at the mouth of the river Göta. The final installment was not paid until 1619. The treaty also referred the dispute over the use of the three crowns in the Danish coat of arms to further negotiations. SPO

KNUD I THE GREAT (DEN STORE) (c. 995-1035). King of England 1014-35, of Denmark 1018-35, and of Norway c. 1027-35. The younger son of King **Svend I Forkbeard**, he accompanied his father on his expedition to England in 1013 and on Svend's death in 1014 was appointed his heir on the English throne, while his elder brother **Harald II** took over Denmark. When driven back to Denmark, he obtained Harald's support for a fresh expedition in 1015, which resulted in a division of England with Edmund, son of King Ethelred. When Edmund died, Knud took over the whole country, where he spent most of the rest of his life, and married Ethelred's widow Emma. The death of his brother Harald in 1018 gave him also the Danish throne, but he exercised his authority in Denmark through a series of viceroys. He was the first Danish king to go on pilgrimage to Rome and in 1027 was present there at the coronation of the emperor Conrad II, to whose son Henry he married his daughter Gunhild. He tried to extend his empire further by laying claim to Norway and allied himself with the enemies of King Olaf Haraldsson (St. Olaf), whom he drove into exile in 1027. Olaf was defeated and killed in battle when he returned in 1030 and Danish rule was restored. But in 1035 the Norwegians chose Olaf's son Magnus (the Good) as their king. Knud died in Shaftesbury and was buried in Winchester. Following his death his North Sea empire broke up, his son **Hardeknud** taking the Danish throne while England went to his illegitimate son Harald "Harefoot". SPO

KNUD II, DEN HELLIGE (SAINT) (1043-1086). King of Denmark 1080-86. Born the illegitimate son of King **Svend II Estridsen**, he took part in raids on the England of William the Conqueror and was elected king of Denmark on the death of his brother **Harald III** "**Hén**." His attempts to create a strong monarchy made him many enemies among the nobility and common people alike. In 1086, while attempting in **Jutland** to form a fleet for an invasion of England, a revolt forced him to flee to Odense, where he was murdered by peasants in St.Alban's Church. He was buried in St. Knud's church in the same town. His canonization in 1101 was the result partly of a reaction against the rule of his brother and successor

Oluf I "Hunger" but is also the reflection of support for his efforts to create a strong government. He married Edele of Flanders, by whom he had two daughters, who married Swedish noblemen, and a son killed in Flanders. SPO

KNUD III MAGNUSSEN (c.1129-1257). King of Denmark 1146-57. Son of Magnus, the son of King **Niels**, he was elected king in **Jutland** in 1146 while his cousin **Svend III Grathe** was elected in **Zealand** and **Scania**. In the civil war which resulted, Knud was defeated, but the intercession of emperor Frederick Barbarossa resulted in the crown being granted to Svend, while Knud took Zealand as an imperial fief. In 1154, however, Svend was driven out and Denmark divided between Knud and **Knud Lavard's** son **Valdemar**. As the result of a fresh settlement in 1157, Knud gained **Zealand**, but at a meeting of the three kings in **Roskilde**, Knud was murdered by Svend's followers. He was unmarried. SPO

KNUD IV (also counted VI if the two Hardeknuds are included) (1163-1202). King of Denmark 1182-1202. Eldest son of King **Valdemar I**, he became co-regent with his father in 1170 before succeeding him. During his reign Danish power was extended along the southern coast of the Baltic to include Mecklenburg and Pomerania and strong government ensured peace in the country. But traditionally Knud has been seen as a rather weak ruler, who owed much of his success to his Archbishop **Absalon**. He is buried in Ringsted. He married Gertrud, daughter of Henry the Lion of Saxony, but had no children and was succeeded by his brother **Valdemar II**. SPO

KNUD LAVARD (c. 1096-1131), son of King **Erik I Ejegod** and father of King **Valdemar I**. Still a minor at the time of his father's death in 1103, Knud was bypassed in the election to the throne by **Niels**. He was raised at the court of Lothar, duke of Saxony and in 1115 was appointed *jarl* (viceroy) in the border province of Slesvig, where he successfully restored order with the aid of his *hird* (bodyguard), who entitled him "Lavard" or "bread-giver." In 1129, Lothar, now emperor, granted him territories in Mecklenburg. His double loyalties and extensive power caused jealousy and suspicion among the Danish **nobility**, in particular his cousin Magnus, who suspected him of designs on the Danish throne after the death of

King **Niels**. Knud spent the Christmas of 1130 in the royal palace at **Roskilde** and on January 7 was invited to meet Magnus in the nearby wood, where he was murdered. He married Ingeborg of Russia. His son Valdemar had him canonized. SPO

KNUDSEN, PETER CHRISTIAN (1848-1910). **Social Democrat** (SD) politician. Born in Randers, where he qualified as a glove-maker, he moved to **Copenhagen** 1868 and joined the general section of the Socialist Internationale 1872. He helped to start glove-makers' unions in Copenhagen, Malmö, Nyborg, **Odense**, Lund and Hälsingborg, becoming founder-chairman of the Danish Glove-makers' Union, editing its journal until 1903. As a delegate to the 1876 Gimle Congress he helped draw up the first Danish SD party program and joined the Trade Union Central Committee in Copenhagen, 1877. Following internal divisions (*see* **PIO**), he drafted rules for the SD Federation 1878. As its manager/chairman 1882-1909 he tightened the link between party headquarters and branches and was a regular contributor to *Socialdemokraten* newspaper from 1881.

Knudsen's work had three themes: close collaboration of party and unions; the importance of recruiting agricultural workers; and that the state should care for the ill, the old, and the disabled. He linked the party to the **trade union** movement as vice-chairman from 1886 of the Cooperating Trade Unions of Copenhagen, then of the National Confederation of Trade Unions (later LO) 1898-1909, making the link personal rather than organic. He actively promoted SD growth in rural areas, while as a member from 1883 of a committee of sick funds and funeral funds he strongly influenced its statistically based 1888 report on Sickness Insurance and Care of the Elderly, on which SD campaigned extensively.

Knudsen was elected to the **Landsting** in 1890, and to the **Folketing** 1898-1901 and 1903-09, arguing strongly for lower sales taxes and excise duties, steeply progressive income and capital taxes, and a local land-value tax. Elected also to **Copenhagen** City Council in 1898, he became "mayor of the poor," heading the Poor Law Department from 1902. As party chairman he was on the board of major **cooperatives** and represented SD at international congresses in Brussels 1891, 1893, and 1899, London 1896, Paris 1900, and Amsterdam 1904. On his initiative the 1910 congress was held in Copenhagen, a month before his death.

Knudsen steadily supported SD cooperation with the **Liberals**, and from 1905 the **Radical Liberals**, while vigorously opposing the Socialist Left opposition. He characterized SD's "matter-of-fact" reformism from the 1880s onward. Under his leadership 1882-1909, SD became a nationwide organization with 230 branches, 44,000 active members, and 98,700 votes. With **Th. Stauning** he was one of the two leaders of Danish social democracy in over 50 of its formative years. AHT

KNUDSEN, WILLIAM S. (1879-1948), industrial leader. The son of a cooper, he emigrated to the United States in 1900, where he worked in various industrial and transport companies. He was production director for Ford Motors 1918-21. He later moved to General Motors, of which he was president 1937-40. Franklin D. Roosevelt appointed him to administer the supply of war materiel to the United States and its allies during **World War II**. AHT

KØBKE, CHRISTEN (1810-1848), painter. He studied at the **Academy of Art** from 1822, as **Christoffer Wilhelm Eckersberg**'s pupil from 1828. His many paintings of **Frederiksborg Castle** were influenced by national romanticism. His fresh treatment of light, especially in his earlier work, points forward toward impressionism. AHT

KOCH, BODIL (1903-1972). **Social Democratic** (SD) politician. She graduated *cand. theol.* from Copenhagen University 1929 and was a member of the **Folketing** 1947-71. As minister for church affairs in 1950 and 1953-1966 under four SD prime ministers, she pursued the interests of the national church with enthusiasm and sympathy, initiating revisions of church structure to open new avenues for its work. She gained unusually wide respect in both the church and politics for her pursuit of greater equality, greater spiritual freedom, and flourishing arts. In Jens Otto **Krag**'s 1966-68 cabinet she moved to the Ministry of Culture, but made little of this wider field. She opposed German membership of **NATO**, nuclear weapons, and the US war in Vietnam, but argued keenly for the interests of developing countries. She married **Hal Koch** and their two children, Ejler and Dorte (see **Bennedsen**), both succeeded politically. **EJLER KOCH** (1933-1978) graduated *cand. jur.* 1957 and was a civil servant and university lecturer in public administration from 1957, represented SD in the **Folketing** 1973-77, and then was director of the Environment Administration. AHT

KOCH, HAL (1904-1963), church historian and social theorist. The son of a priest, he graduated *cand. theol.* in 1926 and *dr. theol.* in 1932, and was appointed professor of church history in **Copenhagen** in 1937. As chairman 1940-46 of the Danish Youth Union (*Dansk Ungdomssamvirke*) he defended parliamentary democracy but opposed the illegal methods of the **Resistance** during the German occupation. After the war he opposed the trials of collaborators based on retrospective legislation. His publications include *Danmarks kirke gennem tiderne* (1939, The History of the Danish Church), *Grundtvig* (1943), vols. I & IV of *Den Danske kirkes historie* (1950, 1954), and *Luther* (1958). AHT

KOCK, JØRGEN (?-1556), merchant and politician. Originally from Westfalen, he ran an extensive merchants business from Malmö and was appointed Master of the Mint 1518-23 by **Christian II**. As mayor in 1523 he led the defense of Malmö against Christian II's enemies, but surrendered the city to **Frederik I** in 1524. He continued as mayor and protected reformers against the Catholic Church. In 1534-36 he took the side of Christian II but in 1536 he capitulated to **Christian III**, who pardoned him, and he resumed as mayor in 1540. AHT

KOFOED, HANS CHRISTIAN (1898-1952), philanthropist. From a landowning family, he wanted to be a priest but had to be content with the post of parish clerk. In 1928 in **Copenhagen** he founded Kofoed's School, which developed into a welfare institution for the reintegration of social misfits. AHT

KOFOED, JENS (1628-1691), officer. In 1658 he led the successful revolt against Swedish forces on **Bornholm** which resulted in the Swedish commandant J. Prinzenskiöld being captured and shot by Kofoed's brother-in-law. Kofoed was rewarded by **Frederik III** with the rank of *landskaptajn* and later became known as the liberator of Bornholm. AHT

KOLD, KRISTEN (or CHRISTEN) MIKKELSEN (1816-1870), education reformer. The son of a shoemaker in Thisted, as a private tutor he organized evening meetings of young farmers with singing and discussions. With the help of **N.F.S. Grundtvig** he opened a **folk high school** in Ryslinge on **Funen** in 1851 which later became the model for many similar schools. In 1853 he moved to Hindsholm in northeast Funen and opened the first Danish free school. In 1862 he became principal of the folk high school in Dalum near **Odense**, where he died. The folk high school movement acquired such popularity largely due to Kold. SPO

KRAG, JENS OTTO (1914-1978). **Social Democrat** (SD) politician and prime minister 1962-68 and 1971-72. He graduated *cand. polit.* in 1940 and worked as a civil servant. He was active in his party in the 1930s, helped to draft its radical 1945 manifesto *Fremtidens Danmark*, was elected to the **Folketing** 1947-73, and was minister of trade 1947-50, minister of finance and labor 1953-57, minister of international trade 1958-62, and foreign minister 1962-63 and in 1966-67. His first cabinet, which he took over in 1962 when **Viggo Kampmann** fell ill, was a majority coalition of SD and **Radical Liberals**. He lost this majority in the 1964 elections but continued without the Radicals. In the hope of increased Folketing support Krag called the 1966 election. SD losses were outweighed by gains by the **Socialist People's Party**, which was keen to use its new strength to influence the SD cabinet. This was the first Danish **election** to produce a socialist majority (the only other one being in 1971-73). Late in 1967, however, the government was defeated when the Socialist Peoples Party refused to back a wage freeze. In the 1968 election SD losses compelled Krag to resign. He returned to office in 1971-73 at the head of a minority SD government and negotiated the terms of Danish membership of the **European Community** actively supported by the **Conservatives, Liberals,** and **Radical Liberals**, an action which left SD divided, since many **trade unionists** were opposed. As soon as the **referendum** result was announced he resigned and was succeeded by **Anker Jørgensen**. His memoirs were entitled *Ung mand fra trediverne* (1969, Young man of the 30s), *Travl tid, god tid* (1974, Busy times, good times), and *Dagbog 1971-72* (Diary, 1971-72). SPO, AHT

KRAK, OVE (1862-1923). Publisher. He graduated *cand. med.* in 1889 and practiced as a doctor 1892-1903. On his father's death he took over the publication of a road map of the **Copenhagen** area and expanded its coverage to all Denmark in 1905, with many later editions. From 1910 he also published *Kraks Blå Bog,* an annual biography of prominent people. AHT

KRISTENSEN, KNUD (1880-1962). Liberal Party politician and prime minister. Raised in a household with a strong attachment to the **Liberal Party** (*Venstre*), he worked in the youth wing of the party before being elected to the **Folketing** in 1920 and rose to be vice-chairman of the party. After the **German Occupation** in April 1940, he joined **Th. Stauning**'s coalition government as minister without portfolio and from July 1941 as minister of the interior. He had to resign in November 1942 under German pressure after having strongly criticized Danish membership of the Anti-Comintern Pact. Kristensen was again minister of the interior in V. **Buhl**'s 1945 liberation government. After gains by the Liberals in the October election he headed a Liberal minority government 1945-47. His support for a proposed referendum to reunify southern **Slesvig** with Denmark lost him the support of the **Radical Liberals**, and in October 1947 he resigned following a vote of no confidence. In 1954 he left the Liberal Party to form his own **Independent Party**, opposed to the 1953 constitution. He published his memoirs in 1954. SPO

KRISTENSEN, THORKIL (1899-1989). Politician. He graduated *cand. polit.* in 1927 and held appointments as professor of business economics (*driftsøkonomi*) at Århus University 1938-45 and at the Copenhagen School of Economics and Business Administration (Handelshøjskolen) 1948-60. He was elected to the **Folketing** 1945-60 for the **Liberals** and was finance minister 1945-47 and 1950-53, pursuing a tight economics and savings policy with **Social Democratic** support, which conflicted with Liberal collaboration with the **Conservatives**. His restrictive policy earned him the nickname Thorkil Tight-belt (*livrem*). In 1960 he became secretary-general of Organization for European Economic Cooperation and in 1961-66 of its successor, the Organization for Economic Cooperation and Development (OECD). AHT

KRISTENSEN, TOM (1893-1974), poet and novelist. Born in London but raised in a middle-class milieu in **Copenhagen**, he rebelled in his youth. Majoring in Danish he graduated *cand. mag.* in 1919, then made a career as an author. He published his first collection of poems in 1920 but is better known for his novels. Beginning with *Livets arabesk* (1921, Arabesque of Life), his most significant novel was *En Anden* (1923, Another). *Hærværk* (1930, *Havoc*, 1968) was a critical reflection on intellectual life in Copenhagen in the 1920s. He was also influential as literary critic of the Radical newspaper *Politiken*. 1924-27 and 1931-63. SPO

KROGAGER, EILIF (1910-1992), travel agent. The son of a bricklayer, he graduated *cand. theol.* in 1934 and was a priest 1935-72 in the village of Tjæreborg, **Jutland**. In 1951 he started the travel business Nordisk Bustrafik, which became the Tjæreborg travel business, taken over by Simon Spies in 1989. He also started Sterling Airways, which was for a time the world's largest charter airline. AHT

KROGH, AUGUST (1874-1949), physiologist. Majoring in zoology he graduated *magister* in 1899 and *dr. phil.* in 1903, and was professor of physiology at Copenhagen University 1916-45. His original research was in animal and human respiration, metabolism, and blood circulation. He was awarded the **Nobel Prize** for physiology and medicine in 1920 for his discovery of the importance of capillaries for the flow of blood through the muscles. AHT

KRONBORG CASTLE in **Elsinore** was built on the orders of King **Frederik II** in 1574-85 by the Dutch architects Hans van Paeschen and Anthonis van Opbergen. It stands on the site of the earlier fortress of Krogen (The Hook) which was built by King **Erik "of Pomerania"** c.1410 to help enforce the collection of the **Sound** tolls. It was built in Renaissance style in red brick faced with sandstone from **Scania** and Gotland. Gutted by fire in 1629, it was carefully restored, with some additions, by King **Christian IV**. Damaged during occupation by the Swedes in 1658, it was again restored. Queen **Caroline Matilde** was imprisoned in the "Queen's Apartment" in 1772 and the castle served as a barracks between 1785 and

1922, after which further restoration was carried out with the assistance of the **Carlsberg Foundation**. SPO

KRØYER, PEDER SEVERIN (1851-1909). Painter. He was brought up by an aunt in **Copenhagen**, studied at the **Academy of Art** 1864-70, and traveled abroad 1877-81, visiting Paris and Rome. From 1882 he was a member of the artists' colony at **Skagen**, living there permanently from 1894. His paintings, admired for their mixture of realism and late-romantic colorism, include *Fishermen on Skagen beach* (1883), *At lunch* (1883), the monumental *Burmeister & Wain's iron foundry* (1884-85), and *A meeting of the Scientific Society* (1896-97). His many portraits include **Holger Drachmann** (1895), **Georg Brandes** (1902) and **Niels Finsen** (1903). AHT

KUHLAU, (DANIEL) FRIEDRICH (FREDERIK) (RUDOLPH) (1786-1832). Composer. Born near Hamburg the son of a military bandsman, he moved from Hamburg to Denmark in 1810 to avoid conscription into the French army. He established himself in **Copenhagen** as a pianist and composer, became a Danish national in 1812, and in 1813 was appointed court chamber musician. He did much to enliven Danish music during the Romantic era, and is best remembered in Denmark for his operas and chamber music, in which the flute is prominent. Best known is the music, based on Scandinavian folk ballads, which he composed for Johan Ludvig **Heiberg**'s Elf Hill (*Elverhøj*) libretto of 1828 to mark a royal wedding, and which contains "King Christian Stood By Lofty Mast," one of Denmark's two **national anthems**. However, some of his most important music was for the piano, especially his seven large-scale sonatas. His C major piano concerto, first performed in 1811, thrillingly emulated Beethoven rather than Mozart. He died in Copenhagen after a fire in his house destroyed all his unpublished manuscripts. *See also* **Music; National Anthem**. SPO, AHT

KUNZEN, FRIEDRICH LUDWIG AEMILIUS (1761-1817). Composer. Born in **Lübeck**, he worked in **Copenhagen**, attaining immediate success as a salon pianist and setting songs by Jens **Baggesen**. He developed a substantial European reputation as concert organizer, publisher and opera conductor, in 1795 succeeding Johann Abraham Peter Schulz (1747-1800) as principal conductor in the **Royal Theater** in Copenhagen. His opera, *Holger Danske*, was written with Jens Baggesen, who based his libretto on Wieland's Oberon but managed to include exotic scenes at the court of Sultan Buurman in which Almansaris attempts to seduce Holger. Kunzen used an unusually fluid structure of arias, recitatives, dramatic scenes and dance interludes with music reminiscent of Gluck and Mozart. But it was controversial and was only performed six times. He was more successful with performances of Mozart's *Don Giovanni*. Hailed as "the Nordic Cherubini," he opened a **Golden Age** of culture in Denmark and raised the standard of professional music. AHT

- L -

LABOR MOVEMENT *see* **SOCIAL DEMOCRATIC PARTY; TRADE UNIONS**

LA COUR, PAUL (1902-1956). Poet, essayist, critic, and translator. Without formal education, he lived in France 1923-30 and made his debut as an expressionist poet with his collections *Den tredie dag* (1928, The Third Day), *Leviathan* (1930), *Menneskets hjem* (1931, The Home of Mankind), and *Regn over verden* (1933: Rain over the World). Some of his aphorisms, printed in *Heretica*, provoked debate. Later he abandoned expressionism for the general humanistic ethic which is evident in the poems *Dette er vort liv* (1936, This is Our Life) and *Alt kræver jeg* (1938, I Want It All). His theoretical reflections on inspiration and the poet's work *Fragmenter af en dagbog* (1948, Fragments of a Diary) guided many young writers. AHT

LÅLE, PEDER (lived about 1350), collector of proverbs. Nothing is known of his life, but he is credited with the oldest collection of about 1,200 proverbs, which were used into the 17th century as a Latin schoolbook, with each proverb given in Latin and Danish. First printed in 1506, it was collected into *Danmarks gamle ordsprog* (1979, Old Danish Proverbs). AHT

LANDER, HARALD (1905-1971). Dancer and choreographer. As ballet master at the **Royal Theater** in 1932-51 he built on the fine traditions already established in the 19th and early 20th century to make the Danish **ballet** admired throughout the world. His most important ballets include *Bolero* (1935), *La Valse* (1940), and *Quarrtsiluni* (1942) to music by **Knudåge Riisager**. He worked closely with Riisager in ballets such as *Études* of 1948, which brought him international fame. From 1952 to 1963 he was ballet master at the Paris Opéra. He was married 1932-46 to the ballerina Margot Lander (1910-61), and then to **Toni Lander Marks**. SPO. *See also* **Ballet**.

LANDER MARKS, TONI (1931-1985). **Ballet** dancer. After attending the Royal Ballet School from 1939 she danced at the **Royal Theater** 1949-51 and then abroad, including in the London Festival Ballet, before becoming prima ballerina in the American Ballet 1960-61 and 1963-70. After her husband **Harald Lander** died she returned to the Royal Theater in 1971, mainly as a teacher. From 1976 she taught at Ballet West in Salt Lake City. She took leading roles in *Études*, as Teresina in *Napoli*, as Svanilda in *Coppelia*, and as the princess in *Swan Lake*. AHT

LAND OWNERSHIP. At the time of the **Reformation**, most church lands in Denmark were seized by the Crown, which as a result owned over half the total. Only a small proportion was owned by peasants, and the rest was held by the **nobility**. After the introduction of **Absolute Monarchy** in 1661 the Crown began to sell off much of its land to solve its financial problems. Much of this land was bought by the nobility, but the bourgeoisie, now enabled to buy estates for the first time, also benefited and held some 16 percent as early as 1688. The peasantry's share increased little until the end of the 18th century, when they began to acquire freehold rapidly until by 1835 some half of all farms were owned by those who worked them. SPO

LANDSORGANISATIONEN (LO) *see* **TRADE UNIONS**

LANDSTING was the upper house of the bicameral Danish **parliament** or Rigsdag, set up under the **Constitution** of 1849. Unlike the lower chamber (**Folketing**), it was elected indirectly, but originally by the same electors. The 1866 constitution ensured a conservative majority: 12 of its 66 members were chosen by the Crown, 1 by the Faroese parliament, and of the remaining 53, half were to be elected by the Folketing electors and half by those paying the highest taxes. The Constitution of 1915 replaced the 12 crown appointees with 18 members chosen by the outgoing Landsting. The Landsting was abolished by the Constitution of 1953. When Home Rule was granted, the name was revived for the **Greenland** legislative assembly. SPO, AHT

LANGAARD, RUED (1893-1952). Composer. Educated mainly by his pianist parents, he conducted and gave organ recitals until appointed organist in Ribe cathedral in 1940. His compositions include 16 symphonies, choral, organ, and chamber works, and the large-scale biblical opera *Antichrist* (1921-36). His ornate late-romantic style isolated him from the modernism of his time. AHT

LANGEN, JOHANN GEORG von (1699-1776). Forester. The son of a Thüringian landowner, he served as a hunt page. After travels in Germany he was appointed forest master in Norway in 1737, court hunt-master (*hofjægermester*) in 1739, and head of the general Forest Office 1739-46 with the task of surveying and mapping Norwegian forests. In 1763 he was appointed to plan the development of sustainable and productive forests in North **Zealand**. He introduced new species, including conifers. Although his system was dropped in 1776, he is considered the father of planned forestry. AHT

LANGUAGES *see* **DANISH, FAROESE, GREENLANDIC**

LARSEN, AKSEL (1897-1972). Communist politician and founder of **Socialist People's Party**. He joined the **Social Democratic** Party in 1919 but in 1920 transferred his allegiance to the newly created **Communist Party**. He spent 1925-29 in the Soviet Union. He became Communist Party chairman in 1932, when he was one of two Communists elected to the **Folketing**, of which he remained a member until 1972. During **World War II** he became a **Resistance** leader but was imprisoned in 1941. For six months he was in Vilhelm **Buhl**'s liberation coalition cabinet as minister without portfolio. In 1958 he was expelled from the Danish Communist Party for "revisionism" and proceeded in 1959 to found the Socialist People's Party, which first contested elections in 1960. Larsen came closest to influencing policy in 1966-68, when there was the first ever socialist majority, but when this fell apart he retired from the party leadership. SPO, AHT

LARSEN, EIGIL (1903-1972). **Resistance** member. As a **Communist** he fought as a volunteer in the Spanish Civil War in the late 1930s. In June 1941 he was interned in Horserød camp but escaped a year later. He organized the sabotage group BOPA and led it until January 1944, carrying out the first derailment of a German ammunition train near Espergærde on 6 November 1942. He assembled the first "cook book" of sabotage methods. AHT

LARSEN, JOHANNES (1867-1961). Painter, trained by Kristian Zahrtmann and others. His oil paintings include *Bathing Boys* (1890) and *April Showers* (1901-07). His importance as a graphic artist is evident from his woodcuts for a 1914 edition of **Steen Steensen Blicher**'s book *Trækfuglene* (1837, Migratory Birds) and his illustrations for *De islandske sagaer* I-III (1930-32, The Icelandic Sagas), *De danskes øer* I-III (1926-28, Islands of the Danes), *De jyders land* I-II (1932-34, Land of the Jutes), and *Danmarks store øer* I-II (1936-37, Denmark's Big Islands). His vast production is a meticulous depiction of Danish landscape, especially of **Funen** and makes him a prime example of the group of Funen artists called *fynboerne*. AHT

LARSEN-LEDET, LARS (1881-1958). Temperance propagandist. The son of a farmer, from the age of 14 he was a journalist for various. **Jutland** papers. He edited *Afholdsdagbladet* (Temperance Daily) during 1906-40, taking up temperance work internationally via the Good Templar order. He was vice-president (1919-58) of the World League against Alcoholism and active in its political work. Without question he was the most prominent and uncompromising Danish abolitionist of the 20th century. AHT

LASSEN, ANDERS FREDERIK EMIL VICTOR SCHAU (1920-1945). Soldier. He was educated at **Herlufsholm School** then went to sea in the merchant navy. In 1941 he was among the first Danish volunteers in the British forces. Following a hunt in a trawler for U-boat bases in West Africa in 1942 he was recommended for the Military Cross. Transferred to the Special Boat Service in the Mediterranean, he took part in numerous landings and captures of Greek islands. Informal in his methods, he was always first if a risk was to be taken, and became a legend among the Greeks. He was awarded two bars to his MC, was promoted to major and was killed in a raid on Lake Comacchio, Northern Italy, on 9 April. Posthumously he was awarded the Victoria Cross (Britain's highest military decoration), the only foreigner in **World War II** to receive this honor. AHT

LAUENBURG. A small duchy east of Hamburg awarded to Denmark in compensation for the loss of Norway to Sweden in the **Treaty of Kiel** of 1814. At the same time the Danish monarch had to allow Lauenburg and adjoining **Holsten** to join the newly established Confederation of German States. The territory was lost to Denmark in the Second **Slesvig-Holsten** War of 1864. AHT

LAURITZEN, KNUD (1904-1978). Shipowner. After advanced management studies in Denmark and several European cities, following his father's death in 1935 he and his brother took over the family shipping firm, which specialized in passenger and refrigerated shipping in Denmark and abroad. In 1964 he inherited a majority shareholding in **DFDS**, with its important North Sea ferry business, but in his last years financial difficulties imposed retrenchment. AHT

LAURITZEN, LAU (1878-1938). Film director. A merchant's son, in 1907 he ended a military career to become an actor, from 1911 in films. At Nordisk Films in 1914-19 he directed some 200 single-reel films, mostly farces. Working for Palladium 1920-37 he developed the characterization for films such as *Han, Hun og Hamlet* (1922, Him, Her and Hamlet). His son, Lau Lauritzen, Jr. (1910-77) also directed films, including *De røde Enge* (1945, The Red Meadows) about the resistance movement, in which **Poul Reichhardt** made his debut. AHT. *See* **Film Industry**.

LAW *see* **DANISH LAW**

LAXMAND, HANS (?-1443). Archbishop. Of noble birth, he studied abroad in Prague and Erfurt, and was appointed archbishop in 1436. As a member of the Council of State (*rigsrådet*) he represented the **nobility** of state and church in their efforts to limit the power of the monarchy, and actively opposed the rebellious peasantry. In 1443 he crowned **Christoffer of Bavaria** as king. AHT

LAXMAND, POUL (?-1502) politician. Born into a very rich noble family, he owned over 900 farms. He was appointed to the Council of State (*rigsrådet*) in 1483 and chancellor of the realm (*rigshoffmester*) in 1489. He was accused by the archbishop of conspiring against King **Hans**. He was murdered by two noblemen and the king confiscated his lands on the allegation of his treasonable contacts with Sweden. Claims that the king ordered the murder have never been proved. AHT

LEFT REFORM PARTY (Venstrereformparti) was a group of the parliamentary **Liberal Party** (*Venstre*) formed in 1895 in opposition to the agreement reached between moderate Liberals under **Frede Bojsen** and the **Conservative** government. Its chairman was **Sofus Hogsbro**, but its true leader was **J.C. Christensen**. In the election of 1898 it won 63 seats and became the largest party in the **Folketing**. It had even greater success three years later, when it increased its representation to 76 and formed a government in the so-called **Change of System**. In 1910 it united with the Moderate Left to form the United Left. SPO

LEFT SOCIALISTS (Venstresocialisterne), a political party formed in 1967 by six members of the **Socialist People's Party** in protest at the latter's support for a proposal to intervene in labor disputes. Their defection caused an election in which they won four seats. Two of the new members, however, soon resigned to form the Socialist Working Group (Socialistisk Arbejsgruppe). The Party increased its seats to five in 1977 and to six in 1979, but was back to five in 1981 and disappeared in 1987. It opposed Denmark's membership of both **NATO** and the **European Community**. SPO

LEGO is a children's play-system based on studded plastic bricks in primary colors, which fit together to build an infinite variety of models, and can be reused repeatedly. The name is a contraction of *leg godt* (play well in Danish). Made at Billund in mid-**Jutland**, it has been exported very widely. Its origins lie in the wood-working business started in 1932 by **Ole Kirk Christiansen** and continued by his son and grandson. Plastic "automatic binding bricks" were introduced in 1949 and were improved over the next decade. Since then the range of components and models has expanded greatly. So has the organization, with sales companies in Europe, the Americas, the Asia Pacific region, and Japan and a net turnover in 1997 of 7.6 billion Danish kroner. Legoland theme-parks opened at Billund in 1968, at Windsor Castle in England in 1996, and in Carlsbad, California in 1999. AHT

LEHMANN, ALFRED (1858-1921). Psychologist. He graduated *cand. polyt.* in 1882 and *dr. phil.* in 1884 and was a professor from 1910. He introduced experimental psychology to Denmark and founded one of the world's first psychological laboratories in the University of Copenhagen. He emphasized the link between psychic and physiological phenomena. His books include *Overtro og trolddom* I-IV (1893-96, Superstition and Sorcery) and *De sjælelige tilstandens legemlige ytringer* (1898, Bodily Expressions of the Condition of the Soul). AHT

LEHMANN, (PETER MARTIN) ORLA (1810-1870). Lawyer and **National Liberal** politician. In spite of a home which was strongly Germanic in spirit, in the first meeting of the Jutland Consultative Assembly in **Viborg** in 1836 he emerged as a fervent Danish nationalist. An impressive speaker and writer, in 1839 he co-founded the liberal daily paper *Fædrelandet* and presented a student petition for a **constitution** to the new King **Christian VIII**. In 1841 he was sentenced to three months in prison for a speech critical of monarchical rule. In 1842 in **Copenhagen** he first proposed the Ejder Program (see *SLESVIG-HOLSTEN*), adopted at the **Roskilde Consultative Assembly** in 1846. In March 1848 Lehmann penned the address to the king which led to the fall of **absolute monarchy**. He joined the cabinet formed under Count Moltke but resigned the following November to become governor (*amtmand*) of the county of

Vejle. He was a member of the **Folketing** in 1851-3 and of the **Landsting** from 1854. In 1861 he was minister of the interior in C.C. **Hall**'s cabinet and was responsible for drawing up the abortive 1863 constitution which proposed uniting Slesvig to Denmark and precipitated the Second **Slesvig-Holsten** War. He resigned in December 1963 having failed to get support for his program of **Scandinavianism**. Although a persuasive and attractive personality, he was not a practical statesman. SPO

LEONORA CHRISTINA (1621-1698). Countess of **Slesvig** and Holsten, and author. Born in **Frederiksborg Castle** as the daughter of King **Christian IV** and his second wife **Kirstine Munck**, she was married at the age of 15 to the courtier **Corfitz Ulfeldt**, who in 1643 became Chancellor of the Realm (*rigshoffmester*). Her social and intellectual talents made her the center of a glittering court circle. She accompanied her husband into exile in 1651 and stayed loyally by his side during his subsequent travels. Suspected of implication in his treasonous activities, Leonora Christina was brought a prisoner from London to Copenhagen in 1663 and imprisoned in the Blue Tower of **Copenhagen Castle** for 22 years. While there she began to compose *Jammersminde* (*Memoirs by Leonora Christina, Daughter of Christian IV of Denmark*, 1929) one of the greatest works of Danish literature, in which she described her experiences and protested her innocence. She was finally pardoned in 1685 and granted an apartment in Maribo Convent, where she completed *Jammersminde*, the manuscript of which was discovered in Austria only in 1868 and was published in 1869. A modern edition of another biographical work, *Hæltinners Pryd* (Heroines' Adornments) was published in 1977. SPO

LEUNBACH, JONATHAN HØEGH (1884-1955). Doctor and sexologist. He graduated *cand. med.* in 1912 and advocated the establishment of public sex clinics. Not meeting success, he set up several consulting rooms to educate poor women in contraception. In 1936 he was imprisoned for three months for illegal abortion, but is considered a pioneer in the fight for free abortion and sex education. AHT

LIBERAL PARTY (Venstre, Danmarks liberale Parti). **National liberals** achieved the 1849 **constitution** which reduced the powers of the monarchy, but saw this ground lost again in 1867. The modern Danish Liberal Party traces its origins from 1870, when various liberal groups in parliament, including the **Farmers' Friends**, formed the United Left to fight for a restoration of the June Constitution of 1849 and parliamentary government. However in 1878 they split into a Moderate group under **Frede Bojsen** and a more radical group under **Chresten Berg** and **V.L.B. Hørup**. Franchise extension and the question of relations with **J.B.S. Estrup**'s government of the **Right**, which remained in power during this period, led to further divisions. After the conservative government reached agreement with the **Moderate Left Party** in 1895, liberals who opposed the agreement united in the **Liberal Reform Party** with **J.C. Christensen** as its leading figure. It was they who achieved the 1901 **Change of System**. The more radical wing within this party broke away in 1905 to form the **Radical Liberal** Party. In 1910 the **Reform Liberals**, then in the cabinet led by **Klaus Berntsen**, and the Moderate Liberals united to form the United Liberals *(samlede Venstre)*. Three years later they lost power to the **Radical Liberals** *(see also* **Alberti**) and did not form a ministry again until 1920 under **Niels Neergaard**.

Venstre was out of power from 1926 until 1945, when **Knud Kristensen** formed a two-year minority cabinet which fell on the issue of the frontier with Germany. **Erik Eriksen** headed a minority coalition of Liberals with Conservatives in 1950-53 which carried through extensive changes of the **constitution.** Merger with the **Conservatives** was later discussed but rejected. Liberal ministers were members of the Radical Liberal-led coalition of 1968-71. Following the chaos of the 1973 "earthquake" election **Poul Hartling** led a very narrowly based minority cabinet 1973-75 and doubled the party's strength in the 1975 election, but failed to form a broader-based government when the **Progress Party** withdrew its support at the last moment. *Venstre's* leader **Henning Christophersen** took the party into coalition with the **Social Democrats** in 1978-9 but this was opposed by the **trade unions** and lasted less than 14 months. The party was an important component of all the cabinets of 1982-93 under **Poul Schlüter**, with Uffe Ellemann-Jensen as foreign minister, Bertel Haarder as minister of education, and several other portfolios. *See also* Appendix 2: Cabinets.

After working with the Social Democrats to achieve social and constitutional reform in 1915, the Liberals became a center-right party, retaining a strong base in the farming community until the 1970s. The party's share of the popular vote declined from over a third at the end of **World War I** to around 20 percent in the years following **World War II**, then fell to about 12 percent in 1977-90. Adopting clear free-market positions in the 1980s, the party contributed core support and intellectual leadership to the Schlüter cabinets. Led in 1984-98 by Uffe Ellemann-Jensen, the Liberals obtained 23 percent of the vote in September 1994 despite his advocacy of a coalition with the Conservatives and the far-right Progress Party. Venstre did not make expected gains in 1998 and Ellemann-Jensen resigned as leader. His successor was Anders Fogh Rasmussen. The party's Danish name, *Venstre*, means the Left but this is in contrast to the reactionary Right of the 19th century rather than in sympathy with socialism. While officially entitled *The Left, Denmark's Liberal Party*, it is also variously termed Agrarian Liberal, Liberal Democrat, or Liberal Left. SPO, AHT

LIBRARIES. The most important library in Denmark is the Royal Library, Det kongelige Bibliotek, in Copenhagen with some 2,300,000 volumes. It was founded in 1660 and made a deposit library in 1697. It was reorganized in 1997 to incorporate Copenhagen University Library, with the Fiolstræde building housing books on sociology, economics, politics, and law, and the Amager building housing humanities books. The Slotsholmen building is being extended and reopens in 1999. It has a research reading room and houses the national library's special collections of manuscripts, including those of the writer **Georg Brandes**. There are also university departmental libraries. The main newspaper collection in Denmark is housed in the State Library in **Århus**, another deposit library which serves Aarhus University. The Karen Brahe Library in **Odense** has a valuable collection of early books and manuscripts.

The rural clergy encouraged popular literacy and in 1885 there were 1,068 parish libraries. Since a law of 1920, modern public libraries run by local government districts (*kommuner*) have offered a free service throughout the country, including to schools, hospitals, and other institutions, as an important part of public (self-)

education. Copenhagen Main Library (Hovedbibliotek) moved in 1994 into specially converted premises on four floors at Krystalgade 15. The Danish Library Bureau (Bibliotekscentralen) provides a central catalog of Danish book production and edits the Danish Book List, *Bogfortegnelse*. SPO, AHT

LIEBE, OTTO (1860-1929). Advocate. He graduated *cand. jur.* in 1882 and in 1889 became a supreme court lawyer with the royal court among his clients. After **Christian X** dismissed the Zahle government in 1920 (*see* **Easter Crisis**) he formed a caretaker government supported by **Liberals** and **Conservatives**, but the threat of a general strike forced its dismissal after only five days. AHT

LILLELUND, JENS (1904-1981). **Resistance** organizer. A bank worker, from the end of 1942 he became active in the resistance, from June 1943 in the Holger Danske group. He fled to neutral Sweden from December 1942 to June 1944. He reorganized **Holger Danske**, which carried out about 50 sabotage actions in **Jutland** during the fall. In November he went via Sweden to England for military training returning to Denmark on 7 May 1945 as liaison officer to the British General Dewing. AHT

LINDHART, POUL GEORG (1910-1988). Theologian and priest. He graduated *cand. theol.* in 1934 and *dr. theol.* in 1939. In 1942-80 he was the first professor in the history of the church and dogma at the University of Århus and in 1945-80 an assistant priest. In his book *Vækkelser og kirkelige retninger i Danmark* (1951, Revivals and Church Directions in Denmark) he argued that the religious life is historically conditioned. In 1953 his lecture (published in *Det evige liv*) started the debate of the century in Denmark about Christianity by rejecting belief in life after death. His other books include *Den nordiske kirkes historie* (1945, The History of the Nordic Church) and *Morten Pontoppidan* I-II (1950-53). AHT

LITERATURE. The **Danish language** has supported a large and varied literature considering the small population who speak it. Peder Låle's 14th-century collection of proverbs in Latin and Danish is one of the oldest known books and was used as a schoolbook into the 17th century. **Christiern Pedersen** translated and printed

Saxo's history of Denmark and contributed to the translation of the **Bible**. With the **reformation**, availability of the Bible in a "plain Danish" style was highly influential for the development of the language, while the hymns of **Thomas Kingo** compare favorably with contemporary English metaphysical poetry.

The Norwegian-born **Ludvig Holberg** helped to exclude Germanic linguistic influences from Danish. His prolific dramas, essays and history-writing make him the most important Nordic writer of the 18th century, with a reputation even surpassing that of Molière, with whom he is often compared. Among the Romantic writers of the Golden Age, **Adam Oehlenschläger**'s poetry and dramas were widely influential, while **N.F.S. Grundtvig**'s poetry, hymns and use of mythological source material (together with extensive writing on religious and social themes) laid the ground-work for a national cultural revival. The philosopher **Søren Kierkegaard** was little considered in his time but has since become seen as a founder of existentialism and an experimental novelist, with many volumes published in English translation in the 1960s. **Hans Christian Andersen**, eight years older and trying to come to terms with many of the same perplexities, achieved recognition in his own lifetime and has had his universally popular tales translated into all major and many minor languages.

Jens Peter Jacobsen is one of the greatest writers of Danish Modernism, without committing himself fully to the program outlined by **Georg Brandes**. He was widely read abroad, by Freud, Rilke and Musil among others, and has had a powerful influence on other writers. Only three Danes have won the **Nobel Prize** for literature: in 1917 it went to **Karl Gjellerup** and **Henrik Pontoppidan** jointly, and in 1944 to **Johannes V. Jensen**. **Gustav Wied**, a contemporary of Gjellerup, is one of the greatest humorists in Danish literature. Humour is often lost in another language, but **Piet Hein**'s poems and aphorisms have been widely and successfully translated.

Women's writing is well represented in Danish, from **Leonora Christina**'s *Jammersminde* and **Thomasine Gyllembourg** onward. **Dorothea Biehl** wrote plays in the style of Holberg and retailed the scandals of court life. **Mathilde Fibiger** is taken as a pioneer of the feminist movement. **Amalie Skram**'s main theme is woman's position in marriage, but she also wrote on poverty and alcoholism and on mental health care in the 1890s. **Thit Jensen,** sister of Johannes

V. Jensen, wrote to explore feminist concerns with the conflicts between work and love, tradition and freedom. **Tove Ditlevsen** wrote poems, short stories and aphorisms, as well as novels depicting childhood and marriage in a realistic mode.

Karen Blixen (*pseud.* Isak Dinesen), a mistress of the short story, wrote in both English and Danish. Films of *Babette's Feast* and *Out of Africa* have enjoyed great success, as has **Martin Andersen Nexø**'s *Pelle the Conqueror*. Blixen was part of the *Heretica* group of writers who combined a serious interest in artistic form with the disturbing political and moral issues raised by **World War II** and the new nuclear weapons. **Martin A. Hansen**, an editor of the journal, is one of the first important novelists of the postwar period. Another, H.C. Branner (1903-66) used a Freudian-inspired stream-of-consciousness in *Rytteren* (1947; *The Riding Master* 1951, *The Mistress* 1953) which paved the way for the realism of many mainstream novels that followed. The communist **Hans Scherfig** developed a fierce line in political satire, while **Leif Panduro**'s often very funny studies of manic and neurotic behaviors were widely seen on television in the 1970s.

Klaus Rifbjerg and **Villy Sørensen** were responsible for a decisive new direction in writing through their editorship in 1959-63 of *Vindrosen*, publishing some talented new writers. Rifbjerg's long series of novels are remarkable for the vitality of his recollective powers, while his provocative attitude has kept him at the center of press attention. Sørensen is an important intermediary of philosophy and fiction, with an authorship ranging from translations to a retelling of Norse mythology and to a much-discussed utopian political manifesto (*Revolt from the Center*, 1981). Ebbe Kløvedal Reich (1940-) has also been politically engaged, with a series of historical novels mirroring present-day conditions. For example, his biography of **N.F.S. Grundtvig**, entitled *Frederik* (1972), became a powerful argument against membership in the **European Economic Community**. By contrast, Benny Andersen (1929-) experiments with quiet humor in verse and short stories, playing on words and juxtaposing metaphors in a low-key celebration of Danish culture. The poet Henrik Nordbrandt (1945-) has used his great lyrical talent to produce a beautiful set of poems, inspired by Turkey and the eastern Mediterranean.

Writers who extend the tradition for tales and grotesque stories established by H.C. Andersen include Frank Jæger (1926-1977), briefly a coeditor of Vindrosen, Villy Sørensen himself, Sven Holm (1940-) with his book *Termush* (1969), and Peter Seeberg (1925-). The tradition of writers who describe proletarian childhood and working life, pioneered by **Martin Andersen Nexø**, was carried forward by Ditte Cederstrand (1915-), Åge Hansen-Folehavn (1913-1979) and John Nehm (1934-). Two of Nehm's books were the basis of the film *Johnny Larsen*. Tove Ditlevsen's memoirs and novels made a powerful contribution to feminist writing.

Documentary literature is an important genre in recent Danish writing, ranging from autobiography and history to the political manifesto. For example, **Thorkild Hansen**'s work has attracted widespread attention both in Denmark and abroad. Examples of writers of neorealistic novels include Anders Bodelsen (1937-), Henrik Stangerup (1937-), and Christian Kampmann (1939-). Many of Bodelsen's criminal novels have been published in English. Stangerup followed an autobiography with a huge novel about **P.W. Lund** that was an artistic adaptation of biographical material. Kampmann wrote a massive four-volume work on the Gregersen family. In the 1980s there developed a strand of ecological realism: novels by Vagn Lundbye around the story of Jonah are absorbed in nature and the cosmos, while Ib Michael's (1943-) writing evinces an interest in peoples — the Sami, Greenlanders, Indians — with more affection and insight for nature than is generally found in Western industrialized culture. **Peter Høeg**'s *Miss Smilla's Feeling for Snow* shares this characteristic, but his two other books have a psychological perspective. AHT

See also **Abell, Kjeld; Arrebo, Anders Christensen; Baggesen, Jens; Bang, Herman; Becker, Knuth; Berntsen, Arent; Blicher, Steen Steensen; Bording, Anders; Brandes, Edvard; Cavling, Ib Henrik; Christmas, Walther; Claussen, Sophus Niels Christen; Drachmann, Holger; Dreier, Frederik; Ewald, Johannes; Fibiger, Mathilde Lucie; Frisch, Hartvig; Goldschmidt, Meïr Aron; Groes, Else; Grundtvig, N.F.S.; Heiberg, Johan Ludvig; Heiberg, P.A.; Heinesen, William; Henningsen, Poul; Hertz, Henrik; Ingemann, Bernhard Severin; Jørgensen, Johannes; Kirk, Hans Rudolf; Kristensen, Tom; la Cour, Paul; Møller, Poul Martin; Munk, Kaj; Nathansen, Henri; Nielsen, Morten; Paludan, Jacob; Petersen, Nis; Sandemose, Aksel; Schade, Jens**

August; Smith, Henrik; Sneedorff, Jens Schelderup; Sønderby, Knud; Soya, Carl Erik; Wessel, Johan Herman ; Winther, Christian.

LOCAL GOVERNMENT. From 1060 until the **Reformation** Denmark was divided into eight bishoprics (*stifter*) and subdivided into *herreder* with coterminous civil and ecclesiastical administrations. The *herred* was the smallest administrative unit, with a court of first instance in which the *foged* (bailiff) was judge. But some estate owners were allowed their own court, *birkeret*, and appointed the judge. In a parallel feudal system the king "loaned" land (called a *len*) to nobles with the obligation of military service by the *lensmand*, but the Danish system differed from elsewhere in Europe in that a *len* was not hereditary. This system was replaced in 1662 by *amter* (counties) each administered by a royally appointed *amtmand*; many of these offices were held by landowning counts and barons and carried administrative, judicial, and military responsibilities analogous to those of a French *prefect*. In 1794-1809 the counties were reorganized as 18 *amter*, and in 1841 they were subdivided into *amtsrådskredser* (county districts) and further into 1021 self-governing civil parishes *(sognekommuner)*. The more populous of these were subdivided until by 1965 there were 1,257, plus 88 self-governing market towns *(købstadskommuner)*.

A major reform in 1970 amalgamated these units into 277 *kommuner* and 14 *amter* (counties), in the process ending the distinctive status of market towns. Legal and police districts were revised to have the same boundaries. Only **Copenhagen** and neighboring **Frederiksberg** kept unitary municipal councils. The *kommuner* raise taxes and are responsible for most local services, including schools, **libraries**, medical and dental services, homes for the elderly, land planning, rubbish collection and disposal, and district heating systems. The counties are responsible for major roads, **hospitals**, further education, and some supervision of social services. AHT

LOLLAND is a low-lying island in southeast Denmark, wooded, with excellent beaches. Maribo, the administrative center, is attractively situated on the Søndersø and is bypassed by the main E4 road from **Copenhagen** heading for Rødby Havn, the port developed in the 1960s for ferry traffic to Puttgarden in Germany. Nakskov, at the head of a wide fjord, had strategic naval importance; in the 19th century it was a port for the grain trade to Germany and in the 20th century the sugar factory processes beet from the surrounding fields. A shipyard flourished until the 1980s. AHT

LONDON PROTOCOL see SLESVIG-HOLSTEN.

LONGOMONTANUS, CHRISTEN SØRENSEN (1562-1647). Astronomer trained by **Tycho Brahe** 1589-97 and 1599-1600. From 1607 he was professor of mathematics at Copenhagen University and from 1621 also of astronomy. His *Astronomia Danica* (1622), which carries forward Brahe's work, became the main 17th century text on the subject in Denmark. He established the observatory in the **Round Tower** in **Copenhagen**. AHT

LORCK, MELCHIOR (1526/7-c. 1583). Painter and graphic artist. Educated in **Lübeck**, he traveled widely to perfect his copper engraving technique and was portraitist in 1580-2 to **Frederik II**. His portraits included Luther (1548), Dürer (1550), Sultan Suleiman the Great (c.1559), and **Frederik II** (1582). A major journey to Turkey (1555-59) produced many well-known paintings, drawings, and etchings, not least an incomplete series of drawings of *Views over the Roofs of Constantinople*. AHT

LORNSEN, UWE JENS (1793-1838). Civil servant and liberal politician. In 1830 he was appointed to a minor post on the island of Sild from where he founded the "**Slesvig-Holsten** Movement" for the union of the two duchies, to be administered from Kiel and only linked to Denmark by the king. He was dismissed from his post, imprisoned, and exiled, a "martyrdom" which fueled his cause. SPO, AHT

LOUISIANA MUSEUM is a museum of modern art opened in 1958 at Humlebæk on the shores of the **Sound** north of **Copenhagen**. Founded by Knud W. Jensen, who has also served as its director, the building, itself a fine example of the best of Danish 20th-century architecture, was designed by Jorgen Bo and Vilhelm Wohlert. It houses a permanent collection of modern Danish art and changing exhibitions of modern art from outside Denmark. SPO

LØVENØRN, POUL VENDELBO (1686-1740). Officer and politician. He served in the Russian army from 1707, first as a private then as a major and lieutenant colonel. From 1711 he was in Danish service, becoming colonel and company commander of the Horse-Guards, and was ennobled. He was employed as a diplomatic envoy, including to the Stockholm negotiations which resulted in the end of the **Great Northern War** in 1720. In 1730 **Christian VI** appointed him secretary for war and deputy for land and sea forces. When adscription (*see* **stavnsbaand** and **peasant reforms**) was introduced, he was one of those who took the initiative to reintroduce the land militia which **Frederik IV** had disbanded in 1740. AHT

LÜBECK, PEACE OF (8 May 1629) was a treaty, signed in the German city of Lübeck, between Denmark and German emperor Ferdinand II, which ended Denmark's participation in the **Thirty Years' War**. After failing in 1628 to secure a foothold on the Baltic coast and faced with ruin in an enemy-occupied Denmark, the Danes agreed to open peace negotiations on 6 January. In March the emperor presented harsh terms which included an enormous war indemnity, the surrender of **Jutland**, and the closure of the **Sound** to the emperor's enemies. But with the Swedes about to enter the war against the German empire, these demands were dropped in order to regain peace, and King **Christian IV** finally had only to surrender all his claims in northern Germany and not to reenter the war. Even so, Christian compelled the Council of State to pay him 10 barrels (*tønder*) of gold (one million rigsdaler) in compensation for his personal losses, before he would ratify the treaty. SPO, AHT. *See also* **Buxtehude, D.; Hanseatic League; Valdemar IV "Atterdag".**

LUMBYE, HANS CHRISTIAN (1810-1874). Composer and musical performer. Trained as a military trumpeter, and influenced by the elder Johann Strauß, his widely popular polkas, waltzes, marches, gallops, and other light pieces are particularly associated with the **Tivoli** Gardens, where as director of the orchestra for nearly 30 years from 1843 he often performed them. He also wrote songs, the idyll *Drømmebilleder* (Dream Pictures) for orchestra, and ballet music. As a popularizer, he introduced many people to music of substance. His sons Carl (1841-1890) and Georg (1843-1922) continued their father's tradition as composers and performers. SPO

LUND, PETER WILHELM (1801-1880). Naturalist. He studied medicine and natural history at the University of Copenhagen, graduating *dr. phil.* in 1829 with a thesis on comb-gilled snails. He lived in Brazil 1825-29 and from 1833, in the village Lagua Santa from 1835. He explored many underground caves and found the late tertiary and early quaternary age remains of 147 species of mammals, 53 of them extinct. These included a giant armadillo, giant sloth, and the sabre-cat *Machærodus*. A pioneer paleontologist, he published *Blik på Brasiliens dyreverden før sidste jordomvæltning* (A View of the Animal World of Brasil before the Last Upheaval of the Earth) and his scientific results in the journal *Videnskabernes Selskabs Tidsskrift* (1837-46). He is the chief character in Henrik Stangerup's novel *Vejen til Lagua Santa* (The Road to Lagua Santa). AHT

LUNDBYE, JOHAN THOMAS (1818-1848), painter, was one of the leaders of the Romantic school of painters who, influenced by the landscapes of Christen Købke (1810-48), broke away from the influence of Christoffer Wilhelm **Eckersberg** to indulge in the beauties of the **Zealand** countryside. He trained in the **Academy of Art** in 1832-42 and spent 1845-46 in Italy. He was also a fine animal painter, and illustrated H.V. Kaalund's *Fabler for børn* (1845, Children's fables). Most of his smaller pieces are housed in the **Hirschsprung Collection**. He was killed by an accidental shot during the campaign of 1848 in the First **Slesvig-Holsten** War. SPO. *See also* **Painting; Romanticism.**

LUR is a a bronze-age musical wind-instrument consisting of a long, slightly tapering and curved tube with a patterned disk at the wider end and a mouthpiece at the narrower end. It makes a distinctive, resonant sound with a musical range restricted to five natural notes, though a skilled player can extract many more. Small metal clappers hanging near the mouthpiece may have supplemented their sound. About 36 have been found in Denmark, Sweden, and northern Germany, almost always in pairs, identical except that the curves mirror each other like the horns of an ox. Their frequent depiction in rock engravings suggests a sacred or ceremonial use. In the 20th century they have been adopted as the trademark for Danish butter. AHT

LUTHERANISM is the Protestant Christian faith established in Denmark by royal decree in 1536 and professed by an overwhelming majority of Danes since then. In the 16th century, tolerant with respect to belief, in the 17th century, Danish Lutheranism became rigidly orthodox under the influence of Hans Paulsen Resen (1561-1638), largely responsible for the first Danish **Bible**. Strongly influenced by German **Pietism** at the beginning of the 18th century, in the 19th it was faced with the contrast of **N.F.S. Grundtvig**'s liberal theology and the new pietism represented by the Inner Mission. SPO. *See also* **Church; Religion; Tausen, Hans.**

LUTTER-AM-BARENBERG in the Harz foothills was the site of a battle during the **Thirty Years' War** in which an army led by King **Christian IV** was defeated on 17 August 1626 by the army of the Catholic League under Tilly. Christian had entered the war the previous year at the invitation of the other German princes of the Lower Saxon Circle, of which Holstein was a member. He advanced cautiously across the Elbe, but was met by the Catholic forces. The defeat forced him to retire to his own dominions and eventually to evacuate **Jutland**. SPO

LYNGSIE, MICHAEL CHRISTIAN (1864-1931). Trade unionist. As a young workman in the 1880s he joined the **Social Democrats** (SD), as a result losing his job at the army cartridge factory in 1890. He recruited many unskilled workers into the labor movement, and was the driving force behind the establishment in 1897 of Dansk arbejdsmands forbund (DAF, Danish Laborer's Union), uniting unskilled laborers from all parts of the country. In 1896-97 he helped found the successful **cooperative** dairy, *Enigheden* (Unity), becoming chairman, but an attempt in 1897 to found the cooperative Svendborg Margarine Factory failed disastrously in 1906. He was one of the leaders of De samvirkende fagforbund (DsF), the national confederation of **trade unions**, which later became Landsorganisationen, LO.

Lyngsie was a member of **Copenhagen** City Council 1900-14 and chairman of its tramways committee. He negotiated an agreement among Scandinavian labor unions which was important in later conflicts. A member of the 1908 committee which set up the labor courts, from 1910 he was a member of the permanent court of arbitration. He energetically opposed the syndicalism of 1908-10 and the **communism** which later attracted many of his members. A member of the SD party executive and general purposes committee 1896-1914, he was elected to the **Folketing** 1898-1906 and to the **Landsting** from 1925, but made no great contribution in parliament.

By 1918 Lyngsie was a member of the Currency Council, the Nutrition Commission, the Interior Ministry's Labor committee, and the board of the Workers' Bank (Arbejdernes landsbank) 1919-31. During the 1925 labor dispute he called a general strike of transport workers that was vigorously opposed by the other leaders of DsF. As a result, DAF left DsF until 1929. The scale of his achievement is indicated by the threefold division of the union in 1925 into transport, factory, and general laborers' branches, each with their own leader. His reputation was as a leader of working men and his often very aggressive policies brought important gains for the union movement. Probably the trade unionist most feared by employers, his vigorous promotion of the interests of unskilled over skilled workers made him enemies elsewhere in the union movement and the SD party. AHT

- M -

MAASTRICHT TREATY *see* **EUROPEAN UNION**

MADSEN, THORVALD (1870-1957). Medical doctor. He graduated *cand. med.* in 1893 and *dr. med.* in 1896, and was director of the State Serum Institute 1910-40, gaining for it an international reputation for tackling epidemic diseases including diphtheria, tuberculosis, and polio by vaccination. He traveled extensively to gain support for his work. AHT

MADSEN-MYGDAL, THOMAS (1873-1943). **Liberal Party** politician, prime minister 1926-9. After qualifying as a teacher and then in agronomy, he became a farmer and was active in the leadership of agricultural organizations. He was a member of the **Landsting** 1920-25 and of the **Folketing** 1926-33, and national chairman of the Liberal Party 1929-41. He became minister of agriculture in **Niels Neergaard**'s second and third **cabinets** in 1920-24, continuing while prime minister. Madsen-Mygdal tried to tackle the economic depression by a policy of free trade and by reducing the costs of production by lowering wages and limiting the power of **trade unions**. He had to resign after the success of the **Social Democrats** in the April 1929 election. SPO

MADVIG, JOHAN NICOLAI (1804-1886). Politician and linguist. He passed the civil service examination in languages in 1825, and graduated *magister* in 1826 and *dr. phil.* in 1828. He was appointed professor of languages 1829-48 and of classical languages 1851-79 in Copenhagen University. In 1841 he wrote *Latinsk sproglære*, the text used for teaching Latin for decades. He was a member of the constitutive assembly in 1848, of the **Folketing** 1849-53 and of the **Landsting** 1853-74. He was minister for education and the church (*Kultusminister*) 1848-51. Madvig was a moderate Liberal who supported the partition of Slesvig, but on **Slesvig-Holsten** in the early 1860s he supported the **Ejder** policy, which he later regretted. After the defeat of 1864 he supported the 1866 **constitution** and opposed democratic parliamentarism. AHT

MAGNÚSSON, ÁRNI (1663-1730). Archivist. The son of an Iceland priest, he graduated *cand. theol.* in 1685 and was appointed to the state archive in 1697, as its director from 1725, combining this with appointments as professor of philosophy, history, and geography at Copenhagen University. His collection of Norse manuscripts from Norway and especially **Iceland** was left to Copenhagen University where it became known as the Arnamagnæan Collection and was used as the basis for Old Norse and Old Icelandic linguistic studies. AHT

MALLING, OVE (1747-1829). Civil servant and author. After graduating *cand. theol.* in 1766 he held a series of important customs, banking, and poor-law offices from 1771 until his death, including first minister 1824-29. He is best known for writing, at the request of **Ove Høegh-Guldberg**, *Store og gode Handlinger af Danske, Norske og Holstenere* (1777, Great and Good Deeds by Danes, Norwegians, and Holsteners), a history text book very widely read for many decades. AHT

MALLING-HANSEN, RASMUS (1835-1890). Inventor. A teacher and son of a teacher, his work with the deaf and efforts to improve their sign alphabet led him to invent the writing ball, the first mass-produced typewriter in the world. AHT

MALTHE-BRUN, KIM (1923-1945). **Resistance** member. After completing school, in September 1944 he joined the underground Students Intelligence Service. In December 1944 he was arrested by the Gestapo, sentenced to death on 4 April 1945, and executed on 6 April, a month before Denmark was liberated. In autumn 1945 the book *Kim: Uddrag af dagbog og breve* (Kim: A Selection from Diaries and Letters) was published, widely read, and translated into seven languages. AHT

MARCH PATENT *see* **SLESVIG-HOLSTEN**

MARGRETHE I (1353-1412). Regent of Denmark 1375-97, of Norway 1380-97, and of Sweden 1388-97. The younger daughter of King **Valdemar IV**, she was born in Søborghus and was married at age 10 to King Haakon VI of Norway. Until the age of 16 she lived most of the time in Sweden, where she was raised by one of the daughters of St. Bridget. In 1370 she gave birth to a son, **Oluf (II)**, and on the death of her father in 1375, she arranged the election of her son to succeed him on the Danish throne with herself as regent. Five years later Oluf also succeeded his father in Norway. Having deposed king Albert of Mecklenburg in 1388, the nobles of Sweden negotiated with Margrethe for her son's accession also to the throne of Sweden, but before this was agreed Oluf died. Margrethe was subsequently granted the title in Sweden of "powerful lady and master" and in 1396 persuaded all three countries to recognize her nephew **Erik of Pomerania** as their king. This implicit agreement on the government, which was reached the following year at Kalmar, laid the basis of the **Kalmar Union**. While Margrethe lived, it was she rather than Erik who administered the countries and dictated policy. A woman of great ability, she sought to strengthen the power of the monarchy, but sowed the seeds of future trouble by appointing her own agents to key positions while ignoring the rights of the national nobilities, which had been guaranteed when the Union was established. She died of the plague while on board ship in

Flensborg fjord and was first interred at **Sorø** but finally in **Roskilde**. SPO

MARGRETHE II (1940-   ). Margrethe Alexandrine Þorhildur Ingrid, Queen of Denmark from 1972. She is the daughter of King **Frederik IX** and Queen Ingrid. As a result of the law of succession passed with the **constitution** of 1953 she is the first queen to *inherit* the Danish throne (but see also **Margrethe I**). In 1967 she married the French aristocrat Henri-Marie-Jean-André, comte de Laborde de Montpezat (Prince Henrik of Denmark). They have two sons: Crown Prince **Frederik**, born in 1968 and Prince **Joachim**, born in 1969. Margrethe has two sisters, Princess Benedikte and Princess Anne Marie.

Queen Margrethe is academically the most highly qualified ruler of Denmark, having studied law and archaeology at the universities of **Aarhus**, **Copenhagen**, London, Cambridge, and Paris. She and Prince Henrik have translated Simone de Beauvoir's novel *Tous les hommes sont mortels* into Danish (1981, *Alle mennesker er dødelige*). She is also a talented artist and designer: she designed costumes for the 1987 television performance of **Hans Christian Andersen**'s *The Shepherdess and the Chimney Sweep* and sets for the 1991 performance of **Bournonville**'s ballet *A Folk Tale*. The 1970 charity Christmas stamp-seals were her design, and she has designed church vestments for **Viborg** and **Fredensborg**.

Her duties as monarch have taken her on state visits abroad and involve receiving visiting heads of state and ambassadors. She is present at the opening of the **Folketing** and presides over the Council of State (*rigsråd*), at which ministers formally place acts of **parliament** before her for signature; but these are only valid if also countersigned by a minister. In theory she could exercise a veto by withholding her signature for 30 days, but by the conventions of limited **monarchy** this is not done. The 1953 constitution (para. 42 [1]) allows for one-third of the members of the Folketing to request, within three weekdays of the passage of a Bill, that it be subject to **referendum**, unless parliament resolves to withdraw the Bill. In effect, this postpones royal assent to the Bill until the electorate has had its say, a procedure only used once, in 1963. SPO, AHT

MARSELIUS, GABRIEL (1609-1673). Merchant and landowner. He learned the trade of merchant in his Dutch father's firm in Amsterdam, where in 1638 he became the Danish resident and factor for trade with the Danish state, including the supply of weapons. During the Swedish wars of 1643-45 and 1657-60 he was one of the chief suppliers to the Danish navy and army, also lending large amounts to the Danish state. These were repaid with grants of land in Denmark and Norway, and he was ennobled in 1665, although he continued to live on his estate at Elzwoud near Haarlem in Holland. AHT

MARSHALL PLAN AID was granted to Denmark by the United States under an agreement ratified in July 1948. Over the following four years 1,500,000,000 kroner in aid was spent mainly on the purchase of grain, animal feed, raw material, and machinery. SPO

MARSTRAND, WILHELM (1810-1873). Painter. An apprenticeship with Christoffer Wilhelm **Eckersberg** in 1826 was followed by studies at the Academy and periods residing abroad, including Italy. He was appointed professor at the **Academy of Art** in 1848. His paintings include genre pieces such as *Removal Day* (1831), *Street Scene in the Dog Days* (1833), and *An Italian Hostelry* (1847) and numerous portraits of the more prosperous citizens of his time, such as *H.C. Ørsted* (1850-51), *Johanne Luise Heiberg* (1858-59) and *The Waagenpetersen Family* (1836). He is also known for his historical pictures such as *Christian IV on Trinity Day* and *The Judgment of Christoffer Rosenkrantz* (1864-66) in **Christian IV's** chapel in **Roskilde** Cathedral. AHT

MARSVIN, ELLEN (1572-1649). Noblewoman. In her widowhood from 1611 she managed and added to her estates, brought up the children fathered by **Christian IV** with her daughter Kirsten Munk, and administered their fortunes. When Kirsten left the king in 1630, Ellen distanced herself from her daughter, but from 1635 she supported her and maintained against the king's denial that he was the father of Kirsten's youngest daughter, Dorothea Elisabeth. AHT

MATHISEN, LEO (1906-1969). Jazz musician. The son of a confidential clerk, he started playing as an amateur in 1922-23 and then in various dance and jazz groups in Denmark and abroad. He had his own band 1936-51 and became the leading jazz pianist, conductor, and composer, especially in the golden era of swing during the German wartime occupation, with the nickname "Leo the Lion". AHT

MEASURES *see* **WEIGHTS AND MEASURES**

MELCHIOR, ARNE (1924-). Politician. He is the son of chief rabbi Marcus Melchior and his wife Meta. After experience as a director of clothing and paint companies, he was a management consultant and an advisor on business policy to the Social Democrats. In 1973 he was a co-founder of the **Centre Democrats,** serving as party group chairman and political spokesman. He was elected to the **Folketing** 1973-75 and from 1977, and was on Folketing committees for Culture, Foreign Policy, Defense, and Finance. He was minister for public works (1982-86) in the Schlüter government and minister of communications and tourism (1993-94) in the Nyrup Rasmussen government, and was a member of the Nordic Council 1981-82 and 1986-87. From 1987 he was chairman of the Tourist Council. His publications include *Danmark under ockupationen* (Sweden, 1975, Denmark During the Occupation); *Noget om herretøj* (1963, A Bit About Men's Clothes); *De danske textilerhverv* (1965, The Danish Textile Trade); *Palestina/Israel* (1978), *There is Something Wonderful in the State of Denmark* (USA, 1987), *New York* (1991), *Det bedste ved at have et barnebarn* (1995, The Best Thing About Having A Grandchild). AHT

MELCHIOR, BENT (1929-). Rabbi. The brother of Arne, he taught in the Jewish religious school in **Copenhagen** (1949-58), qualified as a rabbi at Jews' College, London in 1963, and held the post of rabbi in Copenhagen 1963-70, when he became chief rabbi until 1996. He also taught Jewish literature at Copenhagen University 1971-84. He was president of the World Congress for Soviet Jews 1971-89. He has published *Begyndelsen: Bibelens første del genfortalt* (1976, The Beginning: The First Part of the Bible Retold); *Jødedommen - en tekstcollage* (1977, Judaism: Collected Texts), and *De fem Mosebøger* (new Danish translations of The Five Books of Moses, vol. I, 1977; II, 1978; III, 1980; IV, 1984; V, 1987). AHT

MELCHIOR, LAURITZ (1890-1973). Opera singer. From studies at the **Royal Theater** where he made his debut as a baritone in 1913 and as a tenor in 1918, he led an international singing career from 1921, principally in Wagner roles, during 1926-50 at the New York Metropolitan Opera. In 1947 he became a US citizen. His son Ib (1917-) directed over 500 television shows for CBS and NBC and became a Hollywood script-writer; in 1976 he was awarded the Science Fiction Academy's prize. AHT

MELDAHL, FERDINAND (1827-1908). Architect. The son of a foundryman, he was apprenticed as a moulder but qualified in 1844 as a bricklayer and later qualified from the **Academy of Art** where he became professor 1864-1905. He designed numerous buildings, using elements from earlier styles. He was responsible for the restoration in 1860-75 of **Frederiksborg Castle** after the 1859 fire and of **Rosenborg Castle** (1866-90). In 1876-94 he also completed the building of Frederik's Church (the Marble Church) in **Copenhagen**. AHT

MERCANTILISM is the title given by historians to the economic policy pursued by most Western European governments in the early modern period. It was never an internally consistent economic doctrine. It was based on the assumption of a finite amount of world trade which had to be fought for by individual countries and involved extensive state control to encourage home production and discourage imports, especially of expensive luxury goods, in order to boost the country's balance of trade. It involved the creation of overseas colonies, high customs barriers, and powerful navies. In Denmark such policies were pursued with particular rigor in the early 17th century under King **Christian IV**, who founded a number of monopoly trading companies and encouraged the foundation of industries. In 1742 the **Wholesale Merchants' Society** was formed to develop trade abroad. In the 18th century, mercantilist ideas began to be undermined by liberal doctrines associated in particular with the French *physiocrates* and more attention was paid to **agriculture** than in the past. The sudden withdrawal of state subsidies by **J.F. Struensee** during his brief period in office caused economic chaos, but a lowering of tariffs begun in 1792 started a process of deregulating the Danish economy which continued until the middle of the 19th century. SPO

METHODISM was introduced to Denmark by Christian B. Willerup (1815-1886) who had joined the movement in the United States and began preaching in **Copenhagen** in 1856. The first Danish Methodist congregation was formed in the capital in 1859 and legal recognition came six years later. By the end of the 19th century there were 3,440 Methodists in Denmark in 22 congregations. SPO

MEYER, ADOLPH CHARLES (1858-1938). Politician and journalist. Apprenticed as a smith, in 1878 he cofounded the **Social Democrats** and was the first chairman for a few months. He was elected to the **Folketing** 1895-1932 and founded *Arbejdernes Idrætsklub* (1895), the Labor Sports Club, and its youth counterpart, *De unges Idræt* (1905). AHT

MEYER, JOHANNE (1838-1915), feminist. The daughter of a customs official, she became active in the labor movement, founding and leading Kvindelig Fremskridsforening, the Women's Association for Progress, 1886-93. She also worked for peace, for prohibition of alcohol, for well-fed schoolchildren and for animal protection. AHT

MEZA, General CHRISTIAN DE (1792-1865) was commander-in-chief of the Danish army from December 1863, at the outbreak of the Second **Slesvig-Holsten** War. After he ordered the retreat from the defensive line on the **Dannevirke** on 5 February, Meza was removed from his command and replaced by General Gerlach. SPO

MISSIONARIES. Christianity touched Denmark from North Germany through the activities of **Ansgar** (c. 801-865). **Asser** (c. 1059-1137) was the first Nordic archbishop with his seat in Lund, then in the kingdom of Denmark. A College of Missions was founded in 1714 after two German Pietists had been at work in Tranquebar and in 1716 a mission to the Lapps led to the founding of a seminarium at Trandheim to continue the work. The most famous missionary work of modern times was by the Norwegian **Hans Egede** among the inhabitants of **Greenland** from 1721 for 15 years. The first Danish missionary in Africa was Christian Prosten, who arrived in the Danish fort of Christiansborg on the coast of what is now Ghana in 1737. He was followed by five further missionaries under Jacob Meder in 1763.

The Inner Mission (Indre Mission) flourished in the 1890s, with revivalist preachers warning against the radical decadence of the times and supporting the temperance movement, led by **Lars Larsen-Ledet**. Employing 150 preachers, it developed close links with the YMCA (founded as the KFUM in 1878) and YWCA (KFUK, founded in 1883) and gained most support in western **Jutland**. SPO, AHT

MODEWEG, JOHAN CARL (1782-1849). Clothing manufacturer. In 1810 he was granted the royal privilege to run a clothing factory, from 1831 located in Brede near Lyngby north of **Copenhagen**, where the water power of the Møllåen could be used. On his death the factory was one of the largest industrial activities in Denmark. It ceased operations in 1956 and the building was sold to the **National Museum**. AHT

MOE, LOUIS (1859-1945). Painter and illustrator. The son of a Norwegian dentist, he studied at the **Academy of Art** 1876-82. He is best known for his imaginative illustrations for children's books such as *Oldemors fortællinger om Nordens guder* (1890, Great Grandmother's Tales of the Norse Gods) and *Eventyret om Hans og Grethe* (1892, Hansel and Gretel), and for *Danmarks historie i billeder* (1892-98, Illustrated Danish History), *Saxos krønike* (1896-98, Saxo's Chronicle), and **Hans Christian Andersen**'s Tales (1926). AHT

MODERATE LEFT PARTY *see* **LIBERAL PARTY**

MØLLER, ARNOLD PETER (1876-1965). Shipowner. Trained in shipping, in 1905 he and his father founded a shipping line in Svendborg and then the Steamship Company of 1912 which later took the name AP Møller, trafficking abroad with liners and tankers. In 1918 he founded Odense Steel Shipyard, later named Lindøværftet. In 1962 he secured the concession for prospecting underground in Denmark, for which he formed Dansk Undergrunds Consortium. AHT

MØLLER, JOHN CHRISTMAS *see* **CHRISTMAS MØLLER, J.**

MØLLER, POUL MARTIN (1794-1838). Author. Educated by his father, a priest, he graduated *cand. theol* in 1816 and was appointed professor of philosophy 1828-31 in Kristiania (Oslo) and from 1831 at Copenhagen University. His main work, the incomplete *En dansk students eventyr* (1843, The Adventures of a Danish Student) takes on sentimental romanticism and foreshadows poetic realism. Others of his works are *Scener i Rosenborg Slotshave* (1819-21, Scenes from the Garden of Rosenborg Castle) and two collections of poetry. He wrote with a deftness and humor long absent from Danish writing. AHT

MOLTKE, Count ADAM GOTTLOB (1710-1792). Politician. Originating from Mecklenburg, Moltke was in 1746 appointed Court Chamberlain (*overhofmarskal*) on the accession of King **Frederik V** As the link between the king and his ministers, this effectively gave him the power of the king's first minister for over 20 years, especially as the king was little interested in day-to-day administration. Although a member of the king's council only from 1763, to all intents he shared with **J.H.E. Bernstorff** the most decisive say in policy throughout the reign. He fell from power soon after the accession of King **Christian VII** in 1766, returned to the council in 1767, but was ousted in 1770 by **J.F. Struensee**. He was an enlightened landowner, on whose estates some of the earliest reforms to benefit the peasant tenants were conducted. He improved agricultural productivity by adopting the practice from Holstein of sowing clover. SPO, AHT

MOLTKE, ADAM WILHELM (1785-1864). Of noble family, he graduated *cand. jur.* and was appointed to the central administration. He was prime minister (*gehjimestatsminister*) 1831-48 and 1848-52. In the three first administrations after the end of **absolutism** he sought to bridge the gap between the **National Liberals** and the **Right**. In 1849-60 he was a member of the **Landsting**. AHT

MOLTKE, CARL (1798-1866). Politician. The son of a Holsten count, he graduated *cand. jur* and from 1834 held an appointment in the central administration in **Copenhagen**. In 1846 he was appointed president of the chancellery for Slesvig-Holsten-Lauenburg.

On **Frederik VII**'s accession in 1848 he was appointed prime minister and wrote the constitutional ordinance of 28 January, but resigned in March. He was an uncompromising advocate of the single state (*helstat*) policy toward **Slesvig-Holsten**. Under German pressure he was appointed minister without portfolio in July-October 1851 and 1864-65, and as minister for **Slesvig** 1852-54. AHT

MØN is one of three large islands south of **Zealand**. Its eastern coast has the only chalk cliffs in Denmark and the island has numerous Neolithic burial-places, the best being *Kong Asger's Høj*. The island is also noted for its unique whitewashed churches, many with 14th century frescoes showing rural life. AHT

MONARCHY has been the system of government in Denmark throughout historical times. In the early days the king was elected by the leading men of the community from a small group of families. Only with the **Oldenborg** dynasty beginning with **Christian I** (king 1448-81) was the principle of primogeniture (succession by the eldest son) firmly established. Even so, the system of election, which enabled the nobility to impose conditions on the new king in the form of an **Accession Charter** was maintained until 1660. The crown was then declared hereditary in the male line and in 1661 the king was declared to have **absolute** powers as defined later in the **King's Law**. This remained the position until 1848, when **Frederik VII** conceded to liberal demands for a constitutional monarchy. He retained considerable powers under the **Constitution** of 1849, including that of choosing his ministers. But after the Second **Slesvig-Holsten** War of 1864, which ended in disastrous loss of territory to Prussia, **Christian IX** reverted to monarchical rule, choosing politicians of the **Right** for his advisors despite rising liberal strength in the **Folketing**.

Only in 1901, when the Right was reduced to 7 percent of the seats in the Folketing, was the **Change of System** made to parliamentary democracy, with ministers responsible to the Folketing majority. The Constitution of 1915 recognized the principle of parliamentary government under a constitutional monarchy. Although challenged in the **Easter Crisis** of 1920, the principle has been upheld ever since, despite occupation during **World War II** by Nazi Germany. Under the law of accession of 1953 women may inherit the Danish throne, as **Margrethe II** did in 1972; but between siblings, males take precedence over females, regardless of age.

The present royal house of **Glücksborg** traces its ancestry from King **Gorm the Old**, the 10th century monarch, and thus claims to be the oldest monarchy in Europe. A gold and bejeweled crown, made in 1670 to symbolize the absolute monarchy, was worn by the kings during the next 170 years, but is now placed on the coffin of a monarch when lying in state. It is on show to the public at **Rosenborg Castle**. Modern monarchs are proclaimed from the balcony of **Christiansborg** by the prime minister, and there is no coronation ceremony.

As a constitutional monarch, Queen Margrethe II is present at the annual opening of the Folketing and presides over the council of state which gives formal assent to laws after they have been passed by the Folketing. After an **election** or the fall of a government she is advised by the party leaders and commissions one of them to try to form a cabinet, but success in this depends on the ability to obtain the confidence of a Folketing majority. The monarch also holds audiences for her subjects and as head of state receives ambassadors and other dignitaries. SPO, AHT. *See also* Appendix 1 and entries for each monarch.

MONRAD, DITLEV GOTHARD (1811-1887). Liberal politician, bishop, and prime minister 1863-64. Born in Norway, when his father became mentally ill he was brought up by an uncle in Randers. He graduated *cand. theol.* in 1836 and became active as a **National Liberal**. He was appointed minister of education and ecclesiastical affairs (Kultusminister) in the first ministry after the end of absolute monarchy formed under Count **Moltke** in March 1848. The author of the first draft of the June **Constitution** of 1849, Monrad was largely responsible for the wide **franchise** which it allowed. In 1849-54 he was bishop of **Lolland-Falster**. He took up his old ministerial post in **C. C. Hall**'s first cabinet in 1859 and in Hall's second cabinet, formed in 1860, was also interior minister until 1861. In this capacity he oversaw the first national **railroad** plan.

In December 1863 Monrad was appointed prime minister by the new King **Christian IX** to secure a peaceful settlement of the dispute with Prussia over the new constitution for Denmark and the duchies. Monrad was also minister of finance and (until the beginning of 1864) minister for foreign affairs. Early in 1864 he bound his ministry to suspend the constitution: nevertheless Prussia declared the Second **Slesvig-Holsten** War a few days later. Monrad was blamed for Denmark's military defeats and dismissed in July. He emigrated to New Zealand but returned to Denmark in 1869 and was again bishop of Lolland-Falster 1871-87. He was a member of the **Folketing** 1849-65 and 1882-86. SPO, AHT

MØNSTED, OTTO (1838-1916). Manufacturer. In 1865 he established a wholesale firm trading in grain, butter, and animal feeds and in 1883 founded the first Danish margarine factory, known from 1909 as Otto Mønsted A/S. AHT

MORTENSEN, RICHARD (1910-1993) is one of Denmark's leading abstract painters. After studies at the **Academy of Art**, he painted during 1932-40 in a surrealist style, and after living in France 1947-64 later going over to a simpler nonfigurative mode of expression. He was a professor at the Academy 1964-80. AHT. *See also* **Jorn, Asger.**

MØSTING, JOHAN SIGISMUND von (1759-1843). Civil servant and politician. He graduated *cand. jur.* in 1781 and was appointed prefect (*amtmand*) in Haderslev east. He was president in the German Chancellery in 1804-13, Danish finance minister 1813-31, and prime minister (*gehejmestatsminister*) 1814-42. After the bankruptcy of the state in 1813 he was chiefly responsible for the recovery of the currency and the bank system. When Holsten, as a member of the German federation, demanded a **consultative assembly**, he advised **Frederik VI** to establish similar assemblies for the rest of the kingdom. AHT

MÜLLER, HENRIK (1609-1692). Merchant, landowner, and civil servant. In 1632 he was appointed **Christian IV**'s confidential clerk responsible for purchases. In 1634 he began trading on his own account, bringing in vast amounts to the state and the court from deals on port dues with **Corfitz Ulfeldt**. He mortgaged crown lands and excise income, becoming one of the largest creditors of the state by 1660. In 1641-51 he was customs officer in **Copenhagen**, in 1651-55 he was general administrator of customs. After 1660 the state paid its debts to him in farm land, making him the country's largest landowner. His many businesses and estates proved unprofitable, and when an audit commission in 1680 charged him a large sum for defrauding the state, he was virtually bankrupted. AHT

MÜLLER, PETER ERASMUS (1840-1926). Naturalist. The son of a numismatist, he qualified in agriculture in 1861 and forestry in 1867; studied in Germany, Switzerland, France, and Italy; graduated *dr. phil.* in 1871; and taught at Copenhagen Agricultural College 1873-82. In 1882-1911 he was chief forester for the southern part of north **Zealand**. As a member of the Natural History Association (Naturhistorisk Forening) 1905-25 and its chairman 1912-17 he was one of the chief designers of the first Danish conservation law of 1917. His theoretical studies of forest cultivation achieved international recognition. AHT

MÜLLER, SOPHUS (1846-1934). Archeologist. A pupil of **J.J.A. Worsaae**, he did much both as writer and as director of the **National Museum** to popularize archaeology in Denmark. SPO

MUNCH, PETER ROCHEGUNE (1870-1948). Radical Liberal politician and historian. He graduated *cand. mag* in history, French, and Latin in 1895 and *dr. phil.* in 1900. He first attracted public attention in 1903 in a newspaper article when he called on the **Liberal Party** to be more radical in its social policy and not tie itself so closely to the agrarian interest. These ideas led him to cofound the **Radical Liberal Party** in 1905. A member of the **Folketing** in 1909-45, he was interior minister 1909-10 and minister of defense 1913-20 in Carl Theodore **Zahle**'s second cabinet. On the left of the Radical Liberals, Munch always favored close collaboration with the **Social Democrats** and as successor to **Ove Rode** as leader of his party in 1927 was well placed to take this line. In the Social-Democrat-Radical coalition of 1929-40 led by **Th. Stauning** he was foreign minister. As such he favored a low military budget, neutrality and a cautious policy toward the great powers. He was responsible for the Nonaggression Treaty with Germany signed in May 1939. Because of his commitment to neutrality and his strong opposition to rearmament, Munch was widely accused of appeasement toward the fascist dictatorships. Conservative opposition led him to give way to **Erik Scavenius** in July 1940. As a historian, in 1907 he wrote a widely used high school text on world history. His memoirs, *Erindringer*, were published in eight volumes 1957-67. SPO, AHT

MUNCK, EBBE (1905-1974). **Resistance** activist, journalist, diplomat, and royal court official. He graduated *cand. polit.* in 1928 and became foreign correspondent of *Berlingske Tidende* in Berlin and London, in Spain in the civil war and in Finland in the Winter War of 1939-40. He also took part in several expeditions to **Greenland**. Based in Stockholm, Sweden, during the 1940-45 German occupation of Denmark, he passed intelligence to Britain and from 1943 represented the **Freedom Council**. He helped to form the Danish Brigade, set up escape routes, purchased weapons in Sweden, and established contact between the Freedom Council and the USSR. He returned to journalism 1945-47 then joined the diplomatic service, as ambassador to Bangkok 1959-67 and as chief of staff (*hofchef*) 1967-72 to **Margrethe II** before she succeeded to the throne. AHT

MUNK, JENS (1579-1628). Explorer. In 1610 he was sent by King **Christian IV** on an expedition to discover a North-East passage to India but was halted by ice. In 1619 he was sent to find a North-West Passage, reaching Hudson's Bay that summer. While the two ships over-wintered, all but two of the party of 67 died of cold and scurvy. Munk sailed back to Denmark with these two in the fall of 1620 to a hero's welcome and published an account of his voyage. As a squadron commander he took part in the naval war of 1625-29 during Denmark's involvement in the **Thirty Years' War**. He is portrayed in Thorkild Hansen's documentary novel *Jens Munk* (1965). SPO, AHT

MUNK, KAJ (1898-1944). Playwright. Born in a country parsonage in Maribo, he graduated in theology in 1923 and secured a living in Vederso, West Jutland. His first published play, *En Idealist* (1928, *Herod the King* 1953) portrayed his admiration for the strong leader. In the 1930s he was strongly drawn to the fascist dictators, as is evident from *Sejren* (1936, The Victory) and *Diktatorinden* (1938, The Dictator). In *Han sidder ved smeltediglen* (1938, *He Sits at the Melting-Pot*, 1953) he criticized Nazi persecution of the Jews but was still attracted to the Leader (*der Führer*). His strong religious faith is revealed in *Ordet* (1932, *The Word* 1953), and after the German occupation of Denmark he openly condemned the occupiers. Munk was arrested in 1944 and killed by the Gestapo near Silkeborg on 4 January. Although he became a national hero, his plays soon lost their topicality. SPO

MUSEUMS. The first museum in Denmark was Ole **Worm**'s collection of natural history and ethnography. On his death in 1654, these went to the Royal Museum in **Copenhagen Castle**, where they augmented a collection of paintings, weapons, and applied art. In 1821 these collections were broken up to form the nucleus of more specialized museums of Ethnography, Classical Antiquities, and Coins and Medals. These in 1892 became the **National Museum**.

As prosperity grew in and since the 1870s, so did interest in preserving evidence of the past, and numerous museums of general history were founded outside Copenhagen, as well as museums on specialized themes of historical and natural history. Some are owned by the state or local government but most are self-governing or belong to art societies, and a few are owned privately. They are financed by state and local government grants, by charitable and commercial donations and from admission charges.

In **Copenhagen** and **North Zealand** thematic museums include: **Applied Arts and Design** (Kunstindustrimuseet); the Aquarium; Architecture (the Architectural Center, Christianshavn, and the Open-Air Museum, *see* **National Museum**); the Arsenal (weapons: Tøjhusmuseet); Astronomy (**Ole Rømer**'s Museum and the **Tycho Brahe** Planetarium); the **Karen Blixen** museum at Rungstedlund; Brewing (**Carlsberg**); Coaches and Stables (Kongelige Stalde og Kareter); Crafts (Håndværksmuseet in **Roskilde**); Customs (Toldmuseum); Eksperimentarium (science); Erotica; Film; the Freedom Museum (Frihedsmuseet, about the 1940-45 **resistance** to German occupation of Denmark); Geology; Glass (Holmgaard Glass Works near Næstved, 80 km south of Copenhagen); the Guiness World of Records; Holography; Hunting and Forestry (at Hørsholm); the Labor Movement (Arbejdermuseet); the Lifeguards' Historical Collection (military uniforms, weapons, etc.); Literature (Bakkehusmuseet, 1800-50); Medical History; Musical History; National History (at **Frederiksborg**); Porcelain (**Bing & Grøndahl**), the Postal and Telegraph Museum; Puppets (Dukketheatre Museum); Ripley's Believe It or Not Museum (curiosities and erotic rarities); the Royal Naval Museum (Orlogsmuseet); Ships and diesel engines (**Burmeister & Wain**); Silver (**Georg Jensen**); Technical

Museum (Danmarks Tekniske Museum at Elsinore, with comprehensive natural history and technical collections, including motor vehicles and transport); Telephones (at Hellerup); Theater; Tobacco and Pipes (W.Ø. Larsens Pipe Museum); Toys (Legetøjsmuseet); Trams and Buses (HT Museum); L. Tussaud's Wax Museum; Veteran Cars (Sommers Museum at Nærum); Zoology.

Other major buildings open to the public include: **Christiansborg (parliament)**; Copenhagen City Hall (Rådhuset, with Jens Olsen's Astronomical Clock); **Frederiksborg Castle**; **Kronborg Castle**; **Rosenborg Castle**; the **Round Tower**.

District museums include: Amager; Brøste's Collection on the Christianshavn district; Copenhagen City, with a room on **Kierkegaard**; Dragør (also Mølsteds Museum); Gilleleje; Køge; Søllerud (local prehistory and archaeology).

Art collections: C.L. **Davids** Samling (furniture, paintings, porcelain, and Islamic art); the **Glyptothek**; the **Hirschsprung Gallery**; Kastrupgård (changing exhibitions of modern drawings); **Louisiana**; Marienlyst Palace (changing exhibitions); Nivågård Malerisamling (paintings of the Danish Golden Age, 1800-50 plus Italian and Dutch Renaissance); Ordrupgaard (at Charlottenlund: Danish and French impressionists); Sophienholm (at Lyngby: changing exhibitions); the **State Museum of Art** (Statens Museum for Kunst: 13th to 18th century Danish and European art); Rudolf **Tegner**; **Thorvaldsen** (sculpture); the Willumsen Museum (paintings by **J.F. Willumsen**).

Museums in southwest **Zealand** include: the Open-Air Museum (Frilandsmuseet) at Maribo; Gavnø Park and Castle (rose gardens and a large collection of paintings). On **Bornholm** there are local historical archives, a defense museum, and a museum of local history and art at Rønne. Near Hasle, Melstedgaard is a working museum of farming history.

On **Funen** there are several museums in **Odense**, a collection of Ships in Bottles at Ærøskøbing, and a town museum in Fåborg. The largest vivarium in Scandinavia is Terrariet at Vissenbjerg.

In **Jutland**, **Ålborg** has Jens Bang's Renaissance merchant's house; an Art Museum which displays 20th century paintings; and a Zoological Garden. Ålestrup has a Cycle Museum. **Århus** has Botanical Gardens; Den Gamle By is an "old town" of translocated original buildings; Moesgård Museum displays archaeological finds;

the Women's Museum (Kvindemuseet) is near the cathedral; the Museum of Natural History is in the University park; and there is a History of Science Museum, a Viking Museum and an Art Museum. Dybbøl Mølle is the most important battlefield in modern Danish history. **Esbjerg** has a Fishing and Maritime Museum. Herning has a museum of the work of artists Karl-Henning Pedersen and Else Alfelt. Hirtshals has a Museum of the North Sea. Hjerl Hede has a museum with reconstructions of village life, which also illustrates the settlement of this heathland area after 1866. In Hjørring there is a Museum of Local History for the Vendsyssel region. Holsterbro has an art museum. In Kolding the 13th-century Koldinghus Castle has recently been restored. Silkeborg has an art Museum and a Museum of Cultural History. The Old Village (Den gamle Landsby) is a collection of old buildings to illustrate themes in cultural history, established in 1915 on a piece of protected heathland beside Lake Flynder, south of Skive. It was paid for by the Hjerl Fund, established in 1915 by H.P. Hjerl Hansen (1870-1946), a businessman who made his money from the Siberian Company, which exported dairy and butter-making machinery. Trapholt has an art museum.

The museums mentioned are only a selection of the most significant to be found in Denmark. This reflects the interests of a well-educated population and the desire to cater to the many visitors to the country. It also reflects the generosity of the state, municipalities, organizations, and individual benefactors. AHT

MUSIC. The music played in Denmark during the Bronze Age is unknown, but some of the instruments on which it was played have come to light in the shape of the *lur* or curved horns, usually found in pairs, of which the first emerged near Hillerød in 1797. A large collection of medieval ballads, probably influenced by French and German examples, has survived. These originated in the royal court and were sung to round dances, and later taken up by the peasants. After the **Reformation**, the courts of Kings **Christian III, Frederik II,** and **Christian IV** became the main centers of musical activity in the country. **Christian IV** continued the appointment of **Mogens Pedersen** as deputy *kapelmester* and attracted a number of leading foreign musicians, including the German Heinrich Schütz and the Englishman John Dowland to Denmark. This tradition was continued by the Danish court in the 18th century, when the German Johan Ernst Hartmann (1726-93) composed music for Johannes

Ewald's operas. In the Baroque period the organist and composer **Buxtehude**, an admired contemporary of J.S. Bach and G.F. Handel, began his career in Denmark but ended in **Lübeck**.

Inaugurating a golden age of music of the classical and romantic eras, the Berlin composer Johann Abraham Peter Schulz conducted at the **Royal Theater** in 1787-95, introducing French *opéra comique* and works by Gluck. He was succeeded by **Kunzen**, who introduced Mozart's operas as well as his own compositions. Inspired by the classical composers of Vienna, **Weyse** is seen as the originator of a Danish national musical style. **Kuhlau** was important in paving the way for the fully fledged romanticism with a strong classicist background and specific national characteristics which followed his death.

In the Romantic era of the early 19th century, Denmark began to produce significant composers of its own. **J.P.E. Hartmann** was strongly influenced by the folk ballad tradition. **Heise** set to music many of the Danish poets of the period. Above all **Niels W. Gade** was highly influential in Denmark and gained a European reputation. **C.F.E. Hornemann** was considered Gade's natural successor. On the lighter side **Lumbye** composed numerous dances and popularized a repertoire ranging from Johann Strauss to the classics at his concerts in the **Tivoli** Gardens. Johannes Frederik Frøhlich (1806-60) composed the scores for several of **Bournonville's** ballets, including *Valdemar* (1835), *Menveds Barndom* (1843), *Festen i Albano* (1839), and *Rafaello* (1845).

A music society *Musikforeningen* was founded in 1836, to which Gade devoted much effort as conductor, composer, and organizer, using Lumbye's Tivoli orchestra as the core of a strategy to widen the musical education of both performers and the Danish public. In 1867 the Royal Danish Academy of Music (Det kgl. danske Musikkonservatorium) was founded in Copenhagen, with Gade involved in its teaching and management. Subsequently conservatoires have been founded for **Jutland** (in **Århus**), North Jutland (in **Ålborg**), West Jutland (in **Esbjerg**), and **Funen** (in **Odense**).

In the 20th century **Carl Nielsen** gained an international reputation for Danish music to match those of Edvard Greig in Norway and Jean Sibelius in Finland, and established the standard against which his successors such as **Rued Langaard** and **Knudaage Riisager** are measured. That reputation has been extended by Hermann

D. Koppel (1908-), **Svend Erik Tarp, Vagn Holmboe, Per Nør-gård** who trained under him, **Ib Nørholm**, and a more recent generation which includes **Niels Viggo Bentzon**, Poul Ruders (1949-) and Hans Abrahamsen (1952-). Neoromantic Danish composers include **Hakon Børresen** and **Ludolf Nielsen**.

The professional orchestras are state-funded, with a remit that requires them to include new Danish music in their repertoire. The concert season is mainly in winter, but there is a program of summer concerts in Tivoli concert hall in **Copenhagen** and an Århus Festival in September.

Copenhagen has a jazz festival in early July which manifests the strong following for jazz in Denmark and the popularity of the city with American musicians, some of whom were regular visitors or settlers. The Danish Radio Big Band was founded in 1964 and has nurtured a generation of Danish musicians that includes saxophonist Jesper Thilo, bassist Niels-Henning Ørsted Pedersen, and trumpeters Palle Mikkelborg and Jens Winther. There is a folk-rock movement with a distinctive Danish flavor that supports summer festivals in **Roskilde** (established in 1970) and Tønder and sales of recordings, with Kim Larsen's *Midt om Natten* (1984, The Middle of the Night) holding a sales record for over a decade. The rock-group Shu-bi-dua has been popular in the 1990s. SPO, AHT. *See also* **National Anthems**.

MUUS, FLEMMING BRUUN (1907-1982). Resistance soldier. He received a commercial education and was working abroad when Germany occupied Denmark. In April 1942 he arrived in England and was recruited into the Special Operations Executive (SOE). After training he was chosen to lead the SOE in Denmark and parachuted into **Jutland** on 11 March 1943. In **Copenhagen** he represented British forces to politicians and the resistance movement, joining the **Freedom Council** in September until recalled to London in December 1944. AHT

MYLIUS-ERICHSEN, LUDWIG (1872-1907). Author and polar researcher. The son of a policeman, he worked as a journalist. In 1902-04 he led the "literary expedition" of writers and artists to **Greenland**. In 1906 he led the Danish expedition to northeast Greenland, dying with his two companions in Lambertsland. AHT

MYNSTER, JAKOB PETER (1775-1854). Bishop. Orphaned, he was brought up in the family of a **Copenhagen** professor and graduated *cand. theol.* in 1794 and *dr. theol* in 1815. He held appointments as a parish priest, chaplain and royal confessor, and in 1834-54 as bishop of **Zealand**. Rejecting both romantic and nationalistic interpretations of the **Bible**, he took a conservative view of the state church and started a high-church movement which conflicted with both **N.F.S. Grundtvig** and **Søren Kierkegaard**. He was a member of the **Consultative Assembly** for the Islands 1835-44 and voted against the **constitution** in the **Constitutional Assembly** of 1848-49. He published eight volumes of sermons. AHT

- N -

NACHTEGALL, FRANZ (1777-1847). Gymnastics teacher. After teaching gymnastics at military colleges, in 1799 he founded an institute for physical education, the first in Europe. In 1804 he was appointed professor of gymnastics at Copenhagen University and was instrumental in having gymnastics included as a school subject in the law of 1814. He failed to get acceptance of women's gymnastics in 1838. AHT

NANSEN, HANS (1598-1667). Born in Flensborg, he undertook trading trips to **Iceland** and Muscovy as a young man and learned Russian. He was one of the founders of the Caribbean Company in 1652 after a successful Danish expedition to the West Indies. As borgmester of **Copenhagen** from 1644, he led the Burgher Estate in the Diet of 1660 against the nobility and played an important role in the offer to King **Frederik III** of hereditary monarchy. In 1660 he was appointed to the statskollegiet (privy council) and in 1661 to the High Court. SPO

NAPOLEONIC WARS. Denmark tried to maintain a policy of neutrality, but twice suffered ruthless retaliation from Britain. In 1794 Denmark and Sweden renewed their alliance of neutrality, but when this was extended in 1801 to include Russia and Prussia, Britain regarded the move as a challenge, and demanded that Denmark withdraw. Denmark refused, so the British fleet was deployed. Despite gallant resistance in the 1801 Battle of **Copenhagen**, admiral Horatio Nelson sank the Danish fleet, and Denmark had to withdraw from the Armed Neutrality. Britain declared war on France in 1803. The French Continental Blockade followed in 1806, and Denmark's vital sea communications were at the mercy of the British fleet, even more so when Britain began a counter-blockade. The Treaty of Tilsit (1807) brought peace between France and Russia, and their covert intention was to bring Denmark and Sweden into the Continental Blockade.

Denmark faced British pressure for an alliance, with delivery of the Danish fleet to Britain as a condition. Denmark faced a dilemma: concession to such pressure would bring a French invasion of **Jutland**. Equally, a Danish alliance with France would have disastrous effects on Danish trade. Denmark played for time, but the British grew impatient, and in September 1807, with the Crown Prince in Kiel with his army, Copenhagen surrendered after three days of bombardment and destruction by British forces, who then sailed off with the entire Danish fleet. These events were felt to be deeply humiliating in Denmark and gave impetus to Danish nationalism. The Danes took sides with the French, although this was neither a popular nor a wise move. Attempts to break with France and to join the alliance against Napoleon were thwarted by Sweden, where the new King Carl Johan, the former Marshall Bernadotte in Napoleon's army, had been promised Norway, provided that Denmark was on the losing side when the war ended. In turn Russia gained Finland. Denmark declared the state bankrupt in 1813 and, in the Treaty of **Kiel** in 1814 had to sign away Norway to Sweden. The award of **Lauenburg** lands to the east of Hamburg, proved small compensation. AHT. *See also* **Copenhagen, battles of; Slesvig-Holsten.**

NATHANSEN, HENRI (1868-1944) was the leading Danish-Jewish author (with **M.A. Goldschmidt**). He illustrated the collision between Danish and Jewish life in his frequently performed play *Indenfor murene* (1912, Within the Walls) and in his novels *Af Hugo Davids liv* (1917, From Hugo David's Life) and *Mendel Philipsen og søn* (1932, Mendel Philipsen and Son). AHT

NATHANSEN, MENDEL LEVIN (1780-1868). Merchant and author. The son of a merchant in Holsten, he prospered as a businessman in **Copenhagen**, but went bankrupt in 1820. He was very active in obtaining education for Jewish children and was an important influence on the 1814 law granting citizenship to Jews. After 1820 he wrote extensively on political economy and edited *Berlingske Tidende* 1838-58. AHT

NATIONAL ANTHEMS. The text of the song *Kong Christian stod ved højen mast* (King Christian Stood by Lofty Mast), used as the royal anthem, was written by **Johannes Ewald** for the ballad opera *The Fishermen* (1780). It relates to **Christian IV**'s part in **Torstensson's War**. **J.E. Hartmann's** original tune was simplified and popularized by **Kuhlau**. Regarded by many as the national anthem, the text of the patriotic song *Der er et yndigt land* (This Is a Lovely Land) was written by **Adam Oehlenschläger** and set to music by H.E. Krøyer (1798-1879), Thomas Laub (1852-1927) and **Carl Nielsen**. AHT

NATIONAL BANK (Nationalbanken) was the title adopted by the former Rigsbanken (Bank of the Realm) when it became independent of State control in 1818. SPO. *See also* **Banking**.

NATIONAL LIBERALS were advocates of limited rather than absolute government and of national self-determination, the doctrine that state boundaries should coincide with (linguistically determined) nations. This ideology led to the unification of Germany (1871) and Italy (1870) but the disintegration of the multinational Austro-Hungarian Empire (1918). In Denmark National Liberals in the 1840s such as **Orla Lehmann**), advocated the incorporation of the part Danish-, part German-speaking duchy of **Slesvig** into the Danish kingdom with a frontier on the river **Ejder**, as a counter to the pan-Germanic nationalism which wanted Slesvig and Holsten to be included in greater Germany. This Danish nationalism was coupled with advocacy of constitutional reforms which would end the **absolute monarchy** and introduce a representative **parliament**. At the same time Capt. A.F. **Tscherning**'s critique of Danish defense recommended a citizens' army as more democratic than conscription, which rested on the peasants alone. Their main achievement was the

1849 June **Constitution**, but this provoked the two **Slesvig-Holsten** Wars, a reassertion of monarchy in the 1867 constitution, and postponement of democracy until the **Change of System** in 1901. AHT

NATIONAL MUSEUM is Denmark's principal historical museum. It originated in the collections formed from 1807 by the Royal Commission for the Preservation of Antiquities and was housed in the loft of Trinity Church in **Copenhagen**. In 1832 these were moved to the palace of **Christiansborg**. In 1853 they finally joined **Christian J. Thomsen**'s Ethnographic Collection and the Collection of Oriental and Classical Antiquities in the Prince's Palace, across Frederiksholm Canal from Christiansborg, where they are still housed. All the collections there, plus the Royal Collection of Coins and Medals brought from the palace of **Rosenborg**, became the National Museum (Nationalmuseet) in 1892, with a program of modernization and expansion culminating in 1992.

The collections span from prehistory to the modern age of 1660 to the 1890s. Especially interesting are copies of the **Gallehus Horns**, the **Gundestrup Bowl,** and the **Trundholm Chariot**. The Danish Folk Museum (started in 1885) and the Open-Air Museum (Frilandsmuseet) at Lyngby (8 km. from Copenhagen) were added in 1920. The latter is a 34.8 hectare (86 acre) site onto which original 17th- to 19th-century farm and rural buildings have been relocated. These give a good impression of the diversity of vernacular building styles from all parts of Denmark, ranging from the prosperity of **Funen** to the poverty of the west **Jutland** heath or the **Faroes**. Traditional craft tools are also displayed and demonstrated and there are performances of folk music. SPO, AHT. *See also* **Archaeology; Museums**.

NATO, the North Atlantic Treaty Organization, is a military and political alliance concluded in 1949 between the United States of America, Canada, and most of the countries of Western Europe (but not the Nordic countries of Finland and Sweden). After the failure of negotiations for a Nordic Defense Pact, Denmark joined reluctantly on 4 April 1949. In the parliamentary debate in March, NATO was opposed by the **Communists**, the traditionally pacifist **Radical Liberals**, a majority in the **Justice Party**, and one Liberal, but supported by a majority led by Prime Minister **Hans Hedtoft**.

Subsequently there was agreement on membership and the military budget by a broad majority comprising **Conservatives, Liberals,** and **Social Democrats,** while the Radicals and the **Socialist People's Party** have expressed reservations, especially during the 1980s when they considered that US President Reagan's "twin-track" strategy toward the USSR should give less emphasis to deployment of Cruise and Pershing missiles and more emphasis to negotiated arms limitation and confidence-building measures. In 1988 a parliamentary majority required the government to remind visiting warships that Denmark has never allowed nuclear weapons on its territory in peacetime (although this did not apply to Greenland). Danish military expenditure as a percentage of gross national product was 2.7 per cent in 1960, 2.4 per cent in 1970 and 1980, and 2.0 per cent since 1990, about average for most NATO members (although lower than in neutral Sweden or the US, United Kingdom, Greece, or Turkey). SPO, AHT

NAVY. Given Denmark's geographical position and long coastline, the navy has been of great importance for much of the country's history. The first regular naval force was formed by King **Hans I** at the beginning of the 16th century to counter the force employed by the **Hanseatic League**. He also developed coastal strong points such as Nakskov on Lolland to command the southern entrance into the Great Belt. During the **Northern Seven Years' War**, Denmark maintained a navy of some 30 large ships. In the early 17th century, King **Christian IV** took an unprecedented interest in his fleet, which acquitted itself well against its main rivals, the Swedes. The king himself commanded it at the drawn battle of Kolberger Heide in 1644 during **Torstensson's War**. The Danish navy held its own against the Swedes also in the war of 1674-79, but found its task more difficult in the **Great Northern War**. Units under the command of the great Norwegian admiral Peder Wessel (**Tordenskjold**) were nevertheless able to force Charles XII to abandon his first Norwegian campaign.

Danish neutrality for nearly a century after the end of this war left the navy only escort duties to perform. Its role in the Napoleonic Wars was a humiliating one: after suffering an honorable defeat at the first Battle of Copenhagen in 1801, nearly all Danish warships were seized by the British after the second Battle of Copenhagen in 1807. The new Prussian navy won most of the honors in the **Slesvig-**

Holsten Wars of 1848 and 1865. In the first, one of Denmark's greatest ships, the *Christian VIII*, was sunk by German coastal batteries in Eckenförde and its accompanying gunboat captured. In 1940, as with the army, the Danish navy survived the German occupation, and at the time of the "take-over" in August 1943 its units were either scuttled or escaped to Sweden.

The defense agreement of 1950-51 envisaged a navy of light units such as coastal destroyers, escort and patrol vessels, submarines, motor torpedo boats, mine-layers and mine-sweepers, etc. In 1996 its 6,000 personnel included 1,800 civilians and 500 conscripts, supported by 5,000 reservists. The fleet comprised 5 coastal submarines, 3 corvettes, 5 ocean patrol vessels with 8 Lynx helicopters operated by the Naval Air Arm, 12 patrol vessels, 14 multi-role ships, 10 fast patrol ships, 6 minelayers, 1 minesweeper, 2 light auxilliary oilers, and the Royal Yacht. The naval Home Guard operates 35 inshore patrol craft. The two main naval bases are at Frederikshavn and Korsør. SPO, AHT. *See also* **Cort Adeler; Copenhagen Battles of 1801 and 1807; Olfert Fischer; Niels Juel; Søren Norby; Peter Tordenskiold.**

NAZIS *see* **DANISH NATIONAL SOCIALIST WORKERS' PARTY**

NEERGAARD, NIELS (1854-1936). Liberal politician and historian; prime minister 1908-09, 1920-22, 1922-24. He graduated *magister* in history in 1879 and *cand. polit.* in 1881. He was elected to the **Folketing** for the **Liberal Party** 1887-90 and 1892-1932 and fought to interest his party in social reform. He succeeded **Frede Bojsen** as leader of the Moderate Liberals on the latter's retirement in 1901 and was in **J.C. Christensen**'s cabinet in 1908 as minister of finance. He formed his first government, in which he was also defense minister, when J.C. Christensen retired later in the year as a result of the **Alberti** scandal. His proposal to build new forts as part of the defense of **Copenhagen** split his cabinet and forced an election in 1909 that brought considerable gains for the **Radical Liberal Party**, which led him to hand over the government to Count **Holstein-Ledreborg**. His 1920-24 cabinet was formed after the election following the **Easter Crisis** of 1920, and he also took responsibility for the finance portfolio. He served as minister of finance in Thomas **Madsen-Mygdal**'s cabinet of 1926-29. As a historian his most important work was *Under Junigrundloven* (1892-1916, Under the June Constitution). SPO, AHT

NEIIENDAM, ROBERT (1880-1966). Theater historian. He was trained as a bookseller but had an acting career 1899-1926 and was principal of the **Royal Theater**'s Drama School 1930-50. As a historian he founded (1922) the Theater Museum in the rooms of the Court Theater in **Christiansborg Castle**. His books include *Johanne Luise Heiberg* (1917 and in an expanded edition in 1960), *Det kongelige Teaters historie I-V* (1921-30, The History of the Royal Theater), and *Bogen om grevinde Danner* (1956, The Book about Countess Danner). AHT

NEW CARLSBERG FOUNDATION *see* **CARLSBERG FOUNDATION**

NEWSPAPERS *see* **PRESS**

NEXØ, MARTIN ANDERSEN (1869-1954). Novelist, poet and short-story writer. Born in **Copenhagen** to a large and impoverished family, his father moved when Martin was eight to the town of Nexø on the island of **Bornholm**. After a brief **folk high school** education, he began to teach, but was taken ill and to improve his health traveled in southern Europe, where his political radicalism was reinforced. He added Nexø to his family name of Andersen. His earliest publication was a collection of short stories in 1898. From 1901 he devoted himself to writing and lecturing. His first novel appeared in 1901. Four years later came the first part of his monumental *Pelle Eroberen* (Pelle the Conqueror), followed by his five-volume *Ditte Menneskebarn* (Ditte, Son of Man) in 1917-21, in which his sympathy for the proletariat is eloquently expressed. He traveled widely, again to southern Europe but also to the Soviet Union, for which he entertained a lifelong admiration. During **World War II** he lived for two years in Sweden before moving to the Soviet Union. He finally settled in Dresden in the German Democratic Republic, and died there. SPO

NIEBUHR, CARSTEN (1733-1815). Explorer. The son of a marsh peasant in Hanover, he qualified as a land surveyor. He was invited to join a 1761-67 Danish expedition to south Arabia which wound up in considerable hardship. He published his observations in a series of scientific works which laid the basis for deeper understanding of the Sumerian, Babylonian, and Assyrian cultures. AHT

NIELS (c. 1064-1134). King of Denmark 1104-34, and the last son of **Svend II Estridsen.** On the death of **Erik Ejegod,** Niels was chosen by the Danish fleet in preference to Erik's sons, one of whom was a minor. His subsequent reign was both long and peaceful, enabling Niels to develop the power of the Crown with the help of local officials dependent on it and the Church. In 1131 **Knud Lavard**, Erik Ejegod's son was murdered at the instigation of Niels's only son Magnus, who regarded Knud as a threat to his succession to the throne. Civil war consequently raged between the supporters of the king and the supporters of Knud's half-brother **Erik Emune**, who inherited Knud's claims. Niels turned to the German emperor for support and swore allegiance to him, but this lost him the support of the Church in Denmark under Archbishop **Asser**, and in 1134 he was defeated at the battle of **Fodevig**, in which Magnus was killed. Niels was murdered shortly afterward, and Erik ascended the throne as **Erik II**. SPO

NIELSEN, ANNE MARIE CARL (1863-1945). Sculptor. Daughter of a landowner from Southern Jutland, she studied in **Copenhagen** from 1882 and at the **Academy of Art** in 1889-90, and developed a style of plastic realism well suited to her animal subjects. Her larger works include an equestrian statue of **Christian IX** (in **Christiansborg** riding school), *The Fisherman and His Rescuer* (Skagen 1934), and the monument to her husband **Carl Nielsen** (in Grønningen, Copenhagen, 1934). AHT

NIELSEN, ASTA (1881-1972). Actress. After training at the **Royal Theater** Drama School and a 1902 theater debut, her first film role in 1910 was in *Afgrunden* (The Abyss), which at once made Danish film known abroad. During 1910-14 and in the 1920s she filmed in Germany and became one of the greatest stars of silent films, for example in *The Little Angel*, Amorous Rapture (*Elskovsrus*), *Hamlet*, and *Miss Julie*, but her career ended with the introduction of sound. AHT

NIELSEN, CARL (1865-1931). Composer and a leading figure in 20th century Nordic music. The son of a village fiddler in **Funen** who taught him the violin, Nielsen joined a regimental band in **Odense**, playing the cornet. He studied violin, piano, and theory at the Royal Danish Conservatory in **Copenhagen** and in 1889-1905 was a violinist in the royal chapel, gaining experience of Wagner's music. From 1905 he received a state income, which allowed him to concentrate on composing. He completed the first of his symphonies in 1892 and the sixth and last, *Sinfonia semplice*, in 1925. In these he pioneered the transition from one key to another as the work developed. His compositions also include concertos for violin and clarinet, three string quartets, a wind quintet, three violin sonatas, the operas *Saul and David* (1902) and *Maskarade* (1906), the *Helios* overture (1904), music for the drama *Aladdin* (1919) by Adam **Oehlenschläger**, various pieces for piano, and a range of choral works. He composed 29 Preludes for organ in 1929, while *Commotio* (1931) is the greatest Danish organ work since **Buxtehude**. Nielsen wrote an autobiography, *Min fynske barndom* (1929, My Childhood in Funen) and *Levende musik* (1925, Living Music). While building bridges from **romanticism** to modernism, his music also expresses a distinctive Danish voice, and he is considered the greatest of 20th-century Danish composers. He was married to the sculptor **Anne Marie Carl Nielsen**. *See also* **National Anthems**. AHT

NIELSEN, KAI (1882-1924). Sculptor. Trained at the **Academy of Art** 1902-06 and 1912 and influenced by French sculpture, his works include *The Nude* (1908) and *The Marble Girl* (1909). His later works, such as the *Memorial to Mylius Eriksen's Polar Expedition* (Langelinie, Copenhagen, 1912) and the 18 groups of figures which decorate Blågards Plads, Copenhagen (1913-15) are in more monumental style. Others of his works include the *Water Mother* (1920, Ny Carlsberg **Glyptotek**), and the *Århus Girl* (1921, Århus). AHT

NIELSEN, LUDOLF (1876-1939). Composer. From a farming family like his namesake Carl, he won a scholarship to the Royal Danish Music Conservatoire where he studied violin, piano, and theory. In 1897 he found work playing the viola in the **Tivoli** orchestra, formed a quartet, and started composing. Grants allowed him to study in Leipzig and to travel in Germany, Austria, and Italy. His ballet, *Lackschmi* (1922) was a success in the **Royal Theater**. He was music advisor 1926-32 to the new Statsradiofoni (radio orchestra), developing its repertoire and writing many small pieces. Half his 200 compositions were lieder, but he also wrote orchestral pieces and three symphonies, the second (1910) being best known. AHT

NIELSEN, MARIE (1875-1951). Politician. The daughter of a smallholder, she worked in domestic service as a maid, then qualified as a teacher in 1908. She joined the **Social Democrats** but in 1918 left under the influence of the Russian revolution. In December 1919 she was sentenced to six months in prison for revolutionary activity and was dismissed from her teaching job. In August 1920 she took part in the second congress of the Comintern and in 1921 was a founder of the **Communist Party**, but was excluded 1929-32 and from 1936 as a Trotskyist and for criticizing a new restrictive sexual policy. Her chief contribution was as a feminist, especially 1925-34 in the newly formed Arbejderkvindernes Oplysningsforbund (Working Women's Educational Association), which worked for free abortion and sex education. AHT

NIELSEN, MORTEN (1922-1944). Writer and **Resistance** fighter. His poems, *Krigere uden våben* (1943, Warriors without Weapons) and *Efterladte digte* (1945, Posthumous Poems, published by P. la Cour) on love and death in the somber conditions of the German occupation came to symbolize the feelings of the youthful resistance movement. He was shot dead accidentally. AHT

NOBEL PRIZE WINNERS, DANISH. The *Peace Prize* was won in 1908 by **Fredrik Bajer**. The prize for *physics* was won in 1922 by **Niels Bohr** and in 1975 by his son Aage Bohr jointly with Ben R. Mottelson (US-Danish). The prize for *physiology and medicine* was won in 1903 by **Niels Finsen**, in 1920 by **August Krogh**, in 1926 by **Johannes Fibiger**, in 1943 by **Henrik Dam**, and in 1984 by Niels K. Jerne (British-Danish). The prize for *literature* was won in 1917 by **Karl Gjellerup** and **Henrik Pontoppidan** jointly, and in 1944 by **Johannes V. Jensen**. The prize for *chemistry* was won in 1997 by **Jens Christian Skou**, the other half going to Paul D. Boyer (USA) and John D. Walker (UK). AHT

NOBILITY. In their constant rivalry with the king for power, in 1282 the nobles forced King **Erik V** to sign an **Accession Charter** (*Håndfæstning*) and established an annual parliament as a check on the king, who had to reign with the advice of a Council of State (Rigsraad). This relationship between king and nobles was renewed at each accession. Never numerous, by the 14th century the Danish nobility numbered about 350 families. By the beginning of the 16th century three fourths of the land was owned by the Church or the nobility, and the nobles had developed a closed aristocracy of about 250 families who also monopolized the offices of state. With the **reformation** the state took over church lands, and from the mid-16th century the landed nobility prospered from their export of cattle, while the monarchy levied dues on the rich trade passing through the **Sound**. With the Catholic bishops removed, the power of the king was countered only by the nobility.

    Christian IV (king 1588-1648) was at odds with the nobility for much of his reign, and it became clear that the nobility lacked the skills to defend their privileges. In 1660 **Frederik III** was able to use the clergy and burghers to outflank the nobility and assert the principle of **absolutism**. In 1647 **Christian V** introduced the titles of count (*greve*) and baron (*friherre;* baroness, *friherreinde*) to distinguish the higher nobility, as part of the absolute monarch's policy of creating a new nobility dependent on the crown. Recruited largely from Holstein and other foreign parts and largely awarded for services rendered to the crown, the holders were awarded large grants of land and tax exemptions, and *arrivistes* might outrank inactive members of more ancient title. The aristocracy tried to improve its financial situation by becoming involved in the trading monopolies to East India, the West Indies, **Greenland**, etc. From the mid-18th century the large landowners interested themselves in agricultural improvement, consolidating land holdings and, from 1788, emancipating the peasants from their close ties to the land. (*See* **Peasant Reforms**).

    Titles of nobility survive, but carry no political privileges and none have been created in modern times. The crown-prince could marry someone of neither royal nor noble birth and would retain his right to the throne, provided that the monarch assents to the match by formal resolution in the council of state. There are two non-hereditary knightly orders, the **Order of the Elephant** and the **Order of the Dannebrog**. AHT

NORBY, SØREN (? -1530). Naval officer. He first served King **Hans** as a sea warrior and privateer. **Christian II** made him supreme naval commander and he defended Christian against the Swedes and the Danish council of **nobles** (*rigsråd*). In February 1525 he led an unsuccessful peasant uprising in **Scania** and had to seek reconciliation with **Frederik I**. He returned to serve Christian II but in 1526 was defeated by Frederik I's troops and fled to Russia. In 1528 he joined Christian in exile in the Netherlands, but in 1529 served in the army of Emperor Charles V and was killed in battle outside Florence, Italy. AHT

NORDENTOFT, INGER MERETE (1903-1960). School head and politician. The daughter of a doctor, she qualified as a teacher in 1923 and was appointed head of Katrinedal's School in **Copenhagen** in 1945. That year she announced that she would have a baby, but would not marry. A sensational scandal followed but three-quarters of the children's parents chose for their children to remain at the school. She was elected to the **Folketing** as a **Communist** 1945-53, but resigned in 1957 in protest at the Soviet invasion of Hungary in 1956. AHT

NORDIC COUNCIL first met in **Copenhagen** in March 1952 with participants from the parliaments of Denmark, **Iceland**, Norway, and Sweden. Finland joined in 1955 and national delegations included representatives of the **Faroes**, the Åland Islands (from 1969/70) and **Greenland** (from 1984). The initial impetus came from **Hans Hedtoft** as a way of strengthening Scandinavian cooperation after the collapse of a proposed Nordic Defense pact and the formation of **NATO**, which divided Denmark, Iceland and Norway as members from neutral Sweden and Finland. At the start based on discussions seeking consensus, cooperation was regulated by the Treaty of Helsinki (1962). Each member state appoints a Minister for Nordic Cooperation, but most work is done by direct contact (para-diplomacy) in committees of officials in the relevant ministries. Attempts in 1969-70 (Nordek) to include economic cooperation came to nothing when Danish membership of the European

Community (EC) (*see* **European Union**) became possible. But the Nordic Council of Ministers was created in 1971 with powers to discuss all matters except defense and security. Decisions are taken by unanimous consent and may only become effective if parliamentary approval is required.

Even so, a "web of integration" has been developed which encompasses a passport union and freedom of movement throughout the Nordic region, with mutual recognition of benefit rights and harmonization of much commercial and family law. Close cooperation in science, research, education, culture, and trade has given reality to the ideals of **Scandinavianism**. Since the end of the Cold War this has extended through the Council of Baltic States into coordinated policies toward central and eastern Europe. The **West Nordic Council** brings together Iceland, the Faroe Islands and Greenland to further their interests and counter the emphasis in the 1990s on the Baltic interests of the larger Nordic countries.

The 89 voting parliamentary delegates and about 80 nonvoting government representatives meet in annual plenary sessions of the Nordic Council in the national parliaments by rotation, with five party groups reflecting national parties. Much of the work is done between plenaries in subject committees, coordinated by the 10-member presidium on which each country has two representatives. The secretariat at Store Strandgade 18, Copenhagen, gives administrative support, publishes reports, and supplies information. AHT

NØRGÅRD, PER (1932-). Composer. He trained at the Royal Danish Music Conservatoire under **Vagn Holmboe** and in Paris under Nadia Boulanger, and his teaching (culminating as professor of composition 1987-95) and cultural criticism has influenced a host of Danish and other Scandinavian composers. His fourth (1980-81) and fifth (1990) symphonies are fragmented, the abstract origins of the latter giving rise to unpredictable moments of consonance, peculiar percussive eruptions, prominent piano and tubular bells, and references to the fifth symphonies of Jean Sibelius, Carl Nielsen, and the composer's own earlier symphonies. His other compositions include the operas *The Labyrinth* and *Gilgamesh*, music for a ballet, *The Young Man Shall Marry*, concertos for 'cello, violin, piano, and viola, solo and chamber music, and music for the **film** *Babette's Feast* and the BBC television film *Hedda Gabler*. AHT

NØRHOLM, IB (1931-). Composer. After study at the Royal Danish Music Conservatoire with **Vagn Holmboe** he was organist at **Elsinore** and in Copenhagen, becoming professor of composition at the Conservatoire in 1981. His compositions, including several operas and 9 symphonies, have been described as "a kaleidoscope of stylistic quotations." They vary considerably in style and medium, including late **romanticism**, strict serialism, intimate chamber music, and simple ballads reminiscent of Danish folk song. AHT

NORMANN ANDERSEN, KAI (1900-1967). Composer. He worked in a bank until 1919 while studying music, then worked full time as a choirmaster, pianist, and composer, producing film scores and a stream of entertaining dances, ballads, and songs to catchy but not banal tunes. AHT

NORTH ATLANTIC TREATY ORGANIZATION *see* **NATO**

NORTHERN SEVEN YEARS' WAR (1563-1570) was fought between Sweden on one side and Denmark, **Lübeck,** and Poland on the other. Its fundamental causes were the rivalries of Denmark and Sweden in the southeastern Baltic, where a power vacuum had been created by the collapse of the Livonian knights. The new rulers of the two countries, **Frederik II** in Denmark and **Erik XIV**, both wished to take advantage of the situation and Erik XIV even hoped to revive the **Kalmar Union** under his leadership. Denmark gained an early success with the capture of Älvborg at the mouth of the Göta, Sweden's only outlet to the West, but its troops were unable to secure a decisive victory in central Sweden, and the new Swedish navy proved superior to the Danish at sea. Peace was finally concluded at Stettin under Imperial mediation. By it each side restored its conquests, but Sweden was to grant its possessions in Livonia to the Danish king as an Imperial fief and to pay 150,000 daler as ransom for Älvsborg. To avoid the costs of recurrent conflict, any future dispute would be settled by delegations from the Councils of the two kingdoms or, if they failed, foreign princes would be asked to arbitrate. SPO, AHT

NORWAY, DANISH RELATIONS WITH. Following the union of the Danish and Norwegian crowns under the young **Oluf III** in 1380 and the subsequent **Kalmar Union**, Norway was administered as a component of the Danish kingdom until 1814. Until the **Thirty Years' War** Danish control extended along the entire west coast of modern Sweden except for the port of Göteborg, but Denmark lost these territories to Sweden in 1658. The *len* of Trondhjem was also lost in 1658 but was recovered in 1660 by **Christian IV**, after whom the Norwegian capital was named **Christiania**. In 1683 **Christian V** established a uniform code of law for Denmark and Norway. A Swedish invasion of Norway in 1716 was foiled by the Danish navy. A fresh Swedish invasion of Norway in 1718 ended with the death of Charles XII, the king of Sweden.

Christian VIII went to Norway as viceroy (*statholder*) in 1813 and supported the Norwegian bid for independence after the 1814 Treaty of **Kiel** transferred their country to Sweden. He was elected King of Norway but had to step down after a reign of only three months, and Norway was united with Sweden for the next 90 years, a relationship which rankled increasingly. The 1849 Danish **constitution** drew on the precedents of the 1814 Norwegian constitution drawn up at Eidsvol.

When Norway attained independence from Sweden in 1905, Prince Carl, the second son of King **Frederik VIII**, became the first modern king as Håkon VII. **Greenland, Iceland** and the **Faroe Islands** had been part of the Norwegian kingdom since the 13th century, but they were ignored in the Treaty of Kiel and remained Danish. In 1921 Greenland was finally recognized internationally as under Danish sovereignty. In 1931 Norway laid claim to north eastern Greenland and occupied part of it, but this claim was rejected by the International Court in The Hague in 1933.

Danes who influenced events in Norway include the forester **Johann Georg von Langen**, appointed Forest Master in Norway in 1737; **Erik Pontoppidan**, the Bishop of Bergen 1748-64; the author **Aksel Sandemose**, who emigrated to Norway and wrote in Norwegian; and **Hannibal Sehested** who was regent in Norway and mediated between Denmark and Sweden after the war of 1658-60.

Many Norwegians pursued distinguished careers in Denmark, including **Cort Adeler, Peter Anker, Arent Berntsen, J.F. Classen, Christian Colbjørnsen**, the missionary **Hans Paulsen Egede**, the architect **Edvard Heiberg**, **D.G. Monrad**, the great Norwegian admiral Peder Wessel (**Tordenskjold**), **F.A. Schleppegrell**, the author **Amalie Skram**, the philosopher **Henrich Steffens**, and the poet and dramatist **Johan Herman Wessel.**

The **Danish language** strongly influenced the development of Norwegian. In **Ludvig Holberg**'s time they were indistinguishable, and the language of Henrik Ibsen (1828-1906) is fully intelligible to Danes, but in the 19th and 20th centuries Norwegian *rigsmål* developed some distinctions from Danish, while *nynorsk* was developed from Norwegian dialects as a conscious initiative to assert a distinctive national identity.

In 1914 the kings of Denmark, Norway, and Sweden met at Malmö, reaffirming their neutrality in the face of the threats posed to all three countries by **World War I**, a claim that was respected. Both Denmark and Norway were occupied by Germany in **World War II.** Subsequently both negotiated with Sweden for a Nordic defense pact, but when this collapsed, both became founder members of **NATO** in 1949. Both countries, with Sweden, have contributed to the success of the airline **Scandinavian Airline System, SAS.** Both joined EFTA in 1960, but when the Danes joined the European Community (EC) in 1972, the Norwegians voted to remain outside and did so again in 1994. The **Nordic Council**, of which both Denmark and Norway were founder members in 1952, has been important to both for the web of integrative links which it has helped them to build. Denmark, as a member of the European Union (EU), has acted as a bridge to keep Norway in touch with EC/EU developments. Thus both have contributed to and gained from the implementation of the ideals of **Scandinavianism.** AHT

NY CARLSBERG GLYPTOTEK *see* **GLYPTOTEK**

NYROP, MARTIN (1849-1921). Architect. The son of a priest, he was trained as a carpenter, then studied in 1870-76 at the **Academy of Art**, where in 1906-19 he was professor of building design. Inspired by national **romanticism**, his architecture includes such important Copenhagen buildings as the City Hall of 1892-1905, the Land Registry (Landsarkivet) of 1892-1919, the Elias Church (1905-08), and Bispebjerg Hospital of 1906-13 and 1916-18. AHT

NYRUP RASMUSSEN, POUL *see* **RASMUSSEN**

- O -

OCCUPATION, GERMAN *see* **WORLD WAR II**

ODENSE is the third-largest city of Denmark, with a population in 1990 of 138,986 and the main urban center on the island of **Funen**. Deriving its name from the god Odin, of whom it was a sanctuary (*vi*), it became the seat of a Christian bishop in the 9th century and is first mentioned in a charter of 988. The murder of King **Knud II** in St. Alban's Church in the town in 1086 made it a place of pilgrimage in the Middle Ages. It was burned down in 1247 by **Abel** during his civil war with King **Erik IV Ploughpenny**, but quickly revived, and in the 16th century was an important economic center. Its prosperity suffered during the wars of the 17th century and in the 18th it languished. In 1804 a canal was built to link the city with the nearby fjord, and during the 19th century it became an important port and industrial and shipbuilding center.

The Cathedral, dedicated to St. Knud, is the finest Gothic brick building in Denmark. Constructed to replace a 12th-century stone building destroyed in the fire of 1247, a tower was added in the 16th century and the whole building reconstructed in 1754 and 1874. It contains a fine wooden triptych commissioned by the wife of King **Hans** from the 16th-century German artist Claus Berg for the Franciscan church which has now disappeared. **Odense** is particularly associated with Hans Christian **Andersen**. The house in which he is thought to have been born in 1805 was bought by the city one hundred years later and in 1930 a museum to house Andersen relics was built beside it. Other sons of Odense include the industrialist **C.F. Tietgen**. Odense University was founded in 1964 and admitted its first students in 1966.

In Odense is the Danish Graphic Arts Museum; an Art Museum (Kunstmuseum) showing the work of Danish painters; a museum of prehistory (Stiftsmuseum); a reconstructed Iron Age village (Jernalderlandsby); a Railroad Museum; and a Museum of Photography. There are also museums commemorating Hans Christian Andersen and **Carl Nielsen**. A short distance from the city is a fine open-air museum (Den Fynske Landsby), founded in 1941 and containing buildings from all over the island. SPO, AHT

OEDER, GEORG CHRISTIAN (1728-1791). Botanist and economist. The son of a Bavarian priest, he studied medicine and botany at the University of Göttingen, qualified *dr. med.* in 1749, and started his practice in the town of **Slesvig**. **Frederik V** appointed him royal professor of botany in 1754. He prepared the definitive botanical text *Flora Danica* (1761-71, but see also **Simon Paulli**), extensively illustrated with copper engravings *(see also* **Porcelain**). In a pamphlet published anonymously in 1769 he pleaded for an end to the *Stavnsbaand* which tied peasants to the land. He was appointed to important offices by **J.F. Struensee**, but on the latter's fall he left **Copenhagen** and ended as a bailiff in Oldenburg. AHT

OEHLENSCHLÄGER, ADAM GOTTLOB (1779-1850). Poet and dramatist. Born in **Copenhagen**, where his father was organist in **Frederiksberg** Church, his family soon moved to Frederiksberg Castle on his father's appointment as steward there. He appeared on the stage of the **Royal Theater** in his late teens but was persuaded by the **Ørsted** brothers to study for the university, which he entered in 1800 to read Law. But he became distracted by a love affair and by a desire to write. In 1802 he attended lectures by the Dano-German scientist and philosopher Heinrich Steffens on Goethe and German Romanticism. These inspired him to write the poem *Guldhornene* (1803, The Golden Horns,) on the theme of the **Gallehus Horns**, generally regarded as the debut of the **Romantic** Movement in Denmark. The success of his later production enabled him to travel to Germany and to meet some of its great cultural figures, including Goethe. After traveling on to Italy, he returned to Denmark in 1809 to be named professor of Aesthetics at the University.

Oehlenschläger's other works include *Hakon Jarls død* (The Death of Earl Hakon), *Sankt Hans Aftens spil* (A Midsummer Night's Play), and *Aladdin* (1805). He continued to write extensively but unevenly, met with fierce criticism from the leading critics of his day, **Jens Baggesen** and **Johan Ludvig Heiberg,** and lost something of his earlier popularity. His fortunes changed again and in 1829 he was crowned "Poet-king of the North" in Lund by the great Swedish poet Esaias Tegner, and he is now seen as the leading

Danish romantic poet and dramatist. His statue sits beside the entrance to the Royal Theater. SPO, AHT. *See also* **National Anthems**.

OLDENBORG DYNASTY is the name of the royal house of Denmark between 1448, when the count of Oldenburg was elected King **Frederik I**, and the death without direct heirs of King **Frederik VII** in 1863. Frederik I's successors were also elected until the crown became hereditary in the male line from 1660. After a challenge from the **Augustenborgs**, the crown passed to the **Glücksborg** dynasty. SPO, AHT. *See also* Appendix 1.

OLDENBURG-DELMENHORST were counties in northwestern Germany, whose ruler in 1448 was elected king of Denmark as **Frederik I**, the founder of the **Oldenborg** Dynasty. Six years later Frederik bequeathed the lands to his brother **Gert** (Gerhard), whose grandson **Christoffer** gave his name to the **Count's War**. In 1702 the administration of the counties was resumed by the Danish Crown. In 1767 the latter agreed (in the so-called *mageskifte*) with Catherine II of Russia that when her son Paul should come of age the counties would be exchanged for the lands in **Holsten** to which he had claims as duke of Holstein-Gottorp. In 1773 Frederick Augustus, bishop of **Lübeck**, a kinsman of Paul, became count. SPO

OLUF I ("Hunger") (c. 1052-1095). King of Denmark 1086-95. Son of King **Svend Estridsen**, Oluf was elected to the throne after the murder of King **Knud II**. His reign was marked by a series of crop failures, for which he was blamed and which earned him his epithet. They were seen as divine vengeance for the murder of Knud by the supporters of a strong monarchy, which Oluf did little to achieve. SPO

OLUF (?-1143). A son of Harald Kesja, the opponent of King **Erik II**, who managed to have his brothers killed. He gained recognition as king (c. 1140-1143) in **Scania** but was murdered at the instigation of **Erik III**. AHT

OLUF II (1370-1387). King of Denmark 1376-87 and of Norway (as Olav IV) 1380-87. Son of King **Haakon VI** of Norway and Queen

Margrethe I, he was elected king of Denmark in 1376 and succeeded to the throne of Norway on the death of his father in 1380. He died just after also being elected to the Swedish throne. SPO. *See also* **Kalmar Union**; **Podebusk, Henning**.

OMBUDSMAN. The 1953 **constitution** provided for the **Folketing** to elect "one or two persons, who shall not be members of the Folketing, to scrutinize the civil and military administration of the state", adapting the idea from the Swedish *Justitieombudsman* established some 150 years earlier, to provide protection for "the man in the street against injustice, despotism and misuse of power by the authorities." When all channels of appeal are exhausted, the *ombudsmand* is the neutral intermediary between the individual (citizen or foreigner) and officialdom, whether in central or local government. The number of cases has grown , especially since 1982, to an annual figure over 3,166 in 1994. The highest frequency of complaints concern the Ministries of the Interior, of Justice, and of Social Affairs. Cases commonly concern decisions on social security, family law, asylum (see **Tamil Affair**), or taxation. Prisoners complain about decisions relating to conditional release or leave of absence. Where cases are rejected, it is most often because other channels of appeal have not been exhausted.

As well as receiving complaints, the ombudsman has power to investigate on his own initiative, which may involve institutional visits to children's homes, mental hospitals, or prisons — wherever the weakest members of society need protection or citizens are deprived of their liberty — often following up a press story. The ombudsman can require the production of files and other information, and his findings are reported to the complainant. His main powers are of criticism and recommendation, but if necessary a court case may be brought.

The first office-holder 1955-71, **Stephan Hurwitz** did much to develop the role. He was succeeded by Lars Nordskov Nielsen (1971-81), Niels Eilschou Holm (1981-87), and Hans Gammeltoft-Hansen (1987-). In 1974 an Ombudsman for Consumer Affairs was added. The 1991 Treaty of European Union requires the European Parliament to appoint an ombudsman to investigate complaints about the **European Union**. AHT

ØRESUND *see* **SOUND, THE**

ØRSTED, ANDERS SANDØE (1778-1860). Lawyer and politician. The brother of H.C. Ørsted, he graduated *cand. jur.* in 1799 and served in various senior state offices, including as a deputy in the Chancellery 1813-48, attorney-general 1825-48, royal commissioner 1835-44 at both the **constituent assemblies** of the kingdom, as prime minister 1842-48, as prime minister and *kultusminister* (minister for education and the church) 1853-54 and also interior minister 1853-54, and as minister of justice in 1854. He was the principal driving force in the closing phase of absolute monarchy. In the 1840s he opposed the Ejder policy (*see* **Slesvig-Holsten**) and voted against the June **Constitution** of 1849. As prime minister he carried through the 1853 law of hereditary succession to the **monarchy** which later secured the succession to **Christian IX**. His extensive legal writings, in which he emphasized practicalities before theory, include *Håndbog i den danske og norske lovgivning I-VI* (1822-35, Handbook of Danish and Norwegian Legislation). AHT

ØRSTED, HANS CHRISTIAN (1777-1851). Physicist and philosopher. The son of an apothecary and brother of **A.S. Ørsted**, he graduated *cand. pharm.* in 1797 and *dr. phil.* in 1799, then studied in Germany and France 1801-03. He was professor of physics in Copenhagen University 1806-51, starting the Society for the Spread of Natural Science in 1842, and cofounding the Polytechnic Institute (Den polytekniske Læreanstalt, *see* **Universities and Higher Education**) in 1829. He discovered electromagnetism in 1820 and his many other important discoveries include the element aluminum. He combined his activities in natural science with philosophical considerations, seeking the organic unity, interrelationship and harmony of nature, a view which found expression in his collected talks, scientific papers, and dialogues, *Ånden i naturen* (I-II, 1850, The Spirit in Nature). AHT

OUTZE, BØRGE (1912-1980). Journalist. Born in **Odense**, he trained at *Fyns Venstreblad* and from 1936 was a journalist on *Nationaltidende*. During the German occupation he founded and edited the underground news agency *Information*. From 5 May 1945 this became the newspaper *Information*, with Outze as editor 1945-80 developing a reputation for sharp leaders and impartial reporting. AHT

- P -

PAINTING in Denmark followed the same stylistic trends as in the wider Europe, while emphasizing a quiet intimacy and a love of nature and of the placid Danish landscape. Numerous religious murals were painted in the c. 2000 medieval churches. Renaissance and baroque artists in Denmark were principally Dutch, however, and Danish painting needed the foundation of the **Academy of Art** in 1754 before it could flourish. **Jens Juel**, and **Nikolaj Abildgaard**, two of Denmark's most important 18th-century artists, played important parts in this development. **C.W. Eckersberg** pioneered naturalism and influenced a generation of Danish painters of the **Golden Age**, including his pupils **Christen Købke**, **Constantin Hansen**, and Wilhelm Marstrand.

About 1835 a romantic reaction against Eckersberg's rather rigid naturalism was pioneered by Jørgen Sonne (1801-90), Johan Thomas **Lundbye**, Dankvart Dreyer (1816-52), and P.C. Skovgaard (1817-75). Their subjects were often idylls of the Danish landscape, while Lundbye was also a superb animal painter. Another genre is of paintings of popular life, in which Christen Dahlsgaard (1824-1907), Julius Exner (1825-1910), and Frederik Vermehren excelled. **L.A. Ring** began a new trend of realism with pictures of the **Zealand** landscape and peasants of a unique intensity and warmth. Denmark's outstanding Impressionist is Theodor Philipsen (1840-1920), influenced by Paul Gaugin while he lived in **Copenhagen**. The period from 1870 also saw the development of the **Skagen School** of painters, who included **Michael** and **Anna Ancher, P.S. Krøyer**, and **Lauritz Tuxen**.

At the turn of the century the Symbolists used large unbroken surfaces in their meditations on universal religious and moral values. Among them were **Vilhelm Hammershøi** and Ejnar Nielsen (1872-1956). Their contemporary, the painter and sculptor, Jens Ferdinand **Willumsen**, became a central and controversial figure in Danish art for three generations, although without attracting many followers. **Joakim Skovgaard** was brought up in the fervent biblical **Grundtvig**ian doctrine and developed a monumental style reminiscent of Byzantine art, well displayed in the cathedrals of Viborg and Lund (Sweden). His pupil Niels Larsen Stevns (1864-1941) developed an even bolder and more dramatic style for his depictions of the life of **Hans Christian Andersen** in the museum at **Odense**. A group of Impressionist painters (*Fynboerne*) are associated with **Funen** and have a museum of their work in Fåborg. They include Peter Hansen (1868-1928), Fritz **Syberg**, and **Johannes Larsen**.

Modernism, influenced by French impressionism and Fauvism, emerged in great diversity in Denmark from 1905, with work on show in many places, including Den Frie Udstilling (the Free Exhibition). A small group of Romantics has as its outstanding representatives **Oluf Høst** and Jens Søndergaard (1895-1957), whose paintings glow with an eruptive and romantic relation to nature. Nonfigurative painters have held to the Danish tradition of the sensitive color range originally established by Eckersberg. A "fabulous" tendency is represented by the painting of **Asger Jorn** and Carl-Henning Pedersen (1913-), the former a very active member of the COBRA movement. Others such as Else Alfelt (1910-), Ejler Bill (1910-), and Egill Jacobsen have combined constructive stringency with coloristic delicacy. Social art has never had much following in Denmark: an artist such as John Christensen (1896-1940) has been driven by personal reactions rather than propaganda directives. AHT. *See also* **Bach, Otto; Bloch, Carl; Drachmann, Holger; Frølich, Lorenz; Høyer, Cornelius; Larsen, Johannes; Lorck, Melchior; Moe, Louis; Mortensen, Richard; Sikker Hansen, Aage; Syberg, Fritz; Zahrtmann, Kristian**.

PALLADIUS, PEDER (1503-1560). Bishop. He studied at Wittenberg under Martin Luther and Melanchton, graduated *dr. theol.* in 1537 and became the first Lutheran bishop of **Zealand**, 1537-60. His many writings included a Danish edition of Luther's little catechism and *En Visitatz Bog* (1925), based on supervisory journeys through his diocese, which sets out Lutheran principles for how children should live and how the church should function. AHT

PALUDAN, JACOB (1896-1975). Novelist and essayist. Son of a literary historian, he graduated as a pharmacist in 1918. A visit to the United States of America in 1920-21 resulted in a distaste for the culture there and a conservatism that is reflected in his novels, which include *De vestlige veje* (1922, The Western Ways), *Fugle* *omkring fyret* (1925, Birds around the Light-House), and *Markerne modnes* (1927, The Fields Ripen). His greatest novel, *Jørgen Stein* of 1933, was also his last. Its eponymous hero seeks refuge from modern materialism in old values. Thereafter Paludan devoted himself solely to essay writing. His writing has a pessimistic and skeptical view of what he saw as the superficial and meaningless modern world. SPO, AHT

PALUDAN-MÜLLER, CASPAR (1805-1882). Historian. He graduated *cand. theol.* in 1827 and *dr. phil.* in history in 1840 and was professor of history at Copenhagen University 1872-82. In his view the nation's history was a necessary and organic development in the context of a universal history. His books included two volumes on the **Count's War** (1853-54, *Grevens Fejde*), a study of King **Valdemar**'s land-book (1869-72), and a study of the first **Oldenborg** kings (1874). AHT

PANDURO, LEIF (1923-1977). Novelist and television dramatist. The son of an insurance official who was executed as a Nazi sympathizer by the Resistance, he spent 1924-30 in a children's home and from 1934 at boarding school. After various factory jobs he qualified as a dentist in 1947, and became an author full time only in 1965. His large literary output in a clear and unpretentious style is written from the perspective of a psychoanalytically inspired humanism, with a sharp eye to the hollow falsity of the comfortable middle class. His 13 novels include *Rend mig i traditionerne* (1958, *Kick Me up the Traditions*, 1961) and *Fern fra Danmark* (1963, Far from Denmark). Thirteen television plays include *Farvel Thomas* (1968, Good-bye Thomas), *Bella* and *Et godt liv* (1970, A Good Life), *Hjem hos William* (Home at William's) and *Rundt om Selma* (1971, Around Selma), *I Adams verden* (1973, In Adam's World), and *Louises hus* (1974, Louise's House). For television he wrote *Harry og kammertjeneren* (1961, Harry and the Waiter), *Støvsugerbanden* (1962, The Vacuum-Cleaner Gang), and *Naboerne* (1966, The Neighbors), as well as crime series including *Ka' De li' østers* (1967, Do You Like Oysters?), *Smuglerne* (1970-71, The Smugglers) and eight episodes of *Huset på Christianshavn* (1967-75, The House in Christianshavn). AHT

PAN-SCANDINAVIANISM *see* **SCANDINAVIANISM**

PARLIAMENT. The **Danehof** and its successors were assemblies through which the **nobility** asserted their influence on the king, a relationship which was ended by the transition to **absolute monarchy** in 1661. Alarmed by the European revolutions of 1830 and the divisive potential of liberalism and nationalism in a Denmark of Danish- and German-speakers, and without conceding the absolutist principle, **Frederik VI** set up four consultative assemblies of **Estates**, in Itzehoe for the duchy of Holsten (including **Lauenburg**), in **Slesvig** for that duchy, in **Viborg** for **Jutland**, and in **Roskilde** for the Islands (stænderforsamling). During the following three years their composition was debated between **P.C. Stemann**, for the landowners, who wanted a franchise tightly limited by land ownership requirements, and **A.S. Ørsted,** who wanted a broad franchise with special representation for officials and scientists; eventually Stemann came closest to achieving his aims. The minimum voting age was 25 and the minimum age of candidates was 30. There were three electoral rolls: landed proprietors, owners of town property, and landowning peasants. Professor C.N. David warned against the over-representation of landed interests.

A **constituent assembly** (Den grundlovgivende Rigsforsamling) of 1848-9 drew up the liberal June **Constitution** of 1849 which established a **Rigsdag** of two chambers of equal power, the lower **Folketing** and the indirectly elected **Landsting**, the former elected for a three-year term and the latter for eight years. The Folketing and Landsting were located in **Christiansborg** from 1849.

In 1854-55, as an expression of the *helstat* ideal of incorporating the duchies of **Slesvig** and Holsten into a greater Denmark, which had been agreed in the London Protocol of 1850, a Council of the Realm (*Rigsraad*) was established, with representation from the provinces of Denmark together with the two duchies (and **Lauenburg** with Holsten). This comprised 30 directly elected members, 30 indirectly elected by the provincial councils, and 20 nominated by the Crown, and was to act in parallel with the Rigsdag, some of whose powers were reduced. A short-lived joint constitution for Denmark and Slesvig precipitated the disastrous Second **Slesvig-Holsten** War and the loss of both the duchies in 1866.

The two-chamber Rigsdag continued, with the composition of the Landsting amended to ensure conservative control. Only with the

Change of System in 1901 did the king accept the parliamentary principle, whereby **governments** are expected to have the support of a parliamentary majority. Further amendments to the composition of the Rigsdag were made in 1915 and 1920. **Elections** to the Folketing thereafter were by proportional representation with a universal franchise. Constitutional reform was attempted in 1939 but failed narrowly when put to **referendum**. The 1953 **constitution** abolished the Landsting and fixed the expanded Folketing membership at 179, including two representatives each from the **Faroe Islands** and **Greenland**. Since then the unicameral parliament has been known as the Folketing (which avoids confusion between the Danish Rigsdag and the Swedish Riksdag). AHT

PASSER, DIRCH (1926-1980). Actor. Beginning in repertory in 1944-46, he built a stage career as a comic of the totally absurd, for a time in partnership with Kjeld Petersen as the Kellerdirk Brothers. AHT

PAULLI, SIMON (1603-1680). Doctor and botanist. After studies in Denmark and abroad he graduated *dr. med.* in 1630 and was appointed professor in anatomy, surgery, and botany at Copenhagen University 1639-48. In 1645 he gave the first public anatomical demonstration in Denmark. In 1648 he worked out the extensively illustrated *Flora Danica*. In 1650 he was appointed court *medicus* and in 1656 until his death he was the king's personal physician. AHT

PEASANT REFORMS. At the close of the Middle Ages the proportion of land in peasant ownership was down to about one-eighth in Denmark (compared to a half in Sweden); the church and the nobility each owned one-third and the crown about one-fifth. After the **Count's War** (1534-36) most freeholds were confiscated by the crown. Many of the new lords and their bailiffs were from **Holsten** or elsewhere in Germany, and introduced more stringent practices. Week-work was expected of a peasant living on or near the noble's manor, while a tenant farmer was expected to pay rent in kind, so that the lord benefited from rising prices. The newly installed lord often also acted as magistrate, making conditions for the peasants additionally hard.

Christian VI decreed in 1733 that the peasants were bound to the soil, so that landlords should have no difficulty in providing one man per hundred acres to serve in the militia. Manpower was also retained on the land at a time when agricultural depression made migration attractive. Subsequent enactments during 1735 to 1764 developed this system of *stavnsbaand* or *adscriptio glebae* to apply to all males aged between four and 40 and made acceptance of a tenancy compulsory, even if completion of military service left a peasant otherwise free to leave the estate.

In addition to owners of tax-assessed property and tenants (who until 1702 were subject to *vornedskab*), there were smallholders (cottars or *husmænd*). A smallholder had a cottage and a small piece of land which he was only free to cultivate when he had done the work required by the farmer whose land it was. A fourth category, laborers, were allowed a small patch of land but led a precarious existence unless they acquired a craft. Often they were forced into the militia.

From the 1730s a rise in corn prices encouraged landlords (led by the **Bernstorffs** and the **Reventlows**) to consider improved agricultural methods. The **Great Agriculture Commission** was formed in 1786 and aimed to set a legal framework for general agricultural reform. Its first measure (1786-7) forbade landlords or their bailiffs from imposing such physical punishments on peasants as the use of the long whip or fetters, or making them ride the wooden horse, or go about in a barrel (known as the Spanish mantle), the use of which showed the power of the landlords and the degraded conditions of the peasants. The second stage was to encourage tenants to improve their holdings by giving independent tribunals power to award compensation for disturbance. The third and most important stage was abolition of the *stavnsbånd*. This was phased out from 1788, so that all age-groups were freed from 1800.

From 1790 the minimum duration of a tenancy was fixed as the lifetime of the tenant and his wife. By 1799 all work-rents had to be clearly defined, and as a result they were soon an uncommon element of tenancy agreements. The results of these changes were that, within about 20 years, three-fifths of the land worked by peasant farmers was owned by peasants, and about the same proportion had been enclosed (*see* **Enclosure**). Improved methods had doubled yields, so that during the war years of the early 19th century when prices rose, Danish farmers were able to get good prices for their corn, bacon, and butter. To commemorate these reforms the Column of Liberty (*Frihedsstøtten*), designed by N.A. **Abildgaard** was erected in 1792-97: it stands on Vesterbrogade near **Copenhagen's** main rail station. AHT

PEDERSEN, CHRISTIERN (c. 1480-1554). Author. In 1511 he was named as a master of the liberal arts. He served as a cannon of Lund cathedral 1505-25 and was attached to **Christian II**'s court in exile in the Netherlands 1526-31. In 1532-36 he was a printer of books in Malmö. In 1514 in Paris he published the first collected and printed edition of Saxo's history of Denmark, and later translated it into Danish, but this was lost in the Copenhagen University library fire of 1728. A **Lutheran**, he translated into Danish the New Testament in 1529 and later the rest of the **Bible**. This edition became known as *Christian III's Bible* of 1550. AHT

PEDERSEN, MOGENS (c. 1585-c. 1623). Composer in the Danish court from 1603 except during periods of study in Venice and Sienna (1605-08) and Holland (1611-14). His compositions included madrigals and *Pratum spirituale* (1620), a collection of church music which is the oldest existing substantial text in Danish by a Danish composer. AHT

PENSIONS, RETIREMENT. Provision for the elderly outside the Poor Law dates from 1891, when people over 60 who met a liberal means test were eligible for support. The two main principles, then and since, are that (1) the aim should be full maintenance, making poor-relief or help from relatives unnecessary, and (2) benefits are universal, without qualifying contribution and with all costs met through taxation. A true old-age pension was introduced in 1922. In 1956 a general retirement pension made the pension entitlement universal, extending it to all including those on higher incomes. Arrangements were revised in 1965 and 1970, since when all Danish citizens aged over 67 and resident in the country became eligible for the basic pension (*folkepension*), regardless of income. From 1973 eligibility depended on residence in the country for at least 40 years between the ages of 15 and 67. A shorter residence entitles to a proportional pension equal to one-fortieth of the full amount for each year of residence. The amount paid is automatically adjusted to keep pace with the cost of living. The amount has three elements: the basic pension, a supplement, and a special supplement for single pensioners. A pensioner can also apply for allowances for heating and housing. A supplement is paid to those with no other source of income.

An early pension (*førtidspension*) may be drawn on health grounds for persons aged 18 to 66, or on social and health grounds for those aged 50-66. Farmers and fishermen aged 55-66, on certain conditions, can receive closure support (*ophørsstøtte*), in effect an early pension. Employed people aged 60-66 can on certain conditions receive redundancy pay (*efterløn*). Alternatively they can combine part-time work with a part-pension. Although standard retirement age has long been fixed at 67, these various schemes mean that the average age of retirement in 1996 was 61½.

From legislation in 1964, all employees are also paid a supplementary retirement pension (ATP, Arbejdsmarkedets Tillægspension) from the age of 67, the full ATP again depending on 40 years of employment. Employees who have been a member of the fund for at least three years can retain membership if they become self-employed. A widow is paid this pension at the age of 62 after being married for at least 10 years, provided her husband was a member for 10 years. The ATP is funded from contributions paid by employers and employees; any surplus from the fund is applied to raising pensions.

Disability Pensions began relatively late, in 1921, and initially depended on voluntary membership of an insurance fund. From 1933 they were brought largely into line with retirement pensions. Since 1965 eligibility has been conditional on more than 50 percent loss of capacity, for physical or psychological cause. Supplements are paid for more severe disability and for single people, and there are reductions if the pensioner has other income. Pensions are adjusted in line with the cost of living. Eligibility is decided by the Disablement Insurance Court (Invalideforsikringsretten).

Widow's Pension (Enkepension) has been paid since a 1959 Act to widows of 55 and over who have been widowed after the age of 55, and to widows of 45 and over while they have two or more children under 18 to support. The amount is equivalent to a single person's retirement pension and is reduced if the pensioner has other income.

Retirement, disability, and widow's pensions are administered by municipal government. Disputes can be appealed to county level and finally to the Social Security Appeals Board (*Den sociale Ank-estyrelse*). Pensioners are encouraged to stay in their own homes, and there is help to adapt them. Pensioners also have a right to a place in a pensioners' home. AHT. *See also* **Elderly Care; Family Allowance.**

PEOPLE'S PARTY (FAROESE) (Fólkaflokkurin) is a conservative political party formed in 1939 by the leading Faroese nationalist Jóannes Patursson after breaking with the **Home Rule Party**, largely over economic policy. It won a quarter of the seats in the Løgting in 1940 and began to fight for full independence for the islands. In the elections of August 1943 and September 1945 it increased its representation to nearly half the seats, but an inconclusive **referendum** in 1947 led eventually only to home rule in 1948. In the 1984 elections it won 21.6 percent of the popular vote and seven of the 32 seats in the Løgting. In the 1988 election it finally became the largest party and its chairman Jógvan Smedsten led a coalition with the Center Party. When the coalition collapsed at the beginning of 1991, the People's Party formed a coalition with the **Social Democrats** but withdrew from this in 1993. The party stands for a Christian culture, a just society, and democracy, and seeks an independence for the Faroe Islands which would give the Lagting legislative authority on all policies and membership of NATO independently of Denmark. (See under **Faroe Islands** for the consequences of the 1998 elections). In the **Folketing** the party's representative is attached to the **Conservative People's Party**. SPO, AHT

PETERSEN, EGMONT HARALD (1860-1914). Printer and magazine publisher. The son of a single mother, at the age of 18 he started an independent printing business which expanded rapidly and in 1914 became Guttenberghus, one of the largest Danish printers and publishers of the 20th century. From 1904 one of his most successful titles was the weekly magazine *Hjemmet* (Home). AHT

PETERSEN, NIS (1897-1943). Novelist and poet. Raised by his grandmother in the northwest **Jutland** town of Herning after the early death of his parents, he worked as a journalist in Holbæk on **Zealand** and in **Copenhagen**. His first collection of verse was published in 1926, but the novel *Sandalmagernes gade* (1931, The

Street of the Sandalmakers), set in Ancient Rome, won him international fame. A later novel and collections of verse did not attract so much popularity, although his verse had considerable influence on younger Danish poets. His writing has an almost desperate nihilism set in a divided world. He led the life of a vagabond and died of overwork and alcoholism. SPO, AHT

PETRUS DE PHILOMENA DE DACIA (PEDER NATTERGAL) (lived c. 1300). Astronomer. He appears to have been a canon of **Roskilde** cathedral and to have taught in Paris university. He worked out an astronomical calendar which became of central importance in the development of the church's calendar. He also described an instrument for calculating eclipses and tabulated the movements of the moon. AHT

PIETISM. Toward the end of his reign, **Frederik IV** adopted a pietistic religious perspective, a view which his son **Christian VI** (king 1730-46) implemented extensively. His successor, **Frederik V**, swept away all such strictures. In a theological climate of stifling orthodoxy which led many of the clergy to look askance at the new movement, the spread of pietism from Germany brought a spiritual revival which enabled the individual to seek a way of salvation for himself and his fellows, along with strict Sabbath observance and an Ordinance to prevent dissenting congregations and discourage religious activities under lay leadership. The Schools Ordinance of 1739 encouraged reading as a means of understanding the catechism and a preparation for confirmation: although countered by farmers and landowners, its long-term effect was beneficial. Pietist ideas gave rise to pietist individualism and opened the way for **Enlightenment** thinking. AHT

PIO, LOUIS ALBERT FRANÇOIS (1841-1894) worked as a teacher, army officer, and postal clerk, then helped to start *Socialisten* (The Socialist) newspaper and the Danish branch of the International Association of Workers in 1871, of which he was elected chairman (Grand Master). An able writer and editor and organizer of mass meetings, Pio's moderation on strikes and near-dictatorial leadership was increasingly opposed. In 1872 he was sentenced to six years in prison (with five years for **Paul Geleff** and four for Harald Brix) but was released in 1875 and became chairman of the

Free **Trade Unions'** Central Executive, formed in July 1875. Otherwise critical of the **Liberals**, he encouraged labor to support their fight for democracy. Pio visited Marx and Engels in London in May 1876 with plans to revive the First International, but British unions were apathetic. The June 1876 Gimle Congress of the **Social Democrats** criticized his personal leadership.

In poor health, Pio feared further prison and the police "encouraged" him to emigrate to the United States of America with 10,000 kroner — more if he took Geleff and other labor leaders. He left with Augusta Jørgensen and their daughter and Geleff, with whom he soon fell out. He tried to form a socialist colony at Smoky Hill River, Kansas, but it soon failed and he found work as a typographer, clerk, and customs official in Chicago, Illinois. Complex and charismatic, he adapted elements of international socialism to Danish conditions, and his analysis of the agrarian problem won international recognition. His writings include *Sagnet om Holger Danske, dets Udbredelse og Forhold til Mythologien* (1869, The Legend of Holger Danske, Its Extent and Relation to Mythology), numerous articles on socialism including translations from Karl Marx, *En biografisk Skitse* (1873, A Biographical Sketch), and *Erindringer fra Redaktionskontoret og Fængslet* (1877, Memoirs from Editor's Office and Prison). His daughter Sylvia returned to Denmark, was deeply loved by **Th. Stauning** and was active on **Social Democrats'** women's committee until her death in 1932. AHT

PLESSEN, CHRISTIAN SIEGFRIED von (1646-1723). Politician and civil servant. In 1677 he was appointed to the court of **Christian V**'s brother prince Jørgen to take care of his Danish interests after the prince's marriage to the British princess Anne. As president of the finance office 1692-1700 and member of the council until 1793 he pursued a policy of forced loans and state savings so as to reduce the tax burden. His diplomatic policy was to bring together Denmark, Sweden, Britain, and the Netherlands. In 1703 he left the service of the state and lived in Hamburg, but was still used as an envoy by the Danish government. AHT

PLOUG, CARL (1813-1894). Politician, author, and song writer. The son of a head teacher from Kolding, in the 1830s and 1840s he supported **national-liberalism** and **Scandinavianism**. He edited *Fædrelandet* (The Fatherland) 1841-81, was a member of the constitutional convention 1854-58, the **Folketing** 1854-58, and the **Landsting** 1858-90. He supported the 1866 constitution, which restored to the monarch many of the powers conceded to **parliament** in 1849. In the 1870s and 1880s, as a member of the **Right,** Ploug opposed the **Liberal Party** and majority parliamentarism. AHT

PODEBUSK, HENNING (?-c. 1388). Politician. Originally from Mecklenburg, he entered the service of **Valdemar IV "Atterdag"** in 1350 and was with his campaign in Gotland in 1361. He governed Denmark 1368-70 while Valdemar was out of the country under the threat of his enemies. His was the main initiative behind the Peace of Stralsund, which made possible the king's return. He retained his position under King **Oluf II,** and on Oluf's death he took the initiative which secured **Margrethe I**'s power as regent. AHT. *See also* **Kalmar Union**.

POLICE. In the 15th century, the towns were policed by the royal bailiff *(kongens foged)*, who had powers of distraint and could be asked to restrain antisocial conduct. In larger towns he was helped by a number of *bysvende*. The *foged* held a weekly town court *(byting)* to decide legal disputes. Between 1661 and 1690 **Copenhagen** doubled its population from 30,000 to 60,000. To deal with the growing number of poor people and increasing criminal activity, the first police chief *(politimester)* was appointed, with oversight of the city's morals, virtue, and law and order. In the 1720s Hans Hammerich, as holder of this office, actively punished prostitutes. Amid fears of revolution, police powers of censorship were transferred to the courts in 1790 and were further tightened in 1799 and again in 1810. On the evidence of police informers, Dr. Jacob Jacobsen **Dampe** was sentenced to death in 1821 for advocating opposition to the absolute monarchy. The peasant reforms of 1786-7 transferred authority in the country from landlords to parish bailiffs *(sognefoged)*, and from 1793 they were also given responsibility for roads.

Amid growing pressure for farmers' rights (*see* **Farmers' Friends**), in 1845 permission from the local police chief was required for any public meeting on this issue. In 1848 press freedom was achieved, with the repeal of the 1799 law and all the subsequent additions, but restoration of monarchic rule in 1866 saw police measures against the pioneer socialists (**Pio** and **Geleff** among others) and a large public meeting on 5 May 1871 broken up by police and hussars. Tensions between **Estrup**'s unrepresentative conservative government and the growing opposition of **Liberals** and farmers led to the formation in 1885 of a short-lived corps of "blue gendarmes" to oppose political unrest and class conflict. Again in 1918, with near-revolution in Germany after **World War I**, the Socialist Labor Party and the syndicalist movement *Fagoppositionens Sammenslutning* (FS) called a meeting in Grønttorvet in Copenhagen in the hope of spreading revolution to Denmark. An initially peaceful meeting was followed by three days of fighting with the police.

In 1937 the system of local police forces was replaced by a single national force under the jurisdiction of the Ministry of Justice. During **World War II** the police continued to keep order until August 1943, when the Danish government ceased to function and the Germans rounded up **Jews** and members of the **resistance** movement. The police worked closely with the resistance movement, and about 7,000 went "underground" but on 19 September 1944 some 2,000 policemen were arrested by the Germans and transported to concentration camps, where about 100 died. An unarmed force of guards attempted to keep order, but there was a rapid growth of criminal activity, especially on the black market. The occupying power allowed the formation of a HIPO-corps (from *HilfsPolizei*) of Danish Gestapo-sympathizers who used informers, murder and torture to terrorize the population and pursue the resistance movement. The Danish police were back in action within a week of the country's liberation in 1945, and played an important part in dealing with informers and restoring civil law.

The student uprising of 1968 brought confrontations of police and public in protest against the US war in Vietnam and in 1970 against a meeting in **Copenhagen** of the World Bank, which was opposed for its exploitation of Third World countries. In May 1993, following the **referendum** approval of the Maastricht Treaty (*see* **European Union**) there was a street fight on Nørrebro in Copenhagen: for the first time since 1945 the police drew their pistols and shot into the crowd, wounding eleven people. In 1996-7 the police had to deal with armed warfare (with deaths and other casualties) between two motorcycle gangs of Hell's Angels and Bandidos, the weapons involved including rocket launchers.

In the 1960s there were 72 police districts *(politikredse)* each headed by a *politimester*, but many of these were amalgamated, in line with the 1970 **local government** reform. The police force numbered some 8,500 in 1974, by 1985 increased to 9,350, and by 1995 to 10,300, with a further 2,150 office staff. AHT

POLITICAL PARTIES. The Danish party system originated in 1848 when King **Frederik VII** conceded a **constitution** — previously there was press **censorship** and it was an offense to question the principle of **absolute monarchy.** Initially the **Right** and the **National Liberals** shared cabinet office, then alternated it between them. In 1864-1901 monarchical rule was reasserted, and during this period King **Christian IX** chose his ministers from among a conservative group of large land owners, state officials and professionals which from 1876 organized as the United Right *(Højre)* and dominated the **Folketing.** But support steadily grew for liberal ideas of a government representative of popular opinion. In 1892 a minority of Moderate Liberals declared themselves willing to compromise with the Right, and from 1895 the larger group of liberals took the name **Liberal** Reform Party. By 1901, when the Right held only 7 percent of the Folketing seats, the liberal aim of constitutional and democratic government responsible to the popularly elected chamber of parliament was finally conceded in the **Change of System.** Moderate and Reform wings of the liberals persisted until the 1910 election, when they united as *Venstre* (literally "the Left", but in 20th-century terms they are ideologically on the right, with the conservatives). Although complicated by this division and by the early stages of **Social Democrat** (SD) growth, the party system at this stage was essentially bi-polar.

The **Radical Liberals** broke from the Liberals in 1905, primarily because they wanted more rapid reform of land holdings to improve conditions for smallholders. By 1906 the Social Democrats had 25 percent of the vote and the four-party system was in place which would characterize Danish politics for the next half-century. From left to right, the "four old parties" were the Social Democrats, supported by urban and rural working-class voters. Their long-term allies, the Radical Liberals, were supported by smallholders, teachers, and other professionals. The *Venstre* Liberals had a mainly agrarian electorate. The Conservatives were supported by proprietors of urban businesses and large estates.

The Social Democrats became the largest party in 1924 and from 1929 they have predominated in office. They gained their largest ever share of votes (46.1 percent) in 1935 and have always needed the support of one or more other parties. During 1929-64 this support came from the Radical Liberals. Largely antagonistic relationships between *Venstre* and the Conservatives persisted from 1901 until the 1940s, but warmed sufficiently for them to form a joint cabinet in 1950-53 led by **Erik Eriksen**. They have since worked together closely.

The Danish **Communist Party** first gained Folketing representation at a minimal level in 1932. It took a leading part in the **Resistance** and was represented in the 1945 liberation government, doing well at the election that year but declining thereafter. It was largely replaced in 1959 by the **Socialist People's Party**, and from then on there was a five-party system. Despite the leading importance of the Social Democrats, there has only been a numerical majority for the socialist block of parties for two brief periods, 1966-68 and 1971-73. On both occasions the Socialist People's Party could not agree with SD cabinet policy, first on management of the economy and then on the EEC (*see* **European Union**) and **NATO**.

There were times when a fifth party did play a significant role. The **Justice Party** was included in the Social Democratic plus Radical Liberal coalitions of 1957-60 to give them minimum winning status, but otherwise has not been important. When it lost representation, one **Greenland** representative was brought into the cabinet to make a minimal winning majority in 1960-64. From 1966 the Radical Liberals opposed the tendency toward a two-block pattern. Initially they took the lead in forming the 1968-71 coalition with the *Venstre* Liberals and the Conservatives, and subsequently have played a pivotal role at the center whenever the electoral arithmetic and the policy issues have allowed.

The 1973 "earthquake" election sharply disrupted the five-party system. The number of parties in the Folketing doubled and all the parties with experience in government lost heavily. In the highly fragmented Folketing since then, electoral opinion has been volatile, continuity of parliamentary membership has been reduced, and for a decade protracted negotiations were needed to secure support for a government program. As leader of the party retaining most credibility, **Poul Hartling** formed a very narrowly based and short-lived *Venstre* Liberal government. The Social Democrats, led by **Anker**

Jørgensen, were in office 1975-82 with the parliamentary acquiescence of shifting majorities from the center-right — Radical Liberals, **Christian People's Party**, **Center Democrats**, and sometimes *Venstre* and Conservatives. In 1978-79 SD and *Venstre* Liberals formed a non-closed coalition which omitted the three small parties of the center, but *Venstre's* influence on economic policy was highly unpopular with the trade unions and this experiment lasted less than 14 months.

The governments of 1982-93 were formed by the Conservative leader, **Poul Schlüter**. He was supported by *Venstre*, led by Uffe Ellemann-Jensen as foreign minister, with Center Democrats and Christian People's Party also in the cabinet until 1989, in what were termed *firkløver* ("four-leaf-clover") governments. These were all minority coalitions and faced over one hundred defeats on issues concerning foreign policy, defense, and the environment from an opposition majority comprising Radical Liberals, Social Democrats and Socialist People's Party. This was the period of "foot-note politics" because of the reservations to international agreements which the opposition imposed on Danish representatives. But the Radical Liberals supported the government's economic and social policy, so a no-confidence vote against the government would not have a majority. This phase ended when the Radicals were brought into the 1989-90 government. Schlüter's premiership ended in the **Tamil Affair**, and the center parties switched their support to the Social Democrats.

Poul Nyrup Rasmussen formed his first government in January 1993 with majority support from Radical Liberals, Christian People's Party and Center Democrats, and the Radical Liberal Niels Helveg Petersen as foreign minister. In the 1994 elections the Social Democrats lost seven seats, the Christian People's Party lost its Folketing representation, and the government continued as a minority coalition. The Center Democrats resigned in 1996 and the two-party SD and Radical Liberal government had then to rely on parliamentary support from the Socialist People's Party and the Unity List.

After 1973 a core of "responsible" parties formed governments, while a periphery of non-coalitionable parties formed bilateral oppositions. The Progress Party, formed in protest against high taxation and bureaucracy, was peripheral throughout the subsequent two decades. On the left wing the Communists, Left Socialists, Common

Course, and the Red-Green Unity List were peripheral parties, as was the Socialist People's Party. After the 1992 referendum which narrowly rejected the Maastricht Treaty of European Union (TEU), however, the Socialist People's Party took a lead in formulating the "national compromise". This was a list of reservations agreed to by all the core parties, which was accepted by the EU summit meeting in Edinburgh in December 1992 and formed the basis of the campaign that secured referendum support for the TEU in May 1993.

In 1982 Schlüter hoped to form a majority coalition of Conservatives, *Venstre* Liberals, and Social Democrats, rather than the Conservative-center minority coalition. This failed, and the alternation again in 1993 to a Social Democratic-led center-left coalition illustrates a weak bi-polarity, with Social Democrats and Conservatives or Liberals forming the two poles within the responsible core.

On a left/right scale the parties in the 1990s can be ordered: Red-Green Unity List, Socialist People's Party, Social Democrats, Radical Liberals, Center Democrats, *Venstre* Liberals, Christian People's Party, Conservatives, Danish People's Party, and Progress Party. Of these, the parties between and including the Social Democrats and the Conservatives are broadly pro-European. In contrast with Germany, no Green party has gained representation, but the parties with the "greenest" policies are the **Red-Green Unity** List, the Socialist People's Party, and the Radical Liberals. AHT

POLITIKEN is a newspaper founded in 1884, with **Viggo Hørup** as editor until 1901. It advocated liberal policies, including the responsibility of the cabinet to the popularly elected lower house of parliament, a principle achieved with the **Change of System** in 1901, and a pacifist **defense** policy, which recognized the indefensibility of Denmark's boundaries against the might of Germany. **Henrik Cavling**, the editor 1905-28, gave the paper an accessible style and expanded its circulation. AHT. *See also* **Press**.

PONTOPPIDAN, CLARA (1883-1975). Actress. She was educated at the **Royal Theater** and made her debut in 1901. She became known for her psychological identification with her characters in modern plays, playing the title role in Kjeld Abell's *Anna Sophie Hedvig* (1939), the Widow Tang in Knud Sønderby's *En kvinde er overflødig* (1942, A Woman Is Superfluous), and in many films and television plays. AHT

PONTOPPIDAN, ERIK (1698-1764) was a bishop and author, court priest, professor of theology in Copenhagen University from 1738, and Bishop of Bergen 1748-64. He wrote the official explanation of the catechism (1737), used until the 1790s, and the two first volumes of *Danske Atlas I-VII* (1763-81, The Danish Atlas). He published *Danmarks og Norges oeconomiske Magazin* I-VIII (1757-64, The Economic Magazine of Denmark and Norway), which anticipated the agricultural reforms later in the century. AHT

PONTOPPIDAN, HENRIK (1857-1943). Novelist and short story writer. The son of a pietistic clergyman, he spent most of his childhood in Randers. In 1874 he began studying in **Copenhagen** to be an engineer, but broke off his course before taking his final examination in order to join his brother's **folk high school** in Hillerød as a teacher. He published his first collection of short stories in 1881 and, unable to reconcile himself to the school's Christian ethos, decided to try to live by his pen alone. *Det forjættede land* (1891-95, The Promised Land) was the first of his great multivolume realist novels. But his fame rests largely on the two which followed, *Lykke-Per* (1898-1904, Lucky Per) and *De dødes rige* (1912-16, The Realm of the Dead). He lived in Copenhagen after 1910 and shared the **Nobel Prize** for literature with his fellow-countryman **Karl Gjellerup** in 1917. SPO

PONTOPPIDAN, KNUD (1853-1916). Medical doctor. In 1887-97 he was consultant in charge of Copenhagen district mental hospital and from 1901 was professor of legal medicine at Copenhagen University. He wanted a scientifically based psychiatry, and set clinical observations before theory. He wrote the first Danish textbook of neurology (1887). He also founded the Medico-Legal Institute (Retsmedicinsk Institut) in Copenhagen in 1910. His brother was **Henrik Pontoppidan**. AHT. *See also* **Amalie Skram**.

POPPO. Monk. In c. AD 960 he convinced King **Harald "Bluetooth"** of the strength of **Christianity** by carrying glowing iron in his hand. The king allowed himself to be baptized and ordered the Christian faith to be adopted in Denmark. AHT

POPULATION. In 1991 there were 5,146,469 Danes, of whom 1.7 million lived in the **Copenhagen** region, 47,449 in the **Faroe Islands,** and 55,533 in **Greenland.** The average density was 119.4 per square kilometer in Denmark itself, 33.9 in the Faroe Islands, and 0.2 on the ice-free areas of Greenland.

In the 1769 census the population was 797,584 of whom 80,000 were in Copenhagen. The growth rate over the next two decades was very low, at 0.3 percent per annum. This built up to a maximum rate of 1.37 between 1850 and 1860, and by 1860 the total population was 1.6 million, with only 155,000 living in Copenhagen. Reunification with Southern **Jutland** in 1921 added only 163,622 people, making the total 3,267,831, while the average population density fell slightly to 7.6 per square km. At this stage about 606,000 lived in Copenhagen, **Frederiksberg** and Gentofte (the area of the capital). In the 1920s the growth rate fell to 0.96 percent. Although it rose above 1 percent in the 1940s, in the 1950s it was 0.71 percent. By 1960 the total population was 4.585 million, with 844,504 living in the extended capital region. (*See also* Appendix 6).

Infant mortality dropped sharply from over 130 per thousand live births at the start of the 20th century to 7.4 in 1990. The latter figure was only bettered by Finland, Japan, and Sweden among the 24 OECD member states. Life expectancy exceeded 60 for the first time in the early 1920s and 70 in the early 1950s. In 1991 it was 71.9 for males and 77.7 for females. The Nordic characteristics of blond curling hair and blue eyes are well represented, but so are other features, as the Danish population has been racially mixed since the New Stone Age and as a result of various small **immigrations** since. In 1991 there were about 164,000 foreign nationals living in Denmark, including 29,000 Turks, about 10,000 each ex-Yugoslavians, Norwegians, and Britons, and about 8,000 Germans. AHT

PORCELAIN, ROYAL DANISH. Founded privately in 1775, the Royal Danish Porcelain factory was soon handed over to the king, who imported A.C. Luplau from Fürstenberg to be artistic manager. In 1788 the crown prince (later **Frederik VII**) commissioned a 2,600-piece dinner service as a gift to Catherine the Great of Russia decorated with *Flora Danica* motifs from the engravings of **Georg Christian Oeder.** When the work was finished the empress had died so the dinner service stayed in the Danish royal collection, but it and a blue fluted dinner service have remained in production. In

1888 Arnold Krogh introduced a naturalistic underglaze technique which proved very popular, characterized by the cobalt blue, chrome-green, and yellow-red colors which resist the high kiln temperatures that the technique requires. Collections of Danish porcelain are on show in the Bing & Grøndahl Museum, in C.L. Davids Samling, and at the factory shop near **Frederiksberg** town hall. AHT

POSTAL SERVICES. Christian IV appointed **Poul von Klingenberg** as his postmaster general in 1653, and reorganized and made effective the postal service started in 1624. **Hannibal Sehestad** as regent of Norway started a postal service from Oslo to **Copenhagen**, Bergen and Trondheim in 1647. Inland postal services depended heavily on the development of main roads (*hovedlandeveje*), largely in 1820-60. A steamship service between **Copenhagen** and Kiel in **Holsten** was started in 1819, with further services across the Great Belt in 1828 and between **Århus** and Kalundborg in 1836. The first postage stamps were issued in 1851. In 1852 letter collection places were established, and postal routes were fixed in 1860. A telegraph service was started in 1852 and the cable line from Hamburg via Fredericia to Copenhagen completed in 1854. By 1863 there were 2,100 km of cable laid. The postal service is administered by Generaldirektoratet for Post- og Telegrafvæsenet, under the Ministry of Transport. It included the profitable Giro Bank until that was fully privatized in the early 1990s. There were 856 telephones per thousand Danes in 1989, substantially more than the c. 540 in other Nordic countries. The state sold 49 percent of the telephone system incorporated as TeleDanmark in 1997-98. AHT

POULSEN, VALDEMAR (1869-1942) Physicist. In 1893-98 he was employed by Copenhagen Telephone Company and in 1898 invented the telegraphone, the forerunner of wire- and tape-recorders. In 1903, using the Poulsen electric arc, he found a way to generate electric waves, which made possible radio-telegraphy and telephony, and eventually radio broadcasting. AHT

PREHISTORY. Denmark was covered by glaciers during the ice-ages, but flint tools and signs of habitation have been found near Christiansfeld in Southern Jutland dating from the interglacial period 250,000 years ago. When the ice receded northwards to clear

Denmark and southern Sweden (about 11,000 BC), nomadic hunters of the Old Stone Age left flint arrowheads and knives as evidence of their presence in Bromme, Trollesgave, and Bro. The New Stone Age (c. 3000-1500 BC) was marked by the start of agriculture, while flint-work produced excellently crafted, long, polished ax blades, daggers, and sickle blades. The people lived in wooden longhouses with many partition walls. Megalithic dolmen and passage graves are evidence of ancestor worship. From c. 3500 BC there are the first signs of use of the ard, an early wooden plow, and of domesticated animals. Sheep's wool was used for clothing, and animals were milked for food. The Bronze Age (c. 1500-500 BC) left some remarkable artifacts, including several pairs of long, curved **lur**-horns, and the Trundholm sun-chariot, which depicts a gilded disk about 26 cm in diameter drawn by a horse. Clothing and household goods have been excavated from the many tumuli of this period to give a good idea of its material culture, such as the corded skirt and jacket of the girl found at Egtved. The graves of warriors included their weapons, while richer graves of their overlords reveal more ornate but less used weapons symbolic of their status.

From the Early (or Celtic) Iron Age (c. 800 BC to AD 100) come discoveries of bodies well-preserved in bogs, such as the **Grauballe** and **Tollund** men, though whether they got there as religious sacrifices or in punishment is debated. External contacts declined until about 200 BC, but then there are some magnificent finds such as the **Gunderstrup** bowl, while silver cups found in a grave at Hoby, each weighing over a kilo, are evidence of riches worthy of a Roman senator. Bog-iron was extracted and smelted, and this activity may explain the presence of defense works and large stores of weapons found south of Limfjord in **Jutland**. Two four-wheeled wagons with bronze mountings were found at Dejbjerg, indicating the beginnings of wheeled land transport. By AD 200-350 lighter wagons were being made, and the forerunners of Viking boats: two of which were excavated in 1859-63 at Nydam Mose on Als, dating from AD 300-400. One was 23 m long and could have held 30 men. The Horns of **Gallehus** also date from about this time. The period AD 500-800 was characterized by the dissolution of the Roman Empire and major population movements: including the colonization of southeast England by Saxons from northwest Germany and by Jutes from **Jutland**. By the time we reach the **Viking** period (generally taken to be AD 800-1100) there are written records in runic inscriptions to add to the archaeological evidence. AHT

PRESS. The first newspapers were published in **Copenhagen** in the 1720s, with two or three issues weekly, written in Danish or more often German. The forerunner of *Berlingske Tidende* was published in 1749. A law of 1799 restricted press freedom, forbidding criticism of the monarchy on pain of exile, a penalty which was applied to **P.A. Heiberg.** **Censorship** was tightened further in 1810 when the privilege of publishing foreign news was granted on condition that nothing should be reported which might offend foreign powers. In 1814 police chiefs were given powers to censor all prints of fewer than 24 sheets — although introduced as a wartime measure, these powers remained in force until 1848. They were challenged by increasingly organized pressure for press freedom from 1835 onward, and by liberal critics of monarchy and the limited franchise of the consultative assemblies. In the 1840s, official censorship was challenged by a flurry of satirical publications, including Meir Goldschmidt's *Corsaren.* At this stage, *Berlingske Tidende* (Berling's Times) was the paper for loyal officials; *Corsaren* (The Pirate). was read both by gentlemen and their servants; *Fædrelandet* (The Fatherland), founded in 1834, appealed to young liberal intellectuals; the more radical *Kjøbenhavnsposten* (The Post of Copenhagen) addressed craftsmen and artisans. *Flyveposten* (The Fly Post) was a scandal-sheet, while the little-read *Aftenposten* (Evening Post) was subsidized by **Christian VIII**'s Secretariat for Favors (*nådessager*), set up for this purpose. There was a liberal interlude 1848-1864, during which press **censorship** was repealed, then a reversion to conservatism.

Popular demand for news grew rapidly, and became the basis for newspaper growth. In 1864 Christian Ferslew founded *Dags-Telegrafen* as the first of many conservative Copenhagen papers. By about 1870 it was the biggest paper in the country, with an evening edition from 1876 published as *Nationaltidende* (National Times). At the same time **Chresten Berg** was developing his empire of a dozen **Liberal** papers, including *Morgenbladet* (The Morning Paper) started in 1873 with **Viggo Hørup** as editor, and then the very successful *Politiken* (Politics), founded in 1884. The Paris Commune gave an impetus to Danish socialism and in 1871 **Louis Pio** began publishing *Socialistiske Blade*, later *Socialisten* (The Socialist). Technical developments saw newspaper circulations triple 1880-1900 to almost half a million papers daily. Seven or eight new provincial papers were started each year, as well as weeklies such as *Illustreret Familie Journal* (The Illustrated Family Journal), founded in 1877. In 1866 **Ritzau**'s Bureau (RB) was founded and later became the news-agency serving the whole Danish press.

The four-party system, which had taken shape by 1905, was mirrored by a flourishing provincial and national press, and many towns had four newspapers, with expansion continuing until **World War I**. In the 1920s **Poul Henningsen**'s *Kritisk Revy* (Critical Review) was the model for a string of journals of cultural debate in the 1930s. During the war the news was censored by the German occupying power, but accurate information was an important means of resistance and some 250 news-sheets with a total circulation of 26 million appeared in 1941-45. The **Communist Party** published *Politiske Maanedsbreve* (Political Monthly Letters) from 1941, changing its name to *Land og Folk* (Country and People) in 1942. *Information* was published with the intention of providing reliable and unbiased news; both continued in publication into the 1990s.

Over the twenty years from 1945 the number of papers halved, while those that remained, consolidated. Even so, a 1965 study counted 63 daily papers with independent staffs: ten **Conservative**, 28 *Venstre* **Liberal**, eight **Radical Liberal**, eight **Social Democrat**, one Communist (*Land og Folk*), one for the German minority and seven independent. Of the latter, *Jyllands-Posten* (The Post of Jutland) and the finance-oriented *Børsen* (The Exchange) were clearly liberal, while *Information* and *Kristeligt Dagblad* (Christian Daily Paper), founded in 1896, were more clearly independent and pragmatic. There is also a flourishing sector of weekly or monthly journals, many catering for specialized trade, hobby, or current affairs interests, but with a high turnover of titles. The process of concentration continued and in 1996 the major Danish broadsheet newspapers (with their circulations) were: *Politiken* (150,346; Sundays 203,946), *Morgenavisen Jyllands-Posten* (165,523; Sundays 253,150), *Berlingske Tidende* (133,147; Sundays 192,978), *Weekendavisen Berlingske* (Fridays, 49,664), *Dagbladet Børsen* (40,372), *Information* (22,963), *Kristeligt Dagblad* (15,495), *Det Fri Aktuelt* 939,522). The tabloid papers were *Ekstra Bladet* (167,922, Sundays 187,246) and *B.T.* (154,992; Sundays 189,687). *Jyllandsposten* is published from Viby near **Århus**, and all the others in Copenhagen. AHT

PROGRESS PARTY (Fremskridtspartiet) was started in 1972 on a platform of demands for an end to taxation, bureaucracy, and "paper-shuffling jacks-in-office". Its anti-tax stance was emphasized by a defense policy comprising a phone-answering machine with the message, "We surrender!" in Russian and the proposal to sell off the **Faroe Islands** and **Greenland** "to the highest bidder." The founder of this overtly populist protest movement was a tax lawyer, **Mogens Glistrup**, who claimed that he and many of his clients paid no income tax at all. In the 1973 election the party drew 16 percent of the vote from all the "four old parties" in what is referred to as the earthquake election. With 28 seats it was the second-largest party in the **Folketing**, with policies well to the right of both *Venstre* **Liberals** and the **Conservatives**. Largely ostracized, the party was never in cabinet: its proffered support for a coalition to be led by Poul Hartling in 1975 was withdrawn at the last moment. Thereafter it was regarded as an unreliable ally. Although its support fell away, the party's presence over the following twenty years compelled the other parties to take notice of its demands, not least via its string of amendments to annual Finance Bills. In 1995 the party split — see **Danish People's Party**. In 1988 it lost 7 seats, retaining a parliamentary foothold with only four representatives. AHT

PROSTITUTION was one of the offenses which police chiefs (*politimestre*) were specifically enjoined to combat (*see* **Police**). By the 1850s over 10 percent of children were born outside marriage and, since life as a single mother in a rural community was almost impossible, many pregnant unmarried women moved to the towns where they sought work, often in the clothing industry and sometimes as prostitutes. In 1863 brothels were legalized under medical and police supervision. In addition to some 400-500 prostitutes there were many women "on the street" more casually. In the 1990s prostitution remains illegal, but much is impelled by the need to support a drug habit. AHT

- R -

RADICAL LIBERAL PARTY (Det radikale Venstre, RV) is one of the "four old parties," sometimes labeled "social liberals." The Radicals split from the *Venstre* **Liberals** in 1905 with three objectives: abolition of vested interests, a more just distribution of land and the tax burden, and lower military expenditure. Largely as a result of the efforts of **Karl Hansen (-Ankerstræde)**, the party secured the support of the smallholder movement. It soon formed cabinets led by **C.T. Zahle**, first in 1909-10 and then in 1913-20. In intermittent alliance with the **Social Democrats** (SD) in 1929-64, the Radicals contributed to the substantial reform of Danish society, exerting a liberal influence on the socialism of the Social Democrats. The two parties agreed on the reduction of social inequalities and, until 1940, on neutrality — the Radical **P.R. Munch** was Foreign Minister 1929-40. **Bertel Dahlgaard** and **Kristen Kristensen** placed the party with a pivotal role between Left and Right. Radicals were again in government 1957-64 with a succession of SD prime ministers, taking cabinet responsibility for education, agriculture, finance, trade and Nordic affairs. When SD and the **Socialist People's Party** (SPP) totaled a socialist parliamentary majority following the 1966 election, the Radicals reacted by putting together the 1968-71 majority coalition with the Venstre Liberals and the **Conservatives**, led by the Radical **Hilmar Baunsgaard**. Since then the Radicals have resumed their balancing strategy between socialist and non-socialist blocs. In 1973-82 the **Center Democrats** and **Christian People's Party** tried a similar strategy, and Radical influence declined. From 1982 Radical support for the economic policies of Poul Schlüter's Conservative-led cabinet was crucial. At the same time RV joined with SD and SPP in opposing payment of the costs of **NATO** deployment of Cruise and Pershing INF missiles (elsewhere) in Europe, and in pressing for more stringent environmental policies, inflicting over 100 government defeats. This episode ended when RV joined the 1988-90 Conservative and *Venstre* Liberal government, with Niels Helveg Petersen as finance minister and Radicals responsible for energy, culture, environment, and social policy ministries. From 1993 the Radicals contributed to **Poul Nyrup Rasmussen**'s SD-led government's majority, with Marianne Jelved as economics minister, Niels Helveg Petersen as foreign minister, and Radicals heading the ministries of education and Nordic cooperation. This government continued in office after the 1994 and 1998 elections.

Although small, with a vote between 10 and 4 percent between 1975 and 1998, the Radicals have used their pivotal position to influence both SD and the parties of the moderate right, and to oppose the **Progress Party** and the **Danish People's Party** on the right and the **Socialist People's Party** on the left. Despite the fractionalized Danish party system since 1973, RV has helped to maintain a center-based consensus and to oppose tendencies to polarization. AHT. *See also* **Political Parties**.

RADIO AND TELEVISION. Initially there were many competing radio broadcasters, but in 1923 the parliament legislated to regulate this and in 1925 the state took control by establishing Statsradiofonien. By the end of the 1920s it had over 250,000 license-payers and many more listeners. In 1926 a four-party election meeting was transmitted, an early instance of the equal-time principle which still operates at elections. **Julius Bomholt** argued for a cultural policy which would use radio to develop a socialized working culture that could take over from the predominant middle-class culture, but the latter also attracted the aspirations of many workers. During the wartime occupation, transmissions were heavily censored, and many people preferred to listen (illegally) to BBC programs from London. In the 1950s the broadcast media out-competed the **press**, and the 105 newspapers that were published in 1947 were reduced to 66 titles by 1962.

Television began a regular but limited service in 1953 and by 1968 there were about one million viewers. Color transmissions began the following year. From 1958 Radio Mercur challenged the state radio monopoly by transmitting popular music and advertising from a ship in international waters off Copenhagen. Although the Danish and Swedish governments acted together to prevent this, Danmarks Radio met the challenge with near-continuous music on its Program 3. In 1972 **Erhard Jakobsen**, the founder of the **Center Democrats**, set up an association of Active Listeners (renamed Active Listeners and Watchers in 1976 and closed in 1992) with the aim of securing broadly representative coverage and countering left-wing influence in radio and television. A second channel, TV2, independent of and competing with Danmarks Radio, began sending in 1988. The power of television was questioned when a local channel, TV-STOP, transmitted coverage of the policing of violent disturbances following the May 1993 EU **referendum**. The state monopoly could no longer be maintained against satellite channels; but there remains the wish to keep a Danish culture alive in competition with imported programs. Television plays by **Leif Panduro** in the 1970s and the series *The House in Christianshavn* showed that this was possible. AHT

RAILROADS. The first Danish railroad was laid between **Copenhagen** and **Roskilde** in 1847, but further work was halted first by the First **Slesvig-Holsten** War and then by worries that a rail network might encourage trade from **Jutland** southward, and might also be of strategic use to Germany in a future war. A track from the Limfjord in north Jutland southward could be extended to Hamburg, while east-west track would serve growing trade with Britain, although it would need ferry crossings of the Great and Little Belts. **Frederik VII** suggested using a different gauge from the Germans, but this was rejected. An east-west plan was partly implemented in 1852 with a Flensburg-Tønning line in **Slesvig**. A British contractor, Sir Morton Peto, proposed a zigzag route crossing and recrossing Jutland, but the War Ministry opposed this. The military decided, however, that they could use their garrison in Fredericia to defend a Jutland line along the east coast. By 1875 (after the **Second Slesvig-Holsten** War) the main network of tracks was laid, with a line from Esbjerg via Fredericia to Copenhagen, from Fredericia to Frederikshavn in north Jutland, and lines from Copenhagen northward to **Elsinore** via Hillerød, westward to Kalundborg, and southward to Nykøbing Falster and Nakskov. The ferry to take railwagons across the Great Belt was inaugurated in 1883. It was replaced by the fixed link of tunnel and bridge, which opened to rail traffic in 1997. A similar link across the **Sound** from Kastrup near Copenhagen to Sweden is due to open in 2000.

From 1870 many smaller lines and stations were built to link market towns and communities to the network. In the 1930s many of these were disbanded as the roads were improved and motor vehicles grew in number. But new **bridges** were built, and the first red express (*lyntog*) service began in 1934 when the Little Belt bridge was opened. In the same year the Copenhagen S-train electric service started. This suburban service was expanded in the 1950s and 1960s, and in 1963 the main-line network was extended to Rødbyhavn on Lolland to provide an express service (*fugleflugtslinien*) to Germany via the ferry to Fehmarn.

The main service was developed and run by Danish State Railways (*Danske Statsbaner*, DSB), operating routes with a total length of 2,344 km (1990), up from 1,984 km in 1970, but there are also 13 private companies operating on 494 kms of line. DSB converted from steam to diesel power and modernized signaling and stations. Many of its ferry operations have been replaced by bridges. About half its revenue derived from passenger transport, one-third from ferries, and the rest from conveying mail, operating coach services, etc. DSB received a state subsidy (of about one billion kroner in 1990) to cover its operating losses. Losses on the private railways are subsidized by local government and the state. Operating as a government agency, DSB was Denmark's chief state-owned industry. In November 1997 the Minister of Transport, Bjørn Westh, announced that on 1 January 1999 it would become an independent public corporation and would lose its monopoly on goods traffic. The monopoly on passenger traffic would go a year later. There is a Railroad **Museum** in **Odense**. AHT

RANTZAU, HENRIK (1526-1598), son of **Johan**. As the king's regent in the duchies of **Slesvig** and **Holsten** from 1556 until his death, he did much to keep them together and attached to Denmark. Influenced by German humanism, he kept contact with the leading European scholars of his time, collected an extensive library, and wrote on astrology and topography. AHT

RANTZAU, JOHAN (1492-1565). Military officer. He used his military training to helped Frederik duke of Holstein defeat **Christian II** and secure election in 1523 as King **Frederik I** Rantzau became court chamberlain in the duchies of **Slesvig** and **Holsten**. During the **Count's War** he led the army which suppressed peasant risings in **Jutland** and **Funen**. When unsuccessful in supporting the division of the duchies in 1544, he resigned his court position and retired, but in 1559 led the forces that suppressed **Ditmarsken**. AHT

RASK, RASMUS (1787-1832). Linguistics researcher. As a school-boy he studied Old Norse and wrote an Icelandic grammar and dictionary. From 1808 he was attached to the library of Copenhagen University, as chief librarian from 1829. From 1825 he was also professor of Asiatic languages. He traveled to Sweden, Finland, Russia, Persia, India, and Ceylon, where he collected manuscripts and investigated some 50 languages. The founder of modern comparative linguistics, he emphasized grammatical similarities over word-likenesses. AHT

RASMUSSEN, GUSTAV (1895-1953). After graduating *cand. jur.* in 1921 he entered the diplomatic service. Independent of party, he was foreign minister in **Knud Kristensen**'s **Liberal** government of 1945-47 and in **Hans Hedtoft**'s Social Democratic government 1947-50, undertaking the practical arrangements for Danish membership of **NATO** in 1949. AHT

RASMUSSEN, KNUD (1879-1933). Polar researcher. The son of a missionary in **Greenland**, from the age of 12 he was educated in **Copenhagen**. In 1902-04 he took part in the literary Greenland expedition under Ludwig **Mylius-Erichsen**. After two further expeditions he founded the polar station Thule in 1910. In the period to 1933 this was the base for seven expeditions which gathered 16,000 artifacts for the ethnological collection of the **National Museum**'s ethnological collection. He wrote literary and textbooks and published Eskimo songs and sayings. His books include *Min rejsedagbog* (1915, My Travel Diary), *Myter og sagn på Grønland* (1921-25, Myths and Legends of Greenland), *Den store slæderejse* (1932, The Great Sledge Journey), and his principal scientific work, *Intellectual Culture of the Hudson Bay Eskimos*, I-III (1929-32). An area of North-West Greenland is named after him and there is a cottage museum of his activities at Hundested, North **Zealand**. AHT

RASMUSSEN, LOUISE *see* **DANNER**

RASMUSSEN, <u>POUL NYRUP</u> (1943-). **Social Democratic (SD)** prime minister from 1993. Born in **Esbjerg**, he graduated in economics from Copenhagen University in 1971, then worked as an economist for the Danish Trade Union Council 1971-86, as chief economist 1980-86, and then as managing director of the Employees Capital Pension Fund and of Lalandia Invest, 1986-88. As deputy SD leader from 1987, he was elected to the **Folketing** in 1988 and became leader and chairman of the parliamentary group from 1992. He was chairman of the parliamentary Committee on Commerce, Industry, and Shipping 1988-92 and a member of the Committees on the Labor Market, on Economic Policy, and on Standing Orders. From 1992 he was vice-president of the Socialist International. Following the fall of Conservative prime minister **Poul Schlüter** on the **Tamil Affair**, Rasmussen became prime minister in January 1993, heading a four-party majority coalition supported by his own Social Democrats plus **Radical Liberals**, and initially the **Center Democrats** and **Christian People's Party**. A leading figure in the negotiation of the "national compromise" of opt-outs from the Maastricht Treaty which were agreed to at the **European Union** (EU) Edinburgh summit of December 1992, his party's advocacy persuaded the **referendum** electorate to support ratification of the Treaty in 1993. In the September 1994 election the Christian People's Party lost representation and the other government parties lost support but he continued at the head of a minority coalition which retained its majority in the March 1998 election. In May 1998 his government intervened to impose a settlement on an 11-day general strike. In the 1998 referendum on the Amsterdam Treaty he was credited with a successful campaign to persuade SD voters to vote "Yes." AHT

RASMUSSEN, STEEN EILER (1898-1990), architect. On leaving the **Academy of Art** he set up in independent practice in 1919, traveling to London and elsewhere to study town planning. As professor of architecture at the Academy 1938-68 he was a decisive influence on Danish town planning, through both his teaching and his books, *London* (1934), *Byer og bygninger* (1949, Towns and buildings), *Dejlige stæder* (1964, Nice places), and *København* (1969). His greatest building is the housing development at Brøndshøj, **Copenhagen**. AHT

RED-GREEN UNITY LIST (Enhedslisten - De rød-grønne) was formed in 1989 following discussions between the Left Socialists, the (dwindling) Danish **Communist Party** and the Socialist Labor Party. It also attracted unattached left-wingers and others advocating post-materialist values. It achieved some local election successes, including four on **Copenhagen** city council. Its first parliamentary success was in the 1994 election when it obtained 3.1 percent of the vote and six representatives. It lost one of these in 1998. The List represents libertarian socialist policies to the left of the **Socialist People's Party**. Its leaders supported **Poul Nyrup Rasmussen**'s formation of a **Social Democratic (SD)** government, with implied qualified parliamentary support for SD policies, but this was mainly a tactical move to avoid a bourgeois government. The List uses electoral law to give public voice to the extraparliamentary activities of "popular" movements, but claims not to be intransigent and to be willing to support policy changes which will bring ecological gains or improvements in conditions for ordinary people. AHT

RED-STOCKINGS (Rødstrømper) is the name (chosen for its social-ist connotations and to contrast with the earlier intellectual blue-stockings) of an informally organized militant feminist movement mainly active in the 1970s. They saw class struggle and fundamen-tal social change as essential to the achievement of sexual equality. Their activities included demonstrations, women's communes, and in 1971 a summer study-camp on the island of Femø. In 1979 Red-Stockings occupied the Grevinde **Danner** Foundation, which had been sold for redevelopment, raised the large sum necessary to buy it back, and established it as a center for women who are victims of violence. Drude Dahlerup published an extensive account of the movement in 1998. AHT. *See also* **Women's Movement**.

REEDTZ-THOTT, TAGE (1839-1923), landowner and politician. A member 1886-1910 of the **Landsting** for the **Right**, he was foreign minister 1892-97 and in 1894-97 also prime minister (in succession to **J.B.S. Estrup**) following political agreement between the **Right** and the Moderate **Liberals**. He was ousted by Estrup's faction, which opposed the agreement. From 1902 he joined the Free **Con-servatives**. AHT

REFERENDUM. A referendum has been required to confirm consti-tutional changes since 1915 and it was used for this purpose in 1920, 1939 (narrowly unsuccessful), and 1953. Its use was further extended by the 1953 **constitution**, which provides for referendums in four circumstances:

1. If sovereignty is delegated to an international authority, either a five-sixths majority vote is required in parliament, or a bare majority vote in parliament must be followed by a referendum (Constitution paragraph 20 section 2)

2. A change in the voting age must be put to referendum (Constitution para. 29 section 2.)

3. One third of the members of parliament may request, within three weekdays of the passage of a Bill, that it be subject to referendum (Constitution para. 42 [1]) unless parliament resolves to withdraw the Bill. In effect, royal assent to the Bill is postponed by this procedure until the electorate has had its say by referendum, which must be held not less than 12 nor more than 18 days after the prime minister has published the Bill with notice of the referendum. This functions like a legislative veto and replaces the delaying power of a second chamber. Financial, expropriation, and naturalization (citizenship) Bills are exempted from this referendum, as are Bills discharging *existing* treaty obligations.

In each of these cases the rules are set out in the constitution, para. 42. A Bill must first have been passed by **parliament**, and for the Bill to be rejected at referendum a majority of the voters and not less than 30 percent of the electorate shall have voted against.

4. Amendment of the constitution requires that a Bill is passed by parliament, a **Folketing** election is held, and that the Bill is passed unamended by the new parliament. Within six months a referendum is held. If a majority of voters and at least 40 percent of the electorate vote in favor of the Bill as passed by parliament, and if the bill receives the royal assent, it forms an integral part of the Constitution Act (1953 Constitution para. 88).

In each of these cases use of the referendum is constitutionally regulated, and in case 3 its effect is to intervene before the Bill goes for royal signature. The referendum in 1986 on the Single European Act was advisory or consultative and was held under specific legislation at Prime Minister **Schlüter**'s initiative.

In the 45 years following the confirmation by referendum of the 1953 constitution, there have been 15 referendums. Six were on reduction of the voting age in stages from 25 to 18. Four simultaneously in 1963 rejected a set of land laws. The remaining five concerned Danish relations with the **European Union**, joining the European Economic Community in 1972, ratifying the Single European Act in 1986, narrowly defeating the (Maastricht) Treaty of

European Union in 1992, and passing it with four important reservations in 1993; and ratifying the Amsterdam Treaty in 1998. AHT

REFORMATION. **Lutheran** teachings came to Denmark in 1519, only two years after Luther nailed his 95 theses to the church door in Wittenberg. **Christian II** invited a preacher from Saxony, Martin Reinhardt, to preach in **Copenhagen**, where he converted upper class followers. Christian's slaughter of over 600 Swedish opponents and his policy of extortionate taxation in Denmark drove 18 **Jutland** nobles, including four bishops, to offer the throne to Christian's uncle, Frederik duke of Holstein, who ousted his nephew in 1523 and ended the **Kalmar Union** of the three crowns. **Frederik I** pursued a policy of tolerating Lutheranism, and in 1527 forbade the bishops from making payments to or obtaining confirmation of appointments from the papal Curia. **Hans Tausen** developed a strong following for reformed ideas in **Viborg**, then was called by Frederik to **Copenhagen** in 1529 to continue his preaching. At the same time the new ideas were spread via **Hanseatic** trade links to Malmö, where there was also a printing press. In Copenhagen twenty-one preachers presented a Danish version of the new faith in summer 1530, at the same time as, but independently of, the confession of Augsburg, but no decision was taken by the Council. **Frederik I**'s death gave rise to the **Count's War** (1534-36), as the result of which he was succeeded by **Christian III**, a Lutheran, in preference to his Catholic elder brother Hans duke of Slesvig-Holsten. By 1537 a **Church** Ordinance in Latin had been drafted and proclaimed, and that year seven new bishops (at first called "superintendents") were consecrated, including Hans Tausen and **Peder Palladius**. In its Danish version of 1539 the Ordinance fixed the order of service, with Luther's catechism as its standard of doctrine. An obelisk with bronze relief panels in Bispetorvet, **Copenhagen**, commemorates these events.

The Reformation allowed the king to seize the lands held by the bishops, who thus lost a status equivalent to the **nobility** (see **Johan Friis***)*, while the king came to own almost half of the country's land, though much of it was then granted to noblemen in fief. Priests were allowed to marry and have families, but also became more dependent on noble patronage. Bishops and priests became officials of the state. Many state officials had been priests: they were replaced by laymen, often foreigners, whose careers depended on their loyalty.

The Lutheran ethos emphasized respect for those in authority — in effect the king and the state — and opened the way to **absolute monarchy**. At the same time, the Danes made the Reformation their own: with the **Bible**, hymns, services and sermons in Danish, the new **religion** brought a profound national revival. AHT

REICHHARDT, POUL (1913-1985), began as a singer in operetta in the 1930s in the role of Count Danilo in *The Merry Widow*, but in the 1940s he broke into films in the role of a freedom fighter in *De røde Enge* (The Red Meadows), directed by **Lau Lauritzen, Jr**. Later he took the role of the hero in the Morten Korch series of films of the 1950s. From 1950 he was also a member of the **Royal Theater**, with roles in modern plays by Osborne, Abell, Branner, and **Klaus Rifbjerg**, as well as in plays by Shakespeare and Ludvig Holberg. He was in the television series *Huset på Christianshavn* (The House in Christianshavn) as the removals man Olsen and was one of the most popular Danish actors of his time. AHT

RELIGION. In **Viking** times a pantheon of gods was honored, of whom the greatest (in western Scandinavia) was Thor the Thunderer, who defended heaven from the giants, mankind from monsters, and Viking communities from attack from the White Christ. His symbol was Thor's hammer, considered a powerful counter to the magic sign of the cross. With Tyr and Woden, they gave their names to the three middle days of the week in English. Beside these warlike gods, Freyr, the god of the World, and his voluptuous sister Freyja were gods of fertility. A rich mythology includes Valhall, the hall of the slain, and Ragnarok, the doom of the world, the wolf-time "twilight of the gods" which will lead on to a new Golden Age. These stories, recorded in the early 1200s by Snorri Sturlason (1179-1241) in the younger Edda and in runic inscriptions, were extensively adapted in the 19th century to provide the plots for Richard Wagner's operas.

Where the Vikings settled, in Britain for example, they generally converted to Christianity. The papacy sent a mission to Denmark from Holstein in 822, but **Ansgar** made little impact, and not until c. 965 were the Danes "made Christian." Even then, the conversion by **Poppo** owed much to King **Harald "Bluetooth"** Gormson's fear that religion might become the pretext for foreign intervention. His successor **Sven I Forkbeard** reverted to the old religion but tolerated Christian **missionaries** if based in Britain, fearing political intervention from Hamburg-Bremen. The succession in 1016 of **Knud I** (Canute) to the English and later also the Danish and Norwegian thrones marks Scandinavia's effective **conversion to Christianity**.

The **Reformation** installed evangelical **Lutheranism** in Denmark (and throughout the Nordic region) as the doctrine of the national church early in the 16th century. With services and hymns in Danish it gave impetus to a much greater sense of national identity. The **Bible** was published in Danish in 1550 and was highly influential on the language, both because its orthography was largely consistent and because it used a "plain Danish" which avoided learned Latinisms and Germanisms. In the later years of **Frederik IV**'s reign he took to **Pietism**, a movement fully implemented during the reign of his son **Christian VI** (1730-46). The Conventicle Act of 1741 forbade religious assemblies without the permission of the local Lutheran pastor, and religious toleration was only attained in 1849.

The philosopher **Søren Kierkegaard** was little-regarded in his own time but was later widely considered as a forerunner of existentialist thought. A much greater impact on the church and education was made by Bishop **N.F.S. Grundtvig**, whose liberal influence on the intellectual and spiritual life of Denmark continued long after his death.

Freedom of religion is established in Denmark, but most Danes are members of *Folkekirken* (*see* **Church**). In addition there are 24 recognized faith communities with a total of about 87,000 members (at end-1994) and about 74,000 Muslims. A recognized faith community stands outside the national church but its church actions, such as marriage, have civil validity. AHT. *See also* **King's Law.**

RENAISSANCE in Denmark followed some way behind the **reformation** because there was little middle-class wealth to replace the patronage of the Catholic foundations. The nobility sent their sons to universities abroad, but then they returned acquainted with a knowledge of developments in the arts and architecture. **Frederik II** completed **Kronborg Castle** in 1584 and his son **Christian IV** (1577-1648) employed Dutch architects to embellish **Copenhagen** by the addition of **Rosenborg Castle, the Exchange, Frederiks-**

borg Castle and other buildings. Christian took up the doctrine of mercantilism, and the country's wealth gained from trade with **Africa, East India**, and the **Danish West Indies. Historiography** benefited from new interest and scholarship. Thomas **Kingo**'s hymns and his contemporary, the organist Diderik **Buxtehude**'s compositions represent the culmination of the Baroque. These modest developments were taken further in the **Enlightenment** period which followed. AHT

REPUBLICAN PARTY, Tjóðveldisflokkurin, is a Faroese political party founded in 1948 that wants a republican constitution for the islands, arguing that no foreign power should have the right to own or dispose of the country's resources. In 1994, led by Finnbogi Ísakson, it took four seats in the Løgting. In 1998, led by Høgni Hoydal, it doubled its representation and, with 23.8 percent of the vote, was the largest Faroese party. See also **Introduction** and **Faroe Islands**. AHT

RESEN, PEDER HANSEN (1625-88), historian and topographer. After graduating *cand. theol.* in 1645, he was appointed professor of ethics in 1657 and professor of law in 1658 at Copenhagen University. He published ancient Danish laws and collections of papers on **Copenhagen**'s history, and wrote *King Frederichs II Chronicles* in 1680. His greatest contribution was his work on the large illustrated *Atlas Danicus* in 40 folio volumes, later reduced to seven. The manuscript was lost in the 1728 university library fire, but at long intervals since 1925 surviving transcripts of his regional descriptions have been published. AHT

RESISTANCE MOVEMENT. Throughout **World War II** Denmark was technically neutral: despite the German occupation of Denmark from 9 April 1940 to 5 May 1945, the two countries were never formally at war, so resistance activities were illegal under Danish as well as German jurisdictions. Nevertheless passive resistance grew and incidents of sabotage became more frequent in 1941 and 1942. The **Stauning, Buhl**, and **Scavenius** governments made only such concessions to the German occupying power as were necessary to allow the government to remain in office, and this policy secured a parliamentary election in March 1943. In an 89.5 percent poll the four main parties held 93 percent of the vote, while the **Danish Na-**

tional Socialist (Nazi) vote increased only marginally from 1.8 to 2.2. percent. This reassertion of national unity also brought more acts of resistance, supported by some increase in British supplies of weapons. A wave of sabotage incidents in August 1943 brought a German ultimatum which the Danish government rejected, submitting its resignation on 29 August.

Thereafter the Resistance movement was in clear-cut conflict with the occupying forces. It was thoroughly reorganized, with separate structures for the underground press, sabotage, communications, arms reception and distribution, the escape service, etc., with the **Freedom Council** to coordinate these activities and manage relations with politicians and the armed forces.

The underground **press** was an important source of factual information and a counter to propaganda. The number of titles reached 538 and the circulation grew from 1,200 in 1940 to almost 11 million in 1944, served by the *Information* news agency which kept two-way contact with the free world via Stockholm. Letter and telegraphic communication via Sweden began on a small scale but built up as the construction of equipment improved. Large-scale security arrangements were developed to protect the operators. Separately from civilian communications, the intelligence service regularly reported on troop movements, etc., and the network sent the first detailed description of the V-1 flying bomb to London, after a testflight landed on **Bornholm**. The escape service initially took a trickle of traffic to Sweden, but successfully handled the major task of conveying almost all the 7,000 Danish **Jews** to Sweden in October 1943. A total of some 18,000 escapes were organized, with many of the escapees becoming members of the well-organized Danish Brigade in Sweden.

From 1943 aerial bombing of industrial targets ceased, but incidents of ground-based sabotage grew in number and effectiveness and were directed increasingly at military as well as industrial targets. In **Jutland** especially, sabotage and derailments seriously disrupted transport links between Germany and Norway. An underground army was built up under the command of **Ebbe Gørtz**, to be deployed together with Allied invasion forces. By the end of 1944 it numbered 25,000, and by May 1945 its strength was 45,000. Supplies of arms came by air or sea from the Special Operations Executive in Britain (and from its US counterpart the OSS from 1944). Other weapons, including submachine guns, were bought and smuggled from Sweden or were homemade, or obtained from robberies.

German terror methods deployed in retaliation for sabotage and other Resistance activities included deportations, executions, and random shootings, but they proved counterproductive, sparking a general strike in summer 1944 which paralyzed the city for a week, as well as many lesser strikes. The Resistance movement was hard-pressed by the Gestapo, and many leaders and members were arrested. It avoided collapse because three Gestapo headquarters in Århus, Odense, and Shell House in Copenhagen were bombed with great precision by the British Royal Air Force in early 1945 to destroy records and allow the escape of prisoners.

The Freedom Museum (Frihedsmuseet) in Churchillparken, Copenhagen, depicts the 1940-45 struggle for freedom. AHT. *See also* **Andersen, Alsing; Christmas Møller, John; Communist Party; Copenhagen; Døssing, Th.; Fædrelandet; Faurschou-Hviid, Bent; Fiil, Marius; Fog, Mogens; Foss, Erling; Freedom Council; Frit Danmark; Hansen, Chr. Ulrik; Hjalf, Viggo; Holger Danske; Houmann, Børge; Information; Jakobsen, Frode; Kampmann, Viggo; Koch, Hal; Larsen, Aksel; Larsen, Eigil; Lassen, Anders; Lauritzen, Lau; Lillelund, Jens; Malthe-Brun, Kim; Munck, Ebbe; Muus, Flemming Bruun; Nielsen, Morten; Police; Press; Rottbøll, M. Chr.; Seidenfaden, Erik; Vedel, Aage Helgesen; Wichfeld, Monica.**

REUMERT, POUL (1883-1968), actor. From 1902 he played at the **Royal Theater** and on tours which included France, where he played Molière in French. In 1911-18, 1922-30, and 1937-67 he was a member of the Royal Theater company in roles by Shakespeare, Molière, **Holberg**, Hostrup, Ibsen, Strindberg, **Kaj Munk**, **Nathansen**, and Shaw. From an operetta hero he developed into the greatest male Danish character actor of the mid-20th century. AHT

REVENTLOW, CHRISTIAN DITLEV (1748-1827), politician and prime minister. After study abroad and travel in England, he held various state appointments concerned with trade, customs, and banking. As a landowner he introduced many modernizations and improved conditions for the peasants (*see* **Peasant Reforms**). During 1797-1827 he was a member of the Council of State, although without attending meetings from 1813. As a member of the **Great**

Agricultural Commission of 1786 he helped to draft the reform legislation of 1786-1813 which released the peasants from ties to their landlords. From 1789 Reventlow was a leading member of the School Commission which developed the 1814 School Law and actively developed teachers' colleges. He pioneered a forestry system of intensive thinning and started a policy of forestry protection. He was also responsible for granting Jewish civil rights. He resigned from state service in 1813 in protest against policy on the bankruptcy of the state. AHT. *See also* **Jews**

RIFBJERG, KLAUS (1931-). Novelist, poet, dramatist and critic. Both his parents were teachers, and he studied literature at Copenhagen University but broke off in 1955 to direct films and work as a journalist. With Villy **Sørensen** he coedited *Vindrosen*, the literary journal, in 1959-63. His prolific writing in various genres (poems, film-scripts, plays for stage, radio and television, short stories, children's books as well as novels) brought many prizes and membership of the Royal Danish **Academy** in 1967 in recognition of his outstanding position in Danish literature. Significant examples of his poems include *Konfrontation* (1960, Confrontation), *Camouflage* (1961), the collections *Amagerdigte* (1965, Amager poems) and *Selected Poems* (1976). Among his most important novels are *Den kroniske uskyld* (1958, Chronic Innocence), *Operelskeren* (1966; *The Opera Lover*, 1970), and *Anna (jeg) Anna* (1969; *Anna (I) Anna*, 1982). AHT

RIFBJERG, SOFIE (1886-1981), child-psychologist. She trained as a teacher in 1911 and graduated master of psychology in 1925. She headed the **Copenhagen** school psychology service in 1938-45 and in 1945-54 was head of the Copenhagen auxiliary schools. In 1930 she developed the first Danish intelligence tests. She supported the free school movement and ways of raising children that built on the thinking of the educationalist Maria Montessori, which emphasizes child-centered activities. A pioneer in child and educational psychology, she wrote *Udviklingshæmmede børn* (1935, Children with Developmental Limitations), *Børnenes kår i storbyen* (1946, The Conditions of Children in the City), and *Træk af den moderne opdragelses historie* (1966, Outline History of Modern Upbringing). AHT

RIGHT, THE, was the political party formed in 1876 under the leadership of **J.B.S. Estrup** to bring together the land-owners and their upper-class supporters that predominated in the **Landsting** but were increasingly being challenged by the Liberals in the **Folketing**. Although lacking a Folketing majority from the 1880s, the Right retained cabinet power on the choice of **Christian IX** until the **Change of System** in 1901. In 1916 they became the **Conservative People's Party**. AHT

RIGSDAG see **PARLIAMENT**

RIIS, JACOB AUGUST (1849-1914). Writer and photographer. Apprenticed as a carpenter, in 1870 he went to the United States of America. In 1877-99 he wrote police reports for the New York papers, illustrated with his own photographs of the city's poor. He tried to win support for social reforms with his books and slide shows. In 1901 he opened a house for the homeless in New York. New York governor, later president, Theodore Roosevelt named him "New York's most useful citizen." AHT

RIISAGER, KNUDÅGE (1897-1974), composer. Born in Estonia, the son of a Danish engineer, he graduated *cand. polit.* in 1921 and spent most of his working life (1926-50) in the Danish Ministry of Finance. He studied music, for a time in France with Roussel, and developed a glittering and rhythmic style of composition. In addition to orchestral and chamber works and the opera *Susanne* (1950), he composed the music for the ballets *Quarrtsiluni* (1942), *Tolv med posten* (1942, The Twelve Passengers), and *Études* (1948), all choreographed by **Harald Lander**. He also wrote the music to *Danmarks frihedssang* (1945, The Song of Danish Freedom) to words by Svend Møller-Kristensen. AHT

RING, LAURITZ ANDERSEN (1854-1933). Painter. The son of a smallholder in south **Zealand**, he was largely self-taught, despite attending the **Academy of Art** and visits to Italy in 1893-95 and 1899-1900. He depicted village life in Zealand with a detailed realism in such paintings as *Beggar Children Outside a Farmyard* (1893), *Spring* (1895), *Grandparents' Sunday* (1898), *Smallholders* (1898), and *The Sower* (1910). AHT

RITZAU, ERIK NICOLAJ (1839-1903), started a news agency in 1866 which soon had 29 newspapers as subscribers. In 1947 the Danish daily press took over Ritzau's Bureau (RB) from his son under cooperative ownership, and it has become the principal source of foreign news in the Danish press. AHT

RODE, OVE (1867-1933). Politician and writer. The son of a Copenhagen high school head, he lived as a child in Norway. He was a journalist with *Politiken* 1892-1913, from 1905 as political editor and in 1927-33 as its legally responsible editor. He exposed the 1908 scandal surrounding Justice Minister Alberti, and was a member of the Folketing 1909-27. He carried through the crisis legislation of World War I as interior minister 1913-20 in Carl Theodore Zahle's government. AHT

ROMANTICISM. Classical styles were followed by the romantic school in art and literature, while in music form was subordinated to theme and was characterized by imagination and passion. The beginning of romanticism in Denmark dates from the early 19th century — the 1801 Battle of Copenhagen (Slaget på Reden) perhaps. Adam Oehlenschläger, inspired by the philosophy of Henrich Steffens, wrote his poem on the Golden Horns. *See* The Horns Of Gallehus. He was critical of the materialism of his times and proposed several new themes for literature and thought, including the God-given muse to be found in the spirit of nature, and a patriotic emphasis on the history and landscape of one's own country. A people, a nation's history, would grow and change in response to its inner characteristics and to external change — so historical themes took on a new current significance. Pietism had given way to rationalism in theology: this in turn was attacked, for example by N.F.S. Grundtvig in his ordination sermon which argued that the church had lost its spirituality. After initial turbulence, romanticism sought harmony, beauty, and the wisdom of nature.

In the national romanticism of a generation later, Steen Steensen Blicher founded a whole new poetic realism which emphasized the dramatic and often tragic aspects of human nature. As economic conditions improved, there was less escapism, and writers mixed fantasy with the realism of life observed around them. Poul Martin

Møller illustrates contemporary **Copenhagen** in his writing, as indeed do **Hans Christian Andersen** and **Søren Kierkegaard**. Another lasting consequence was a renewed interest in the Nordic past, in prehistoric burial mounds and runic inscriptions, in folklore and peasant culture which led **C.J. Thomsen** to start what became the Museum of Nordic Antiquities. Grundtvig published Danish-language translations of **Saxo**, of Snorre's sagas, and the Anglo-Saxon Beowulf, and plans were made to publish the Icelandic sagas. For Danish painting this was a **Golden Age**.

Inspired by Sir Walter Scott, **B.S. Ingemann** wrote *Valdemar Sejr* as the first of a series of popular medieval historical novels which appealed to an awakening Danish national self-consciousness. This flourish of literature contrasted with the economic disaster which followed the **Napoleonic wars**. By the 1840s national romanticism began to inspire the **national liberals**, while the Grundtvigians were forming a literary **Scandinavianism** which began to alarm the king. The motif of Oehlenschläger's play *Aladdin* was that certain people are chosen to achieve greatness and that nothing will prevent this, however weak or unsuited they may otherwise seem: despite Aladdin's poverty and the sorcerer's wiles, he gets his princess. The motif inspired both Oehlenschläger and Hans Christian Andersen personally, while **Carl Nielsen** later wrote an Aladdin suite.

In **music Niels W. Gade** brought romanticism to Danish life, making his mark both as a composer and in musical education, while one of the leaders of the Romantic school of painters was Johan Thomas **Lundbye**. The art critic **N.L. Høyens'** program for a Nordic art based on motifs of home life inspired a whole generation of artists and led to the foundation in 1847 of the Society for Nordic Art (Selskab for nordisk Kunst).

Romanticism generally and the Aladdin theme particularly helped to develop a climate of opinion that the destiny of individuals and indeed of the Danish nation could prevail against the growing might of Prussia — an aspiration that was fed by success in the First **Slesvig-Holsten** War and reflected in the 1849 June Constitution. After the disastrous defeat of the second Slesvig-Holsten war of 1866 Romanticism came under attack by **Georg Brandes'** advocacy of realism and naturalism and soon afterward by the **labor movement**, whose knowledge of the reality of working-class life had little time for romantic idealism. In music, Carl Nielsen struck out in new directions, but Hakon Børresen continued the romantic tradition. AHT

RØMER, OLE (1644-1710). Astronomer and physicist. He studied at Copenhagen University from 1662, then worked during 1664-70 on a planned edition of **Tycho Brahe**'s observations. He lived in Paris 1672-81 and became a member of the French Royal Academy of Science. In 1677 he was awarded a professorship in astronomy at Copenhagen University which he took up in 1681. At the same time he was appointed to lead technical reforms which included a national survey, a new system of **weights and measures**, paving and lighting of **Copenhagen** streets and improving the city's water supply and fire services. As an astronomer Rømer gained a world reputation for observations of the darkening of Jupiter's moons, which led to the discovery of a method of calculating the speed of light. His many discoveries included the construction of meridians and a revolving telescope for determining the placing of heavenly bodies, of decisive importance for the science of astronomy. His work is illustrated in a Museum at Taastrup. AHT

ROSENBORG CASTLE, Copenhagen. Christian IV had the southern part built in 1606-07 and then considerably extended it in 1613-17 by the addition of the square west tower. In 1633-34 the octagonal staircase tower was added. The palace is in Dutch Renaissance style and intended as the spring and autumn residence of the Danish kings, and was used as such for about 120 years. Since 1833 it has been used to display furniture, pictures, and other items associated with Danish monarchs. In the vaults the Treasure Chamber has been used since 1975 to display to the public the royal regalia and jewels, including the golden crown made in 1670 and used over the next 140 years to symbolize the absolute monarchy. Surrounding the Palace is Kongens Have (The King's Garden), the oldest park in Copenhagen. It is open to the public and contains many statues, including one of **Hans** Christian **Andersen.** The barracks of the Royal Guards are also located in the park. AHT

ROSENKRANTZ, HOLGER (1574-1642), politician and theologian. After studies at the universities of Rostock and Wittenberg 1590-95 he took over the farm which his father had established at Rosenholm in Djursland. In 1616-27 he was a member of the council of state. He acquired the nickname "the learned," breaking off his service of the state to study theology. Rosenkrantz was critical of **Lutheran** orthodoxy and was charged with supporting not only justification by grace but also by works. He corresponded with theologians throughout Europe and assembled a large library at Rosenholm, which was also a private college. AHT

ROSKILDE (population 39,924 in 1990) is an ancient town 32 km (20 miles) west of **Copenhagen**, located on rising ground at the south end of the long Roskilde fjord. Founded by the **Vikings** in AD 980, it became the seat of the **Zealand** bishops in 1020 and of royal power until the court moved to Copenhagen in 1416. **Absalon**, the founder of Copenhagen, was elected bishop at age 29 in 1157. **Knud III Magnussen** was assassinated here in the same year by his co-regent, **Sven III Grathe**. **Abel** was crowned here after the mysterious death of his brother **Erik IV Plovpenning.** The theologian **Niels Hemmingsen** was a cannon of the cathedral for 20 years, to his death in 1600. The **Consultative Assembly** for the Islands met in Roskilde in 1834.

Always an important market town, the **railway** brought commercial and industrial development and residents commuting to Copenhagen. Roskilde University Center began teaching in 1972 and has grown substantially since.

The imposing red-brick cathedral is considered the finest church in Denmark. It was begun in 1170 and extended in 1200 in Northern French Gothic style. Two west towers were added in the 14th century and the copper-covered roofs date from 1635-36. It is the final resting place of Danish kings and queens for the past 400 years, from **Margrethe I** (d. 1412) to **Frederik IX** (d. 1972). Many of their tombs are elaborate expressions of the artistry of their time. The height of each king is marked on a pillar.

The Viking Ship Museum on the outskirts of the town displays the five **Skuldelev** ships recovered from the sea in 1962 and preserved. These include a merchant ship, a deep-sea trader, a warship, a longship and a ferry. The Crafts Museum (Håndværksmuseet) displays traditional tools. The Palæ Collections display 18th and 19th century paintings and furniture. Lejre Historical and Archaeological Research Center is nearby. AHT

ROSKILDE, TREATY OF (1658). **Frederik III** unwisely started a war against Sweden in 1657 and the following year had to accept the humiliating terms of the treaty drafted at **Roskilde,** which ceded his possessions in **Scania** to Charles X Gustavus. The treaty was signed at Taastrup. AHT. *See also* **Ulfeldt, Corfitz.**

ROTTBØLL, MICHAEL CHRISTIAN (1917-1942). **Resistance** fighter. He trained as a gymnastics teacher and in July 1941 joined the Special Operations Executive (SOE) in Britain. In April 1942 he was parachuted to Jyderup, **Zealand,** to lead SOE activities in Denmark. He made radio contact and planned some sabotage operations, but in an exchange of fire was killed by the Danish police in their attempt to arrest him. AHT

ROTWITT, CARL EDUARD (1812-1860). Politician and prime minister. He graduated *cand. jur.* in 1834 and was a member of the **Folketing** 1849-60 with links to the **Farmers' Friends.** Frederik **VII** appointed him prime minister (*konseilspræsident*) in 1859 when the **C.C. Hall** government resigned because the king refused to dismiss his adviser **Ernst Heinrich Berling** or limit the influence of his wife, Countess **Danner.** Because of his sympathy for the Farmers' Friends, Rotwitt's government is considered to be the first Danish forerunner of a **Liberal** government. AHT

ROUND TOWER *(*Rundetårn*)* was built on Købmagergade, **Copenhagen,** by **Christian IV** in 1642. At 35 meters (115 feet) high it gives excellent views of the old town from the open gallery at the top, which is reached by a spiral ramp. This was to allow heavy equipment to be pulled up to the astronomical observatory which was the original purpose of the tower, and which was established by **Longomontanus.** There is now a "planet machine" which illustrates the movement of the sun and six planets against the stars of the northern sky. The adjoining Trinity Church (Trinitatis kirke), of which the tower is a part, was designed by Hans von Steenwinckel the Younger, begun in 1637 and consecrated in 1656, with the intention that the university library would be housed in the roof. The library suffered a fire in 1728 and has since been housed in Fiolstræde. The observatory was moved to Østervold in 1862. AHT

ROYAL DANISH ACADEMY OF ART *see* **ACADEMY OF ART**

ROYAL DANISH ACADEMY OF SCIENCE *see* **SCIENCE**

ROYAL DANISH PORCELAIN *see* **PORCELAIN**

ROYAL LAW *see* **KING'S LAW**

ROYAL THEATER (Det Kongelige Teater). The original building on Kongens Nytorv in **Copenhagen** opened its doors in December 1748, marking the revival of theatrical life in Denmark after the puritanical reign of **Christian VI**. In the 19th century it became the home of Danish opera and **ballet** as well as drama. A projected new opera house was under discussion in 1998. SPO, AHT. *See also* **Theater**.

RUSSIA, DANISH RELATIONS WITH. Russia first played an important role in the Baltic following the **Great Northern War** of 1700-21. With war between Britain and France, in 1780 Denmark joined with Russia, Prussia, and Sweden in a pact of armed neutrality aimed at preserving their rights to trade with both sides and with America. Copenhagen prospered, again becoming the center of the Baltic trade. This lasted only until the 1807 Treaty of Tilsit between France and Russia, following which Denmark and Sweden were to be pressed into Napoleon's continental blockade. For Denmark the result was the second **Battle of Copenhagen**, alliance with France, and the loss of **Norway** to Sweden in 1814.

Britain and France had guaranteed the status of **Slesvig** in 1720 and Russia did likewise in 1773. In the First **Slesvig-Holstein** War Russian intervention persuaded Prussia to withdraw, contributing to the Danish victory in 1849. Denmark and Prussia signed an unconditional peace in 1850 and the London Protocol of 4 July reestablished the unified Danish kingdom over the signatures of Britain, France, Russia, Sweden-Norway, and later Austria. Russia also pressed Prussia to agree not to fight and to oppose Slesvig-Holsten nationalism. Russia feared nationalist movements generally and was interested in continuing freedom of passage to and from the Baltic.

The Russian Revolution of 1917 was followed with interest by socialists in Denmark, but the **Communist Party** remained tiny in the 1920s and 1930s. During **World War II** the Germans tried to persuade Danes to join a Danish Free Corps to fight against the Soviet Union on the German Eastern Front, as Finland's experience in the Winter War of 1939-40 had sharpened Danish dislike of Russians, but only some 1,500 did so. At the end of the war the German garrison on **Bornholm** refused to surrender: following heavy bombardment of the towns of Rønne and Nexø, Russian troops occupied the island for a few months.

NATO membership aligned Denmark against the Soviet Union in the Cold War. Subsequently Denmark has been active in the Baltic Council, mainly with a view to developing closer links with Latvia, Lithuania, and Estonia on the south Baltic coast, but contacts with St. Petersburg have also been made. AHT

RYBERG, NIELS (1725-1804), trader. The son of a feudal peasant, he learned to trade in his uncle's business in **Ålborg**. In the 1750s he founded a general trading firm in **Copenhagen** to import goods from the East and West Indes, to export Danish agricultural produce, and to trade in slaves in Guinea. In 1764 he was a cofounder of the insurance company De private Assurandører and was one of the first to reassure risks abroad. He also founded a spinning and weaving business in Køng, south **Zealand**, and held various public appointments, including Poor Law director for Copenhagen in 1771. AHT

- S -

SABROE, PETER (1867-1913). Politician and journalist. He was editor 1895-1908 of the social democratic paper *Demokraten* in **Århus** and worked 1910-13 for *Social-Demokraten* in **Copenhagen**, vigorously attacking the mistreatment of servants, the poverty of conditions in orphanages and child-care homes, and the use of beatings and corporal punishment in schools. This brought him a national reputation as a spokesman for better conditions for the worst-placed in society. His son Povl became a journalist, writing mildly humorous articles for the conservative tabloid *BT* and the liberal *Politiken* under the pen-name *Den Gyldenblonde* (the golden blond). From 1933 he developed a very successful series of radio conversations. AHT

SANDEMOSE, AKSEL (1899-1965). Author. The son of a smith from Nykøbing Mors, he worked as a gardener, seaman, and laborer and in the 1920s as a journalist. In 1930 he emigrated to Norway and wrote in Norwegian. His books include *En sømand går i land* (1931, A Seaman Goes Ashore), *En flygtning krydser sit spor* (1933, A Fugitive Crosses His Tracks, 1936), *Varulven* (1958, *The Werewolf*, 1966) and *Murene omkring Jeriko* (*The Walls around Jericho*, 1960). His prolific writing sought psychological explanations for otherwise inexplicable actions. In *En flygtning ...*, he was the author of the "Jante-law": "don't believe that you are something," that describes the small-society values, said to be widespread in the Nordic societies, which pit the individual against the collective. His bitter tone softens in his later autobiographical work. AHT

SAXO GRAMMATICUS (c. 1145-?). Historian. Little is known about Saxo's life, except that his father was a housecarl to **Valdemar the Great** and was himself a clerk of Bishop **Absalon**. According to his own account, at the bishop's instigation he began to compose the 16 volumes of his great *Gesta Danorum*, a history of Denmark in Latin from the earliest times to the reign of King **Knud VI** in the later 12th century. Its early books are mythical (including the story of **Hamlet**), but the later ones were based on written sources. He acquired the epithet *Grammaticus* ("grammarian") only in the 14th century. The work dates from around 1200 but was first published in Latin in 1514 by **Christiern Pedersen**. Its **historiographical** importance is clear from the several translations into Danish, by Anders Sørensen Vedel (1575, reproduced in 1967), **N.F.S. Grundtvig** in 1818-22, and Frederik Winkel Horn (in 1898, reprinted photographically in 1977). SPO

SCANDINAVIAN AIRLINE SYSTEM (SAS) was formed in 1946 from the existing national airlines of Denmark, Norway, and Sweden to operate between Europe and North America. The Danish component Det Danske Luftfartsselskab was responsible for two-sevenths of the capital with the state owning at least half. The airline now makes major use of **Copenhagen** and Stockholm airports to operate an extensive service in all the Nordic countries, providing an essential link to the small cities of the north and to the Faroes and Greenland. Its European and world-wide network is supplemented by the Star Alliance, formed in 1997, of partnership arrangements with Air Canada, Lufthansa, Thai Airways International, United Airlines, Varig Brazilian Airlines, and, from 1988, Air New Zealand and Ansett Australia. It has additional partnership agreements with Air Baltic, British Midland, Cimber Air, Icelandair, Skyways, Spanair, and Wideroe. SPO, AHT

SCANDINAVIANISM is the ideal that emphasizes the similarities of Denmark, Norway, Sweden (and Iceland) in language, culture, religion, and shared history. Disregarding Denmark's centuries of conflict with **Sweden,** and Sweden's uneasy union with **Norway,** 1814-1905, it looks to the **Kalmar Union** as a precedent. In reaction to the **Slesvig-Holsten** problem, **Orla Lehmann** argued for a Nordic federation. In the late 1830s the followers of **N.F.S. Grundtvig** began to emphasize Scandinavian literary and cultural affinities. In 1843 **Carl Ploug,** editor of **Fædrelandet,** led a student march to **Kalmar** and spoke in terms indicating that Russia and Germany were Scandinavia's enemies. A Scandinavian Society was formed in **Copenhagen,** holding a large meeting in 1845 at which Orla Lehmann called on the students present to defend Scandinavia, a call which Russia interpreted as critical of its 1809 acquisition of Finland from Sweden. In the form of national romanticism, it found early expression in the music of **Niels W. Gade,** while the art critic **N.L. Høyen** looked to themes from home life as the inspiration of Nordic art. Since its formation in 1952 the **Nordic Council** is seen as embodying the Scandinavianist ideal. AHT

SCANIA (Skåne), the southernmost province of modern Sweden and including the towns of Hälsingborg, Lund, and Malmö, across the **Sound** from **Copenhagen.** Together with the provinces of Bohuslän, Halland, and Blekinge, they formed "East Denmark" and gave Denmark command of the entire western and southern coastline (except for the port of Göteborg with its inland river and canal connections) from the Norwegian border to north of **Bornholm** until 1654, when King Karl X Gustav annexed them for Sweden. The **Scanian War** failed to recover the territory. Denmark made a last attempt to recover the Scanian territories in 1709-10, during the **Great Northern War**.

In modern times a large transnational urban Øresund region (see the **Sound**) has developed which includes Swedish Scania and Danish **Zealand**, centered on Copenhagen and its airport and linked by ferries, with a rail and road **bridge** scheduled to open by 2000. This region includes 41 percent of the Danish population and 12.5 percent of Swedes, and its development was encouraged by Swedish membership of the **European Union** from 1 January 1995. AHT

SCANIAN WAR (1675-1679). A Swedish defeat by French forces allied to the Elector of Brandenburg in 1675 encouraged **Christian V** to attack Gottorp and then Swedish-held Pomerania. In 1676 Gotland was captured by Admiral **Niels Juel** and the Dutch-Danish fleet ejected the Swedes from Øland, took Ystad and Landskrona, and went on to capture the three old east-Danish provinces of **Scania**. Dissatisfied by the burdens laid on them by their recent Swedish rulers, the peasants supported the Danes. The Swedish King Karl XI regrouped his troops and in a bloody battle outside Lund on 4 December 1676 about 5,000 Danes and 3,000 Swedes fell, but the conflict continued. Juel split the Swedish fleet at the battle of Køge Bight in 1 July 1677, sinking 20 Swedish ships. On land, however, Swedish troops advanced and Danish forces had to withdraw, burning villages as they went. The two sides met in Lund in 1679 but could not agree.

The Scanian War was ended at the Peace of Fontainebleau of 23 August 1679, with Louis XIV taking the initiative on Sweden's behalf and the territorial holdings restored to the status quo ante. At Lund a month later Denmark agreed to leave all the conquered land and a defense union with Sweden bound the two countries not to intervene in each other's affairs, nor to ally with third powers without each other's knowledge and agreement. In 1700 a Swedish army landed in North **Zealand** but soon withdrew. AHT

SCAVENIUS, ERIK (1877-1962). Politician. The son of a land owner, he graduated *cand. polit.* and pursued a career in the diplomatic service which included postings in Vienna (1912-13), Rome, and Stockholm (1924-32). During 1918-20 and 1925-27 he represented the **Radical Liberals** in the **Landsting**. He served as foreign minister 1909-10 and 1913-20, when he gained a reputation as an able negotiator with Germany, and from 8 July 1940 to 29 August 1943, from 9 November 1942 also as prime minister. As an unconditional supporter of Danish neutrality Scavenius worked during **World War I** to keep Denmark out of the war. During **World War II** he took Denmark into the Anti-Comintern Pact. His policy was to make only such concessions to the German occupying power as were necessary to allow his government to remain in office. Germany presented an ultimatum on 28 August 1943 requiring the government to introduce the death penalty for sabotage, declare martial law, ban all strikes and meetings, and accept German censorship. The government rejected these demands, supported by all the political parties and with the king's approval. Turned out of office, the government presented its resignation to the king, who however did not accept it until 5 May 1945, so a non-functioning constitutional government remained in existence for the remainder of the war. Scavenius came to be seen as the most consistent proponent of appeasement and later ably defended this policy although he was widely hated for it. AHT

SCHADE, JENS AUGUST (1903-1978). Author. He started as a student but led a bohemian life and became known as "the poet of light" because of his erotically colored and subtle verse, published as *Den levende violin* (1926, The Living Violin), *Sjov i Danmark* (1928, Fun in Denmark), *Hjertebogen* (1930, The Book of the Heart), *Jordens største lykke* (1949, The World's Greatest Happiness), *Schades højsang* (1958, Schade's Hymn), and *Overjordisk* (1973, Supernatural), and his novel *Mennesker mødes og sød musik opstår i hjertet* (1944, People Meet and Sweet Music Springs Up in the Heart). AHT

SCHALBURG, CHRISTIAN FREDERIK von (1906-1942). Officer. He grew up in Russia, the son of a Danish land owner and a Russian mother, but after the Russian revolution he came to Denmark and joined the army. He joined the Nazi Party and in 1941 was in the Russian campaign as a member of the Waffen-SS. He became an *SS-Sturmbannführer* and chief of the Danish Free Corps in 1942, but was killed that summer by Lake Ilmen in Russia. The Schalburg Corps, founded in 1943 and named for him, specialized in actions against the Danish **resistance**, including murders of randomly chosen citizens, of whom **Kaj Munk** is best remembered, and the bombings of **Tivoli** and the **East Asiatic Company**'s (ØK) building. AHT

SCHAUFUSS, FRANK (1921-1997). Ballet dancer. He trained at the Royal Danish **Ballet** School, entered the company in 1941, and was named solo dancer in 1949. He was ballet master 1956-58 and remained with the company until 1970, when he and his ballerina wife Mona Vangsaae founded the Danish Academy of Ballet in **Copenhagen**. He danced in major roles in the Danish repertory and in ballets by Massine and Lichine, and as Mercutio in Frederick Ashton's *Romeo and Juliet*, extending the reputation of Danish ballet to London and Paris. AHT

SCHERFIG, HANS (1905-1979). Author. The son of a director, he did not complete his studies but lived from his writing, journalism and painting. He is best known for his socially critical satirical stories, including *Den døde mand* (1937, The Dead Man), *Den forsvundne fuldmægtig* (The Disappeared Executive), *Det forsømte forår* (1940, Neglected Spring), *Idealister* (1945, Idealists), *Skorpionen* (1953, The Scorpion), and *Frydenholm* (1962, Island of Delight). AHT

SCHIMMELMANN, Count ERNST (1747-1831). Politician. After studies abroad that included national economics, from 1773 he held various state offices but in 1783 was dismissed from most of them by **Ove Høegh-Guldberg** and took part the following year in the coup against the latter. From 1788 until his death he was a member of the Privy Council (gehejmestatsrådet). He achieved the abolition of **slavery** in 1792 and the Customs Law of 1797. As finance minister 1784-1813 he tried to pursue a firm monetary policy, but in 1813 was dismissed for not having prevented the bankruptcy of the state that year. He was foreign minister 1824-31. AHT

SCHIØTZ, AKSEL (1906-1975). Singer. The son of an architect, he graduated *cand. mag.* in Danish and English and held various appointments in high schools. At the same time he studied singing and made his opera debut at the **Royal Theater** in 1939. He was a valued interpreter of *lieder* by Schubert and Schumann, but during the German occupation specialized in Danish songs. In Denmark and abroad he sang roles in the operas of Mozart, Gounod, **Hartmann**, Britten and Reesen. In 1955-68 he was a professor at universities in the United States of America and Canada and in 1968-75 at the Danish Teachers' College (Lærerhøjskole). AHT

SCHLEPPEGRELL, FRIEDRICH ADOLPH (1792-1850). Officer. Born in Norway, from 1804 he served in the army there but was dismissed in 1815 when he refused to swear allegiance to the Swedish king after Norway's union with Sweden. He continued his career in the Danish army, becoming major general in 1848. When the First **Slesvig-Holsten** War started in 1848, he took part as corps commandant in the battles of Bov, **Slesvig**, Sunderved, and Isted, where he was hit by an enemy shot and died on 26 July 1850. AHT

SCHLESWIG-HOLSTEIN see **SLESVIG-HOLSTEN**

SCHMIDT, ALFRED (1858-1938). Cartoonist. He studied at the **Academy of Art** 1874-82 and submitted drawings to *Folkets Nisse* (Gnome of the People) from the 1870s. When *Blæksprutten* (Octopus) started in 1889 he was its chief cartoonist and from 1899 he also contributed to *Klods Hans*. He was well known for his caricature of politicians and of such typical characters as the confirmand, the farmer, the soldier, and the priest, all from a conservative perspective. AHT

SCHOLTEN, PETER von (1784-1854). Governor. The son of a colonial officer, he joined the army. He was appointed governor of St. Thomas in 1823 and governor-general of the **Danish West Indies** 1827-48. After an uprising in 1848, on his own initiative he ended Negro slavery on the islands, and then resigned. In 1851 a judicial commission found that he had breached his office, but the Supreme Court acquitted him. He did not return to the islands but retired to Altona. AHT

SCHLÜTER, POUL HOLMSKOV (1929-   ). Conservative prime minister. He graduated *cand. jur.* from Copenhagen University in 1957 and practiced as an advocate with the right to appear in the Supreme Court. Active in the **Conservative Party** as a student, he was a member of its executive committee 1952-55 and from 1971, national chairman from 1974-77 and from 1981, a member of the

Folketing from 1964 and of Gladsakse *kommune* council 1966-71. His leadership in the 1970s stabilized the party after bitter leadership disputes. As prime minister 1982-93 he headed a series of minority coalitions with the Liberals which also included **Center Democrats** and the **Christian People's Party**. Until 1988 these governments had the support on economic policy of the **Radical Liberals**, but faced a series of over one hundred adverse votes on foreign, defense, and environmental policies by an opposition majority of Radical Liberals, **Social Democrats** and **Socialist People's Party**. These often required the foreign minister, **Uffe Ellemann-Jensen** (Liberal) to enter reservations to **NATO** or European Community (see **European Union**) resolutions, e.g., on the Danish share of infrastructure costs for the deployment of Cruise and Pershing missiles, or the reminder to visiting ships that Denmark did not allow nuclear weapons within its territory. This phase ended when the Radical Liberals were brought into the cabinet in 1988. His period in office saw economic prosperity, a stabilization of spending on **welfare**, and a gentle trend toward market neoliberalism. It ended in the **Tamil Affair** and his cabinet's resignation in face of charges of maladministration. He was elected a member of the European Parliament for 1994-99. He was the first Conservative to hold office as prime minister since the **Change of System** in 1901. AHT

SCHOOLS *see* **EDUCATION**

SCHOUW, JOACHIM FREDERIK (1789-1852). Politician of the moderate wing of the **National Liberals**. He graduated *cand. jur.* in 1811 but also studied botany, in which he graduated *dr. phil.* in 1816. After studies in Germany, Italy, Switzerland, and France he was appointed professor of botany in Copenhagen University in 1821. In 1835-40 and 1848 he was chairman of the **Consultative Assemblies** of both the Islands and North Jutland. In 1848-9 he was chairman of the **Constituent Assembly**, and was a member of the **Landsting** in 1849-50. AHT

SCHULIN, JOHAN SIGISMUND (1694-1750). Politician. The son of a priest and born in Germany, he studied at German universities. In 1730 he entered Danish service, becoming foreign minister from 1735, a member of the council from 1737, and a privy councillor (*gehejmeråd*) from 1738. He was the most influential Danish politician during 1730-50. In foreign policy he strove for good relations with Sweden and for neutrality in the conflicts between the European powers, laying the ground for Danish foreign policy in the 1700s. AHT

SCHUMACHER, PEDER *see* **GRIFFENFELD, P.S.**

SCIENCE, ROYAL DANISH ACADEMY OF (Det kongelige danske videnskabernes Selskab) was founded in 1742, and from the first published its proceedings in Danish rather than German, a symptom of linguistic and cultural resurgence. Its first volume reported an excavation in 1744 by Crown Prince Frederik (V) and the court chaplain, Pontoppidan, of an early Stone Age grave with a metal age grave above it at Jægerspris. In 1755 the Academy published the findings of Captain F.L. Norden (1708-1742), who had been sent by **Christian VI** to explore along the Nile to Ethiopia. He did not achieve this objective, but returned with extensive drawings, maps and notes of Egypt's "antiquities." The academy sponsored the first modern land survey by triangulation in 1757-1842. Appointment to the Academy is an important academic honor, and a few are made annually. The Academy also runs a series of public lectures. AHT

SCULPTURE. Archaeological finds include small Ice Age figures in amber and, from the Early Bronze Age (about 1000 BC) the Sun Chariot of Trundholm, on display in the **National Museum**. From the Viking Age there are relief carvings on rock, of which the **Jelling** Stone is the most famous. Christianization at the start of the second millennium gave opportunities to decorate the newly built churches: the resulting Romanesque stone carvings have a rugged and primitive power. The 13th-century work which followed shows a strong French Gothic influence, for example in the **Herlufsholm** Church ivory crucifix. Much of this work was imported, but around 1500 artists worked more in Denmark. The Reformation put an end to the commissioning of wood carvings, but scope remained for tomb stones for the nobility, on which Renaissance themes began to appear. Excellent examples include the memorial to Archbishop Absalon in **Sorø** Abbey, executed in 1536 by Martin Bussert, and work such as **Christian III**'s monument in **Roskilde** Cathedral by the Amsterdam sculptor Cornelius Floris (1514-1575). Other 16th- and

17th-century pieces were the work of Dutch, German, Walloon, and French artists.

The foundation in 1754 of the Royal Danish **Academy** of Art was an important turning point in the development of Danish sculpture. An equestrian statue of **Frederik V** was commissioned from the eminent French sculptor J-F-J Saly (1717-76); one of the finest examples of the genre in Europe, it stands in the square formed by the four **Amalienborg** palaces. The first generation of Danish sculptors were pupils of Saly's such as Hartmann Beeken (1743-1781) and Nicolai Dajon (1748-1823). Their work can be seen in the Royal Museum of Art. **Johannes Wiedewelt** was the leading 18th-century Danish neoclassical sculptor. He studied in Paris but developed a heavy neoclassical style, examples of which are Frederik V's tomb in Roskilde Cathedral and sculptures in the parks of **Fredensborg** and Jægerspris Castle. Nikolaj **Abildgaard** designed the Column of Liberty (*Frihedsstøtten*) in **Copenhagen**.

Widely appreciated in his time and eventually welcomed back to Copenhagen in 1838 as its first freeman, **Bertel Thorvaldsen** went on a scholarship from the academy to Rome, where he studied and worked from 1796. His restrained classicism is well represented in the Thorvaldsen Museum beside Christiansborg where he is buried. Other items by him are displayed in Our Lady's Church in Copenhagen and in Lucerne, Warsaw, Mainz, Cambridge, and Rome. His pupils included H.E. Freund (1786-1840), J.A. Jerichau (1816-1883), and **H.V. Bissen** whose work includes the equestrian statue of Bishop Absalon (1902) in Højbro Plads and the statue of **Hans Christian Andersen** in Kongens Have, Copenhagen. **Georg Jensen** began as a sculptor but made his reputation as a **silver**smith.

From the 1880s the painter and sculptor, Jens Ferdinand **Willumsen** broke away from the prevailing naturalism to pioneer symbolism, and Jean Gaugin (1881-1961) made a series of bronze statuettes of figures in rapid motion from about 1915. **Kai Nielsen** developed a new monumental style, as did **Anne Marie Carl Nielsen**. The Swedish-born **Gerhard Henning** (1888-1967) worked on a small scale in the early years of the century on subtle little groups in porcelain but after **World War I** his finest works are of monumental female figures such as his *Reclining Girl* (1942, Grønningen, Copenhagen). Other notable sculptures from between the wars include: the *Sailors' Memorial* on Langelinie, Copenhagen by Svend Rathsack (1885-1941); the memorial to the politician **Ove Rode** (1937, Copenhagen) by Adam Fischer (1888-1968); the statue of the painter **Anna Ancher** (1939, **Skagen** Museum) by Astrid Noach (1889-1954); and the statue of a young man, *Josef*, by Jørgen Gudmundsen-Holmgreen (1886-1966).

Post-**World War II** Danish sculptors have worked in a wide range of styles. Mogens Bøggild (1901-) stayed close to nature with his two fountains in the form of a Bear (Nykøbing Falster, 1936-38) and a Pig (Århus, 1941-50), as did Gottfred Eikhoff (1902-) and Knud Nellemose (1908-). The work of Henrik Starcke (1899-1973) and Henry Heerup (1907-93) shows a fantastic individualism. Others cultivated abstract forms, such as **Robert Jacobsen, Asger Jorn**, Erik Thommesen (1916-), Søren Georg Jensen (1917-), Willy Ørskov (1920-), and Bent Sørensen (1923-). Gunnar Westmann (1915-) represents a new realism that springs from delight in everyday beauty, while Svend Wiig Hansen (1922-) expresses a feeling for the elemental forces in human life. The Ny Carlsberg **Glyptotek** in Copenhagen has one of the largest assemblages of ancient Egyptian, Greek, Roman, and Etruscan sculpture in northern Europe, as well as a good collection of modern Danish sculptures. AHT

SEHESTED, HANNIBAL (1609-1666). Politician. After studies at **Sorø Academy** and abroad, in 1640 he was appointed to the cabinet and in 1642 regent (statholder) in Norway. He founded a peasant army for use in the border skirmishes with the Swedes in 1644-45, known as the "Hannibal feud." In 1647 he started a postal service, initially run as a private business under royal charter, with a service to **Copenhagen**, Bergen and Trondheim. Following allegations of fraud, he resigned as regent in 1651 and traveled abroad. In the war of 1658-60 he mediated between Sweden and Denmark. In October 1660 he was appointed master of taxes for the kingdom and a member of the council of state. In his last years he acted as a diplomat to the, by then, absolutist **Frederik III**. In 1636 he married Christiane, daughter of **Christian IV** with Kirsten Munk. AHT

SEHESTED, HANNIBAL (1842-1924). Politician. Graduated *cand. jur.* in 1869 and was a member of the **Landsting** 1886-1910. As prime minister *(konseilspræsident)* in 1900-01 he was the last member of the **Right** (conservatives) to hold this office before the 1901 **Change of System**. AHT

SEIDENFADEN, ERIK (1910-1990). Journalist. After studies of comparative literature in **Copenhagen** and France, in the 1930s he worked as a foreign correspondent for Danish newspapers. During World War II he made contact with the **resistance**. In January 1943 he became *Politiken's* Swedish correspondent and leader of the Danish press service. In 1946-65 he was a member of the editorial board of *Information*. In 1966-82 he was director of the Danish Student House in Paris. He supported Danish membership of **NATO** and the **European Union**. AHT

SEPTEMBER AGREEMENT of 5 September 1899 between the Danish Employers' Association (Dansk Arbejdsgiverforening, DA) and the **trade unions** recognized the right of each side to organize, and that the employers had the right to direct and allocate employment. It ended a three-month industrial dispute. The opposing sides bound themselves to reach collective agreements on wages and working conditions lasting two years. Disputes would be negotiated, and there would be a "cooling-off" period before a strike. The Agreement regulated the conduct of disputes, acting as the "constitution of the labour market", until in 1960 it was replaced by a new agreement (*hovedaftalen*) which laid down that the employers' right to direct and allocate employment must be exercised with responsibility to employees. A new agreement in 1973 between employers (DA) and unions (Landsorganisationen, LO) emphasized that the right of leadership by employers must be exercised in collaboration with wage earners and their union representatives. A change in 1981 required an employer to reemploy a worker fired unreasonably. AHT

SHIPPING. After heavy losses in **World War II** the Danish merchant fleet grew steadily in size, although not as fast as the world growth rate, reaching 556 ships and 1.36 million gross registered tons (g.r.t.) in 1953. Growth continued until 1972 when the fleet comprised 1,011 ships of 100 g.r.t. and over, totaling 3.81 million g.r.t.. Tonnage continued to increase until 1978, largely by the addition of tankers, but thereafter the fleet declined in both number and tonnage to 1988, when there were 605 ships and 4.27 million g.r.t. By 1993 there had been some increase, to 671 ships totaling 5.11 million g.r.t. These figures show the Danish fleet to be bigger than the fleets of Finland or Sweden, but a half to a third the size of the Norwegian fleet. In proportion to population, Denmark in 1972 was third after Norway and Greece in tonnage per inhabitant. However, the growth of "flags of convenience" has resulted in large fleets nominally registered in Liberia, Panama, etc.

A large proportion of Danish cargo shipping world-wide is carried by the Maersk Line (founded by **A.P. Møller**), the **East Asiatic Company** (ØK), and **DFDS**, the private-sector United Steamship Company, but there are also half a dozen smaller shipping companies. Maersk has a large new head-quarters building on the Esplanade in Copenhagen, has major oil interests and also operates an airline, but most of its shipping activity is in the Asia-Pacific region. ØK operates mainly from Singapore. Most external passenger routes are served by DFDS, which runs services from **Copenhagen** to Oslo and to the **Faroes, Iceland**, and **Greenland**, and from **Esbjerg** to Harwich or Newcastle in England. Ferry services (where they have not been superseded by **bridges**) are operated by DSB, the state **railroads** company, which operates services between **Århus** and Kalundborg and (until about 2000) between Copenhagen and Malmö. In the cargo it handles, Copenhagen is by far the largest port, with the private oil refinery harbors at Stigsnæs, Kalundborg, and Fredericia next in size. The major provincial ports in order of size are Århus, **Ålborg, Fredericia, Esbjerg**, and **Odense**. AHT

SIBBERN, FREDERIK CHRISTIAN (1785-1872). Philosopher. He graduated *cand. jur.* in 1810 and *dr. phil.* in 1811 then traveled for two years in Germany before taking up the professorship in philosophy at Copenhagen University which he held until 1870. His philosophy is based on organic development, that existence consists of contradictory elements which strive toward order and harmony. Otherwise conservative, he published *Nogle meddelelser af indholdet af et skrift fra året 2135* (I-II, 1858-62, Reports on the Content of Writings from the Year 2135) in which he outlines a communist society which has the harmony that he advocated philosphically and psychologically. AHT

SIGSGAARD, JENS (1910-1991). Author and psychologist. He qualified as a teacher in 1932 and *cand. psych.* in 1945, and was principal of the Frøbel Education College 1941-74. He considered children's play and creative activity as central to their development. This thinking was widely influential, especially in preschool education theory. These ideas were published in his *Barnets verden. Træk af barnets sjælelige udvikling* (1945, The Child's World: Lines of the Child's Mental Development) and *Folkebørnehave og socialpædagogik* (1976, The People's Preschools and Social Pedagogy). He also wrote over 30 children's books, many translated into other languages, the best known being *Palle alene i verden* (1945, Palle Alone in the World), and numerous children's rhymes, jingles, and games. AHT

SIKKER HANSEN, AAGE (1897-1955). Artist/draughtsman. He trained as a painter, learned lithography, and then drew posters and illustrations for the magazine supplement of *Politiken*. His depictions of ordinary people and animals won a wide public. AHT

SILVER, DANISH *see* **DESIGN; GEORG JENSEN**

SINGLE-TAX PARTY *see* **JUSTICE PARTY**

SIUMUT is a Greenlandic political party whose name means "Forwards." With origins in 1971, it became a full-fledged political party in 1977 with the long-term aim of maximum autonomy for the island, although in the 1990s it has supported the Home Rule law of 1979. In the 1979 elections it won 13 of the 21 seats in the **Greenland Landsting** and a government was formed under the Siumut chairman, the **Lutheran** pastor Jonathan Motzfeldt. In 1982 it successfully campaigned for **Greenland** to leave the European Community (see **European Union**) in 1985. Its representative in the **Folketing** has been a member of the **Social Democrats'** parliamentary group. Motzfeldt remained prime minister until 1991, when he was replaced by Lars Emil Johansen. In the 1991 elections the party won 37.3 percent of the vote and 11 of the 27 seats. SPO, AHT.

SJÁLVSTYRISFLOKKURIN *see* **HOME-RULE PARTY (FAROES)**

SKAGEN SCHOOL is named after the village at the northern tip of **Jutland** where artists gathered from the 1870s onwards. The poet

Holger Drachmann and the composer **Hakon Børresen** were leading members, as were the painters **P.S. Krøyer** and **Michael** and **Anna Ancher**. The Ancher's house has been a museum open to the public since 1967, and more paintings of the Skagen School are displayed in Skagen's Museum. AHT

SKOU, JENS CHRISTIAN (1918-). Chemist. His studies of crab tissues at the University of Århus from 1957 led to fundamental discoveries concerning the mechanism which pumps potassium ions into and sodium ions out of cells, and the energy-transporting enzyme ATP. These research results were important to the later development of medical treatments of the heart and of stomach ulcers. He was awarded the 1997 **Nobel Prize** for chemistry, the other half being shared between Paul D. Boyer (American) and John E. Walker (British). AHT

SKOVGAARD, JOAKIM (1856-1933), was a painter whose brilliant and monumental frescoes dominate the interior of the cathedral in **Viborg**, while others of his paintings are in the Skovgaard museum nearby. Taught his art by his landscape-artist father Peter Christian Skovgaard (1817-1875), he studied at the **Academy of Art** in **Copenhagen** 1871-76 and traveled in Italy, Greece, and France, returning to the Academy as professor in 1909-21. AHT

SKOVGAARD, PETER CHRISTIAN (1817-1875). Painter. He studied at the **Academy of Art** in 1831 and became a trained painter in 1835. His landscape paintings are in a decorative architectural romantic style which shows pleasure in the countryside. His son was Joakim **Skovgaard**. AHT

SKRAM, AMALIE (1846-1905). Author. Born in Bergen, Norway (where there is a statue of her), she went to sea as the new young wife of a ship's captain. Following divorce, she worked as a journalist in Norway, but moved with her second husband, the writer Erik Skram to **Copenhagen** in 1884. Her continuing theme is the woman's position in marriage, in *Constance Ring* (1885, trans. 1985), *Bøn og anfægtelse* (1886, Prayer and Temptation), and *Forrådt* (1892, *Betrayed*, 1987). In her main work, *Hellemyrsfolket* I-IV [1887-98, The People of Hellemyr: *Sjur Gabriel* (1887), *To Ven-*

ner (1887, Two Friends), *S.G. Myre* (1890), and *Afkom* (1898, Offspring] she describes the inheritance of poverty and alcoholism. In two novels from 1895, *Professor Hieronimus* (Eng. trans. 1899) and *På Sct. Jørgen* (1895, At St. Jørgen's), she attacked Danish mental health care and especially the psychologist **Knud Pontoppidan**, contrasting the passivity expected of a woman patient by a male doctor with the affection and concern shown by female nurses. As autobiography thinly veiled as fiction, these are exceptions to the usually tragic themes of her work. AHT

SKRAM, PEDER (c. 1503-1581). As a naval officer, he took part in expeditions in 1523 against the deposed **Christian II**, against the **Hanseatic** towns, and at the side of **Christian III** in the **Count's War**. He was a member of the Council of State from c. 1539/40 and was an admiral 1535-55, as supreme commander of the navy at the start of the **Northern Seven Years' War**. He was later named "Denmark's daredevil" for his bold conduct of war at sea. AHT

SKULDELEV SHIPS are five **Viking** ships that were sunk about AD 1000 in **Roskilde** fjord, apparently as a defensive barrier. Excavated and restored, they are on display in the specially built Viking Ship Hall at Roskilde. There is a 16.5-meter (54 feet) ocean-going ship, a 28-meter (92 feet) longship, a 13.3-meter (44 feet) trading ship, an 18-meter (59 feet) warship, and a 12-meter (39 feet) ferry in a display of Viking shipbuilding second only to its Oslo counterpart. AHT

SLAVERY developed with the acquisition of the **Danish West Indies** (now US Virgin Islands) from 1666 and the transport there of slaves from the Gold Coast (now Ghana) to work the sugar plantations. Slavery under Danish law was abolished in 1792 by Count **Ernst Schimmelmann** but continued in practice in the Danish West Indies until ended by **Peter von Scholten** in 1848. **Thorkild Hansen** uncovered this suppressed dimension of Danish history in his trilogy of historical novels. AHT. *See also* **Africa, Danish Possessions in.**

SLESVIG *see* **SLESVIG-HOLSTEN**

SLESVIG PARTY represented in the **Folketing** the German-speaking minority in southern **Jutland** following the 1920 **referendum** which established the Danish-German border and transferred territory and population to Denmark. The minimum for representation was relaxed to allow a single representative to sit in the **Folketing** 1920-35 and 1953-64. Subsequently the **Center Democrats** nominated a German-speaking candidate in the South Jutland district. AHT

SLESVIG-HOLSTEN (in German, Schleswig-Holstein. *See the map in the* **Introduction***).* Slesvig and Holsten were two small, sparsely populated duchies which had been ruled by Denmark since 1460. Holsten was wholly German-speaking. Slesvig, half Danish and half German-speaking and referred to in Denmark as Southern Jutland (*Sønderjylland*), had been closely associated with Holsten since medieval times. With the end of the Holy Roman Empire in 1806, Denmark incorporated the duchy of Holsten under the Danish crown. **Frederik VI** remained duke of Holsten while allowing Holsten and **Lauenburg** to join the newly established Confederation of German States. Slesvig did not join. The stage was set for a complex conflict with dynastic and territorial dimensions against pan-Germanism.

Consultative Assemblies were established in 1831 in the dukedoms of Holsten and Slesvig (and in the Danish kingdom), and these were the arenas for debate between conservative supporters of **absolute monarchy** and **national liberal** advocates of **constitutional** reform. **Christian VIII** wanted the unified solution of a "whole state" (*helstad*) with the kingdom and the duchies of Slesvig, Holsten, and Lauenburg under a single head of state. Within the kingdom the **Ejder** Program gained wide support, ably advocated by **C.C. Hall** and **Orla Lehmann**. This would set the frontier at the Ejder River and incorporate Slesvig into the kingdom, and break with Holsten and Lauenburg. But Schlesvig-Holstein was seen in Germany as a single and indivisible unit, a view not shared in Denmark but increasingly attractive to German national liberals and to Bismarck with his aim to unify Germany. The issue complicated constitutional change and was complicated by the question of succession to the Danish throne, since it seemed clear that **Frederik VII** would be the last of the **Oldenborg** dynasty.

In 1846 a wave of German national feeling was directed against Denmark. In July **Christian VIII** declared that the Danish law of female succession applied without doubt to Slesvig and even to parts of Holsten, an act portrayed in Germany as "Danish aggression." In Holsten a resolution was adopted demanding independence and indivisibility under the house of **Augustenborg**, an outcome which would end all ties of Slesvig and Holsten to Denmark.

The issue came to a head when **Frederik VII** succeeded to the throne and granted the 1849 June **constitution**. Although this gave the duchies equal status in a unified kingdom, suspicions remained when C.C. Hall and other National Liberals were included in the cabinet. The upsurge of German national feeling following the 1848 Revolution in France strengthened demands for a provincial government in Slesvig-Holsten and the inclusion of Slesvig in the German Confederation. The Danish government offered a free constitution for Holsten and Lauenburg and continued membership of the German Confederation, but Slesvig would be united with Denmark, with its own assembly and administration — in effect implementing the Ejder Program. A Slesvig-Holsten provisional government was hastily formed in Kiel, war was immanent, and Denmark mobilized.

In the **FIRST SLESVIG-HOLSTEN WAR** (1848-50, also called the Three Years' War), the Danes outweighed the Slesvig-Holsten forces and **Frederik VII** entered Flensborg. Prussia and the other German states mounted a large army, forced the Danish army back into **Funen**, and themselves entered **Jutland**. Under the **Frederiksborg Treaty** of 1720 the status of Slesvig had been guaranteed by Britain, France and Russia. Denmark appealed only to Britain for support, but was offered mediation instead. Russia pressed Prussia to withdraw and attacked the other German troops with Swedish help. Denmark accepted a cease-fire and British mediation. Britain and most of the other great powers proposed a frontier along the language border but the Danes wanted Slesvig as an integral part of Denmark. On 26 February 1849 Denmark ended the truce and in early April recommenced hostilities, this time with an army increased to 41,000 by universal conscription. A German/Slesvig-Holsten force of 65,000 imposed an initial defeat and withdrawal to Fredericia, but in the battle of Fredericia on 6 July the Danes roundly defeated the Germans (*see also* **Friedrich Adolph Schleppegrell***). A new truce was signed and a commission comprising one Prussian, one Dane, and one Englishman was appointed to govern

Slesvig, the northern part of which was occupied by Norwegians and Swedes and the southern part by Prussians. A proposal to give Slesvig its own constitution, without ties to either Denmark or Holsten, was unacceptable to the Slesvig-Holsteners, who fought on alone.

Denmark and Prussia signed an unconditional peace in 1850, and the London Protocol of 4 July acknowledged the indivisibility of the Danish kingdom, in theory reestablishing the unified-state (*helstat*) policy. The protocol was also signed by Russia, Britain, France, Sweden-Norway, and later Austria. Unsupported by Prussia, the Slesvig-Holsten army was defeated in battles at Isted and again at Dannevirke. Under Russian pressure, Prussia agreed to refrain from fighting and to oppose Slesvig-Holsten nationalism, and the provisional government was dissolved in 1851.

The agreements of 1851 and 1852 determined that Denmark would consist of three parts: the kingdom, Slesvig, and Holsten with Lauenburg. Nothing should be done to tie Slesvig closer to either Denmark or Holsten. Holsten and Lauenburg should be free to continue in the German Confederation. The Danish **constitution** would not apply in the duchies, which would each have legislative assemblies. The 1852 Treaty of London decided the succession to the Danish throne: if **Frederik VII** should die without a male heir, the throne would go to Prince Christian of **Glücksborg** (who became **Christian IX** in 1863) and his male heirs. These terms were enacted in the 1855 Danish constitution. Strategically, Prussia accepted this outcome under Russian pressure and knowing that, with Holsten in the Confederation, Slesvig would be more easily gained than if it was fully incorporated into Danish jurisdiction.

Although Prussia and Austria accepted the 1855 constitution, the following year they complained that the 1851 and 1852 agreements were not being kept, and opposition grew. In 1858 the German Confederation assembly declared that the 1855 constitution did not apply in Holsten and Lauenburg. Faced by this ultimatum, Denmark annulled it for the two duchies, which briefly quieted German objections and was also acceptable in Denmark as a return in effect to the Ejder Program. Although British prime minister Palmerston promised help to Denmark in July 1863, Queen Victoria soon changed this to a pro-German policy. Denmark rejected all complaints and, relying on Swedish-Norwegian support, prepared for war. In March 1863 Slesvig was incorporated into Denmark, while Holsten and Lauenburg were separated from the kingdom. Germany reacted by threatening to occupy Holsten and Lauenburg if the constitution was not restored. Denmark responded with the November **constitution**, implementing the March decision with a single bicameral **Rigsdag** representing Slesvig and Denmark together, despite grave warnings. The Danish parliament passed the new constitution on 13 November 1863. Two days later **Frederick VII** died without having signed it. **Christian IX** ascended the throne and, in an excited atmosphere of nationalism but against his better judgment, was persuaded to sign it.

THE SECOND SLESVIG-HOLSTEN WAR. Bismarck recognized **Christian IX**'s succession but again demanded enforcement of the other terms of the 1851 and 1852 agreements, and obtained Austrian support. On 23 December 1863 Saxon and Hanoverian troops entered Holsten and were reinforced on 21 January 1864 by Prussian and Austrian forces. Without support, even from Sweden, Denmark withdrew to Slesvig. Prussia advanced into Slesvig and the Danes retreated to the **Dannevirke** fortifications, and then to **Dybbøl** and Als. A peace conference was called in London but Denmark, with false hopes of British support, was intransigent. Bismarck maneuvered adroitly to prevent a coalition of Britain, Russia, and France in support of Denmark, and Prussia invaded Denmark proper in June. Denmark hoped for but did not receive Swedish help, and had only the aid of some Swedish-Norwegian volunteers. Prime minister **D.G. Monrad** was blamed and dismissed, and his successor Christian Albrecht **Bluhme** obtained peace on humiliating conditions that included the loss of all three duchies. About a third of the territory and population was lost and Denmark was reduced to its smallest size since the consolidation of the kingdom, with a frontier in Jutland running just south of Ribe, Askov, and Kolding.

After **World War I** a **referendum** was held in 1920 with Slesvig divided into three zones. North Slesvig and the island of Als had a majority for Denmark, but majorities in the middle zone, which included Flensborg, and the southern zone opted for Germany. This settled the subsequent Danish-German frontier, a decision only challenged unsuccessfully by **Knud Kristensen** in 1947. AHT

SMITH, HENRIK (c. 1495-1563). Author. He was attached to the exiled King **Christian II**, then lived in Malmö from 1536 until his death. He published the first book on the treatment of plague, *En bog om pestilens* (1536, A Book about the Plague); the first Danish evangelical catechism, *En liden dialogus eller katekismus* (1537, A Little Dialogue or Catechism); and a medicinal herbal, *En skøn lystig urtegård* (1546, A Fine Vigorous Herb Garden). His collected medical works were published as *Henrick Smids lægebog* (1577, Henrick Smids Medical Book, much reprinted, including in facsimile, 1976). AHT

SNEEDORFF, JENS SCHELDERUP (1724-1764). Author. He graduated *magister* in 1746, studied French and constitutional law in France and Germany, and was professor of law and politics at **Sorø Academy** from 1751. Inspired by the French **Enlightenment**, he supported enlightened **absolute monarchy** and emancipation of peasants. His writings included *Om den borgerlige regering* (1757, On the Citizens' Government) and the journal *Den patriotisk tilskuer* (1761-63: The Patriotic Observer). AHT

SOCIAL DEMOCRATIC PARTY (FAROESE) (Javnaðarflokkurin). Founded in 1925, the party believes that the **Faroe Islands** and their resources belong to their people. It wishes to retain the link with Denmark but with full freedom for either side to decide on the transfer of policy responsibility to the Faroes home government. It supports national self-determination and Nordic cooperation. After a change of leader from Marita Petersen to Joannes Eidesgaard, in 1998 it increased its representation in the Lagting from five to seven. AHT

SOCIAL DEMOCRATIC PARTY IN DENMARK (SD, Socialdemokratiet i Danmark) was founded in 1871 on Marxist principles, although there was little initial contact with such parties in other countries. In its early years it concentrated on **trade union** organization and achieved its first two parliamentary representatives in 1884. By 1913 the party had more votes than any other, in a still-disproportionate voting system. **Thorvald Stauning**'s acceptance of observer status in the cabinet in 1916-20 and the predominance of the party over the union wing from the 1920s attracted a wider range of voters than just industrial workers. These developments have made SD the largest party in the **Folketing** since 1924. Effective leadership by Stauning and an expanding organization in the

1920s limited **Communist** influence and consolidated SD as the only significant socialist party, appealing to middle-class voters as well as workers. From the 1960s SD has been challenged from the left by the **Socialist People's Party**.

SD formed its first brief cabinet in 1924-26, while the coalition with the **Radical Liberals** 1929-40 carried through extensive social reforms, led by **K.K. Steinke**, and laid the foundation of the **welfare** state. The collaborative link between SD and Radicals lasted to the mid-1960s and was revived in 1993. SD has given Denmark eight of its 15 prime ministers: Thorvald Stauning (1924-26, 1929-42), **V. Buhl** (1945), **Hans Hedtoft** (1947-50, 1953-55), **H.C. Hansen** (1955-60), **Viggo Kampmann** (1960-62), **Jens Otto Krag** (1962-68, 1971-72), **Anker Jørgensen** (1972-73, 1975-82), and **Poul Nyrup Rasmussen** from 1993. (*See also* Appendix 2).

Throughout the period since the late 1920s, although it has never had more than 46 percent of the vote (in 1935) and has usually governed from a minority **cabinet**, SD has been the predominant party in government and has given a more egalitarian and democratic shape to Denmark's political culture and policies. SD claims credit for reducing class-based social divisions and building a society with equal access to publicly provided education, health, and social services. These achievements have rested on center-oriented pragmatism rather than dogmatic ideology. AHT

SOCIALIST PEOPLE'S PARTY (Socialistisk Folkeparti, SF) was founded in 1959. **Aksel Larsen**. had been leader of the Danish **Communist Party** since 1933, but he and others who formed SF were expelled for advocating socialism on Danish lines rather than on the lines laid down from Moscow. The new party eclipsed the Communists and has won between 3.9 and 13.0 percent of the votes and substantial **Folketing** representation ever since. SF has never participated in cabinet, taking a stance critical of Social Democratic compromises, **NATO**, and **European Union**. In only two brief periods (1966-68 and 1971-73) has there been a socialist majority. In the first of these SF operated a close consultative arrangement (known as "the red cabinet") with the minority SD government, but the **Left Socialists** split away when SF was asked to support deflationary economic policies. In 1971-73 the minority SD government was supported from the center and right in its negotiations for European Community membership, outvoting SF's opposition.

SF demonstrated its responsible opposition by negotiating and voting for Finance Bills until 1982, but then refused to do so until 1996 because of concessions to **Liberal, Conservative** and **Progress Party** priorities. In 1992, after the **referendum** result which opposed the Treaty of European Union, SF helped to broker the "national compromise" of exceptions which paved the way for the Yes referendum vote in 1993. SF also helped to keep SD in office during 1996-98. These are reasons to see SF as part of the "core" of responsible **political parties** in the party system, rather than of the anti-consensual periphery where it has been located for most of the 40 years of its existence. AHT

SØNDERBY, KNUD (1909-1966). Author. He graduated *cand. jur.* in 1935 but from 1937 he made his living as a journalist and author. His socially critical writing includes *Midt I en jazztid* (1931, In a Jazz Age, filmed in 1968) and the love story, *To mennesker mødes* (1932, Two People Meet). In *En kvinde er overflødig* (1936, A Woman Is Superfluous, dramatized in 1942 and filmed in 1956), he depicts the generation gap. He also wrote essays, many autobiographical, collected in *Grønlandisk sommer* (1941, Greenland Summer), *Forsvundne somre* (1946, Lost Summers), *Hvidtjørnen* (1950, The Whitethorn), *Gensyn med havet* (1957, Meeting the Sea Again), *De blå glimt* (1964, The Blue Glimpses), and *De danske havne* (1969, The Danish Harbours). AHT

SØRENSEN, ARNE (1906-1978). Politician. On leaving school he worked as a journalist and high school teacher. In 1936 he helped to found Dansk Samling, the **Danish Rally** (or Unity) Party. Ideologically it opposed both conservatism and socialism, standing instead for a popular renewal growing out of the Danish cultural heritage. This so-called Third View was seen at the time as an ultra-nationalistic uprising from the political right. He was a member of the **Folketing** 1943-47, joined the **Freedom Council** in December 1943 and was minister of church affairs in **V. Buhl's** liberation cabinet of 1945. He left the party in 1949 and worked as an educationalist. He stated his views in the book *Det moderne menneske* (1936, Modern Man). AHT

SØRENSEN, CARL THEODORE (1893-1979). Landscape architect. Educated as a gardener, from the 1920s he had his own studio from which he developed a close working relationship with the leading architects in the development of play areas and recreational spaces near the large social housing developments such as Ryparken (1932), Voldparken (1952), and Bellahøj (1957), all suburbs of **Copenhagen**. He also designed the Hans Christian **Andersen** garden in **Odense** (1939) and the University Park in **Århus** (1953). In 1940 he built the world's first adventure playground at Emdrup. He was a professor at the **Academy of Art**, 1954-63. AHT

SØRENSEN, RASMUS (1799-1865). Politician. He trained as a teacher and pursued this career 1818-44. Working with Peder Hansen-Lundby, he led the farmers' and smallholders' movement in the early 1840s. His social program put him in conflict with the absolutist government, even though he supported it. He also opposed the Ejder program. He was a member of the **Folketing** 1849-52, then emigrated to the United States of America. AHT

SØRENSEN, VILLY (1929-) is a writer and critic, the recipient of many literary prizes including the 1974 **Nordic Council** prize for literature, a member of the Royal Danish Academy, and holder of an honorary doctorate from the University of Copenhagen. His writing includes short-stories, translations of Seneca (1979), Erasmus (1979), Kafka (1960), and Hermann Broch (1960, 1966-67). He has edited **Søren Kierkegaard**'s The Concept of Dread (*Begrebet Angst*, 1944, ed. 1960), Kafka's collected stories (1967-68), and anthologies of Karl Marx (1962) and Richard Wagner (1983), tales of the Nordic gods and their doom (*Ragnarok*, 1982; The Downfall of the Gods, 1989), as well as six volumes of his own essays. *Oprør fra midten* (1971, *Revolt from the Center*, 1981), written with Niels I. Meyer and Helveg Petersen, sets out a more utopian modern political system. AHT

SORGENFRI is a castle just north of **Copenhagen** built in 1705 for Count Ahlefelt and enlarged in 1743 by **Laurids de Thurah** as a summer residence for the crown prince, later **Frederik V**. It was later used as his residence by **Frederik IX**'s brother, Prince Knud. The fine surrounding park is open to the public. AHT

SORØ ACADEMY is a school of high prestige, originally a Cistercian monastery founded c. 1160 by Bishop **Absalon**. **Frederik II** transferred the royal school here in 1586 and new buildings were completed in 1747, funded from estates left by the dramatist **Ludvig Holberg**. Since 1849 the school has been run by the state, with about 170 *alumner* (boarding pupils) among its 400 students. Unusually for a Danish school, the students wear a navy blue uniform like naval cadets. AHT

SOUND, THE (ØRESUNDET), is the narrow stretch of water between **Scania** and southern Sweden to the east and **Funen** and **Copenhagen** to the west. **Kronborg Castle** at **Elsinore** (Helsingør) was built on the orders of King **Frederik II** in 1574-85 on the site of an earlier fortress to help enforce the collection of Sound tolls from the rich trade passing through the narrow waterway. The 1720 Treaty of **Frederiksborg** gave Denmark the right to levy tolls on Swedish ships sailing through the Sound. **Nina Bang** researched 16th-century shipping and trade in the Sound. The tolls were abolished in 1846 to make **Copenhagen** more attractive and prevent further loss of trade to Hamburg. Crossed hitherto by ferry, a 'fixed link' of tunnel, causeway and **bridge** across the Sound between Malmö in Sweden and Copenhagen opens to traffic by 2000. AHT

SOYA, CARL ERIK (1896-1983). Author. The son of an artist, he supported himself from an early age as a writer. With often brutal openness he depicts middle-class untruthfulness and dual sexual morality in his plays *Parasitterne* (1929, The Parasites) and the four plays jointly entitled *Blindebuk, eller: Sådan kan det gå!* (1940-40, Blind Man's Buff, or That's How It Happens). He also wrote a series of short stories and radio plays, the novel *Sytten: I-III* (1953-4, Seventeen), and the memoirs, *Min farmors hus,* (1943, My Grandfather's House). AHT

SPIES, SIMON (1921-1984). Businessman. Starting by selling chocolates in a cinema, he learned commerce. During the German occupation he was a delivery man, then graduated *cand. psych.* and *cand. polit.* in 1951. From 1953 he ran bus tours and in 1956 started the travel firm Spies, with its own charter airline, Conair. The firm expanded and profited from the subsequent growth in holiday sales. AHT

STAGE, MADS (1922-). Artist. He was educated at the **Academy of Art** as a painter, and at the School of Graphics. His pencil and color-wash illustrations have sold widely and he has illustrated many books, including H.D. Thoreau, *Walden*; Turgenyev, *A Hunter's Diary*; Palle Lauring, *Synderjylland* (Southern Jutland); and many children's books. He has designed many commemorative stamps including one for **Carl Nielsen**, and stamp-series of Danish birds and castles. His recent work includes the design of posters, textiles, glass and porcelain, and drawings of Danish and European architecture. AHT

STARCKE, CARL NICOLAE (1858-1926). Politician. He graduated *mag. phil.* in 1881 and *dr. phil.* in 1883. Initially he supported the **Radical Liberals**, was a member of the **Folketing** 1913-18, at first as an independent then from 1914 as a **Liberal**. He chaired the Henry George Society 1913-16, arguing for a single tax on land values, and was a founder of the **Justice Party** in 1919. His publications on this theme include *Det økonomiske livs hoved love og grundværdiskatten som eneste skat* (1912, The Chief Laws of Economic Life and the Land Value Tax as the Only Tax) and *Jordskyld* (1914). Father of **Viggo Starcke**. AHT

STARCKE, VIGGO (1895-1974). Politician. The son of Carl Nicolae Starcke, he graduated *cand. med.* in 1921 and practiced as a doctor until 1946. He represented the **Justice Party** in the **Folketing** 1945-60 and was minister without portfolio in **H.C. Hansen**'s three-party coalition 1957-60. He was one of the most energetic political opponents of rationing and other economic restrictions. AHT

STATE MUSEUM OF ART (Statens Museum for Kunst) displays a representative collection of European Art from the 13th to the 18th century, in 104 rooms on two floors. It was originally derived from the royal collections of paintings and sculptures housed in **Christiansborg**, but after the 1894 fire there a new museum in Italian Renaissance style was built at Sølvgade 48-50 in 1889-96. Italian painting is represented by Titian Bassano and Tintoretto; there is a strong collection of Dutch/Flemish paintings; and notable French paintings are by Poussin and Fragonard, plus a 20th-century collection including pictures by Braque, Matisse, Rouault, and Picasso. The Danish collection is strong in Biedermeyer paintings and work up to the first decade of the 20th century, including **Nicolai Abildgaard** and **Jens Juel** (18th century), **C.W. Eckersberg, Constantin Hansen,** and **Christen Købke** (the **Golden Age** of the early 19th century); and the landscapes of Johan Thomas **Lundbye** and **Peter Christian Skovgaard** (of the second half of the 19th century). There is also a gallery of about 100,000 European engravings. AHT

STAUNING, THORVALD MARINUS (1873-1942). Prime minister 1924-26 and 1929-42. Educated in a council school, he worked as a cigar-sorter until 1899, joining the **Social Democrats** (SD) in 1890 not long after their foundation by **Louis Pio, Paul Geleff,** and others. He was active on the executive of the Tobacco Workers' Congress as chairman and editor of its journal 1896-1908, and treasurer and secretary of the SD Federation from 1898, working well with chairman Peter Christian **Knudsen**. Elected to the **Folketing** in 1906, Stauning continued as a member until his death, serving as SD chairman from 1910 and chairman of the SD parliamentary group. He was elected concurrently to **Copenhagen** City Council 1913-25 and was chairman 1919-24.

As a reformist party leader Stauning united party and trade unions but opposed the temperance movement or close links to the **cooperatives**, fearing that diversity would harm the party and that cooperatives would harm the SD voters who ran small businesses. After the government sold the **Danish West Indies** (Virgin Islands) to the United States of America in 1915, he joined **Zahle**'s **Radical Liberal** cabinet in 1916 as an observer, staying as social affairs minister 1918-20. His attempts to secure peace included abortive plans for a 1917 Stockholm peace conference. In the 1920 **Easter Crisis** he led a delegation which persuaded the king to hold to the parliamentary principle adopted in the 1901 **Change of System**, using labor unrest to avert a coup d'état (*see also* **F.J. Borgbjerg, Aksel Larsen**). He was critical of rising unemployment 1920-24 and advocated policies prophetic of Keynesian counter-cyclical macroeconomics. SD grew in members and voters, extending a broad appeal from its urban base to provincial and rural areas, and expanding from a working-class party into a broad-based popular party.

Stauning formed the first SD minority cabinet 1924-26 with Radical Liberal support, and then a majority cabinet 1929-42 in coalition with the Radicals. With patient skill he built broad consensus for the 1933 **Kanslergade Agreement**. The 1935 election, fought under the slogan "Stauning or chaos," won SD its best share of the poll and, with the Radicals, a majority in both Folketing and **Landsting**. He was revered as father of his country and guarantor of its political stability, but constitutional reforms were narrowly defeated at **referendum** in 1939. Danish neutrality seemed possible in 1939, as in 1914-18, so the German **World War II** occupation on 9 April 1940 was a serious blow: Stauning stayed in office to forestall nonparliamentary rule (by a proposed cabinet to be headed by Prince **Axel**) and broadened his government. His first priority was to retain the labor movement's organizational base (by contrast to its fate in Germany; *see also* **Alsing Andersen**), so collaboration with the occupiers rankled but seemed unavoidable. His health declined and he died on 3 May 1942 and was succeeded by **V. Buhl**, with a younger stratum of leaders also in place (see **Hans Hedtoft, H.C. Hansen, Viggo Kampmann, Jens Otto Krag**). He and his Swedish contemporary, Per Albin Hansen, were the leaders of the European labor movement. AHT

STAVNSBAAND, adscription: the law by which feudal serfs or peasants were attached to the land and transferred with it. *See also* **Løvenørn; Oeder; Peasant Reforms.** AHT

STEFFENS, HENRICH (1773-1845). Philosopher. Born in Stavanger in southwest Norway to a German doctor from Holstein and a Danish mother, he moved with his family to Denmark in 1779. He studied natural science in **Copenhagen** and was the first Danish graduate in the subject in 1794. He earned his doctorate at the University of Kiel in mineralogy. In Germany he was influenced by Schelling, Goethe, and other leading figures of German Romanticism. A series of lectures in Copenhagen in 1802-3 inspired **Adam Oehlenschläger, N.F.S. Grundtvig, A.S.** and **H.C. Ørsted** and the entire **Golden Age** of thinking and art. Steffens' view was that the earthly was a reflection of the godly, which man could recognize by mystic insight, the highest expression of which was philosophy and art. Nine of the lectures were published with the title *Indledning til filosofiske forelæsninger* (1803, Introduction to Philosophical Lectures). From 1804 he lived in Germany where he held chairs in Halle and Breslau. AHT

STEINKE, KARL KRISTIAN (1880-1963). **Social Democrat** (SD) politician and social reformer. He joined SD as a student and edited *Socialisten* 1903-14. After graduating *cand. jur.* in 1906 from Copenhagen University he worked 1907-21 in Fredriksberg local council, in 1917-21 as head of the municipal (*kommune*) Department of the Poor. He published *Offentlig Hjælp* (1910, Public Assistance), expanded as *Haandbog i Forsørgelsesvæsen* (1916, Handbook on the Maintenance Service), the standard work on social administration of the time. His pioneering book *Fremtidens Forsørgelsesvæsen* (1920, The Income Maintenance Service of the Future) covered welfare theory in volume 1 and proposed legislative reforms in volume 2.

On the SD national executive committee 1913-19 Steinke often opposed **Th. Stauning** and **F.J. Borgbjerg**, having argued in his *Kulturbetragtninger* (1912, Cultural Considerations) that SD and its press had adopted bourgeois narrow mindedness and distorted the facts. He presided 1921-24 and 1926-28 over the new court determining invalidity pension disputes. He was minister of justice 1924-26 when extensive reforms of criminal law were proposed but not passed, but passed laws in 1925 to give marriage partners economic equality. He was a member of the **Landsting** 1918-52, directly elected 1918-40, then elected by the **Folketing**. In 1927 he controversially advocated acceptance of couples living together without legal consequences while childless, arguing that SD ideology went beyond welfare and working conditions.

As minister for social policy 1929-35, in 1933 Steinke carried through the extensive social reforms planned in the 1920s. They rested on the principle that public assistance should not be charitable but be given by right according to uniform simple rules administered by a single office in each municipality and funded from compulsory national insurance to cover illness, accident, invalidity, etc. The **Kanslergade Agreement** secured **Liberal** and **Radical Liberal** support to meet the problem of youth unemployment, with "institutions" (to avoid the German overtones of labor camps) organized with mornings of work, afternoons of education and sport, and evenings of entertainment and discussion. In the social unrest of the 1930s he was shot at from the public gallery in **parliament** and physically attacked at home and at work, but was admired for his calmness under fire. As minister of justice, 1935-39 he continued with social reforms, granting an illegitimate child the right to its father's name and inheritance and to maintenance from him. Abortion was legalized in 1937 on medical and narrow social grounds, and he joined extensively in the public debate on this controversial issue. A single national **police** force was introduced in 1937, and security police in 1939 to deal with numerous spying incidents.

Steinke vigorously defended democracy and parliamentary responsibility in controversial debate, and brought several cases of defamation in defense of his integrity, but left office in 1939 after a dispute with **Stauning**. As a member of the Foreign Policy Council he several times sought to stop persecution of **Jews**, but was criticized for his responsibility for the rights of interned communists during the German occupation. He was chairman of the **Landsting** 1948-50 and 1951-52. As minister of justice again briefly in 1950 in **Hedtoft**'s cabinet he gave amnesty to minor traitors during the **World War II** occupation. An important administrator and legislator, as a politician his quick tongue and inability to foresee possibilities and implications had damaging consequences for his party and colleagues. AHT

STENSEN, NIELS (STENO)(1638-1686). Natural scientist and bishop. The son of a goldsmith, he studied natural science from 1656 at Copenhagen University, 1660-64 in the Netherlands, 1665 in France and 1666 in Florence, Italy. In 1667 he converted to Catholicism and after further travels returned to Denmark in 1672-4. Ordained a priest in 1675, from 1677 until his death he was a Catholic bishop in northern Germany. He was beatified in 1988. As a scientist Stensen investigated the salivary glands and the passageways between ear and mouth, and demonstrated that the heart was a muscle. His studies of stone formation and geological strata showed their different ages, and he is therefore counted as the founder of geology. His studies of the form and growth of rock crystals also make him the founder of crystallography. AHT

STETTIN, PEACE OF (1570) *see* **NORTHERN SEVEN YEARS' WAR**

STORM PETERSEN, ROBERT (1882-1949). Cartoonist and actor. His 1903-33 acting career was mainly in comic roles. He painted early expressionist and ofte socially critical pictures, but is best known for his cartoons and humorous tales, published from 1914 in *BT* and *Berlingske Tidende*. He published an annual *Album* 1913-48, *Storm Petersens Dagbog* (diary) from 1917, and *Dagens flue* (*Fly of the Day* from 1939). His collected baroque tales and monologues were published in nine volumes (1949-50). A museum and library of his work at Frederiksberg Runddel opened in 1977. AHT

STRUENSEE, JOHANN FRIEDRICH (1737-1772). Politician. The son of a German priest, he graduated *dr. med.* in 1757. As doctor to **Christian VII** from 1769 and as queen Caroline Mathilde's lover his influence at court grew rapidly and in 1770 he issued his first two cabinet orders in the name of the mentally ill king. On 10 December that year he abolished the Council and introduced a cabinet system, becoming the king's only minister from 17 December. In March 1771 he became cabinet secretary and in July minister in the Privy Council, with the right to sign and issue cabinet orders as if they were signed by the king himself. He used these extraordinary powers to introduce reforms which included freedom of the press, inspired by the French **Enlightenment**. Another of his reforms was to amalgamate the many saints days into a single public holiday, Store Bededag (Great Prayer Day) on the second Friday in May. As a result of a court conspiracy led by the dowager Queen Juliane Marie and **Ove Hoegh-Guldberg,** he was arrested on 17 January 1772, condemned for lese-majesty, and executed on 28 April 1772. AHT

SUFFRAGE *see* **FRANCHISE**

SVEND I FORKBEARD (?-1014) was king of Denmark from about 987 until his death. He deposed his father, King **Harald Bluetooth,** to gain the crown and joined Olaf Tryggvason's **Viking** expedition to England. But Olaf converted to Christianity and soon afterwards seized power in Norway, so Svend changed allegiance. He married Gunhild, the mother of the Swedish king Olof Skötkonung, and joined with the Norwegian jarl Håkon's sons. In a famous sea-battle near the lost island of Svold, Olaf Tryggvason was killed by united Danish-Norwegian-Swedish forces. This placed Svend in such a strong position throughout the Nordic region that he allowed Harald's round fortifications to decay. He decided to conquer England and take the *danegeld*, a tax which the English paid to the competing Viking chief Thorkil the Tall for protection from Viking raids. Svend's vikings landed in England in the summer of 1013 and England was conquered by Christmas, but Svend died a few months afterward. His elder son succeeded as **Harald II** in Denmark and his younger son **Knud I the Great** (Canute) in England. AHT

SVEND II ESTRIDSEN (c. 1020-1074). King of Denmark 1047-74. Son of **Harald II**'s sister Estrid, he was chosen as king at **Viborg** five years after the death of King **Hardeknud**, and only after the death of King Magnus of Norway, and the Danish coast was under attack by the new Norwegian king Harald Hårderåde in 1048, 1050, and 1060. In a sea battle with Harald Hårderåde near Nisås off the Halland coast in 1062, Svend Estridsen was allowed to escape with his life, but in 1064 the two met at Gøtaelven where Denmark, Norway, and Sweden joined, and concluded a ceremonial peace for their lifetimes. About 1070 Svend Estridsen and the Swedish king Edmund commissioned the setting of six stones to mark the border between their lands. In 1060 Denmark was divided into bishoprics and during Svend's reign contact with Rome became rare. He died leaving many progeny but no legitimate sons and was succeeded by **Harald III Hén**. AHT

SVEND III GRATHE (?-1157). King of Denmark 1146-57, son of **Erik II Emune**. He was chosen king in **Zealand** and **Scania**, while in **Jutland, Knud III Magnussen** was chosen. Briefly they agreed on a crusade against the **Wends** in 1147, but this lasted only until a battle on the Mecklenburg coast, when Knud's warriors looked on while the **Wends** slaughtered Svend's men of Scania. Knud asked the German king Frederik Barbarossa to intervene in the dispute, and at a meeting at Merseberg in 1152 Frederik ruled that in future only Svend should have the title of king, but Svend gave allegiance to Frederik. Knud gained Zealand, and Valdemar was given the duchy of **Slesvig**. Seeing the danger that the affairs of Denmark and its church would be determined in Germany, the leading Danes forced a settlement which gave Scania to Svend, Zealand and **Funen** to Knud, and Jutland to **Valdemar**. The agreement was to be sealed at a feast in **Roskilde** on 9 August 1157, but Svend had Knud killed. Valdemar escaped to Jutland in the night. Svend gained his nickname at the decisive battle on **Grathe Heath** near **Viborg**, which was won by the Jutlanders. Svend fled but was recognized and killed by peasants. AHT

SVENNINGSEN, NILS (1894-1985). Civil servant. He graduated *cand. jur.* in 1917 and in 1920 joined the Foreign Ministry, of which he was director 1941-45 and 1951-61. In the period of German rule after the cabinet had resigned (29 August 1943 to 5 May 1945) he led the Heads of Departments. His diplomatic appointments included legation secretary in Berlin 1924-30 and envoy and ambassador in Stockholm 1945-50, Paris 1950-51, and London 1961-64. AHT

SWEDEN, DANISH RELATIONS WITH. The Kalmar Union, formed in 1397 and finally dissolved in 1521, united the kingdoms of Denmark, Norway, and Sweden under **Margrethe I** and her successors. At its height it was the largest kingdom in Europe. Denmark under **Frederik II** (1559-88) still dominated the Nordic region, but Sweden posed a growing challenge. There followed almost a century of wars between Denmark and Sweden. The **Kalmar War** (1611-1613) was followed by Danish involvement in the **Thirty Years' War**. This ended in 1629 with the Peace of **Lübeck,** from which Denmark was fortunate to obtain more advantageous terms than were justified by Sweden's successes in battle. **Torstensson's War** (1643-45) was the third in this series of wars. It ended with the **Treaty of Brømsebro**, following which Denmark no longer levied **Sound** tolls on Sweden, and Sweden gained the province of Halland and the islands of Gotland and Ösel. In 1657, while Sweden was preoccupied in quelling a nationalist uprising in Poland, **Frederik III** unwisely started a further war, the **Swedish-Danish War** of 1657-60. He had to accept humiliating terms in the 1658 **Treaty of Roskilde,** ceding all Danish possessions in **Scania**. This gave Sweden the entire western coastline as far as the Norwegian border and, temporarily, a province in central Norway. The latter was recovered in 1660 by the Treaty of Copenhagen, but Denmark lost command of the entry to the Baltic and lost the income from Sound tolls on Swedish ships.

Denmark tried to regain Scania in 1675. While Sweden was attacking Brandenburg in alliance with France, Denmark landed an army and won the **Scanian War**. Despite heavy losses, French pressure ensured no lasting territorial gains to Denmark. The **Great Northern War** (1700-1721) brought further Danish-Swedish conflict, from which Denmark's only gains were the lands of the duke of Holstein-Gottorp in **Slesvig** and the abolition of Sweden's exemption from the Sound tolls.

With Britain and France at war, in 1780 Denmark joined with Russia, Prussia, and Sweden in armed neutrality. When Britain again went to war with revolutionary France, Denmark rejoined the armed neutrality but had to withdraw following the **1801 Battle of Copenhagen**. Denmark was caught between pressure from France, threatening invasion of Jutland, and British demands for an alliance. The **1807 Battle of Copenhagen** pushed the Danes into joining France, while Sweden, led by Marshall Bernadotte (the future King Karl XIV Johan) succeeded in disengaging. In 1814 Sweden gained **Norway** in the Treaty of Kiel, the reward that had been promised to Sweden provided that Denmark was on the losing side. The allocation of previously Swedish **Lauenburg** to Denmark proved to be small compensation.

In the First **Slesvig-Holsten** War, in the spirit of **Scandinavianism** Sweden sent a contingent of soldiers which were instrumental in the successful Danish attack on German troops in Jutland in 1848. King Oscar I of Sweden-Norway responded to a congress of Scandinavianist students in 1856 by saying that: "From now on war between the Scandinavian brothers is impossible," but a Danish appeal for assistance from Norway-Sweden a decade later was only answered by a few volunteers, and Denmark suffered the disaster of the Second **Slesvig-Holsten** War. Scandinavianism advanced commercially, however, with the Danish-Swedish gold-based currency union of 1873, which lasted until **World War I**. As this threat loomed, the kings of Denmark, Norway (independent of Sweden since 1905) and Sweden met at Malmö and resolved that their countries would remain neutral — a hope that was fortunately fulfilled.

The interwar years saw the rapid growth of **social democracy** in both countries. In 1929 **Thorvald Stauning** became prime minister

398 / The Dictionary

of a majority coalition, and in 1932 Per Albin Hansson inaugurated a period of government by Socialdemokratiska Arbetarepartiet that lasted unbroken to 1976, while in Norway the Labour Party began 30 years of continuous government in 1935. The parties and their leaders collaborated closely to build political, social and economic democracy in their countries. As this grand project gathered momentum, the three countries (and later also Finland and **Iceland**) came to resemble each other increasingly, a process which was enhanced by formal cooperation in the **Nordic Council** from 1952.

Denmark and Norway were occupied by Germany in 1940, but Sweden remained neutral throughout **World War II** and provided refuge for many Danes and Norwegians, including almost all the Danish **Jews** — although there were later dark questions about Swedish-German wartime relations. After the war a Scandinavian Defense Pact was proposed, but Norway and Denmark opted for founder-membership of **NATO** in 1949, while Sweden remained neutral. In compensation, the Nordic Council was founded to provide a framework of cooperation between its five member states. It developed a "web of integration" which drew the five countries into a close community of collaboration on commercial, social, cultural, academic, and educational policies. Denmark and Sweden remained distinct, however, in their economic, defense, and foreign policies. Although all the Nordic countries joined **EFTA**, Denmark left to join the European Community (EC) in 1972, while Sweden (and Finland) waited until 1994 to join the **European Union**. During this period Denmark saw a role in maintaining a diplomatic bridge between its EC partners and its Nordic neighbors.

The **bridge** between Denmark and Sweden takes concrete form with the opening in 2000 of the "fixed link" between **Copenhagen** and Malmö. Close collaboration in the development of infrastructure is expected to contribute further to the growth of a single Øresund economic region which once again brings together **Zealand** and **Scania**. AHT

SWEDISH-DANISH WAR (1657-60). In a succession of brilliant campaigns the Swedes advanced steadily to occupy **Jutland** and later the Danish islands. In 1660 Denmark was obliged to sign a Treaty in **Copenhagen** which limited her to territory west of the **Sound**, the sole exception being **Bornholm**, while the rich provinces of **Scania**, Halland, and Blekinge (at the southern end of the Swedish peninsula) passed to Sweden. Intervention on Denmark's behalf by the Netherlands, who wished to safeguard their trading interests in the Baltic, retained **Zealand** for Denmark. The war left the Danish state bankrupt and the country laid waste, and the way was open for **Frederik III** to assume **absolute** power for himself and his heirs. AHT

SYBERG, FRITZ (1862-1939). Painter. The son of a distillery manager, he had various jobs while receiving drawing lessons. He was a pupil in **Kristian Zahrtmann**'s painting school in 1885-91. From 1894 he lived in **Funen**, and its landscape became his ongoing subject and led him into the *"Fynboer"* group of Impressionist painters. Many of his pictures are of domestic subjects, with the sense of daily life indicated by such titles as *The Death* (1890-2), *Mother and Daughter* (1898-99), *View of Svanninge* (1899), *Evening Game* (1900), *The First Snow* (1905), *The First Day of Spring* (1910), *The Snow Melting* (1925-27), and illustrations for **Hans Christian Andersen**'s *The Story of a Mother* (1895-98). AHT

SYV, PEDER (1631-1702). Language researcher. He qualified as a priest in 1664 and was appointed royal philologist in 1683. He published the first Danish grammar in Danish, *Den Danske Sprog — Kunst eller Grammatica* (1685, The Danish Language, Art or Grammar). His *Almindelige Danske Ord-Sprog og Korte Lærdomme I-II* (1682-88, General Danish Proverbs and Wise Sayings) contained about 15,000 sayings, proverbs, etc. He also published *Viser om konger, kæmper og andre* (1695, Songs of Kings, Warriors and Others) containing 200 songs. AHT

- T -

TAMIL AFFAIR. Tamil refugees who had fled the conflict in Sri Lanka obtained asylum in Denmark. They then applied for permission for their wives and children to join them. Erik Ninn-Hansen was Conservative minister of justice in **Poul Schlüter**'s government during 1982-89, before becoming chairman (speaker) of the

Folketing in January to October 1989. As such he was politically responsible for the operation of immigration law. It was alleged that in 1987-89 he had illegally instructed officials to delay decisions in the cases of the Tamils, while other applications were processed normally. The affair was investigated by the Folketing Justice Committee and then by the **Ombudsman**, who reported on 1 March 1989 that the Foreigners' Directorate had used more resources to delay the applications than were needed to process them.

Amid threats to activate the impeachment procedure (the 1953 **Constitution** paragraph 16 provides for a minister to be tried before the High Court of the Realm (*rigsret*) by the King or the Folketing on a charge of maladministration of office), the case was investigated by an independent court of inquiry chaired by a Supreme Court judge. The court also inquired whether the affair had been covered up by other ministers, and particularly by the prime minister. The long-awaited report was published in January 1993 and stated unambiguously that Ninn-Hansen's administrative decisions had been illegal and that statements by Schlüter to the Folketing had been "highly misleading" and "directly incorrect." Five leading Conservative members of the Folketing were also seriously criticized in the report.

Schlüter immediately announced his cabinet's resignation, hoping to retain the initiative and avoid the expected election — only twice, in 1950 and 1982, had a prime minister resigned without calling an election. The **Social Democrat** leader **Poul Nyrup Rasmussen** then formed a majority government with support from the Radicals, the **Center Democrats,** and the **Christian People's Party**. AHT

TANG KRISTENSEN, EVALD (1843-1929) Teacher and collector of folklore. He collected about 35,000 tunes, songs, tales, and legends, published as *Danske sagn som de har lydt I folkemunde*, I-VI (1892-1901, Danish Legends As They Sounded in the Mouth of the People, republished in eight volumes in 1980); *Danske børnerim, remser og lege* (1896, Danish Children's Rhymes, Jingles, and Games), and *Gamle folks fortællinger om det jyske almueliv I-VI* (1891-1902, Old People's Tales of Jutland Peasant Life). AHT

TARP, SVEND ERIC (1908-1994) composed symphonies, a piano concerto and other orchestral music, chamber music, operas, and many film scores. His choral music included a *Te Deum* in an eclectic style reminiscent of Stravinsky. Although he was influenced by the French group, *Les Six*, the seventh symphony is neoclassical in feeling. AHT

TAUSEN, HANS (1494-1561). Religious reformer and Bishop. Born on **Funen**, he entered the monastery at Antvorskov, but also journeyed in Europe and was strongly attracted to the teaching of Luther. In 1525 he was sent to **Viborg**, where his sermons led to a break with his order. He gained the protection of King **Frederik I** as a royal chaplain with permission to preach in **Copenhagen**. There he formed the first **Lutheran** congregation in Denmark. In 1529 Tausen was given charge of St. Nicholas church and was soon seen as the leading Protestant. In 1536-7 he helped draft the Church Ordinance, effectively the constitution for the evangelical Lutheran state church. He also helped write *En håndbog for sognepræster* (1535, reprinted 1970, A Handbook for Parish Priests) and published the first **Lutheran** hymn book. He was bishop (entitled 'superintendent') of Ribe from 1542 until his death. SPO, AHT

TELEVISION *see* **RADIO AND TELEVISION**

THAILAND, DANISH RELATIONS WITH *see*
H.N. ANDERSEN; EAST ASIATIC COMPANY

THEATER. The earliest theater in Denmark, as elsewhere in western Europe, is represented by religious "miracle" and "morality" plays performed in town squares and churchyards. These were succeeded after the **Reformation** by equally didactic dramas in Latin and Danish performed by scholars and students, sometimes with music and dance to accompany them. These were also performed at court. In the 17th century, spectacular court festivals were popular. At the same time visiting players from outside Denmark were influential, and it was a French company which stimulated the opening of the first permanent playhouse in Denmark, on Lille Grønnegade in Copenhagen, in 1722. For this **Ludvig Holberg** produced his earliest comedies. During the reign of the **Pietist** King **Christian VI**, theaters were discouraged as ungodly, but after his death, the **Royal Theater** opened on Kongens Nytorv to become the center of Danish drama ever since. In the 1770s *singspiel* were introduce there, and in the 19th century Danish theater, with actors and actresses like **Johanne Luise Heiberg** enjoyed a European reputation. Luise's husband **Johan Ludvig Heiberg** dominated the critical scene as his wife dominated the stage, but his romantic *Elverhøj* (Elf Hill) was one of the most popular productions. Denmark has produced no great international dramatists since Holberg to match Norway's Ibsen or Sweden's Strindberg, but in the 20th century the works of **Kjell Abell**, **Kaj Munk** and **Leif Panduro** have enjoyed great popularity within their own country. SPO

THIRTY YEARS' WAR (1618-48). Danish involvement was limited. Following the **Northern Seven Years' War**, Swedish influence in the Baltic expanded to include Ingria, southwest Karelia and the entire eastern Baltic coast, and then also Livonia, Riga, and important Prussian ports on the southern Baltic coast. **Christian IV** wanted to limit this expansion and secure the north German coast. The Council of the Realm opposed his plans, so in 1625 as duke of **Holsten** he was elected supreme commander in Lower Saxony. British and French support was promised. Christian's army faced General Tilly's at **Lutter-am-Barenberg** (1626). The result was catastrophic for Christian. Meeting in January 1627, the Estates voted a war tax and the otherwise untaxed nobility promised one-fifth of their income. The Saxons suffered further defeat by General Wallenstein, whereupon some landowners and cities went over to the German Emperor. Tilly and Wallenstein advanced northward, and by October had captured and plundered all Jutland. Peace negotiations in **Lübeck** were opened on 6 January 1629 with the Duke of Gottorp and the Elector of Saxony as arbiters. At the same time Christian met the Swedish King Gustav Adolf, but to the latter's great disappointment, no alliance was achieved: Christian's motive was to influence the peace talks. Initial heavy German demands were moderated and, considering the weak Danish military position, very advantageous terms were obtained in the **Peace of Lübeck** on 8 May 1629. AHT

THOMSEN, CHRISTIAN JÜRGENSEN (1788-1865). Archaeologist. The son of a merchant, while working as a businessman 1804-40 he collected coins and later copperplates. As director from 1816 he built up with other collectors the Museum of Nordic Antiquities, and had it moved in 1853 to the Prince's Palace in **Copenhagen**. This became the basis for the foundation in 1892 of the **National Museum**. His division of prehistoric times into Stone, Bronze, and Iron Ages became internationally accepted. AHT

THOMSEN, EWALD (1913-1993). Musician. As a 13-14-year-old he began playing the violin at folk dances. In 1951 he founded the fiddler's museum at Rebild, and from 1971 he was consultant to Folkemusikhuset (Folk Music House) at Hogager by Holsterbro. For several decades he had the highest reputation in Denmark as a folk musician. AHT

THORKIL nicknamed "THE TALL" (?-1024), the son of a jarl of **Scania**, was one of the most prominent **Viking** leaders about AD 1000. He led the army in England 1002-12, in the service of **Knud the Great** 1013-14, and was in charge of East Anglia from 1016. Knud sent him back to Denmark in 1021, which he governed from 1023. AHT

THORVALDSEN, BERTEL (1770-1844). Sculptor. The son of a carver, he was educated from 1781 at the **Academy of Art**. He lived in Rome during 1797-1819, 1820-38 and 1841-42 and, inspired by classical sculpture, became one of the leading neoclassical sculptors in Europe. His major works include *Jason* (1803), *Amor and Psyche* (1807), the Alexander frieze (1812), *Venus* (1816), the *Three Graces* (1818), *Christ and the Twelve Apostles* (1821-27) for Copenhagen Cathedral, and a large number of statues and portrait busts of contemporary and historical figures such as Gutenberg, Copernicus, **Christian IV**, Schiller, **Eckersberg**, Byron, Adam **Oehlenschläger**, **Frederik VI**, his own family, and his patron Christine Stampe. In 1837 he gave his collections and his own works to Denmark, and these form the basis of the Thorvaldsen **Museum** in **Copenhagen**. Some of his sculptures are also displayed at Nysø Manor House, Præstø. AHT

THREE-YEARS' WAR (1848-1850) *see*
FIRST **SLESVIG-HOLSTEN** WAR

THRIGE, THOMAS BARFOED (1866-1938). Manufacturer. The son of a teacher, he trained as a smith and a machinist. In 1888-93 he was in the United States of America, working for some of that time in Thomas Edison's laboratory. In 1894 he started his own firm in Denmark to produce electric motors and dynamos, and is considered the pioneer of electrification in Denmark. AHT

THURAH, LAURIDS DE (1706-1759) was the leading Danish architect of the late Baroque period. The son of a priest, he pursued a career as a military engineer, then traveled as an architect in 1729-31 in Germany, Italy, France, the Netherlands, and England. Appointed court building master in 1733, his greatest works include **Eremitagen** (1734-36), the spire of Vor Frelsers Kirke (1752, Our Saviour's Church), parts of Frederik's Hospital (now the Museum of Industrial Design, Kunstindustrimuseet) in **Copenhagen**, and additions to **Sorø Academy** and to the castles of **Sorgenfri** and **Fredensborg**. He published the definitive book of architectural history, *Den danske Vitruvius* (I, 1746; II, 1749). AHT

TIETGEN, CARL FREDERIK (1829-1901). Businessman and industrialist. The son of a cabinet-maker, he trained as a draper, and in 1855 established the firm C.F. Tietgen & Co. in **Copenhagen** to trade in drapery, metalware, and telegraph supplies. As director of Privatbanken (*see* **banking**) from its foundation in 1857 until 1896, he was decisive in the development of Danish industry and commerce, forming the shipping line **DFDS** in 1866, the Great Northern Telegraph Company (1869), the Danish Sugar Factories (1872), Tuborg Breweries (1873), the Danish Spirit Distilleries (1881), Copenhagen Telephone Company (KTAS)(1882), United Breweries (1891), and many other enterprises. AHT

TIVOLI pleasure gardens in central **Copenhagen** are a fairground and cultural center combined. They were founded by **Georg Carstensen** in 1843, when he persuaded **Christian VIII** that "If the people are kept amused they do not get involved in politics." The 8-hectare (20-acre) site on part of the old city moat and ramparts is close to the central rail station and Town Hall Square (Rådhuspladsen). An immediate success, it soon (unusually at the time) became a place where all social classes could mix and is still a unique combination of amusing and exciting entertainment with architectural beauty and a spirit of artistic adventure. Many of the original buildings survive, inspired by the oriental influences of the founder's childhood, and are lit in the evening to form a magical dream world which culminates in fireworks displays midweek and at weekends.

Attractions include many fairground rides, boats on the lake, and 28 restaurants offering everything from gastronomic delicacies to simple sandwiches and beer. Uniquely, the Italian pantomime tradition of *commedia dell'arte* continues with performances every evening by the classic characters, Pierrot, Colombine, and Harlequin. The concert hall features orchestral, wind instrument, and jazz performances by Danish and international artists. There are covered and open-air stages for theatrical and cabaret entertainments. A Tivoli Guard of boys aged 9-16, drawn from all classes, parades every Saturday and Sunday in uniforms modeled on the Royal Guards. All these features combine to make Tivoli the most famous and popular attraction in the city for both tourists and residents. AHT

TOLERATION, RELIGIOUS, *see* **CONVENTICLE ACT**

TOLLUND MAN was a body found in 1950 in a bog at Tollund, west of Silkeborg, and dated to about 500 BC. He had been strangled with a leather noose and then thrown into the bog as a sacrifice to the mother goddess. His fine features and hooked nose are extraordinarily well-preserved and similar in appearance to the modern inhabitants of central **Jutland**, while his stomach contents showed that his last meal was a porridge of barley and flax seed. Similar finds, studied by P.V. Glob, of bodies of a 14-year-old girl at Windeby in **Slesvig** and a man at **Grauballe** made important contributions to understanding Iron Age and **prehistoric** life in Denmark. AHT

TORDENSKIOLD, PETER (1690-1720). Officer. The son of a merchant of Trondheim, Norway, he went to **Copenhagen** in 1704 to begin a naval career. In 1706-10 he joined merchant expeditions to Africa and the West and East Indies. During the **Great Northern War** of 1709-20 he took part as a captain in several naval encounters, in one of which he destroyed a Swedish cargo fleet near Dyneskilen, south of Frederikshald, in 1716, whereupon he was appointed Commander. In 1719 he captured and occupied Marstrand, north of Göteborg, Sweden, and forced the capitulation of the fort of Karlsten nearby. In 1716 he was ennobled, changing his name from Wessel. He was killed in a duel abroad. AHT

TORSTENSSON'S WAR (1643-1645). This was the third in a series of wars between Sweden and Denmark, following the **Kalmar War** (1611-1613) and Danish involvement in the **Thirty Years' War** which ended in 1629 with the Peace of **Lübeck**. Christian IV tried to recover his military and financial fortunes by raising the **Sound** tolls and blockading the **Hanseatic** city of Hamburg to enforce a toll on the Elbe. In December 1643 without warning the Swedish general Lennart Torstensson (1603-51) marched northwards into the duchies of **Slesvig** and **Holsten**, capturing them within two weeks. In January 1644 his troops attacked and occupied **Jutland**, and in February **Scania**, only Malmö holding out. But a Swedish attack on Norway failed, and on 16 May a Dutch and Swedish fleet was defeated in Listerdyb off the Slesvig coast. On 1 June the main Swedish fleet sailed from Stockholm to collect Torstensson's troops and carry them to Zealand. When they were not to be found, the fleet captured Femern instead. On 1 July the Swedish and Danish fleets joined battle off Kolberger Heath in the waters between Kiel and Femern, and the Swedes had to remain in the fjord for a month. **Christian IV** had Admiral Peder Galt executed for allowing them to slip away, but it also became known that the king had been wounded in the battle and had lost his right eye. This scene was depicted in Johannes **Ewald**'s poem "King Christian Stood by Lofty Mast" which became one of the two Danish **national anthems**. The Danish fleet was heavily defeated on 13 October between **Lolland** and Femern by a Swedish-Dutch fleet. The Dutch did not want to see Danish command over the Baltic and the **Sound** replaced by Swedish control, so peace talks were opened on 8 February 1645 at **Brömsebro** and concluded in August with major Danish losses of territory and income. AHT

TOWN GOVERNMENT *see* **LOCAL GOVERNMENT**

TRADE UNIONS originated after the Free Trade Act of 1857 dissolved the **guilds**, while the growth of industry and population movement into the towns worsened working and housing conditions for the workers. Inspired by the Paris Commune, in 1871 a Danish section of the Workers International was formed by **Louis Pio** and others, out of which grew the **Social Democratic Party** and the trade unions, the two wings of the labor movement. A bricklayers' strike in 1872 led to the International being banned, but union sections continued independently. From 1878 the party and the unions developed separately but in close association. Early union gains included making child labor illegal (from 1873) and aid for destitute people over 60 (from 1891) without loss of voting rights. With consolidations and growing strength (to about 70,000 members) a Danish national federation of trade unions (now known as Landsorganisationen, LO) was formed in 1898. The **Employers' Federation** was formed in 1899 to combat union power. The strike which followed involved 40,000 workers and lasted almost four months, but was conducted peacefully and resulted in the **September Agreement**.

The guild background led to a predominance of craft-based unions but unskilled workers were organized in what became Specialarbejderforbundet i Danmark, SiD, from 1890. In 1997 LO had about 1,502,000 individual members organized in 24 unions, of which the three largest are Handels- og Kontorfunktionærernes Forbund, HK (Union of Shop and Office Workers) with 361,000 members, SiD with about 307,000 members, and *Forbundet af Offentlig Ansatte* (the Union of Public Employees) with about 202,000. In 1997 LO regrouped the unions into six sector-related cartels: industry; public employees; trade, transport and service; municipal employees; building, construction and timber; and the graphics and media industry. These cartels will gradually take over negotiations in their sectors, while LO negotiates on issues affecting workers generally. The Metal Union and the Electricity Union remain outside this controversial structure.

In addition to LO there are four other collective workers' organizations, the two largest being Fællesrådet for danske Tjenestemands- og Funktionærorganisationer, FTF (Joint Council of Danish Public Servants' and Salaried Employees' Organizations) with 332,000 members, and Akademikernes Centralorganisation, AC (Central Organization of Professional Employees), founded in 1972 and with about 132,000 members. LO is very closely aligned with the Social Democratic Party, but FTF and AC are independent of party politics. Brewery workers are independent of LO, doctors left AC in 1982, and journalists remain outside FTF. AHT. *See also* **Jørgensen, Anker; Lyngsie, M.C.**

TRANKEBAR was a Danish trading post in India, south of Madras (*see* **East India Company, Gjedde, Ove***)* and also the name of a design of Royal Copenhagen **Porcelain**, blue painted on a pale gray base. AHT

TRAP, JENS PETER (1810-1885). Civil servant and author. He was appointed cabinet secretary 1857-84, and took part in many royal journeys. His topographical interest led to publication of *Statistisk-topographisk beskrivelse af kongeriget Danmark* I-IV (1858-60, Statistical and Topographical Description of the Kingdom of Denmark), later published in many updated editions as *Trap Danmark*. A similar description of the duchy of **Slesvig** followed (1861-64). He also wrote the very gossipy memoirs, *Fra fire konges tid* I-III (1966-7, From the Time of Four Kings, edited by H. Jørgensen). AHT

TRELLEBORG Viking fortress, 6 km west of Slagelse, **Zealand**, was constructed in 980 as a circular military camp with ramparts and moats, capable of housing 1,000. Excavated in 1934-42, a 1:100 model is on show and a barrack-house has been reconstructed full scale outside the perimeter. A similar fortress at Fyrkat, near Hobro at the head of Mariager fjord 48 km south of **Ålborg**, was excavated and reconstructed in 1951-59. It lacks the outer ward and the ditch is comparatively insignificant. Both are thought to have been built by **Sven II "Forkbeard"** before his invasion of England. Another Viking fort at Aggersborg on the north shore of Limfjorden where it narrows at Løgstør was destroyed in 1086; it was excavated in 1945-52, then covered again. AHT

TROELS-LUND, TROELS (1840-1921). Historian. His book, *Dag-ligt liv i Norden i det 16. århundrede I-XIV* (1879-1901, Daily Life in the North in the 16th Century) locates him as a major Danish cultural historian. He also wrote *Christian 4.s skib på Skanderborg sø* I-II (1893. Christian IV's Ship on Skanderborg Lake), *Livsbe-lysning* (1898, Life's Illumination), and *Bakkehus og Solbjerg. Træk* *af et nyt livssyns udvikling i Norden,* I-III (1910-22, Hill-House and Sun-Mountain: Features in the Development of a New Outlook on Life in the North). AHT

TROLLE, HERLUF (1516-1565). Politician and officer. From a noble family, he studied in Wittenberg (1536-37) then entered the service of **Christian III**, becoming a member of the Council of State in 1557 and chief admiral 1559-62 and 1564-5. With his wife **Brigitte Gøye** he founded **Herlufsholm** school. AHT

TSCHERNING, ANTON FREDERIK (1795-1874). Army officer and politician, interspersed with periods as an engineer and merchant. In 1833 he was effectively exiled by **Frederik VI** for an article in a liberal paper which criticized Danish defense and foreign policy. An advocate of a citizen army, as minister of war in March-November 1848 during the First **Slesvig-Holsten** War he brought in general conscription. In 1846 he was a cofounder of the Society of **Farmers' Friends** and its chairman to 1848. He was a member of the **Constituent Assembly** 1848-49 and of the **Folketing** 1849-66. He supported the Ejder program in 1848 but in the 1850s advocated the "Whole State" policy (*see* **Slesvig-Holsten**) on grounds of "European necessity." As a proponent of universal **suffrage** he opposed the 1866 **Constitution**. AHT

TUXEN, LAURITS (1853-1927). Painter. After an education at the **Academy of Art** (1868-72) and travel in England and France he worked as a teacher and then in 1909-16 as a professor at the Academy. Working at first in a naturalistic and then an impressionistic style, his paintings include *From the West Coast of Jutland* (1875), ceiling paintings in **Frederiksborg Castle**, including the *Triumph of Venus* (1882), *Denmark Receiving the Tribute of the Estates* (1883), group portraits such as *The Royal Family at Fredensborg* (1883-86), and various other royal portraits and historical scenes. He was a contemporary of the **Skagen School**. AHT

- U -

ULFELDT, CORFITZ (1606-1664). Politician. Of noble birth, he studied during 1617-29 in Switzerland, Germany, France and Italy. In 1636 he married **Leonora Christina**, daughter of **Christian IV** and Kirsten Munk and was appointed to the Council of State. The following year he was appointed regent of **Copenhagen** and in 1643 Court Chamberlain, negotiating a number of international agreements. In 1650 he resigned the post as a result of disagreements with **Frederik III**, fleeing to Sweden the following year for fear of a court case alleging that he had misused his office. At the Peace of **Roskilde** of 1658 between Denmark and Sweden Ulfeldt was the negotiator for Sweden. In 1659 a Swedish court convicted him of high treason. He fled to Denmark and was imprisoned 1650-51 in Hammershus on the island of **Bornholm**. Pardoned, in 1662 he traveled to Brandenburg and offered the Danish throne to the Elector. As a result he was charged by **Frederik III** with *lèse-majesté*, condemned to death, and hanged in effigy. He died in a boat on the river Rhine. AHT

UNEMPLOYMENT. National unemployment INSURANCE is administered by unemployment funds (arbejdsløshedskasser) attached to each **trade union**. This system developed from the original role of trade unions, with most of the insurance benefits deriving from contributions by union members and only a small proportion from employer contributions.

An ACTIVE LABOR MARKET POLICY has been continually emphasized. From 1969 the government established employment offices (arbejdsformidlingskontorer, AF) to take over from the unemployment funds the service of channeling people to jobs and providing occupational advice and training. This service is free, but a charge is made to employers for special services. AF also helps with business plans, job training, job rotation, establishment costs, etc., and is responsible for arrangements for child care and educational and sabbatical leave. Trade unions with recognized unemployment funds can also be approved as providers of employment services. As part of an active employment policy the employment offices analyze developments in the labor market. If retraining is not sufficient, there are state grants for work for state, county, or local government organizations and sometimes for private-sector bodies. Employment tribunals (arbejdsmarkedsnævn) in each county are responsible, with the employment offices, for developing plans for work that can be started at short notice when unemployment threatens to increase.

In the years 1994-96 an experiment in HOME SERVICE was tried, and was made permanent from 1997. The state pays a subsidy for the purchase of housekeeping services from value-added-tax (VAT, or MOMS in Danish) registered organizations by householders (not businesses). This can cover shopping, cleaning, cooking, washing, gardening, snow-clearing, and similar activities. The subsidy equals half the invoiced total (including VAT) and the householder pays the other half, plus materials. The organizations must include environmental policies in their objectives and must follow national wage-policy guidelines. By 1997 some 2,900 such organizations had been established. The 1997 Finance Act committed 500 million kroner during 1997-2000 for "green jobs" in the following areas: urban ecology, traffic, renewable energy, energy saving, sewer renewal, recycling, organic foods, and landscape restoration.

UNEMPLOYMENT BENEFIT is paid on condition that: 1. the person is registered with the employment office (AF); 2. s/he has been a member of an unemployment fund at least a year; and 3. s/he has worked at least 52 weeks (1,924 hours) within the past three years, if registered as a full-time worker, or 34 weeks (1,258 hours) as a part-time worker. In 1997 the 52-week rule replaced a 26-week requirement, and the 34-week rule replaced a 17-week requirement. Those who do not qualify under these rules can apply for assistance benefits (*bistandshjælp*).

Unemployment benefit levels since the 1960s have amounted to a maximum of 90 percent of average earnings in the previous three months, with a maximum cash limit (set at 2,625 kroner per week in 1997). Self-employed people and wage earners with three years of full employment before they became unemployed always get a minimum benefit of at least 82 percent of the highest welfare rate. If one is insured as a full-time worker but works less than the 37-hour full week, a supplementary payment is made, provided that the employer certifies that the employee may leave without notice to move to a full-time job.

Employers must pay an insured worker for the first two days of unemployment following dismissal or redundancy, etc. Claimants of unemployment benefit must be available for work, which means actively seeking work and taking courses which improve employment prospects. They are expected to accept "appropriate" work within their own trade, but after a year's unemployment they are expected to accept "reasonable" employment, i.e., work that they are physically capable of doing, regardless of educational or trade qualifications and within a wider geographical area. Refusal to accept a job offer without valid reason may incur exclusion ("quarantine") from entitlement to any benefit for a week. Leaving a job without acceptable reason or being fired for misconduct can be penalized with five weeks quarantine. Refusal to cooperate in an employment reactivation plan means that one only becomes entitled to benefits again by meeting the 52-week rule. Although the benefits are generous by comparison to many **European Union** countries, there are substantial penalties for failure to seek employment.

Workers' CONTRIBUTIONS were about 14 percent and employers' contributions were about 5 percent of the cost of unemployment benefits, and the state paid the remainder from tax revenue (1970-71 figures). Average annual unemployment among insured persons fell from 8.7 percent in 1950 to 4.2 percent in 1960 and 2.9 percent in 1970. From 1975 onward the average was nearer the 1980 figure of 11 percent. In 1990 the average was 8.8 percent. It was up to 10.3 percent in 1995 but was down below 8 percent in 1998 and falling steadily, a trend shared with Finland and Sweden but contrasting with Germany. AHT. *See also* **Elderly Care; Health Insurance; Pensions; Welfare State**.

UNIONIST PARTY (FAROESE) Sambandsflokkurin. Founded in 1906, this is a liberal party which pursues progressive policies on the basis of Christian cultural values. It wishes to retain the link of the **Faroe Islands** with the Danish kingdom and, within this, to work for the stable development of the Faroese people, constitutionally, economically, and culturally. In the 1995 Lagting it held eight seats. In the **Folketing** it was represented by its chairman, Edmund Joensen, who was attached to the **Liberal** (*Venstre*) parliamentary group. AHT

UNITED STATES OF AMERICA, DANISH RELATIONS WITH. After the Napoleonic Wars, Denmark's possessions in **Africa** rapidly declined in value and in 1818 the Danish Crown tried unsuccessfully to sell them to the USA as a home for freed slaves. The **Danish West Indies** also became a liability that the government offered to sell to the US. A treaty was concluded in 1867 but was not ratified by the Senate. A similar treaty in 1902, with a price of $5 million, also failed to be ratified, this time by the **Landsting,** but in 1917 after a **referendum** (*see* Appendix 5) the islands passed to US control for a price of $25 million.

The export of cheap US grain to Europe in the 1860s led to severe difficulties for Danish farmers and impelled them to change to livestock and dairy farming. The capture of **Slesvig** by Germany in 1864 brought the requirement of an oath of allegiance to the Prussian constitution, which many officials and potential conscripts were unwilling to swear. Many Danish speakers emigrated from Slesvig, some to Denmark but most to the USA. The US Homestead Act of 1862 provided an attractive alternative to the discouraging tasks of trying to farm the **heath** land of western **Jutland,** or of finding work in the towns where as many as one-third were unemployed. Between 1866 and 1900 172,000 Danes emigrated, about one in ten of the **population.** *See* Appendix 7.

Emigration also gave the conservative Danish regime a convenient answer to the challenges posed by the rising agricultural and **labor movements. Rasmus Sørensen** led the farmers' and smallholders' movement in the early 1840s, but emigrated to the US in 1852. As a result of activities for the **social democrats, Louis Pio** became hopelessly indebted and in 1877 was "encouraged" by the police and bribed with money from **Burmeister & Wain** to emigrate to the US, with more money if he took **Paul Geleff** and other labor leaders with him. Pio tried to found a socialist colony in Kansas, but it soon failed and he found work in Chicago.

An example of the success achieved by many Danish emigrants to the US is the career of **William S. Knudsen**: he emigrated in 1900, and by 1918-21 was production director for Ford Motors. He moved to General Motors and was president 1937-40, then was appointed by F.D. Roosevelt to administer the supply of war materiel during **World War II**.

In 1918 US president Wilson advocated self-determination as the principle on which Europe should be restructured after **World War I**. This opened the way for the 1920 referendum that returned north **Slesvig** to Denmark. But US rejection of membership of the League of Nations, which Denmark joined in 1920, doomed to failure the neutrality and collective security upon which Denmark built its foreign policy in the 1920s and 1930s, and when Germany occupied Denmark in 1940-45, there was no-one to come to Denmark's aid.

Outside occupied Denmark, many Danes, including most of the Danish merchant marine, became actively involved with the Allies. About 600 Danish seamen lost their lives and 60 percent of the ships were sunk, and another c. 1,000 Danes served in US or British forces. **Henrik Kaufmann**, the ambassador to Washington, stated that he no longer felt bound by the government in Copenhagen and agreed in 1941 to US bases in **Greenland**. The **Faroe Islands** were occupied by Britain in April 1940, while **Iceland** (Danish until 1944) was occupied initially by British and later by US forces.

After World War II **Marshall Plan Aid** from the US was spent mainly on the purchase of grain, animal feed, raw material, and machinery to reestablish Danish agriculture. Denmark joined in negotiations to form a Nordic Defense Pact, but after these failed, the country reluctantly joined **NATO** in 1949. Although willingly contributing a fair share to the NATO budget, nuclear weapons and foreign forces have always been excluded from Danish territory (except Greenland), and many Danes were skeptical of the wilder US claims of Soviet aggressive intentions. In the mid-1980s the **Schlüter government** was repeatedly required by a Folketing majority to enter reservations ("footnotes") to NATO policies. Denmark also differs from the US in its development aid policy: while the US has been minimalist, Denmark has increased its aid to over one percent of gross national product.

Danish ideas on social reform have won some American interest. The writer and photographer **Jacob A. Riis** wrote police reports for the New York papers, illustrated with his own photographs of the city's poor in 1877-99, and tried to win support for social reforms with his books and slide shows. In 1901 he opened a house for the homeless in New York. This work led Theodore Roosevelt, then New York governor, to name him "New York's most useful citizen." In Denmark in 1933 the social reforms were passed which laid the foundations of the **welfare** state. The resources to implement these fully only became available after World War II, but the commitment did much to advance Danish social solidarity in the 1930s, when economic depression in the United Kingdom and the US was highly divisive. The Danish welfare model was sometimes the inspiration for those who sought alternative policies. Conversely, the ideas of a free economy and a single land-tax, propounded by the American economist Henry George, impressed **J.L. Bjørner** and his wife Signe, who co-founder the **Justice Party** in 1919.

Danish **design** and production attracted American attention, as a few of many examples will show. **Thomas Barfoed Thrige** worked for a time in Thomas Edison's laboratory before returning to Denmark in 1894 to produce electric motors and dynamos, and to pioneer electrification in Denmark. **Georg Jensen**'s success in the US was assured when Randolph Hearst bought his whole exhibit of silver at the San Francisco Exposition in 1915. In the mid-1950s a three-year tour of the US created a huge new market for the 'Danish Modern' style in furniture design. The ingenuity and primary colors of **Lego** sold well to American children, and the high quality of design of B&O hi-fi equipment sold well to their parents. (*See* **Bernhard Bang**.)

Experience in the **film industry** and the performing arts in Denmark has led to successful careers partly or wholly in America for performers such as the opera singer **Lauritz Melchior**, whose son Ib Melchior directed television shows for CBS and NBC, and became a Hollywood script-writer. **Victor Borge** developed a successful concert and radio career as a pianist and comic. **Aksel Schiøtz** sang *lieder* and opera roles before becoming a professor of music at universities in the USA and Canada in 1955-68. The ballet master **Flemming Flindt** introduced the American style of dance to Denmark, then spent much of his time in the 1980s and 1990s in the US. **J. F. Willumsen**'s travels in the United States inspired some of his painting. The artistic work by **Bjørn Wiinblad** in ceramics, silver, bronze, textiles, and graphics has been widely shown and sold in the US. *See also* **Methodism; Paludan, Jacob**. AHT

UNIVERSITIES *and* **HIGHER EDUCATION.** The University of Copenhagen was founded with papal agreement by **Christian I** in 1479 but it was closed at the time of the **Count's War** 1534-36 and achieved importance only after the **Reformation**: in 1569 a college (Kommunitetet) to maintain 100 students was endowed, but almost all read theology. The 1601 building was burned down in 1728 (*see also* **Round Tower**), when many priceless manuscripts were lost, but it was rebuilt in 1732. In 1736 a law examination was started as a training for civil servants, who previously had been sent abroad to study by their noble parents. A new charter in 1788 finally established its educational purpose, expanded the staff, and introduced final written examinations. In the 1820s an annual entry of 100-200 students read theology, classics, law, or medicine. From the mid-19th century the university was maintained by the state. The university has faculties of theology, medicine, arts, science, and social science, the latter including law, political science, and sociology/anthropology. Some of its c. 150 departments or institutes are still located in the city center, but many are housed on a campus in Amager. Copenhagen University library has merged with the Royal Library. The national hospital (Rigshospitalet) is used, with others, for clinical teaching. Commercial education is provided by the Copenhagen Business School (Københavns Handelshøjskolen), in impressive buildings designed by Henning Larsen, and by Niels **Brock** College.

Aarhus University in **Århus** began teaching in 1928 but only became a state university in 1970. It is housed in buildings designed by **Kay Fisker** in University Park in the north of the city and has a faculty structure similar to Copenhagen's but is distinctive in awarding degrees of *cand. oecon.* in economics and *cand. scient. pol.* in political science. The State Library (Statsbiblioteket) on the same site also serves as the university library. Although not part of the university, its staff also teach at the nearby Danish College of Nurse Education (Danmarks Sygeplejerskehøjskole), the Institute of Home Economics (Specialkursus i Husholdning), the Danish College of Journalism (Danmarks Journalisthøjskole), the Occupational and Physiotherapy School (Institut for Terapiassistenter), and the School of Social Work (Den sociale Højskole i Aarhus).

Universities were founded in **Odense** in 1966 and in **Ålborg** a decade later. **Roskilde** Universitetscenter (RUC) was founded in 1972 but was soon charged with being one-sidedly left-wing in its teaching. It came close to closure under **Conservative** pressure and only survived when in 1975 the education minister, **Ritt Bjerregaard** imposed an external rectorate. There is also a university in **Greenland**. A responsibility of the Ministry of Education, the universities have extensive self-government. Until the 1960s they were ruled by the professors, but since the protests of 1968 students have been represented on the management committees.

The Danish *candidatus* degree requires a minimum of six years of study and a substantial thesis. It is broadly equivalent in the UK or US systems to B.A. plus M.A. or to B.Sc. plus M.Sc. Its possessor is usually qualified to practice the relevant profession. The qualification is placed before the name, e.g., *cand. jur.* Hans Jensen (a lawyer); *professor, cand. scient pol.* Mogens Pedersen (a professor of political science). Students use *stud. jur., stud. med.*, etc. A bachelor's degree may be gained after three years of study but is treated as an interim award. The degree of *licenciatus* is an advanced postgraduate degree approximately equivalent to Ph.D. in the UK or the US. This degree can be obtained in all faculties. The Danish doctorate degree requires many years of preparation and research and is obtained by writing a thesis, which is judged by an expert committee, published, and publicly defended. A graduate in any faculty may be admitted to study for *dr. phil.*, which is awarded by both Arts and Science Faculties. Other faculties award the degrees of *dr. theol.* (Theology), *dr. jur.* (Law), *dr. polit.* (Social Science), *dr. scient. soc.* (Sociology), or *dr. med.* (Medicine). Holders of a doctorate have the right to lecture in their subject at the university. See also *exam., mag.*, and other degree titles in the List of Abbreviations.

In 1829 a polytechnic, the Polyteknisk Læreanstalt, was founded on the initiative of the scientist **H.C. Ørsted**, initially offering two-year courses in mechanics and "applied natural sciences." By 1857 it was educating engineers and had opened its doors to women, as had the veterinary and agricultural college (Den Kongelige Veterinær- og Landbohøjskole), founded in 1856. The latter is housed in Frederiksberg, close to the center of **Copenhagen.** The polytechnic moved to Lyngby, to the north of the capital, and became Danmarks Tekniske Universitet (DTU) in 1995. In 1830 the Royal Military High School for officers was founded to give a science-based extension to the education provided by the Cadet Academy. The college of pharmacy, founded in 1892, in 1941 became the Royal Danish School of Pharmacy (Danmarks Farmaceutiske Højskole). The Royal Dental College (Danmarks Tandlægehøjskole) also dates from 1941. A second dental college was founded in 1959 in Århus.

In 1883 radical staff and students founded Studentersamfundets Arbejderoplysning to bring together the university and the rising labor movement, leading to the start of *Folkeuniversitet* in 1898. The labor movement founded its own high school in Esbjerg in 1909 and a counterpart in Copenhagen the following year, and the work of widening access to education was continued when *Arbejdernes Oplysningsforbund* (AOF), the workers' educational association, was started in 1923-4. AHT. *See also* **Education, Folk High Schools**.

URANIBORG *see* **BRAHE, TYCHO; VEN**

UTZON, JØRN (1918-). Architect. He was educated at the **Academy of Art** in **Copenhagen**, and inspired by the organic architectural influences of the Finn Alvar Aalto and the American Frank Lloyd Wright. He developed one of the most original talents in 20th-century Danish architecture, and pioneered the open-plan family home with his own house in Hellebæk in 1952. He gained world renown when he won the international competition for Sydney Opera House, built under his supervision 1959-66 and completed by others in 1973. His other designs include the Kingo houses in **Elsinore** (Helsingør, 1958-59), the collective Terraces housing in Fredensborg (1962-63), and Bagsværd Church (1976). His design for the Art Museum in Silkeborg also won a prize. AHT

- V -

VALDEMAR I "THE GREAT" (1131-1182). King of Denmark 1157-1182, son of **Knud Lavard** and his wife Ingeborg. He married Sophie of Novgorod. Their two sons became **Knud IV** and **Valdemar II**. With the kingdom divided between **Knud III Magnusen**, king of **Jutland** and **Funen**, and **Sven III Grathe**, king of the regions east of the Great Belt, during a reconciliation ceremony in **Roskilde** Knud was murdered. Valdemar was wounded, escaped, and aroused the Jutlanders. Valdemar's victory at **Grathe Hede** united the kingdom and began the golden age of the Valdemars. Danish power was extended along the Baltic coast and the Jutland Code was enacted, with its introduction by Bishop Gunner of **Viborg** beginning "With law shall a land be built." Valdemar ensured the appointment as Bishop of Roskilde of his foster-brother **Absalon**, who was his chief advisor throughout his reign. Under Valdemar the Slavic **Wends** were defeated and the southern border was fortified by reinforcing the old **Danevirke** line, a brick-built section of four km that became known as Valdemar's Wall, which helped to exclude German incursions into Denmark. AHT. See also **Saxo Grammaticus**.

VALDEMAR II "THE VICTORIOUS" (Sejr) (1170-1241). King of Denmark 1202-41 in succession to his elder brother **Knud IV**; his second marriage was to Berengaria of Portugal, and their children included the future kings **Erik IV**, **Abel**, and **Christoffer I**. As Duke of **Slesvig** he conquered **Holsten** in 1201, and Hamburg and **Lübeck** the following year. His influence extended southward to the river Elbe and eastward to the Oder and the Vistula. With papal blessing he partially conquered and Christianized Estonia in 1219. The Danish flag, **Dannebrog**, dates from then, and the name of the Estonian capital, Tallinn, derives from "Danish Castle." These conquests secured Danish trading interests right along the southern Baltic coastal territories. While hunting, Valdemar and his eldest son were captured by Count Heinrich of Schwerin and held to ransom, a widely condemned act of treachery. Denmark remained peaceful during his capture and the large ransom was raised. On his release Valdemar II led a large army against the north German forces. But due to the treachery of the **Ditmarshers** he was defeated in 1227 at the battle of Bornhöved. Although losing an eye and thousands of followers, he retained part of Estonia and control of the Baltic trade. As a result Denmark remained the strongest power in the Baltic throughout the Middle Ages. In his later years Valdemar II established an ordered government through a well-organized royal Chancelry, and his court roll is a valuable record of the condition of his kingdom. He held court assemblies (**Danehof**) to which nobles and clergy were called, where laws were promulgated and judgments issued, strengthening national unity at the expense of the provincial assemblies *(ting)*. He gave his sons feudal dukedoms in the border regions to secure strong local rule and protection from attacks from the south. AHT

VALDEMAR (III) ABELSEN (c. 1238-1257) was King **Abel's** eldest son by Mechtilde of **Holsten**. When his father fell in a military expedition against the Frisians he was imprisoned by the archbishop of Cologne (Köln), who wanted him ransomed by Abel. The usual rule of succession was therefore broken when instead the third son of Valdemar Sejr and Berengaria let himself be acclaimed King **Christoffer I**. The political price for agreement to this was that much power passed to the **Danehof**, an assembly of the spiritual and secular leaders of the kingdom, which met regularly during the

1250s. Nevertheless Christoffer excluded Valdemar Abelsen by securing the succession for his own five-year-old son Erik, later **Erik V**. AHT

VALDEMAR III (c. 1315-1364). King of Denmark 1326-1330, interrupting **Christoffer II**'s reign. The son of Duke Erik II of **Slesvig** and great grandson of King **Abel**, he ascended the throne at the age of 12 in a deal made by his patron Gert III Count of **Holsten**, who held effective power as regent. With a large army Gert conquered **Jutland** and **Funen** and gained the support of leading landowners. Christoffer's defense failed and he left for Germany with the recently gathered taxes to raise an army, with help from the Duke of Mecklenburg, but soon the money ran out, and the country was divided between the unpopular Holsten nobility. In 1330 Gert reached an agreement with Christoffer which restored him to the throne. Valdemar was forced to abdicate but regained the dukedom of Slesvig. AHT

VALDEMAR IV "ATTERDAG" (1320-1375). King of Denmark 1340-75, son of **Christoffer II** and father of **Margrethe I**. After eight years without a king, he was installed with the support of Ludwig of Bavaria, in whose family he had grown up, and of **Lübeck**, as the **Hanseatic** towns felt the want of a king to control the large **Scania** market and protect their trade from attack from the Danish coastal castles. But in Denmark he was welcomed as a liberator and with popular support eliminated **Holsten** influence and recovered lost lands. He built some 50 castles, compelling lords of manors to supply the labor to do so, and replacing vassals, who had hereditary title, with stewards, who could be dismissed at will. An energetic monarch, Valdemar also encouraged the building of watermills. His attempt to limit **Hanseatic** influence led to defeat, the loss of revenues from Scania, and rebellion in **Jutland**, which he quelled. An attempt to recover **Slesvig** also met failure. *See also* **Henning Podebusk**. AHT

VALKENDORF, CHRISTOFFER (1525-1601). Politician. He entered the king's service in 1553, holding posts as vassal (*lensmand*) of **Iceland** in 1569-70 and of Gotland in 1571-73. In 1574-84 he was master of finances (*rentemester*) and from 1576 was a member of the council of state. In 1588-1590 he was a member of the administration during King **Christian IV**'s minority. In 1589 he had the **Faroe Island** freebooter Mogens Heinesen condemned to death and executed, although the judgment was set aside by the council of **nobility** in 1590. **Christian IV** appointed him Chancellor of the Realm (*rigshofmester*) in 1596. AHT

VEDEL, AAGE HELGESEN (1894-1981). Naval officer, and son of the director of the Naval Dockyard. He was appointed vice admiral and chief of the naval staff in 1941. With Denmark occupied by German forces, on 29 August 1943 he gave the order to sink the Danish fleet, then worked with the **Resistance** movement. After **World War II** he saw to the revival of the **navy** and retired in 1958. AHT

VEDEL, ANDERS SØRENSEN (1542-1616). Historian. Born in Vejle, he went to school in Ribe, where he met the future bishop, **Hans Tausen**. He traveled abroad as tutor with the astronomer **Tycho Brahe** before being appointed court chaplain to King **Frederik II**. The historian **Arild Huitfeldt** was one of those who persuaded Vedel of the need for a better translation into Danish of the Latin history of Denmark by **Saxo Grammaticus**. In 1575 Vedel produced a "translation" which was in fact a rewriting in simple prose. In 1581 Vedel was appointed Historiographer Royal and began a continuation of **Saxo**'s work. But so thorough was he that in 15 years he got no further than the first book, and the task was given to professor Niels Krag. As important as his historical writings was the collection of Danish folk songs which he produced at the behest of the queen in 1591 (republished in 1926-1927). SPO

VEDEL, PETER (1823-1911). Civil servant. He was professor of law at Copenhagen University 1852-1857 before a career in the foreign ministry, of which he was director 1864-1899. He is considered the chief proponent of Denmark's policy of neutrality from 1866 onward (*see* **Slesvig-Holsten**). AHT

VEN (Hven), an island in the **Sound** 8 km (5 miles) off the **Zealand** shore, granted by **Frederik II** to **Tycho Brahe** as the base for his observatory. For more than two decades this was the most important center for the study of **astronomy** in the Western world. The islanders accused Brahe of neglecting his estate, harrassing the islanders, and "living in sin with a woman who was not a noble." The young King **Christian IV** disapproved and Brahe left for Prague. The island was the scene of a naval battle in 1700, providing shelter for the English and Dutch fleet which supported the transfer of Swedish forces under the 18-year-old Karl XII from **Scania** to Zealand, forcing **Frederik IV** to recognize and respect the rights of the duke of Gottorp. The island is now Swedish. AHT

VENSTRE *see* **LIBERAL PARTY**

VIBORG is an administrative center and market town in northern **Jutland** with a population of 29,455 (1990). Its name derives from *Vibjerg*, sacred hill. It lies beside a lake at the meeting-place of roads from all parts of Jutland, and was an important place of pagan worship before, in 1065, it became the seat of a bishop, with the foundation of a cathedral following c. 1130 at the initiative of Bishop Eskil. Here national assemblies were held, laws were issued, and all the kings from **Knud** in 1027 to **Christian V** in 1655 were crowned. By the **Viking** period it was a notable market, and the first Danish coins were struck here in the reign of **Knud the Great**. The 12th century charter was renewed by **Christoffer III** in 1440. Viborg was among the first places affected by the **Reformation**: in 1523 the future King **Frederik I** welcomed the new faith and received the homage of **Jutland**. **Hans Tausen** preached Martin Luther's protestantism here, eight years before Denmark officially converted from Roman Catholicism, and he obtained the dissolution of the six local monasteries and the destruction of 10 of the 12 ancient churches.

The largest town in Jutland until the mid-17th century, it then declined, suffering successive fires, the worst in 1726 when most of the old buildings were lost. The cathedral was later rebuilt in baroque style and its interior decorated in 1901-13 with vast fresco paintings by **Joakim Skovgaard**. In 1834 **Frederik VI** established a **consultative assembly** in Viborg, with another in **Roskilde** for the Danish islands, to recommend revisions of the 1660 constitution. Its economy revived as the **Heath Society** improved the surrounding heathland in the last third of the 19th century. Since 1919 the city has been the seat of the *Vestre Landsret*, the High Court for Jutland. The **Greenland** explorer **Ludvig Mylius-Erichsen** (1872-1907) was born in Viborg, and the **Nobel Prize**-winning author **Johannes V. Jensen** attended the Latin School in 1891-1893 and began his medical studies here. AHT

VIKINGS. The Viking era runs from the early 9th century to the mid-10th century, during which Norsemen (or Normans) plied the coastal waters of Europe in their open, square-rigged ships and landed as buccaneers, traders, or colonizers.

The first recorded Viking raid was made on Lindisfarne Monastery, on an island off northeast England in 793, contributing to the destructive Viking reputation. The major trading town of Dorestad in Friesland was pillaged several times, as were Rouen and Paris in France: the latter was devastated on 28 March 845 and a vast ransom of 7,000 pounds of silver was exacted. The 9th century raids extended along the west European coast as far south as the Mediterranean.

The Vikings were impelled partly by the technical superiority of their navigation and partly by a northward shift of trade patterns between Byzantium and western Europe following the Arab advance into the Mediterranean. Norwegians headed to Scotland, Ireland, the **Faroe Islands, Iceland, Greenland**, and on to Vinland in North America. Swedes settled the southern Baltic and traveled along the Russian rivers to the Caspian and Black Seas. The Danes followed the west European coast to Normandy and east England. As Normans they won the Battle of Hastings in 1066. During the era Denmark developed from an almost unknown heathen region to a well-defined kingdom within Christendom.

Around 987, Gorm's son **Harald** was ousted from the throne by his son **Svend I Forkbeard**. In 1013 he conquered England, with its lucrative tax revenue from the Danegeld, but he died the following year. **Harald II** held the Danish throne for four years, but then Svend I's son **Knud the Great** held the thrones of both England and Denmark. His domain included all of England, Scotland (except the west Highlands), Denmark (including Slesvig), Norway, and the western and southern Swedish coast east of Karlskrona.

There were three classes in Viking society: the warrior elite, free farmers, and thralls without legal rights. They lived mainly in farm-based villages, but Ribe and Hedeby (**Slesvig**, founded in 808 by **Godfred**) developed as important towns, with the ramparts of the **Danevirke** as a defense against invasion into **Jutland** from the south. Other Danish towns were founded in the AD mid-1000s. Although missionaries had been attempting for some 200 years to convert the Danes, it was during the reign of King **Gorm the Old** that the **religion** of the Norse gods was replaced by Christianity.

For the tourist, the most interesting Viking sites include the **Trelleborg** fort, the **Roskilde** ships, the **Jelling** rune-stones and the burial ground at Lindholm Høje, Nørresundby just north of **Ålborg**. A museum of the Viking era and the Middle Ages opened in Ribe in 1995. AHT

VILHELM (c. 1127-1203). Abbot. Possibly from a noble French family, he studied in Paris where he met **Absalon**, who in c. 1165 called him to Denmark to reform the Augustinian monastery at Eskilsø near **Roskilde**. About 1175 the monastery, one of the largest in the country, moved to North **Zealand** and took the name Æbleholt. Vilhelm also acted as a diplomat for the Danish king in France and to the pope. A keen proponent of monastic discipline, he was canonized in 1224 by Pope Honorius III. AHT

VIRGIN ISLANDS *see* **DANISH WEST INDIES**

VORNEDSKAB was a system under which a tenant farmer's son could be compelled to take over a tenancy, and therefore in effect a form of serfdom. By the beginning of the 15th century this had been widely adopted in the eastern Danish islands, where there had been a rapid increase in medium-sized farms rented from the **nobility**. In 1702 **Frederik IV** freed subjects born since his accession in 1699 from *vornedskab*, for which he was very popular. **Christian VI** compensated the nobles for his father's action. *See also* **peasant reforms**. AHT

- W -

WALTER, CAROLINE (1756-1826). Singer and the leading Danish actress of the 18th century. The daughter of an ensign, she was educated in the dance school of the Comedy House, where she took children's roles, going on to much admired **Ludvig Holberg** roles and as a soprano in works by **Johannes Ewald** and J.P.E. Hartmann. Involvement in intrigues meant that she had to continue her career in Sweden in 1781-1806. AHT

WEIGHTS AND MEASURES. Until the 17th century measures varied in different parts of the country, a situation which **Christian IV** tried to remedy in a statute of 1615, although uniformity throughout the country was not achieved until statutes of 1683 and 1698, under the leadership of **Ole Rømer**. The metric system was adopted in 1907 and is universal, though coloquially units such as *tomme, tønde land, pund* are still used.

The system used in the 18th and 19th centuries had an *alen* (= 62.8 cm) as the unit of **length**, with submultiples of a foot (*fod* = ½), a *kvarter* (= 15.7 cm), and an inch (*tomme*, 1/12 = 2.6 cm) and multiples of 3 (= 1 *favn*, 188 cm) and a mile (*mil* = 12,000 alen = 7.532 km = 4.68 UK miles).

The unit of **area** was 1 *tønde land* (= 14,000 *kvadratalen* = 5516 m^2 = 0.55 hectares); a *skæppe* (= 689.5 m^2) was 1/8 of this, a *fjerdingkar* (= 172.4 m^2) was ¼ of a *skæppe*, and an *album* was 1/3 of a *fjerdingkar* (= 57.5 m^2).

The unit of **volume** was a *pot* (= 1/32 cubic *fod* = c. 0.968 litre during 1698-1835, then 0.966 litre); a *pægl* was ¼ *pot* (= 0.24 litre), a *kande* was 2 *potter* and 1 *ottingkar korn* was 2¼ *pot* (=2.17 litre), a *fjerdinkar korn* was twice this and 1 *skæppe korn* was 18 *potter* (= 17.4 litre). A *balle* of herring was 28 *potter*. An *anker* of beer was 34 *potter*, and an *anker* of wine was officially 39 and actually 40 *potter* (= 38.7 litres). Rhine wine was measured by the *amme* (= 4 *ankre*), the *oksehoved* (oxhead = 6 *ankre* = 240 *potter* = 232.3 litre), the *pibe* (pipe = 3 *ammer* =480 *potter* = 464.6 litre), and the *fad* (vat = 960 *potter*). A *tønde* corn was 144 *potter* (= 139.4 litres).

The unit of **weight** was the Danish *pund* (pound = the weight of 1/62 cubic *fod* of water = 498.6 grams, from 1839 rounded to 500 grams). A *(bismer)mark* was ½ pund, a *lod* was 1/32 *pund* (= 15.6 gram), a *kvintin* was ¼ *lod* (= 3.9 grams), and an *ort* was ¼ *kvintin* (= 0.97 gram). 12 *pund* was a *bismerpund* (= 6 kg), 16 *pund* was a *lispund*, 100 *pund* was a *centner* (= 49.9 kg), 208 *pund* was 1 *tønde* (= 103.7 kg), 320 pund was a skippund. A *læst korn* was 42 *tønder* (= 4355.4 kg), and a *læst* of iron was 12 *skippund* (= 3840 *pund* = 3717.1 kg).

Units were subdivided by 2 (*hælvt*), 3 (*treding* or *tierts*), 4 (*fjerding*), and 8 (*otting*). Multiples were a *par* (2); a *læg* or *tal* of pigs (6); a *degger, deger, ring,* or *balle* of linen or canvas (10); a *dusin, tylvt, vrad* of pigs, *stod* of horses, *hjord* of cattle (12 = dozen); a *mantel* of leather or hides (15); a *snes* (20 = score); a *tømmer* or *zimmer* (40 hides or dried pike); a *skok* (60); an *ol* (80); a *gros* (gross, 144 = 12 *dusin*). AHT

WELFARE. Provision for those in need was made as early as the 1849 **constitution**, though more specific forms of support awaited enactment of the Poor Law and the Law on Support in Old Age, both of 1891: separating the two categories was an important advance. Many piecemeal changes followed until in 1933 **K.K. Steincke**, as social minister, negotiated the social reform which replaced all existing social legislation by four simplified and comprehensive laws covering general insurance, accident insurance, unemployment, and public welfare. In its time this was one of the most progressive sets of social welfare provision anywhere, and its aim to move from covering the bare necessities to maintaining the dignity of those in need was an advance of which Danes were justly proud.

The resources to implement it fully only became available after **World War II**, but the commitment did much to advance social solidarity in the 1930s, when economic depression in the United Kingdom and the United States of America was highly divisive. The 1953 constitution (paragraph 75) promised: "In order to advance the public weal efforts should be made to afford work to every able-bodied citizen on terms that will secure his existence. Any person unable to support himself or his dependants shall, where no other person is responsible for his or their maintenance, be entitled to receive public assistance, provided that he shall comply with the obligations imposed by statute in such respect."

In 1961 a Welfare Act replaced the 1933 Social Reform package. Finally the principle of poor-aid was replaced by the principle of insurance, with benefits paid as of right to those who needed them. Moreover, those needing assistance should not have their standard of living drastically reduced. When **local government** was restructured in 1970, so were social services: the sickness benefit societies were abolished in 1971, and health insurance became a local responsibility, with flat-rate contributions replaced by taxation proportional to income. Employers were expected to pay for the first five weeks of illness, with sickness benefits taking over after that. The principle of universality has been applied in all areas of social security except **unemployment** benefits, for which it remains necessary to be a member of one of the unemployment funds, most of which are run by **trade unions**.

The Social Security Act (bistandslov) was passed in order to simplify and rationalize social security provision and took effect in 1975. This located all social security services with the local (*kommune*) authority, giving an applicant a single focus for services, whether mother's help, or rehabilitation, or public assistance, or home help, or child and youth care: all are available from the *kommune*'s social and health administration, whether in the form of advice, counseling or financial assistance. From 1975 until 1987 the determining factor was the applicant's need, as estimated by a social worker. Since 1987 payments have been made according to entitlement, and at fixed rates. The underlying principle is that cash help is payable to a person who, because of a change in circumstances, is unable to obtain the necessities for his own or his family's support.

To a person with a child-care commitment the monthly payment in 1997 was 9,100 kroner, corresponding to 80 percent of the maximum unemployment payment. A person without a child-care commitment was paid 6,825 kroner, equivalent to 60 percent of the maximum unemployment payment. The 1996 Finance Act tightened the conditions for payments to people aged under 25: if they lived at home they were paid 2,144 kroner, or 4,384 kroner if they had left home. They would qualify for the full adult rate if for 18 continuous months they had earned a monthly income of at least 6,825 kroner. Previously the qualifying period was 12 months. Pregnant women regardless of age were paid the over-25 rate from the 12th week of pregnancy. These payments were intended to cover all fixed costs (including housing) and all personal necessities. A tax-free supplement was payable to people with difficulties because of high housing or care costs. Conversely, payments were reduced by the extent to which payments exceed 90 percent of the claimant's previous taxed income.

After 12 months on benefit, the maximum payable (regardless of previous income) was set at the maximum unemployment payment (of 11,376 kroner per month). Within three months of starting to receive benefit, the claimant's family finances are reviewed to see whether commitments can be reduced and to see whether non-cash assistance would be more appropriate, such as education, occupational training, or retraining. A person who has received benefit for at least three months may earn up to 2,000 kroner per month (before tax) in each of six months, without the benefit being reduced. AHT. *See also* **Education; Elderly Care; Employment Supplementary Pension; Health Insurance; Pensions; Unemployment.**

WENDS were the Slavic people of the Baltic coast near Stetin, to the south and east of Denmark. In 1043 they attacked Jutland but were thrown out by the Norwegian King Magnus. Still pagan, they used the period of division and conflict in Denmark to colonize Danish lands, plunder the coast, and take Danes captive. A consequence was that the defensive **round churches** of **Bornholm** were built. **Valdemar the Great** and Bishop **Absalon** led a successful conquest of the island of Rügen in 1169, capturing Arkona and requiring their king Tetislaw to submit to Valdemar. But further conquests were limited by the interests of the duke of Saxony and the king of Bavaria. In 1440 King **Christoffer** added *King of the Wends* to the titles of the Danish monarchs, symbolized by a heraldic wyvern (dragon) which remained in the royal coat of arms until it was simplified on the accession of **Margrethe II**. AHT

WESSEL, JOHAN HERMAN (1742-1785). Poet and dramatist. Born on the Oslofjord in Norway, Wessel entered the University of Copenhagen in 1761, but soon abandoned his studies to earn his living as a teacher of English and French. He became the central figure in a lively group of Norwegians living in the Danish capital. In 1772 these founded the Norske selskab (Norwegian Society), which was antipathetic to the preromanticism then beginning to appear in **Copenhagen**. In 1773 the play was produced which above all earned Wessel his place in Dano-Norwegian literature, the satirical *Kærlighed uden Strømper* (Love without Stockings), a parody of contemporary French tragedy or its Scandinavian imitators. His lifestyle and poverty brought ill-health. In 1778 he secured a post at the **Royal Theater** and continued to write, including two further satirical comedies and satirical verse. In 1784 he published his "Comical Tales" in verse as a poetical journal, but was never able to repeat his early success. SPO

WESSEL, PETER (1690-1720) *see* **TORDENSKIOLD, PETER**

WESSEL, THEODORE (1842-1905). Businessman. As a salesman he traveled to England and to the Paris Exhibition. In 1868 he started a business under the name of his partner, Emil Vett, which developed branches throughout Denmark, trading mainly in linen. From 1879 it took the name Magasin du Nord. In the 1890s this became the department store in Kongens Nytorv, **Copenhagen**, which was still in business a century later. AHT

WEST INDIA COMPANY *see* **DANISH WEST INDIES**

WEST NORDIC COUNCIL brings together six representatives each from **Iceland**, the **Faroe Islands**, and **Greenland**. It was started in 1985 to bring together parliamentarians for cooperative action on environmental, cultural, fisheries, communications, and trade policies. It meets annually. The leaders of the three delegations meet as a presidium four times each year, and a secretariat headed by Pàll Brynjarsson is based in Reykjavik. It is financed by contributions from the three governments and has an interest in the allocations of the West Nordic Fund, started in 1987 and with a capital in 1998 of 91 m. kroner, which is intended to develop competitive commerce in the region, and Nordic Atlantic Cooperation (NORA) financed by the **Nordic Council** of Ministers to support industrial and trade initiatives. AHT

WEYSE, CHRISTOPH ERNST FRIEDRICH (1774-1842). Composer. Born in Altona in the duchy of Holstein and educated as an organist and violinist, he held appointments as organist in **Copenhagen** churches, inlcuding Our Lady's. A noted pianist, he introduced Mozart's piano concertos to Copenhagen. He composed from the age of 10, and in 1819 he was appointed court composer. Weyse's works include seven symphonies (1795-99) reminiscent of

Haydn's, the operas *Sovedrikken* (1809, The Sleeping Draught) to a libretto by **Adam Oehlenschläger** and *Et eventyr i Rosenborg have* (1827, An Adventure in Rosenborg Garden), plus more than 30 cantatas. Many of his songs from his larger works attained lasting popularity, as did his settings of **B.H. Ingemann's** morning and evening songs (2 vols., 1837 and 1838), notable for their purity and simplicity. Inspired by the classical composers of Vienna, he is seen as the originator of a Danish national musical style. *See also* **Music**. AHT

WHOLESALE MERCHANTS, SOCIETY OF (Grosserer-Societetet) was founded by King **Christian VI** in 1742 to organize the leading **Copenhagen** merchants and shipowners, and to advise the government on matters of trade. At the same time, the monarchy made it attractive for the merchants to give up retail trade and concentrate on large-scale wholesale trade and trading voyages abroad. By raising their social status, the monarchy strengthened itself, both by developing the country's economy and by building up a prosperous and independent middle class. In 1857 the Society took over the **Exchange** and now performs the functions of the Copenhagen Chamber of Commerce. In pursuit of its object of protecting its members' interests in relations with the government and other organizations, the Society often works closely with the **Conservative People's Party**. It had about 2,500 members in 1977, including 164 trade associations. There is an executive committee, a representative council of 144 members, and a general assembly with final authority. A journal, *Handel* (Trade), is published. AHT

WICHFELD, MONICA (1894-1945). **Resistance** activist. From a Scottish-Irish landowning family, she and her Danish husband settled on Engerstofte estate in Denmark in 1941. She was the main resistance organizer in **Lolland**, sheltering British parachutists. In January 1944 she was imprisoned by the German authorities and the following month was the first woman during the occupation to be sentenced to death. The sentence was commuted to life imprisonment but she soon died in a German prison. AHT

WIED, GUSTAV (1858-1914). Author and one of the greatest humorists in Danish literature. Until 1889 he worked as a bookseller, teacher, and actor. His writing takes a superficially merry view, with underlying sharp satire and melancholy, of small town and country life, for example in *Adel, gejstlighed, borger og bonde* (1897, Nobility, Clergy, Citizens and Peasants), *Skærmydsler* (1901, Quarrels), and *Dansemus* (1901, Dancing Mice). He also wrote the novels *Slægten* (1898, Kin), *Livsens ondskab* (1899, Life's Malice), later dramatized as *Thummelumsen* (1901), *Knagsted* (1902), and *Fædrene æde druer* (1908, The Fathers Ate Grapes). AHT

WIEDWELT, JONHANNES (1731-1802) was the leading 18th century Danish neoclassical sculptor. He learned his trade in his father's workshop and at the **Academy of Art**. He was in France and Italy until 1758 and was appointed court sculptor 1759-1802, combining this with an appointment as professor at the Academy 1761-1802. His major works include **Christian VI**'s sarcophagus and **Frederik V**'s grave stone, both in **Roskilde** cathedral, sculptures for **Fredensborg Castle** garden, **Ludvig Holberg**'s tomb in **Sorø** church, and the figure of Faith on the freedom memorial commemorating the **peasant reforms**. AHT

WIEHE, MICHAEL (1820-1864). Actor. He entered the **Royal Theater** school in 1837, made his debut the same year, and remained at the Theater until 1864, except for 1855-1856 when he left in protest at **Johan Ludwig Heiberg**'s management. Considered the leading male actor of the Romantic period, he began as a lyrical lover, including roles opposite **Johanne Luise Heiberg**, but later took tragic character roles in plays by Shakespeare, Ludvig **Holberg**, Schiller, **Adam Oehlenschläger** and **Henrik Hertz**. AHT

WIETH, MOGENS (1919-1962). Actor. The son of actors, he trained at the **Royal Theatre** school and made his debut in 1939, remaining there in leading roles until 1955 except for periods in England in 1950-54 and 1962. AHT

WIINBLAD, BJØRN (1918-). Artist in ceramics, silver, bronze, textiles, and graphics. His work has been shown widely in Europe, in the United States of America first in 1954 and in Japan, Australia and Canada in 1968. He was attached to the US Embassy in Paris in 1947 as a poster designer. Later his posters illustrated **Tivoli** and many other activities in Denmark, as well as the Olympic Games for the Handicapped at Seoul, the New World Symphony, Miami, and the Royal Danish Ballet at the Metropolitan Opera House, all in 1988. His textile work produced the costumes for numerous ballets and stage presentations. His large ceramics and tapestries have been used for hotel decorations in Japan and the USA; for example, he designed the large Sheherazade tapestry for the Dallas World Trade Center. He was Man of the Year in New York in 1985 and was awarded the American-Scandinavian Foundation's Cultural Prize of 1995. AHT

WILLEMOES, PETER (1783-1808). Naval officer. In the Battle of Reden of 1801 he was in charge of a fleet battery and attacked the British flagship but had to retreat after heavy losses. He fell in a sea battle off Sjællands Odde between the Danish ship of the line *Prince Christian Frederik* and the British fleet, and came to be seen as a symbol of Danish national consciousness. AHT

WILLUMSEN, JENS FERDINAND (1863-1958). Painter and sculptor. The son of an innkeeper, he was a pupil at the **Academy of Art**, 1881-1885. He traveled in France, Norway, the United States, Italy, Spain, Greece, and North Africa during 1888-94 and 1901-16, then settled in the south of France. His creations, often monumental in scale, full of experimental color, symbolism, and movement, include the paintings *Jotunheim* (1892-93), *A Woman Mountaineer* (1904), *Sun and Youth* (1902-10), *Evening Soup* (1918), *Self-Portrait in a Painter's Blouse* (1933), and the trilogy *Titian Dying* (1933-38). As a sculptor he made the statue of **Hørup** in Kongens Have, **Copenhagen**, and *The Grand Relief* (1893-1928) for the **Willumsen Museum** in Frederikssund. His work also included graphics, ceramics, drawings, photographs, and architecture. AHT

WIMMER, LUDVIG FRANDS ADALBERT (1839-1920). Linguist. He graduated *magister* in Nordic languages in 1866 and *dr. phil.* in 1868 amd was professor of Nordic languages at Copenhagen University 1886-1910. His original research on runes, the script of the **Vikings**, was published as *De danske Runemindesmærker* (1893-1908, The Danish Memorial Runes). AHT

WINTHER, CHRISTIAN (1796-1876). Author. The son of a priest, he graduated *cand. theol.* in 1824, then taught, but later lived from his writing. A lyricist of nature and love in the Romantic style, he published volumes of poems in 1828 and 1832, and a collection, *Samlede digtninger I-IX* (1859-60, Collected Poems). He was also well known for his verse drama, *Hjortens flugt* (1855, The Flight of the Deer). AHT

WOMEN'S MOVEMENT. The modern women's movement grew out of the student movement of the late 1960s. One of its militant manifestations was the **Red-stockings**. During the 1970s the movement gained support from women in all sections of society. Demands for equal pay were accepted in principle by unions and employers, and in 1976 a law was passed to enforce equality, and the Equality Council (Ligestillingsrådet) was established. As an illustration of women's progress in public careers, in the **Folketing** elected in 1968 there were 18 women (10.1 percent) and one of the seventeen cabinet ministers was a woman. After the 1990 election 33.7 percent of Folketing members and four of the 19 ministers were women, while the 1994 and 1998 cabinets of 20 each had seven women ministers. Other manifestations of greater equality include a lower value set on marriage, evident in a high divorce rate (divorces as a proportion of marriages were 18 percent in the 1950s and 1960s but 43 per cent in the 1970s and 50 per cent in the 1980s) and an increase in "paperless marriages" — couples living in a lasting but undocumented relationship. A consequence has been that illigitemacy has lost its stigma. Women increasingly keep their surname on marriage, and by law children are called by their mother's name unless a specific request is made to give them the father's surname.

Activities in the Women's House (Kvinder Huset) in Copenhagen give a snapshot of the movement in 1998. They include: an InfoShop, covering benefits advice, recycling and clothes exchange. Re-Design gives motivation and training in design to unemployed women. An artists' cooperative produced a museum exhibition on the design of brassieres. FemØlejr continues the island summer camps for women, begun in the 1960s. Vagina Dentata militantly defends the rights of women and lesbians to decide for themselves, with the motto: 'We never gained anything by good behavior'. A women's choir sings ballads, rock, jazz and women's songs; a chamber orchestra gives concerts several times a year, and a group arranges women's dances. 'Dykes on Bikes' has a club night and a cycle tour each month. 'Brunhilde' gives a psychological counseling service. The group 'Thit & Ofte' (named after **Thit Jensen**) arranges a monthly debate or cultural event. AHT

WOMEN'S SUFFRAGE, NATIONAL ASSOCIATION (Landsforbundet for kvinders valgret) was founded in 1907. Its vigorous liberal campaign was also supported from the Right, because women were expected to be more conservative than men. Women over age 29 gained the vote in 1915 and the general voting age was reduced to 25 from the third election of 1920 (*see* **Franchise**). As a safeguard against the increased power of the poor, the **Liberals** and **Conservatives** brought in a rule that municipal tax could not be increased without the agreement of the Interior Ministry. AHT

WORKERS' FRONT, FAROESE (VERKMANNAFYLKINGIN) was a political party which contested its first election in 1994. In its view the old parties had lost all connection with or respect for **trade unions** and wage earners. It argued that the exceptional economic difficulties facing the Faroes required broad political cooperation to get their society functioning again, since social cohesion was threatened by current social changes. The party sought to secure the people's rights, economically, politically, socially and generally. Led by Óli Jacobsen, it obtained three seats in the Løgting, but lost representation in 1988. *See also* **Faroe Islands**. AHT

WORLD WAR I (1914-1918). At the beginning of the war, Denmark issued a declaration of neutrality, but Germany demanded that the Great Belt between the islands of **Zealand** and **Funen** should be mined to prevent British naval incursions into the Baltic. After securing sympathetic British assurances, the mining proceeded. To meet the internal economic situation, prices of essential goods were controlled and some rationed. In spite of these and similar measures, there was much speculation, most notoriously by the so-called "gulash barons" who made considerable profits by selling canned meat to Germany. Inflation was met in 1916 by supplementary payments to employees on fixed incomes, and Europe's first value-added tax was introduced to help pay for the additional expenses incurred as a result of the emergency. The opening in 1917 of unrestricted submarine warfare, which led to the loss of 180,000 tons of Danish shipping, worsened the economic situation; unemployment increased and with it social unrest. The latter grew in the early months of 1918, when syndicalists organized a series of strikes and demonstrations. The end of the war by German surrender in November raised the question of the future of **Slesvig**, lost by Denmark after the Second **Slesvig-Holsten** War. In accordance with the Treaty of Versailles (para. 109) a **referendum** was held there in 1920 which resulted in the return of the northern part of the province to Denmark. SPO. *See also* **Britain; Germany, Danish Relations with; Erik Scavenius; Slesvig-Holsten**.

WORLD WAR II (1939-1945). Thorvald **Stauning**'s foreign minister **V. Buhl** pursued a policy of neutrality during the 1930s, and there were repeated assurances from Germany of respect for that neutrality. Alone of the Nordic countries, Denmark signed a nonaggression pact with Germany in May 1939. The 1937 Defense Act allowed some modernization of the armed forces, but in April 1940 only 14,000 men were under arms. The **navy** had only two coastal defense vessels, built in 1906 and 1918, and the air forces, divided between **army** and navy, had about 50 aircraft, most obsolete. So when the German forces occupied Denmark on 9 April 1940 they caught the Danes by surprise and they could only resist for a few hours. The government ordered a cease-fire and, under protest, accepted German occupation of the country, but continued in office in an attempt to prevent German interference in Danish administration, justice, etc. Control of Danish territory, waters, and airspace was strategically necessary to operation Weserübung, the German invasion of Norway. Denmark provided a land route for forces and equipment to Norway and its agriculture was an additional source of food for Germany.

The opposition parties joined the cabinet to form a national government, on the condition that Thorvald Stauning acknowleged that it was his cabinet that had agreed to capitulate. **Eric Scavenius** became foreign minister and took the line that cooperation with the Germans was necessary to the extent that it kept the country's administration in Danish hands. The Germans stated that they would not interfere in Danish internal affairs, but then made repeated demands for military equipment, the removal of ministers they found awkward, etc. About 100,000 Danish workers were encouraged to go to Germany, rather than be conscripted. After the German invasion of the USSR in June 1941 the **Communist Party** was banned. In November Denmark was obliged to join the Anti-Comintern Pact, but only did so on condition that in no circumstances would Denmark be drawn into the German-Soviet war. In 1942 the German ambassador was recalled and replaced by a Nazi official, Werner Best, with a more conciliatory policy than the "iron rule" which Hitler expected. Elections were held in March 1943 with a turnout of 89.5 percent, the highest ever, and 95 percent of the votes were for parties in the cabinet. The **Danish National Socialist** (Nazi) vote was only 2.2 per cent.

Resistance activity increased sharply, in frequency and effectiveness. Joachim von Ribbentrop ordered Best to make the Danish government declare a state of emergency, and on 28 August the Danish government was faced with an ultimatum with demands including the death penalty for sabotage, the declaration of martial law, a total ban on strikes and meetings, and direct German **censorship**. But instead it resigned and the country was administered by Danish civil servants led by Nils **Svenningsen** under German direction. The **Freedom Council** began to coordinate resistance groups such as BOPA (*see* **Communist Party**) and *Holger Danske*. It also served as a link with the British Special Operations Executive (SOE) and organized an underground **press**. In October 1943 most Danish **Jews** were moved to safety in Sweden. German communications to Norway were sabotaged. In June 1944 there was a general strike in **Copenhagen** against German brutality, and resistance activity increased greatly thereafter.

Outside Denmark, many Danes became actively involved with the Allies. **Henrik Kaufmann**, the ambassador to Washington, agreed to US bases in **Greenland**. The **Faroe Islands** were occupied by Britain in April 1940, while Iceland was occupied initially by Britain and then by the United States of America. Much of the Danish merchant marine, some 200 ships totaling 1.1 million tons and with about 5,000 crew (more than 90 per cent of the total) joined the Allies and took part mainly in Atlantic and Arctic convoys. Some 600 Danish seamen lost their lives and 60 percent of the ships were sunk. About another 1,000 Danes served in US or British forces, including the Royal Navy, the Royal Air Force, and the Special Operations Executive, which trained people for the **resistance**.

In Sweden a Danish Brigade of 5,000 awaited a possible Allied invasion or a German capitulation. In the event, the latter came at

Lüneburg Heath on 4 May 1945 and included German forces in Denmark as well as Germany. The German commander on **Bornholm** refused to surrender to the Russians and the towns of Rønne and Neksø were bombed on 7 and 8 May by Soviet aircraft, with few casualties but much damage. Soviet warships arrived on 9 May, whereupon the Germans surrendered, but Soviet troops remained on the island until April 1946. The **resistance** movement, increasingly active from 1943, was important in transforming Denmark's status from collaborative neutral to de facto Ally, with important implications for United Nations membership and pation in Marshall Plan Aid. One of the tasks of the governments of **Vilhelm Buhl** and **Knud Kristensen** of 1945-47 was to deal with the 34, 000 collaborators who were arrested and tried under civil law. AHT. *See also* **Gørtz, Ebbe; Scavenius, Erik; Stauning, Th**.

WORM, OLE (1588-1654). Scientist and doctor. He lived abroad, attending various European universities during 1605-1613, and graduated *dr. med.* in Basel in 1611. In 1613 he was appointed a professor at Copenhagen University, becoming professor of medicine in 1624. He founded research in antiquities by securing an order in 1622 which required Danish and Norwegian bishops to collect artefacts. His special interest in runic inscriptions resulted in his book *Danicorum Monumentorum libri sex* (1643-1651, Monuments of the Danes in Six Volumes), a complete record of the then known runic inscriptions. In 1641 he wrote a little book on the golden horn of **Gallehus**, found in 1639. He started an extensive collection of worldwide archaeological and ethnographic objects, which he described in his book *Museum Wormeanum* (1655). AHT

WORSAAE, JENS JACOB ASMUSSEN (1821-1885). Archaeologist. As a boy he took part in excavations and later worked as an assistant at the Ancient Nordic Museum. In 1847 he was appointed Inspector of Ancient Monuments for Denmark and in 1866 Director of the Ancient Nordic Museum, the Ethnographic Museum, and the Royal Chronological Collection in **Rosenborg Castle**. His books include *Prehistoric Denmark Illustrated by Ancient Objects and Grave Mounds* (1843), *Relics of the Danes and Northmen in England, Scotland and Ireland* (1851), and *Nordic Prehistory from Contemporary Monuments* (1881). He pioneered empirical comparative archaeology and was the founder of scientific archaeology in Denmark. In 1874-75 he was minister of culture in C.A. Fonnesbech's cabinet of the Right. *See* **Archaeology**. AHT

- Z -

ZAHLE, CARL THEODORE (1866-1946). Lawyer and politician. The son of a shoemaker, he graduated *cand. jur.* in 1890 and was elected to the **Folketing** 1895-1928 and then elected by the Folketing to the **Landsting** 1928-1939, serving as its chairman 1936-1939. Initially a member of the Reform **Liberals** (Venstre reformparti), he was a co-founder in 1905 of the **Radical Liberals**, of which he was chairman except while he was a minister. He was prime minister and minister of justice 1909-1910 and again in 1913-1920. When the **Danish West Indies** were sold to the United States of America in 1916 three "control" ministers were brought into the cabinet, including the **Social Democrat** leader **Thorvald Stauning**, which strengthened cooperation between the two parties. A revised constitution was passed in 1916 with broad parliamentary support, and in 1918 the law to give Iceland home rule. His cabinet wanted to reclaim all the land in Southern Jutland/ North Slesvig lost in the Second **Slesvig-Holstein** War, but encountered some popular opposition to this, and the issue was settled by referendum in 1920. In March 1920 the king asked Zahle to call an election, but when Zahle declined until the new proportional electoral rules were extended to rural areas, the king dismissed him, provoking the **Easter Crisis**. In 1923-1929 he was director of a credit association (savings and loan society). As justice minister in Stauning's 1929-1935 government he passed the penal code of 1930 which extensively reformed the system of justice. AHT

ZAHLE, NATALIE (1827-1913). Educator. The daughter of a priest, she taught from 1843. In 1851 she opened a private teachers college and in 1860 a college for peasant women teachers which became officially recognized in 1894. She introduced such subjects as housekeeping, physiology, health education, and gymnastics and is considered a pioneer throughout the Nordic region for the education of women and especially of teachers. AHT

ZAHRTMANN, KRISTIAN (1843-1917). Painter. He was educated at the **Academy of Art** 1864-68 and traveled in Italy and Greece in 1875-78, 1883-84 and 1888-89. His narrative and psychological style is evident especially in his many historical paintings, which include *Scenes from Christian VII's Court* (1873 and 1881), *The Death of Queen Sophie Amalie* (1882), and Italian scenes such as *A Sabine Woman Nursing Her Child* (1877), and *Lovisa* (1912). He is best known for a series of paintings of **Christian IV**'s daughter *Leonora Christina* (1870-97). AHT

ZEALAND (Sjælland) is the large island of eastern Denmark, just west of southern Sweden. Its 1991 population with adjacent small islands was 2,138,278. It is dominated economically by **Copenhagen**, in the north-east of the island, with its major airport at Kastrup on the island of Amager just to the east. The fixed-link bridge and tunnel over the **Sound** (Øresund) to Sweden (**Scania**) opens in 2000 and is stimulating the new Ørestad urban development on Amager. A **bridge** over the Great Belt to the west connects it to **Funen**, while a bridge over Storstrømmen to **Falster** carries traffic south over **Lolland** to ferries across the Femer Belt to Germany. In addition to Copenhagen, there are county (amt) administrations for Frederiksborg and West Zealand. Southern Zealand is administered with the islands of **Lolland**, **Falster**, and **Møn** as Storstrøms Amt. **Elsinore** (Helsingør), **Roskilde**, Slagelse, and Næstved are other important towns. AHT

THE BIBLIOGRAPHY

This bibliography includes principally English-language publications selected to give readers the information necessary to follow up a topic of interest. Most were published since 1965, though some earlier items of lasting interest are also included.

The **Danish Cultural Institute** was formerly Det danske Selskab.

I.	GENERAL	IV.	HISTORY
1.	Bibliographies and Dictionaries	1.	General
2.	General Information and Interdisciplinary Studies	2.	Prehistory
		3.	Viking and Medieval
3.	Guides and Yearbooks	4.	16th Century
4.	Statistical Abstracts	5.	17th Century
5.	Geography, Travel and Description, Environment	6.	18th Century
		7.	19th Century
		8.	20th Century
II.	CULTURE	V.	LAW
1.	General		
2.	Architecture	VI.	POLITICS
3.	Painting and Sculpture		
4.	Crafts and Design	VII.	SCIENCE
5.	Language and Linguistics		
6.	Literature	VIII.	SOCIETY
7.	Music, Dance, Theater, Film	1.	Demography
8.	Philosophy	2.	Emigration
		3.	Education
III.	ECONOMICS	4.	Religion
1.	General	5.	Sociology
2.	Agriculture		

I. GENERAL

1. Bibliographies and Dictionaries

Alenius, Marianne (ed), *The Royal Danish Library, Today and in the Future.* Copenhagen: Museum Tusculanum Press, 1990.

Anderson, Ralph J.B., *Anglo-Scandinavian Law Dictionary of Legal Terms Used in Professional and Commercial Practice.* Oslo: Universitetsforlaget, 1977.

Axelsen, Jens (comp), *Dansk-engelsk Ordbog.* 9th ed. Copenhagen: Gyldendal, 1984.

Axelsen, Jens (comp), *Engelsk-dansk Ordbog.* 10th ed. Copenhagen: Gyldendal, 1979.

Becker-Christensen, Christian, *Politikens forkortelsesordbog* [dictionary of abbreviations]. Copenhagen: Politiken, 1991.

Bredsdorff, Elias, *Danish Literature in English Translation: A Bibliography.* Copenhagen: Munksgaard, 1950.

Bruun, Henry, *Dansk historisk bibliografi 1913-1942.* 3 vols. Copenhagen: Den danske historiske forening, 1966-8.

Danica Polyglotta. Repertoire bibliographique des ouvrages, études, articles etc. en languages étrangères parus en Danemark de 1901-1944. 3 vols., 1947-50. Copenhagen: Royal Library.

Danica Polyglotta. Repertoire bibliographique annuel des ouvrages, articles, resumés etc. en languages étrangères parus en Danemark. 1946-. Copenhagen: Royal Library.

Dania Polyglotta: Literature on Denmark in Languages Other Than Danish and Books of Danish Interest Published Abroad. Copenhagen: Royal Library, 1969- annual.

Danish Data Archive 1993. Odense University Press, 1993.

Danish Ecological Abstracts, edited by Hans-Henrik Schierup & Vagn Juhl Larsen. Copenhagen: National Agency for the Protection of Nature, Monuments and Sites. 1981- annual.

Danish Family Studies of Medical Genetic Disorders 1927-1980, an Annotated Bibliography, edited by Bodil Broeng-Nielsen et al. Odense: Odense University Press, 1982.

Danish Literature in English Translation: A Bibliography. Copenhagen: The Royal Library, 1981.

Dansk Sprognævn, *Retskrivningsordbogen.* [Correct Danish]. Copenhagen: Gyldendal, 1989.

Den Danske Historiske Forening, *Dansk historisk bibliografi 1943-1947.* Copenhagen: 1956.

Denmark: Literature, Language, History, Society, Education, Arts: A Select Bibliography. Copenhagen: Royal Library, 1966.

Dollerup, Cay & Inge Padkær Nielsen, *Dansk Grundbog. Basic Disctionary of Danish. Shortcut to the Danish Language.* Copenhagen: Høst & Søn, 1994.

Excerpta Historica Nordica. International Committee of Historical Sciences. 1955-.

GADS engelsk, engeslsk-dansk, dansk-engelsk ordbog. Copenhagen: G.E.C. Gads Forlag and Glasgow, William Collins Sons & Co Ltd, 1987.

Ginsburg, Ruth Bader, *A Selective Survey of English Language Studies on Scandinavian Law.* S.Hackensack: N.J.Rothmann, 1970.

Groennings, Sven, *Scandinavia in Social Science Literature: An English-Language Bibliography.* Bloomington: Indiana University Press, 1970.

Hansen, Peter Allan, *A Bibliography of Danish Contributions to Classical Scholarship from the Sixteenth Century to 1970.* Copenhagen: Rosenkilde & Bagger, 1977.

Haugen, Eva L., *A Bibliography of Scandinavian Dictionaries.* White Plains, New York: Kraus International Publications, 1985.

Henriksen, Liselotte, *Isak Dinesen: A Bibliography.* Copenhagen: Gyldendal, 1977.

Holtermann, Henrik (ed.), *Denmark in International Affairs: Publications in Languages Other than Danish 1965-1995.* Copenhagen: Danish Institute of International Affairs (DUPI)/Jurist- og Økonomforbundets Forlag, 1997.

Høsts engelsk-dansk og dansk-engelsk lommeordbog 6th ed. [pocket dictionary]. Copenhagen: Høst & Søn, 1978.

Ilsøe, Harald, *On Parchment, Paper and Palm-Leaves: Treasures of the Royal Library, Denmark: A Presentation in Pictures and Words on the Occasion of the 200th Anniversary of the Opening of the Library to the Public.* Copenhagen: Museum Tusculanum Press, 1993.

Iuul, Stig et al., *Scandinavian Legal Bibliography.* Stockholm: Almqvist & Wiksell, 1961.

Jacobsen, Henrik Galberg & Peter Stray Jørgensen, *Håndbog i Nudansk.* 3rd edition. Copenhagen: Politiken, 1996.

Jørgensen, Aage, *Contributions in Foreign Languages to Danish Literary History 1961-1981: A Bibliography.* Ballerup, Denmark: Bibliotekscentralens Forlag, 1982.

Kay, Ernest (ed.), *Dictionary of Scandinavian Biography*. Cambridge, England: International Biographical Centre, 1976.

Kvavik, Robert B., *Scandinavian Government and Politics: A Bibliography of Materials in English*. Minneapolis: University of Minnesota, 1984.

LaPointe, François (comp.), *Søren Kierkegaard and His Critics: An International Bibliography of Criticism*. Westport, Connecticut: Greenwood, 1980.

Lewkowicz, Mieczyslaw, *Holocaust Literature in Denmark, 1945-88*. Copenhagen: Museum Tusculanum Press, 1991.

Miller, Kenneth E. (comp.), *Denmark* (World Bibliographical Series). Oxford; Santa Barbara, California; Denver, Colorado: Clio Press, 1987.

Mitchell, P.M., *A Bibliographical Guide to Danish Literature*. Copenhagen: Munksgaard, 1951.

——, *A Bibliography of English Imprints of Denmark through 1900*. Lawrence: University of Kansas Library, 1960.

——, *A History of Danish Literature*. New York: Kraus-Thomson, 1971.

Munch-Petersen, Erland, *A Guide to Danish Bibliography*. Copenhagen, Royal School of Librarianship, 1965.

—— (ed.), *Guide to Nordic Bibliography*. Copenhagen: Nord, 1984.

Nordstrom, Byron J. (ed.), *Dictionary of Scandinavian History*. Westport and London: Greenwood Press, 1986.

Oakley, Stewart P., *Scandinavian History 1520-1970: A List of Books and Articles in English*. London: The Historical Association, 1984.

Politikens store ny NUDANSK ordbog, editor-in-chief: Christian Becker Christiansen. 2. vols. [In Danish only; includes new words and changed meanings]. Copenhagen: Politiken, 1997.

Possing, B. & B. Svindborg (eds.), *The Royal Library, Manuscript Department Acquisitions 1924-1987. Guide to Users*. 2 vols. Copenhagen: Museum Tusculanum Press, 1995.

Regional Problems and Policies in OECD Countries: vol 1, France, Italy, Ireland, Denmark, Sweden, and Japan. Paris: OECD, 1976.

Schroeder, Carol L., *A Bibliography of Danish Literature in English Translation 1950-1980 with a Selection of Books about Denmark*. Copenhagen: Det danske Selskab, 1982.

Skarsten, Trygve R., *The Scandinavian Reformation: A Bibliographical Guide*. St. Louis, Missouri: Center for Reformation Research, 1985.

US Bureau of the Census, *Bibliography of Social Science Periodicals and Monograph Series: Denmark, 1945-61*. Washington, DC: Government Printing Office, 1963.

US Department of the Army, *Scandinavia: A Bibliographic Survey of Literature*. Washington, DC: Government Printing Office, 1975.

Vexler, Robert I., *Scandinavia: A Chronology and Factbook, 1319-1974*. Dobbs Ferry, New York: Oceana, 1977.

Zuck, Virpi (ed.), *Dictionary of Scandinavian Literature*. Chicago and London: St. James Press, 1990.

2. General Information and Interdisciplinary Studies

Allardt, Erik, Nils Andrén, Erik J. Friis, Gylfi P. Gislasson, Sten Sparre Nilson, Henry Valen, Frantz Wendt, and Folmer Wisti, *Nordic Democracy: Ideas, Issues, and Institutions in Politics, Economy, Education, Social and Cultural Affairs of Denmark, Finland, Iceland, Norway and Sweden*. Copenhagen: Det danske Selskab, 1981.

Bure, Kristjan, *Greenland*. 3rd rev. ed. Copenhagen: Royal Danish Ministry of Foreign Affairs, 1961.

Connery, Donald S., *The Scandinavians*. New York: Simon & Schuster, 1966; London: Eyre and Spottiswoode, 1967.

Daedalus, vol. 13(1), The Nordic Enigma; vol. 13(2) Nordic Voices. Spring and Winter 1984.

Danish Ministry of Foreign Affairs, Royal. Press and Cultural Relations Department, *Denmark: An Official Handbook*. Ed. Bent Rying. 15th ed. Copenhagen: Krak, 1974.

Himmelstrup, Per (ed.), *Discover Denmark: On Denmark and the Danes, Past, Present and Future*. Copenhagen: Danish Cultural Institute/Systime, 1995.

Lauwerys, J.A. (ed.), *Scandinavian Democracy: Development of Democratic Thought and Institutions in Denmark, Norway and Sweden*. Copenhagen: Det danske Selskab, 1958.

Malmström, Vincent H, *Norden: Crossroads of Destiny*. Princeton, New Jersey: Van Nostrand, 1965.

Reddy, J. Prakash, *Danes are Like That*. Mørke, Denmark: Grevas, 1993.

Scott, Franklin D., *Scandinavia*. Cambridge, Massachusetts & London: Harvard University Press, 1975.

Spink, Reginald, *The Land and People of Denmark*. Rev. ed. London: Macmillan, 1959.

Strange, Morten, *Culture Shock! Denmark, a guide to customs and etiquette*. London: Kuperard, 1996.

Stubbekjær, Jens, *Facts about Denmark*. Copenhagen: Ministry of Foreign Affairs with Forlaget Aktuelle Bøger, 1992.

Thomasson, Eric, *Danish Quality Living*, Copenhagen: Forlaget Folia, 1985.

Vedel, P.V. (ed), *Hello Denmark*. Stout. 1993. [176 pages & 3 audiotapes].

Warburton, Ann, *Signposts to Denmark*. Copenhagen: Hernov, 1992

Williamson, Kenneth, *The Atlantic Islands: A Study of the Faroe Life and Scene*. 1st ed. London: Collins, 1948. Reprinted London: Routledge & Kegan Paul. New York: Fernhill House, 1970.

Wuorinen, John H, *Scandinavia*. Englewood Cliffs, New Jersey: Prentice-Hall, 1965.

3. Guides and Yearbooks

AA/Baedeker, Copenhagen. Stuttgart: Baedeker; London: Jarrold & Sons Ltd., Automobile Association, 1995.

Aistrup, I., *Denmark*. [74 pages of color photos]. Copenhagen: Høst, 1995.

Birkebæk, Frank, et al., (eds)., *Museumsguide Danmark: Dansk English Deutsch*. Viborg: Museumstjenesten, 1994.

Boesen, Gudmund, *Danish Museums*. Copenhagen: Committee for Danish Activities Abroad, 1966.

——, *Copenhagen*. Leipzig: Edition Leipzig, 1967.

Constance, P. & H., *The Visitor's Guide to Denmark*. Cincinnati Ohio: Moorland Publishing and Seven Hills Book Distributors, 1993.

Davidsen, L. (ed), *Welcome to Denmark*. Copenhagen: Dansk Flygtningehjælp (Danish Refugee Council), 1984.

Fodor's Scandinavia 97: The complete guide to denmark, Finland, Iceland, Norway, and Sweden, edited by Åke Gille. New York and London: Fodor's Travel Guides, 1996.

Hardy, Hathaway, "The collectors: The Danish royal family — a dynasty's treasures at Rosenborg Castle," *Architectural Digest* 41 (1): 62-69. 1985.

Himmelstrup, Per (ed.), *Discover Denmark: On Denmark and the Danes, Past, Present and Future*. Copenhagen: Den danske Selskab/Systime, 1992.

Jones, W. Glyn and Kirsten Gade (eds.), *Blue Guide Denmark*. London: A & C Black; New York: W.W. Norton, 1992.

Nelson, Nina, *Denmark*. London: Batsford, 1974.

Nye, D.E., *Denmark and the Danes*. [40 pages.] Copenhagen: Danish Society for the Advancement of Business Education, 1992.

Roussel, Aage (ed.), *The National Museum of Denmark*. Copenhagen, National Museum, 1957.

Samson, J. *Denmark*. London: Automobile Association, & Copenhagen: Gad. 1993.

Shirer, William L., *The Challenge of Scandinavia: Norway, Sweden, Denmark, and Finland in our Time*. London: Robert Hale, 1956.

Siegner, Otto, *Scandinavia: Denmark, Sweden, Norway*. New York, Scribner's, 1971.

Simpson, Colin, *The Viking Circle: Denmark, Greenland, Norway, Sweden, Finland*. New York: Fielding Publications, 1968.

Skaarup, Kirsten (trans from Danish by David Hohnen), *Danmark. De fire årstider (Denmark: The Four Seasons)*. Copenhagen: Høst & Søn, 1980.

Swaney, Deanna, *Iceland, Greenland and the Faroe Islands*. London: Lonely Planet, 1991

Taylor-Wilkie, Doreen (ed.), *Denmark* (Insight Guides). London: APA Publications (HK) Ltd, 1996.

Warner, Oliver, *A Journey to the Northern Capitals*. London: Allen & Unwin. 1968.

4. Statistical Abstracts

Statistisk Årbog [Statistical Yearbook. Subheadings in English.]. Copenhagen: Danmarks Statistik, annual.

Yearbook of Nordic Statistics 1995, vol. 33 (and other years), eds. Marianne Mørch and Harry de Shàrengrad. Copenhagen: Nordic Statistical Secretariat, 1995 and annually.

5. Geography, Travel and Description, Environment

Belloc, Hillaire, *Return to the Baltic* (illustrated by Edmund L. Warre). London: Constable, 1938.

Bure, Kristjan (ed.), *Greenland*. Ringkjøbing, Denmark: A. Rasmussen, for Royal Danish Ministry of Foreign Affairs, 1961.

Caie, Graham D. and Caie, Ann (trans.), *Funen: The Heart of Denmark*. Copenhagen: Det danske Selskab, 1980.

Church, R.J. Harrison et al., *An Advanced Geography of Northern and Western Europe*. London: Hulton, 1967.

Danish Physical Planning Acts:

vol. 1: National and Regional Planning Act for the Metropolitan Region. vol. 2: Municipal Planning Act. vol. 3: Urban and Rural Zones Act. Copenhagen: Ministry for the Environment and National Agency for Physical Planning, 1983.

Degn, Ole, *Denmark: Ribe 1500-1950* (Scandinavian Atlas of Historic Towns). Odense University Press, 1993.

Environment Denmark: Denmark's National Report to the United Nations on the Human Environment. Copenhagen: Royal Ministries of Foreign Affairs, Housing, Cultural Affairs and Environmental Protection, 1972.

Freuchen, Peter, ed. by Dagmar Freuchen, *The Peter Freuchen Reader*. New York: Julian Messner, 1965.

Fullerton, Brian, *Scandinavia: An Introductory Geography*. New York: Praeger, 1972.

—— and Richard Knowles, *Scandinavia* (Western Europe: Economic and Social Studies Series). London: Paul Chapman Publishing, 1991.

Gosse, Edmund, *Two Visits to Denmark, 1872, 1874*. London: J. Murray, 1911.

Greiffenberg, Tom (ed.), *Sustainability in the Arctic*. Aalborg University Press, 1993.

Humlum, Johannes and Knud Nygård (eds.), *Danmark Atlas*. Copenhagen: Gyldendal, 1976.

Jensen, C. Haagen, *The Law and Practice Relating to Pollution Control in Denmark*. London: Graham and Trotman for the Commission of the European Communities, 1976.

Kort over København og omegn (Map of Copenhagen and Surroundings). Copenhagen: Politiken, 1973.

Lyck, Lise, (ed), *Nordic Arctic Research on Contemporary Arctic Problems*. Aalborg University Press, 1992.

—— and P.O. Berg, *The Øresund Region building*. Copenhagen: New Social Science Monographs, Institute of Organization and Industrial Sociology, Copenhagen Business School, 1997.

Millward, Roy, *Scandinavian Lands*. New York: St. Martin's. 1965.

Scandinavian Atlas of Historic Towns. 4 vols. Odense: Odense University Press, 1977-83.

Sømme, Axel (ed.), *A Geography of Norden: Denmark, Finland, Iceland, Norway, Sweden*. London: Heinemann, 1968.

Svensson, Ole, *Danish town planning guide*. Copenhagen: Ministry for the Environment and National Agency for Physical Planning, 1983.

Tuxen, Poul, *Stege 1500-1950.* (Scandinavian Atlas of Historic Towns). Odense University Press, 1987.

II. CULTURE

1. General

Anker, Peter, *The Art of Scandinavia.* Vols. 1-2. London: Hamlyn, 1970.

Benzon, Gorm, *Art Treasures in Denmark.* Odense: Skandinavisk Bogtryk, 1966.

Garde, Roger de la, William Gilsdorf, Ilja Wechselmann and Jørgen Lerche Nielsen, *Small Nations, Big Neighbor: Denmark and Quebec/Canada Compare Notes on American Popular Culture.* London: John Libbey, 1993.

Harrison, K.C., *Libraries in Scandinavia.* London: Andre Deutsch, 1969.

Kaalund, Bodil, *The Art of Greenland: Sculpture, Crafts, Painting.* Berkeley, Los Angeles, and London: University of California Press, 1983.

Laurin, Carl G., Emil Hannover and Jens Thiis (eds), *Scandinavian Art.* New York: American-Scandinavian Foundation, 1922.

Poulsen, Vagn and H.E. Nørregaard-Nielsen, *Danish Painting and Sculpture.* Copenhagen: Det danske Selskab, 1976.

——, *Illustrated Art Guide to Denmark.* Copenhagen: Gyldendal, 1959.

Thorsen, Leif, *Public Libraries in Denmark.* Copenhagen: Det danske Selskab, 1972.

2. Architecture

Faber, Tobias, *Danish Architecture.* Copenhagen: Det danske Selskab, 1964.

——, *A History of Danish Architecture.* Copenhagen: Det danske Selskab, 1964.

——, *New Danish Architecture.* London: Architectural Press. New York and Washington DC: Praeger; Teufen: Arthur Niggli, 1968.

——, *Jorn Utzon: Houses in Fredensborg Photographed by Jens Frederiksen.* Berlin: Ernst & Sohn, 1991.

Hartung, Martin, "Arne Jacobsen: Danish architect of the international style," *Scandinavian Review* 72 (3): 5-13. 1984.

Lind, Olaf and Annemarie Lund, *Copenhagen Architecture Guide*. Copenhagen: Arkitektens Forlag, 1996 [well illustrated with plans and photographs; also in Danish or German].

Olsen, Robert Dahlmann, *Art in Architecture and Townscape: Denmark*. Copenhagen: Ministry of Foreign Affairs, 1969.

Paulsson, Thomas, *Scandinavian Architecture: Buildings and Society in Denmark, Finland, Norway and Sweden, from the Iron Age until Today*. London: Leonard Hill, 1958; Newton, Massachusetts: Charles T. Branford, 1959.

Skovgaard, Joakim A., *A King's Architecture: Christian IV and His Buildings*. London: Evelyn, 1973.

Skriver, Poul Erik (et al., eds.), *Guide to Modern Danish Architecture*. 4th ed. Copenhagen: Arkitektens Forlag/Krohn, 1973.

3. Painting and Sculpture

Andreasen, Erik, *Carl-Henning Pedersen: Paintings, Watercolors, Drawings*. Pittsburgh, Pennsylvania: Museum of Art, Carnegie Institute, 1968.

Arvidsson, Mats, and Bent Irve, "The art of the Faroe Islands," *Scandinavian Review* 73 (1): 74-78. 1985

Atkins, Guy, *Asger Jorn: The Crucial Years, 1954-1964*. New York: Wittenborn Art Books. Copenhagen, Borgens Forlag, 1977.

——, *Jorn in Scandinavia 1930-1953*. London: Lund Humphries; Copenhagen: Borgens Forlag; New York, George Wittenborn, 1968.

Bramsen, Henrik, *Danish Marine Painters*. Copenhagen: Nyt Nordisk Forlag, 1962.

—— and Alastair Smith, *Danish Painting in the Golden Age*. London: National Gallery, 1984.

Johansen, Ejner, *Richard Mortensen*. Copenhagen: Munksgaard, 1962.

Poulsen, Vagn and H.E. Nørregaard-Nielsen, *Danish Painting and Sculpture*. 2nd rev. ed. Copenhagen: Det danske Selskab, 1976.

Sleeping Beauty — Art Now. New York: Solomon R. Guggenheim Foundation, 1982.

Varnedoe, Kirk (ed.), *Northern Light: Realism and Symbolism in Scandinavian Painting 1880-1910*. Brooklyn: Brooklyn Museum, 1982.

Voss, Knud, *The Painters of Skagen*. Stockholm: Stok-Art, c.1990.

Weschler, Lawrence, "Louisiana in Denmark," *New Yorker* 58: 36-42, 52-56, 58-61. 30 Aug. 1982.

Zibrandtsen, Jan, *Moderne Dansk maleri* (Modern Danish painting). Copenhagen: Gyldendal, 1967.

4. Crafts and Design

Andersen, Finn & Ian O'Riordan, *From the Golden Age to the Present Day*. Copenhagen: Det danske Selskab, 1995 [A catalogue of the most significant exhibition of arts and crafts ever shown in Britain].

Beer, Eileene Harrison, *Scandinavian Design: Objects of a Life Style*. New York: Farrar, Straus & Giroux, 1975.

Dal, Erik, *Scandinavian Bookmaking in the Twentieth Century*. Urbana: University of Illinois Press, 1968.

Georg Jensen Silversmithy: 77 artists, 75 years. Washington, DC: Smithsonian Institution Press, 1980.

Grandjean, Bredo L., *The Flora Danica Service*. Copenhagen: Forum, 1973.

——, *Kongelig Dansk Porcelain, 1775-1884*. Copenhagen: Thanning & Appel, 1962.

Hayden, A., *Royal Copenhagen Porcelain: Its History and Development from the Eighteenth Century to the Present Day*. London, 1941.

McFadden, David Revere (ed.), *Scandinavian Modern Design, 1880-1980*. New York: Harry N. Abrams, 1982.

McFate, Patricia, "The art of simplicity: An interview with Vibeke Klint," *Scandinavian Review* 71 (3): 31-40. 1983.

Møller, Svend Erik (ed.), *Danish Design*. Copenhagen, Det danske Selskab, 1974.

Nielsen, Edith, *Scandinavian Embroidery, Past and Present*. New York: Scribner's, 1978.

The Scandinavian Touch: Contemporary Scandinavian Textiles. New York: American-Scandinavian Foundation, 1982.

Segerstad, Ulf Hård af, *Scandinavian Design*. London: Studio Books, 1961.

Vedel-Rieper, Joan, "Danish design in the 1980s," *Scandinavian Review* 73 (10): 11-18. 1985.

Victoria and Albert Museum, *Two Centuries of Danish Design*. Copenhagen: Danish Society of Arts and Crafts and Industrial Design, 1968.

Worsaae, J.J.A., *The Industrial Arts of Denmark from the Earliest Times to the Danish Conquest of England*. London: Chapman & Hall, 1882.

Zahle, Erik (ed.), *A Treasury of Scandinavian Design*. New York: Golden Press, 1961.

5. Language and Linguistics

Bredsdorff, Elias, *Danish: An Elementary Grammar and Reader*. 2 rev ed. Cambridge: Cambridge University Press. 1979.

Haugen, Einar, *The Scandinavian Languages: An Introduction to Their History*. Cambridge, Massachusetts: Harvard University Press, 1976.

—— and Thomas L. Markey, *The Scandinavian Languages: Fifty Years of Linguistic Research (1918-1968)*. The Hague: Mouton, 1972.

Jones, W. Glyn and Kirsten Gade, *Danish: A Grammar*. Copenhagen: Gyldendal, 1981.

Norlev, Erling, and H.A. Koefoed, *The Way to Danish: A Textbook in the Danish Language Written for Americans*. Copenhagen: Munksgaard, 1968.

Stemann, Ingeborg with Angus MacDonald and Niels Haisund, *Danish: A Practical Reader*. Copenhagen: H. Hagerup, 1969.

Stølen, Marianne, *Harmonien: An Ethnohistorical Sociolinguistic Analysis of a Danish-American Organization*. Odense University Press, 1994.

Viktør, Lars S., *The Nordic Languages: Their Status and Interrelations*. Oslo: Novus Press for Nordic Languages Secretariat, 1993.

Walshe M. O'C., *Introduction to the Scandinavian Languages*. London: Deutch, 1965.

White, James R. (comp.), *Danish Made Easy: Phrases and Useful Information for Your Stay in Denmark*. Copenhagen: Høst & Søn, 1978.

6. Literature: a selection

(See also Carol L. Schroeder, *A Bibliography of Danish Literature in English Translation, 1950-1980 with a Selection of Books about Denmark*. Copenhagen: Det danske Selskab, 1982.)

Allwood, Martin (ed.), *Modern Scandinavian Poetry 1900-1975*. New York: New Directions; Mullsjö, Sweden, 1982.

Andersen, Benny, *Selected Poems*. Princeton, New Jersey: Princeton University Press, 1975.

——, *Selected Stories*. Willimantic, Connecticut: Curbstone Press, 1982.

——, *The Pillows*. Willimantic, Connecticut: Curbstone Press, 1983.

Andersen, Hans Christian, [Collections and Selections].

——, *The Best of Hans Andersen*. Godalming: Treasure Press, 1984.

——, translated by Erik Christian Haugaard, *The Complete Fairy Tales and Stories*. Garden City, New York: Doubleday. London: Victor Gollancz, 1974.

——, *Complete Illustrated Works*. London: Chancellor Press, 1994.

——, *An Anniversary Edition of the First Four Tales*. Cambridge University Press, 1986.

——, *Andersen's Fairy Tales*. [Selection] Teaneck: Sharon Publications, 1981. New York: Wanderer Books, 1983. New York: NAL Books, 1987.

——, *The Complete Hans Christian Andersen's Fairy Tales*. New York: Avenel Books, 1981.

——, *Eighty Fairy Tales*. New York: Pantheon, 1982. Copenhagen: Hans Reitzel Publishing, 1994.

——, *Fairy Tales*. New York: Viking Press, 1981. New York: Omeg Press, 1984. Cambridge: Hardy Books, 1985.

——, *Favourite Tales of Hans Christian Andersen*. London: Faber & Faber, 1986.

——, *Hans Andersen's Fairy Tales*. London and New York: Penguin (Puffin Classics), 1981. Oxford University Press, 1987.

——, *Hans Christian Andersen's Fairy Tales*. New York: Buccaneer Books 1982.

——, *His Classic Fairy Tales*. London: Gollancz, 1984.

——, *The Penguin Complete Fairy Tales and Stories of Hans Christian Andersen*. London & New York: Penguin Books, 1985.

——, *The Stories of Hans Andersen*. Englewood Cliffs: Silver Burdett, 1985.

——, *Tales from Hans Andersen* London: Longman, 1989.

——, *Tales and Stories by Hans Christian Andersen*. Conroy, Patricia and Sven H Rossel (eds. & trans.). Seattle: University of Washington Press, 1980.

——, *Three Hans Andersen Fairy Tales*. London: Dent & Sons, 1980.

Andersen, Hans Christian [Single tales, in alphabetical order]

——, *Big Claus and Little Claus*. London: Hodder & Stoughton, 1983.

——, *The Emperor's New Clothes*. (Kejserens nye klæder) London: Hodder & Stoughton, 1980.

New York: Harper & Row (Trophy Picture Books), 1982.

New York: Thomas Y. Crowell, 1982.

London & New York: Macmillan, 1983.

Boston: Little Brown, 1984.

London: Piccolo (Pan Books), 1984.

New York: Holiday House, 1985.

London: Hutchinson, 1985.

London: Abelard-Schuman, 1986.

New York: H.Holt & Co, 1986.

New York: Harper & Row (Trophy Picture Books), 1987.

London: Methuen Children's Books, 1987.

Waco: Tex, Word Inc, 1987.

Nashville: Ideals, 1988.

Fremont: Worlds Wonder (Tell Me A Story), 1988.

——, *Father Knows Best* (Hvad fatter gør er altid det rigtige) London: Hodder & Stoughton, 1983.

——, *What the Old Man Does is Always Right* (Hvad fatter gør er altid det rigtige). Waco: Tex. Word Inc., 1988.

——, *The Flying Chest and Other Tales* [Selection]. (Den Flyvende kuffert). London: Burke, 1983.

——, *The Flying Trunk and Other Stories* [Selection]. (Den Flyvende kuffert). London: Andersen Press, 1986.

——, *The Fir Tree* (Grantræet) London: Kaye & Ward, 1980.

Mankato: Creative Education, 1986.

New York: Harper & Row (Trophy Picture Books), 1986.

New York: Random House, 1988.

——, *It's Absolutely True*. Waco: Tex. Word Inc., 1987.

——, *It's Perfectly True*. New York: Holiday House, 1988.

——, *The Little Match Girl* (Den lille pige med svovlstikker) London, Kaye and Ward, 1981.

London: Abelard-Schuman, 1983.

Milwaukee: Gareth Stevens, 1987.

London: Hodder & Stoughton, 1987.

New York: Putnam Publishing, 1987.

Waco: Tex Word Inc., 1988.

——, *The Little Mermaid* (Den lille havfrue)
Loughborough: Ladybird Books, 1980.
Vero Beach: Arthur Vanous, 1981.
London: Methuen Children's Books, 1983.
Princeton: Neugebauer Press, 1984.
Waco: Tex Word Inc., 1988.
——, *The Nightingale* (Nattergalen)
Princeton: Neugebauer Press, 1984.
New York: Crown Publications, 1985.
San Diego: Harcort Brace Jovanovich, 1985.
New York:Harper & Row (Trophy Picture Books), 1985.
New York: Barron, 1986.
Waco: Tex Word Inc., 1988.
London: Methuen Children's Books, 1989.
——, *The Emperor and the Nightingale.* (Nattergalen)
London & New York: Macmillan, 1982.
Loughborough: Ladybird Books, 1987.
Saxonville: Picture Book Studio, 1988.
——, *The Emperor's Nightingale.* (Nattergalen)
London: Moonlight Publishing Ltd, 1980.
London: Piccolo Books (Pan Books) 1981.
——, *The Old House,* London: Abelard-Schuman, 1984.
New York: H. Holt & Co, 1986.
——, *The Princesse and the Pea* (Princessen på ærten)
New York: Holiday House, 1982.
London: Abelard-Schuman, 1984.
Droitwich: Hanbury Plays, 1984.
New York: H. Holt & Co, 1985.
London: Methuen Children's Books, 1985.
Englewood Cliffs: Silver Burdett, 1985.
London & New York: Puffin Books (Penguin), 1986.
Saxonville: Picture Book Studio, 1987.
New York: Tuffy Books, 1987.
Fremont: World's Wonder, 1988 (with cassette)
——, *The Red Shoes* (De røde sko).
Princeton: Neugebauer Press, 1983.
Oxford: Oxford University Press, 1983.
——, *The Shadow and Other Tales* [Selection](Skyggen og andre
fortællinger). University of Wisconsin Press, 1983.

——, *The Snow Queen* (Snedronnningen).
London & New York: Puffin Books (Penguin), 1981.
New York: Dial Books Young, 1982.
Loughborough: Ladybird Books, 1982.
New York: Harper & Row, 1985.
London & New York, Macmillan, 1985.
New York: Barron, 1986.
Hempstead: Beehive Books, 1986.
Mankato: Creative Education, 1986.
London: Abelard Schuman, 1987.
New York: H. Holt & Co, 1988.
London: Walker Books, 1988.
——, *The Steadfast Tin Soldier* (Den standhæftige tinsoldat).
Boston: Little Brown, 1983.
Mankato: Creative Education, 1986.
——, *The Tin Soldier* (Den standhæftige tinsoldat).
Oxford University Press, 1983.
——, *The Swineherd* (Svinedrengen).
New York: William Morrow, 1982.
New York: H. Holt & Co, 1987.
——, *Thumbelina* (Tommelise).
New York: William Morrow, 1980.
Loughborough: Ladybird Books, 1982.
London: Pan Books (Piccolo Picture Books), 1983.
New York: Dial Books Young, 1985.
Saxonville: Picture Books Studio, 1985.
Waco: Tex. Word Inc., 1987.
——, *The Tinderbox* (Fyretøjet). London: Hodder & Stoughton, 1980.
Loughborough: Ladybird Books, 1984.
London & New York: Macmillan, 1988.
New York: McElderry, 1988.
——, *The Ugly Duckling* (Den grimme ælling).
Suffolk: Brimax Books, 1981.
London: Hamilton, 1982.
Englewood Cliffs: Silver Burdett, 1985.
New York: Alfred A. Knopf, 1986.
New York: Barron, 1986.
Loughborough: Ladybird Books, 1986.
London: Longman, 1987.
London & New York: Macmillan, 1987.

New York: Tuffy Books, 1987.

New York: Western Publishers, 1987.

New York: Scholastics Inc, 1988.

Waco: Tex Word Inc, 1988.

——, *The Wild Swans* (De vilde svaner).

New York: Dial Books Young, 1981.

Mahwah: Troll Associates, 1981.

London: Ernest Benn, 1984.

New York: Barron, 1986.

New York: Julia MacRae Books, 1986.

London: Hutchinson, 1987.

London & New York: Macmillan, 1988.

Andersen, Hans Christian [autobiography, poems, travel]

——, *The Fairy Tale of My Life: An Autobiography.* New York: Paddington Press, Two Continents Publishing Group, 1975.

——, *Brothers, Very Far Away.* [27 poems].

Seattle: Mermaid Press, c.1992

——, (translated by Grace Thornton), *A Visit to Portugal: 1866* London: Peter Owen, 1972.

——, *A Poet's Bazar: A Journey to Greece, Turkey, and up the Danube.* New York: Kesend 1987.

Allen, W. Gore, *Renaissance in the North.* Freeport, New York: Books for Libraries Press, 1970.

Asmundsen, Doris R., *Georg Brandes: Aristocratic Radical.* New York: New York University Press, 1981.

Bain, R. Nisbet, *Hans Christian Andersen: A Biography.* New York: Dodd Mead. London: Lawrence & Bullen, 1895.

Billsskov Jansen, F.J. and P.M. Mitchell (eds.), *Anthology of Danish Literature.* Carbondale & Edwardsville, Illinois: Southern Illinois University Press, 1971.

Blicher, Steen Steensen, *The Diary of a Parish Clerk and Other Stories* (En Landsbydegns Dagbog) trans. Paula Hostrup-Jessen and Poul Christensen. London: Athlone, 1996

Blixen, Karen (see also Isak Dinesen), *Anecdotes of Destiny.* London: University of Chicago Press, 1976.

——, *The Angelic Avengers.* Chicago, Illinois: University of Chicago Press, 1976.

——, *Carnival: Entertainments and Posthumous Tales.* London: Heinemann, 1977.

——, *The Caryatids — An Unfinished Tale* trans. Sonia Brandes. Copenhagen: Gyldendal, 1993.

——, *Daguerreotypes and Other Essays.* Chicago, Illinois: University of Chicago Press, 1979.

——, *The Dreaming Child and Other Stories.* London: Penguin, 1995.

——, *Ehrengard.* New York: Vintage Books, 1975.

——, *Last Tales.* London: University of Chicago Press, 1976.

——, *Letters from Africa, 1914-1931.* Chicago, Illinois: University of Chicago Press, 1981.

——, *Out of Africa.* Harmondsworth: Penguin, 1979. New York: Random House, 1992

——, *Seven Gothic Tales.* St. Albans: Triad, 1979.

——, *Shadows on the Grass.* London: University of Chicago Press, 1976.

——, *Winter's Tales.* London: University of Chicago Press, 1976. New York, Vintage Books, 1993.

Bjørby, Pål, "The prison house of sexuality: Homosexuality in Herman Bang scholarship," *Scandinavian Studies* 58 (3): 223-55. 1986.

Bjørnvig, Thorkild, *The Pact: My Friendship with Isak Dinesen.* Baton Rouge, Louisiana: Louisiana State University Press.

Bodelsen, Anders, *Consider the Verdict.* New York: Harper & Row, 1976.

——, *Freezing point.* London: Joseph, 1971.

——, *Hit and Run, Run, Run.* Harmondsworth: Penguin, 1971.

——, *Operation Cobra.* London: Pelham, 1976.

——, *The Silent Partner.* Harmondsworth: Penguin, 1978.

——, *Straus.* New York: Harper & Row, 1974.

Borum, Poul, *Danish Literature.* [a short critical survey]. Copenhagen: Det danske Selskab, 1979.

Brandt, Jørgen Gustava, *Tête à Tête.* Willimantic, Connecticut: Curbstone Press, 1978.

Branner, H.C., *Anguish.* Copenhagen: The Wind-Flower Press, 1980.

——, *No Man Knows the Night.* London: Secker & Warburg, 1958.

——, *The Poet and the Girl.* Copenhagen: The Wind-Flower Press, 1980.

——, *The Riding Master.* London: Secker & Warburg, 1951.

——, *The Story of Börge.* New York: Twayne, 1973.

——, *Two Minutes of Silence: Selected Short Stories* (trans. by Vera Lindholm Vance). Madison and London: University of Wisconsin Press, 1966.

Bredsdorff, Elias, *Danish Literature in English translation, with a Special Hans Christian Andersen Supplement.* Copenhagen: Munksgaard, 1950, reprinted Westport, Connecticut: Greenwood, 1973.

—— (ed.), *Contemporary Danish Prose.* Copenhagen: Gyldendal, 1958, reprinted Westport, Connecticut: Greenwood, 1974.

——, "A critical guide to the literature on Hans Christian Andersen." *Scandinavica*, 6 (2), 1967.

——, et al., *An Introduction to Scandinavian Literature from the Earliest Times to Our Day.* Copenhagen: Munksgaard, 1951. Westport, Connecticut: Greenwood, 1970 .

——, *Hans Christian Andersen: The Story of His Life and Work 1805-75.* New York, Scribner's. London: Phaidon Press, 1975.

Brøgger, Suzanne, *Deliver Us from Love.* New York, Delacorte, 1976.

——, *A Fighting Pig's Too Tough To Eat.* (En gris som har været oppe at slås kan man ikke stege.) Trans. Marina Allemano. Norwich: Norvik Press, 1997.

Brønner, Hedin (ed.), *Faroese Short Stories.* New York: Twayne and American-Scandinavian Foundation, 1972.

——, *Three Faroese Novelists: an Appreciation of Jørgen-Frantz Jacobsen, William Heinesen and Hedin Brú.* New York: Twayne, 1973.

Byram, Michael, *Tom Kristensen.* Boston, Massachusetts: Twayne, 1982.

Dinesen, Isak (Karen Blixen), *Isak Dinesen's Africa: Images of the Wild Continent from the Writer's Life and Words.* San Francisco: Sierra Club Books, 1985.

——, *Seven Gothic Tales.* Harmondsworth: Penguin, 1934. New York: Vintage Books, 1972.

——, *Out of Africa.* Harmondsworth: Penguin, 1937, 1954.

——, *Out of Africa. Shadows on the Grass.* New York: Vintage Books, 1985.

——, *Winter's Tales.* Harmondsworth: Penguin, 1942, 1983. New York, Dell, 1957. New York: Books for Libraries Press, 1972. London: University of Chicago Press, 1976.

——, *The Angelic Avengers.* Harmondsworth: Penguin. 1947, 1986.

——, *Last Tales.* Harmondsworth: Penguin. 1955, 1986. New York: Random House. London: Putnam, 1957.

——, *Anecdotes of Destiny.* Harmondsworth: Penguin. 1958.

——, *Shadows on the Grass.* Harmondsworth: Penguin. 1960.

——, *Letters from Africa 1914-31* (ed. Frans Lasson, trans Anne Born. Chicago & London: University of Chicago Press, 1981.

Dinesen, Thomas, *My Sister, Isak Dinesen*. London: Michael Joseph, 1975.

Ditlevsen, Tove, *Complete Freedom and Other Stories*. Willimantic, Connecticut: Curbstone Press, 1982.

Fenger, Henning, *The Heibergs*. New York: Twayne, 1971.

Gosse, Edmund, *Northern Studies*. London: Walter Scott, 1890.

Grønbech, Bo, *Hans Christian Andersen*. Boston, Massachusetts: Twayne, 1980.

Gustafson, Alrik, *Six Scandinavian Novelists: Lie, [Jens Peter] Jacobsen, Heidenstam, Selma Lagerlöf, Hamsun, Sigrid Undset*. New York: Biblo & Tannen, 1969.

Hallmundsson, Hallberg, *An Anthology of Scandinavian Literature from the Viking Period to the Twentieth Century*. New York: Collier Books, 1965.

Hannah, Donald, *'Isak Dinesen' and Karen Blixen: the Mask and the Reality*. New York: Random House, 1971.

Hansen, Martin A., *The Liar*. New York: Twayne, 1969. Sun and Moon Press, 1995.

——, *Lucky Kristoffer (Lykkelig Kristoffer)* (trans. John Jepson Egglishaw). New York: Twayne and American Scandinavian Foundation, 1974.

——, *The Book*. Copenhagen: Wind-Flower Press, 1978.

——, *Against the Wind*. New York: Ungar, 1979.

Hansen, Thorkild, *Arabia Felix: The Danish Expedition of 1761-1767*. London: Collins, 1964.

——, *North-West To Hudson Bay: The Life and Times of Jens Munk*. London: Collins, 1970.

Hein, Piet, *Words - Grooks and Gruk*. Copenhagen: Borgen, 1995.

Heinesen, William, *The Lost Musicians (De fortabte spillemænd)* (trans. Erik J. Friis). New York: Hippocrene Books, 1971.

——, *The Black Cauldron* (Den sorte gryde), (trans. W. Glyn Jones.) London: Daedalus. New York: Hippocrene Books, 1992.

Høeg, Peter, *Borderliners (De måske egnede)*. (trans. Barbara Haveland). London and New York: Harvill, 1995.

——, *Fortællinger om Natten*. Copenhagen: Munksgaard/ Rosinante, 1990. *Tales of the Night*. London: Harvill, 1997.

——, *The History of Danish Dreams (Forestilling om det tyvende århundrede)*. New York: Doubleday. London: Harvill, 1995.

——, *Miss Smilla's Feeling for Snow (Frøken Smilla's fornemmelse for sne)*. London: HarperCollins, 1993.

——, *Smilla's Sense of Snow* New York: Doubleday, 1994.

——, *The Woman and the Ape (Kvinden og aben)*. New York: Farrar, Straus & Giroux. London: Harvill, 1996

Holbek, Berryl, *Interpretation of Fairy-Tales: Danish Folklore in a European Perspective*. Helsinki: Suomalaisen Tiedeakalemia, 1987.

Holberg, Ludvig, (trans. Bergliot Stromsoe), *Peder Paars*. Lincoln: Nebraska University Press, 1962.

Holm, Sven, *Termush*. London: Faber & Faber, 1969.

——, (ed.), *The Devil's Instrument and Other Danish Stories*. London: Owen, 1971.

Ingwersen, Faith and Niels Ingwersen, *Martin A. Hansen*. Boston, Massachusetts: Twayne, 1976.

Ingwersen, Niels (ed.), *Seventeen Danish Poets: A Bilingual Anthology of Contemporary Danish Poetry*. Lincoln, Nebraska: Windflower Press, 1981.

Jacobsen, Jens Peter, *Mogens and Other Stories* (trans. Tiina Nunnally). Fjord Press, 1994.

——, *Niels Lyhne* (trans. Hanna Astrup Larsen). New York: Twayne & American-Scandinavian Foundation, 1967. Fjord Press, 1994.

Jensen, Johannes V., (trans. A.G. Chater). *The Long Journey (Den lange rejse)* 3 vols. New York: Alfred A Knopf, 1923-24.

Jensen, Line (ed.), *Contemporary Danish Poetry: An Anthology*. Boston, Massachusetts: Twayne, 1977.

Jensen, Niels Lyhne, *Jens Peter Jacobsen*. Boston, Massachusetts: Twayne, 1980.

Johannesson, Eric O., *The World of Isak Dinesen*. Seattle: University of Washington Press, 1961.

Jones, W. Glyn, *Johannes Jörgensen*. Boston, Massachusetts: Twayne, 1969.

——, *William Heinesen*. Boston, Massachusetts: Twayne, 1974.

Juhl, Marianne and Bo Hakon Jørgensen, *Diana's Revenge: Two Lines in Isak Dinesen's Autobiography*. Odense, Denmark: Odense University Press, 1985.

Langbaum, Robert, *Isak Dinesen's Art: The Gayety of Vision*. London & Chicago: University of Chicago Press, 1975.

Larsen, Marianne, *Selected Poems*. Willimantic, Connecticut: Curbstone Press, 1982.

Lasson, Frans and Clara Svendsen, *Life and Destiny of Isak Dinesen.* London & Chicago: University of Chicago Press, 1976.

Lederer, Wolfgang, *The Kiss of the Snow Queen: Hans Christian Andersen and Man's Redemption by Woman.* Berkeley, Los Angeles & London: University of California Press, 1986.

Lindsay, Jack, *Decay and Renewal: Critical Essays on Twentieth Century Writing.* Sydney: Wild and Woolley. London: Lawrence & Wishart, 1976.

Literature from Denmark. Copenhagen: Danish Literature Information Centre. 1991. [Especially quality Danish literature available in English].

Malinovski, Ivan, *Critique of Silence.* Copenhagen: Gyldendal, 1977.

Marker, Frederick J. and Lise-Lone Marker, *The Scandinavian Theatre: A Short History.* Oxford, 1975. Lotowa, New Jersey: Rowman & Littlefield.

Markey, T.L., *H.C. Branner.* New York: Twayne, 1973.

Marx, Leonie, "Literary experimentation in a time of transition: The short story after 1945," *Scandinavian Studies* 49 (2): 131-54. 1977.

Migel, Parmenia, *Titania: The Biography of Isak Dinesen.* New York: Random House, 1967.

Mitchell, P.M., *A History of Danish Literature.* 2nd rev. ed. New York: Kraus-Thomson, 1971.

—— and Kenneth H. Ober (ed. & trans.), *The Royal Guest and Other Classical Danish Narrative.* Chicago & London: University of Chicago Press, 1977.

——, *Henrik Pontoppidan.* Boston, Massachusetts: Twayne, 1979.

Nexø, Martin Andersen, *Pelle the Conqueror (Pelle erobreren).* New York: Henry Holt, 4 vols., 1913-16. Gloucester, Massachusetts: Peter Smith, 2 vols., 1963.

Nielsen, Marion L., *Denmark's Johannes V. Jensen: Translations from His Works and an Introductory Essay.* Logan: Utah State Agricultural College, 1955.

Nordbrandt, Henrik, *Selected Poems.* Willimantic, Connecticut: Curbstone Press, 1978.

——, *God's House.* Willimantic, Connecticut: Curbstone Press, 1979.

Nolin, Bertil, *Georg Brandes.* Boston, Massachusetts: Twayne, 1976.

Ober, Kenneth H., *Meïr Goldschmidt.* Boston, Massachusetts: Twayne, 1976.

Ørum, Poul, *Scapegoat.* New York: Pantheon, 1975.

——, *Nothing but the Truth.* London: Gollancz, 1976.

Paludan, Jacob, *Jørgen Stein* (trans. Carl Malmberg), Madison: University of Wisconsin Press, 1966.

Panduro, Leif, *Kick Me in the Traditions*. New York: Erikson-Taplinger, 1961.

——, *One of Our Millionaires Is Missing*. New York: Grove Press, 1967.

Rasmussen, Halfdan, *Halfdanes Nonsense and Nursery Rhymes*. Illustrated by Ernst Claussen, Ib Spang Olsen & Arne Ungermann. Copenhagen: Schønberg, 1973.

——, *Hocus Pocus: Nonsense Rhymes*. Illustrated by Ib Spang Olsen. London: Angus & Robertson, 1973.

Review of Contemporary Fiction 15(1), special issue "New Danish Fiction," Spring 1995.

Rifbjerg, Klaus, *Selected Poems*. Willimantic, Connecticut: Curbstone Press, 1976.

——, *Anna (I) Anna*. Willimantic, Connecticut: Curbstone Press, 1982.

Rossel, Sven H., *A History of Scandinavian Literature, 1870-1980*. Minneapolis: University of Minnesota Press, 1982.

——, *Johannes V. Jensen*. Boston, Massachusetts: Twayne, 1984.

Sarvig, Ole, *Late Day*. Illustrated by Palle Nielsen. Willimantic, Connecticut: Curbstone Press, 1976.

Scandinavian Studies. Urbana, Illinois: Society for the Advancement of Scandinavian Study, 1928- quarterly.

Scherfig, Hans, *The "Idealists."* London: Paul Elek, 1949.

Schou-Hansen, Tage, *The Naked Trees*. London: Cape, 1959.

Schroeder, Carol L., *A Bibliography of Danish Literature in English Translation 1950-1980*. Copenhagen: Det danske Selskab, 1982.

Sonne, Jørgen, *Flights*. Willimantic, Connecticut: Curbstone Press, 1982.

Sørensen, Villy, *The Soldier's Christmas Eve*. Illustrated by Victoria Schaaf. Willimantic, Connecticut: Trekroner Press, 1973.

——, *Tiger in the Kitchen and Other Strange Stories*. Freeport, New York: Books for Libraries Press, 1969.

Spink, Reginald, *Hans Christian Andersen*. London: Thames and Hudson. New York: G.P. Putnam, 1972.

Stangerup, Henrik, *The Man Who Wanted to Be Guilty*. London: Marion Boyars, 1982.

Sterling, Monica, *The Wild Swan: The Life and Times of Hans Christian Andersen*. New York: Harcourt, Brace & World, 1965.

Stork, Charles Wharton (trans.), *A Second Book of Danish Verse*. Freeport, New York: Books for Libraries Press, 1968.

Svendsen, Clara (ed.), *Isak Dinesen: A Memorial*. New York: Random House, 1965.

Thorup, Kirsten, *Baby*. Baton Rouge: Louisiana State University Press, 1980.

———, *Love from Trieste*. Willimantic, Connecticut: Curbstone Press, 1980.

Thurman, Judith, *Isak Dinesen: The Life of a Storyteller*. New York: St. Martin's, 1982.

Topsoe-Jensen, H.G., *Scandinavian Literature from Brandes to Our Day*. London & New York: American-Scandinavian Foundation, W.W. Norton, 1929.

Wamberg, Bodil (ed), *Out of Denmark: Karen Blixen 1885-1985 and Danish Women Writers Today*. [Portraits of 20th century women writers, including Karen Blixen, Suzanne Brøgger, and Dea Trier Mørch] Copenhagen: Det danske Selskab, 1985.

Whissen, Thomas Reid, *Isak Dinesen's Aesthetics*. Port Washington, New York: Kennikat Press, 1973.

Willumsen, Dorrit, *If It Really Were a Film*. Willimantic, Connecticut: Curbstone Press, 1982.

Young, G.V.C. and Cynthia R. Clewer, *The Faroese Saga Freely Translated with Maps and Genealogical Tables*. Belfast: Century Services, 1973.

Zuck, Virpi (editor), *Dictionary of Scandinavian Literature*. Chicago & London: St. James Press, 1990.

7. Music, Dance, Theater, Film

Andersen, M., "Holmboes epitaph," *Dansk musiktidsskrift* XXXIV trans. in Nytida Musik, 3/6, 1959-60 (6). 1959.

Argetsinger, Gerald, *Ludwig Holberg's Comedies*. Carbondale, Illinois: Southern Illinois University Press, 1983.

Balslev-Clausen, P. (ed), *Songs from Denmark*. Copenhagen: Det danske Selskab. 2ed., 1992.

Balzer, Jürgen (ed.), *Carl Nielsen 1865-1965: Centenary Essays*. Copenhagen: Nyt Nordisk Forlag, 1965. New York: Dover. London: Dennis Dobson, 1966.

Bates. Alfred, James P. Boyd and John P. Lamberton, *Scandinavian Drama*. 1903 reprinted New York: AMS Press, 1970.

Beyer, Anders (ed.), *The Music of Per Nørgård: Fourteen Interpretive Essays*. Aldershot: Scolar, 1996.

Billeskov Jansen, F., *Ludvig Holberg*. New York: Twayne, 1974.

Bondebjerg, Ib, Jesper Andersen & Peter Schepelern, *Dansk Film 1972-97*. Copenhagen: Munksgaard/Rosinante, 1997.

Bordswell, David, "Carl-Theodor Dreyer: discoveries and rediscoveries," *Scandinavian Review* 70 (2): 60-70. 1982.

———, *The Films of Carl-Theodor Dreyer*. Berkeley, California: University of California Press, 1981.

Borge, Victor and Robert Sherman, *My Favourite Intervals*. London: Sphere, 1977.

Bournonville, August (trans. Patricia McAndrew), *My Theater Life*. Middleton, Connecticut: Wesleyan University Press, 1979.

Bredsdorff, Elias (ed.), *Contemporary Danish Plays: An Anthology*. Freeport, New York: Books for Libraries Press, 1970.

Breitbart, Eric, "Man in motion: The films of Jørgen Leth," *Scandinavian Review* 74 (1): 68-75. 1986.

Cowie, Peter, "Scandinavian cinema: Denmark," *Scandinavian Review* 72 (2): 76-84. 1984.

Dreyer, Carl-Theodor Dreyer, *Four Screenplays*. London: Thames & Hudson. Bloomington: Indiana University Press, 1970.

Fabricius, Johannes, *Carl Nielsen 1865-1931*. Copenhagen: Berlingske, 1965.

Fog, Dan, *The Royal Danish Ballet 1760-1958 and August Bournonville: A Chronological Catalogue of the Ballets and Ballet-Divertissements Performed at the Royal Theatre of Copenhagen and a Catalogue of August Bournonville's Works, With a Musical Bibliography*. Copenhagen: Dan Fog Musikforlag, 1961.

Gruen, John, *Erik Bruhn: Danseur noble*. New York: Viking, 1979.

Haven, Mogens von, *The Royal Danish Ballet*. Copenhagen, Gyldendal, 1964.

Holberg, Ludvig, trans. Henry Alexander, *Four Plays by Holberg*. 1946, New York: Kraus Reprint Company, 1971.

Holmboe, Vagn, *Danish Street Cries: A Study of Their Musical Structure and a Complete Edition of Tunes with Words Collected Before 1960*, trans. Anne Lockhart. Copenhagen: Kragen (Acta ethnomusicologica danica) 5. 1988.

———, *Experiencing Music*, 1991.

———, and Meta Holmboe, *Samklang* [music examples and photographs].

Horton, John, *Scandinavian Music: A Short History*. London: Faber, 1963.

Kappel, Vagn, *Contemporary Danish Composers against the Background of Danish Musical Life and History*. Copenhagen: Det danske Selskab, 1967.

Ketting, Knud (ed.), *Music in Denmark*. Copenhagen: Det danske Selskab, 1987.

Larsen, Peter H., "Copenhagen blues," *Scandinavian Review* 72 (2): 85-90. 1984.

Lawson, Jack, *Carl Nielsen*. London: Phaidon, 1997.

Marker, Frederik J., *Kjeld Abell*. Boston, Massachusetts: Twayne, 1976.

—— and Lise-Lone Marker, *The Scandinavian Theatre: A Short History*. Oxford: Basil Blackwell, 1975.

Martins, Peter, with Robert Cornfield, *Far from Denmark* [autobiography]. Boston, Massachusetts: Little, Brown, 1982.

Meier, Ellen Bick, "You can't keep a good thing down," *Scandinavian Review* 67 (4): 48-55. 1979 [on children's theater].

Milne, Tom, *The Cinema of Carl Dreyer*. New York: A.S. Barnes, 1971.

Nash, Mark, *Dreyer*. London: British Film Institute, 1977.

Olsen, Peter (intro.), *Modern Nordic Plays: Denmark. H.C. Branner: Thermopylae. Ernst Bruun Olsen: The Bookseller Cannot Sleep. Klaus Rifbjerg: Developments. Peter Ronild: Boxing for One*. Oslo: Universitetsforlaget. Boston, Massachusetts: Twayne, 1974.

Rapoport, P., *Vagn Holmboe: A Catalogue of His Music, Discography, Bibliography*. London: Triad Press, 1974.

——, *Vagn Holmboe's Symphonic Metamorphoses*. Doctoral Dissertation: University of Illinois, 1975.

Schrader, Paul, *Transcendental Styles in Film: Ozu, Bresson, Dreyer*. Berkeley: University of California Press, 1972.

Searl, Humphrey and Robert Layton, *Twentieth Century Composers: Britain, Scandinavia and the Netherlands*. New York: Holt, Rinehart & Winston, 1973.

Simpson, Robert, *Carl Nielsen, Symphonist*. London: Kahn & Averill. New York: Taplinger, 1979.

Soila, Tytti, Astrid Söderberg Widding and Gunner Iversen, *Nordic National Cinemas*. London & New York: Routledge, 1998..

Skollar, Donald (ed.), *Dreyer in Double Reflection: Translation of Carl Th. Dreyer's Writings* About the Film *(Om filmen)*. New York: E.P. Dutton, 1973.
Terry, Walter, *The King's Ballet Master: A Biography of Denmark's August Bournonville*. New York: Dodd, Mead, 1979.
Wells, Henry W., (intro.), *Five Modern Scandinavian Plays*. New York: Twayne and American-Scandinavian Foundation, 1971.
Yoell, John H., *The Nordic Sound: Explorations into the Music of Denmark, Norway and Sweden*. Boston, Massachusetts: Crescendo Publishing, 1974.

8. Philosophy (*see also* **Religion**)
Olson, Raymond E. and Anthony M. Paul, *Contemporary Philosophy in Scandinavia*. Baltimore, Maryland & London: Johns Hopkins Press, 1972.

III. ECONOMICS

1. General (including Accounting)
Alban, Anita & Terkel Christiansen (eds), *The Nordic Lights: New Initiatives in Health Care Systems*. Odense University Press, 1995.
Andersen, Jørgen Goul, "Sources of Welfare-State Support in Denmark: Self-Interest or Way of Life?" pp. 25-48 in Erik Jørgen Hansen et al. (eds.), *Welfare Trends in the Scandinavian Countries*. New York: M.E. Sharpe, 1993.
Andersen, Poul Houmann, *Collaborative Internationalization Of Small and Medium-Sized Enterprises: SME's Participation in the International Division of Labour*. Copenhagen: Jurist- og Økonomforbundets Forlag, 1995.
Amoroso, Bruno, "Development and Crisis of the Scandinavian Model of Labour Relations in Denmark," pp. 71-96 in Guido Baglioni and Colin Crouch (eds.), *European Industrial Relations: The Challenge of Flexibility*. London: Sage, 1990.
Bendixen, Kirsten, *Denmark's Money*. Copenhagen: The National Museum, 1967.
Björkman, Ingmar and Mats Forsgren (eds.), *The Nature of the International Firm: Nordic Contributions to International Business Research*. Copenhagen: Handelshøjskolens Forlag, 1997.

Braendgaard, Asger, "International Technology Programmes and National Systems of Production: ESPRIT and the Danish Electronics Industry," pp. 184-202 in Christopher Freeman and Bengt-Åke Lundvall (eds.), *Small Countries Facing the Technological Revolution*. London: Pinter Publishers, 1988.

Buksti, Jakob, "Policy-making and unemployment in Denmark," pp. 217-237 in J.J. Richardson and Roger Henning (eds.), *Unemployment*. London: Sage, 1984.

Christiansen, Peter Munk, "A Negotiated Economy? Public Sector Regulation of the Manufacturing Sector in Denmark," *Scandinavian Political Studies* 17 (4): 305-319. 1994.

Damgaard, Erik, P. Gerlich and J.J. Richardson, *The Politics of Economic Crisis*. Aldershot: Avebury, 1991.

Danish Accounting Standards 1-11. [parallel texts, English translation by KPMG C Jespersen]. Copenhagen: Forlaget FSR, 1998.

Danish Ministry of Foreign Affairs, Royal, *Economic Survey of Denmark*. Annual.

Due, Jesper, Jørgen Steen Madsen, Carsten Strøby Jensen and Lars K. Petersen, *The Survival of the Danish Model: A Historical Sociological Analysis of the Danish System of Collective Bargaining*. Copenhagen: Jurist- og Økonomforbundets Forlag, 1994.

Elvander, Nils, "Collective bargaining and incomes policy in the Nordic countries: A comparative analysis," *British Journal of Industrial Relations* 12(3): 417-437. 1974.

Esping-Andersen, Gösta, "Government responses to budget scarcity: Denmark," *Policy Studies Journal* 13 (3): 534-546. 1985.

——, *The Three Worlds of Welfare Capitalism*. Cambridge: Polity Press, 1990.

Ferner, Anthony and Richard Hyman (eds.), *Industrial Relations in the New Europe*. Oxford: Blackwell Publishers, 1992.

Fløistad, Brit, "Greenland's international fisheries relations: a coastal state in the 'North' with problems of the 'South,'" *Cooperation and Conflict* 24: 35-48. 1989.

Gjerding, Allan Næs, Björn Johnson, Lars Kallehauge, Bengt-Åke Lundvall and Poul Thøis Madsen, *The Productivity Mystery: Industrial Development in Denmark in the Eighties*. Copenhagen: Jurist- og Økonomforbundets Forlag, 1995.

Gustafsson, Bo (ed.), *Post-industrial Society*. New York: St. Martins, 1979.

Hansen, Finn Kenneth, "Redistribution of Income in Denmark," pp. 139-160 in Robert Erikson, Erik Jørgen Hansen, Stein Ringen and Hannu Uusitalo (eds.), *The Scandinavian Model: Welfare States and Welfare Research.* Armonk, New York & London: M.E. Sharpe, Inc., 1987.

Hedegaard, Birthe, *The Financing of Continuing Training in Denmark.* Luxembourg: Office for Official Publications of the European Community, 1991.

Johansen, Hans Christian, *The Danish Economy in the Twentieth Century.* London: Croom Helm, 1987.

Jonsson, Ivar, *West-Nordic countries in crisis; new-structuralism, collective entrepreneurship and microsocieties facing global systems of innovation.* New Social Science Monographs. Copenhagen: Copenhagen Business School, 1995.

Katzenstein, Peter, *Small States in World Markets: Industrial Policy in Europe.* Ithaca, New York & London: Cornell University Press, 1985.

Korst, Mogens, *Industrial Life in Denmark: A Survey of Economic Development and Production.* Copenhagen: Det danske Selskab, 1976.

Korst, Mogens, *Industrial Life in Denmark, the Faroe Islands and Greenland.* Copenhagen: Det danske Selskab, 1987.

Kosonen, Pekka, "Public expenditure in the Nordic Nation States: the source of prosperity or crisis?" pp. 108-123 in Risto Alapuro, Matti Alestalo, Elina Haavio-Mannila and Raimo Vayrynen (eds.), *Small States in Comparative Perspective — Essays for Erik Allardt.* Oslo: Norwegian University Press, 1985.

Kuemel, Bernd, Stefan Krüger Nielsen and Bent Sørensen, *Life-cycle analysis of energy systems.* Roskilde University Press, 1997.

Lauersen, Finn and Søren Riishøj (eds.), *The EU and Central Europe: Status and Prospects* (TKI International Political Economy Series 1). Esbjerg: Sydjysk Universitetsforlag, 1997.

Lookofsky, Joseph, *Understanding the CISG in Scandinavia.* [CISG = UN Convention on Contracts for the International Sale of Goods] Copenhagen: DJØF Publishing, 1996.

Lyck, Lise (ed.), *Socio-Economic Development in Greenland and the Other Small Nordic Jurisdictions.* New Social Science Monographs. Copenhagen: Copenhagen Business School, 1997.

Mjøset Lars, "Nordic economic policies in the 1970s and 1980s," *International Organization* 41 (3): 403-456. 1987.

Mogensen, Gunnar Viby (ed.), *Work Incentives in the Danish Welfare State: New Empirical Evidence*. Aarhus University Press, 1995.

Nannestad, Peter, *Danish Design or British Disease? Danish Economic Crisis Policy 1974-79 in Comparative Perspective*. Aarhus University Press, 1992.

Nielsen, Klaus, "Learning to manage the supply-side — flexibility and stability in Denmark," pp. 282-313 in Bob Jessop, Hans Kastendiek and Klaus Nielsen (eds.), *The Politics of Flexibility — Restructuring State and Industry in Britain, Germany and Scandinavia*. Aldershot: Edward Elgar, 1991.

Notermans, Ton, "The abdication from national policy autonomy: Why the macroeconomic policy regime has become so unfavourable to Labor," *Politics and Society* 21(2): 133-167. 1993.

OECD *Economic Surveys, Denmark*. Paris, OECD, 1997 and about every two years previously.

Ølgaard, Anders, *The Danish Economy*. Brussels, Luxembourg: Commission of the European Communities, 1980.

Olsen, Ole Jess, *Competition in the Electricity Supply Industry: Experience from Europe and the US*. Copenhagen: Jurist- og Økonomforbundets Forlag, 1995.

Olsen, Poul Bitsch, *Six Cultures of Regulation: Labour Inspectorates in Six European Countries*. [Covers Denmark, Finland, Norway, Sweden, Britain and Italy]. Copenhagen: Handelshøjskolens forlag, 1992.

Paldam, Martin and Friedrich Schneider, "The macro-economic aspects of government and opposition popularity in Denmark 1957-78," NOTAT 1980-4, Institute of Economics, University of Aarhus, Århus, 1980.

Paldam, Martin and Hans E. Zeuthen, "The expansion of the public sector in Denmark — a post festum?" pp. 157-186 in Johan A. Lybeck and Magnus Henrekson (eds.), *Explaining the Growth of Government*. Amsterdam: North-Holland, 1988.

Paldam, Martin, *Economic Development in Greenland*. Aarhus University Press, 1996.

Pedersen, Clemens (ed.) *The Danish Co-operative Movement*. Copenhagen: Det danske Selskab, 1977.

Peters, B. Guy and David Klingeman, "Patterns of expenditure development in Sweden, Norway and Denmark," *British Journal of Political Science* 7: 387-412. 1977.

Sainsbury, Diane, "The Scandinavian model and women's interests: The issues of universalism and corporatism," *Scandinavian Political Studies* 11 (4): 337-346. 1988.

——, "Analysing welfare state variations: The merits and limitations of models based on the residual-institutional distinction,' *Scandinavian Political Studies* 14 (1): 1-30. 1991.

Scandinavian Economic History Review. Copenhagen: Scandinavian Society for Economic and Social History and Historical Geography. 1953-. Semi-annual.

Schiff, Eric, *Income Policies Abroad, Part II: France, West Germany, Austria, Denmark*. Washington, DC: American Enterprise Institute for Public Policy Research, 1972.

Schmidt-Andersen, Johannes, *The Postage Stamps of Denmark 1851-1951*. Copenhagen: Royal Danish Post Office, 1951.

Swenson, Peter, "Bringing capital back in, or Social Democracy reconsidered: Employer power, cross-class alliances, and centralization of industrial relations in Denmark and Sweden," *World Politics* 43 (4): 513-544. July 1991.

Thomsen, Birgit Nüchel and Brinley Thomas, *Anglo-Danish Trade, 1661-1963: A Historical Survey*. Århus: Universitetsforlag, 1966.

Tillotson, Amanda R., "Open States and Open Economies — Denmark's Contribution to a Statist Theory of Development," *Comparative Politics* 21 (3): 339-354. 1989.

Uhr, C.G., "Economic development in Denmark, Norway, and Sweden," pp. 219-48 in Karl H. Cerny (ed.), *Scandinavia at the Polls: Recent political Trends in Denmark, Norway and Sweden*. Washington, DC: American Enterprise Institute for Public Policy Research, 1977.

Winther, Gorm, *Employee Ownership: A Comparative Analysis of Growth Performance*. Aalborg University Press, 1995.

Worm, Verner, *Vikings and Mandarins; Sino-Scandinavian Business Co-operation in Cross-Cultural settings*. Copenhagen: Handelshøj-skolens Forlag/Copenhagen Business School Press/Munksgaard International Publishing, 1997.

2. Agriculture

Baak, Lawrence J., *Agrarian Reform in Eighteenth Century Denmark*. Lincoln: University of Nebraska, 1977.

Buksti, Jacob A., "Bread-and-butter agreement and high policy disagreement: Some reflections on the contextual impact on agricultural interests in EC policy-making," *Scandinavian Political Studies* 6 (4): 261-80, 1983.

Carter, Tony, "Danish and Norwegian land ownership and land use," pp. 65-81 in Clive Archer and Stephen Maxwell (eds.), *The Nordic Model: Studies in Public Policy Innovation.* Farnborough, England: Gower, 1980.

Commission of the European Communities. Directorate-General for Agriculture. *Factors Influencing Ownership Tenancy, Mobility and Use of Farmland in Denmark.* Brussels: Commission of the European Communities, 1981.

Hansen, Christian Aagaard, *Educational and Vocational Orientation for the Adult Unemployed and Long-Term Unemployed in Denmark.* Luxembourg: Office for Official Publications of the European Community, 1989.

Institute of Farm Management and Agricultural Economics, *Technical and Economic Changes in Danish Farming: 40 Years of Farm Records 1917-1957* Copenhagen: Landhusholdningsselskabet, 1959.

Jensen, Einar, *Danish Agriculture, Its Economic Development: A Description and Economic Analysis of the Free-trade Epoch, 1870-1930.* Copenhagen: J.H. Schultz, 1937.

Jensen, S.P. and Kjeld Ejler, *Agricultural Production and Marketing.* Copenhagen: Agricultural Council of Denmark, 1986.

Knudsen, P.H. (ed.), *Agriculture in Denmark.* London: Land Books, 1967.

Knudsen, P.H. and Hans Vedholm, *Farmers' Organisations and the Co-operative Movement.* Copenhagen: Agricultural Council of Denmark, 1986.

Manniche, Peter, *Rural Development and the Changing Countries of the World: A Study of Danish Rural Conditions and the Folk High School with its Relevance to the Developing Countries.* Oxford & New York: Pergamon Press, 1969.

Mitchison, Naomi, *Karensgaard: The Story of a Danish Farm.* London: Collins, 1961.

Nash, Erik Francis and E.A. Attwood, *The Agricultural Policies of Britain and Denmark: A Study in Reciprocal Trade.* London: Land Books, 1961.

OECD, *Agricultural Policy in Denmark.* Paris: OECD, 1974.

Skovgaard, Ib and K.B. Andersen, *Research Advisory Services and Education.* Copenhagen: Agricultural Council of Denmark, 1986.

Statistics on Danish Agriculture, 1985. Copenhagen: Agricultural Council of Denmark, 1986.

Thestrup, Poul, *The Standard of Living in Copenhagen 1730-1800: Some Methods of Measurements.* Copenhagen: Københavns Universitets fond for Tilvejebringelse af Læremidler/Gad, 1971.

US Department of Agriculture. *Food Marketing in Denmark.* Washington, DC: Government Printing Office, 1971.

IV. HISTORY

1. General
a) Scandinavia

Barton, H. Arnold, *Scandinavia in the Revolutionary Era, 1760-1815.* Minneapolis: University of Minnesota Press, 1986.

Bukdahl Jørgen and Aage Heinberg, *Scandinavia Past and Present* 3 vols. Odense: Arnkrone, 1959.

Butler, Ewan, *The Horizon Concise History of Scandinavia.* New York: American Heritage Publishing Co, 1973.

Derry, T.K., *A History of Scandinavia: Sweden, Denmark, Finland, Iceland and Norway.* London: Allen & Unwin. Minneapolis, University of Minnesota Press. 1979.

Dovring, Folke, "Scandinavia," pp. 139-162 in Raymond Grew (ed.), *Crises of Political Development in Europe and the United States.* Princeton: Princeton University Press, 1979.

Elting, John R., *Battles for Scandinavia.* (World War II Series, vol. 28). New York: Time-Life, 1981.

Jacobsen, Helge Seidelin, *An Outline History of Denmark.* Copenhagen: Høst. 1986, reprinted 1995.

Kent, H.S.K., *War and Trade in the Northern Seas: Anglo-Saxon Economic Relations in the Mid-18th Century.* Cambridge: Cambridge University Press, 1973.

Kjersgaard, Erik, *History of Denmark.* Copenhagen: Ministry of Cultural Affairs, 1990.

Knudsen, Tim and Bo Rothstein, "State building in Scandinavia," *Comparative Politics* 26 (2): 203-220. 1994.

Lauring, Palle, trans. David Hohnen, *A History of Denmark.* 4th ed. Copenhagen: Høst, 1986.

Lindström, Ulf, *Fascism in Scandinavia, 1920-40.* Stockholm: Almqvist & Wiksell, 1985.

Nissen, Henrik (ed.) (trans Thomas Munch-Petersen), *Scandinavia during the Second World War*. Minneapolis: University of Minnesota Press. Oslo: Universitetsforlaget, 1983.

Nordstrom, Byron J. *Dictionary of Scandinavian History*. Westport, Connecticut: Greenwood Press, 1986.

Scandinavian Journal of History. Stockholm: Almqvist & Wiksell. 1976-, quarterly.

Scott, Franklin, *Scandinavia*. Cambridge, Massachusetts; London: Harvard University Press, 1975.

Toyne, S.M., *The Scandinavians in History*. Port Washington, New York: Kennikat Press, 1970.

Wilson, David M (ed.), *The Northern World: the History and Heritage of Northern Europe*. London: Thames & Hudson, 1980.

b) Denmark

Andrup, Otto, trans John R.B. Gosney, *Bonds of Kinship Between the Royal Houses of Great Britain and Denmark*, 1948. 2nd ed. Copenhagen: Royal Danish Ministry of Foreign Affairs and Gyldendal, 1957.

Birch, J.H.S., *Denmark in History*. London: John Murray, 1938, reprinted Westport, Connecticut: Greenwood Press, 1975.

Danstrup, John, *A History of Denmark*. 2 ed. Copenhagen, 1949.

Gad, Finn, *The History of Greenland*. Vol. 1: *Earliest Times to 1700*. Vol. 2: *1700-1782*. Vol. III: *1782-1808*. London: C. Hurst, vol. I, 1970. Montreal: McGill-Queen's University Press, vols. II & III, 1973, 1982.

Hill, Charles E., *The Danish Sound Dues and the Command of the Baltic: A Study of International Relations*. Durham, North Carolina: Duke University Press, 1926.

Jacobsen, Helge Seidelin, *An Outline History of Denmark*. Copenhagen: Høst, 1986.

Jones, W. Glyn, *The Norse Atlantic Saga, Being the Norse Voyages of Discovery and Settlement to Iceland, Greenland and America*. London: Oxford University Press, 1964.

——, *Denmark*. (Nations of the Modern World series). London: Ernest Benn Ltd. New York: Praeger. 1970.

——, *Denmark: A Modern History*. London; Sydney; Dover, New Hampshire: Croom Helm, 1986 [Revised edition of the previous item].

Kjærgaard, Thorkild (trans. David Hohnen), *The Danish revolution, 1500-1800: An Ecohistorical Interpretation*. Cambridge: Cambridge University Press, 1994.

Kjersgaard, Erik, trans. Reginald Spink, *A History of Denmark*. Copenhagen: Royal Danish Ministry of Foreign Affairs, 1974.

Lauring, Palle, trans. W. Glyn Jones, *History of Denmark in Pictures*. Copenhagen: Hasselbalch. 1963.

——, (trans. David Hohnen), *A History of the Kingdom of Denmark*. 4th ed. Copenhagen: Høst, 1973.

Oakley, Stewart, *A Short History of Denmark*. New York: Praeger, 1972.

——, *The Story of Denmark*. London: Faber & Faber, 1972. [A different title for the previous item].

Rying, Bent (trans. Reginald Spink), *Denmark History (Danish in the South and the North*, Vol. 2). Copenhagen: Royal Danish Ministry of Foreign Affairs, 1988.

2. Prehistory

Blankholm, Hans Peter, *On the Track of a Prehistoric Economy: Maglemosian Subsistence in Early Postglacial South Scandinavia*. Aarhus University Press, 1996.

Froncek, Thomas et al. (eds.), *The Northmen*. New York: Time-Life Books, 1974.

Glob, P.V. (trans. R. Bruce-Mitford), *The Bog People: Iron-Age Man Preserved*. London: Faber. Ithaca, New York: Cornell University Press, 1969.

——, (trans. Jane Bulman), *Denmark: An Archaeological History from the Stone Age to the Vikings*. Ithaca, New York: Cornell University Press, 1971.

——, (trans. Jane Bulman), *Danish Pre-historic Monuments: Denmark from the Stone Age to the Vikings*. London: Faber, 1971.

——, (trans. Joan Bulman), *The Mound People: Danish Bronze-Age Man Preserved*. London: Faber. Ithaca, New York: Cornell University Press, 1974. London: Paladin, 1983.

Jensen, Jørgen, *The Prehistory of Denmark*. London: Methuen, 1982.

Jørgensen, Lise Bender, *North European Textiles Until AD 1000*. Aarhus University Press, 1992.

Klindt-Jensen, Ole (trans. Eva Wilson), *Denmark Before the Vikings*. London: Thames & Hudson, 1957. New York: Praeger, 1969.

Kristiansen, Kristian (ed.), *Archaeological Formation Processes: the Representatiivity of Archaeological Remains from Danish Prehistory.* Aarhus University Press, 1985.

Moltke, Erik, *Runes and Their Origin: Denmark and Elsewhere.* Copenhagen: National Museum of Denmark, 1985.

Munksgaard, Elizabeth, *Denmark: An Archaeological Guide.* London: Faber. New York: Praeger, 1970.

Ramskou, Thorkild, *Prehistoric Denmark.* Copenhagen: National Museum, 1970.

3. Viking and Medieval

Almgren, Bertil, Charlotte Blindheim and Kristján Eldjárn, *The Viking.* Gothenburg, Sweden: Nordbok, 1975.

Brøndsted, Johannes, *The Vikings.* London: Penguin, 1960, 1965.

Foote, Peter and David M. Wilson, *The Viking Achievement.* London: Sidgwick & Jackson, 1969, 1980. New York: Praeger, 1970.

Friis-Jensen, Karsten, *Saxo Grammaticus: A Medieval Author between Norse and Latin Culture.* Copenhagen: Museum Tusculanum Press, 1982.

Graham-Campbell, James, *The Viking World.* New Haven, Connecticut: Ticknor & Fields, 1980.

Hansen, William F., *Saxo Grammaticus and the Life of Hamlet: A Translation History and Commentary.* Lincoln: University of Nebraska Press, 1983.

Jacobsen, Lis, and Erik Moltke, *The Runic Inscriptions of Denmark,* 1947.

Jones, Gwyn, *A History of the Vikings.* London & New York: Oxford University Press, 1973, rev. ed. 1985.

Kendrick, T.D., *A History of the Vikings.* New York: Barnes and Noble, 1968.

Kirkby, Michael Haslock, *The Vikings.* Oxford: Phaidon. New York: E.P. Dutton, 1977.

Klindt-Jensen, Ole, *The World of the Vikings.* Washington: Luce, 1970.

Krogh, Knud J., *Viking Greenland: With a Supplement of Saga Texts.* Copenhagen: The National Museum, 1967.

Larson, Laurence Marcellus, *Canute the Great and the Rise of Danish Imperialism during the Viking Age.* 1912, reprinted New York: AMS Press, 1970.

Levy, Janet E., *Social and Religious Organization in Bronze-age Denmark: An Analysis of Ritual Hoard Finds*. Oxford: B.A.R, 1982.

Loyn, H.R., *The Vikings in Britain*. London: Batsford. New York: St. Martin's, 1977.

Magnusson, Magnus, *Vikings!* New York: E.P. Dutton, 1980.

Nørlund, Poul, trans. W.E. Calvert, *Viking Settlers in Greenland and Their Descendants during Five Hundred Years*. 1937, reprinted New York: Kraus Reprint Co, 1971.

Pálsson, Hermann and Paul Edwards, *Knytlinga Saga: The History of the Kings of Denmark*. Odense University Press, 1986.

Pendlesonn, K.R.G., *The Vikings*. New York: Windward Books, 1980.

Pratt, Fletcher, *The Third King* [Valdemar IV "Atterdag"]. New York: William Sloan Associates. Toronto: George J. McLeod, 1950.

Randsborg, Klaus, *The Viking Age in Denmark: The Formation of a State*. London: Duckworth. New York: St. Martin's, 1980.

Roesdahl, Else (trans. Susan Margeson, Kirsten Williams), *Viking Age Denmark*. London: British Museum Publications, 1982.

——, *The Vikings*. London: Penguin, 1987. 2nd ed., 1998.

Sawyer, P.H., *The Age of the Vikings*. 2nd ed. London: Arnold, 1971.

Saxo Grammaticus, ed. Hilda Ellis Davidson, trans. Peter Fisher, *The History of the Danes*. 2 vols. Cambridge: D.S. Brewer. Totowa, New Jersey: Rowman & Littlefield, 1979-80.

Saxo Grammaticus, *The History of the Danes*, books 1-9. (Gesta Danorum). trans. Peter Fischer. D.S. Brewer, 1996.

Simpson, Jacqueline, *The Viking World*. New York: St. Martin's, 1980.

Skyum-Nielsen, Niels and Niels Lund, *Danish Medieval History: New Currents*. Copenhagen: Museum Tusculanum Press, 1981.

Starcke, Viggo, *Denmark in World History: The External History of Denmark from the Stone Age to the Middle Ages with Special Reference to the Danish Influence on the English-Speaking Nations*. Philadelphia: University of Pennsylvania Press. Oxford: Oxford University Press, 1963.

Wernick, Robert, *The Vikings*. Alexandria, Virginia: Time-Life Books, 1979.

Wilson, David M., *The Vikings and Their Origins*. London: Thames & Hudson. New York: McGraw-Hill, 1970.

Wilson, David M. and Ole Klindt-Jensen, *Viking Art*. Minneapolis: University of Minnesota Press, 1980.

4. Sixteenth Century

Ady, Julia Cartwright, *Christina of Denmark, Duchess of Milan and Lorraine, 1522-1590*. New York: E.P. Dutton, 1913. Reprinted New York: AMS Press, 1973.

Christianson, J.R., "The reconstruction of the Scandinavian aristocracy, 1350-1660," *Scandinavian Studies* 53 (3): 289-301. 1981.

5. Seventeenth Century

Council of Europe, *Christian IV and Europe: the nineteenth art exhibition in the Council of Europe, Denmark* [catalogue], 1988.

Molesworth, Robert, *An Account of Denmark As It Was in the Year 1692*. 1694, reprinted Copenhagen: Rosenkilde & Bagger, 1976.

Riis, Thomas, *Should Auld Acquaintance Be Forgot: Scottish-Danish Relations, c.1450-1707*. Odense: Odense University Press, 1988.

Westergaard, Waldemar. *The Danish West Indies under Company Rule (1671-1754), with a supplementary chapter, 1755-1917*. New York: Macmillan, 1917.

Williams, Ethel Carleton, *Anne of Denmark: Wife of James VI of Scotland, James I of England*. London: Longmans, 1970.

6. Eighteenth Century

Chapman, Hester W., *Caroline Matilda, Queen of Denmark 1751-75*. London: Cape, 1971. New York: Coward, McCann & Geoghegan, 1972.

Feldbæk, Ole, *India Trade under the Danish Flag, 1772-1808: European Enterprise and Anglo-Indian Remittance and Trade*. Lund, Sweden: Studentlitteratur, 1969.

Fischer, Raymond H., *Bering's Voyages: Whither and Why*. Seattle: University of Washington Press, 1977.

Hall, Nevill A.T. (ed. B.W. Higman), *Slave Society in the Danish West Indies: St Thomas, St John and St Croix*. Aarhus University Press/University of West Indies Press, 1993.

Lauridsen, Peter (trans. Julius E. Olson), *Vitus Bering: The Discoverer of the Bering Strait*. 1889, reprinted Freeport, New York: Books for Libraries Press, 1969.

Wolstonecraft, Mary (ed. Carol H. Poston), *Letters Written during a Short Residence in Sweden, Norway and Denmark (1759-1797)*. Lincoln: University of Nebraska Press, 1983.

7. Nineteenth Century

Carr, W., *Schleswig-Holstein 1815-48: A Study in National Conflict.* Manchester: Manchester University Press, 1963.

Gold, Carol, *Educating Middle-Class Daughters: The Education in Private Girls' School in Copenhagen 1790-1820.* Copenhagen: Museum Tusculanum Press, 1996.

Halicz, Emanuel, *Danish Neutrality during the Crimean War (1853-56): Denmark between the Hammer and the Anvil.* Odense: Odense University Press, 1977.

Hansen, S.A., *Early Industrialization in Denmark.* Copenhagen: Gad, 1970.

Hjelholt, Holger, *Great Britain, the Danish-German Conflict and the Danish Succession 1850-1852.* Copenhagen: Munksgaard, 1971.

Holborn, Hajo, *A History of Modern Germany.* London: Eyre and Spottiswoode, 1969.

Nørregaard, Georg (trans. Sigurd Mammen), *Danish Settlements in West Africa, 1658-1850.* Boston, Massachusetts: Boston University Press, 1966.

Miller, Kenneth E., "Danish Socialism and the Kansas Prairie" [Louis Pio], *Kansas Historical Quarterly* 38 (2): 156-68. 1972.

Nielsen, J. Schioldan, *The Life of D.G. Monrad, 1811-1887: Manic-Depressive Disorder and Political Leadership. (Odense University Studies in Psychiatry and Medical Psychology 4).* Odense University Press, 1988.

Pope, Dudley, *The Great Gamble: Nelson at Copenhagen.* London: Weidenfeld & Nicolson, 1972.

8. Twentieth Century

Battiscombe, Georgina, *Queen Alexandra.* London: Constable. Boston, Massachusetts: Houghton Mifflin, 1969.

Bennett, Jeremy, *British Broadcasting and the Danish Resistance Movement 1940-45.* Cambridge: Cambridge University Press, 1966.

Blüdinkow, B., "Denmark during the First World War," *Journal of Contemporary History* 24: 693-703. 1989.

Due-Nielsen, Carsten and Nikolaj Petersen (eds.), *Adaptation and Activism: The Foreign Policy of Denmark 1967-1993.* Copenhagen: DJØF Publishing, 1995.

Einhorn, Eric S., *National Security and Domestic Politics in Post-War Denmark: Some Principal Issues, 1945-61.* Odense: Odense University Press, 1975.

Eriksen, Knut Einar, "Great Britain and the Problem of Bases in the Nordic Areas 1945-1947," *Scandinavian Journal of History* 7 (2): 135-163. 1982.

Hæstrup, Jørgen, (trans. Alison Borch-Johansen), *Secret Alliance: A Study of the Danish Resistance Movement*. 3 vols. Odense: Odense University Press, 1976-77.

——, *Passage to Palestine: Young Jews in Denmark, 1932-45*. Odense University Press, 1983.

Hong, Nathaniel, *Sparks of Resistance: The Illegal Press in German-Occupied Denmark, April 1940-August 1943*. Odense University Press, 1996.

Joesten, Joachim, *Rats in the Larder: The Story of Nazi Influence in Denmark*. New York: G.P. Putnam's, 1939.

Kaarsted, Tage, *Great Britain and Denmark, 1914-20*. Odense: Odense University Press, 1979.

Kirmmse, Bruce H., "Your neighbour: Reflections on the 50th anniversary of the rescue of the Danish Jews," *Scandinavian Review* 81 (2): 37-45. 1993.

Lampe, David, *The Danish Resistance*. New York: Ballantine, 1957.

——, *The Savage Canary: The Story of Resistance in Denmark*. London: Cassel, 1957.

Levine, Daniel, "Conservatism and tradition in Danish social welfare legislation 1890-1933," *Comparative Studies in Society and History*: 54-69. 1978.

Lundestad, Geir. *America, Scandinavia and the Cold War, 1945-1949*. New York: Columbia University Press, 1980.

Nevakivi, Jukka, "Scandinavian talks on military cooperation in 1946-1947: A prelude to the decisions of 1948-1949," *Cooperation and Conflict* 19 (3): 166-75. Sept 1984.

Outze, Børge (ed.), *Denmark during the German Occupation*. Copenhagen: Scandinavian Publishing Co, 1946.

Petersen, Nikolaj, "Danish and Norwegian Alliance Policies 1948-49: A Comparative Analysis," *Cooperation and Conflict* 14: 193-210. 1979.

Petrow, R., *The Bitter Years: The Invasion and Occupation of Denmark and Norway, April 1940-May 1945*. London & New York: William Morrow, 1974.

Reilly, Robin, *The Sixth Floor*. London: Leslie Frewin, 1969.

Schiller, Bernt, "At Gun Point: A critical perspective on the attempts of the Nordic Governments to achieve unity after the Second World War," *Scandinavian Journal of History* 9 (3): 221-38. 1984.

Seymour, Susan, *Anglo-Danish Relations and Germany, 1933-1945*. Odense: Odense University Press, 1982.

Tansill, Charles Callan, *The Purchase of the Danish West Indies*. New York: Greenwood Press, 1968.

Thomas, John Oram, *The Giant-Killers: The Story of the Danish Resistance Movement, 1940-45*. London: Michael Joseph, 1975. New York: Taplinger, 1976.

Thomsen, Birgit Nüchel, "Democracy in Crisis. A Research Project on Danish Politics 1945-1985," *Scandinavian Journal of History* 14: 93-96. 1988.

Tisdall. E.E.P., *Unpredictable Queen: The Intimate Life of Queen Alexandra*. London: Stanley Paul, 1953.

——, *Alexandra: Edward VII's Unpredictable Queen*. New York: John Day, 1954.

Werstein, I., *That Denmark Might Live: The Saga of Danish Resistance in World War II*. Philadelphia: Macrae Smith, 1967.

Yahil, Leni, *The Rescue of Danish Jewry: Test of a Democracy*. Philadelphia: The Jewish Publication Society of America, 1969.

V. LAW

Aaron, Thomas J., *The Control of Police Discretion: The Danish Experience*. Springfield, Illinois: Charles C. Thomas, 1966.

Axmark, Flemming and Hans Gammeltoft-Hansen (eds.), *The Danish Ombudsman: Essays and Articles*. Copenhagen: Jurist- og Økonomforbundets Forlag, 1995.

Berlin, Knud Kugelberg, *Denmark's Right to Greenland, Iceland and the Faroe Islands in Relation to Norway and Denmark*. London: Oxford University Press, 1932.

Blaustein, Albert P. and Gisbert H. Flanz (eds.), *Constitutions of the Countries of the World*. 17 vols. Dobbs Ferry, New York: Oceana Publications, 1986.

Bradley, David, *Family Law and Political Culture* (Scandinavian Laws in Comparative Perspective). London: Sweet & Maxwell, 1996.

Brief Account of the Administration of Justice in Denmark. Copenhagen: Ministry of Justice, 1992.

Clausen, Nis Jul and Karsten Ensig Sørensen, *Takeover Bids: The Danish, Norwegian and Swedish Regulation.* Copenhagen: Jurist- og Økonomforbundets Forlag, 1998.

Criminal Procedure in Denmark: An Outline. Copenhagen University, 1991.

Ginsburg, Ruth Bader, *A Selective Survey of English Language Studies on Scandinavian Law.* South Hackensack, New Jersey: Fred B. Rothman, 1970.

Herlitz, Nils, *Elements of Nordic Public Law.* Stockholm: P.A. Norstedt & Söner, 1969.

Hurwitz, Stephen, *The Ombudsman, Denmark's Parliamentary Commissioner for Civil and Military Administration.* Copenhagen: Det danske Selskab, 1961, 1968.

Jensen, Søren Stenderup, *The European Convention on Human Rights in Scandinavian Law.* Copenhagen: Jurist- og Økonomforbundets Forlag, 1992.

Jørgensen, Ellen Brinck, *Union Citizens: Free Movement and Non-discrimination.* Copenhagen: Jurist- og Økonomforbundets Forlag, 1995.

Knutsson, Johannes, et al. (eds.), *Police and the Social Order: Contemporary Research Perspectives.* Stockholm: National Swedish Council for Crime Prevention, 1979.

Lønberg, Arne, *The Penal System of Denmark.* Copenhagen: Ministry of Justice, 1975.

Petersen, Lars Lindencrone and Niels Ørgaard, *Danish Insolvency Law: A Survey.* Copenhagen: Jurist- og Økonomforbundets Forlag, 1996.

Rehof, Lars Adam and Clans Gulmann (eds.), *Human Rights in Domestic Law and Development — Assistance Policies of the Nordic Countries.* Dordrecht: Nijhoff, 1989.

Scandinavian Studies in Criminology. Oslo: Universitetsforlaget, 1965-.

Scandinavian Studies in Law. Stockholm: Almqvist & Wiksell, 1957-.

Staccy, Frank, *Ombudsmen Compared.* Oxford and New York: Oxford University Press. 1978.

Sturup, Georg Kristoffer, *Treating the "Untreatable": Chronic Criminals at Herstedvester.* Baltimore, Maryland: Johns Hopkins Press, c.1968.

Svarlien, Oscar, *The Eastern Greenland Case in Historical Perspective*. Gainesville: University of Florida Press, 1964.

VI. POLITICS

Aardal, Bernt Olav, "Economics, ideology and strategy: An analysis of the EC-debate in Norwegian and Danish organisations 1961-72," *Scandinavian Political Studies* 6 (ns) (1): 27-49. 1983.

Anckar, Dag, "Political Science in the Nordic Countries" in David Easton, John G. Gunnel and Luigi Graziano (eds.), *The Development of Political Science — A Comparative Survey* London: Routledge, 1991.

Andersen, Gert, *The Danish Parliament*. Copenhagen: Folketingets Presidium, 1975.

Andersen, Heine, "Organisation, classes and the growth of state interventionism in Denmark," *Acta Sociologica* 23: 113-31. 1980.

Andersen, Jørgen Goul, "Decline of class voting or change in class voting? Social classes and party choice in Denmark in the 1970s," *European Journal of Political Research* 12 (3): 243-259. 1984.

——, "Electoral trends in Denmark in the 1980s," *Scandinavian Political Studies* 9 (2): 157-74. 1986.

——, "Denmark: environmental conflict and the 'greening' of the Labour movement," *Scandinavian Political Studies* 13 (2): 185-210. 1990.

—— and Tor Bjørklund, "Structural changes and new cleavages: The Progress Parties in Denmark and Norway," *Acta Sociologica* 33 (3): 195-217. 1990.

——, "Denmark — the Progress Party — populist neo-liberalism and welfare state chauvinism," pp. 193-205 in Paul Hainsworth (ed.), *The Extreme Right in Europe and the USA*. London: Pinter, 1992.

——, "The Scandinavian welfare model in crisis? Achievements and problems of the Danish welfare state in an age of unemployment and low growth," *Scandinavian Political Studies* 20 (1): 1-31. 1997.

Anderson, Stanley V., *The Nordic Council: A Study of Scandinavian Regionalism*. Seattle: University of Washington Press, 1967.

Arter, David, *The Nordic Parliaments: A Comparative Analysis*, London: Hurst. New York: St. Martin's, 1984.

——, "The Nordic parliaments: patterns of legislative influence," *West European Politics* 8 (1): 55-70. 1985.

———, "One *ting* too many — the shift to unicameralism in Denmark" in Lawrence D. Longley (ed.), *Two into One — the Politics and Processes of National Legislative Cameral Change*. Boulder, San Francisco and Oxford: Westview Press, 1991.

Bach, H.C. and Jørgen Taagholt, *Greenland and the Arctic Region: Resources and Security Policy*. 2nd ed. Copenhagen: Information and Welfare Service of the Danish Defence, 1982.

Benoit, France and Gunnar Martens, "Municipal government in Greenland," *Polar Record* 165: 93-104. April 1992.

Bentzon, Karl-Henrik, "The process of politicization of the Danish local elections, 1909-1958," *International Journal of Politics* 4 (1-2): 174-206. 1974.

Berglund, Sten and Ulf Lindström, *The Scandinavian Party System(s)*. Lund: Studentliteratur, 1978.

———, "The Scandinavian party system(s) in transition (?) — A macro-level analysis," *European Journal of Political Research* 7 (2): 187-204. 1979.

Bernstein, Harry and Joan Bernstein, *Industrial Democracy in 12 Nations*. Washington, DC: Bureau of International Labor Affairs, US Department of Labor, 1979.

Berrigan, A. John, "Antecedents of realignments and the case of secular realignment in Denmark," *Scandinavian Political Studies* 5 (ns) (3): 261-81. 1982.

Bierring, Ole, "Denmark: A champion of multilateral diplomacy," *Scandinavian Review* 73 (3): 48-54. Autumn 1985.

Bille, Lars, "Denmark: The oscillating party system," *West European Politics*, 42-57. 1989.

———, "The 1988 election campaign in Denmark," *Scandinavian Political Studies* 14 (3): 205-18. 1991.

Birch, Jens Christian and Henrik Christoffersen (eds.), *Citizen Participation and Local Government in America and Scandinavia*. Gentofte: Erling Olsens Forlag, 1981.

Bjøl, Erling, "Denmark: Between Scandinavia and Europe?" *International Affairs* 64 (4): 601-17. 1986.

Bogason, Peter, "Denmark," pp. 4-15 in Edward Page and Michael J. Goldsmith (eds.), *Central and Local Government Relations: A Comparative Analysis of West European Unitary States*. London: Sage, 1987.

———, "Danish Local Government — toward an effective and efficient welfare state," pp. 261-290 in Joachim Jens Hesse (ed.), *Local*

*Government and Urban Affairs in International Perspective —
Analyses of Twenty Western Industrialised Countries.* Baden:
Nomos Verlagsgesellschaft, 1991.

Boolsen, R. Watt, *Security in the North: Report from a Seminar in
Iceland, April 1982, Concerning Security and Arms Control in the
Northern European NATO Region.* Oslo: Alumni Association of the
Norwegian Defence College, 1982.

Borberg, Preben and Mogens Espersen, *Military Intelligence Service
As Part of Crisis Management.* Copenhagen: Information and
Welfare Service of the Danish Defence, 1980.

Borre, Ole, "Recent Trends in Danish Voting Behavior," pp. 3-37 in
Karl H. Cerny (ed.), *Scandinavia at the Polls: Recent Political
Trends in Denmark, Norway and Sweden.* Washington, DC:
American Enterprise Institute, 1977.

——, "The social basis of Danish electoral behaviour," pp. 241-82 in
Richard Rose (ed.), *Electoral Participation: A Comparative
Analysis.* London: Sage, 1980.

——, "Electoral instability in four Nordic countries 1950-77,"
Comparative Political Studies 13 (2): 141-71. 1980.

——, "Critical electoral change in Scandinavia" in Russell J. Dalton
et al., *Electoral Change in Advanced Industrial Democracies:
Realignment or Dealignment?* Princeton: Princeton University
Press, 1984.

——, "Denmark," pp. 372-399 in Ivor Crewe and David Denver
(eds.), *Electoral Change in Western Democracies: Patterns and
Sources of Electoral Volatility.* London: Croom Helm, 1985.

——, "Economic voting in Danish electoral surveys 1987-94,"
Scandinavian Political Studies 20 (4): 347-65. 1997.

Bregnsbo, Henning and Niels Sidenius, "Adapting Danish Interests to
European Integration," *Scandinavian Political Studies* 16 (1): 73.
1993.

Browne, Eric C., John P. Frendreis and Dennis W. Gleiber,
"Dissolution of governments in Scandinavia: A critical events
perspective," *Scandinavian Political Studies* 9 (2): 93-110. 1986.

Bruun, Finn and Carl-Johan Skovsgaard, "Local self-determination
and central control in Denmark," *International Political Science
Review* 1 (2): 227-44. 1980.

Buchert, E. and H. Mammen, "Regional development problems and
policies in North Jutland," *Acta Sociologica* 21 (4): 381-84. 1978.

Buksti, Jacob A., "Corporate structures in Danish EC policy," *Journal of Common Market Studies* 19 (2): 140-59. Dec 1980.

——, and Lars Norby Johansen, "Variations in organisational participation in government: the case of Denmark," *Scandinavian Political Studies* 2: 197-219. 1979.

Butler, David and Austin Ranney, *Referendums around the World*, London: Macmillan, 1994.

Buzan, Barry, Morten Kelstrup, Pierre Lemaitre, Elzbieta Tromer and Ole Wæver, *The European Security Order Recast: Scenarios for the Post-Cold War Era.* London: Pinter, 1990.

Callesen, Gerd and John Logue, *Social-demokraten and Internationalism: The Copenhagen Social Democratic Newspaper's Coverage of International Labor Affairs 1871-1958.* Gothenborg, Sweden: University of Göteborg Department of History, 1979.

Carlsen, Hanne Norup, J.T.Ross Jackson and Niels I.Meyer (eds.), *When No Means Yes: Danish Visions of a Different Europe.* London: Adamantine Press. New York: New York University Press. Mørke, Denmark: Grevas Forlag, 1993.

Carstairs, A.M., *A Short History of Electoral Systems in Western Europe*, Part 3, pp. 75-122: The Nordic Countries. London: Allen & Unwin, 1980.

Castles, F.G., *The Social Democratic Image of Society: A Study of the Achievements and Origins of Scandinavian Social Democracy in Comparative Perspective.* London: Routledge, 1978.

Christensen, Dag Arne, " Foreign Policy Objectives: Left Socialist Opposition in Denmark, Norway and Sweden," *Scandinavian Political Studies* 21 (1): 51-70. 1998.

Christensen, Jørgen Grønnegård, "Blurring the international-domestic politics distinction: Danish representation at EC negotiations," *Scandinavian Political Studies* 4 (3): 191-208. 1981.

——, "Blurring the international-domestic politics distinction: Danish representation at the EC negotiations," *Scandinavian Political Studies* 4(ns) (3): pp. 190-208. 1981.

——, "In search of unity: Cabinet committees in Denmark," pp. 114-37 in Thomas T. Mackie and Brian W. Hogwood (eds.), *Unlocking the Cabinet: Cabinet Structures in Comparative Perspective.* (Sage Modern Politics Series vol. 10). London: Sage, 1985.

Christensen, Rolf Buschardt, "Denmark: consequences of EC membership," *Scandinavian Political Studies* 3(ns) (1): 79-94. 1980.

Christiansen, Niels Finn, "Denmark: End of the idyll," *New Left Review* 144: 5-32. 1984.

——, "The Danish No to Maastricht," *New Left Review* 195: 97-100. 1992.

Co-operation and Conflict: Nordic Journal of Intenational Politics. Oslo Norwegian University Press, 1965-. quarterly.

Cornell, Richard, "K.K. Steinke's notion of *personlig kultur* and the moral basis of Danish social democracy," *Scandinavian Studies* 54 (3): 220-38. 1982.

Dahl, Hans F., "Those Equal Folk," *Daedalus* 113 (1): 93-108. 1984.

Dahlerup, Drude, "Women's entry into politics: The experience of the Danish local and general elections, 1908-20," *Scandinavian Political Studies* 1 (2-3): 139-62. 1978.

——, "Is the new women's movement dead? Decline or change in the Danish movement," pp. 217-244 in *The New Women's Movement: Feminism and Political Power in Europe and the USA*. London: Sage, 1986.

——, "From a Small to a Large Minority: Women in Scandinavian Politics," *Scandinavian Political Studies* 11 (4): 275-98. 1988.

Dahlsgard, Inga, *Women in Denmark, Yesterday and Today.* Copenhagen: Det danske Selskab, 1980.

Damgaard Erik, "The parliamentary basis of Danish governments: The patterns of coalition formation," *Scandinavian Political Studies* 4: 30-57. 1969.

——, "Stability and change in the Danish party system over half a century," *Scandinavian Political Studies* 9: 103-25. 1974.

——, "The political role of non-political bureaucrats in Denmark," pp. 275-291 in M. Dogan. (ed.), *The Mandarins of Western Europe: The Political Role of Top Civil Servants.* London: Sage, 1975.

—— and Jerrold G Rusk, "Cleavage structures and representational linkages: A longitudinal analysis of Danish legislative behavior," *American Journal of Political Science* XX (2): 179-205. 1976.

—— and Kjell A. Eliassen, "Corporate pluralism in Danish law-making," *Scandinavian Political Studies* 1 (4): 285-313. 1978.

—— and Jerrold G. Rusk, "Cleavage structures and representational linkages: A longitudinal analysis of Danish legislative behaviour," pp. 169-188 in Ian Budge, Ivor Crewe and Dennis Fairlie (eds.), *Party Identification and Beyond.* Chichester, New York, Brisbane, Toronto, Singapore: John Wiley & Sons, 1979.

——, "The function of parliament in the Danish political system: results of recent research," *Legislative Studies Quarterly* 5 (1): 101-21. Feb. 1980.

—— and Kjell A. Eliassen, "Reduction of party conflict through corporate participation in Danish law-making," *Scandinavian Political Studies* 3 (2): 105-21. 1980.

——, "The public sector in a democratic order: Problems and non-solutions in the Danish case," *Scandinavian Political Studies* 5(ns) (4): 37-58. 1982.

——, "The importance and limits of party government: Problems of governance in Denmark," *Scandinavian Political Studies* 7 (2): 97-110 June 1984.

——, "The public sector in a democratic order: Problems and non-solutions in the Danish case," *Scandinavian Political Studies* 5 (ns) (1): 337-58. 1982.

—— and Palle Svensson, "Who Governs? Parties and Policies in Denmark," *European Journal of Political Research* 17 (6): 731-46. 1989.

——, (ed.), *Parliamentary Change in the Nordic countries.* Oslo: Scandinavian University Press, 1992.

DANIDA, *The Nordic Way — the Nordic Countries and the Developing World.* Copenhagen: Danida, 1995.

Danish Political Parties — In Their Own Words. Copenhagen: Ministry of Foreign Affairs, 1994.

Dreyer, H. Peter, *Scandinavia Faces Europe.* Paris: Atlantic Institute for International Affairs, 1973.

Due-Nielsen, Carsten and Nikolaj Petersen (eds.), *Adaption and Activism: Denmark's Foreign Policy 1967-1993.* Copenhagen: Jurist- og Økonomforbundets Forlag, 1995.

Early, Barry, "Local government reorganisation in Denmark: Some comparisons with Ireland," *Administration* (Dublin) 22 (2): 128-140. 1974.

Einhorn, Eric S., "Danish politics in the 1980s: The habit of muddling through," *Current History* 81 (479): 412-16, 434, 448. 1982.

——and John Logue, *Welfare States in Hard Times: Problems, Policies and Politics in Denmark and Sweden.* Rev. ed., Kent, Ohio: Kent Popular Press, 1982.

——and John Logue, *Modern Welfare States: Politics and Policies in Social Democratic Scandinavia.* New York: Praeger Publishers, 1989.

Elder, N.C.M (1975), "The Scandinavian States," in Finer, S.E. (ed.), *Adversary Politics and Electoral Reform.* London: Anthony Wigram, 1975.

Elder, Neil, "Denmark," pp. 73-91 in Juliet Lodge (ed.), *Direct Elections to the European Parliament 1984.* London: Macmillan, 1986.

Elder, Neil, Alastair H. Thomas and David Arter, *The Consensual Democracies: The Government and Politics of the Scandinavian States.* Rev. ed. Oxford: Blackwell, 1988.

Eliason, L.C., "Reading the cards on the table: Danish politics in the era of European Integration," *Scandinavian Studies* 64: 544-81. 1992.

Eliassen, Kjell A. and Pedersen, Mogens N., "Professionalisation of legislatures: Long-term changes in political recruitment in Denmark and Norway," *Comparative Studies in Society and History* 20 (2): 286-319. 1978.

—— (eds.), *Skandinaviske politiske institutioner og politisk adfærd 1970-1984. En kommenteret bibliografi.* [Scandinavian political institutions and political behavior 1970-1984: An annotated bibliography]. Odense: Odense University Press, 1985.

Eliassen, Kjell A., "Professionalisation of legislatures: long-term change in political recruitment in Denmark and Norway," *Comparative Studies in Society and History* 20 (2): 286-318. 1978.

Elklit, Jørgen, "Sub-national election campaigns: The Danish local elections of November 1989," *Scandinavian Political Studies* 14 (3): 219-319. 1991.

——, "The Best of Both Worlds? The Danish Electoral System 1915-1920," *Electoral Studies* 11 (3-9): 189. 1992.

——, "Simpler than its reputation — the electoral system in Denmark since 1920," *Electoral Studies* 12 (1): 41-58. 1993.

Elvander, Nils, "The role of the state in the settlement of labour disputes in the Nordic countries: A comparative analysis," *European Journal of Political Research* 2: 363-83. 1974.

——, *Scandinavian Social Democracy: Its Strengths and Weakness.* Uppsala: Almqvist & Wiksell International, 1979.

Espersen, Mogens, *The Baltic: Balance and Security.* Copenhagen: Information and Welfare Service of the Danish Defence, 1982.

Esping-Andersen, Gösta, *Politics against Markets: The Social Democratic Road to Power.* Princeton, New Jersey: Princeton University Press, 1985.

Fagerberg, Jan and Lars Lundberg (eds.), *European Economic Integration: A Nordic Perspective.* Aldershot: Avebury, 1993.

Faurby, Ib, "Party System and Foreign Policy in Denmark," *Cooperation and Conflict* 14: 159-70. 1979.

——, "Government by Opposition: Denmark and the New Missiles in Europe," *Scandinavian Review* 72 (2): 47-53. 1984.

Fitzmaurice, John, "National Parliaments and European Policy-making: the Case of Denmark," *Parliamentary Affairs* 29 (3): 281-92. 1976.

——, "Denmark," in Stanley Henig (ed.), *Political Parties in the European Community.* London: Allen & Unwin, 1979.

——, *Politics in Denmark.* London: Hurst. New York: St. Martin's, 1981.

——, "Coalitional Theory and Practice in Scandinavia," pp. 251-277 in G. Pridham (ed.), *Coalition Behaviour in Theory and Practice: An Inductive Model for Western Europe.* Cambridge: Cambridge University Press, 1986.

——, "The Politics of Belgium and Denmark: A Comparative Perspective," *Government and Opposition* 22 (1): 33-48. 1987.

——. *Security and Politics in the Nordic Area.* London: Gower, 1987.

——, *The Baltic — A Regional Future.* London: Macmillan, 1992.

Flanagan, Robert J., David W. Soskice and Lloyd Ulman, *Unionism, Economic Stabilization and Incomes Policies: European Experiences.* Washington, DC: Brookings Institution, 1983.

Flynn, Gregory, *NATO's Northern Allies.* London: Croom Helm, 1985.

Foighel, Isi, "Home rule in Greenland: A framework for local autonomy," *Common Market Law Review* 17 (1):90-109. 1980.

——, "A framework for local autonomy: The Greenland case," *Israel Yearbook on Human Rights* 9: 82-105. 1979.

Franklin, Mark N., Thomas T. Mackie and Henry Valen et al., *Electoral Change: Responses to Evolving Social and Attitudinal Structures in Western Countries.* Cambridge & New York: Cambridge University Press, 1992. [includes chapter on Denmark by Ole Borre.]

Gellhorn, Walter, *Ombudsmen and Others: Citizens' Protectors in Nine Countries.* Cambridge, Massachusetts: Harvard University Press, 1962. pp. 5-47, "Denmark's Ombudsman," by I.M. Pedersen.

Georg, Anders, Niels-Peter Albertsen and John Host Schmidt (eds.), *Denmark's Presidency of the European Community.* Copenhagen: Royal Danish Ministry of Foreign Affairs, 1978.

Gilberg, Trond, "Communism in the Nordic Countries: Denmark, Norway, Sweden and Iceland," pp. 205-59 in David Childs (ed.), *The Changing Face of Western Communism*. New York: St. Martin's, 1980.

Graham, John, *A Comparative Study of Firefighting Arrangements in Britain, Denmark, the Netherlands and Sweden*. London: HMSO, 1992.

Grimsson, O.R., "Peripheries and nationalism: The Faroes and Greenland," *Scandinavian Political Studies* 1 (4): 315-26. 1978.

Gulmann, Claus, "The Single European Act — some remarks from a Danish perspective," *Common Market Law Review* 24: 31-40. 1987.

Gundelach, Peter and Ole Riis, "Value Changes in Denmark: A New Conservatism?" *Scandinavian Review* 81 (3): 29-33. 1993.

Haagerup, Niels J., *A Brief Introduction to Danish Foreign Policy and Defense*. Copenhagen: Information and Welfare Service of the Danish Defence, 1980.

——, "Denmark's views on NATO and other security issues," *Scandinavian Review* 72 (4): 35-41. 1984.

Haahr, Henrik, "European Integration and the Left in Britain and Denmark," *Journal of Common Market Studies* XXX (1-3): 77-100. 1992.

Haahr, Jens Henrik, *Looking to Europe: The EC Policies of the British Labour Party and the Danish Social Democrats*. Århus: Aarhus University Press, 1993.

Haarder, Erik, *Local Government in Denmark*. Copenhagen: Det danske Selskab, 1973.

Haavio-Mannila, Elina et al., (eds.), *Unfinished Democracy: Women in Nordic Politics*. New York: Pergamon, 1985.

Hagel-Sørensen, Karsten and Hjalte Rasmussen, "The Danish administration and its interaction with the Community administration," *Common Market Law Review* 22 (2): 273-300. 1985.

Hansen, Erik Jørgen, "The Progress Party in Denmark is a class-party — but which class?" *Acta Sociologica* 25 (2):167-76. 1982.

Hansen, Peter, "Adaptive behavior of small states: The case of Denmark and the European Community," pp. 143-74 in Patrick J. McGowan (ed.), *Sage International Year Book of Foreign Policy Studies*. Beverly Hills, California: Sage, 1974.

Hansen, Povl, "The Danish ombudsman directives and relation to parliament," *Cambrian Law Review* 3: 43-53. 1972.

Harder, Margit, and Keith Pringle (eds.), *Protecting Children in Europe: Towards a New Millennium.* Denmark: Aalborg Universitetsforlag. 1997. [Includes contributions from Denmark, Finland, England, Ireland and Italy].

Haskel, Barbara G., *The Scandinavian Option: Opportunities and Opportunity Costs in Postwar Scandinavian Foreign Affairs.* Oslo: Universitetsforlaget, 1976.

Heckscher, Gunnar, *The Welfare State and Beyond: Success and Problems in Scandinavia.* Minneapolis: University of Minnesota Press, 1984.

Heisler, Martin O., "Denmark's Quest for Security: Constraints and Opportunities within the Alliance," pp. 57-112 in Gregory Flynn, (ed.), *NATO's Northern Allies: the National Security Policies of Belgium, Denmark, the Netherlands and Norway.* Totowa, New Jersey: Rowman & Allanheld, 1985.

——, (ed.), The Nordic Region: Changing Perspectives in International Relations. Special issue of the *Annals of the American Academy of Political and Social Science* vol. 512. 1990.

Hernes, Helga Maria, *Welfare State and Woman Power: Essays in State Feminism.* Oslo: Norwegian University Press, 1987.

Holbraad, Carsten, *Danish Neutrality.* Oxford: Clarendon Press, 1991.

Holm, Hans-Henrik, "A democratic revolt? Stability and change in Danish security policy, 1979-1989", *Cooperation and Conflict* 24: 179-197. 1989.

Janda, Kenneth, *Political Parties: A Cross-National Survey.* New York: Free Press. London: Collier Macmillan, 1980. [pp. 404-25 covers Denmark.]

Jarlov, Carsten, and Ole P. Kristensen, "Electoral mobility and social change in Denmark," *Scandinavian Political Studies* 1(ns) (1): 61-78. 1978.

—— and Lise Togeby, "Political involvement and the development of political attitudes," *Scandinavian Political Studies* 2(ns) (2): 121-40. 1979.

Jenkins, David, *Job Power: Blue and White Collar Democracy.* Harmondsworth and Baltimore, Maryland: Penguin Books, 1974.

Johansen, Lars Nørby, "Denmark," in Geoffrey Hand, Jacques Georgel and Christoph Sasse (eds.), *European Electoral Systems Handbook.* London: Butterworth, 1979.

―― and Ole P. Kristensen, "Corporatist traits in Denmark, 1946-1976," pp. 189-218 in Gerhard Lehmbruch and Philippe C. Schmitter (eds.), *Patterns of Corporatist Policy-Making*. Beverley Hills, California: Sage, 1982.

Karvonen, Lauri and Jan Sundberg (eds.), *Social Democracy in Transition*. Aldershot: Dartmouth, 1991.

Kelstrup, Morten (ed.), *European Integration and Denmark's Participation*. Copenhagen: Political Studies Press for the Institute of Political Science, 1992.

Kienetz, Alvin, "Ethnonationalism and Decolonialization in Greenland and Northern Eurasia," *Canadian Review of Studies in Nationalism* XIV (2): 247-60. 1987.

Klausen, Kurt Klaudi, "Danish Local Government: Integrating into the EU?" pp.16-38 in M.J.F. Goldsmith and K.K. Klausen (eds.), *European Integration and Local Government*. Cheltenham, UK & Brookfield, US: Edward Elgar, 1997.

Knudsen, Tim, "A Portrait of Danish State-Culture: Why Denmark needs two National Anthems," pp. 262-97 in Morten Kelstrup (ed.), *European Integration and Denmark's Participation*. Copenhagen: Institute of Political Science, 1992.

Krasner, Michael A. and Nikolaj Petersen, "Peace and politics: The Danish peace movement and its impact on national security policy," *Journal of Peace Research* 23 (2): 155-73. 1986.

Lane, Jan-Erik, Tuomo Martikainen, Palle Svensson, Gunnar Vogt and Henry Valen, "Scandinavian exceptionalism reconsidered," *Journal of Theoretical Politics* 5 (2): 195-230. 1993.

Lafferty, William M., *Economic Development and the Response of Labor in Scandinavia*. Oslo: Universitetsforlaget, 1971.

Laursen, Finn, "Parliamentary bodies specializing in European Union affairs: Denmark and the Europe Committee of the Folketing," pp. 43-60 in Finn Laursen and Spyros A. Pappas (eds.), *The Changing Role of Parliaments in the European Union*. Maastricht, Netherlands: European Institute of Public Administration, 1995.

Lerhard, Mogens (ed.), *The Danish Ombudsman 1955-1969: Seventy-five Cases from the Ombudsman's Reports*. Copenhagen: Schultz, 1972.

Leni, Yahil, "National Pride and Defeat — a comparison of Danish and German nationalism," in Jehuda Reinharz and George L. Mosse (eds.), *The Impact of Western Nationalisms*. London: Sage, 1992.

Lerhard, Mogens (ed.), *The Danish Ombudsman 1955-1969*. Copenhagen: Schultz, 1972.

Lindström, Ulf, "The changing Scandinavian voter: When, where, how, who, why?" *European Journal of Political Research* 10: 321-32. 1982.

——, *Fascism in Scandinavia 1920-1940*. Stockholm: Almqvist & Wiksell, 1985.

Listhaug, Ola, S.E. Macdonald and G. Rabinowitz, "A comparative spatial analysis of European party systems," *Scandinavian Political Studies* 13 (3): 227-54. 1990. [Compares Denmark, France, Netherlands, Norway, Sweden, West Germany].

Logue, John, *Socialism and Abundance: Radical Socialism in the Danish Welfare State*. Minneapolis: University of Minnesota Press, 1982.

——, "Social welfare, equality, and the labour movement in Denmark and Sweden," *Comparative Social Research* 6: 243-77. 1983.

——, "Stable Democracy Without Majorities? Scandinavian Parliamentary Government Today," *Scandinavian Review* 73 (3): 39-47. 1985.

—— and Eric Einhorn, "Restructuring the Governors — The Nordic Experience with Limiting the Strong State," *Scandinavian Political Studies* 11 (1): 45-68. 1988.

Lundestad, Geir, *America, Scandinavia and the Cold War 1945-1949*. New York: Columbia University Press, 1980.

Lyck, Lise (ed.), *Denmark and EC Membership Evaluated*. London: Pinter Publishers. New York: St. Martin's Press, 1992.

——, *The Nordic Countries and the Internal Market of the EEC*. Copenhagen: Handelshøjskolens forlag & Nyt Nordisk Forlag Arnold Busck, 1990.

Lykketoft, Mogens, "Towards economic democracy: Wage earners' funds," *Scandinavian Review* 65 (2): 40-45. 1977.

Mackie, Thomas T. and Richard Rose (eds.), *The International Almanac of Electoral History*. 3rd ed. London: Macmillan, 1991.

—— (eds.), *A Decade of Election Results: Updating the International Almanac*. Glasgow: University of Strathclyde, Centre for the Study of Public Policy, 1997.

Maor, Moshe, "The 1990 Danish election: An unnecessary contest?" *West European Politics* 14 (3): 209-14. 1991.

McDaniel, Gerald (1983), "Denmark," pp. 157-183 in Vincent E McHale and Sharon Skowronski (eds.), *Political Parties in Europe*. London: Greenwood Press, 1983.

Meyer, Niels, Villy Sørensen and K. Helveg Petersen, *Revolt from the Centre*. London: Marion Boyars, 1981.

Miles, Lee (ed.), *The European Union and the Nordic Countries*. London: Routledge, 1996.

Miljan, Toivo, *The Reluctant Europeans: The Attitudes of the Nordic Countries towards European Integration*. London: Hurst. Montreal: McGill-Queens University Press, 1977.

Miller, Kenneth E., "The Danish electoral system," *Parliamentary Affairs* 18 (1): 71-81. 1964/65.

——, *Government and Politics in Denmark*. Boston: Houghton Mifflin, 1968.

——, "Parliament and local government reform in Denmark," *Parliamentary Affairs* 24 (4): 321-37. 1971.

——, "Policy-making by referendum: the Danish experience," *West European Politics* 5 (1): 54-67. 1982.

——, *Denmark: A Troubled Welfare State*. Boulder, San Francisco, Oxford: Westview Press, 1991.

——, *Friends and Rivals: Coalition Politics in Denmark, 1901-1995*. Lanham, New York & London: University Press of America, 1996.

Møller, J. Ørstrøm, "Danish EC decision-making: An insider's view," *Journal of Common Market Studies* 21 (3): 245-60. 1983.

Mouritzen, Hans, "The two musterknaben and the naughty boy: Sweden, Finland and Denmark in the process of European integration," *Cooperation and Conflict* 28 (4): 373-402. 1993.

——, "The Nordic Model as a foreign policy instrument: Its rise and its fall," *Journal of Peace Research* 32 (1): 9-21. 1995.

Mouritzen, Hans, Ole Wæver and Håkon Wiberg, *European Integration and National Adaptations: a Theoretical Inquiry*. Commack, New York: Nova Science Publications, 1996.

Nannestad, Peter, *Reactive Voting in Danish General Elections*. Århus: Aarhus University, 1989.

Neumann, Iver B., "A region-building approach to Northern Europe," *Review of International Studies* 20: 53-74. 1994.

Nielsen, Flemming Schroll, *AMF — NATO's Crisis Force*. Copenhagen: Information and Welfare Service of the Danish Defense, 1982.

Nielsen, Hans Jørgen, "The uncivic culture: Attitudes towards the political system in Denmark, and vote for the Progress Party 1973-75," *Scandinavian Political Studies* 11: 147-54. 1976.

—— and Steen Sauerberg, "Upstairs and Downstairs in Danish Politics: An analysis of political apathy and social structure," *Scandinavian Political Studies* 3 (ns) (1): 59-78. 1980.

——, "Size and evaluation of government: Danish attitudes towards politics at multiple levels of government," *European Journal of Political Research* 9 (1): 47-58. 1981.

——, "The Danish election of 1981," *West European Politics* 5 (2): 305-8. 1982.

——, "Electoral politics and the corporate system: The question of support," *Scandinavian Political Studies* 5 (1): 43-65. 1982.

——, "Ambiguities in attitudes towards interest group influence," *Scandinavian Political Studies* 8 (1-2): 65-84. 1985.

——, "The Danish Voters and the Referendum in June 1992 on the Maastricht Agreement," pp. 365-80 in Morten Kelstrup (ed.), *European Integration and Denmark's Participation*. Copenhagen: Institute of Political Science, 1992.

Nielsen, Lars Nordskov, "The Danish Ombudsman," *Administration, Journal of the Institute of Public Administration of Ireland* 21 (3): 355-364. 1973.

Nilson, Sten Sparre, "Norway and Denmark," pp. 205-34 in Peter H. Merkl (ed.), *Western European Party Systems: Trends and Prospects*. New York: Free Press. London: Collier Macmillan, 1980.

Nissen, Henrik (ed.), *Scandinavia during the Second World War*. Minneapolis: University of Minnesota Press, 1983.

Nissen, Ove, "Key issues in the local government debate in Denmark," pp. 190-197 in Richard Batley and Gerry Stoker, *Local Government in Europe — Trends and Developments*. Basingstoke: Macmillan, 1991.

Noraagerup, Niels Jørgen, *A Brief Introduction to Danish Foreign Policy and Defence*. 2nd rev. ed. Copenhagen: Information and Welfare Service of Danish Defence, 1980.

Nordeval, Ingunn, "Party and legislative participation among Scandinavian women," *West European Politics* 8 (4): 71-89. 1985.

Noreen, Erik, "The Nordic Balance: A security policy concept in theory and practice," *Co-operation and Conflict* 18 (1): 43-56. 1983.

Nørgaard, Asbjørn Sonne, *The Politics of Institutional Control: Corporatism in Danish Occupational Safety and Health Regulation and Unemployment Insurance, 1870-1995.* Århus: Forlaget Politica, 1997.

Nørgaard, Ole, Thomas Pedersen and Nikolaj Petersen (eds.), *The European Community in World Politics.* London: Pinter, 1993.

Øberg, Jan (ed.), *Nordic security in the 1990s: Options in the changing Europe.* London: Pinter Publishers for TFF, The Transnational Foundation for Peace and Future Research, 1992.

Olsen, Thorsten B (ed.), *Interdependence versus Integration: Denmark, Scandinavia and Western Europe, 1945-60.* Odense: Odense Universitetsforlag, 1996.

Open to the World: Local Government in Denmark. Copenhagen: National Association of Local Authorities, 1990.

Örvik, Nils, "Greenland: The politics of a new northern nation," *International Journal* 39 (4): 932-961. 1984.

Pallesen, Thomas, *Health Care Reforms in Britain and Denmark: The Politics of Economic Success and Failure.* Århus: Forlaget Politica, 1997.

Paterson, William E. and Alastair H. Thomas (eds.), *Social Democratic Parties in Western Europe.* London: Croom Helm, 1977.

——, *The Future of Social Democracy.* Oxford: Oxford University Press, 1986.

Pedersen, I.M., "Denmark's Ombudsman," pp. 75-94 in Donald C. Rowat (ed.), *The Ombudsman: Citizen's Defender.* London: Allen & Unwin, 1968.

Pedersen, Klaus Carsten, "National views on Western Europe's security policy — Denmark," pp. 117-124 in Mathias Jopp (ed.), *Integration and Security in Western Europe — Inside the European Pillar.* Boulder: Westview Press, 1991.

Pedersen, Lars Dahl, *The Politics of Cost Containment in Public Services. Hospital Budgeting in Denmark, Germany, and the Netherlands, 1978-92.* Århus: Forlaget Politica, 1997.

Pedersen, Mogens N., "Preferential voting in Denmark: The voters' influence on the election of Folketing candidates," *Scandinavian Political Studies* 1: 167-87. 1966.

——, "Consensus and conflict in the Danish Folketing 1945-65," *Scandinavian Political Studies* 2: 143-166. 1967.

——, Erik Damgaard and P. Nannestad Olsen, "Party distances in the Danish Folketing 1945-1968," *Scandinavian Political Studies* 6: 87-106. 1971.

——, "The geographical matrix of parliamentary representation: A spatial model of political recruitment," *European Journal of Political Research* 3: 1-19. 1975.

——, "The circulation of a legislature: The Danish Folketing 1849-1968," pp. 63-101 in William O. Aydelotte (ed.), *The History of Parliamentary Behavior*, Princeton: Princeton University Press, 1977.

——, *Political Development and Elite Transformation in Denmark.* London, Thousand Oaks, New Delhi: Sage, 1976.

——, "The dynamics of European party systems: Changing patterns of electoral volatility," *European Journal of Political Research* 7: 1-26. 1979.

——, *The Defeat of All Parties: The Danish Folketing Election, 1973.* Odense: Odense University Department of Public Finance and Policy. 1983.

——, "A. John Berrigan on Realignment in Denmark: A critical comment," *Scandinavian Political Studies* 6(ns) (1): 99-103. 1983.

——, "The Danish 'Working Multiparty System': Breakdown or Adaptation?" pp. 1-60 in Hans Daalder (ed.), *Party Systems in Denmark, Austria, Switzerland, the Netherlands, and Belgium.* London: Pinter, 1987.

——, "Incumbency Success and Defeat in Times of Electoral Turbulences: Patterns of Legislative Recruitment in Denmark 1945-1990," pp. 218-250 in Albert Somit et al. (eds.), *The Victorious Incumbent: A Threat to Democracy?* Aldershot: Dartmouth, 1994.

Pesonen, Pertti and Alastair H. Thomas, "Coalition formation in Scandinavia" in Vernon Bogdanor (ed.), *Coalition Government in Western Europe.* London: Routledge, 1983.

Petersen, Nikolaj, "Danish Security Policy in the Seventies: Continuity or change?" pp. 7-38 in Johan-Jørgen Holst (ed.), *Five Roads to Nordic Security.* Oslo: Universitetsforlaget, 1973.

——, "Attitudes towards European integration and the Danish Common Market referendum," *Scandinavian Political Studies* 1 (1): 23-41. 1978.

——, "The Scandilux experiment: Towards a transnational social democratic security perspective?" *Co-operation and Conflict* 20: 1-22. 1985.

——, "Abandonment vs Entrapment: Denmark and Military Integration in Europe 1948-1951," *Co-operation and Conflict* XXI: 169-186. 1986.

——, "The security policies of small NATO countries: Factors of change," *Cooperation and Conflict* 23 (3): 145-63. 1988.

——, *Danish Security Policy after the Cold War: Adaptation and Innovation.* Århus: Institute of Political Science, 1994.

——, "Denmark and the European Union 1985-96: A two-level analysis," *Co-operation and Conflict* 31 (2): 185-210. 1996.

Picard, Louis A., "Decentralization, 'recentralization' and 'steering mechanisms': Paradoxes of local government in Denmark," *Polity* 15 (4): 536-54. 1983.

Piven, Frances Fox (ed.), *Labor Parties in Postindustrial Societies.* Cambridge: Polity Press, 1991.

Postel-Vinay, Olivier, "L'éternité sociale-democrate: L'éxemple danois," *Le Debat* 7 (Dec.): 37-57. 1980.

Rasmussen, Hans Kornø, *No Entry: Immigration Policy in Europe.* Copenhagen: Handelshøjskolens Forlag. 1996.

Regulski, Jerzy, *Decentralization and Local Government — a Danish-Polish Comparative Study in Political Systems.* New Brunswick: Transaction Publishers, 1998.

Rohde, Peter P., "The Communist Party of Denmark," pp. 3-33 in A.F. Upton (ed.), *The Communist Parties of Scandinavia and Finland.* London: Weidenfeld & Nicolson, 1973.

Rusk, Jerrold G. and Ole Borre, "The changing party space in Danish voter perceptions, 1971-73," pp. 137-61 in Ian Budge, Ivor Crewe and Dennis Fairlie (eds.), *Party Identification and Beyond: Representations of Voting and Party Competition.* London: John Wiley, 1979.

Sainsbury, Diane, "Class voting and left voting in Scandinavia: The impact of different operationalizations of the Working Class," *European Journal of Political Research* 15 (5): 507-26. 1987.

Särlvik, Bo, "Coalition politics and policy output in Scandinavia: Sweden, Denmark and Norway," in V. Bogdanor (ed.) *Coalition Government in Western Europe.* London: Routledge, 1983.

Sauerberg, Steen, "The general election in Denmark 1988," *Scandinavian Political Studies* 11 (4): 361-71. 1988.

——, "The Danish Parliamentary Election of December 1990," *Scandinavian Political Studies* 14 (4): 321-34. 1991.

Scandinavian Journal of History "Scandinavianism" [Whole issue devoted to this subject], 9 (3): 171-253. 1984.

Scandinavian Political Studies. Annual, 1966-77. Quarterly, 1978-. Oslo: Universitetsforlaget.

Scheuer, Steen, "Denmark: Return to decentralization," pp. 168-197 in Anthony Ferner and Richard Hyman (eds.), *Industrial Relations in the New Europe*. Oxford: Blackwell Publishers, 1992.

Schlüter, Poul, "Denmark facing the challenges of the 1990s," *International Affairs* (Moscow) 9 (9): 26. 1991.

Schmidt, Kristian, *Collective Western European Resort to Armed Force: Lessons from Danish, Italian and British Experience in the Gulf and Former Yugoslavia*. Copenhagen: Jurist- og Økonomforbundets Forlag, 1994.

Schou, Tove-Lise, "Denmark" chapter in Jean Blondel and Ferdinand Müller-Rommel (eds.), *Cabinets in Western Europe*. London: Macmillan, 1988.

Schüttenmeyer, Suzanne S., "Denmark: 'De Grønne,'" pp. 55-60 in Ferdinand Müller-Rommel (ed.), *New Politics in Western Europe*. Boulder: Westview, 1989.

Schwerin, Don S., "Norwegian and Danish incomes policy and European monetary integration," *West European Politics* 3 (3): 388-405. 1980.

——, "The Danes said 'No' to the Maastricht Treaty: The Danish EC referendum of June 1992," *Scandinavian Political Studies* 16 (1): 93-103. 1992.

—— and Palle Svensson, "The Danes and the Maastricht Treaty: The Danish EC referendum of June 1992," *Electoral Studies* 12 (2): 99-111. 1993.

—— et al., "The European Union: The Danes Said 'No' in 1992 but 'Yes' in 1993: How and Why?" *Electoral Studies* 13 (2): 107-116. 1994.

Sjöblom, Gunnar, *The Roles of Political Parties in Denmark and Sweden, 1970-1984*. Copenhagen: University of Copenhagen Institute of Political Studies, 1985.

Skovsgaard, Carl-Johan, *Reforms and Central-Local Relations: The Changing Role of Local Government in Denmark*. Århus: University of Aarhus: Institute of Political Science, 1983.

Solem, Erik, *The Nordic Council and Scandinavian Integration*. London, New York: Praeger, 1977.

Sørensen, Carsten Lehmann, "Danish party policies on European and Nordic cooperation," *Cooperation and Conflict* 14: 171-191. 1979

——, "The Danish experience with the European Communities," *Österreichishe Zeitschrift für Politikwissenschaft* 16 (2): 159-65. 1987.

Sørensen, Georg, "Peace and security in Europe: the context for Denmark's choices," *Cooperation and Conflict* 21 (4): 219-240. 1985.

Stehouwer, Jan, "Long-term ecological analyses of electoral statistics in Denmark," *Scandinavian Political Studies* 2: 94-116. 1967.

Stephens, John D., "The Scandinavian welfare states: Achievements, crisis, and prospects" pp. 32-65 in Gøsta Esping-Andersen (ed.), *Welfare States in Transition: National Adaptations in Global Economies*. London, Thousand Oaks. New Delhi: Sage/UNRISD, 1996.

Stokke, Olav (ed.), *Western Middle Power and Global Poverty — The Determinants of the Aid Policies of Canada, Denmark, the Netherlands, Norway and Sweden*. Uppsala: The Scandinavian Institute of African Studies, 1989.

Strøm, Kaare, "Minority governments in parliamentary democracies: The rationality of non-winning cabinet solutions," *Comparative Political Studies* 17 (2): 199-227. 1984.

——, "Party goals and government performance in parliamentary democracies," *American Political Science Review* 79: 738-754, 1985.

——, "Deferred gratification and minority governments in Scandinavia," *Legislative Studies Quarterly*, 11 (4): 583-605. 1986.

——, *Minority Government and Majority Rule*. Cambridge & New York: Cambridge University Press, 1990.

Sundberg, Jan, "Exploring the basis of declining party membership in Denmark: a Scandinavian comparison," *Scandinavian Political Studies* 10 (1): 17-38. 1987.

Sundelius, Bengt, *Managing Transnationalism in Northern Europe*. Boulder, Colorado: Westview Press, 1978.

——, (ed.), *Foreign Policies of Northern Europe*. Boulder, Colorado: Westview, 1982.

Svensson, Palle, "Support for the Danish Social Democratic Party 1924-39 — growth and response," *Scandinavian Political Studies* 9: 127-146. 1974.

——, "The lowering of the voting age in Denmark: The referendum of September 1978," *Scandinavian Political Studies* 2 (1): 65-71. 1979.

——, "Party cohesion in the Danish parliament during the 1970s," *Scandinavian Political Studies* 5 (1): 17-42. 1982.

——, "Class, party and ideology: A Danish case study of electoral behaviour in referendums," *Scandinavian Political Studies* 7 (3): 175-196. Sept 1984.

—— and Lise Togeby, "The political mobilisation of the new middle class in Denmark," *West European Politics* 14 (4, October): 149-68. 1991.

——, "The Danish 'Yes' to Maastricht and Edinburgh: The EC Referendum in May 1993," *Scandinavian Political Studies* 17 (1): 69-82. 1994.

——, "Denmark: the referendum as minority protection," pp. 33-51 in Michael Gallagher and Pier Vincenzo Uleri (eds.), *The Referendum Experience in Europe*. Basingstoke: Macmillan. New York: St. Martin's, 1996.

Taylor, William J. and Paul M. Cole (eds.), *Nordic Defense: Comparative Decision-Making*. Lexington, Massachusetts: Lexington Books 1985.

Thomas, Alastair H., *Parliamentary Parties in Denmark 1945-72*. (Strathclyde University Occasional Papers no. 13.) Glasgow, 1973.

——, "Danish Social Democracy and the European Community," *Journal of Common Market Studies* 13 (4): 454-68. 1975.

——, "Denmark: Coalitions and minority governments," pp. 109-41 in Eric C. Browne and John Dreijmanis (eds.), *Government Coalitions in Western Democracies*. New York: Longman, 1982.

——, "The Danish Folketing elections of 1984," *West European Politics* 8 (1): 113-5. 1985.

——, "The 1987 Danish Election," *West European Politics* 11 (2): 114-18. 1988.

——, "Local coalitions in Denmark: A preliminary approach," in Bert Pijnenberg and Colin Mellors (eds.) *Political Parties and Coalitions in European Local Government*. London: Routlege, 1988.

——, "Denmark," in Juliet Lodge (ed.), *The 1989 Election of the European Parliament*. Basingstoke: Macmillan, 1990.

——, "Changes in the Danish Communist Party (DKP)," *Journal of Communist Studies* 6 (4): 208-12. 1990.

Thomsen, Birgit Nüchel, *The Odd Man Out: Denmark and European Integration 1948-92*. Odense: Odense University Press, 1993.

Thomsen, Søren Risbjerg, "The 1994 Parliamentary Election in Denmark," *Electoral Studies* 14 (3): 315-22. 1995.

Tiilikainen, Teija and Ib Damgaard Petersen (eds), *The Nordic Countries and the EC*. Copenhagen: Political Studies Press.1993.

Turner, Barry and G.B. Nordquist, *The Other European Community: Integration and Cooperation in Nordic Europe*. London: Weidenfeld & Nicolson, 1982.

Wæver, Ole, "Nordic Nostalgia: Northern Europe after the Cold War," *International Affairs* 68 (1): 77-102. 1992.

——, Barry Buzan, Morten Kelstrup and Pierre Lemaitre, *Identity, Migration and the New Security Agenda in Europe*. London: Pinter, 1993.

Wendt, Franz, *Co-operation in the Nordic Countries: Achievements and Obstacles*. Stockholm: Almqvist & Wiksell, 1981.

Wiberg, Håken and Keld Jensen, "Military defence in Denmark: Expenditure and conversion problems," *Cooperation and Conflict* 27 (4): 349-375. 1992.

Winter, Søren, "How policy-making affects implementation: The decentralization of the Danish Disablement Pension administration," *Scandinavian Political Studies* 9 (4): 361-385. 1986.

Worre, Torben, "Class parties and class voting in the Scandinavian countries," *Scandinavian Political Studies* 3 (4): 199-320. 1980.

——, "The 1979 European election in Denmark: an analysis of participation, choice of party and attitude towards Europe," *Co-operation and Conflict* 16 (2): 73-90. 1981.

——, "The Danish Euro-Party System," *Scandinavian Political Studies* 10 (1): 79-95. 1987.

VII. SCIENCE

Böcher, Tyge W., et al., *The Flora of Greenland*. Copenhagen: P. Haase & Son, 1968.

Bohr, Niels, *Collected Works*. New York: Elsevier:

Vol. 1: *Early Work 1905-1911*. J.R. Nielsen (ed.), 1973.

Vol. 2: *Work on Atomic Physics 1912-1917*. V. Hoyer (ed.), 1982.

Vol. 3: *The Correspondence 1918-1923*. J. Rud Nielsen (ed.), 1976.

Vol. 4: *The System 1920-1923*. J. Rud Nielsen (ed.), 1977.

Vol. 5: *The Emergence of Quantum Mechanics 1924-1926*. K. Stolzenberg and E. Rudinger (eds), 1984.

Vol. 6: *Foundations of Quantum Physics 1926-1932*. Niels Bohr and J. Kalckar (eds), 1984.

Vol 9: *Nuclear Physics 1929-1952*. R. Peierls (ed.), 1985.

Ferguson-Lees, James et al (eds), *A Guide to Bird-watching in Europe*. New York: Scribner's, 1972. [Includes a chapter on Denmark by Kai Curry-Lindahl.]

French, A.P. and P.J. Kennedy, *Niels Bohr: A Centenary Volume.* Cambridge, Massachusetts: Harvard University Press, 1985.

Fristrup, Børge, *The Greenland Icecap.* Copenhagen: Rhodos. Seattle: University of Washington Press, 1967.

Hagerup, Olaf and Vagn Petersson (trans. Gilbert Carter), *A Botanical Atlas.* Copenhagen: Munksgaard, 1959-60.

Hendry, John, *The Creation of Quantum Mechanics and the Bohr-Pauli Dialogue.* Boston, Massachusetts: D. Reidel, 1984.

Meisen, V. *Prominent Danish Scientists through the Ages, With Facsimiles from their Works,* 1932.

Moore, Ruth, *Niels Bohr: The Man, His Science, and The World They Changed.* New York: Alfred A. Knopf, 1966.

Pais, Abraham, *Niels Bohr's Times in Physics, Philosophy and Polity.* Oxford: Clarendon Press, 1991.

Pauli, W. (ed.), *Niels Bohr and the Development of Physics.* Oxford: Pergamon, 1962.

Rozental, S. (ed.), *Niels Bohr: His Life and Work As Seen by His Friends and Colleagues.* Amsterdam: North Holland Publishing Co. New York: Wiley, 1967.

Thoren, Victor E., *The Lord of Uraniborg: A Biography of Tycho Brahe,* with contributions by John R. Christianson. Cambridge: Cambridge University Press, 1990.

VIII. SOCIETY

1. Demography

Bolander, Anne-Marie, *A Comparative Study of Mortality by Cause in Four Nordic Countries, 1966-1968, with Special Reference to Male Excess Mortality.* Stockholm: National Central Bureau of Statistics, 1971.

Court, Yvonne K., "Recent patterns of population change in Denmark," *Geography* (Sheffield, England), 70 (4) no. 309: 353-356. 1985.

Leeson, Graham W., "Aging and economic welfare," *Genus* (Rome), 41 (3-4): 157-69. 1985.

Matthiessen, P.C. *Some Aspects of the Demographic Transition in Denmark.* Copenhagen: Københavns Universitet, 1970.

Springfeldt, Peter (ed.), *The Sixth Scandinavian Demographic Symposium, 16-19 June 1982 in Kungälv, Sweden: Studies in Mortality.* Stockholm: Scandinavian Demographic Society, 1984.

2. Emigration

Babcock, Kendric Charles, *The Scandinavian Element in the United States.* New York: Arno Press, 1969.

Bille, John H., *A History of the Danes in America.* Reprint of 1896 edition. San Francisco: R & E Research Associates, 1971.

Friis, Eric J. (ed.), *The Scandinavian Presence in North America.* New York: Harper's Magazine Press, 1976.

Furer, Howard B., *The Scandinavians in America, 986-1970.* Dobbs Ferry, New York: Oceana Publications, 1972.

Hale, Frederick (ed.), *Danes in North America.* Seattle: University of Washington Press, 1984.

Hvidt, Kristian, *Flight to America: The Social Background of 300,000 Danish Emigrants.* New York: Academic Press, 1975.

Kuhnle, Stein, "Emigration, democratisation and the rise of the European welfare states," pp. 501-523. in Per Torsvik (ed.), *Mobilization, Centre-Periphery Structures and Nation-Building: A Volume in Commemoration of Stein Rokkan.* Oslo: Universitetsforlaget, 1982.

Lane, James B., *Jacob A. Riis and the American City.* Port Washington, New York: Kennikat Press, 1974.

Mortensen, Enok, *Danish-American Life and Letters.* New York: Arno Press, 1979.

——, *The Danish Lutheran Church in America: The History and Heritage of the American Evangelical Lutheran Church.* Philadelphia: Board of Publications, Lutheran Church in America, 1967.

Nielsen, George R., *The Danish Americans.* Boston, Massachusetts: Twayne, 1981.

Riis, Jacob A., *The Making of an American.* New York, London: Macmillan, 1970.

Skårdal, Dorothy Burton, *The Divided Heart: Scandinavian Immigrant Experience Through Literary Sources.* Lincoln: University of Nebraska Press, 1974.

——, "Danes in the United States," *Scandinavian Review,* 73 (4): 50-59. 1985.

3. Education

Andresen, Arne (ed.), *The Danish Folk High School Today.* Esbjerg, Denmark: Arnold Thomsen, 1985.

Boje, Per and Knud J.V. Jespersen, *Pastures New: Odense University, the First 25 Years.* Odense University Press, 1991.

Borish, Steven M., ed. Paul Clemens, *The Land of the Living. Danish Folk High Schools and Denmark's Non-violent Path to Modernization.* Nevada City, California: Blue Dolphin, 1991.

Brickman, William, W., *Denmark's Educational System and Problems.* Washington, DC: Department of Health, Education and Welfare, 1967.

Christmas Møller, John and Katherine Watson, *Education in Democracy: The Folk High Schools of Denmark.* London: Faber, 1944.

Dixon, C.W., *Society, Schools and Progress in Scandinavia.* Oxford and New York: Pergamon, 1965.

Education for Life [Contributions to an international conference marking the bicentenary of N.F.S. Grundtvig] Copenhagen: Det danske Selskab, 1983.

Great Britain. Department of Education and Science. Inspectorate of Schools. *Education in Denmark: Aspects of the Work of the Folkeskole.* London: HMSO, 1989.

Grundtvig's Ideas in North America: Influences and Parallels. Copenhagen: Det danske Selskab, 1983.

Jensen, Arne (ed.), *Decision, Planning and Budgeting: Studies in Institutional Management in Higher Education.* Paris: OECD, 1972.

Jørgensen, I. Skov (ed.), *Special Education in Denmark: Handicapped Children in Danish Primary Schools.* Copenhagen: Det danske Selskab, 1979.

Knudsen, Johannes (ed.), *N.F.S. Grundtvig: Selected Writings.* Philadelphia: Fortress Press, 1976.

Learning in Denmark. Copenhagen: The Danish Cultural Institute, 1998. [Essays surveying the whole Danish education system, intended for those planning study-visits of all kinds.]

Lund, Ragnar (ed.), *Scandinavian Adult Education.* Westport: Greenwood Press, 1970.

Lykke, Palle, *A Pictorial History of Aarhus University.* Århus: Aarhus University Press, 1992.

Mathiesen, Anders, "Polarization of the qualification structure of the Danish labour force: The role of the education system in post-war Denmark," *Acta Sociologica* 23: 157-172. 1980.

OECD, *"Reviews of National Policy for Education"* [in Denmark]. Paris: OECD, 1980.

OECD *Economic Surveys: Denmark 1997.* Special feature: education, training and labour market reform. Paris: OECD, 1997.

Rørdam, Thomas, *The Danish Folk High Schools.* Copenhagen: Det danske Selskab, 1980.

Schools and Education in Denmark. Copenhagen: Det danske Selskab, 1972.

Struwe, Kamma (ed.), *Schools and Education in Denmark.* Copenhagen: Det danske Selskab, 1981.

Stybe, Svend Erik, *Copenhagen University: 500 Years of Science and Scholarship.* Copenhagen: Bianco Lunos, 1979.

Thanning, Kaj, *N.F.S. Grundtvig.* Copenhagen: Det danske Selskab, 1972.

Thodberg, N.F.S. and A. Pontoppidan (eds.), *N.F.S. Grundtvig: Tradition and Renewal.* Copenhagen: Det danske Selskab, 1983.

Thomsen, Ole B. *Some Aspects of Education in Denmark.* Toronto: University of Toronto Press, 1967.

4. Religion

See also Education for items on N.F.S. Grundtvig.

Allchin, A.M. et al. (eds.), *Heritage and Prophecy: Grundtvig and the English-Speaking World.* Århus: Aarhus University Press, 1993.

Arbaugh, George E. and George B. Arbaugh, *Kierkegaard's Authorship: A Guide to the Writings of Kierkegaard.* Rock Island, Illinois: Augustana College Library, 1967.

Bamberger, Ib Nathan, *The Viking Jews: A History of the Jews in Denmark.* New York: Shengold Publishers, 1983.

Bedell, George C., *Kierkegaard and Faulkner: Modalities of Existence.* Baton Rouge: Louisiana State University Press, 1972.

Brandt, Frithief, *Søren Kierkegaard, 1813-1855: His Life, His Works.* Copenhagen: Det danske Selskab, 1963.

Carnegie, William Alexander, *The Religion of Ancient Scandinavia.* 1906 edition reprinted. Freeport, New York: Books for Libraries Press, 1969.

Collins, James, *The Mind of Kierkegaard.* London: Secker & Warburg. 1954. Chicago: Henry Regnery, 1967.

Crossley Holland, Kevin, *The Penguin Book of Norse Myth: Gods of the Vikings.* London: Deutsch 1980. London: Penguin, 1982.

Davidson, H.R. Ellis, *Pagan Scandinavia*. London: Thames & Hudson, 1967.

——, *Scandinavian Mythology*. London, New York, Sydney, Toronto: Paul Hamlyn, 1969.

Dumezil, Goerges (ed. Einar Haugen), *Gods of the Ancient Northmen*. Berkeley: University of California Press, 1973.

Dunkley, E.H., *The Reformation in Denmark*. London: SPCK, 1948.

Elrod, John W., *Kierkegaard and Christendom*. Princeton, New Jersey: Princeton University Press, 1981.

Fenger, Henning, *Kierkegaard, the Myths and their Origins: Studies in the Kierkegaardian Papers and Letters*. New Haven, Connecticut, and London: Yale University Press, 1980.

Hallencreutz, Carl F. (ed.), *Missions from the North: Nordic Missionary Council 50 Years*. Oslo: Universitetsforlaget, 1974.

Hannay, Alastair, *Kierkegaard*. London: Routledge & Kegan Paul, 1982.

Hartling, Poul (ed.), *The Danish Church*. Copenhagen: Det danske Selskab, 1964.

Hunter, Leslie S. (ed.), *Scandinavian Churches: The Development of the Churches of Denmark, Finland, Iceland, Norway and Sweden*. London: Faber. Minneapolis, Minnesota: Augsburg Publishing House, 1965.

Kierkegaard, Søren, *A Kierkegaard Reader*. London: Fourth Estate, 1989.

——, *The Laughter is on My Side. A Kierkegaard Reader*. Princeton, New Jersey: Princeton University Press, 1989.

——, *The Concept of Anxiety*. (Kierkegaard's Writings 8). Princeton, New Jersey: Princeton University Press, 1980.

——, *The Concept of Dread*. (trans. Walter Lowrie), 2nd ed. Princeton, New Jersey: Princeton University Press, 1967.

——, *The Concept of Irony*. New York: Hippocrene Books, 1983.

——, *The Concept of Irony*. (Kierkegaard's Writings 2). Princeton, New Jersey: Princeton University Press, 1989.

——, *Concluding Unscientific Postscript*. (Kierkegaard's Writings 12). Princeton, New Jersey: Princeton University Press, 1991.

——, *The Corsair Affair*. (Kierkegaard's Writings 13). Princeton, New Jersey: Princeton University Press, 1991.

——, *Eighteen Upbuilding Discourses*. (Kierkegaard's Writings 5). Princeton, New Jersey: Princeton University Press, 1990.

———, *Early Polemical Writings*. (Kierkegaard's Writings 1). Princeton, New Jersey: Princeton University Press, 1990.

——— *Either/Or*.(trans. David F. Swenson, Lillian M. Swenson, Walter Lowrie), (Kierkegaard's Writings 2 & 3). Princeton, New Jersey: Princeton University Press, 1971, 1987.

———*Fear and Trembling: A Dialectical Lyric* (trans. Walter Lowrie). Garden City, New York: Doubleday, Anchor Books, 1954.

———, *Fear and Trembling*. London & New York: Penguin, 1986.

———, *Fear and Trembling; Repetition*. (Kierkegaard's Writings 6). Princeton, New Jersey: Princeton University Press, 1990.

———, *Fear and Trembling, and the Book on Adler*. (trans. Walter Lowrie). London: Everyman's Library, 1994.

———, *For Self-Examination; Judge for Yourself!* (Kierkegaard's Writings 21). Princeton, New Jersey: Princeton University Press, 1990.

———, *Gospel of Sufferings*. Cambridge: James Clarke, 1982.

———, *Papers and Journals: A Selection* ed. Alastair Hannay. London: Penguin, 1996.

———, *Parables of Kierkegaard*. Princeton, New Jersey: Princeton University Press. 1989.

———, *Philosophical Fragments; Johannes Climacus* (Kierkegaard's Writings 7). Princeton, New Jersey: Princeton University Press, 1985.

———, *The Point of View*. (Kierkegaard's Writings 22). Princeton, New Jersey: Princeton University Press, 1991.

———, *Practice in Christianity*. (Kierkegaard's Writings 20). Princeton, New Jersey: Princeton University Press, 1991.

———, *Prefaces*. Florida State University Press, 1989. (Kierkegaard's Writings 9). Princeton, New Jersey: Princeton University Press, 1991.

———*The Sickness unto Death: A Christian Psychological Exposition for Upbuilding and Awakening* (trans. Howard V. Hong and Edna H. Hong). (Kierkegaard's Writings 19). Princeton, New Jersey: Princeton University Press, 1980.

———, *Søren Kierkegaard's Journals and Papers* (trans Howard V. Hong and Edna H. Hong with Gregor Malantschuk), 7 vols. Bloomington, Indiana & London: Indiana University Press. 1978.

———, *Stages on Life's Way*. (Kierkegaard's Writings 11). Princeton, New Jersey: Princeton University Press, 1988.

——, *Three Discourses on Imagined Occasions* (trans Howard V. Hong and Edna H. Hong). Princeton, New Jersey: Princeton University Press. 1993.

——, *Upbuilding Discourses in Various Spirits* (trans Howard V. Hong and Edna H. Hong). Princeton, New Jersey: Princeton University Press. 1993.

——, *Without Authority* (trans Howard V. Hong and Edna H. Hong). Princeton, New Jersey: Princeton University Press, 1997.

——, *Works of Love* (trans Howard V. Hong and Edna H. Hong). Princeton, New Jersey: Princeton University Press, 1995.

Lebowitz, Naomi, *A Life of Allegory*. Baton Rouge: Louisiana State University Press, 1985.

Mackey, Louis, *Kierkegaard: A Kind of Poet*. Philadelphia: University of Pennsylvania Press, 1971.

Melchior, Marcus, (trans. Werner Melchior), *A Rabbi Remembers*. New York: Lyle Stuart, 1968.

Mitchell, P.M., *Vilhelm Grønbech*. Boston, Massachusetts: Twayne, 1978.

Scheifer, Ronald and Robert Markley, *Kierkegaard and Literature: Irony, Repetition and Criticism*. Norman: University of Oklahoma Press, 1984.

Sløk, Johannes, *Kierkegaard's Universe*. Copenhagen: Det danske Selskab, 1994.

Stendall, Brita K., *Søren Kierkegaard*. Boston, Massachusetts: Twayne, 1976.

Thompson, Josiah, *Kierkegaard*. New York: Alfred A. Knopf, 1973. London: Victor Gollancz, 1974.

Thulstrup, Niels, *Kierkegaard and the Church in Denmark*. Copenhagen: C.A. Reitzel, 1984.

Ussher, Arland, *Journey through Dread*. London: Darwen Finlayson, 1955. New York: Biblo & Tanner, 1968.

5. Sociology

Abrahamson, P., "Poverty and welfare in Denmark," *Scandinavian Journal of Social Welfare* 1 (1): 20-27. 1992.

Alestalo, Matti and Stein Kuhnle (1987), "The Scandinavian route: Economic, social, and political developments in Denmark, Finland, Norway, and Sweden," pp. 3-38 in Robert Erikson, Erik Jørgen Hansen, Stein Ringen and Hannu Uusitalo (eds.), *The Scandinavian*

Model: Welfare States and Welfare Research. Armonk, New York, and London: M.E. Sharpe, 1987.

Andersen, Heine, "Organisations, classes, and the growth of state interventionism in Denmark," *Acta Sociologica* 23: 113-31. 1980.

Anderson, Robert Thomas, *The Vanishing Village: A Danish Maritime Community.* Seattle: University of Washington Press, 1964.

——, *Denmark: Success of a Developing Nation.* Cambridge, Massachusetts: Schenkman, 1975.

Andreassen, Tayo (et al., eds.), *Moving On: New Perspectives on the Women's Movement.* Århus: Aarhus University Press, 1991.

Bruun, Kettil (ed.), *Controlling Psychotropic Drugs: The Nordic Experience.* London: Croom Helm. New York: St. Martin's, 1983.

Buckser, Andrew, *Communities of Faith: Sectarianism, Identity and Social Change on a Danish Island (Mors)* (New Directions in Anthropology, vol. 5). Providence, Oxford: Berghahn Books, 1996.

Cave, W. and P. Himmelstrup, *The Welfare Society in Transition.* Copenhagen: Det danske Selskab, 1995.

Dahlsgaard, Inga, *Women in Denmark: Yesterday and Today.* Copenhagen: Det danske Selskab, 1980.

Denmark, Ministry of the Interior, *Health Care in Denmark.* Copenhagen, 1995.

The Elderly in Denmark. Copenhagen: Det danske Selskab, 1989.

Esping-Andersen, Gösta, "Social class, social democracy and the state: Party policy and party decomposition in Denmark and Sweden," *Comparative Politics* 11 (1): 42-58. 1978.

European Union. Commission. DGV-MISSOC. Social Protection in the Member States of the European Union. Situation on 1 July 1995 and Evolution. Brussels: ECSC-EC-EAEC, 1995.

Hansen, Erik Jørgen, Stein Ringen, Hannu Uusitalo and Robert Erikson (eds.), *The Scandinavian Model: Welfare States and Welfare Research.* Armonk, New York, and London, England: M.E. Sharpe, 1987.

Hansen, Erik Jørgen, Stein Ringen, Hannu Uusitalo and Robert Erikson (eds.), *Welfare Trends in the Scandinavian Countries.* Armonk, New York, and London, England: M.E. Sharpe, 1993. [Includes chapters: Jørgen Goul Andersen, "Sources of Welfare State Support in Denmark: Self-Interest or Way of Life?". Poul Christian Matthiessen, "Family Formation in Denmark." Erik Jørgen Hansen, "The Female Factor in the Changing Living Conditions in Denmark."

Hastrup, Bjarne, *Contemporary Danish Society: Danish Democracy and Wellfare* [sic]. Copenhagen: Academic Press, 1995.

Hendin, Herbert, *Suicide and Scandinavia: A Psychoanalytic Study of Culture and Character*. Garden City, New York: Doubleday, Anchor Books, 1965.

Hoff, Jens, and Jørgen Goul Andersen, "The Danish class structure," *Acta Sociologica* 32 (1): 23-52. 1989.

Jamison, Andrew et al., *The Making of The New Environmental Consciousness: A Comparative Study of Environmental Movements in Sweden, Denmark and the Netherlands*. Edinburgh: Edinburgh University Press, 1990.

Johansen, Lars Nørby, *The Danish Welfare State, 1945-1980: Institutional Profile and Basic Tables*. Odense: Institute for Social Science, Odense University, 1982.

Kandel, Denise B. and Gerald S. Lesser, *Youth in Two Worlds: United States and Denmark*. San Francisco: Jossey-Bass, 1972.

Knudsen, Tim (ed), *Welfare Administration in Denmark*. Copenhagen: Institute of Political Science, University of Copenhagen/Ministry of Finance, 1991.

Knutzen, Oddbjørn, "The priorities of materialist and post-materialist values in the Nordic countries — a five nation comparison," *Scandinavian Political Studies* 12 (3): 221-44. 1989.

——, "Materialist and postmaterialist values and social structure in the Nordic countries: A comparative study," *Comparative Politics* 23 (1): 85-104. 1990.

Koch-Nielsen, Inger, *Family Obligations in Denmark*. Copenhagen: Danish National Institute of Social Research, 1996.

Krause, Daniel R., "Institutional living for the elderly in Denmark: A model for the United States," *Ageing*, 321-22: 29-38. 1981.

Kutschinsky, Berl, *Studies on Pornography and Sex Crimes in Denmark: A Report to the US Presidential Commission on Obscenity and Pornography*. Copenhagen: New Social Science Monographs. Copenhagen: Copenhagen Business School, 1970.

Logue, John, "The welfare state: Victim of its success," *Daedalus* 108: 69-87. 1979.

Madsen, Henrik Jess, "Class power and participatory equality: Attitudes towards economic democracy in Denmark and Sweden," *Scandinavian Political Studies* 3 (4): 277-98. 1980.

Manniche, Peter, *Living Democracy in Denmark: Independent Farmers, Farmers' Cooperatives, the Folk High Schools,*

Cooperation in the Towns, Social and Cultural Activities, Social Legislation, a Danish Village. Copenhagen: G.E.C. Gad, 1952.

———, *Denmark: A Social Laboratory.* Oxford: Pergamon Press, 1969.

Marcussen, Ernst, *Social Welfare In Denmark.* 4th rev. ed. Copenhagen: Det danske Selskab, 1980.

Møller, Torgny, "The People's Television Factory: Workers' ownership in practice," *Scandinavian Political Studies* 3(n.s.) 4: 277-98. 1980.

National Identity and International Community. [Contributions to a conference at the Grundtvig Centre, Aarhus University]. Copenhagen: Det danske Selskab, 1993.

Nielsen, Hans Jørgen and Sauerberg, Steen, "Upstairs and downstairs in Danish politics: An analysis of political apathy and social structure," *Scandinavian Political Studies* 3 (1): 59-78. 1980.

Nielsen, Ruth and Erika Szyszczak, *The Social Dimension of the European Union.* 3 ed., Copenhagen: Handelshøjskolens Forlag, 1997.

OECD, *Manpower Policy in Denmark.* Paris: OECD, 1974.

Østergård, Uffe, "Peasants and Danes: The Danish national identity and political culture," *Comparative Studies in Society and History* 34 (1): 3-27. Jan. 1992.

Pedersen, Johannes T., "The relationship between democratic values and norms in the Danish electorate," *Scandinavian Political Studies* 8 (1-2): 23-43. 1985.

Petersen, Nikolaj, "The popular basis of Nordic co-operation: A Danish case study," *Acta Sociologica* 20 (3): 263-85. 1977.

Ploug, Niels and Jon Kvist (eds.), *Recent Trends in Cash Benefits in Europe. Social Security in Europe, vol. 4.* Copenhagen: Danish National Institute of Social Research, 1994.

Rasmussen, Hans Kornø. *No Entry: Immigration Policy in Europe.* Copenhagen: Copenhagen Business School Press/Munksgaard DBK, 1996.

Ribal, Joseph E., *Learning Sex Roles: American and Scandinavian Contrasts.* San Francisco: Canfield Press, 1973.

Rise, Allan, *Employees and Workers: Development and Organization of the Danish Labour Market.* Copenhagen: Det danske Selskab, 1974.

Schested-Larsen, Gunnar, "Social mobility in Denmark," pp. 79-102 in Frederick C. Turner (ed.), *Social Mobility and Political Attitudes — Comparative Perspectives.* New Brunswick, New Jersey: Transaction Publications, 1992.

Schindler, Gordon (ed.), *A Report on Denmark's Legalized Pornography*. Torrance, California: Banner Books, 1969.

Schwartz, Jonathan M., "Vognmandsmarken: A Copenhagen ghetto," *Scandinavian Review* 66 (1): 66-73. 1978.

Svalastoga, Kaare, *Prestige, Class and Mobility*. Copenhagen: Gyldendal. London: William Heinemann, 1959.

Tagil, Sven (ed.), *Ethnicity and Nation-building in the Nordic World*. London: Hurst, 1995.

Tham, Henrik, "Crime, drugs, and suicide in the Scandinavian countries since 1950," *International Journal of Sociology* 23 (2-3): 173-95. 1993.

Togeby, Lise, "The disappearance of a gender gap: Tolerance and liberalism in Denmark from 1971 to 1990," *Scandinavian Political Studies* 17 (1): 47-68. 1994.

——, "Feminist attitudes in times of depolitization of women's issues," *European Journal of Political Research* 27 (1): 47-68. 1995.

Wagner, Marsden and Mary Wagner, *The Danish National Child-Care System: A Successful System As a Model for the Reconstruction of American Child Care*. Boulder, Colorado: Westview Press, 1976.

Walker, Robert, "Denmark: Policies to combat unemployment and low incomes," in Robert Walker, Roger Lawson, Peter Townsend (eds.), *Responses to Poverty: Lessons from Europe*. Rutherford, New Jersey: Fairleigh Dickinson, 1984.

Weiner, Jonathan P., "Primary health care systems in the United States, Denmark, Finland, and Sweden: can the 'Corporatized' learn from the 'Socialized', or vice versa?" *Scandinavian Studies* 61 (2-3): 231-260. 1989

West, John F., *Faroe: The Emergence of a Nation*. London: Benn. New York: Paul S. Eriksson, 1972.

Williamson, Kenneth, *The Atlantic Islands: A Study of the Faeroe Life and Scene*. 1948, reprinted with additional chapter, London: Routledge & Kegan Paul. New York: Fernhill House, 1970.

Wylie, Jonathon, *The Faroe Islands: Social Change and Cultural Continuity*. Lexington: University Press of Kentucky, 1986.

—— and David Margolin, *The Ring of Dancers: Images of Faroese Culture*. Philadelphia: University of Pennsylvania Press, 1981.

Appendix 1:
THE DANISH MONARCHS

Birth	Accession	Death	Name, numeral	Nick-name
			Sigfrid	
		c. 810	Godfred	
			Hemming	
?	? 940	958	Gorm *den Gamle*	the Old
?	958	987	Harald I *Blåtand*	Bluetooth
?	c. 987	1014	Sven I *Tveskæg*	Forkbeard
?	1014	1018	Harald II	
c. 1000	1019	1035	Knud I *den Store*	Canute the Great
1018	1035	1042	Hardeknud	
c. 1024	1042	1047	Magnus *den Gode*	the Good
c. 1020	1047	1074	Sven II Estridsen	
?	1074	1080	Harald III *Hén*	Whetstone
?	1080	1086	Knud II *den Hellige*	the Holy
?	1086	1095	Oluf I *Hunger*	Hunger
?	1095	1103	Erik I, *Ejegod*	Always good
?	1103	1134	Niels	
?	1134	1137	Erik II, *Emune*	Unforgettable
?	1137	1146	Erik III, *Lam*	Meek
?	1146	1157	Sven III reigning)	Grathe
?	1146	1157	Knud III together)	Magnussen
1131	1157	1182	Valdemar I *den Store*	the Great
1163	1182	1202	Knud IV	'the sixth'
1170	1202	1241	Valdemar II *Sejr*	Victorious
1216	1241	1250	Erik IV	Plowpenny

Birth	Accession	Death	Name, Numeral	Nickname
1218	1250	1252	Abel	
c. 1219	1252	1259	Christoffer I	
1249	1259	1286	Erik V	Klipping
1274	1286	1319	Erik IV	Menved
1276	1320-26		Christoffer II	
c. 1315	1326-30	1364	Valdemar III	
	1330	1332	Christoffer II (restored)	
c. 1320	1340	1375	Valdemar IV	Atterdag
1370	1376	1387	Oluf II	
1353	regent 1387	1412	Margrethe I (last of the **Skyldings**)	
c. 1382	1396-1439	1459	Erik VII of Pommerania	
1416	1440	1448	Christoffer III of Bavaria	
			Oldenborg dynasty	
1426	1448	1481	Christian I,	
1455	1481	1513	Hans	
1481	1513-23	1559	Christian II	
1471	1523	1533	Frederik I	
1503	1534	1559	Christian III	
1534	1559	1588	Frederik II	
1577	1588	1648	Christian IV	
1609	1648	1670	Frederik III	
1646	1670	1699	Christian V	
1671	1699	1730	Frederik IV	
1699	1730	1746	Christian VI	
1723	1746	1766	Frederik V	
1749	1766	1808	Christian VII	
1768	1808	1839	Frederik VI	
1786	1839	1848	Christian VIII	
1808	1848	1863	Frederik VII	
			Glücksborg dynasty	
1818	1863	1906	Christian IX	
1843	1906	1912	Frederik VIII	
1870	1912	1947	Christian X	
1899	1947	1972	Frederik IX	
1940	1972		Margrethe II	

Appendix 2: DANISH PRIME MINISTERS AND CABINETS

Dates of Office	First Minister Majority/Minority	Party		Party Composition of Cabinet	
1848-1855	*premierminister*				
1855-1918	*konsejlspræsident*				
22.03.48-16.11.48	A.W.Moltke	Right		Right + National Liberal	'March government'
16.11.48-13.07.51	A.W.Moltke	Right		Right + National Liberal	'November government'
13.07.51-27.01.52	A.W.Moltke	Right		Right + National Liberal	
27.01.52-21.04.53	C.A.Bluhme	Right		Right	
21.04.53-12.12.54	A.S.Ørsted	Right		Right	
12.12.54-18.10.56	P.G.Bang	National Liberal		Right + National Liberal	
18.10.56-13.05.57	C.G.Andræ	National Liberal		National Liberal	
13.05.57-02.12.59	C.C.Hall	National Liberal		National Liberal	
02.12.59-08.02.60	C.E.Rotwitt	No party			
08.02.60-31.12.63	C.C.Hall	National Liberal		National Liberal	
31.12.63-11.07.64	D.G.Monrad	National Liberal		National Liberal	
11.07.64-06.11.65	C.A.Bluhme	Right		Right	
06.11.65-28.05.70	C.E.Krag-Juel-Vind-Frijs	Right		Right	
28.05.70-14.07.74	L.H.C.H.Holstein-Holsteinborg	Right		Right + National Liberal	Minority
14.07.74-11.06.75	C.E.A.Fonnesbech	Right		Right + National Liberal	Minority
11.06.75-07.08.94	J.B.S.Estrup	Right		Right	Minority

Appendix 2: DANISH PRIME MINISTERS AND CABINETS

Dates of Office	First Minister	Party	Party Composition of Cabinet	Majority/Minority
1855-1918	*konsejlspraesident*			
After 1918	*statsminister*			
07.08.94-23.05.97	T.Reedtz-Thott	Right	Right	Minority
23.05.97-27.04.00	H.Horring	Right	Right	Minority
27.04.00-24.07.01	H.Sehested	Right	Right	Minority
	Change of System			
24.07.01-14.01.05	J.H.Deuntzer	Liberal	Liberal	Majority
14.01.05-12.10.08	J.C.Christensen	Liberal	Liberal	Majority
12.10.08-16.08.09	N.Neergaard	Liberal	Liberal	Majority
16.08.09-28.10.09	L.Holstein-Lederborg	Liberal	Liberal	Minority
28.10.09-05.07.10	C.T.Zahle	Radical	Radical	Minority
05.07.10-21.06.13	K.Berntsen	Liberal	Liberal	Majority
21.06.13-29.03.20	C.T.Zahle	Radical	Radical (broadened from 1916)	Minority
29.03.20-05.04.20	O.Liebe	Non party		Caretaker
05.04.20-05.05.20	M.P.Fries	Non party		Caretaker
05.05.20-09.10.22	N.Neergaard	Liberal	Liberal	Minority
09.10.22-23.04.24	N.Neergaard	Liberal	Liberal	Minority
23.04.24-14.12.26	T.Stauning	Social Democrat	Social Democrat	Minority
14.12.26-30.04.29	T.Madsen-Mygdal	Liberal	Liberal	Minority

Appendix 2: DANISH PRIME MINISTERS AND CABINETS

Dates of Office	Prime Minister	Party	Party Composition of Cabinet	Majority/Minority
30.04.29–04.11.35	T.Stauning	Social Democrat	Social Democrat + Radical	Majority coal'n
04.11.35–08.07.40	T.Stauning	Social Democrat	Social Democrat + Radical	Majority coal'n
08.07.40–03.05.42	T.Stauning	Social Democrat	SD+Radical+Liberal+Conservative	Broad coalition
03.05.42–09.11.42	V.Buhl	Social Democrat	SD+Radical+Liberal+Conservative	Broad coalition
09.11.42–30.08.43	E.Scavenius	(Radical) non-party	SD+Radical+Liberal+Conservative	Non-party coalition
30.08.43 resigned.	05.05.45 resignation accepted by King Christian X			
30.08.43–05.05.45	"Departmental Administration" of civil servants			
05.05.45–07.11.45	V.Buhl	Social Democrat	SD+Conservative+Radical+Liberal+Danish Union+Communist	All-party coalition
07.11.45–13.11.47	K.Kristensen	Liberal	Liberal	Minority
13.11.47–30.10.50	H.Hedtoft	Social Democrat	Social Democrat	Minority
30.10.50–30.09.53	E.Eriksen	Liberal	Liberal + Conservative	Minority coal'n
30.09.53–01.02.55	H.Hedtoft	Social Democrat	Social Democrat	Minority
01.02.55–28.05.57	H.C.Hansen	Social Democrat	Social Democrat	Minority
28.05.57–21.02.60	H.C.Hansen	Social Democrat	Social Democrat+Radical+Justice	Majority coal'n
26.09.64–28.11.66	J.O.Krag	Social Democrat	Social Democrat	Minority
28.11.66–31.01.68	J.O.Krag	Social Democrat	Social Democrat	Minority
02.02.68–06.10.71	H.Baunsgaard	Radical	Radical + Liberal + Conservative	Majority coal'n

Appendix 2: DANISH PRIME MINISTERS AND CABINETS

Dates of Office	Prime Minister	Party	Party Composition of Cabinet	Majority/Minority
11.10.71–05.10.72	J.O.Krag	Social Democrat	Social Democrat	Minority
21.02.60–18.11.60	V.Kampmann	Social Democrat	Social Democrat+Radical+Justice	Majority coal'n
18.11.60–03.09.62	V.Kampmann	Social Democrat	Social Democrat+Radical	Minority coal'n
03.09.62–26.09.64	J.O.Krag	Social Democrat	Social Democrat+Radical	Minority coal'n
05.10.72–05.12.73	A.Jorgensen	Social Democrat	Social Democrat	Minority
19.12.73–12.02.75	P.Hartling	Liberal	Liberal	Minority
13.02.75–26.02.77	A.Jorgensen	Social Democrat	Social Democrat	Minority
26.02.77–29.8.78	A.Jorgensen	Social Democrat	Social Democrat	Minority
30.08.78–24.10.79	A.Jorgensen	Social Democrat	Social Democrat + Liberal	Minority coal'n
26.10.79–30.12.81	A.Jorgensen	Social Democrat	Social Democrat	Minority
30.12.81–09.09.82	A.Jorgensen	Social Democrat	Social Democrat	Minority
10.09.82–09.09.87	P.Schlüter	Conservative	Conservative+Liberal+ Christian People's+Center Democrat	Minority coalition
10.09.87–03.06.88	P.Schlüter	Conservative	Conservative+Liberal+Christian People's+Center Democrat	Minority coalition
03.06.88–17.12.90	P.Schlüter	Conservative	Conservative+Liberal+Radical	Minority coal'n
17.12.90–14.01.93	P.Schlüter	Conservative	Conservative+Liberal	Minority coal'n
25.01.93–21.09.93	P.Nyrup Rasmussen	Social Democrat	Social Democrat + Radical +Center Democrat+Christian People's	Majority coalition

Appendix 2: DANISH PRIME MINISTERS AND CABINETS

Dates of Office	Prime Minister	Party	Party Composition of Cabinet	Majority/Minority
21.09.93-21.09.94	P.Nyrup Rasmussen	Social Democrat	Social Democrat+Radical+Center Democrat	Minority coalition
21.01.94-30.12.96	P.Nyrup Rasmussen	Social Democrat	Social Democrat+Radical+Center Democrat	Minority coalition
30.12.96-12.03.98	P.Nyrup Rasmussen	Social Democrat	Social Democrat+Radical	Minority coal'n
12.03.98	P.Nyrup Rasmussen	Social Democrat	Social Democrat+Radical	Minority coal'n

Appendix 3:
PARTY SHARES OF CABINET OFFICE, 1848-1998

| From | 1848 | 1864 | 1901 | 1929 | 1945 | 1973 |
To	1864	1901	1929	1945	1973	1998
Years	**16.3**	**37.1**	**27.8**	**14.9**	**28.1**	**24.2**
Party						
Right	53	100				
NL	81	14				
V			63	25	31	52
Cons				25	23	43
DR					12	
CD						43
KRF						26
RV			27	100	39	34
SD			10	100	69	55
Others				3		

The Table shows the percentage of each period that the party was in cabinet. Columns do not sum to 100 because in coalitions two or more parties are in cabinet together.

Party names: SD, Social Democrats. RV, Radical Liberals. KRF, Christian People's Party. DR, Justice Party. CD, Center Democrats. V, *Venstre* Liberals. NL, National Liberals. Cons, Conservative People's Party. Others: during the liberation government of 5 May to 7 November 1945 the Communists and *Dansk Samling* were also in the cabinet.

Dates of periods:
22/ 3/1848 to 11/ 7/1864.   11/ 7/1864 to 24/ 7/1901.
24/ 7/1901 to 30/ 4/1929.   30/ 4/1929 to 7/11/1945.
 7/11/1945 to 5/12/1973.   19/12/1973 to 12/03/1998.
The period 1929-1945 excludes 1.7 years (30/8/43 to 5/5/45) during the 1940-45 German occupation when cabinet government was suspended.

Appendix 4:
PARTY SHARES OF VOTES, PERCENT

Party	1890	1892	1895	1898	1901	1903	1906
SD	7.3	8.9	11.3	14.3	17.1	20.4	25.4
RL							13.7
Liberal Reform	53.0	28.1	40.5	43.8	42.9	47.9	31.6
Moderate Liberals		28.1	19.4	16.1	12.0	8.1	6.8
Right	39.7	34.8	28.8	25.9	24.0	20.8	22.3
Other					4.0	2.7	0.2

Party	1909	1910	1913	1918	1920 April	1920 July	1920 Sept
DKP					0.4	0.3	0.4
SD	28.7	28.3	29.5	28.7	29.3	29.9	32.2
RL	18.6	19.0	18.7	20.7	11.9	11.5	12.1
Liberals *Venstre*		34.1	29.1	29.4	34.2	36.1	34.0
Liberal Reform	25.8						
Moderate Liberals	5.9						
Right/ **Cons**	20.4	18.6	22.6	18.3	19.7	18.9	17.9
IP				1.3	2.9	2.7	2.3
SP							0.6
Other	0.6	0.0	0.0	1.7	1.6	0.6	0.5

For key to names, see final page. The "four old parties" are in **bold.**

Sources: Møller, Poul (ed.), *Politisk Haandbog: En samling konkrete oplysninger.* Copenhagen: H. Hagerup, 1950, p. 38 (for 1890-1898).
Mackie, Thomas T. and Richard Rose (eds.), *The International Almanac of Electoral History.* 3rd ed. London: Macmillan, 1991.
Politiken, http://www.pol.dk/valg98/lands.htm, 14/3/98.

Appendix 4:
PARTY SHARES OF VOTES, PERCENT

Party	1924	1926	1929	1932	1935	1939	1943
DKP	0.5	0.4	0.3	1.1	1.6	2.4	—
SD	36.6	37.2	41.8	42.7	46.1	42.9	44.5
JP	1.0	1.3	1.8	2.7	2.5	2.0	1.6
RL	13.0	11.3	10.7	9.4	9.2	9.5	8.7
Lib	28.3	28.3	28.3	24.7	17.8	18.2	18.7
FP					3.2	3.0	1.2
Cons	18.9	20.6	16.5	18.7	17.8	17.7	21.0
IP	0.2						
Nazis				0.0	1.0	1.8	2.2
SP	0.6	0.8	0.7	0.6	0.8	0.9	—
DU						0.5	2.2
NC						1.0	

Party	1945	1947	1950	1953	1953	1957	1960
DKP	12.5	6.8	4.6	4.8	4.3	3.1	1.1
SPP							6.1
SD	32.8	40.0	39.6	40.4	41.3	39.4	42.1
JP	1.9	4.5	8.2	5.6	3.5	5.3	2.2
RL	8.2	6.9	8.2	8.6	7.8	7.8	5.8
Lib	23.4	27.6	21.3	22.1	23.1	25.1	21.1
Cons	18.2	12.4	17.8	17.3	16.8	16.6	17.9
SP		0.4	0.3	0.4	0.4	0.4	0.4
DU	3.1	1.2		0.8			
Ind					2.7	2.3	3.3

Appendix 4:
PARTY SHARES OF VOTES, PERCENT

Party	1964	1966	1968	1971	1973	1975	1977
DKP	1.2	0.8	1.0	1.4	3.6	4.2	3.7
LS			2.0	1.6	1.5	2.1	2.7
SPP	5.8	10.9	6.1	9.1	6.0	5.0	3.9
SD	41.9	38.3	34.1	37.3	25.6	29.9	37.0
JP	1.3	0.7	0.7	1.7	2.9	1.8	3.3
RL	5.3	7.3	15.0	14.3	11.2	7.1	3.6
ChP				2.0	4.0	5.3	3.4
CD					7.8	2.2	6.4
Ind		1.6					
LC		2.5	1.3				
Lib	20.8	19.3	18.6	15.6	12.3	23.3	12.0
Cons	20.1	18.7	20.4	16.7	9.2	5.5	8.5
Ind	2.5	1.6	0.5				
PrP					15.9	13.6	14.6
DU	0.4						
SP	0.4		0.2	0.2			

Party	1979	1981	1984	1987	1988	1990	1994
CC				2.2	1.9	1.8	—
DKP	1.9	1.1	0.7	0.9	0.8	—	—
LS	3.7	2.6	2.7	1.4	0.6	—	—
RGU						1.7	3.1
SPP	5.9	11.3	11.5	14.6	13.0	8.3	7.3
SD	38.3	32.9	31.6	29.3	29.8	37.4	34.6
JP	2.6	1.4	1.5	0.5	—	0.5	—
RL	5.4	5.1	5.5	6.2	5.6	3.5	4.6
ChP	2.6	2.3	2.7	2.4	2.0	2.3	1.8
CD	3.2	8.3	4.6	4.8	4.7	5.1	2.8
Lib	12.5	11.3	12.1	10.5	11.8	15.8	23.3
Cons	12.5	14.5	23.4	20.8	19.3	16.0	15.0
PrP	11.0	8.9	3.6	4.8	9.0	6.4	6.4
SP							
Green				1.3	1.4	0.9	—
Other	0.4	0.2	0.1	0.4	0.1	0.3	* 1.0

* In 1994 Jacob Haugaard was elected independently of any party.

Appendix 4:
PARTY SHARES OF VOTES, PERCENT

Party	1998	Party name
CC		Common Course
DKP		Communist Party
LS		Left Socialists
RGU	2.7	Red-Green Unity List
SPP	7.5	Socialist People's Party
SD	36.0	**Social Democrats**
JP		Justice Party
RL	3.9	**Radical Liberals**
ChP	2.5	Christian People's Party
CD	4.3	Center Democrats
LC		Liberal Center
Lib	24.0	*Venstre* **Liberals**
FP		Farmers' Party
Cons	8.9	**Conservative People's Party**
IP		Industry Party
Nazis		National Socialists
Ind		Independents' Party
DP	7.4	Danish People's Party
PrP	2.4	Progress Party
NC		National Cooperation
DU		Danish Union
SP		Slesvig Party
Other	0.3	

The "four old parties" are shown in **bold**.

Appendix 5: REFERENDUMS IN DENMARK

Year	Issue	Result	Per cent of electorate voting Yes	Turnout per cent	Valid votes Yes	Valid votes No
1916	Sale of Danish West Indies (Virgin Islands) to USA (consultative)	Approved	63.2	23.0	57.4	44.1
1920	Constitutional amendment following reunion with northern Slesvig	Passed	47.5	49.0	96.9	3.1
1939	Constitutional amendments (including lower voting age and abolition of Landsting (upper house)	Rejected	44.46 (45% required)	48.4	91.85	8.15
1946	(In the Faroes) on independence	Rejected	48.6	66.4		
1953	New constitution	Passed	45.76	59.1	78.75	21.25
1953	Reduce voting age from 25 to 23 or 21 (all over 21 entitled to vote)					
	For 23	Passed	25.0 voted Yes			
	For 21	Rejected	30.0 voted No			

Appendix 5: REFERENDUMS IN DENMARK

Year	Issue	Result	Per cent of electorate voting Yes	Turnout per cent	Valid votes Yes	Valid votes No
1961	Reduce voting age from 23 to 21	Passed	20.3	36.9	55.0	45.0
1963	Land laws:					
	inheritance of farms	Rejected	27.7	72.2	38.4	61.6
	state small-holdings	Rejected	27.9	72.2	38.6	61.4
	municipal compulsory purchases	Rejected	28.7	72.3	39.6	60.4
	nature conservation	Rejected	30.8	72.3	42.6	57.4
1969	Reduce voting age from 21 to 18	Rejected	13.6	63.4	21.4	78.6
1971	Reduce voting age from 21 to 20	Passed	47.4	83.9	56.5	43.5
1972	Denmark to join European Community	Passed	56.7	89.6	63.3	36.7
1978	Reduce voting age from 20 to 18	Passed	34.2	63.2	53.8	46.2
1986	Danish ratification of Single European Act (advisory)	Passed	42.0	75.4	56.2	43.8
1992	Maastricht Treaty (Treaty of European Union)	Rejected	41.0	83.1	49.3	50.7
1993	Maastricht Treaty with Danish reservations	Passed	49.0	86.5	56.7	43.3
1998	European Union, Amsterdam Treaty	Ratified	41.2	74.8	55.1	44.9

Appendix 5: REFERENDUMS IN DENMARK

Legal basis of referendums

    1916 and 1953 (voting age), 1986: specific legislation.

    1920, 1939, 1953: Constitution of 1920, paragraph 94.

The Constitution of 1953, paragraph 42 (3)-(8), sets out the procedure for holding referendums.

1:    1972, 1992, 1993, 1998: Constitution of 1953, paragraph 20, sections 1 and 2 (concessions of sovereignty)

2:    1961, 1969, 1971, 1978: Constitution of 1953, paragraphs 29 (change of voting age) & 42

3:    1963: Constitution of 1953, paragraph 42 (1) legislative veto.

Sources: Kauffeldt, Carl, *Folkeafstemninger: principper og praksis i Danmark og andre lande.* Copenhagen: Gyldendal,1972. Holt, Elise (ed.), 1988, *Folketingets Håndbog efter valget den 10. maj 1988.* Copenhagen: Schultz Grafisk A/S, 1988. Keesings Record of World Events 1993: 39483. Bille, Lars, "Denmark," *European Journal of Political Research* 24 (4), Political Data Yearbook 1993: 412. 1993. Bille, Lars, "Denmark," *European Journal of Political Research* 26 (3/4), Political Data Yearbook 1994: 281. 1994.

Appendix 6: Economic Data

	1990	1991	1992	1993	1994	1995	1996
Final national consumption (PPS: Purchasing Power Standard)	60,760	65,759	67,322	72,626	78,458	82,291	86,323
Gross domestic product at market prices (billion Danish kroner)	799,109	827,868	856,031	874,910	928,597	970,778	1,013,492
Gross domestic product at market prices (US$ per person)	129,195	130,845	142,026	134,716	146,183	173,189	174,864
Employed, by industry, percent							
Agriculture, forestry, hunting, fishing	6	6	5	5	4	4	4
Mining, manufacturing, electricity and water	21	21	21	19	19	19	19
Construction	6	6	6	5	6	6	6
Wholesale and retail trade, restaurants, hotels	15	14	14	17	17	17	18
Transport and communication	7	7	7	7	7	7	7
Finance, insurance, real estate, busness services	9	9	9	11	11	11	11
Services	36	36	37	35	37	36	35
Unknown				0	1	1	1

	1990	1991	1992	1993	1994	1995	1996
Employed and unemployed on 1 January							
Employed, aged 16-64	2,539,410	2,518,899	2,498,712	2,486,960	2,467,082	2,501,180	2,534,214
Unemployed	232,729	252,069	283,298	299,404	322,457	277,547	221,875
Not in the Labor Force	609,070	625,658	633,324	644,239	652,375	675,598	719,649
Total	3,381,209	3,396,626	3,415,334	3,430,603	3,441,914	3,454,325	3,475,738
Unemployed (percent of total)	6.88	7.42	8.29	8.73	9.37	8.03	6.38
Industrial production indices	1990=100						
Total	100	100	104	101	111	116	117
Intermediate goods (except energy)	100	99	101	97	110	113	114
Capital goods industries	100	99	104	97	108	119	122
Durable consumer goods industries	100	98	100	98	108	113	113
Non-durable consumer goods	100	102	106	107	115	117	118

Appendix 6: Economic data

	1990	1991	1992	1993	1994	1995	1996
Foreign trade (billion Danish kroner)							
Exports	283,786	306,254	309,630	300,108	324,990	335,326	346,727
Imports	240,442	255,567	251,142	238,582	269,059	294,904	302,572
Balance	43,344	50,687	58,488	61,526	55,931	40,422	44,155
Exchange rates, annual average: Danish kroner per 1 US$	6.19	6.33	6.03	6.49	6.35	5.61	5.80

Billion is used in the American and French sense of 10^9, and is equivalent to the English thousand million or the Danish milliard.

Source: Nordic Council of Ministers: Nordic Statistical Yearbook 1993, 1995, 1997.

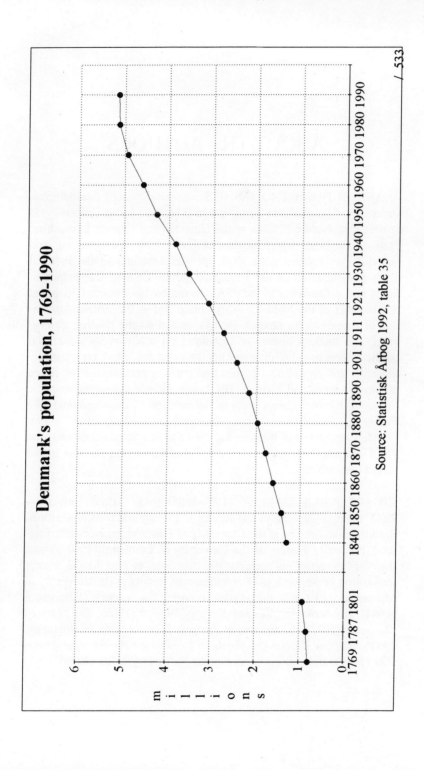

Denmark's population, 1769-1990

Source: Statistisk Årbog 1992, table 35

ABOUT THE AUTHORS

ALASTAIR HUGH THOMAS (B.Sc. Social Sciences Southampton University, Post-graduate Certificate in Education Leeds University) is Professor of Nordic Politics at the University of Central Lancashire, Preston, England, where he has taught British, Comparative, and Scandinavian Politics since 1979. He was Treasurer of the Political Studies Association of the United Kingdom 1978-83. He helped to found and is Convenor of the PSA's Scandinavian Politics Group and is a member of the Nordic History Group and of the British Association of Scandinavian Studies. He has written on the politics, government, and modern history of Denmark; on coalition formation and political consensus-building mechanisms and processes; on social democracy; and on political parties and party systems, including issues of measurement and change. His books include *Social Democratic Parties in Western Europe* (also in German and Chinese editions), *The Future of Social Democracy: Problems and Prospects of Social Democratic Parties in Western Europe* (also in a Spanish edition), and *The Consensual Democracies? The Government and Politics of the Scandinavian States.*

STUART PHILIP OAKLEY (1931-1995) (MA Oxford University, Ph.D. London University) was Reader in History and then Professor of Scandinavian Studies at the University of East Anglia, Norwich, England. He taught History at the University of Edinburgh 1960-69 and then for the rest of his career at the University of East Anglia, except for visiting professorships of Scandinavian History at the University of Minnesota (1966-67) and Gustavus Adolphus College, Minnesota (1984). His books include *The Story of Sweden* (1966), *The Story of Denmark* (1972), *Scandinavian History 1520-1970* (a bibliography, 1984), *William III and the Northern Crowns during the Nine Years' War* (1987), and *War and Peace in the Baltic 1560-1798* (1993).